2195

D0729388

A Theology of Power

5/24/93

For John:
    Another departing brother of the desert.
You have been a pleasure in conversation, in
laughter and in--how shall I say?--silliness. I
will always be
    Yours,

A
THEOLOGY
OF
POWER

Being beyond Domination

——— *Kyle A. Pasewark* ———

FORTRESS PRESS   MINNEAPOLIS

For my father, Richard

Power surrounds him and love emerges.

A THEOLOGY OF POWER
Being beyond Domination

Copyright © 1993 Augsburg Fortress. All rights reserved. Except for brief quotations in critical articles or reviews, no part of this book may be reproduced in any manner without prior written permission from the publisher. Write to: Permissions, Augsburg Fortress, 426 S. Fifth St., Box 1209, Minneapolis, MN 55440.

Interior design: The HK Scriptorium, Inc.
Cover design: Judy Swanson
Cover art: "When We Learn to Come Together We Are Whole" (Intaglio) by Jan Shoger

Library of Congress Cataloging-in-Publication Data

Pasewark, Kyle A., 1959–
    A theology of power : domination and being / Kyle A. Pasewark.
      p.   cm.
    Includes bibliographical references and index.
    ISBN 0-8006-2605-2 (alk. paper)
    1. Power (Christian theology). I. Title.
BT738.25.P37   1993
261 – dc20   92-19343
                                               CIP

The paper used in this publication meets the minimum requirements of American National Standard for Information Sciences – Permanence of Paper for Printed Library Materials, ANSI Z329.48-1984. ∞™

Manufactured in the U.S.A.   AF 1-2605

97   96   95   94   93   1   2   3   4   5   6   7   8   9   10

CONTENTS

ACKNOWLEDGMENTS

Many people have given considerable time and energy to produce this book. To affix a single author's name is, at best, overstatement — the labor and care of many are concealed beneath and throughout these pages. Only a smattering of the debts can be acknowledged, because so few can be remembered with clarity. But almost no one I have spoken with for any length of time has failed to make an impression on me and, therefore, this work. This vast and productive tangle of encounters, in fact, first gave rise to the suspicion that power is omnipresent, unavoidable, and essentially desirable. If it is impossible to recall precisely who said or did what, this is the highest compliment, for such influences have been claimed as my self.

The restless nights of a graduate student, in which years this book originated, are supposed to be due to one's advisor, the insomnia of an author, to one's editor. I slept very well. My advisor, Langdon Gilkey, is a power deep underneath the surface of these pages, and me, in ways I can feel but no longer trace. His candor, gentleness, zest, and subtle guidance made my work more productive, certainly, but above all an enjoyable and relaxed adventure. Tim Staveteig, who walked me through the editorial process, is an all too uncommon blend of efficiency and geniality, and the value of his assistance cannot be overestimated. The careful attention of Maurya Horgan and Paul Kobelski to every facet of the manuscript was astonishing and improved the book immensely. David Lott and Michael Wegs of Fortress Press kept numerous details in order. David Tracy's perceptive comments and accommodating personality were always a pleasure. Jerald Brauer's willingness to work through the manuscript with me will always be appreciated, as will his jovial charm. Robert Scharlemann, the first person outside the walls of the University of Chicago to read the project, gave me the confidence to believe the idea was not limited to a doctoral rite of passage, and I will never forget his exceptional kindness. Generous assistance on the index was provided by my student Ellen Kussow.

Three collaborators deserve special mention. Tom Davis, one of the most courageous people I have ever known, helped inspire the interest in

Reformation theology which turned out to be decisive for this theory of power and also pored over the manuscript. Dean Hammer, a political theorist who writes about religion, kept honest a theologian who writes about political thought. The depth of his love is appreciated more each day. Kelly Morse, who labored over the index, is a truly remarkable woman who has become a steadfast friend. It is my sacred honor to count these three as lifelong companions of my heart. In comparison with their love, beauty, and power, their considerable help with the book pales in importance.

It would be unfair and unkind to express appreciation only to those who have read or contributed the words of the pages. It is not they alone who have sparked the spirit of the book or its author. My many friends are an apt earthly analogy to justification by grace; no one deserves such a rich bounty. The occasional tedium of writing was turned to joy by the love of friends. Barbara Pasewark and Melanie Lane now rest in the bosom of God; I can do no more than cherish their memory. About my father, Richard, to say more than the dedication would say less. My brother Mark; my sister-in-law, Virginia; Karen, my stepmother; and my wife, LeslieAnn have sustained me. My new brother, Michael, and my even newer nephew, Eric, I hope will read this someday. My reestablished contact with my mother, Alice, exemplifies the tortuous but fertile circuits of power. The Brown family, Isaac Catt, Karin Caves, Frank and Kathy Guliuzza, Steve Häggmark, Carol Hammer, Dale Herbeck, Eileen and Jim Fleissner, Nancy Johnson, the Knapp family, Jeff and Julia Pearson, Jeff Pool, John Powers, Martha Wilson, the Pasewark/Gruters clan, my friends at Immanuel Lutheran Church in Chicago, First Lutheran Church in Lynn, Massachusetts, my warm and wonderful colleagues and friends at Gustavus Adolphus College (particularly the Departments of Religion, Philosophy, and Political Science, the Chaplain's Office, and students), and not least of all, our five cats, have given me more than they can ever know.

To say "thank you" to every one of you seems so small, but there are no other words. You are gifts of God. You do not draw breath for me; you do make me alive.

THE UBIQUITY
OF POWER

"Should everybody from Right to Left, from Bertrand de Jouvenel to Mao Tse-tung, agree on so basic a point in political philosophy as the nature of power?"[1] In the three decades since Hannah Arendt asked this question, the broad consensus about the nature of power has less disintegrated than been detonated into tiny fragments. To find even two thinkers who claim agreement on the nature of power is difficult, but what is agreed upon is the need to rethink the meaning of power.

This book reformulates the idea of power by way of three thinkers: Michel Foucault, Martin Luther, and Paul Tillich. Despite their many differences, each sees power as ubiquitous, in contrast to most recent descriptions of power as occasional and discretionary. This inevitability of power's presence leads these three to see power as more productive than other, more orthodox perspectives. Thus, power's ubiquity is assumed from the beginning; later, this assumption is justified.

If being is saturated with power inevitably, a fundamental choice appears immediately: Is the power of being ultimately and finally destructive of beings, or is it fundamentally supportive of them? Generally, political theories of power have understood power either as domination or as the capacity to dominate. Indeed, despite growing discomfort, most recent reformulations of power dispense neither with these categories nor with the central assumptions that produce their identification with power—among them, that power is a possession, that it is applied only externally, and that it is occasional. Not surprisingly, such reflections about power often are restricted solely to politics, conceiving of power by means of a dichotomy between the externally politically powerful and dominating and the externally powerless and dominated.

The confinement of power to the externality of the sociopolitical and its quantification by degrees of dominion cross many of the normal boundary lines of philosophy and theology. They traverse the predominantly Anglo-American empirical tradition of social thought, Continental thought, and

---

[1] Hannah Arendt, *On Violence* (New York: Harcourt, Brace & World, 1970), 38.

1

liberation and political theology.[2] Moreover, such a view is not confined to academic treatments of power; some form of domination or control is also the primary component in most cultural definitions and uses of power. Even though restricting power to domination is losing its hold on some theoreticians of power, little change in everyday cultural understandings of power is visible.

This broad analysis of the dominant conception of power covers several uses of the term. On the one hand, power unalloyed by a preposition such as "to" or "of" is usually defined as domination or control. On the other hand, even "power of" something or someone, or the "power to" do something, equates "power" with domination or control. The "power of reason," for example, typically means reason's ability to control, defeat, and cast out what is unreasonable. Similarly, a doctor's "power to heal" refers to the ability to eradicate disease. Thus, in nonpolitical contexts, the use of "power" is itself

---

[2] For the empirical tradition of social thought, see the essays in *Power,* ed. Steven Lukes (New York: New York University Press, 1986); for a more Continental tinge, see *The Responsibility of Power: Historical Essays in Honor of Hajo Holborn,* ed. Leonard Krieger and Fritz Stern (Garden City, N.Y.: Doubleday & Co., 1967). Nearly all the pieces in these otherwise disparate volumes are identical in dealing with power only as a political and social reality and in reducing power to either the potency or actuality of dominion. For its part, the debt of liberation and political theology to Marx has meant a fairly unreflective borrowing of Marx's notion of power as domination. Especially in the last few years, the danger of this uncritical importation has become clear with the nearly total worldwide collapse of Marxism. It is not too much to suspect that the future of liberation theology depends on whether it can disengage itself from Marxism. However, even non-Marxian political theology maintains this restrictive view of power; see, e.g., Glenn Tinder, *The Political Meaning of Christianity: The Prophetic Stance* (Baton Rouge: Louisiana State University Press, 1989; reprint, San Francisco: HarperCollins, HarperSanFrancisco, 1991), 9, 32, 36 (page references are to reprint edition).

Though dominant, the external imprisonment of power is by no means universal. For an understanding of power that includes an inward dimension, see Starhawk's fascinating work *Truth or Dare: Encounters with Power, Authority, and Mystery* (San Francisco: HarperSanFrancisco, HarperCollins, 1987), 8–26. Oddly, however, insofar as power is political/institutional, at least in contemporary culture, Starhawk still considers it to be strictly external. Thus, there is a significant difficulty in uniting the three "types of power," a problem that appears also in Tillich.

An important exception to this tendency to identify power and domination is Anna Case-Winters, *God's Power: Traditional Understandings and Contemporary Challenges* (Louisville, KY: Westminster/John Knox Press, 1990). Unfortunately, my access to this fine study of power was too late in the editorial process to permit its treatment with the seriousness it deserves. Case-Winters sees clearly the crucial problem — understanding power as domination and control — and is also persuasive in presenting the need to defend the notion of God's omnipotence on philosophical and theological grounds and for reasons of religious life. Our approaches are somewhat different. We take omnipotence in a stronger sense than Case-Winters does and she finds less value in the classical tradition than will be evident here, relying more on process and feminist thought. This difference should be tremendously productive. First, it may aid in a rapprochement between schools of thought often viewed as antagonists by adherents of both and may compel us to begin to overcome the chauvinistic boundaries of "schools." Second, although there remain differences of substance between Case-Winters's conception of power and the one advocated here, the broad common ground enables these differences themselves to initiate a conversation that should serve to clarify and sharpen both views of power and their relation.

controlled and dominated by its political analogue. "Powers to" and "powers of" are indebted to "power" unadorned.[3]

This political root should not obscure differences, largely ethical, attributed to particular exercises of power. How curious that the contemporary world finds political power, domination, and control so abhorrent, while at the same time lionizing a variety of "powers of"—reason, life—and "powers to"—heal, create, learn, act. This is not because what power is understood to be is obscure, but because power is conceived as something exercised by one thing upon another. Power is a medium with effects on an object; thus, power's value is in inverse proportion to the value of the object upon which it is exercised. Power itself is neutral and formal, almost indifferent. It becomes good, bad, necessary, excessive, or abusive only through the object to which it is applied.[4] The value of what is dominated determines the value of dominating power. If applied in order to control or eliminate disease, death, unreason, and the like, power is desirable. Power acts on the exterior of its object—to move it, confine it, destroy it; it does not transform its object but only controls it. This is why political power is feared or is at best seen as a necessary evil. The objects of political power are people with inner lives including freedom, spirit, and subjectivity. Any power that dominates this inner life is undesirable (even if occasionally unavoidable). Power is dangerous at best, evil at worst, because it dominates what is valuable. The more valuable the objects of power are, the more dangerous power becomes; because the greatest human value is humanity, power applied to humans is abusive almost by its very nature.

Two conclusions may be drawn: First, if power is domination, it is ultimately destructive of beings. The perfection or fulfillment of power as domination is "absolute power," the tyrannical enslavement or eradication of whatever opposes such power. Particular uses of power may have temporary value, but if power becomes total and dominates a being entirely, it necessarily destroys all special value of that being.[5] If Tillich is right that the most fundamental description of Being-itself is the "power of being," we are led inevitably to believe that the ground of our existence ultimately and finally opposes us, seeking to destroy beings in their freedom.

---

[3] There is not a claim here, although it might be true, that this colloquial use of "power" originates historically from its employment in political theory. What is suggested is that our common use of the term takes instances of political power as its exemplar. This is clear from the fact that when we speak of "power" without the addition of prepositional phrases to indicate a special manifestation of power, we nearly always refer to political power.

[4] Peter Gay suggests a close association between power's neutrality and that of its agent, the will ("Burckhardt's *Renaissance:* Between Responsibility and Power," in *The Responsibility of Power,* ed. Krieger and Stern, 190–91).

[5] A stark expression of this is Thomas Hobbes, *Leviathan,* ed. C. B. Macpherson (Harmondsworth, England: Penguin, Penguin English Library, 1968), 313–17, 602, in which "person" is a predicate only of the sovereign. Without the sovereign, all others are merely pieces of a body, without intrinsic worth. Indeed, only the sovereign is made in God's image (p. 669).

For Christian theology, the unacceptability of this view of power is manifest; certainly, understanding power as domination is intolerable also for non-Christians. But the principal concern is a theological one. Christian theology has always assumed that God ultimately supports and redeems God's own creation. Simply to destroy created being is not within the purposes of God. If part of this creation is human freedom, then the purpose of God relative to freedom is to fulfill it, perhaps to re-create it but not to destroy it. Yet if Being is fundamentally the power of being, if the Christian God is in any sense an omnipotent God—necessary claims if God is not to become simply a god—and if theology appropriates uncritically the standard political conception of power as domination—as much theology, especially politically oriented theology, has done—it becomes impossible to understand how the Christian God can be said to support beings, rather than destroying them.[6] If power is domination, God can hardly be but despised:

> [God] deprives me of my subjectivity because he is all-powerful and all-knowing. I revolt and try to make *him* into an object, but the revolt fails and becomes desperate. God appears as the invincible tyrant, the being in contrast with whom all other beings are without freedom and subjectivity. He is equated with the recent tyrants who with the help of terror try to transform everything into a mere object, a thing among things, a cog in the machine they control.[7]

The second conclusion introduces a note of caution into attempts to recast the understanding of power. However unappetizing the contemporary world finds political domination and control, this notion remains the fountain from which the various "powers to" and "powers of" are drawn. Few of us are willing to condemn power over disease without hesitation. Moreover, if such a

---

[6] At the very least, God is made capricious. Eberhard Jüngel puts the problem of unreflective theological appropriation of political theory succinctly: "This is the earthly way of thinking of a lord: first he has all power and then perhaps he can be merciful—but then again, perhaps not. God's lordliness and lordship are thought of in the same general way. He is mighty, able, and free to love or not to love" (*God as the Mystery of the World,* trans. Darrell L. Guder [Grand Rapids: William B. Eerdmans, 1983], 21).

[7] Paul Tillich, *The Courage To Be* (New Haven: Yale University Press, 1952), 185. Masculine pronouns in direct quotations in reference to humanity as a whole or to God have not been altered, despite my own convictions regarding inclusive language. If the texts, presented as written, produce a certain discomfort for the reader, as they do for me, this may be more helpful in the end than altering a text so that it may agree with us.

Luther was more than willing to use feminine imagery for the divine. In addition to the examples that appear throughout, see Martin Luther, *Commentary on 1 Corinthians 15,* in *Luther's Works,* vol. 28, *Commentaries on 1 Corinthians 7, 1 Corinthians 15, Lectures on 1 Timothy,* trans. Martin H. Bertram, ed. Hilton Oswald (St. Louis: Concordia Publishing House, 1973), 126 (Martin Luther, *Luthers Werke,* 36 Band [Weimar: Hermann Böhlaus Nachfolger, 1909], 571). Tillich decried "the predominance of the male element in the symbolization of the divine" and hoped to develop female symbols that would "transcend the alternative male-female and which are capable of being developed over against a one-sided male-determined symbolism" (Paul Tillich, *Systematic Theology* [Chicago: University of Chicago Press, 1963], 3:293–94).

condemnation is issued, it is announced in a language that is a product of power, imposed on and reproduced by speakers, a language that can be altered only at its margins. In some instances domination or control is valued. A radical transvaluation of power, defining "real" power as weakness, is neither possible nor desirable. An unyielding transvaluation of power is functionally meaningless outside its own highly abstract and artificial context and has nothing in common with the ways in which the word "power" is used. Instead, an approach to the phenomenon of power must be discovered that steers a course between the irrelevance of a complete transvaluation of power, which eliminates any relation between sovereignty and power, and a complete identification of power with domination.

Within a basic framework that posits power as omnipresent, power must be seen as a broader phenomenon than its traditional confinement to politics allows. The starting point of a constructive theology of power is outside political theory, reentering that field only later. This shift in the point of departure allows power to appear as more than something always external to the human subject. The usual position of political theory, either explicitly or implicitly, has been that power is solely an external phenomenon. This "spatial" restriction has an intimate connection with the identity of power and domination. In opposition to these geographical and substantive decisions, we present two theses. First, power is both an internal and an external event, and yet it is properly neither of these; power is a phenomenon of the borders. Second, at its root, power is a communication of efficacy. These definitional tasks completed, it will be possible to return briefly to the arena of political theory and to suggest some implications for a concrete ethic of power. Neither of these latter two tasks is strictly within the scope of the project, but it is necessary to give some indication of why a reformulation of the definition of power matters.

The procedure will be as follows. First, the tradition of political thought about power will be outlined briefly. Since this exposition is concurrent with an examination of Foucault's innovative theory of power, it relies heavily on his review of Western political theory. Foucault's own understanding of power provides two criteria for a theory of power. Foucault argues persuasively that conditions of the exercise of power include the mutual presence of the "powers" involved, and the body as a medium of the exercise of power. But Foucault also demonstrates the possibilities and limits of confining a discussion of power to a political model. Of politically based conceptions of power, Foucault's is interesting and challenging because it seeks to overcome an identity of power and sovereignty from within the framework of political thought. Foucault tested the outer limits of a political understanding of power and discovered, toward the end of his life, that politics alone cannot provide an adequate concept of power.

"Power" cannot remain captive to political power. This is especially true of a theology of power. The effort to overcome the imprisonment of power within the bars of politics, while still accounting for those forms of power which are political, leads to the thought of Martin Luther. It is from Luther that the principal clues for redefining power in the contemporary world are derived. Both the basic definition of power as a communication of efficacy and what we express in the notion of the "border" are discovered in Luther.[8] In the final two chapters, Paul Tillich's position on the nature of power engages what we have discovered in Luther, and vice versa, and the understanding of power as communication of efficacy at the border of encounter can thereby be evaluated in relation to several contemporary alternatives.

[8] The discussion of Luther is restricted to what is generally agreed to be his "mature" theology; accordingly, the weight of emphasis falls on his writings from approximately 1518 on. A good review of the literature regarding the early Luther is found in B. A. Gerrish, *The Old Protestantism and the New: Essays on the Reformation Heritage* (Chicago: University of Chicago Press, 1982), 69–89. See also Alister E. McGrath, *Iustitia Dei: A History of the Christian Doctrine of Justification,* vol. 2, *From 1500 to the Present Day* (Cambridge: Cambridge University Press, 1986), 5; and the splendid biography, Heiko A. Oberman, *Luther: Man Between God and the Devil,* trans. Eileen Walliser-Schwarzbart (New York: Doubleday, Image Books, 1989), 164, 173. If 1518 is taken as the point of departure, questions about when the Reformation insights took shape are less relevant, because almost all the disputants agree they are in place by this time.

CHAPTER 1

THE CONTEMPORARY QUESTION OF POWER: MICHEL FOUCAULT

The claim that a more productive understanding of power should start in earnest from outside political thought does not mean it is possible to begin a presentation there. To say the political road does not lead where it ought, that a different path should be cut, is not justifiable until we see where the explorations of political thought have and have not brought us. Accordingly it is necessary to approach power from the more conventional angle of theories of political power. The work of Michel Foucault is especially appropriate, for Foucault was a brilliant political thinker who placed his own conception of power in opposition to more orthodox theories. Through his exposure of the weaknesses of this orthodoxy, Foucault was driven to a unique and compelling understanding of power. Until near the end of his life, he retained a political notion of power, but after producing one of the most sophisticated political conceptions of power, he saw its limitations. In his last works, he broke, albeit only partially, from understanding power solely in political terms; therefore, the value of his work for developing a different understanding of power is immense. In the course of his career, he was able to take his readers to the summit of political theory's road and then show it to be partial and inadequate. If the theology of power developed here takes another course than Foucault would have, it is still in traveling with him that this route can be found.

We begin by presenting Foucault's criticism of traditional political theory regarding power. Three themes in Foucault's critique of traditional theories of power are especially important to this study.[1] First, Foucault argues that orthodox domination theory, or the "sovereignty theory" of power,[2] views power as fundamentally occasional. The store of possessed power is used relatively infrequently. Power is a possession of the powerful, and it is at their

---

[1] An excellent summary of the variety of conceptions of power Foucault criticizes is in Gilles Deleuze, *Foucault* (Minneapolis: University of Minnesota Press, 1988), 25–31.

[2] Michel Foucault, "Two Lectures," trans. Kate Soper, in *Power/Knowledge: Selected Interviews and Other Writings, 1972–1977,* ed. Colin Gordon (New York: Random House, Pantheon Books, 1980), 92–108.

discretion whether it is used or not. It is decidedly not an ongoing, ubiquitous aspect of social life. Second, this conception views power as fundamentally tied to the state and as the possession of a few.[3] Even when the analysis concerns the use of power outside the structure of the state, the model of power developed on the basis of state power is carried into the description. Thus, analyses of varieties of social power operate within a framework that sees the powerful few exercising power upon, and dominating, the powerless many.[4] Finally, sovereignty theory places power and knowledge in an external relationship to each other. Knowledge is associated not with power but only with reason. One need only think of Hobbes's inability to find a principle in reason that would limit power to understand how deeply knowledge and reason have been divorced from power. What is significant about this division for Foucault, however, is not the insufficient limitation that is placed upon power by reason, with the effect that power can trample reason without limitation. That is the fear of Acton's aphorism "Power corrupts." Foucault's concern is exactly the inverse problem, namely, that reason and knowledge have no understanding of their own involvement in power. Truth, the voice of reason, knowledge, are all formulated as ineluctably opposed to power. Truth is liberating; power is repressive.[5]

[3] Ibid., 105; Michel Foucault, "The Eye of Power," conversation with Jean-Pierre Barou and Michelle Perrot, trans. Colin Gordon, in *Power/Knowledge*, 156.

[4] Foucault, "Two Lectures."

[5] This concealment of reason's involvement in power is the major point of the history of incarceration in Michel Foucault, *Discipline and Punish: The Birth of the Prison*, trans. Alan Sheridan (New York: Random House, Vintage Books, 1979), esp. 27, 257–308 (orig. *Surveiller et Punir: Naissance de la prison* [Paris: Éditions Gallimard, 1975], 32, 261–315), and is even more prominent in Foucault, *The History of Sexuality*, vol. 1, *An Introduction*, trans. Robert Hurley (New York: Random House, Vintage Books, 1980) (orig. *Histoire de la sexualité, 1: La volonté de savoir* [Paris: Éditions Gallimard, 1976]).

Foucault's assertion of the gordian knot in which reason and power are enveloped has been one of the most criticized aspects of his thought. Many interpreters seek a road back to sovereign "rights of reason." The least satisfactory of these is J. G. Merquior, *Foucault* (Berkeley: University of California Press, 1985), who champions the accomplishments of positive science without ever questioning the possibility of science, which was exactly Foucault's challenge in his archaeologies and genealogies of power and the subject. The weakness of Merquior's argument is exceeded only by the astonishing arrogance of his presentation. A more serious and persuasive argument for reason's rights over and apart from power is forwarded by Michael Walzer, "The Politics of Michel Foucault," in *Foucault: A Critical Reader*, ed. David Couzens Hoy (New York: Basil Blackwell, 1986), 66–67. Walzer tries to reestablish both the importance of the state and the reign of knowledge, the latter of which attempts to control the abuse of power, apparently without being itself involved in power essentially. Reason can and must triumph over power. The need for a rationality beyond power is felt also by Charles Taylor ("Foucault on Freedom and Truth," in *Foucault: A Critical Reader*, ed. Hoy, 69–102), Edward W. Said ("Foucault and the Imagination of Power," in *Foucault: A Critical Reader*, ed. Hoy, 149–55; Said's position appears to end in a desire for Foucault to exempt Foucault's own philosophical standpoint from critique), and Jürgen Habermas (*The Philosophical Discourse of Modernity: Twelve Lectures*, trans. Frederick Lawrence [Cambridge, Mass.: MIT Press, 1987], 238–326). Habermas sees his own theory of communicative reason as a way between the

For Foucault, this analysis of power, with the probable exception of the division of power and knowledge, was at one time a relatively accurate reflection of the way power was exercised. His use of the rather grisly description of the punishment of Damiens, an eighteenth-century regicide, shows that, however severely the sovereign punished, the intervention of power was saved for special occasions.[6] But whatever the adequacy of these theories of power to the historical situation in which they were developed, power in the West has shown a tendency to ever-increasing and more specific interventions in social life. Power has both widened its sphere and deepened its roots. The rise of the human sciences, in particular, has been both an instrument and an effect of this tendency.[7] The "disciplinary technologies" of modern power invade all aspects of social life; they are visible in surveillance and "the gaze" (applied primarily to the lower classes)[8] as well as in the minute interventions of psychoanalysis (applied largely to the bourgeoisie).[9]

The inadequacy of prevailing theories of power produces disastrous consequences. With regard to the occasional nature of power, Foucault thinks that to cling to a theory that sees power as occasional is to mask its increasing interventions in social life.[10] And to view power as the possession of a few has the double effect of concealing the practice of power by a diverse range of social actors and forces, and impeding efforts to analyze strategies of resistance to power. The division between power and knowledge is, however, the point most in need of radical criticism. This division also serves as a mask. It hides the involvement of power with knowledge, allowing knowledge a reign of its own, a royal dress so dangerous precisely because it presents itself as uninterested in power. In such impressive disguise, knowledge's power is nearly absolute. If one resists knowledge, one is accused of resisting not power but truth. The demand of the current situation in the West is to formulate a perspective on power that allows rather than prevents analyses of the mechanisms and strategies of power. One of these strategies is the claim to possess a

---

problems of modern thought Foucault exposes, and what Habermas thinks are Foucault's own aporias. Habermas's road around the impasse at which he believes Foucault has arrived is discussed in some detail in chapter 5 below. For an excellent summary of Foucault's own position and the range of social thought to which it applies, see David Couzens Hoy, "Power, Repression, Progress: Foucault, Lukes, and the Frankfurt School," in *Foucault: A Critical Reader,* ed. Hoy, 123–47.

6 Foucault, *Discipline and Punish,* 3–69 (*Surveiller et Punir,* 9–72).

7 Most of *Discipline and Punish* and *History of Sexuality,* vol. 1, demonstrate this. In addition, see Michel Foucault, "The Politics of Health in the Eighteenth Century," trans. Colin Gordon, in *Power/Knowledge;* idem, "The History of Sexuality," interview by Lucette Finas, trans. Leo Marshall, in *Power/Knowledge,* 190–93; and idem, "Prison Talk," interview by J.-J. Brochier, trans. Colin Gordon, in *Power/Knowledge,* 44, 47–54.

8 Foucault, *Discipline and Punish.*

9 Foucault, *History of Sexuality,* vol. 1.

10 Foucault, "Two Lectures," 104; idem, "Truth and Power," interview by Alessandro Fontana and Pasquale Pasquino, trans. Colin Gordon, in *Power/Knowledge,* 114; idem, *History of Sexuality* 1:86 (*Histoire de la sexualité, 1,* 113).

knowledge and truth uninvolved with power. In turn, Foucault's analyses of mechanisms and strategies are undertaken with a view to resistance against the widening and deepening contemporary circle of power.

To this critique, we add two more points. To begin with, traditional theories of power, because of their tendency to understand power as the possession of a few and as used only occasionally by those few, evaluate choices in regard to the use of power within a framework of "balances of power," which are in turn worked out in a kind of zero-sum game. The quantity of power is assumed to be finite, such that if one person or group has "more" power, its counterpart must have "less." Typically, Hobbes has one of the strongest statements. If the sovereign does not have all power, in effect he or she has none: "For what is it to divide the Power of a Commonwealth, but to dissolve it; for Powers divided mutually destroy each other."[11] Power is understood, in sum, as external power over others and therefore as domination.

Moreover, when domination controls the viewpoint from which the exercise of power is seen, the evaluation of power has, broadly speaking, taken two forms. First, power can be seen as an ethical nonentity. It may be removed entirely from the realm of ethical reflection, in the mode of Machiavelli. Since power as the exercise of domination is accepted as necessary in social life, normal ethical reflections on its legitimacy are removed, and the exercise of power becomes a realpolitik controlled solely by principles of self-interest. Or, in the case of Hobbes, reason is involved in a progressive self-eradication in favor of power. Reason cannot, Hobbes recognizes, conquer power; therefore, he concludes, reason must be mute in power's presence. A second alternative tends to see power as an ethical disaster; power as domination is inherently dangerous. Power's exhaustion in control and domination requires an advance "beyond power."[12] With respect to the identification of power and domination, and the evaluation of power flowing from this equivalence, Foucault's position changed dramatically during the course of his career and took an especially sharp turn near the end of his life. Part of our task is to expose the alterations in Foucault's thought and to determine their implications for a theology of power.

A statement of points of criticism of "sovereignty theory" demonstrates neither its accuracy nor the superiority of an alternative conception. The task of the remainder of this chapter, and the project as a whole, is to satisfy the dual demand to establish more firmly the shortcomings of the identification of power and domination and to develop a more persuasive alternative. Up to now, Foucault's critique of power has been abstracted from his constructive position. It is evident that the two develop together and play off each other. It is to the constructive position that attention must now be turned.

---

[11] Thomas Hobbes, *Leviathan,* ed. C. B. Macpherson (Harmondsworth, England: Penguin, Penguin English Library, 1968), 368.

[12] For a contemporary version of this argument, see Marilyn French, *Beyond Power: On Women, Men, and Morals* (New York: Ballantine Books, 1985).

This involves an exegetical problem, however. Much less than either Luther or Tillich can Foucault be said to have followed a single trajectory of reflection. Any discussion of Foucault must, therefore, be attentive to the changing topography of his thought. There are, it seems, at least four distinguishable periods that can be isolated schematically.[13] (1) In *Madness and Civilization* and before, Foucault was concerned primarily with social practices.[14] (2) Soon, however, he entered what may be termed his "archaeological period," in which the principal focus was on an archaeology of systems of thought. Concern with the use of systems of thought in social practice receded into the background.[15] (3) However, in his third period, nondiscursive practices again received primary attention.[16] As far as a theory of power is concerned, this third phase introduces two important changes: first, power becomes a thematic issue for the first time; second, the treatments of social practices are conducted in opposition to philosophies of the subject. This opposition is an important

[13] The first three distinctions follow the schemata of Hubert L. Dreyfus and Paul Rabinow, *Michel Foucault: Beyond Structuralism and Hermeneutics,* 2nd ed. (Chicago: University of Chicago Press, 1983).

[14] Michel Foucault, *Madness and Civilization: A History of Insanity in the Age of Reason,* trans. Richard Howard (New York: Random House, 1965).

[15] There is something of a bridge between the second and third phases in Michel Foucault, *The Birth of the Clinic: An Archaeology of Medical Perception,* trans. A. M. Sheridan Smith (New York: Random House, Vintage Books, 1975) (orig. *Naissance de la clinique: Une archéologie du regard médical* [Paris: Presses universitaires de France, 1963]). In this work, however, practices of medicine and their significance are no more than background issues. After the first five chapters of the book, discussion of social practices disappears almost entirely, except for a brief reference in the conclusion (*Birth of the Clinic,* 196; *Naissance de la clinique,* 199–200). The point of the work is not to elucidate social practices but to construct a medical discourse that is a witness to "changes in the fundamental arrangements of knowledge" (*Birth of the Clinic,* 199 [translation modified]; *Naissance de la clinique,* 202, reads "changements dans les dispositions fondamentales du savoir . . .").

[16] In an otherwise excellent review of Foucault's archaeologies and their critique of truth, Dreyfus and Rabinow claim that Foucault largely abandons his archaeological interest because of insurmountable methodological problems (*Michel Foucault,* 79–100). Deleuze is more persuasive in his elegant tracing of the persistence of each of Foucault's dominant thoughts through to the end of his life and work, treating them as emphases more than stages (*Foucault*). Arnold I. Davidson takes a similar position ("Archaeology, Genealogy, Ethics," in *Foucault: A Critical Reader,* ed. Hoy, 221–27. To reemphasize nondiscursive practice, as Foucault does in this third phase, does not imply any irremediable difficulty with his archaeological work concerned principally with discursive practice, as Dreyfus and Rabinow suggest. Rather, archaeology simply "stops at this point and does not attempt to deal with a problem that surpasses the limits of 'knowledge'" (Deleuze, *Foucault,* 12).

Dreyfus and Rabinow characterize this third phase as Foucault's genealogical stage (*Michel Foucault,* 104–17). That description is not followed here, primarily because of a fourth line of thought, which developed just prior to Foucault's death, which Dreyfus and Rabinow had seen only in outline. The third period runs roughly from the mid-1970s through *History of Sexuality,* vol. 1. The final phase incorporates both archaeological and genealogical elements and cannot, therefore, be characterized as nongenealogical or nonarchaeological, but to these aspects Foucault adds the ethical self-constitution of the subject. It was obviously impossible for commentators on Foucault prior to the second and third volumes of *History of Sexuality* to account for this ethical

carryover from Foucault's archaeologies.[17] (4) Toward the end of Foucault's life, however, the antagonism to a constructive philosophy of the subject had ebbed, and he began to retrieve the human subject discarded since *Madness and Civilization*. The recovery of the subject is the distinguishing mark of Foucault's final, and uncompleted, phase of thought.

Within this simplified schema of the course of Foucault's thought, a few issues must be addressed in order to understand Foucault's analysis of power.[18] The first task is to trace the concept of power through the changing directions of Foucault's thought. Second, the place of the subject within each of these periods must be discussed. The question of the subject emerges out of Foucault's explication of the "depth of power." Finally, Foucault's reflections on the possibility of truth need to be confronted. It is evident that they present a challenge to any effort to elevate power to the level of an ontological concept.

---

phase, but it is disappointing that many essays published after the appearance of these works suffer from a similar failure. This is especially true of almost all the essays in *After Foucault: Humanistic Knowledge, Postmodern Challenges,* ed. Jonathan Arac (New Brunswick, N.J.: Rutgers University Press, 1988). The treatment of Foucault in this volume does not go beyond the first volume of *History of Sexuality.*

[17] It is not that Foucault eliminates the subject in his archaeologies, but he understands the subject, and especially consciousness, as dependent on its placement in certain ensembles and spaces of discourse. What he opposes about philosophies of the subject is their tendency to make the subject sovereign over, rather than created by, discursive fields. See, e.g., Michel Foucault, *The Archaeology of Knowledge and the Discourse on Language,* trans. A. M. Sheridan Smith (New York: Harper & Row, 1972; reprint, New York: Random House, Pantheon Books, 1972), 12–14, 122 (page references are to reprint edition) (orig. *L'archéologie du savoir* [Paris: Éditions Gallimard, 1969], 21–24, 160–61). See also Michel Foucault, *The Order of Things: An Archaeology of the Human Sciences* (New York: Random House, Vintage Books, 1973), xiii–xiv. Deleuze is especially clear on this point (*Foucault,* 7).

[18] The exposition presented here is somewhat incommensurate with Deleuze's treatment of power in *Foucault.* Because Deleuze's book is so excellent, our lack of fit with it deserves comment. The reason lies in a different emphasis. There is not just one place for power in Foucault's work, but two. There is, first, a lateral dimension, in which power is the means by which discursive and nondiscursive practices capture each other. On the other hand, there is an *application* of the complex or structure of power created in this reciprocal capture. That is, once the web of power relations between discursive and nondiscursive practices is constituted, the web itself moves to "catch" certain objects within its net. Since the employment of the complex of power results in domination, this may be called the "vertical" exercise of power. Through it, the lateral complex achieves a victory over those to and upon whom it is exercised. This may be one of the reasons Foucault insists on the value of genealogy as a way to recover local knowledges excluded from the dominant discourse of truth, a topic treated later. If such knowledges are reinvested, they become capable of their own lateral integrations, creating their own web, which may prove strong enough to resist the incursions of the "prevailing" discourse of truth (or to break the hold of its integrations) and remove the vertical domination of one discourse over another. Whereas Deleuze concentrates primarily on the first, or lateral dimension (see esp. pp. 68–123), the focus here is on the generally vertical application of the lateral net. Systematically, although not temporally, an investigation of vertical, or at least external, applications of power assumes the prior constitution of the horizontal web of relations. In this sense, genealogy presupposes archaeology.

Foucault's Concept of Power

In *Madness and Civilization,* there is no thematization of the issue of power. The absence of an explicit place for power continues until about the mid-1970s and is broken by *Discipline and Punish* and its surrounding work. This is not to say that something like power is not present in Foucault's efforts of the first two phases, only that it is not a topic of reflection. It is true that "what can only be called power"[19] is a theme throughout Foucault's work, even in the early period. Foucault himself comes to realize that he had been speaking about power all along.[20] But since power is an unthematized topic, it is not surprising that there is little innovation with regard to power. In its many manifestations, power is domination.

In contrast to his later explication of power, the equation of power and domination means at least two things. First, at this stage, the fateful connection between power and knowledge has not yet been discovered. Power simply suppresses what society wants to hide. Madness is tamed progressively through the Renaissance and the classical age. Untamed madness, which Foucault sees in art of the late Middle Ages, increasingly becomes isolated and suppressed.[21] The force of power is exhausted in repression. Second, Foucault is interested almost exclusively in how the laws and institutions of the state accomplished this repression of the experience of madness.[22] It is not that the state employed its power, especially the power to confine, infrequently. Foucault points out the astonishing statistic that, within a few months of the opening of the Hôpital General, about 1 percent of the Parisian population had been confined. Power indeed widened the reach of its tentacles with the advent of confinement.[23] But Foucault does not pay attention, at this point, to the systems of thought that might have served as a support to this burgeoning mode of control. Nor

[19] Dreyfus and Rabinow, *Michel Foucault,* 4.

[20] Foucault, "Truth and Power," 115. An excellent and detailed treatment of Foucault's earlier work from the standpoint of the themes that will be central to Foucault's later work on power is in Peter Miller, *Domination and Power* (New York: Routledge & Kegan Paul, 1987), 97–158, although Miller's "reading back" into these sources sometimes tends to obscure the differences between Foucault's various phases. It is one thing to suggest that Foucault already had resources that would enable him to develop his theory of power, and another to assert that his later thought was present all along. It is not quite clear which view Miller supports (see esp. pp. 194–96), but the second is not defensible.

[21] Foucault, *Madness and Civilization,* 24–37.

[22] This applies equally to what Foucault has to say about social practices in *Birth of the Clinic.* There too his focus is on the laws of the state as constitutive of the material conditions for the possibility of clinical medicine (pp. 22–85). The assertion in Miller (*Domination and Power,* 136) that it is "not to 'the State' that Foucault looks to account for the emergence of a politics of health," is deceptive, since Miller purports to be presenting the argument of the *Birth of the Clinic,* while his evidence for this claim comes from the 1976 interview, "The Politics of Health in the Eighteenth Century."

[23] Foucault, *Madness and Civilization,* 38.

does he cast his glance at actors outside the framework of the state and its institutions.

Foucault's point of view does not change a great deal for some time. In the archaeological period, there is little or no explicit reflection on the issue of power. When, through Nietzsche, the genealogical method begins to be formed, however, there are shifts in Foucault's perspective on power. In the early 1970s, there are three important developments.[24]

First, the pivotal relation of knowledge and power is discovered. Knowledge is recognized as an instrument of power; knowledge "is not made for understanding; it is made for cutting." Moreover, Foucault now understands the archaeology of knowledge, which had focused on discontinuity rather than continuity in describing the history of thought and its conditions, as in some sense a history of power. An event in history in general, and in the history of knowledge in particular, "is not a decision, a treaty, a reign, or a battle, but the reversal of a relationship of forces, the usurpation of power, the appropriation of a vocabulary turned against those who had once used it, a feeble domination that poisons itself as it grows lax, the entry of a masked 'other.'"[25] This is as much Foucault's interpretation of Nietzsche as it is Foucault himself, but it is clear from Foucault's own constructive work that he affirms the association of knowledge and power, if not the valorization of power he finds in Nietzsche.

Second, Foucault begins to give the body a place within a theory of power. The "descent" into genealogy also involves a descent into the body;[26] thus Foucault notes in passing in his interpretation of Nietzsche that domination "establishes marks of its power and engraves memories on things and even within bodies."[27]

These are only anticipatory fragments of a developing theory of power. Even though Foucault has found a connection between power and knowledge, their relationship has not been clarified adequately. The link between power and the body is not explicated at all; mention of the body's relation to power occurs only perfunctorily; and power is still repressive domination. Foucault interprets Nietzsche as claiming, "only a single drama is ever staged in this 'non-place,' the endlessly repeated play of dominations."[28] This is not only Nietzsche's view of power; it is also Foucault's.[29] Although he locates the

[24] An excellent discussion of Foucault's understanding of power and its relation to his genealogical method is found in Barry Smart, *Foucault, Marxism and Critique* (London: Routledge & Kegan Paul, 1983), 73–91.

[25] Michel Foucault, "Nietzsche, Genealogy, History," trans. Donald F. Bouchard and Sherry Simon, in *Language, Counter-Memory, Practice: Selected Essays and Interviews,* ed. Donald F. Bouchard (Ithaca, N.Y.: Cornell University Press, 1977), 154.

[26] Foucault, "Nietzsche, Genealogy, History," 147.

[27] Ibid., 150.

[28] Ibid.

[29] See, among other pieces, Michel Foucault, "On Popular Justice: A Discussion with Maoists," trans. John Mepham, in *Power/Knowledge,* 26.

penal system as the place in which power is most purely power,[30] this means only that the penal system is where domination is the most prevalent:

> What is fascinating about prisons is that, for once, power doesn't hide or mask itself; it reveals itself as tyranny pursued into the tiniest details; it is cynical and at the same time pure and entirely "justified," because its practice can be totally formulated within the framework of morality. Its brutal tyranny consequently appears as the serene domination of Good over Evil, of order over disorder.[31]

Foucault will later modify this simple equation between power and repressive domination and will assert that power is not simply repressive and negative, but productive. But he has not yet made this move, primarily because the lock that secures knowledge to power remains vague. Foucault already holds that knowledge is an instrument of power. One might say that for Foucault knowledge is "ideological." But as Marxism has shown, to see knowledge as ideological is consistent with a conception of power as repressive domination. In "Nietzsche, Genealogy, History," knowledge is understood as awaiting its capture by one power or another. Power turns knowledge into its instrument, but the knowledge that is forced into service by power exists, for the most part, before its violent appropriation.[32] It is exactly this preexistence of knowledge in relation to power that Foucault challenges in *Discipline and Punish;* that challenge in turn forces him to reevaluate the equation of power and repressive domination.

There is a third shift in Foucault's early view of power that continues through most of the rest of his career and is substantially in place prior to the groundbreaking work of *Discipline and Punish*. Already in the early 1970s, Foucault realizes that theories and analyses of power cannot be restricted to theories and analyses of the state. The long arm of power cannot be restricted to the long arm of the law of the state. Indeed, the law's arm appears scrawny when compared to the massive and deepening interventions of power. In a discussion in 1972, Foucault wrestles with this problem:

> Isn't this difficulty of finding adequate forms of struggle a result of the fact that we continue to ignore the problem of power? After all, we had to wait

---

[30] Michel Foucault, "Intellectuals and Power," in *Language, Counter-Memory, Practice,* 210.

[31] Ibid.

[32] Foucault does suggest something closer to his later position when he remarks that knowledge is "made for cutting." But this is an isolated comment, and when Foucault discusses this claim, he handles it in such a way as to remove its possibilities. In short, his discussion concerns the appropriation of knowledge rather than its creation. There are, of course, material components of the development of certain kinds of knowledge, which are outlined in the case of clinical knowledge in *Birth of the Clinic,* 22–85 (*Naissance de la clinique,* 21–86). But power's provision of certain conditions for knowledge is not the same thing as power's direct creation of knowledge, as Foucault's disregard of social practices and state power after the fifth chapter of *Birth of the Clinic* shows.

until the nineteenth century before we began to understand the nature of exploitation, and to this day, we have yet to fully comprehend the nature of power. It may be that Marx and Freud cannot satisfy our desire for understanding this enigmatic thing which we call power, which is at once visible and invisible, present and hidden, ubiquitous. Theories of government and the traditional analyses of their mechanisms certainly don't exhaust the field where power is exercised and where it functions . . . . We know that it is not in the hands of those who govern.[33]

Foucault has become aware that power is not exclusively, or even primarily, in the hands of the state and its functionaries. Although the social analyses that would make this hypothesis convincing had not yet been done, Foucault has already assumed the ubiquity of power.

This brings us to *Discipline and Punish*. Until then, Foucault retained a concept of power that took power to be repressive domination. The mechanics of power, particularly the mechanism of the body, which later take center stage, have advanced from nonissues to passing comments. On the other hand, Foucault has prepared the way for dramatic shifts in each of these positions. He has begun to understand the relation of knowledge and power, and when that connection is spelled out more fully, power begins to look much more productive. He has already posited the ubiquity of power, which both severs the identity between theories of power and theories of the state and makes the mechanics of power a more interesting and important phenomenon.

Discipline and Punish is the most convenient benchmark upon which to locate the fruition of a truly different theory of power. It is here that Foucault develops an understanding of power that will be changed only under the pressure of an issue apparently external to power—the question of the subject. Our treatment of Foucault from approximately *Discipline and Punish* to *The Will to Know* will be a thematic one rather than a repetition of the histories provided by Foucault.

However, a question preliminary to that discussion concerns the status of these histories in relation to a theory of power. Foucault presents two apparently conflicting alternatives. For Foucault, the history of penality is in some sense the archetypal history of power; there power reveals itself unconcealed. Similarly, the histories of sex and sexuality are privileged because in them the model of power as repression and law seems to find its most persuasive instance.[34] Against this orthodoxy, a new *theory* of power must be discovered.[35] There is already a difficulty, however. To speak of archetypes seems to begin to pick the pocket of essentialism. But it is a central methodological principle of genealogy that a systematic impulse makes history into

---

[33] Foucault, "Intellectuals and Power," 212–13.
[34] Foucault, *History of Sexuality* 1:90 (*Histoire de la sexualité, 1,* 119).
[35] Ibid. 1:90–91 (Fr. 119–20).

a continuous whole and loses the specificity of each single event.[36] A theory of power makes the mechanics of power invisible, and it is these mechanics that must be analyzed in order to see how power has taken hold, and more, how it can be resisted.[37] Unitary theories oppose genealogical analyses.[38] The methodological restriction to treatments of mechanisms and strategies of power makes Foucault a nominalist in regard to power.[39]

It is not necessary to resolve this tension completely now. Foucault himself comes to a different opinion later in his career. If he remained a nominalist in regard to power, this proved possible only because he became an ontologist elsewhere. At this point, however, Foucault thinks that genealogy and unitary theory are mutually exclusive alternatives for thought. The brilliance of Foucault's discussions of power lies in his exposure of the subtle and not-so-subtle mechanisms and strategies of power in their specificity. Foucault's genealogical method bears an immense harvest, but how does he know which phenomena to choose, which phenomena are instances of power? Foucault chooses instances on the basis of a preexisting conception of the nature of power in general. He operates with an implicit theory of power and then proceeds to elucidate an opposition between genealogical histories and theory which would lead one to believe that this could not have been his procedure. Foucault can discover how power operates precisely because he already has a sense of what power is.

Why then are genealogy and theory so radically opposed? For Foucault, the answer is that theory implies a staticity that obscures the turbulences of history. Theory stabilizes; genealogy shakes and rattles that stability. This presumed opposition has implications for an analysis of power. For Foucault, "theories of power" are theories that understand power in a particular way. Theory is unitary in two senses.[40] There is unity both in a systematic view of the phenomenon under consideration and in the mechanisms which operate that phenomenon. Foucault does not distinguish between the two. The second unity seems to be an inevitable consequence of the first. However, the first type of unity, the systematicity of viewpoint, is a presupposition common

[36] Foucault, "Nietzsche, Genealogy, History," 146, 154; idem, "Truth and Power," 114; idem, "Two Lectures," 78–80.

[37] Foucault believes that power is tolerable only if it masks itself. The implication is that if power were stripped of disguise, resistance would follow. See History of Sexuality 1:86 (Histoire de la sexualité, 1, 113).

[38] Foucault, "Two Lectures," 81–92.

[39] Foucault, History of Sexuality 1:93 (Histoire de la sexualité, 1, 123).

[40] Foucault, "Two Lectures," 83–87. At one point, Foucault suggests that the theoretical enterprise of genealogy might be able to avoid this problem. Genealogy's claim to be a theory might be justified because it entertains "the claims to attention of local, discontinuous, disqualified, illegitimate knowledges against the claims of a unitary body of theory which would filter, hierarchize and order them in the name of some true knowledge and some arbitrary idea of what constitutes a science and its objects." Genealogy, therefore, because of its intrinsic pluralism, can claim to be a superior theory. This is why Foucault lays such emphasis on "local knowledges" and resistance.

both to Foucault's own "definition" of power as a relation between forces and to the theories he criticizes.

The second tendency to unity, though, is of a different nature, despite Foucault's tendency to conflate the two. It attempts to localize power within a particular type of institutional mechanics, namely, the institution of the state and the mechanism of law. It is therefore in this second sense rather than the first that a unitary view of power conceals and masks the multivalent exercises, strategies, and mechanisms of power. It conceals the "event" by positing a smooth contour in which all events disappear.[41] Foucault has already abandoned the most important implication of this unitary understanding of power, the positing of power as an occasional phenomenon. His emphasis on the omnipresence of power continues in the period under consideration.[42]

The philosophical uses of this intuition of the omnipresence of power now are specified much more precisely. Three related aspects of this specification are relevant: (1) the philosophical and historical grounds of the exercise of power; (2) Foucault's shift from the traditional (and also Nietzschean) inquiry centered on the "who" of power to one concentrated on the "how" of power; (3) Foucault's description of the emergence of a depth to the interventions of power. The first two points combine to show that sovereignty theory disguises the breadth of power in the contemporary world, and the problem of depth will lead into the pivotal claims of power's relation to knowledge, the subject, and the body.

The Breadth of Power

If one compares our situation with that in which sovereignty theories of power were put forward, and were appropriate, one must first recognize that the basis of the exercise of power has changed. When sovereignty theory was asserted, the ground of the exercise of power lay primarily in the notion of right. Reflection about power centered on the notion of offense against royal power, which came into play when the dignity or right of the sovereign was attacked. In contract theory's opposition and defeat of monarchial theories of power in western Europe, the attack that justified interventions of power was one against society rather than against the sovereign. Still, contract and monarchial theories of power have the same essential root. In the former, the contract defines the acceptable range of power's exercises.[43] Power—at least legitimate power—is occasional.

---

[41] Michel Foucault, "Questions of Method: An Interview with Michel Foucault," *Ideology and Consciousness* 8 (1981): 6.

[42] Foucault, *Discipline and Punish*, 293–308 (*Surveiller et Punir*, 300–315); *History of Sexuality* 1:93 (*Histoire de la sexualité, 1,* 122).

[43] Foucault, "Two Lectures," 88–95. The bondage of the theory of power to notions of the

Historically, the relative infrequency of the exercise of power is demonstrable. However brutal the mechanics of torture of those offending the sovereign's dignity were, they were at least relatively rare. The body of the sovereign was offended by criminality, and the sovereign had a right and an obligation to inscribe the marks of his power upon the condemned. Until at least the middle of the eighteenth century, the exercise of power in France occurred as the spectacle of a battle in which the criminal was defeated by the infinite power of the sovereign.[44]

By the end of that century, however, objections to torture became increasingly strident. It was argued that torture was inhumane. The protest of the reformers against torture "was first formulated as a cry from the heart or from an outraged nature. In the worst of murderers, there is one thing, at least, to be respected when one punishes: his 'humanity.'"[45] This is the thunder, though not yet the rain, of the invasion of power upon and into the soil it simultaneously creates — the human subject. That is a topic to which we will return. Another objection to the method of torture and the staged battle between sovereign and condemned was that it was an inherently irregular means of exacting punishment. This was, in fact, the major concern of the reformers: "What they were attacking in traditional justice, before they set out the principles of a new penality, was certainly the excessive nature of the punishments; but an excess that was bound up with an irregularity even more than with an abuse of the power to punish."[46] The reformers aimed their arrows at several targets: at gaps in the law itself and at irregularity in its administration. The reformers sought to broaden the definition of illegality, so as to reduce the tolerated forms of popular illegality, and to make the system uniform. This was related to a third variance, which defines the reformers as essentially bourgeois. There was, owing to the superabundance of the monarch's power, inconstancy in who was to be subject to the law.[47] It is here that we see a decisive shift in the basis for the analysis of power. A contest developed between the absolute power of the sovereign and a more "generalized" power: the power of the "social body."[48] The significance of this alteration should not be overestimated, however. The question common to both is still this: Who has the right to punish and to set the bounds of punishment? Finally, an irregularity in the correspondence between crime and punishment had to be remedied. Instead of a sporadic application of punishment to the offender, punishment

---

"right" to power is also present in Marxism, and Foucault's opposition to Marxism goes hand in hand with his rejection of this basis of power.

[44] Foucault, *Discipline and Punish*, 47–73 (*Surveiller et Punir*, 59–77).

[45] Ibid., 74 (Fr. 76).

[46] Ibid., 78 (Fr. 80).

[47] Ibid., 82–89 (Fr. 84–91).

[48] Ibid., 90 (Fr. 92).

must become certain and swift. The tie between the crime and its punishment must become like "a mathematical truth."[49]

What holds these seemingly diverse changes together, so that Foucault can claim that they belong to a common, although brief, era is that the power to punish was generalized.[50] The aim was to make punishment more regular, and this involved an extension of the field of punishment. Irregularity is also a limitation of scope, and the inconsistency of law partly excluded economic offenses from the field of crime. Thus, the elimination of irregularity extended the field of acts that were subject to law. The regularization of administration and the theoretical placement of power within the hands of the social body were designed, in large part, to eliminate the exemption of certain individuals from the law. The elimination of gaps simultaneously extended the field of population subject to the law. Finally, designing punishment as both swift and sure, as an equation between crime and punishment, meant that punishment was represented even to those who had not violated the law but nonetheless might do so. The power to punish not only represented the social body; it was also represented *to* the social body and aimed at preventing the repetition of illegality.[51] In all of these programs, the range of power has expanded.

But power has not yet become ubiquitous, in Foucault's view; it has not yet reached its full depth or breadth. In its most general features, it is the carceral diagram that extends the breadth of intervention begun earlier. Increasing surveillance becomes the hallmark of an age to which we still belong, and which finally merits the title "the carceral age."

In addition, power attempts to guard itself from interference, to become total in its own locale of exercise. Indeed, despite Foucault's reluctance to reflect on the "nature" of power, attempts to "efface all disturbance"[52] characterize power's aim even in the age of the sovereign, albeit with mixed success. Problems of order and chaos troubled the reformers who opposed torture. The spectacle of the scaffold at times created public disorder. The enactment of the battle between the sovereign and the condemned sometimes ended without the vindication of the sovereign's power. This was, for power, intolerable.[53] Similarly, the representation of morality to the social body in the processions of the chain gangs could create both sympathy within the social body for the criminal and a certain reveling in the role of criminal by the offenders themselves.[54]

---

[49] Ibid., 97 (Fr. 100).

[50] The title of the chapter in which these shifts are outlined is, naturally enough, "Generalized Punishment" (*Discipline and Punish*, 73; *Surveiller et Punir*, 75).

[51] Foucault, *Discipline and Punish*, 93–94 (*Surveiller et Punir*, 96).

[52] Michel Foucault, "The Life of Infamous Men," in *Power, Truth, Strategy*, ed. Meaghan Morris and Paul Patton (Sydney: Feral Publications, 1979), 81.

[53] Foucault, *Discipline and Punish*, 59–65 (*Surveiller et Punir*, 63–68).

[54] Ibid., 257–63 (Fr. 261–67).

Disorder is a means of resisting power and is truly what power in the West has been at pains to eliminate. So punishment, in response to public disorder, becomes increasingly secretive. Power tries to hide itself. In the history of punishment, power's desire to conceal itself created the complete and autonomous institution of the prison.[55] The autonomy of the prison is designed to shield power from review and to prevent public disorder (i.e., resistance) from interfering with punishment. Viewed in this way, power increases to the extent that it removes resistance to its work. Foucault believes he has answered the question posed early on:

> How is it that, in the end, it was the third [modality of punishment, the carceral] that was adopted? How did the coercive, corporal, solitary, secret model of the power to punish replace the representative, scenic, signifying, public, collective model? Why did the physical exercise of punishment (which is not torture) replace, with the prison that is its institutional support, the social play of the signs of punishment and the prolix festival that circulated them?

One of the reasons is power's tendency to eliminate its opposition. The field of power has expanded in society at large and tries to become total in the autonomous institution: "in penal justice, the prison transformed the punitive procedure into a penitentiary technique; the carceral archipelago transported this technique from the penal institution to the entire social body,"[56] including, but not restricted to, societies for moral reform, institutions for the care of children, and even the family.

This ubiquitous expanse of power leads Foucault to the second revision in an analysis of power. Sovereignty theory studies particular objects — not the mechanisms of power but its employers. As power becomes broader in scope, more total and unopposed, however, its nature changes and makes the question of the "who" of power less important.[57] The mechanics of power detach from the state. In the extension of the range of power by means of surveillance, and particularly the alliance of criminal informants with the police, it can no longer be said that the state exercises surveillance.[58] In fact, the import of these means of surveillance is precisely their secrecy. Those who are being watched are unaware of it, but they must be suspicious of it. There need not

---

[55] Ibid., 237 (Fr. 239–40).

[56] Ibid., 131, 298 (Fr. 134, 305).

[57] The primacy of the sovereign should not be taken to imply that the mechanics of power are irrelevant even when sovereign power is at its height. In "Life of Infamous Men" (pp. 83–89), Foucault supplements his discussion of *Discipline and Punish* with reflections on the mechanics of power between 1660 and 1760. The importance of power mechanics is due to the need for the sovereign whose power was to be vindicated to become aware of situations calling for power's employment. Thus, the concentration of political theory on the user of power was always somewhat disingenuous.

[58] Foucault, *Discipline and Punish*, 280–83 (*Surveiller et Punir*, 285–89). An alliance is born between the observed and those who do the observing.

be, in fact, a watcher; the potentially watched must watch themselves.[59] Within the total and autonomous institution of the prison, the diagram of the Panopticon reveals this strategy of power.[60] Again, surveillance is anonymous. The prisoner subject to the gaze of the tower does not and cannot know precisely when it focuses on him or her. The threat of constant and invisible surveillance removes the need to actually watch the subject constantly—the anonymity and omnipresence of the mechanism turns surveillance into auto-surveillance.

The anonymity of surveillance increases in yet another way. Not only may the watcher be no one; it may be anyone. Who watches is relatively unimportant. What is important is the mechanism that makes this surveillance possible; the mechanism is designed so that anyone may watch.[61] In carceral institutions and carceral society generally, power's "how" becomes infinitely more important than the "who" of power.[62]

The impact of this shift in emphasis toward the mechanisms and strategies of power is momentous. For Foucault, what is now clear is that power can no longer be conceived as descending from the top of society and spreading downward into society. A pyramid, or "trickle-down" effect, of power is a feature of sovereignty theory's view of power, and it is simply wrong. The law that descends from the state's powerful few remains, to be sure, an aspect of power[63]—but hardly the only one or even the most important one. The true character of power in a carceral society, or in a society of confession,[64] is a power that comes from below, not above. The "who" of power is increasingly vague; power is exercised by anonymous technicians. It is no longer in the control of those whom sovereignty theory considers to be powerful. In the case of crime and punishment, which is only one example of the expanse of power,[65]

---

[59] Foucault, "The Eye of Power," 155; *Discipline and Punish*, 201 (*Surveiller et Punir*, 201–2).

[60] The term "diagram" is borrowed from Deleuze (*Foucault*, 34–44) and is distinguished from a mechanism on one side and metaphor on the other. The diagram lacks the form of the mechanism and contains a materiality the metaphor does not. It is "a map, . . . an abstract machine" (p. 34).

[61] Foucault, *Discipline and Punish*, 201 (*Surveiller et Punir*, 201–2).

[62] Foucault, "Two Lectures," 92–97. Whatever other alterations there are in Foucault's thought, this emphasis on mechanics remains constant, at least until the work surrounding the second volume of *History of Sexuality*. For Foucault's assertion of this basic continuity, see Foucault, "Questions of Method," 4.

[63] Foucault, "Truth and Power," 122.

[64] Foucault, *History of Sexuality*, vol. 1; idem, "The Confession of the Flesh," trans. Colin Gordon, in *Power/Knowledge*, 213–17.

[65] An especially interesting example of widening power, not originally related to punishment, is the early meaning of "police": "Royal power had asserted itself against feudalism thanks to the support of an armed force and by developing a judicial system and establishing a tax system. These were the ways in which royal power was traditionally wielded. Now, 'the police' is the term covering the whole new field in which centralized political and administrative power can intervene. . . . In short, life is the object of the police: the indispensable, the useful, and the superfluous" (Michel Foucault, "Politics and Reason," in *Politics, Philosophy, Culture: Interviews and Other Writings, 1977–1984*, trans. Alan Sheridan and others, ed. Lawrence D. Kritzman [New York:

sovereignty theory asserts that those at the top of the judicial process, the judges, are the ones "in power." Foucault is eloquent in his argument for the opposite thesis:

> the carceral system . . . had a whole series of effects: the internal dislocation of the judicial power or at least of its functioning; an increasing difficulty in judging, as if one were ashamed to pass sentence; a furious desire on the part of the judges to judge, assess, diagnose, recognize the normal and abnormal and claim the honor of curing or rehabilitating. In view of this, it is useless to believe in the good or bad consciences of judges, or even of their unconscious. Their immense "appetite for medicine" which is constantly manifested . . . expresses the major fact that the power they exercise has been "denatured."[66]

If the judges have lost their power, the power to judge has not been lost; on the contrary, it is exercised universally:

> But, conversely, if the judges accept having to condemn for the sake of condemning more and more uncomfortably, the activity of judging has increased precisely to the extent that the normalizing power has spread. Borne along by the omnipresence of the mechanisms of discipline, basing itself on all the carceral apparatuses, it has become one of the major functions of our society. The judges of normality are present everywhere. We are in the society of the teacher-judge, the doctor-judge, the educator-judge, the "social worker"-judge; it is on them that the universal reign of the normative is based; and each individual, wherever he finds himself, subjects to it body, gestures, behaviors, aptitudes, achievements. The carceral network, in its compact or disseminated forms, with its systems of insertion, distribution, surveillance, observation, has been the greatest support, in modern society, of the normalizing power.[67]

The locus of power has changed; it no longer starts at a single point at the top and moves downward but is exercised locally and diffusely.[68] Moreover, this local, diffuse power entraps those usually considered to be at the apex of the pyramid of power. An analysis of power confined to the traditional model in fact misses the most important, because omnipresent, exercises of power.[69] To understand power in terms of sovereignity in contemporary society does little more than conceal the activity of power.

Routledge, Chapman & Hall, 1988], 80–81). See also Michel Foucault, "Governmentality," *Ideology and Consciousness* 6 (1979): 9–10.

[66] Foucault, *Discipline and Punish*, 304 (*Surveiller et Punir*, 310–11). With respect to the "inward" question of conscience, it is remarkable that Habermas (*Philosophical Discourse of Modernity*, 274) insists on forcing a Weberian definition of power upon Foucault and then criticizes Foucault for borrowing such a definition from philosophies of the subject. Such an intentional concept of power, however, is exactly what Foucault attacks, not what he upholds. An interesting comparison of Foucault and Weber is contained in Smart, *Foucault, Marxism and Critique*, 123–37.

[67] Foucault, *Discipline and Punish*, 304 (translation modified; *Surveiller et Punir*, 311).

[68] The "disciplinary technologies" outlined in *Discipline and Punish*, 170–94 (*Surveiller et Punir*, 172–96) are among many examples of this.

[69] Foucault, "Truth and Power," 122.

The Depth of Power

The expansion of the range of power is but one of the effects of a policy of incarceration. Carceral society achieves its real fruition, its evil genius, less in its insatiable appetite for range than in its thirst for depth. Power plants itself in a soil that it has helped create—the soil of the subject—and a tiller of this soil, a mechanism of power's depth, is knowledge. A complex of issues arises at this point. The history of the depth of power involves the subject, knowledge in the human sciences, and the body. We begin with the latter.

When punishment was exacted through torture, the object of punishment was obviously the body, which was crushed and destroyed. Sovereign power was inscribed indelibly on the body.[70] Moreover, the power of the sovereign was, as a whole, based on the ubiquity of the body of the king.[71] But one of the protests of the reformers was against the "inhumanity" of torture. The body of the sovereign loses its importance. The principle of punishment is no longer the protection of the body of the sovereign but the attempt to make punishment a legible sign of the crime. There should be, it was argued, a direct correspondence between punishment and crime. Crime ought to be represented by its punishment. This seems to reduce the emphasis upon the bodies of the sovereign and the criminal. This is only partially true. Punishment, with this new emphasis on the reciprocal representation of crime and punishment, may aim at the "soul" of the members of the social body,[72] but the shift away from the individuality of the bodies of sovereign and offender is a qualified one. The scheme of the punitive city, which serves as the overarching symbol for the era of representative punishment, includes

> a functioning of penal power, distributed throughout the social space; present everywhere as a spectacle, sign, discourse; legible like an open book; operating by a permanent recodification of the mind of citizens; eliminating crime by those obstacles placed before the idea of crime; acting invisibly and uselessly on the "soft fibers of the brain," as Servan put it.[73]

The materiality of the body is hardly eliminated. It remains the indispensable means for making representations "readable" to society in general. Even the result is understood as a recodification of the physical fibers of the brain.

[70] Foucault, *Discipline and Punish*, 28–29 (*Surveiller et Punir*, 33–34).

[71] Foucault, "Life of Infamous Men," 87; see also Michel Foucault, "Body/Power," interview by editorial collective of *Quel Corps?*, in *Power/Knowledge*, 55.

[72] Foucault, *Discipline and Punish*, 104–15, 131 (*Surveiller et Punir*, 106–17, 134).

[73] Ibid., 130 (Fr. 133). This qualifier, which implies the presence of bodies in exercises of power, is not appreciated by Dreyfus and Rabinow (*Michel Foucault*, 147–51, 153), who view this second phase of power as relatively disembodied, perhaps because they associate too closely the exposition of representation in *The Order of Things* and that contained in *Discipline and Punish*. There is certainly a common theme in the two, but the body had become increasingly important to Foucault in the years after *The Order of Things*.

Carceral policy and the problematization of sex, both of which take hold in the nineteenth century, redirect themselves to bodies. It is not that either of these interventions of power claims to seek only the control of bodies. To the contrary, the creation of suppliant and useful bodies in carceral society aims at normalization of the body. The discourses of "reform" and "normalization" assert a result quite different from simple control of bodies. Similarly, attempts to create a normal sexuality, a normal use of the body, maintain that they liberate the whole person from repressive power. There is a reversal of sorts between the age of representation and the carceral age. The era of representation attempted to control the "soul" by means of its use of bodies. In the carceral age, however, the objective is to trap bodies within the claws of power, but power's tactic is indirect. Instead of the direct command of bodies, as in the age of torture, power proceeds to appropriate the body by means of knowledge's creation of the human subject.

We are at the threshold of the central problems of the subject and the relations of knowledge and power, but first we should emphasize the importance of the body to any theory of power. In Foucault's histories of power, the body plays a central role at every turn. It is also clear that the body, in order to be subordinated to power, must be made present to it. Even in the case of the anonymous surveillance of the Panopticon, in which power can be exercised by anyone or by no one, the need for presence does not disappear. At least the mechanism, the executor of power, must be present to the one being watched. The genius of power in the carceral age is that surveillance becomes continuous, at least potentially, so that there can be no escape from power. It is difficult to imagine the exercise of power without these twin features of the presence of power and the body. The only alternative would be a theory that defines power purely in terms of personal interiority, and such a theory would take one so far afield of the ordinary use of the word "power" as to be practically useless. From Foucault we receive, then, two limiting conditions of an adequate conception of power. Any reformulation of the idea of power must include the body and some account of power's presence.

Knowledge, Power, and the Subject

Two issues emerge: (1) the connection between knowledge and power, and (2) the mutual involvements of knowledge, power, and the subject. These two topics are inseparable from each other in Foucault, so that the distinction between them is only for convenience.

The innovation of the carceral age is more an extension of power's depth than of its breadth. Certainly, power became wider in scope also, but for the omnipresence of power to be realized, power had to be made deeper as well as wider.[74] This process of deepening involves, it appears, two aspects — a minute application of power and the engine of knowledge. In the first, the body itself is mechanized. The incredibly specific military drills for handling a weapon are an example of this phenomenon. But it is not mere mechanization; it is also an individualization of power. No longer is the soldier understood in terms of a rhetoric of honor. Instead, "by the late eighteenth century, the soldier has become something that can be made; out of a formless clay, the machine required can be constructed" through ever more specific modes of training. Power has become concentrated upon the minute movements of the individual soldier. What is created is a "'new micro-physics' of power."[75]

This microphysics is not, of course, confined to the military. It invades almost all spheres of social life — factories, schools, orphanages,[76] hospitals,[77] and finally, the family.[78] The disciplinary technologies that were developed aimed at making bodies docile and controllable, useful and productive, and above all, normal.[79] What should be produced by disciplinary technologies is, in modern terms, a collection of smoothly functioning and trouble-free robots. To be successful, what such technologies required was knowledge.

Two types of knowledge, it seems, an informational knowledge and a normative knowledge. Informational knowledge constitutes the individual as the perpetual object of knowledge.[80] Data must be gathered on those who are to be subject to "general formulas of domination."[81] Procedures for gathering information become the subject of investigation and refinement; reports on individuals become more extensive and more precise. In turn, the gathering of information requires the support of more sophisticated and complete methods of surveillance. The architectural designs of institutions are changed to satisfy the demands of this new knowledge/power.

Still, the gathering of information is in a way ineffectual. To gather information is not an exercise of power so much as a condition for its exercise. To make information truly a weapon of power, the second form of knowledge is needed — normative knowledge, which posits, unsurprisingly, a standard of normalcy. This type of knowledge is the target of Foucault's polemic against anthropology. Theories of the subject produce, Foucault argues, two kinds of subjects — the subject that the humanities claim they have

---

[74] This too is merely a schematic division. In fact, the two "dimensions" of power nourish and reinforce each other.

[75] Foucault, *Discipline and Punish*, 135, 139 (*Surveiller et Punir*, 137, 140).

[76] Ibid., 170–78 (Fr. 173–81).

[77] Foucault, "The Politics of Health in the Eighteenth Century."

[78] The careful observation to which children were subjected is outlined in *History of Sexuality* 1:38, 42 (*Histoire de la sexualité, 1*, 53, 57–58).

[79] Foucault, *Discipline and Punish*, parts 3 and 4 (*Surveiller et Punir*, 137–315).

[80] Ibid., 189–92 (Fr. 191–94).

[81] Ibid., 137 (Fr. 139).

discovered and the individual in subjection, which they have created really.[82] Anthropology posits a human condition in the most general terms[83] and then uses and is used by mechanisms of power (of which it is one) in order to produce a comprehensive vision of normalcy for each individual, a normalcy that excludes alternatives from any claim to scientific knowledge or truth.[84]

In the combination of these two types of knowledge, the network of knowledge and power reaches both its all-encompassing width and its most penetrating depth. Power and knowledge gain the ability not only to supervise but also to prescribe. For Foucault, there are many examples of the deadliness of the alliance between knowledge and power. One is the creation of child sexuality as a problem. The sexual habits of children are made problematic ostensibly in order to create "normal" children, but the requirement of parents and schools to supervise the habits of children reveals a different effect. The child's body is made a problem to be solved; the wall of silence around sex is created and then broken in order to impose a power of normalization, not in order to liberate the child. Another example of the conspiracy of knowledge/power is the "hysterization" of women's bodies, which is employed as a support and means for the discipline of women. It is true that sex is dragged from silence, after having first been silenced; discourse about sex has exploded.[85] However, its objective is not a liberating truth, but a disciplinary control:

> Whence the importance of the four great lines of attack [including the two mentioned above] along which the politics of sex advanced for two centuries. Each one was a way of combining disciplinary techniques with regulative methods. . . . Broadly speaking, at the juncture of the "body" and the "population," sex became a crucial target of a power organized around the management of life rather than the menace of death.[86]

It is hardly necessary to recall that this complex of power and knowledge is not restricted to a politics of sex; it includes virtually the entire range of the knowledge of the humanities. We live in a society of judges. What is judged and prescribed is normalcy, and the ubiquity of power is characterized by our inability to escape the panopticism of normalizing knowledge.

It is in this sense that Foucault's claim that power is productive, and not merely repressive, negative domination, must be understood. The "repressive hypothesis" understands power as that which opposes a liberating reason.[87] Theories of power as domination presuppose this basic opposition between

---

[82] Foucault, "Two Lectures," 97–98.

[83] For example, in the emerging science of sexuality, "sexuality" must be defined as being "by nature" in order to become accessible to a truth, which would in turn transmit the effects of power (*History of Sexuality* 1:68–69; *Histoire de la sexualité, 1,* 91–92).

[84] Foucault, "Two Lectures," 81–92.

[85] Foucault, *History of Sexuality* 1:17–42 (*Histoire de la sexualité, 1,* 25–58).

[86] Ibid. 1:146–47 (Fr. 193).

[87] Ibid. 1:36–49 (Fr. 50–67).

power and knowledge or reason. Foucault's reconceptualization of power as a productive phenomenon posits, on the contrary, an internal relation between knowledge and power. It is the productivity of power that makes it acceptable:

> If power were never anything but repressive, if it never did anything but to say no, do you really think one would be brought to obey it? What makes power hold good, what makes it accepted, is simply that it doesn't only weigh on us as a force that says no, but that it traverses and produces things, it induces pleasure, forms knowledge, produces discourse. It needs to be considered as a productive network which runs through the whole social body.[88]

It is not that knowledge is created only as a tool of power; it is not that, for example, "the human sciences emerged from the prison."[89] The creation of knowledge as an effect of power is certainly part of the story, but only a part. Power uses knowledge, but knowledge also employs and creates power.[90] It is impossible to determine which comes first; for Foucault, knowledge and power are copresent in the same matrix.[91] Any employment of knowledge produces effects in power, and vice versa. The two cannot exist without each other.[92] The key point is this: truth cannot be understood as if it exists, or could exist, outside of power.[93] The way of reason as an answer to power— because it would be external to power and therefore in the position of an impartial judge—is forever closed.[94] That way disguised power all along. If reason is to judge at all, and Foucault doubts that this is a legitimate possibility at this point in his career, it must judge from within its own involvement with power and must recognize its effects within power. The cord that allies power and knowledge cannot be cut.[95]

Now one of the truths that is created by the complex of power and knowledge is the notion of the subject. Foucault sees the subject as created historically by knowledge/power. It is not a discovery of philosophy or science but a product of, and a partner in, power. Foucault did not always think this. Early

---

[88] Foucault, "Truth and Power," 119.

[89] Foucault, *Discipline and Punish*, 305 (*Surveiller et Punir*, 312). Deleuze (*Foucault*, 31–33, 74) is correct to argue that discursive and nondiscursive practices lack the direct correspondence in their formation that would permit one to say that the human sciences were simply an effect of the prison. This is perhaps the crucial division between Foucault's viewpoint and a mode of thought which argues that discourse is simply the ideological justification of practices.

[90] Foucault, *Discipline and Punish*, 27 (*Surveiller et Punir*, 32).

[91] Foucault, "Prison Talk," 51; "Confession of the Flesh," 196.

[92] Foucault, "Prison Talk," 52; "Two Lectures," 93.

[93] Foucault, "Truth and Power," 131.

[94] Michel Foucault, "Why Study Power: The Question of the Subject," afterword to Dreyfus and Rabinow, *Michel Foucault*, 210.

[95] This is another reason for Foucault's separation from Marxism, which, particularly in the concept of ideology, does not recognize the cooperation of knowledge and power ("Truth and Power," 110). This suspicion of the notion of ideology also shows the distance Foucault has traversed in his thought. As late as 1972, he used the notion of ideology quite uncritically ("On Popular Justice"). For suggestions of the significance of Foucault's criticism for Marxism from within Marxist thought, see Smart, *Foucault, Marxism and Critique*.

in his career, there was a philosophical ground to the subject. Indeed, the prac-tices of exclusion of the insane were an attempt to suppress the Mirror and Other of madness residing in each of us.[96] The social process of confinement was both a cause and an effect of the effort to suppress this inner other. By the time of the archaeologies, Foucault dismisses this type of claim. Instead, he attempts to demonstrate that the subject was created in a certain ensemble of discourse.[97] In his third phase of thought, the emphasis shifts toward an effort to show how the creation of the subject in the discourse of truth has produced, simultaneously, subjects who are subject to power. The individual, says Foucault, "is not a pre-given entity which is seized on by the exercise of power."[98]

It is useless, therefore, to engage in the kinds of inquiries to which the presupposition of the ahistorical status of the subject directs one. It is not important, for example, to ask who exercises power. Nor is it important to ask about the good or bad intentions of those who exercise power. Power engulfs us all, and it does so because knowledge has made us believe in a sub-ject that will be liberated by more and more knowledge of that subject. Foucault returns to the question of the subject toward the end of his life and answers it quite differently. But two other matters still hover around the theory of power Foucault developed in the mid-1970s: the question of truth and meaning, and its consequences for the practical import of Foucault's understanding of power.

Truth and Practice

For Foucault, truth is a historical production. It is created by discourses that, on the one hand, claim the status of truth for themselves[99] and, on the other, disqualify the claim to truth in other knowledges, particularly local knowledges.[100] These discourses of truth are, moreover, both effects and pro-ducers of power. Power creates knowledge, and the assertion of the truth of knowledge is an exercise in and a condition of increasing power. Truth and power complement, generate, and sustain each other. Immediately, a problem arises. If the import of truth is reducible to its being a creator or an effect of power, how can Foucault claim any measure of truth for his own reflections?

[96] Foucault, *Madness and Civilization*, 277–78, 288–89.

[97] Foucault, *Order of Things*, 344–87.

[98] Michel Foucault, "Questions on Geography," interview by the editors of *Hérodote*, in *Power/Knowledge*, trans. and ed. Colin Gordon (New York: Random House, Pantheon Books, 1980), 74.

[99] In the contemporary world, the claim of knowledge to be "scientific" is the certification of its truth. That this view is alive and well, even in a fairly crude and unreflective form, is shown by the argument of Merquior (*Foucault*).

[100] Foucault, "Two Lectures," 82–84.

Put more precisely, can Foucault claim that his thought is anything more than yet another stage in a history of strategies of control?

In *Madness and Civilization,* there was, it appears, a truth of madness that could be uncovered if the layers hiding the experience of madness were stripped away. An opposition between true knowledge and power was taken for granted. In Foucault's archaeologies, the issue of power falls by the wayside, but the notion of truth is closely scrutinized. Foucault uncovers the historicity of the production of truth. In *The Order of Things,* Foucault analyzes the various historical complexes of truth, but none of these is either true or false; they are simply produced. His attitude to truth is, by and large, a playful one;[101] the seriousness with which people adhered to these views of the world, and especially their reasons for doing so, are suspended. The archaeological attitude lays bare the conditions for certain discourses of truth but steadfastly refuses to judge them as more or less true. Moreover, the play of discourses of truth is ultimately devoid of meaning; it has no significance outside of itself.

By the 1970s, Foucault has given up this playful attitude because it will not allow him to account for his own work. His productions would also be mere sign play, ultimately devoid of significance.[102] Moreover, why should he write at all? If the discourses of truth are meaningless, then an analysis of them is equally meaningless. The recovery of the primacy of social practices in Foucault's thought resolves this problem. Whether discourses of truth are true or not, they produce and condition power, and it is the power effects of truth that now come under Foucault's eye. At the level of a theory of truth, then, the discourses of truth are still without meaning, but at the level of social practices, they are terribly significant and meaningful.[103] The nondiscursive practices that had receded into the background in his archaeologies now reclaim Foucault's attention.

The unmasking of discourses of truth as instruments of power must be understood in order to be combatted. Foucault's vociferous protest against normalization implies that power must be understood not for knowledge's sake but to resist its encroachments. Local knowledges, the alternatives to totalizing knowledge, must be reinvented in order that they may resist

---

[101]   Ibid., 85–90. Foucault is not entirely playful, however, for he thinks *The Order of Things* lies on the threshold between the dissolution of modern thought and new possibilities for thought. If Foucault cannot provide such an alternative, he can at least help apply the wrecking ball to the decaying structure of modernity. His playfulness, therefore, is designed to show the incommensurate character of the thoughts of the past and therefore to deny the truth claims of the sovereign consciousness, tradition, and the like, upon which modern philosophy is based.

[102]   Dreyfus and Rabinow, *Michel Foucault,* 95. Again, Foucault's purpose is to move the process of decay in modern thought forward. The question that arises is why such a contribution is desirable in view of his understanding of truth.

[103]   This is especially clear in "Life of Infamous Men," 78, in which a self-consciously playful approach does not exclude the seriousness of the existential alterations on those affected by power.

totality.[104] The revalorization of these knowledges is a strategy designed to wage war on the dominant strategies of truth. The point is not to understand the world, nor even to change it; it is to resist it as far as knowledge claims to have grasped the world it created.[105]

The need to resist is why power, in this third stage, is conceived on the model of warfare. Foucault reverses Clausewitz's axiom that war is politics by other means. Instead, "power is war," and he sees "politics as sanctioning and upholding the disequilibrium of forces that was displayed in war."[106] An understanding of power based on a model of warfare accounts in part for Foucault's persistent references to power in terms of metaphors of the game.[107] Like wars, games are contests between strategies, struggles of mutual resistances. There is a crucial insight contained in this model. It is not true, despite Foucault's rather gloomy picture elsewhere, that power has succeeded in complete normalization. There are always resistances against power—the disciplinary society's program has not succeeded in creating a disciplined society.[108] Even in the carceral society, even in the prison, power is always battled with more or less frequency, intensity, and effectiveness. There are, in fact, "no relations of power without resistances."[109] Events of resistance are rendered invisible by sovereignty theory, which conceives of power as present only at the peak of the pyramid. Opposition to totalizing power is observable only when analysis descends to witness local and minute struggles against power.[110] These microstruggles are what genealogy is supposed to enable us to notice. Genealogies are, moreover, concrete weapons in such battles,[111] for they make visible the singularity of the event, breaking the self-evidence of discourses of truth, and therefore open the possibility of resistance to such discourses and to the nondiscursive practices to which the production of truth is linked.[112] Once again, the notion of power has been broadened; now an account of the fullness of power must include not only the aggressors but also the resisters, not only the attack of power but also the defense against it.[113]

104 Foucault, "Two Lectures," 81–92; "Intellectuals and Power."

105 Foucault, "Two Lectures," 85; "Truth and Power," 133; "Why Study Power," 211–12.

106 Foucault, "Two Lectures," 90; see also History of Sexuality 1:93 (Histoire de la sexualité, 1, 123).

107 See, e.g., Michel Foucault, "How Is Power Exercised?" afterword to Dreyfus and Rabinow, Michel Foucault, trans. Leslie Sawyer, 225.

108 Smart, Foucault, Marxism and Critique, 115.

109 Michel Foucault, "Power and Strategies," interview by editorial collective of Les révoltes logiques, in Power/Knowledge, 142.

110 Ibid., 142–45. It is false to suggest, as does Walzer ("Politics of Michel Foucault," 60), that Foucault hopes for or thinks possible a global "mega-resistance," which would be accomplished somehow independently of local victories. What would such grand resistance mean, and how would it be possible, without a local beginning? Even Walzer's example of factory revolts in the United States (p. 66) were local resistances before they were anything else.

111 Foucault, "Intellectuals and Power," 212–13.

112 Foucault, "Questions of Method," 6–14.

113 See also Elizabeth Janeway, Powers of the Weak (New York: William Morrow, 1980).

If Foucault's work is itself to be seen as an instance of knowledge/power, has the question of its status relative to resistance been resolved? In part, yes. It is at least clear that Foucault, at this point anyway, does not lay claim to possession of a knowledge that is external to power. Local knowledges are themselves bound to power. But there are still other difficulties with Foucault's affirmation of resistance.

To begin with, what are the criteria for determining whether any particular exercise of power/knowledge deserves resistance? Resistance is possible only from within another complex of power/knowledge. In the contest of two matrices, what allows one network to be affirmed against another? Foucault's answer, it appears, is that whichever knowledge is more normalizing and totalizing is the one that must be opposed,[114] a position that has been called into question by the increasing viciousness of the recent rise of local resistances worldwide. Foucault's response leads directly to another unresolved problem. He protests against normalizing power vehemently, but from what vantage point is this protest possible? Why does normalizing power merit resistance and opposition? Dreyfus and Rabinow put the question sharply:

> What is wrong with carceral society? Genealogy undermines a stance which opposes it on the grounds of natural law or human dignity, both of which presuppose the assumptions of traditional philosophy. Genealogy also undermines opposing carceral society on the basis of subjective preferences and intuitions (or posing certain groups as carriers of human values capable of opposing carceral society). What are the resources which enable us to sustain a critical stance?[115]

In short, in whose name can Foucault's critique of carceral society be launched? On what basis and with what tools can Foucault know that "power is tolerable only on the condition that it mask a substantial part of itself. Its success is proportional to its ability to hide its own mechanisms. Would power be accepted if it were entirely cynical? For it, secrecy is not in the nature of an abuse; it is indispensable to its operation"?[116]

This question ends the presentation of Foucault's theory of power in the mid-1970s. In the final years of his life, he will try to formulate an answer to the question of the ground of resistance. The line between the third and final stage is drawn by the long hiatus between the first and second volumes of *The History of Sexuality*. Although Foucault's suspicion of a depth hermeneutics of the subject continues until the end of his life, his opposition to every philosophy of the subject does not. It is Foucault's own attempt to "promote

---

[114] Foucault, "Intellectuals and Power," 208; Michel Foucault, "Revolutionary Action: 'Until Now,'" discussion with Michel Foucault under the auspices of *Actuel*, in *Language, Counter-Memory, Practice*, ed. Bouchard, 218–33.

[115] Dreyfus and Rabinow, *Michel Foucault*, 206; see also Habermas, *Philosophical Discourse of Modernity*, 280–84.

[116] Foucault, *History of Sexuality* 1:86 (*Histoire de la sexualité, 1*, 113).

new forms of subjectivity through the refusal of this kind of individuality which has been imposed on us for several centuries"[117] that will define, for us, those final years. The framework of the theory of power Foucault has outlined will be altered yet again, and the significance of power will be at once expanded and marginalized.

The Dance of Freedom

If the conception of power developed in and around *Discipline and Punish* and *The Will to Know* opens a variety of hitherto obscured relations of power, it remains troublesome in certain respects. Before proceeding to the late modifications in Foucault's thought, the difficulties with the view presented in the mid-1970s should be clarified. Many of these difficulties are noted by Foucault himself. No matter how self-assured his assertions seemed at almost every stage of his career, he remained flexible and self-critical. In addition, the direction Foucault began to follow toward the conclusion of his life was more a beginning than an end.

Foucault's mature theory of power, as it has developed up to now, is unclear on two important points. First, despite Foucault's claim that he is developing a theory that does not equate power and domination, power is still basically understood according to that model. If power is not domination per se but a relation of forces,[118] then at least the contest concludes in domination. The term "domination" persists in Foucault's descriptions of the results and uses of power. Foucault distinguishes his own thought from sovereignty theory on two grounds: (1) domination cannot be taken as a purely negative and repressive concept; it produces and is produced by knowledge; (2) domination is not a static condition.[119] Still, Foucault's description of social power in contemporary society is replete with the language of domination and control. These are the objectives of power. Moreover, this is not simply a historical description. In *The Use of Pleasure*, the ethical self-constitution of the individual is directed at self-mastery. When Foucault describes this in terms of power, he employs the terms "domination" and "control" regularly.[120] In distinguishing his own conception of power from sovereignty theory,

---

[117] Foucault, "Why Study Power," 216.

[118] For power as "relations of forces," see, e.g., Foucault, "Confession of the Flesh," 196.

[119] Michel Foucault, "The Ethic of Care of the Self as a Practice of Freedom," interview by Raúl Fornet-Betancourt, Helmut Becker, and Alfredo Gomez-Müller, in *The Final Foucault*, trans. J. D. Gauthier, ed. James Bernauer and David Rasmussen (*Philosophy and Social Criticism* 12, nos. 2–3 [1987]; reprint, Cambridge, Mass.: MIT Press, 1988), 3 (page references are to reprint edition); Michel Foucault, "L'ethique du souci de soi comme pratique de liberté," *Concordia* 6 (1984): 100–101.

[120] Michel Foucault, *The Use of Pleasure: Volume Two of the History of Sexuality*, trans. Robert Hurley (New York: Random House, Vintage Books, 1986), 80–81 (orig. *Histoire de la sexualité, 2: L'Usage des Plaisirs* [Paris: Éditions Gallimard, 1984], 93–94).

Foucault's definition of domination is simply very narrow. By the yardstick of a broader conception of domination as, perhaps, an attempt at ongoing control, Foucault's reformulation of power remains suspiciously close to the domination language of sovereignty theory. It is something to be feared and resisted, though it must also be used in that resistance. Foucault's musings that he is simply a permanent critic without constructive purpose (which would also be a purpose of power), express this ambivalence.[121] Power is dangerous, and Foucault's attitude toward its use is ambivalent at best.

A related point is the persistence of a description of power as inevitably a zero-sum game. Foucault denies that his view of power ends in such a consequence.[122] That assertion is based on the same basic premise as his claim to have avoided an understanding of power as domination. The quantity of available power is not finite; it can be increased without limit largely because of the alliance between power and knowledge.[123] To the extent that a zero-sum game means only this, Foucault is correct. He cannot be accused of posing such a view of power. But insofar as power is made analogous with war, insofar as it is described in terms of a game in which there are only winners and losers even after Foucault gives up the metaphor of war, Foucault remains trapped within a zero-sum framework. The fact that one side in a conflict can marshal more and more resources with which to oppress and dominate does not change the final objective. The aim is still victory, and in the conflicts Foucault describes, victory is not something both sides can have. The proximity of totality and resistance to their respective goals must vary inversely. To be sure, the balances of power are more volatile and variable in Foucault's version of the games of power than in many others', but the stubborn alternative of victor and vanquished has not changed.

If power is dangerous, if its balances must be worked out in terms of victory and defeat, and if, additionally, power is ubiquitous, it seems to follow that existence is a perpetual and meaningless battle. This is an intolerable alternative for Christian theology. It also turns out to be inadequate for Foucault. In the end, Foucault cannot but protest against the finality of this battle. He too discovers a principle of meaning which transcends this nihilistic conflict.

---

[121] The "anarchistic/nihilistic" implications of such a position are noted by Walzer, "Politics of Michel Foucault," 61–63. Foucault does not remain a permanent critic, however, at least in regard to self-creation.

[122] Foucault, "How Is Power Exercised?" 217.

[123] The influential essay of Talcott Parsons, "On the Concept of Political Power," *Proceedings of the American Philosophical Society* 107, no. 3 (June 1963; reprint, in *Power,* ed. Steven Lukes [New York: New York University Press, 1986]), has a similar solution to the problem of zero-sum power insofar as it a question of a fixed quantity of power. Like Foucault, Parsons maintains that power is not so limited but, like money, can be "invested" and therefore increased. Parsons, unlike Foucault, does not discuss the conflictual possibilities of the competition for such resources which, though not fixed absolutely, are not infinite either.

The Aesthetic Subject

The previous section ended with the question of the basis on which Foucault justifies resistance against totalizing power. When Foucault begins to formulate an answer, it is cast, surprisingly, in terms of the subject. Not in terms of a "deep" subject perhaps, but a subject nonetheless.[124] The implication of his work in the 1970s had been that, because the subject was constituted historically only in the last two centuries, it was described exhaustively in its association with power. By the early 1980s, however, a period marked by the publication of the next two volumes of *The History of Sexuality,* Foucault distinguishes the notion of the subject in general from the hermeneutic subject of desire. The "history of desiring man"[125] was a historical product, though its history begins much earlier than the nineteenth century, but it does not cover the entire domain of philosophies of the subject. It became necessary for Foucault to undertake a genealogy of the subject. Foucault describes his own career in this way:

> A theoretical shift had seemed necessary in order to analyze what was often designated as the advancement of learning; it led me to examine the forms of discursive practices that articulated the human sciences. A theoretical shift had also been required in order to analyze what is often described as the manifestations of "power"; it led me to examine, rather, the manifold relations, the open strategies, and the rational techniques that articulate the exercise of powers. It appeared that I now had to undertake a third shift, in order to analyze what is termed "the subject." It seemed appropriate to look for the forms and modalities of the relation to self by which the individual constitutes and recognizes the self as a subject.[126]

The object of analysis is now the subject's ethical self-constitution.

It is impossible not to notice the radical alteration of the philosophical question. Instead of an inquiry concentrated on the constitution of the subject from the outside (which effects both subjectivity and subjection), Foucault now seeks to understand how we may constitute, even "liberate,"[127] *ourselves* as subjects, and especially as ethical subjects. Some general features of the "new subjectivity" must be highlighted.

First, Foucault now believes that his reflections on power have been directed toward the genealogy of the subject: "the goal of my work during the last twenty years has not been to analyze the phenomena of power, nor

---

[124] Walzer predicted correctly that Foucault would have to adopt a more positive relation with the categories he criticized if he were to escape the position of permanent criticism ("Politics of Michel Foucault," 67). One of Foucault's earlier formulations of his direction is to say he is searching for a "political *spiritualité*" ("Questions of Method," 11).

[125] Foucault, *Use of Pleasure,* 6 (*Histoire de la sexualité, 2,* 12).

[126] Ibid. (translation slightly modified).

[127] On the latter, see "Politics and Reason," 85.

to elaborate the foundations of such an analysis. My objective, instead, has
been to create a history of the different modes by which, in our culture, human
beings are made subjects."[128]

Second, questions that arise in traditional treatments of the subject re-
appear. The intentions of the acting subject gain significance. Foucault's disdain
for this topic initially softens in his assertion that "people know what they
do; they frequently know why they do what they do; but what they don't
know is what what they do does."[129] In other words, action has consequences
that cannot be anticipated, effects beyond what the actor intends. In short,
action involves risk. But this is not equivalent to a debunking of the subject;
at worst, it only shreds the notion of the absolute, omniscient subject. It also
creates an opening for Foucault's work on ethical self-constitution. What has
been unlocked is the horizon of meaning.

It is now relevant to Foucault what actors intend; ethical constitution is
not a discontinuous process in the Greeks and the Romans. It involves an
aesthetic discipline that continues throughout the subject's entire life.[130] There
is a *telos,* an end, toward which the ethical life orients itself. To be sure, it may
be an aesthetic *telos* rather than a rule-governed supervision of action, but the
ethical life is not devoid of meaning.[131] The project of an "aesthetics of
existence"[132] is, in fact, a project of meaning creation.

There is, nonetheless, a danger, particularly in Greek ethics. Greek sexual
ethics were based in and entailed relations of domination — domination of the
self, certainly, but also domination of women, slaves, and boys. The latter group
of dominations becomes a special moral problem for the Greeks because the
moral judgment of the sexual act was based not on the nature of the act itself
but on the activity or passivity of the participants.[133] Although it was acceptable to dominate slaves and women because of their "intrinsic" passivity, the
boy was a difficult case, because his passivity in the sexual act carried with
it the danger of damaging his ability to become an active participant in the
government of the city in the future. Thus arose a complex practice of erotics
to combat this hazard. Even in posing the question of the love of boys in this

---

[128] Foucault, "Why Study Power," 208.

[129] Personal communication, cited in Dreyfus and Rabinow, *Michel Foucault,* 187.

[130] Michel Foucault, *The Care of the Self: Volume Three of the History of Sexuality,* trans. Robert
Hurley (New York: Random House, Pantheon Books, 1986), 58 (orig. *Histoire de la sexualité, 3:
Le souci de soi* [Paris: Éditions Gallimard, 1984]), 75).

[131] In fact, the temporal and teleological character of ethical conduct is one of the factors which
leads Foucault to conclude that an exclusive concentration on codes is in error (*Use of Pleasure,*
27–28; *Histoire de la sexualité, 2,* 34–36). The discourse of codes obscures the essentially temporal
nature of nondiscursive practices.

[132] Michel Foucault, "On the Genealogy of Ethics: An Overview of Work in Progress," in
Dreyfus and Rabinow, *Michel Foucault,* 231.

[133] Foucault, *Use of Pleasure,* 46–47, 215–25; *Histoire de la sexualité, 2,* 55–57, 237–48. It is not
true that the active, dominating role of male penetration first appears in the third volume of the
History of Sexuality, as Mark Poster claims ("Foucault and the Tyranny of Greece," in *Foucault: A
Critical Reader,* ed. Hoy, 220). See esp. *Use of Pleasure,* 220 (*Histoire de la sexualité, 2,* 242).

way—not to mention enforcing the inferior role of passivity upon women and slaves—"the Greek ethics of pleasure is linked to a virile society, to dissymmetry, exclusion of the other, an obsession with penetration, and a kind of threat of being dispossessed of your own energy, and so on. All that is quite disgusting!"[134] The close link between these seedier aspects of Greek sexual ethics and domination is not hard to uncover. The entire principle of moderation was, according to Foucault, tied to domination. Moderation was the means, a "freedom-power" by which the free Greek man remained free and, accordingly, produced a self-domination that qualified him to dominate others:

> What one must aim for in the agonistic contest with oneself and in the struggle to control [dominer] the desires was the point where the relationship with oneself would become isomorphic with the relationship of domination [domination], hierarchy, and authority that one expected, as a man, as a free man, to establish over his inferiors; and it was this prior condition of "ethical virility" that provided one with the right sense of proportion for the exercise of "sexual virility," according to a model of "social virility." In the case of male pleasures, one had to be virile with regard to oneself, just as one was masculine in one's social role. In the full meaning of the word, moderation was a man's virtue.

Moderation as ethical practice was as essentially male as immoderation was essentially feminine, deriving from passivity.[135]

In Roman culture, however, and especially in the Stoics, Foucault finds an aesthetic of existence that operates largely without uniform codes and also begins to incorporate principles of reciprocity. We need not follow Foucault's sympathetic treatment of this ethic, except to note the aspects he finds deserving of praise: the lack of a uniform, compulsory code; the reliance on an aesthetic rather than a rule-governed ethic; and an emerging reciprocity.[136] The looseness of the codification of pleasure and the trajectory of reflection toward an aesthetic ethic are two sides of the same coin. The secondary importance of the few codified elements in Artemidorus, for example, shows a primary concern "not with . . . the act and its regular or irregular form, but with . . . the actor, his way of being, his particular situation, his relation to others, and the position he occupies with respect to them." The chief subject of thought regarding pleasure is the "style of activity," the application of which produces a new "stylistics of existence." In this shift of emphasis, the order of value in carceral society is reversed:

> The movement of analysis and the procedures of valuation do not go from the act to a domain such as sexuality or the flesh, a domain whose divine,

---

134 Foucault, "On the Genealogy of Ethics," 233.

135 Foucault, Use of Pleasure, 83–86 (Histoire de la sexualité, 2, 97–99).

136 The increasing reciprocity characterizing relationships in Roman culture is due to increasing emphasis on the "shared existence" of the partners (Care of the Self, 78; Histoire de la sexualité, 3, 96). The change from Greek ethics is that marriage is now "interrogated as a mode of life whose value was not exclusively, nor perhaps even essentially, linked to the functioning of the oikos, but rather to a mode of relation between two partners" (Care of the Self, 80; Histoire de la sexualité, 3, 99). This theme is developed in depth in Care of the Self, 147–85 (Histoire de la sexualité, 3, 173–216).

civil, or natural laws would delineate the permitted forms; they go from
the subject as a sexual actor to the other areas of life in which he pursues
his activity.[137]

Not the externally imposed rule of conduct but the style of self-conduct stands
at the center of self-constitution.[138]

We have at last found that by which Foucault grounds his critique of normalizing power. It is aesthetic freedom, through which each person forms his
or her own subjectivity apart from the normalizing gaze of carceral society.
Foucault wants each person to become a work of art. "Why," he asks, "should
the lamp or house be an art object, but not our life?"[139] This aesthetic creation
is where meaning is made; accordingly, Foucault no longer is able to suspend
questions of meaning. He even returns, after a fashion, to Sartre, comment-
ing, "I think the only truly acceptable consequence of what Sartre has said
is to link his theoretical insight to the practice of creativity — and not of authen-
ticity. From the idea that the self is not given to us, I think that there is only
one practical consequence: we have to create ourselves as a work of art."[140]
Foucault maintains that one should care for the self in this sense of making
an aesthetic creation of oneself, and that care of the self is an affirmation and
an extension of freedom.[141] Subjectivity is constituted in a dance of freedom.

[137] Foucault, *Care of the Self*, 35–36, 71 (*Histoire de la sexualité, 3*, 49, 89). It is not that the aesthetic
element is absent in the Greeks; on the contrary, the emphasis on the use of pleasure produces
an art (*Use of Pleasure*, 57; *Histoire de la sexualité, 2*, 68). The difficulty of Greek ethics is again
that the art of existing is based on predetermined status and is therefore exclusive to free men
(*Use of Pleasure*, 59–62; *Histoire de la sexualité, 2*, 70–73).

[138] This distinction appears in *Use of Pleasure*, 26 (*Histoire de la sexualité, 2*, 33) as one of the
possibilities of moral constitution. This focus of Foucault's emerging ethic removes at least some
of the criticism directed against him. It simply misses Foucault's point to argue, as does Martin
Jay, that Foucault's critical impulse is undefended because he never developed an ethic ("In the
Empire of the Gaze: Foucault and the Denigration of Vision in Twentieth-century French Thought,"
in *Foucault: A Critical Reader*, ed. Hoy, 195–96). Although Jay's argument is far superior to a similar
demand on Foucault issued by Merquior (*Foucault*, 146–49), the call, in effect, is for Foucault
to develop a code of ethics. An attempt to do this would, however, contradict Foucault's entire
enterprise. An aesthetic ethic, he believes, forbids any universal claim of content applicable to
all, as Barry Smart notes ("The Politics of Truth and the Problem of Hegemony," in *Foucault:
A Critical Reader*, ed. Hoy, 166–68). One may criticize Foucault's argument, but one cannot simply
ignore it, as Jay tends to do. The source of the problem, again, seems to be in the attempt to
establish a reign of reason divorced from power.
      A slightly different criticism is posed by Poster ("Foucault and the Tyranny of Greece," 216–18),
who argues that *The Care of the Self* in particular shows a decline in Foucault's work because
he fails to give us a history of what ethical practices actually were for the Romans. But this is
exactly Foucault's point. Since "there was never a question of making [morality] an obligation
for all," it is "difficult to know who did participate in it" (Michel Foucault, "The Return of Morality,"
in *Politics, Philosophy, Culture*, ed. Kritzman, 245; orig., "Le retour de la morale," *Les Nouvelles*, 28
June 1984, 38).

[139] Foucault, "On the Genealogy of Ethics," 236.

[140] Ibid., 237.

[141] Foucault, "Care of the Self as a Practice of Freedom"; "Souci de soi comme pratique de
liberté." The liberty of self-care is also a liberty of thought for the philosopher ("Return of Morality,"
249; "Le retour de la morale," 40).

The vision is exhilarating. But what has happened to the question of power? Exactly at the point where Foucault takes up the history of ethical self-constitution prior to the strict imposition of normalizing and uniform codes, his theory of power is recast dramatically. Foucault finds a new locale of power to which he had not attended before—a power placed in relation to the rediscovered dimension of the subject.[142] But what of external, dominating power in Foucault's new vision of a stylistics of existence?

The Sublimation of Power

Power that imposes dominations from outside is deemphasized, inasmuch as this type of power is no longer final and definitive for the individual. It is present in Foucault's analysis of Greek ethics, but primarily as the seamy and dangerous side of that ethic. The power created by the self-constitution of the free man authorizes his dominion over all others, restricting their liberty and ability to constitute themselves as ethical subjects. But the self-constitution of the free man involves his own freedom—which is itself free from normalizing and dominating power. Free self-constitution is separated from, and opposed to, this type of power. Power must leave room for freedom in order to be power,[143] but there is no inversion of this principle. Freedom does not need power.

The simultaneous recession of external dominating power and the exaltation of free self-creation has two important consequences for a theory of power. To begin with, freedom is raised to the level of an ontological principle.[144] It is the inescapable precondition of human fulfillment. Freedom is

---

[142] In his final interview, Foucault says: "I tried to locate three major types of problems: the problem of truth, the problem of power, and the problem of individual conduct. These three domains can only be understood in relation to each other, not independently. What bothered me about the previous books is that I considered the first two experiences without taking the third one into account. By bringing to light this third experience, it seemed to provide a kind of guiding thread which, in order to justify itself, did not need to resort to somewhat rhetorical methods of avoiding one of the three fundamental domains of experience" ("Return of Morality," 243; "Le retour de la morale," 38).

[143] Foucault, "Care of the Self as a Practice of Freedom," 12–13; "Souci de soi comme pratique de liberté," 108–9.

[144] Foucault, "Care of the Self as a Practice of Freedom," 8; "Souci de soi comme pratique de liberté," 105. Deleuze (*Foucault,* 93, 118–32) finds several ontologies in Foucault, culminating in a new vitalism, but Deleuze comes to this conclusion in two especially odd ways. In the first place, he tends to ignore Foucault's writings concerning liberty. He lays little stress on the third volume of *History of Sexuality* and the interviews cited in this chapter. Second, the evidence for Foucault's vitalism is drawn primarily from his emphasis on life as an epistemological construct in *The Order of Things.* But to my knowledge Foucault never argues for "life" as any kind of ontological linchpin for his own thought; he does discuss an ontology of freedom. It is not that "life" and "liberty" are necessarily contradictory concepts, but if Foucault's interest in his later work can be said to be "life," it is a rarified version of life—not life in general so much as the life of

what makes humans human. Repudiating his earlier refusal of the existence of a "primal liberty,"[145] a denial tied to his opposition to philosophies of the subject, Foucault finds the unifying principle of his work in this discovery of the ontological status of freedom. It answers the questions of why the normalizing power of carceral society warrants resistance, and why it would be resisted were it known for what it is — totalizing power constricts liberty wantonly. In addition, the ontology of freedom provides a basis for assessing the importance of his archaeologies. The objective of archaeology, performed from the vantage point of sensing the dissolution of modern thought, is to "open the way to a future thought,"[146] to produce possibilities. Ironically, the justification of the value of new possibilities now discovers its root in the soil of the subject. Finally, if the aesthetics of self-constitution does not retrieve

---

freedom. Therefore, it would seem a better approach to begin with Foucault's treatment of human liberty before attempting to make the ontological generalization to "life." A good, albeit indirect, critique of organic vitalism, from a Foucault-influenced viewpoint, is James W. Bernauer, "Beyond Life and Death: On Foucault's Post-Auschwitz Ethic," *Philosophy Today* 32, no. 2 (Summer 1988): 128–42.

[145] See, e.g., "Power and Strategies," 142. The contrast is striking between the refusal of a primal liberty and the principle Foucault discovers in Epictetus: there the human is the "being destined to care for the self," and we are endowed with reason for the purpose of self-care (*Care of the Self*, 47 [translation slightly modified]; *Histoire de la sexualité, 3,* 61–62).

[146] Foucault, *The Order of Things,* 386; orig., *Les mots et les choses: une archéologie des sciences humaines* (Paris: Éditions Gallimard, 1966), 397–98. It is, in fact, only on the threshold of the disintegration of modern thought that any "archaeology of the present" can be conducted, as Alan Sheridan argues (*Michel Foucault: The Will to Truth* [London: Tavistock Publications, 1980]), 196). As the term "archaeology" indicates, an approach to its subject matter depends upon that matter being sedimented and settled in the past. It is therefore misleading for Deleuze to say, "archaeology does not necessarily refer back to the past. There is an archaeology of the present" (*Foucault,* 50). Strictly speaking, this is not true. *The Order of Things* asserts: "No doubt the Classical age was *no more able than any other culture to circumscribe or name its own general system of knowledge*" (p. 75, emphasis added, translation slightly modified; *Les mots et les choses,* 90). The questions of archaeology are asked only retrospectively (ibid.). Archaeological finds are placed on display in museums of truth. If it is possible to discover some items that are still contemporaneous with our culture in Foucault's museum, it is only because they have already become relics and no longer function usefully. Only if the force of a system of thought has dissipated is an archaeology of it possible.

The introduction of a genealogical approach produces the opening for a "history of the present" (*Discipline and Punish,* 31; *Surveiller et Punir,* 35). Foucault's reflections on the meaning of this phrase continue to develop throughout his career. His most fascinating essay is "Kant on Enlightenment and Revolution," trans. Colin Gordon, *Economy and Society* 15, no. 1 (February 1986), 88–96, in which Foucault actually affirms the significance of the Enlightenment, Kant in particular, for his own philosophical program. Two interesting, and in many respects opposed, uses of Foucault's essays on the Enlightenment are Jürgen Habermas, "Taking Aim at the Heart of the Present," trans. Sigrid Brauner, Robert Brown, and David Levin, in *Foucault: A Critical Reader,* ed. Hoy, 103–8; and Hubert L. Dreyfus and Paul Rabinow, "What Is Maturity? Habermas and Foucault on 'What is Enlightenment?'" in *Foucault: A Critical Reader,* ed. Hoy, 109–21.

the content of the conclusion of *Madness and Civilization*,[147] it does return the eye to the relation between the subject and the work of art.[148]

A second consequence of the escape of freedom from dominating power is that liberty must always hide in order to prevent its recapture. What makes power effective is its presence to its object. But the self-constitution of the ethical subject is precisely that—self-constitution. Foucault has found the aesthetic arena of ethics for which it appears he searched ever since *The Will to Know*. There he contrasts the science of sex with the erotic arts. The former evokes discourse about sex in order to gain power, and the explosion of discourse about sex is a strategy of power. The erotic arts, on the other hand, draw truth from pleasure itself, not from an externally imposed law. More important, "there is formed a knowledge that must remain secret."[149] Of course, the ethic of self-care is not identical with the erotic arts. But in regard to their publicity, erotic arts and the care of the self are similar. Foucault, for example, does not discuss resistance in relation to the care of the self. Resistance becomes an ancillary strategy of self-care, albeit an important one. Self-care resists, but only to eradicate the interference of power, since "liberation" from "states of domination" is required as a precondition for the "practice of liberty."[150] The objective is, finally, the elimination of power. The care of the self seeks only to be left alone, for self-care and liberty guarantee each other.[151]

This radical dissociation of power and the subject applies only to power that imposes and fixes "states of domination."[152] The recovery of the subject, however, opens a new territory in which power can be applied. Foucault introduces the notion of "government," which applies both to the self and others. As government of others, power governs while preserving its openness to fluidities of variation, instability, reciprocity, and the like.[153] In other words, power operates without fixing states of domination. This new concept of government both expands and restricts power. Power's range is increased because it now enters the interiority of the subject. Yet this effort

---

[147] Foucault, *Madness and Civilization*, 288–89.

[148] In fact, aesthetics may have never been far from Foucault's attention. Sheridan comments that in *The Order of Things* "discourse was broken down into three clearly defined periods bearing names drawn, not from the 'science' of historical materialism, but from art history" (*Michel Foucault: The Will to Truth*, 210).

[149] Foucault, *History of Sexuality* 1:57 (*Histoire de la sexualité, 1*, 77).

[150] Foucault, "Care of the Self as a Practice of Freedom," 3–4; "Souci de soi comme pratique de liberté," 100–101.

[151] Foucault, *Care of the Self*, 47 (*Histoire de la sexualité, 3*, 62).

[152] Foucault, "Care of the Self as a Practice of Freedom," 19; "Souci de soi comme pratique de liberté," 114.

[153] Foucault, "Care of the Self as a Practice of Freedom," 19–20; "Souci de soi comme pratique de liberté," 114–16. Foucault's earlier discussions of government do not distinguish it so clearly from domination. They are important, however, because apparently the concept of government is what spurs Foucault to claim that freedom is the precondition of power relations. See, e.g., "Governmentality," 5–21; "Politics and Reason," 83–85; and "How Is Power Exercised?" 221.

to make power truly ubiquitous, to remove its confinement to exteriority common in political theory, comes at a price that compromises the omnipresence of power in another way. Finally, the most distinctive and decisive aspect of Foucault's theory of power is lost: knowledge loses its necessary and inevitable involvement with power. Foucault introduces the possibility of knowledge not constituted by power. If Foucault escapes the tendency of political theory to understand power as only external, in the end it is his inability to separate himself from a political starting point in constructing a theory of power that leads him to cut his thought loose from the knot he had tied between knowledge and power.

As far as the expansion of Foucault's concept of power is concerned, power as the imposition of states of domination requiring resistance no longer covers the whole field of power relations. It is true that the self-constitution of the ethical subject must be executed in a realm relatively free of powers of states of domination. But the retrieval of the subject as a target of philosophy, combined with Foucault's claim that power is everywhere, permits the extension of power into the realm of the subject as an operation within it, a self-relation, and not merely as a force that operates on it from outside. Self-government entails self-mastery, a self-domination which orders and applies the knowledge that is part of self-care and one's ethical constitution.[154] The possibility of interiority is given to power. In addition to this new interiority of power, domination is given a positive ethical value. No longer does domination appear merely as that which is to be resisted, but it is also an instrument of value — the necessity for self-mastery in ethical self-constitution opens Foucault to a notion of legitimate and valuable domination.[155] The productivity of dominating power is now one that is valuable and worthwhile in the exercise of power. Foucault can distance himself further from the simplistic assertion that power is evil.[156] Whereas until now it had been possible to say that the goodness of power was restricted to the purely negative role of resisting normalizing and totalizing power, now power attains a positive status of its own.

Both new elements of Foucault's theory of power are important. The move toward an interiority of power amplifies the range of power; for the first time, power appears to be truly ubiquitous, present "inside" as well as "outside" the subject. Similarly, the recognition that domination is not universally to be feared, but is also necessary, closes the way of a utopian abandonment of power, the positing of a personal or social position in which power would no longer be. This is Foucault's criticism of Habermas:

---

[154] See *Care of the Self*, 58–64 (*Histoire de la sexualité, 3*, 74–81), for examples of the involvement of knowledge as "connaissance" with the practices of self-care.

[155] This is especially clear in *Use of Pleasure*, 63–70 (*Histoire de la sexualité, 2*, 74–82).

[156] Foucault, "Care of the Self as a Practice of Freedom," 18–19; "Souci de soi comme pratique de liberté," 114.

The thought that there could be a state of communication which would be such that the games of truth could circulate freely, without obstacles, without constraint and without coercive effects, seems to me to be Utopia. It is being blind to the fact that relations of power are not bad in themselves, from which one must free oneself.[157]

Foucault is able to recognize these features of power because he is not only a political philosopher, but a philosopher.[158] The customary boundaries of political theory are broken; the exclusive focus on external relations characteristic of political thought cannot understand domination as a positive phenomenon; at best, domination can appear as a lesser of evils in comparison with another power. A political utopia is able to (perhaps it must) abandon power because it has left any relation to inwardness out of account from the beginning. Foucault understood that a merely external political theory of power was inadequate, and he investigated its inward complement.[159]

The self-government of the subject operating below the threshold that establishes fixed dominations does not, however, privatize power. For example, the practice of self-government for the free Greek was a precondition for his effective participation in the government of the city.[160] The ambiguity of Greek ethics lay in its bases in virility and the dichotomy of activity/passivity, which meant that the successful government of the self and others also entailed the establishment of states of domination. The trick ethical constitution must turn is to govern self and others successfully without imposing permanent states of domination. The introduction of notions of reciprocity in Roman culture is an example of relative success in drawing the line between government and domination,[161] and the struggle of contemporary Western culture (one Foucault seems to think we are losing, but is not yet lost for the individual) is precisely

---

[157] Foucault, "Care of the Self as a Practice of Freedom," 18; "Souci de soi comme pratique de liberté," 113; see also "How Is Power Exercised?" 222-23.

[158] Foucault, "How Is Power Exercised?" 224.

[159] The terms "inner" and "outer" do not perhaps mean quite the same thing in interpreting Foucault as they would for most thinkers, as Deleuze tries to explain through his use of "folding" to describe Foucault's meaning (Foucault, 93-123). This is not terribly important at this point. It is sufficient to say that what Deleuze expresses through "fold" is not too distant from "border," a term that appears in chapter 4 below.

[160] See esp. Foucault, Use of Pleasure, 143-84 (Histoire de la sexualité, 2, 158-203). The same is true of the Romans—the activity of self-care constitutes a social practice, not an exercise of solitude (Care of the Self, 51-54; Histoire de la sexualité, 3, 65-69).

[161] The effective demarcation of government from domination frequently involves the avoidance of codification. Foucault notes with a certain wistful reminiscence:

it is remarkable that, with rare exceptions, this desire for rigor expressed by the moralists did not take the form of a demand for intervention on the part of public authority. One would not find in the writings of the philosophers any proposal for a general and coercive legislation of sexual behaviors. They urge individuals to be more austere if they wish to lead a life different from that of "the throngs"; they do not try to determine which measures or punishments might constrain everyone in a uniform manner. (Care of the Self, 40; Histoire de la sexualité, 3, 54)

to prevent legitimate and necessary government from spilling over into states of domination. Between self-government, government of others, and states of domination, the crucial task is to discover the boundary between the second and the third, to govern others without fixing a relation of domination over them,[162] to avoid the "contradiction . . . between, on one hand, the relentless search for a certain style of activity and, on the other, the effort to make it common to all."[163]

Yet Foucault did not overcome completely a political starting point of a theory of power. What is given with his left hand, the interiority of power and the value of mastery and sovereignty, cannot conceal that his right hand takes away an integral feature of his previous understanding of power—the production of knowledge by power. At stake is Foucault's most decisive and distinctive insight, that power is a condition for knowledge and that, therefore, knowledge must take account of its involvement with power. The knowledge of carceral society is supremely dangerous because it denies its involvement with power and pretends to speak in the name of truth itself, thereby exercising a covert and almost total dominion. Were this power understood for what it is, it would be resisted. Conversely, local knowledges, which can resist totalizing and normalizing power, were self-consciously affirmed in their relation to power. If these powers/knowledges were not truth, they were at least truthful in confessing their association with power. The aesthetic of freedom and self-care, however, severs this bond between knowledge and power. The truth of freedom, because it is not a truth of power, risks its own untruthfulness in the rupture.

In large part, both the dissociation of power and knowledge, and the location of the sensitive problematic of power at the division between the government of others and states of domination (rather than in the dimension of the subject) occur because the philosophy of the subject is constructed primarily along the continuum of time, whereas the philosophy of power is mapped out along spatial coordinates. In rediscovering the importance of the subject in philosophical reflection, and being forced to recognize the value of the sovereignty of one force in relation to another, Foucault is led to an impasse that is resolved by divorcing at least one form of knowledge (knowledge involved in the care of the self, and especially the knowledge of freedom) from power.

In his construction of the theory of power in the mid-1970s, Foucault's thought is cast almost entirely in the language of spatial metaphors. He summarizes the spatial character of his usual vocabulary:

---

[162] See esp. "Care of the Self as a Practice of Freedom," 12–19; "Souci de soi comme pratique de liberté," 108–14.

[163] Foucault, "Return of Morality," 244 (translation modified); "Le retour de la morale," 38, reads: "contradiction . . . entre d'une part cette recherche obstinée d'un certain style d'existence et, d'autre part, l'effort le rendre commun à tous. . . ."

Territory is no doubt a geographical notion, but it's first of all a juridico-political one: the area controlled by a certain kind of power. *Field* is an economico-juridical notion. *Displacement:* what displaces itself is an army, a squadron, a population. *Domain* is a juridico-political notion. *Soil* is a historico-geological notion. *Region* is a fiscal, administrative, military notion. *Horizon* is a pictorial, but also a strategic notion.[164]

Regardless of the origin of these terms, they are now spatial terms, and if one thinks by means of them, one thinks spatially. Foucault admits:

People have often reproached me for these spatial obsessions, which have indeed been obsessions for me. But I think through them I did come to what I had basically been looking for: the relations that are possible between power and knowledge. Once knowledge can be analyzed in terms of region, domain, implantation, displacement, transposition, one is able to capture the process by which knowledge functions as a form of power and disseminates the effects of power.[165]

These spatial descriptions are not simply metaphorical. One example should be sufficient to show this. In the construction of systems of surveillance, space structures time. The temporal effect of continuous surveillance is created by means of a particular organization of space.[166] The prison, the classroom, the hospital, among others, all are reconstructed architecturally so that power is made omnipresent. The effect of continuous surveillance is, moreover, less to sustain time than to eliminate it. A properly functioning surveillance assures that each piece of time will be properly organized, which is to say it will be identical with every other segment. No deviation from normalcy is allowed in effective surveillance. The prescribed routine must be repeated; the creativity of time is obliterated as time itself is immobilized under the domination of space.[167] What is normalized under the domination of spatial structuralization is not only the person, but time itself. Time is not a factor in the exercise of power, or, rather, the use of power is tied inextricably to its neutralization of time.

This spatial emphasis of Foucault's thought is also present in his archaeologies. This seems surprising, since the archaeologies are intended precisely as histories of conditions of knowledge. In *The Order of Things*, Foucault analyzes three distinct discourses of truth. But the divisions between these discourses are unusually sharp. After all, archaeology — and genealogy, for that

---

164 Foucault, "Questions on Geography," 68; see also Said, "Foucault and the Imagination of Power," 149.

165 Foucault, "Questions on Geography," 69.

166 Dreyfus and Rabinow, *Michel Foucault,* 154–55.

167 Foucault, *Discipline and Punish,* 160 (*Surveiller et Punir,* 162). Habermas (*Philosophical Discourse of Modernity,* 244) recognizes power's control of time by space in *Madness and Civilization.* Simple confinement of the deviant means "only a spatial segmentation of the wild and the fantastic, which are left to themselves; it does not yet mean a domesticating confrontation. . . ." Spatial division is power, but it is not yet the deeply pernicious power of normalizing society, which confronts in order to alter. To normalize requires the spatialization of time itself.

matter—focus on discontinuity rather than continuity in history.[168] What emerges is a picture of periods (or systems of thought, since it is possible for more than one system to occupy the same time) that are discrete in relation to each other. Systems are placed in separate and self-contained compartments,[169] and little attention is paid to the reasons for transitions between them.[170] It is revealing, to say the least, that Foucault refers to practitioners

[168] This is the primary theme of *The Archaeology of Knowledge*. An index of the distance between *The Archaeology of Knowledge* and the rediscovery of the subject is Foucault's claim in the former that "the theme of a continuity of history [produces] a history that would be not division, but development; not an interplay of relations, but an internal dynamic; not a system, but the hard work of freedom" (*Archaeology of Knowledge*, 13; *L'archéologie du savoir*, 22–23). Here are the essential linkages between space, division, and the archaeological layers on one side, and time, continuity/development, the subject and freedom on the other.

Another graphic indication of Foucault's archaeological spatialization of time through general disregard of transitions is seen if *Madness and Civilization* is compared with the introduction of archaeology in *Birth of the Clinic*. The former does focus on temporal transitions. The opening words of *Birth of the Clinic*, ix (*Naissance de la clinique*, v) are: "This is a book about space, about language, and about death; it is about the act of seeing, the gaze [regard]." Foucault seeks the "decisive line . . . drawn between" periods (*Birth of the Clinic*, xi [translation modified; *Naissance de la clinique*, vii, reads "ligne decisif est donc tracée entre . . ."]); he is not interested in any permeation from one side of the line to the other.

[169] Within the context of the archaeologies, at least, this is understandable. To open the compartments to each other would imply an engagement with "commentary"; that is, the fact of communication between systems would lead one to think that the signified might have an "excess" whose meaning is not exhausted in a spatial measurement of difference from another system. Discussions of commentary are found in *Birth of the Clinic*, xvi–xvii (*Naissance de la clinique*, xii–xiv), and *The Order of Things*, 17–45 (*Les mots et les choses*, 32–59). As Deleuze notes, "a statement has a 'discursive object' which does not derive in any sense from a particular state of things, but stems from the statement itself (*Foucault*, 7–8).

[170] In *The Order of Things*, the use of "thresholds" as a description of the area between systems of thought is an indication of this. The threshold is a demarcation between what is within and what is outside; it does not produce or indicate any continuity between these regions. On Foucault's use of threshold, see Deleuze, *Foucault*, 51–53. Indeed, the metaphor of archaeology itself suggests the presence of layers or strata that are not mutually permeable. Even in the case of the move from representation to the analysis of life, labor, and language, which Foucault presents in two phases, the final step (in the work of Ricardo, Bopp, and Cuvier), incompatible with representation, is presented as a sharp break from both classical representation and from its own first phase. Little or no attention is paid to questions one finds in many intellectual histories (what problem innovating thinkers believed they uncovered, why a new conceptual apparatus is developed, and so on). These questions would require attention to the interior of systems of thought and a thinking subject. As Deleuze puts it, "by the nineteenth century [language] leaps out of its representative functions" (not "flows out" or "struggles out," but "leaps out") (*Foucault*, 56). Foucault's concern is the bottom line, a description of what appears and how it overturns the previous system of truth. Even a continuity of phrases, sentences, and the like, does not establish a continuity of regimes of truth, for the function of the same phrase changes dramatically between discourses of truth (*Archaeology of Knowledge*, 79–87; *L'archéologie du savoir*, 105–15). What is true of phrases in Foucault's archaeologies remains true of codes in his writings on ethics: "the same advice given by ancient morality can function [jouer] very differently in a contemporary style of morality" ("Return of Morality," 247; "Le retour de la morale," 39).

of historians of continuity as "agoraphobics of history and time."[171] Mutation, not transition, is the operative category of archaeology.[172]

Why should this be the case? It is necessary to recall once again Foucault's suspicion of the subject in both the second and third phases of his work. This meant that the reasons which were given for the shifts in definitions of truth by the thinkers themselves are unimportant. Those who produced discourses of truth assumed a meaning to those discourses which Foucault denies. They assumed, in short, that in their discourse there was some advance toward truth, however that was conceived. The term "advance" is a temporal one, even though it is also spatial. Motion from one place to another must occur during some time, while to see archaeological layers in cross-section requires only a single glance. The discovery of meaning also includes, inevitably, a temporal dimension. Even if the meaning one receives is thought to be from eternity, it must still impact the history of those receiving it. The subject lives with a future and a past.

Foucault, however, dispensed with these temporal concepts. Meaning itself was a mask, meaningless in itself, given meaning only through its effects in the spaces of power.[173] A direction toward the future is always a totalizing direction. Foucault's opposition to philosophies of history rests on the presupposition that these are always progressivist and total philosophies of history.[174] Time hides the relations of space:

> Metaphorizing [sic] the transformations of discourse in a vocabulary of time necessarily leads to the utilization of the model of individual consciousness with its intrinsic temporality. Endeavoring on the other hand to decipher discourse through the use of spatial, strategic metaphors enables one to grasp precisely the points at which discourses are transformed in, through and on the basis of relations of power.[175]

Space and time are severed from each other, and with them, power and the subject.

This basic opposition between space and time remains even when Foucault rediscovers the subject and its relation to power. Self-knowledge and the care of the self, since they relate to the ethical constitution of the subject, pertain primarily to time. Aesthetic self-constitution involves advance and progression, a knowledge of what comes next in the construction of the self as a work of art.[176] In short, ethical self-constitution requires practice over time. Power,

---

[171] Foucault, *Archaeology of Knowledge*, 174 (*L'archéologie du savoir*, 228).

[172] Deleuze, *Foucault*, 85–86. A good discussion of the argument of this paragraph is contained in Sheridan, *Michel Foucault: The Will to Truth*, 210–14.

[173] To give a priority to one system or another assumes a "retrospective question," which turns out to be a question of value or truth (*Birth of the Clinic*, xi; *Naissance de la clinique*, vii).

[174] Foucault's discussion of teleology in "Prison Talk," 49, is an example of this.

[175] Foucault, "Questions on Geography," 69–70.

[176] Foucault (*Use of Pleasure*, 57–77; *Histoire de la sexualité*, 2, 68–91), for example, introduces the notions of the *kairos*, or the "right time," as well as "training" over time. Deleuze (*Foucault*,

on the other hand, is understood in spatial terms. Now, of course, the spatiality of power must be incorporated into the temporal framework of the subject, but power itself does not become temporal. The endurance of the assertions that power is a concept of space and that a philosophy of the subject stands under the principle of time explains why ethical self-constitution lacks the sense of ambiguity and danger that pertains to external relations. The danger of fixing states of domination does not apply to the realm of the subject, because there space remains subservient to the principle of time.[177]

Two curious aspects of Foucault's discussions of ethical self-constitution demonstrate the enduring spatiality of power and its consequences. First, the knowledge employed in self-discipline and the care of the self is not subjected to critique except insofar as it authorizes external states of domination. There is not an analysis exposing how the knowledge involved in the constitution of the self is produced by power. Second, there is no hint of a darker side to the self as a work of art. The possibility of self-destruction is not opposed to self-creation. The alternative Foucault presents is not between correct and incorrect self-care, but between self-care and its absence.[178] The disastrous and destructive practices of extreme asceticism, for example, do not find their way into Foucault's discussions of self-constitution.[179] It would be petty and unfair to criticize Foucault for failing to do what he did not set out to do in the first place, and the corpus of work he left does not analyze more questionable modes of self-constitution. But the absence of such a treatment means that he does not correct or modify the unambiguous status he accords self-constitution of an ethical subject.

---

104), quoting Blanchot, goes so far as to say that Foucault creates an "interiority of expectation." It is no longer true that a directedness toward the future inevitably implies efforts at totality.

[177] Indeed, self-care obliterates the risk of domination of others ("Care of the Self as a Practice of Freedom," 8; "Souci de soi comme pratique de liberté," 105). Even in the Greeks, self-mastery made one a better ruler; the tyrant was a tyrant because he could not rule himself, and therefore ruled others badly (*Use of Pleasure*, 81–82; *Histoire de la sexualité, 2*, 94–95).

[178] Foucault, "Care of the Self as a Practice of Freedom," 8; "Souci de soi comme pratique de liberté," 105).

[179] Foucault's own "ascesis," as expected, is directed to new possibility, an "exercise of oneself in the activity of thought" through which "it might be possible to think differently, instead of legitimating what is already known" (*Use of Pleasure*, 9; *Histoire de la sexualité, 2*, 14–15).

To the extent that Foucault suggests how he might treat destructive self-practices, it appears that the blame lies in the reinscription of the "universal code" upon the task of ethical constitution, the "self" of ethical self-constitution being removed thereby (*Care of the Self*, 238–40 [*Histoire de la sexualité, 3*, 272–74]; *Use of Pleasure*, 21 [*Histoire de la sexualité, 2*, 27–28]). "Politics and Reason" conceptualizes this relation as the combination of two games of power, the individualizing "pastoral" power and the "city-citizen game" of power; through their combination, the modern state is "really demonic" (pp. 60–71). It is doubtful, however, whether all practices of self-destruction can be laid at the doorstep of excessive codification applied to the individual, and to his credit Foucault never makes such a large claim. But it is true that Foucault's unwritten assumption appears to be that self-interested liberty can read its own needs with very little difficulty.

The recognition of ambiguity in care of the self would have required yet another alteration in Foucault's conception of power and might have prevented Foucault from tearing asunder what he first brought together— knowledge and power. The government of the self is largely free from the danger attached to government of others, which requires performing a precarious balancing act on the tightrope between government and domination. The reason is that, as long as it is the self-government of the subject that is in question, the spatiality of power is limited by the subject it concerns. Space is surrounded by time and therefore is safely enclosed by it. Liberty is the precondition for power, "since freedom must exist for power to be exerted."[180] In carceral society, power attempts to immobilize time and make every time like every other, but in the realm of the subject, time envelops power and can overcome power's tendency to freeze and capture it. The time of self-care enlists power in its service, but retains its privilege. This means, however, that power is surrounded on each side by something other than itself: on one side, by the knowledge of freedom required for aesthetic self-creation, and on the other, by the self for whom the knowledge is intended. Care of the self certainly involves knowledge.[181] But this knowledge is now based in and transcended by an ontology of freedom, not an analytic of power. Whatever material one has available for ethical self-constitution, and however much it may be part of a complex of power, it is transcended and conditioned by "choice,"[182] by a self-forming activity and *telos*.[183] The knowledge of freedom is no longer produced by power. In fact, freedom does not even involve power; Foucault's positing of the fact of human liberty does not derive from his description of the phenomenon of power, and he does not show how the basic and fundamental postulate of freedom is in any way an affirmation produced by power.[184] There is now knowledge not formed by power, but instead a transcendence and confinement of power. Indeed, it is only when states of domination cease that care

---

[180] Foucault, "How Is Power Exercised?" 221.

[181] Foucault, "Care of the Self as a Practice of Freedom," 5; "Souci de soi comme pratique de liberté," 102; see also "On the Genealogy of Ethics," 243–44.

[182] Foucault, "On the Genealogy of Ethics," 244.

[183] Davidson, "Archaeology, Genealogy, Ethics," 228–30. Davidson's otherwise excellent article suffers from his tendency to place all of the elements of ethics on the same plane. Foucault cannot do this, because liberty would disappear in the play of external determinations upon it. Freedom is the precondition for power, and it is also what limits power, because only freedom can introduce the temporal notions of self-formation and goal.

[184] Deleuze expresses this point well: "a 'subject' must be isolated which differentiates itself from the code and no longer has an internal dependence on it" (*Foucault,* 101). As he explains this claim, however, he argues that "Foucault's fundamental idea is that of a dimension of subjectivity derived from power and knowledge without being dependent on them" (ibid.). In reference to this latter assertion, one must be clear in distinguishing between the contents of subjectivity and the fact of liberty. It is true that the contents through which one exercises liberty are derived from power and knowledge, but this is not the same as saying that subjectivity and liberty themselves are so derived. The fact of liberty itself transcends and limits power, and in this sense, is no more derived from power than dependent on it.

of the self can arise. In this sense, the beginning of freedom requires an absence of power.

On the other side of power stands the self as the work of art. Whatever knowledge is required for adequate self-care, and whatever techniques are employed, the objective is the creation of a beautiful self. If what one must know and be in order to care for oneself is not rooted in power, neither must it seek power. This is part of the difference in value between Greek and Roman political ethics. The Greek free man was in some way obligated to exercise political power. This meant that the self-constitution of the Greek as an ethical subject was from the beginning ordered to political domination; the free Greek governed himself so that he could govern others. This political *telos* is one reason that extrapolitical relations are contaminated by domination—they remain defined by a political end and oriented by a political model.[185] What is new in the ethics of Rome is both a reversal of the order of one's relation to the political and the extrapolitical and an elimination of the necessity of their linkage. Instead of defining one's task of ethical constitution through the position of political power one is obliged to assume, the relation to the self determines the conditions and desirability of political involvement.[186] Self-definition and the relation to oneself are no longer determined by a "system of signs denoting power over others, but through a relation that depends as little as possible on status and its external forms, for this relation is fulfilled in the sovereignty that one exercises over oneself."[187] The corollary of this principle is that entry into political activity becomes a matter of choice rather than obligation attendant on social status.[188] One can seek power, but this relationship between self-government and external power is neither necessary nor full; indeed, the care of the self is a conversion of power, the limiting of power, which prevents its misuse,[189] even in politics, for what one is, is detached from the rank one holds.[190] The beautiful self is the purpose of existence and the guarantee of proper exercise of power, if one chooses to exercise it. In the end, Foucault is driven to the recognition that the positions the subject may occupy are no longer determined by forces external to it; self-constitution is also a self-positioning that transcends, evaluates, and chooses between positions offered.[191]

---

[185] Foucault, *Use of Pleasure*, 83 (*Histoire de la sexualité, 2*, 96). This is so despite the fact that proper self-mastery would prevent one's rule from being tyrannical. Tyranny or no, all those other than the free man remained in a state of subjugation.

[186] Foucault, *Care of the Self*, 86 (*Histoire de la sexualité, 3*, 107).

[187] Ibid., 85 (Fr. 106).

[188] Ibid., 85–95 (Fr. 106–17).

[189] Foucault, "Care of the Self as a Practice of Freedom," 7–8 ("Souci de soi comme pratique de liberté," 104–5).

[190] This double reversal of Greek ethics is largely what Foucault believes produces the reciprocal elements of Roman ethics mentioned above (*Care of the Self*, 93–95; *Histoire de la sexualité, 3*, 114–16).

[191] It might even be said that a limited role for the "author" has returned. Against Foucault's earlier efforts to place the notion of authorship in question, another way to express the subject's

Both the beginning and the end of one's self-constitution as an ethical subject are conceived without requiring recourse to the notion of power. Liberty, freedom, liberation—all these remain opposed to power in the end, even if one cannot eliminate the other but must struggle with and provoke each other.[192] Power has, in fact, been reduced to a means, the switching yard that transmits and applies liberty, through the material of knowledge, to the self. Neither freedom nor its *telos* —the beautiful self—is concerned essentially with power except insofar as they must keep it in check. The brush may indeed be necessary to transfer paint to canvas, but it must be controlled by the artist's freedom, and neither the paint nor the final work of art contains the brush. Power is merely a means between freedom and aesthetic creativity, inessential to the content of their constitution and end. The means of power do not produce the knowledge of freedom necessary for self-care. Nor is the end of that care power; rather, it is the removal of external dominion (an ancillary strategy) so that one may please oneself.[193] If power remains ubiquitous, it is only in a weak sense. Power may be everywhere insofar as it is involved in every relation, including self-relation. But it no longer defines those relations. Truth and the self can be defined independently of power, even if they cannot be accomplished without it. Foucault has discovered a principle that is not power/knowledge, but instead limits power by trapping it between the jaws of freedom's transcendence and the body to which it is applied in the practices of self-care. While the attribution of privilege to a certain kind of truth is precisely what Foucault had opposed in all the discourses of truth, now it has returned in his own thought as the truth of freedom.[194] It may no longer be knowledge that steps in to control and limit power, but power must be caged nonetheless. For the usual philosophical imprisonment of power behind the bars of knowledge and reason, Foucault substitutes transcending freedom. But as soon as power is confined by something other than itself, the insight that had most clearly separated Foucault from sovereignty theories of power has been lost. The individual performs the dance of self-care on a stage of time rather than space, its steps no longer choreographed by power, but chosen by freedom.

---

creation of itself as a work of art is to say that there is now a writer capable of authoring the self as a work.

[192] Foucault, "How Is Power Exercised?" 221–22; see also "Care of the Self as a Practice of Freedom," 3–4 ("Souci de soi comme pratique de liberté," 100–101).

[193] Foucault, *Care of the Self,* 65–67 (*Histoire de la sexualité, 3,* 82–84). It is true that pleasing oneself also is power over the self, but this power is again necessary only to prevent external dominion over one. Power is not the objective of self-care, but the means of its continuance over against the threats of "fortune." This describes the conversion of power from being one's own master to taking pleasure in the self, from an ethics of control to an art of pleasure.

[194] For a similar point, see Habermas, "Taking Aim at the Heart of the Present," 107. While Habermas takes Foucault's movement as desirable and necessary, we take it as regressive.

An Assessment of Foucault

The discussion of Foucault has ended. There are two ways in which Foucault's thought is significant for a theology of power. To begin with, we have seen the ways in which he violates his own intentions in the construction of his theory of power relations. From a consideration of these departures, it should be possible to define a path to the fulfillment of Foucault's stated objective more closely. In a sense, we seek to produce Foucault's theory of power in his absence. We must conceive of a true and strong ubiquity of power without producing the collateral difficulties that forced Foucault to abandon some of his most important insights. In addition, we have garnered several criteria for a more adequate theory of power from Foucault.

Critique

We found Foucault's critique of sovereignty theory persuasive primarily on two grounds. First, Foucault opposed any understanding of power as occasional. His argument was that power is omnipresent in breadth and depth. Moreover, power is in some way universally accessible. It is not the possession of a few. Second, power is productive and not simply repressive. It produces knowledge, and any theory of knowledge has to account for its own involvement with power. In the end, however, Foucault gives up both of these assertions. Liberty splits knowledge/power. Moreover, the knowledge that is involved in freedom is fundamentally removed from power; it is privileged as a criterion of truth.

It is possible to read this project as an attempt to make Foucault's intentions with regard to the ubiquity and productivity of power hold good. It would be necessary to affirm the omnipresence of power. To do so, however, would mean that no realm of life could be opposed to power fundamentally, and this would have to include the dimensions of freedom and the subject. If freedom is understood as having a nonantagonistic relation to power, there are additional implications for how power's productivity can be approached. To begin with, the inevitable involvement of knowledge in power must be conceded, and this cannot allow the exemption of any knowledge or reason from an inner relation to power. Moreover, the internal relation between power on the one side and freedom and the subject on the other implies that an analysis of power's productivity cannot be restricted to the claim that it is productive of and produced by knowledge. Power must also be understood as productive of and produced by freedom.

The attempt to establish an inner relation of knowledge and power has an important methodological consequence. Power is most often discussed within, broadly speaking, the field of political theory. But these discussions generally are restricted to an analysis of power as a phenomenon of external relations. It is unlikely, therefore, that we would be able to clarify the inner relation between power and the subject or between power and freedom, if a confinement to political theory were accepted as a parameter for the construction of a theory of power. Political theory does not apprehend power as related to inwardness. While Foucault's genius in constructing his theory of power is clearest precisely when he sees the inadequacy of a purely political approach to power and escapes its confines partially, he still wears the collar of political theory and cannot, therefore, take power as constitutive of either the art of self-care or the liberty that is its condition. In the end, Foucault is frightened by the ghost that haunts political theory and from which it usually recoils: the possibility that the "critique of power," carried to its extreme, "becomes deprived of the normative yardsticks that it would have to borrow from the [analysis of truth]."[195] Finally, he too blinks at the prospect of power unleashed and attempts to "conceive of a 'power of truth' which would no longer be the truth of power."[196]

But is it so self-evident that a "power of truth" is possible apart from the truth of power? The very phrase "*power* of truth" is sufficient to cast doubt on that possibility. Is it clear, moreover, that the phantom which political theory fears is such a malevolent threat? Is it obvious that power should be treated as derivative of the Fall rather than as constitutive of creation and that, therefore, redemption can be thought possible only through the neutralization (or perhaps elimination) of power? If political thought has been unable, in general, to confront the truth of power, this may be because it does not open the gate to inwardness. If what is sought is a truth of power, and only that, we should begin uncoupled from political theory, although we cannot but merge with politics again at some point in the journey. If power is a condition of freedom, it cannot be or seek domination. Nor can the "game" of power be a zero-sum game. Power's productivity could not be synonymous with the construction of an "iron cage" from which there is no escape. Rather, the ethical valuation of power would be considerably more positive, and less cynical, than it has been in political theory.

There is one final clue to an adequate theory of power that can be gleaned from the critique of Foucault. We saw that, for Foucault, there was a sharp division between space and power, on the one hand, and time and the subject of freedom, on the other. This opposition ended in the restriction of power. We may suspect, then, that a view of power which truly affirms its ubiquity would have to include both temporal and spatial elements — transitions and evolutions must be capable of incorporation in the same understanding of power as mutations and revolutions.

[195] Ibid., 108.
[196] Deleuze, *Foucault,* 94.

Criteria

Foucault has not been discarded simply because he has been criticized. The discussion of Foucault also revealed criteria for a theory of power. These criteria both help define the task of a theology of power and provide standards by which to judge it.

First, any approach to the problem of power must be broad enough to allow for concrete analyses of any and all exercises of power. A second and closely related criterion is the criterion of presence. We saw in Foucault that a condition for the exercise of power was power's presence. These are really alternate ways of saying that power must be understood as a ubiquitous phenomenon that is not a possession, but an event. But they also imply that power is not ubiquitous contingently. This will eventually lead us to an ontological conception of power.

Third, a theology of power must provide criteria for the judgment of concrete manifestations of power. Foucault judges the power of domination, of course, but judges it negatively because he finds a standpoint outside of power from which to level his critique. A positive valuation of power is allowed only on the condition that the spatiality of power is contained adequately by the meaning creation of the subject's temporality. Power, if it is to have positive value, must receive it from elsewhere; its dignity must be reduced to service of a creation essentially alien to it. If power is truly omnipresent, however, there can be no such vantage point, no "elsewhere" outside power. Instead, the criteria for judging manifestations of power must be found within power itself.

Fourth, the body must be included as the place, or at least a place, where power is manifested. A disembodied theology of power is ruled out from the start. In combination with the criterion of presence, this means that any theology of power must include the presence of power to the body prominently.

Fifth, and finally, there is an element in Foucault's argument that must be left in abeyance, somewhere between critique and criterion. This is the question of the public character of power. With respect to power dominated by spatiality, Foucault argues persuasively that a condition for the exercise of power is that it must be public. True, power masks itself and attempts to keep its exercise hidden from view. Secrecy is not an abuse of power, but a necessity internal to power. But this means only that power does not confess its publicity. The exercise of power itself requires an interaction between its object and itself. It is not possible to exercise power over sex, for example, unless there is a discourse of confession, of disclosure—in short, a discourse which makes public. The situation becomes more complex when power is transferred to the subject, when time controls the space of power. A pure privacy of power, under the auspices of the subject, appears to be possible. And yet, if power is a relation between forces, this includes a presence of those forces to each other. The forces themselves cannot be hidden from each other. Moreover, we have seen that the ethics of self-care did not imply a privatization of power. Foucault does not determine the public status of power. One of the tasks that follows is to resolve this question of power's position.

The venture into Foucault's thought has been useful; it has provided a direction and substantive criteria to which a constructive theory of power must adhere. With those boundaries in mind, we can take up another approach to power, that found in the thought of Martin Luther.

CHAPTER 2

LUTHER'S ANTINOMY OF POWER: POLITICS AND EUCHARIST

An attempt to distinguish power from sovereignty should not, it seems, begin with Luther's theology. Luther's thought appears to provide a secure home for an identification of power and domination. But this is true only on the twin assumptions that power is fundamentally political in character and that Luther's political writings are determinative of his entire understanding of power. This chapter questions these suppositions indirectly, while directly it seeks to expose two theologies of power that arise in Luther's thought. One is contained in his sacramental theology, especially his theory of the Lord's Supper. The second is the theology of power tied to Luther's political work.

This chapter is preparatory in two ways. First, the sacramental and political views of power are presented as sharply contrasting, even contradictory. An exposition of the relationship between political power and a wider understanding of power is postponed. Second, both this chapter and the next simply present Luther's position; they do not defend it. Questions about the validity of Luther's understanding are delayed until the fourth chapter.

The Sacrament of the Lord's Supper

Luther's disputes in regard to the Lord's Supper involved two primary sets of opponents, the Roman church and the radical reformers.[1] Of these two,

---

[1] Luther's Protestant opponents (including Karlstadt, Zwingli, Oeclampadius, Schwenkfeld, and others) are placed under the latter banner. There were certainly substantial differences between them, which Luther himself saw, though he frequently did not distinguish this group. See Martin Luther, *The Sacrament of the Body and Blood of Christ—Against the Fanatics*, in *Luther's Works*, vol. 36, *Word and Sacrament II*, trans. Frederick C. Ahrens, ed. Abdel Ross Wentz (Philadelphia: Fortress Press, 1959), 337 (Martin Luther, *D. Martin Luthers Werke: Kritische Gesammtausgabe* [hereafter *Luthers Werke*], 19 Band [Weimar: Hermann Böhlaus Nachfolger, 1897], 484 [hereafter WA]); idem, *Confession Concerning Christ's Supper*, in *Luther's Works*, vol. 37, *Word and Sacrament III*, trans. and ed. Robert H. Fischer (Philadelphia: Fortress Press, 1961), 161–372 (WA 26 Band [1909], 261–509); idem, *Brief Confession Concerning the Holy Sacrament*, in *Luther's Works*, vol. 38, *Word and Sacrament*

the debate with the radical reformers raises the question of the nature of sacramental power more sharply. Insofar as the arguments about the sacrament concern power, the difference can be put this way: Luther's disagreement with Roman eucharistic theology involved the type and mechanics of power available through the Supper, whereas the argument with the radical reformers revolved around the question of whether the sacrament had any power at all.

Attack on Rome

Luther's writings on the sacrament from roughly 1519 to 1524 are the principal texts for elucidating the issues Luther thought were in contest between Rome and himself. There are at least two distinct schemata through which Luther analyzes the sacrament in this period. The first places the sacrament in a tripartite framework of sign, significance or meaning, and faith. This terminology is displayed prominently in the treatises of late 1519, *The Holy and Blessed Sacrament of Baptism* and *The Blessed Sacrament of the Holy and True Body of Christ, and the Brotherhoods;*[2] however, Luther develops a different structure as early as 1520. Then the Lord's Supper is understood principally as a testament. Although the sketches Luther draws of the promissory testament between 1520 and the onset of the radical challenge do not always have the same emphases, the central point remains the same. The Lord's Supper and the sacraments generally are promises made by God to Christians.[3]

IV, trans. and ed. Martin E. Lehmann (Philadelphia: Fortress Press, 1971), 296–98 (WA 54 Band [1928], 149–51). The variety was attributed to the influence of the devil, who cannot permit unity (*Confession Concerning Christ's Supper,* 163–65; WA 26:262–64). But as far as basic issues of the efficacy of the sacrament and the reality of the body and blood within the sacramental elements are concerned, Luther believed all of his opponents were of a single mind (*Sacrament of the Body and Blood of Christ,* 337 [WA 19:484]; Martin Luther, *That These Words of Christ, "This Is My Body," etc., Still Stand Firm Against the Fanatics* (hereafter *This Is My Body*), in *Luther's Works,* vol. 37, *Word and Sacrament III,* trans. and ed. Fischer, 34, 40–41 (WA 23 Band [1901], 97, 105–7); Luther, *Confession Concerning Christ's Supper,* 163–64; WA 26:263).

[2] Martin Luther, *The Holy and Blessed Sacrament of Baptism,* in *Luther's Works,* vol. 35, *Word and Sacrament I,* trans. Charles M. Jacobs, rev. and ed. E. Theodore Bachmann (Philadelphia: Fortress Press, 1960), 29–43 (WA 2 Band [1884], 727–37); idem, *The Blessed Sacrament of the Holy and True Body of Christ, and the Brotherhoods* (hereafter *Blessed Sacrament of the Body*), in *Luther's Works,* vol. 35, *Word and Sacrament I,* rev. and ed. Bachmann, 49–73 (WA 2:742–58). Luther's baptismal theology is not our concern, but his writings on baptism are useful insofar as they expound his more general sacramental structure.

[3] An especially helpful review of the dispute between Luther and Rome, largely because it includes considerable reference to the Roman debaters, is David V. N. Bagchi, *Luther's Earliest Opponents: Catholic Controversialists, 1518–1525* (Minneapolis: Fortress Press, 1991), 118–46. Bagchi also includes the broader sacramental framework in his discussion.

Sign, Meaning, Faith

The first sacramental diagram is divided into three parts: the sacrament consists of a sign, its meaning or significance, and faith. Taken together, these three components are the sacrament fulfilled. The sign (*zeychen*) or token of the sacrament is its external, bodily, and material form. Indeed, the sign is the sacrament proper. The sign of the Lord's Supper is the form of bread and wine.[4] Because the sign is external and outward, in a certain respect it is also empty. Luther protests against the Roman understanding of the sacrament on this ground — for the Roman church, the sacrament is adequate even if it remains "external" to the recipient. Luther believes another, inward aspect is required to bring the sacrament to fruition.

The second component of the sacrament, its meaning or significance (*bedeutung*),[5] effects the transition from the outer to the inward. Meaning is inner and spiritual:[6] as inward, the meaning of the sacrament outlasts the external sacramental act — although the sign itself is temporary and is "quickly over," its meaning continues. Thus is the ephemeral nature of the outward contrasted with the endurance of the inward and spiritual. Put a different way, Luther says that while the "sacrament has taken place, the work of the sacrament has not yet been fully done."[7] In baptism, this work consists in the sacrament's efficacy for one's dying to sin and resurrection in the grace of God.[8] Baptism has a twofold meaning. Eschatologically, it confirms and announces the resurrection; but the sacrament also performs a second, earthly function, namely, to assist the believer in dying to sin more and more in this life.

The worldly significance of baptism, the progressive dying to sin undergone by the believer, is largely duplicated in the Lord's Supper. Luther's treatment of the meaning of the Eucharist in *Blessed Sacrament* is within the context of the "adversity that assails us," which comes first in the form of "the sin that remains in our flesh after baptism." The Lord's Supper assists us in our battle against this sin by signifying our community (*gemeynschafft*) with Christ and all the saints. The communion of the altar is a "sacrament of love."[9]

The transition from outward to inward accomplished by the meaning of the sacrament does not define Luther's early polemic against Rome. What

---

[4] Luther, *Blessed Sacrament of the Body,* 49 (WA 2:742). The spelling and capitalization of Luther's German, both in the text and in the footnotes, conforms to the Weimar edition rather than to contemporary German.

[5] Luther, *Holy and Blessed Sacrament of Baptism,* 30 (WA 2:727); see also *Blessed Sacrament of the Body,* 50 (WA 2:743).

[6] Luther, *Blessed Sacrament of the Body,* 49 (WA 2:742).

[7] Luther, *Holy and Blessed Sacrament of Baptism,* 30, 32 (WA 2:727, 729–30).

[8] Ibid., 30 (WA 2:727). The significance of this double work of baptism will be taken up in more detail in chapter 3.

[9] Luther, *Blessed Sacrament of the Body,* 53, 54 (WA 2:744, 745).

Luther believed was in dispute was not whether the sacraments meant something over and above their signs, but whether and how their meaning was appropriated by the recipient of a sacrament. Meaning is a middle term between the external character of the elements and a third component which fixes the sacramental meaning firmly in one's heart. The meaning of the Lord's Supper, incorporation into and participation with Christ and the saints, is not effected by simple reception of the elements of bread and wine. The elements point to the significance of the sacrament, but do not accomplish it. Rather, the meaning of the sacrament must be activated from the depths of the heart, through faith.

Faith is required in order to lay hold of meaning; it is the yeast by which sacramental meaning becomes mine, by which I partake in it. Faith in the Supper is desire for the blending of our sin and suffering with the righteousness of Christ and belief that one has received this in the sacrament. It is not enough to know what the sacrament means. To knowledge of meaning must be added desire and faith. Only then can sacramental meaning become operative; the benefit of the sacrament, the incorporation of a specific person into the spiritual body, is sparked by faith. Participation in the spiritual body of Christ is nothing other than being changed into another in love, a transformation accomplished through the leaven of faith.[10] As the property of a city is the common possession of all its citizens, so membership in the spiritual body implies "that all spiritual goods of Christ and his saints are shared and become common with who receives this sacrament."[11]

Here, at the intersection of the sacrament's work and the person's faith, Luther speaks of sacramental power. The meaning of the sacrament discloses its proper purpose through the

> divine sign, in which are pledged, granted, and imparted (*zu gesagt, geben und zu geeygent*) Christ and all saints together with all their works, sufferings, merits, mercies, and possessions, for the comfort and strengthening (*sterck*) of all who are in anxiety and sorrow, persecuted by the devil, sins, the world, the flesh, and every evil. And to receive the sacrament is nothing else than to desire all this and firmly believe that it is done.

When the sacrament is received in faith, the gifts promised by God actually are given and possessed by the communicant. The power the sacrament contains for strengthening the recipient explains Luther's position on one's "worthiness" to eat and drink. Desire for sacramental power implies weakness and need on the part of the recipient. Worthy participation requires a troubled and hungry soul, not a pure one; indeed, the Supper is of "little or no benefit

---

[10] Ibid., 49–62 (WA 2:742–50).

[11] Ibid., 51 (translation modified; WA 2:743 reads: "das alle geystlich guter Christi unnd seyner heyligen mit geteyllet und gemeyn werden dem, der dysz sacrament empfeht").

(*nutz*) to those who have no misfortune or anxiety, or who do not sense their adversity."[12]

Faith's appropriation of meaning does not end the work of the sacrament. The communicant cannot rest comfortably in the reception of the strength given in the Eucharist. Just so far as the believer receives the natural body of Christ, and through it is given membership in the spiritual body, the transformed and strengthened Christian must make these benefits available to others. The personal, inward change that is a product of the sacrament proceeds to reach outward. Since receiving the sacrament in faith makes the heart free and strong, "through this same love, we are to be changed and . . . make the infirmities of all other Christians our own; we are to take upon ourselves their form and their necessity, and all the good that is within our power (*vormugen*) we are to make theirs, that they may profit (*genieszen*) from it." Our power is to be offered to others for their benefit—this is the meaning of being "changed into another through love."[13]

Alongside the argument that the Eucharist's power actually accomplishes a transformation of the person lies a second assertion that further delimits Luther's understanding of power. Luther draws a contrast between worthy reception and use of the sacrament, and its abuse. The sacrament is a useful work and pleasing to God not "because of what it is in itself but because of your faith and good use of it." If, however, one concentrates exclusively on what the sacrament is in itself, namely, the natural body of Christ, the consequence is condemnation, just as the misuse of all other good things results in condemnation of the user. Indeed, "the more precious the sacrament, the greater the harm which comes upon the whole community [of saints] from its misuse." What is true of the Word is true of the sacrament of the altar—"it is harmful to me unless in me it pleases God."[14]

There are two important points concerning the abuse of the sacrament. First, its misuse flows from exclusive focus on the external aspect of the sacrament. Rather than understanding the spiritual body, the inner meaning, as the most important aspect of the sacrament, Luther thinks that Rome inverts the order of priority, according the natural body first place. But the natural body without the spiritual is of no help.[15] Moreover, instead of directing attention to the faith of the recipient and the use of the sacrament, Luther believed faith was made to count for next to nothing.

---

[12] Ibid., 60, 55 (WA 2:749, 746).

[13] Ibid., 58, 61–62 (WA 2:748, 750).

[14] Ibid., 64, 63, 64 (WA 2:752, 751, 752).

[15] Ibid., 62–63 (WA 2:751–52). The question of location and order in the Supper is one example, among many others we will see in subsequent chapters (especially the next), of the importance of "the order of things" in Luther. Most of his theological differences with the Roman church and others are not arguments over the elements of those theologies, but about the ordering of the elements.

Second, when Luther claims the Lord's Supper is capable of condemning the recipient as well as strengthening the heart, he accords a double effect to it, an effect of condemnation as well as a power that gives power. But the first of these, use for damnation, is not the meaning of the sacrament. Accordingly, Luther does not often refer to this effect as "power." The Supper is intended for the power and strengthening of the believer, and what "power" it has for condemnation is a distortion of its truth. The more perfect and undistorted power comes not when the sacrament (as external sign) is completed but when it is used in faith; then the power (*crafft*) of the sacrament operates.[16] The two types of power are not equal; only one, the use of the Supper in faith, preserves the proper sacramental meaning, communicating "the fruit of this sacrament [which] is community and love, by which we are strengthened against death and all evil."[17]

Power, then, is essentially teleological. The work of the sacrament, its significance and meaning, is not, properly speaking, power. Power enters the arena when recipients take, or fail to take, this meaning as their own in faith. The meaning of the sacrament is a prelude to its power, indispensable but not sufficient. Power occurs at the point of contact between meaning and faith. This accounts for the two possibilities of power, the intended and perfect power that conforms to their heavenly and worldly purpose, and the distorted power that leads the recipient further along the road to condemnation. Moreover, the appearance of sacramental power at the border of meaning and faith has a double direction—toward both the inner strengthening of the believer through membership in the spiritual community and toward the external strengthening of the community of the holy in works of love for the neighbor.

The teleological nature of power is the first indication of how far Luther's theology of power in the sacrament departs from a model that views power as pure domination. Power is not a static possession of the sovereign but is created when its purpose comes to pass. There are other suggestions of the distance separating Luther from a conception of power as domination. To begin with, a zero-sum understanding of power is broken definitively, as is the need to treat the problematic of power through the rubric of "balances of power" and the attendant deft negotiations to assure that one party does not gain "too much" of this scarce and essentially exclusive thing called power. Sacramental power given to one person does not mean that it is refused to another. No intrinsic limit is placed on the "quantity" of power given by God. The power of the Lord's Supper even compromises an atomistic conception of power. The more participants in the community of the saints there are, the more power is generated. The more who participate in the spiritual body and community of the holy, the more power is available to all. Power, far from varying in inverse

---

[16] Luther, *Blessed Sacrament of the Body*, 63 (WA 2:751–52).

[17] Ibid., 67 (translation slightly modified; WA 2:754 reads: "Ist die frucht diszes sacraments gemeynschaft und lieb, dat durch wir gesterckt werden widder tod und alles ubell.").

proportion to the number of its recipients, varies in direct proportion with the number of believers. Power's aim is not exclusivity but universality.

Finally, the restriction of power to external life is shattered. Indeed, attention to only the outer visage of the sacraments is what distorts their power,[18] making them efficacious for damnation rather than for their intended purpose. Faith, the completion of the inward movement of meaning, must be present in order for sacramental power to be activated. The external dominion of God, who gives the gifts of the sacrament, though maintained strictly by Luther, is not identical with power; power occurs when the communicant is transformed, when the meaning of the sacrament is owned and possessed by the believer, and when the received gift is not retained jealously but moves outward in works of love.

Whatever this understanding of the sacraments contributes to a theology of power, the structure of sign/meaning/faith does not last even through 1520. Luther did not repaint the sacramental picture in order to develop a better understanding of power; he never made any explicit effort to construct a theology of power. Instead, his concern was whether or not the tripartite order and categories of 1519 best represented the sacraments. There is a glaring difficulty. How can that which faith is supposed to apprehend in the sacrament, its meaning and benefits, be present there at all? They cannot be present through the elements, for Luther has already made a distinction between elements and meaning, and there is no indication that he thinks the significance of the sacraments depends on the inherent content of the elements. This separation of the intrinsic content of the sacramental material from its meaning makes Luther's later denial of the radicals' claim that there is a natural analogy between elements and meaning quite unsurprising.

Luther's unwillingness to connect element with significance by means of analogy and his insistence on the distinction between them create a substantial theological problem. If the elements are part of the sacrament—if Luther goes so far as to say that they are the sacrament—and if the sacrament is involved in communication of benefits and efficacy to the believer, he cannot say that the material of the sacrament is irrelevant to the sacramental process. On the other hand, if the elements are a mere sign, if faith is what is essential to the sacrament, and if faith is not related to sign and meaning in any cogent way, why is it necessary to eat at all? Does this mean that the elements are unimportant, in fact worthless, and does this imply further that the sacrament is at best an unnecessary convention? It is obvious that Luther does not think so. It is equally evident that the division between material and meaning hinders any explanation of how the sacrament can mediate real benefits to and for faith.

The crack in Luther's understanding of sacramental operation visible from the side of the sign becomes a canyon if the same problem is considered from the perspective of sacramental significance. Meaning does not emerge from

---

[18] Ibid., 63 (WA 2:751–52).

nowhere. It relies on the sign as its prior condition. Granting that spiritual meaning is more important than sign and that the sign is the least important aspect of the sacrament, this cannot mean that the sign is of no importance. Clearly, Luther believes that the sign is one of three components which make the sacrament effective. The same call arises from the shores of sacramental meaning as from the island of the sign. Without being able to explain why the elements of the sacrament are of any importance, how can Luther maintain "the sacrament is for us a ford, a bridge, a door, a ship, and a stretcher, by which and in which we pass from this world into eternal life"? To say "everything depends on faith"[19] in order that the bridge be crossed and the door opened is not an answer. How can the sacrament be the bridge faith crosses if there is no relation between the sacramental material, which is the sacrament proper, and its meaning? How can faith gain anything from the sacrament, much less be strengthened by it, if sacramental power lacks any basis? How does what faith is supposed to appropriate, the meaning of the sacrament independent of faith, exist in the first place?

Luther's second account of the sacrament tries to remove this problem, but before this structure is considered it is important to note the effects of the atomization of sign and meaning on the question of power. Even if Luther does not intend to develop a conception of power, his sacramental theory involves one anyway, and the intrasacramental problem of sign and meaning reduplicates itself in a theology of power that turns to Luther for assistance. Luther's sacramental thought of 1519 escapes from a purely external conception of power, but the way in which it does so appears to plot a course toward a pure internalization of power. The power of the sacraments appeared at the convergence of faith and meaning, both of which are "inward and spiritual." Yet the meaning of the sacrament is supposed to be related to its sign. How, then, can power be created at the intersection of meaning and faith, if meaning itself lacks a footing allowing its participation in power? On the other hand, if power is produced only through faith, faith would not need to cross the bridge of the sacrament. Such a position would have at least two effects. First, there would be no need for the external sign or, for that matter, the special meaning of the sacrament. Sign and meaning would not only be powerless in themselves (that is, until completed by faith), but powerless even in conjunction with faith. There would remain only the inner power of faith, the external elements being severed from any relation to sacramental power. But if we look ahead to the final act of the sacramental play, Luther's dispute with the radicals, we see that this was exactly the issue: Do the elements of the sacrament have any more than a suggestive, analogical role to play, and, by extension, is the sacrament itself essential? Luther has already laid the foundation by which he will deny any natural analogy between the sign and sacramental meaning. Moreover, he asserts, both then and now, the real, objective, and externally originating power of the sacrament. In a sense, Luther's Protestant opponents internalized the sign by maintaining that the sacrament of the table was both constituted and effective only when taken spiritually and inwardly. Luther objects to this move as an imaginary blasphemy of the real force of the sacrament, reducing it to nothing. His work of 1519, however, seems to open the window to the air of this fantasy. The second effect of the impotence of the sign is that it eliminates any possible ground for the double efficacy of the sacrament. The sacramental material cannot play any role in salvation or condemnation if it is utterly incapable of having any relation to power.

Sacrament and Testament

Luther's first version of the sacrament becomes questionable because of the lack of connection between its three components. This may well have troubled later theologians, without disturbing Luther himself, were it not for his attention to a new question that the first model of the sacrament cannot address. His thought becomes driven by an economic interest in identifying what is and is not essential to a sacrament. For the Lord's Supper, this attention is expressed in an effort to pare down the imposing structure of the mass. Luther does not want to replace or abolish all the practices of the mass, but he does want to clarify what is essential to it and what is merely a supplement.[20] By its sheer mass, the mass had become a mess.

This economic problem presents a target significantly different from that Luther aimed at in 1519. His initial architecture confronted the question of whether the sacrament can be effective without faith, without being related to inwardness. Having answered negatively, he now asks to which practices of the mass *must* faith be related. This inquiry cannot be resolved by recourse to the nature of faith, for it is a problem regarding faith's object, not faith itself. Nor is it possible to produce an economy of the mass by appeal to the meaning of the sacrament, for that is exactly what needs clarification: What is (are) the essential meaning(s) of the sacrament in view of the multiplicity of asserted meanings? What is required is a criterion by which to choose. If such a rule cannot be supplied by the categories of meaning and faith, but is instead to be applied to them, Luther is thrown back upon the only remaining source from which a standard could emerge: the sign.

The sign of 1519 cannot bear the weight of the burden thrust upon it. The sacramental order Luther developed then was not simply an arrangement of equal components but also involved assignments of value. The first part,

---

[20] Martin Luther, *A Treatise on the New Testament, that is, the Holy Mass,* in *Luther's Works,* vol. 35, *Word and Sacrament I,* rev. and ed. Bachmann, 81, 97 (WA 6 Band [1888], 355, 367). See also Martin Luther, *The Babylonian Captivity of the Church,* in *Luther's Works,* vol. 36, *Word and Sacrament II,* ed. Wentz, 52 (WA 6:523), in which Luther suggests, intending all irony, that the mass has been transubstantiated in reverse: the simple substance of the mass has been replaced by "manifold 'accidents' of outward pomp."

the sign, was of questionable import. The meaning of the sacrament, the second part, was more important, while faith, which was treated as the third component of the sacrament but is outside the physical eating and drinking, was the most essential. The problem we raised was how this increasing importance is possible if the foundation, the sign, is narrow and weak. It was hard to comprehend how meaning is possible at all, or how and why faith is related to the sacrament. When Luther attempted to economize faith's relation to the mass, and when the only possibility of success depended on the sign, the inverted pyramid of value and order constructed in 1519 had to be given a stronger foundation or crash to the ground.

The sign itself, being merely an external token, cannot produce criteria to distinguish the essential from the supplemental. If, however, the task at hand must be performed through a theory of the sign, the sign must be related to something that can provide a standard of judgment. The criteriological razor cannot be discovered in front of the sign, in the meaning of the sacrament, because its meaning is the question. Luther is thus forced back behind the sign, prior to it. The sacramental theology of 1520 returns to the beginning, the sign, in order to make it something other than the beginning, to open a road behind it upon which one must travel if the sign is to be reached.[21]

The sixfold edifice of the Eucharist presented in Luther's 1520 *Sermon on the New Testament, that is, the Holy Mass* is less revealing than the title itself, which equates the essence of the mass, the Supper, with the new testament. The sermon is well under way before Luther finally unveils the full structure of the mass. Its first three components are a testator, heirs, and the testament. Relocated into fourth position is the sign, seal, or token, which is the sacrament itself. Finally, in front of the sign are, fifth, the blessing or good which the words of the testament mean, and sixth, the duty of remembrance incurred by the recipient of the meal.[22] The pivotal supplement is the third element, the testament. The parts of the sacrament that endure from his work of the previous year, sign and meaning, are altered considerably by this addition. And although faith continues to have an indispensable function in relation to the sacrament, it is no longer a part of the sacrament itself.

This new conception of the Eucharist has two important results. First, it brings the sacrament into conformity with, and contributes to, Luther's theology of the Word. Second, it produces a strong emphasis on the exclusive

---

[21] Alexander Barclay makes the same division between the 1519 and 1520 treatises, although for him this division is between a second and third stage of sacramental thought (*The Protestant Doctrine of the Lord's Supper: A Study of the Eucharistic Teaching of Luther, Zwingli, and Calvin* [Glasgow: Jackson, Wilie & Co., 1927]). Barclay's exposition of Luther's first period is not relevant for our purposes.

[22] Luther, *Treatise on the New Testament*, 86 (WA 6:359). Bagchi is incorrect to say that the structure of sign, meaning, and faith continues to constitute the sacrament in this sermon (*Luther's Earliest Opponents,* 118).

sovereignty of God, while at the same time providing that the relation between God and persons is the central factor in the efficacy of the sacrament.

With respect to Luther's emphasis on the Word, his interpretation of the sacrament as a testament meets his requirement of scriptural warrant.[23] Now, if the Supper is the "new testament," Luther must explain what a testament is. It is, he maintains, a promise activated by the death of the one who promises, the testator.[24] The Eucharist, therefore, is promissory. Promise and testament are not new categories in Luther's theological repertoire,[25] but they had not been applied as a criterion for discerning the essence of the Lord's Supper. The promise may have been one of the features of sacramental meaning, but it was not the basic meaning, from which all else must derive. Now, however, Luther conceives of the promissory testament as constituting the essence and center of the Eucharist. Furthermore, the formal criterion of testament drives Luther toward a restriction of the content of the Supper. A will or testament makes its promise through the words of the testator. This means that the biblical words of institution supply the essential content of what is given in the sacrament: "We must turn our eyes and hearts simply to the institution of Christ and this alone, and set nothing before us but the very word of Christ by which he instituted the sacrament, made it perfect, and committed it to us."[26] As important as the words of institution are for supplying a positive standard which tells us what is given in the sacrament, they are equally significant as a negative criterion. What is not contained in these words is not a part of what

---

[23] Matt. 26:28; Mark 14:24; 1 Cor. 11:25. See esp. Martin Luther, *The Misuse of the Mass*, in *Luther's Works*, vol. 36, *Word and Sacrament II*, ed. Wentz, 162–63 (WA 8 Band [1889], 506–7). Although Luther frequently collapses the relevant sacramental texts into one, he does recognize their differences. In *Confession Concerning Christ's Supper*, 307–60 (WA 26:448–98), the texts are discussed individually, with Luther expressing a preference for Luke and especially Paul, although he suggests that the Scriptures should be coordinated so that they speak as one voice (*Confession Concerning Christ's Supper*, 336; WA 26:477).

[24]Luther, *Babylonian Captivity*, 38 (WA 6:513).

[25]At least as early as his lectures on Hebrews, Luther said, "in the sacraments of grace we have the promise of Christ." He had even recognized the promissory element in a testament, and linked the "testament," albeit vaguely, with the "cup":

> One should note that where it is recorded in the Holy Scriptures that God makes a will, there it is pointed out somewhat obscurely that at one time or another God will die and arrange the inheritance, as . . . "Where there is a testament, the death of the testator must intervene." This has been fulfilled in Christ. Hence the words "testament," "inheritance," "part," "portion," "cup," etc., occur so frequently in Scripture. All this points to the death of Christ and to faith in His resurrection. (Martin Luther, *Lectures on Hebrews*, in *Luther's Works*, vol. 29, *Lectures on Titus, Philemon, and Hebrews*, trans. Walter A. Hansen, ed. Jaroslav Pelikan [St. Louis: Concordia Publishing House, 1968]), 193, 194–95; WA 57 Band [III] [1939], 192, 193)

I thank Thomas Davis for directing my attention to these lectures.

In addition, Luther's 1519 treatise on baptism had touched on the role of the covenantal pledges made by God and the recipient (Luther, *Holy and Blessed Sacrament of Baptism*, 33–34; WA 2:730–31).

[26] Luther, *Babylonian Captivity*, 36 (WA 6:512). *Misuse of the Mass*, 163 (WA 8:507), ties the institution to divine power and wisdom.

is promised.[27] The axe for clearing the overgrowth of missive practices has been supplied:

> When Christ himself first instituted this sacrament and held the first mass, there was no tonsure, no chasuble, no singing, no pageantry, but only thanksgiving to God and the use of the sacrament. According to the same simplicity the apostles and all Christians for a long time held mass, until there arose the various forms and additions, by which the Romans held mass one way, the Greeks another. And now it has finally come to this: the chief thing in the mass has been forgotten, and nothing is remembered except the additions of men.[28]

Again, it is not that Luther demands that such "added" practices be eliminated, but his focus on the promise contained in the words of institution does mean, "All the rest is the work of man, added to the word of Christ, and the mass can be held and remain a mass just as well without them."[29]

The economic sufficiency of the words, located prior to the sign, explains why Luther can and must derive the blessings of the sacrament from those words. By fortifying the foundation below the sign, Luther has solved the problem of how meaning can arise through the sign. The meaning of the Supper, its goods or blessings, is communicated not on the basis of the arbitrary sign alone but by the promise of the testament through the sign. The whole mass, Luther emphasizes, is contained in the words of institution, without which nothing is gained; in the words of Christ lie "the whole mass, its nature, work, profit, and fruit."[30] The principal blessing is, therefore, also to be found

---

[27] Luther, *Misuse of the Mass,* 148 (WA 8:494).

[28] Luther, *Treatise on the New Testament,* 81 (WA 6:354–55).

[29] Luther, *Babylonian Captivity,* 36 (WA 6:512). On the other hand, if these supplementary practices are turned into requirements, "it is an addition of the devil. For no one changes, adds to, or takes away from a man's testament, as Paul says; much less should one add anything to God's testament or change it" (*Misuse of the Mass,* 142; WA 8:489).

[30] Luther, *Treatise on the New Testament,* 82 (translation slightly modified; WA 6:355 reads: "die mesz gantz mit all ymrem weszen, werck, nutz und frucht"). See also *Babylonian Captivity,* 37–38: "if we enquire what a testament is, we shall learn at the same time what the mass is, what its right use (*usus*) and blessing (*fructus*), and what its wrong use (*abusus*)" (WA 6:513). Luther used this language of use and fruit several times and laid great emphasis on it in two important sermons: *A Beautiful Sermon on the Reception of the Holy Sacrament* (hereafter *Reception of the Sacrament*), in *Sermons of Martin Luther,* vol. 2, *Sermons on Gospel Texts for Epiphany, Lent, and Easter,* trans. John Nicholas Lenker and others, ed. John Nicholas Lenker (Minneapolis: Lutherans in all Lands, 1906; reprint, Grand Rapids, MI: Baker Book House, 1988), 223–37 (page references are to reprint edition) (WA 12 Band [1891], 476–93) (1523); and *Confession and the Lord's Supper,* in *Sermons of Martin Luther,* vol. 2, *Sermons on Gospel Texts for Epiphany, Lent, and Easter,* ed. Lenker, 193–214 (page references are to reprint edition)(WA 15 Band [1899], 481–504) (1524). Although his schematic of the Eucharist in these sermons, a triptych of elements, use, and fruit, might appear to constitute a third topography of the sacrament prior to the battle with the radicals, it depends on the words of institution and is already present in 1520. Luther's employment of the categories of use and fruit relates to the presence or absence of the communicant's faith.

in the words of institution—the forgiveness of sin.[31] All the other goods of the sacrament either derive from, or are contained in, the promise of forgiveness. This is an important shift. The absence of a foundation of sacramental meaning in his earlier work was not merely a formal difficulty but produced vagueness with regard to the content of the sacramental benefits. The several meanings Luther discovered in the Supper were not related to a unifying principle. But when Luther discovers that the formal character of the Lord's Supper is a testament and lays exclusive stress on the words of institution proclaiming forgiveness of sin as the purpose of the meal, whatever else the sacrament confers must flow from this primary meaning. The fruits implied in sacramental forgiveness are connected intimately with a second facet of Luther's sacramental theology, a vigorous defense of the sovereignty of God, to which attention must now be turned.

In the sacramental writings of 1520, Luther identifies a number of abuses of the sacraments. In one way or another, each of his objections is relevant to a theology of power. The protest against the sequestering of the words of the Supper[32] concerns the publicity of power. His displeasure with the practice of withholding the cup is largely a question of the authority of the church.[33] The emerging dissatisfaction with transubstantiation[34] is important for Luther's view of the mechanics of power. However, the most serious abuse of the Supper, Luther believes, is its interpretation as a sacrifice by the officiant, given to God as a good work.[35]

Luther's conviction that the overwhelming issue for sacramental theology is this question of whether the mass is a sacrifice by the church is a direct implication of his argument that a sacrament is a promise. To make the mass a sacrifice to God inverts the roles of giver and receiver. Far from being a sacrifice offered to God, the sacrament is actually reception of a gift from God.[36] This is because of its promissory character. A promise is made solely at the discretion of the one who promises. The promiser, especially in a testament, does nothing other than give and is the only one who does give. As the testator is dead, there can be no question of the testator's receiving anything back. The opposing claim, that the sacrament is a sacrifice made to God, is an attempt

---

[31] Luther, *Treatise on the New Testament*, 82 (WA 6:355); *Babylonian Captivity*, 38–40 (WA 6:513–15). *Misuse of the Mass*, 176–83 (WA 8:518–25), contains a sustained exposition of the promise of forgiveness given in the Supper. On this point see also Hermann Sasse, *This Is My Body: Luther's Contention for the Real Presence in the Sacrament of the Altar* (Minneapolis: Augsburg Publishing House, 1959), 113–14.

[32] Luther, *Treatise on the New Testament*, 90 (WA 6:363).

[33] Luther, *Babylonian Captivity*, 23–27 (WA 6:504–7).

[34] Ibid., 27–35 (WA 6:507–12).

[35] Luther, *Treatise on the New Testament*, 94 (WA 6:365); *Babylonian Captivity*, 35 (WA 6:512). A good discussion of Luther's position is in Barclay, *Protestant Doctrine of the Lord's Supper*, 31–33.

[36] Luther, *Babylonian Captivity*, 54 (WA 6:525).

to make the priest "omnipotent (*omnia posse*) with God."[37] This cannot be tolerated, for "God will accept no other mediation and no other mediator" than Christ.[38] The power of the mass emerges exclusively through God's words of promise,[39] because the Word itself is all-powerful (*allmächtig*).[40] What is at stake in this "most heretical"[41] abuse of the mass is nothing less than God's exclusive omnipotence.[42] Luther will brook no power beginning elsewhere than with God. Those who interpret the mass as sacrifice "deny God and insult the sacrifice that Christ has made and disgrace his blood, because they try thereby to do what only Christ's blood can do."[43] Power produced in the mass has its source in God and God alone. The priest's "sacrifice" and God's "gift" are mutually exclusive acts.[44]

The sharpness of Luther's defense of God's sovereignty in the sacrament has a collateral effect. His work of 1519 escaped a purely external conception of power, but in so doing seemed to leave open the possibility that sacramental power would become purely inward. That door has now been closed. The power of the Supper is now based externally, in the promise of God communicated through the Word. It is true that the blessing of the Eucharist is still given to recipients and is intended to transform inner life. As in his earlier work, the meaning of the sacrament is focused on the intention of God in instituting it. Moreover, faith is still required in order to appropriate this true meaning, and the relation of faith to the Supper remains the ground for the double efficacy of the sacrament.

But it is a startling reversal that faith is no longer a part of the sacrament.[45]

---

[37] Ibid., 47 (WA 6:520).

[38] Martin Luther, *The Abomination of the Secret Mass*, in *Luther's Works*, vol. 36, *Word and Sacrament II*, trans. and ed. Wentz, 313 (WA 18 Band [1908], 23).

[39] Martin Luther, *Receiving Both Kinds in the Sacrament*, in *Luther's Works*, vol. 36, *Word and Sacrament II*, trans. and ed. Wentz, 257 (WA 10 Band [II] [1907], 32).

[40] For one of Luther's many statements to this effect, see Martin Luther, *The Adoration of the Sacrament*, in *Luther's Works*, vol. 36, *Word and Sacrament II*, trans. and ed. Wentz, 278 (WA 11 Band [1900], 433).

[41] Luther, *Adoration of the Sacrament*, 288 (WA 11:441).

[42] The mercy of God is also at stake, for one "who sacrifices wishes to reconcile God. But he who wishes to reconcile God considers him to be angry and unmerciful (*ungenedig*). And whoever does this does not expect grace and mercy from him, but fears his judgment and sentence" (*Misuse of the Mass*, 175; WA 8:517).

[43] Luther, *Abomination of the Secret Mass*, 313 (WA 18:24).

[44] Luther, *Adoration of the Sacrament*, 288 (WA 11:442).

[45] The interesting treatment of the sacramental debates by Reinhold Seeberg (*Text-Book of the History of Doctrines*, vol. 2, *History of Doctrines in the Middle and Early Modern Ages*, trans. Charles E. Hay [Grand Rapids: Baker Book House, 1966], 318–31) is somewhat damaged by Seeberg's interest in showing that almost all changes in Luther's thought can be accounted for as evolutions or developments of his previous positions. While there is a substantial element of this in Luther, Seeberg's treatment tends to obscure the magnitude of Luther's alterations. Perhaps the best example of this is that Seeberg does not even note that faith, once part of the sacrament, is finally removed from it.

The exclusion of faith from the sacrament proper puts an exclamation point on the contention that the mass is entirely the gift of God and does not involve a human contribution. Sacramental meaning now functions as a proclamation of what is promised by the sovereign God. Certainly the promise is to us and for us, but the sacrament itself no longer involves one's response to the promise or meaning.[46] Even the sixth part of the sacrament, the duty of remembrance, is a demand placed on the communicant, the fulfillment or abandonment of which is not included in the sacrament's nature. The Supper, strictly speaking, is what it is without the recipient.

Although the Eucharist is an independent entity, the power emerging from it is not. The sacrament intends and establishes a relationship with its recipient. If faith is not required in order that the sacrament be constituted, it is involved in how the meal is used. The external sacrament drives toward the inner life of faith. It is true that Luther believes if one understands the nature of the testament proclaimed by the Supper, one also comprehends the use and fruit of the sacrament. On the other hand, it is equally true that the use or abuse of the Eucharist is not determined simply by its nature. Luther maintains the position he took against the independent efficacy of the mass in 1519. An assertion that the mass is powerful (vi) simply because it is performed is the other side of the effort to make the officiant omnipotent with God.[47] Despite the external nature of the sacrament, its work cannot occur without an inward complement.

The continuing emphasis on the inward thrust of the sacraments explains Luther's persistent return to their twofold efficacy. The whole efficacy (efficatia) of the sacrament, he argues, consists in faith.[48] If the work of the sacraments is sought apart from faith, they are used for condemnation.[49] Instead of communicating their intended blessing, they act as poison and death, despite the fact that the sacraments were instituted as comforts.[50] The Word upon which

---

[46] This is especially clear in *Adoration of the Sacrament,* in which Luther argues that "participation in Christ" is not part of the sacrament itself but is instead what the sacrament gives to the faithful. To become "'one loaf' . . . does not say what the bread is (*sey*) but what it bestows (*gebe*)." The nature of the sacrament does not change according to its user, but its efficacy does: "not all who 'break' [bread] have spiritual participation in the body of Christ, even though they all have participation in the sacrament" (*Adoration of the Sacrament,* 285, 286; WA 11:439, 440).

[47] Luther, *Babylonian Captivity,* 37–47 (WA 6:513–20).

[48] Ibid., 65 (WA 6:532). This part of the *Babylonian Captivity* is an extremely important presentation of Luther's view of sacramental power. It occurs within his discussion of baptism, but the contrast he draws between the "old signs" of the Hebrew Scriptures and the "new signs" of the New Testament is applicable to the Lord's Supper also.

[49] Luther, *Babylonian Captivity,* 67 (WA 6:533).

[50] In relation to baptism, see *Adoration of the Sacrament,* 300 (WA 11:452); in the case of the Eucharist, see *Confession and the Lord's Supper,* 208 (WA 15:496). *Confession and the Lord's Supper* is presented as a single piece in the Lenker edition, but is actually the combination of two sermons delivered on March 20 and 24, 1524. See Kurt Aland, *Hilfsbuch zum Lutherstudium* (Gütersloh: Carl Bertelsmann Verlag, 1956), 151–52, for the various editions of these two sermons.

sacramental power depends is powerful inasmuch as it produces some effect on the communicant, but what is effected depends upon the presence or absence of faith. The sacrament works according to its intention in the believer, but in an alien way (*alienum opus*) in the unbeliever.[51] Neither promise nor faith can be properly effective without the other, because there is no efficacious power (*vim efficacem*) in the sacrament itself; rather, sacraments are effective "in the sense that they certainly and effectively impart (*conferant*) grace where faith is unmistakably present."[52] The Word of promise is the unavoidable condition of sacramental power, but this single condition produces two varieties of power, a distorted power flowing from the misuse of the sacrament, and the real power emerging from the meeting of the sacrament and the recipient's faith.

The double efficacy of the sacrament is retained in Luther's work, but removing faith from the sacrament changes it. Both effects more clearly depend upon the sovereignty of God. The two possibilities of efficacy, alien and proper, are rooted solely in the promise made at the exclusive discretion of Christ the testator. Whereas the intersection that actually produced power in 1519 was the meeting of two parts of the sacrament (meaning and faith), now power emerges at the border between sacrament and faith.

Luther's emphasis on God's sovereignty does not impair his claim that the proper efficacy of the sacraments occurs in God's relation to the recipient. To a conception of power tied to the notion of a zero-sum game, this is a strange position. How is it possible for Luther to claim that the omnipotence of God, far from eradicating the power of creatures, is actually the condition for their power? For an understanding of power which holds that one participant's power in an encounter reduces the power of all others, Luther's assertion is startling. If power is primarily a possession of the powerful, as it tends to be for political theory, it is nonsense. Luther's position hinges on the teleological character of power. He maintained that the sacrament is truly fulfilled when it reaches its end. Sacramental power was intrinsically teleological. In the first diagram of sacramental operation, the power created at the border of meaning and faith drove in two directions. First, it pushed inward, to strengthen and nourish faith. Even this was not the final objective. A new inner power of faith is inadequate without a drive to externality, to love.[53] Luther retains these convictions in his second topography.

The sacrament is intended as a comfort for faith and believers, not for their torture.[54] Luther says repeatedly that the sacrament strengthens and

---

[51] Luther, *Babylonian Captivity,* 56 (WA 6:526).

[52] Ibid., 66–67 (WA 6:533).

[53] "Inadequate" is a vague term. It does not specify why and in what way inward faith is unsatisfactory. For the moment, it will have to do. Chapter 4 will show that Luther himself is not clear on just what the "inadequacy" of a purely inward faith means.

[54] Luther, *Confession and the Lord's Supper,* 207 (WA 15:496).

nourishes faith.[55] The possibility of strengthening faith implies, however, a weakness of faith. In fact, the sacraments would cease if their purpose were fulfilled,[56] that is, if faith were full, complete, unshakable. The frequent use of the metaphor of the "hungry soul" expresses the simultaneous presence and absence of faith brilliantly. The Supper "requires a hungry, thirsty, oppressed, and anxious soul, that comes of its own accord, conscious of its own need and thirst, with utter confidence";[57] "it delights to enter a hungry soul, which is constantly battling with its sins and eager to be rid of them. He who is not thus prepared should abstain for a while from the sacrament, for this food will not enter a sated and full heart, and if it comes to such a heart, it is harmful."[58] Worthy reception of the sacrament presupposes only the knowledge of one's need. The sacrament communicates spiritual power to battle the death of unbelief, and the altar becomes a "table for me against all my affliction (anfechtung)"[59]; on the other hand, only a living and real faith can feel its hunger.

The power that appears when faith and sacrament meet pushes itself into the inner realm of faith. There it becomes a weapon of conquest against two primary temptations:

> The first is that we are sinners, and unworthy of such great things because of our utter worthlessness. The second is that, even if we were worthy, these things are so high that our fainthearted nature does not dare to aspire to them or hope for them. For who would not simply stand awe-struck before the forgiveness of sins and life everlasting rather than seeking after them, once he had weighed properly the magnitude of the blessings which come through them, namely, to have God as father, to be his son and heir of all his goods![60]

In 1519, Luther made the same point with respect to the hungry soul, although less often. Now, however, he is more specific about the temptations to which the soul is subject, against which the food of the sacrament must contend. The right use of the sacrament and the temptations the recipient must battle are related to the new unifying principle, the promise proclaimed in Jesus'

---

[55] Some of the many examples are the following: Luther, *Treatise on the New Testament*, 105–6 (WA 6:373); *Babylonian Captivity*, 61 (WA 6:529); Martin Luther, *Eight Sermons at Wittenberg*, in *Luther's Works*, vol. 51, *Sermons I*, trans. and ed. John W. Doberstein (Philadelphia: Muhlenberg Press, 1959), 95 (WA 10 Band [III] [1905], 55); *Reception of the Sacrament*, 230 (WA 12:484).

[56] Luther, *Babylonian Captivity*, 125 (WA 6:572).

[57] Luther, *Receiving Both Kinds in the Sacrament*, 264 (WA 10[II]:38).

[58] Luther, *Eight Sermons at Wittenberg*, 94 (WA 10[III]:52–53). In view of the multiplicity of texts like this, Barclay's denial (*Protestant Doctrine of the Lord's Supper*, 100) that Luther's sacramental theology has anything to do with the sacrament as "food for the soul" is incomprehensible.

[59] Luther, *Treatise on the New Testament*, 109–10 (WA 6:376–77).

[60] Luther, *Babylonian Captivity*, 45 (WA 6:519); see also *Treatise on the New Testament*, 89 (WA 6:361). The term "goods"—*bonorum* in *Babylonian Captivity* and *güter* in the *Sermon on the New Testament*—is often translated in the American edition as "blessings," the fifth part of the sacrament in this period.

words of institution.[61] The communicant's faith is strengthened not just against any temptation but against the temptation to unbelief in the promise of forgiveness and everlasting life.[62] Confidence in the promise's power to overcome one's own sinfulness, to grant forgiveness in spite of the horrible condition of the self, is both what is under siege in the contest between the flesh and the spirit, and the special object of sacramental power.[63] Only the person who needs forgiveness needs the sacrament, which "has no other purpose than that your sins may be forgiven."[64] Confidence in God's exclusive sovereignty is itself the ground, and the only ground, upon which the sacrament can be efficacious. God's omnipotence does not rob the communicant of power; instead, it gives power to faith.

On the soil of the proper use of the sacrament, consisting in the feeding and strengthening of faith's confidence in the promises of God, arises the sacrament's external impetus to love. As in Luther's earlier work, a theology of the Supper cannot cease when it describes the benefit, fruit, and use of the sacrament for the recipient alone. The sacrament is not fulfilled in the strengthening of inward faith, for faith itself is not only inward.[65] Love of the neighbor is the guarantee that we have partaken of the sacrament fruitfully and is the goal toward which the power of the sacrament drives. The presence or absence of love after receiving the Lord's Supper has a double power attached to it also. Lack of love shows that the sacrament is received without fruit, and under these conditions the sacrament injures the recipient. The perversion of the sacrament is not simply neutral, rendering the meal powerless; rather, it produces condemning power, positive injury to the recipient.[66]

Despite these similarities between Luther's treatment of the Supper in 1519 and those under consideration now, an important shift of emphasis occurs. Again, it is related to the testamental character of the sacrament. The effect of this alteration on the love produced through the sacrament is clearest when Luther returns to the theme of the single body of Christians. In *The Blessed Sacrament,* Luther maintained that love of neighbor was possible because we are changed into each other through love and incorporated into the spiritual body; by receiving the strength of Christ and the saints in the Supper, one

---

[61] In *Reception of the Sacrament,* 224 (WA 12:477), Luther criticizes his own earlier work on the Supper on the grounds that he did not show "to what end we should desire it." It is not desire for the sacrament itself that is significant, but for the Supper's purpose.

[62] See the quotation earlier in this paragraph, as well as *Babylonian Captivity,* 40 (WA 6:515).

[63] Luther, *Eight Sermons at Wittenberg,* 92 (WA 10[III]:49). Unbelief also has its object in God's promise. Luther's frequent description of the act of unbelief as calling God a liar expresses this.

[64] Luther, *Confession and the Lord's Supper,* 206 (WA 15:494); see also *Misuse of the Mass,* 181 (WA 8:522).

[65] The relation between these two fruits of the sacrament is expressed most clearly in Luther's sermons of March 20 and 24, 1524, *Confession and the Lord's Supper.* The first sermon closes when Luther has "said enough" about the profit, fruit, and use of the Supper "for ourselves," and the second sermon opens with the "other part" of the Supper, "Christian love" (WA 15:497).

[66] Luther, *Confession and the Lord's Supper,* 208–14 (WA 15:498–504).

could communicate that strength to the neighbor. Luther repeats several of these claims now. On the basis of 1 Corinthians 10, he draws a twofold conclusion. First, we become one cake with Christ, we participate (*teilhafftig*) in the body of Christ together.[67] Second, we become one with each other. Because of the believer's participation in Christ, we may (indeed, we must) turn from our "devotions and thoughts" to our neighbor, for "God's word and work do not intend to be idle," that is, for ourselves alone.[68]

If the emphasis on the "one body"[69] of communing Christians is carried over from Luther's earlier work, this should not obscure its new basis.[70] In 1519, baptismal power already involved a theory of the two realms. Baptism made its recipient pure, but only through God's gracious imputation (*gottis gnediges rechnen*) to us. The impurity remaining in our living person is not counted (*nicht rechnen*) against us; grace is the assurance that the sin remaining in our flesh does not harm us eternally.[71] Baptism itself does not eradicate this sin. Yet baptism has a second aspect, which does effect a real change in the believer. With the recognition that sin remains, even while it is ultimately conquered by God's decree, baptism reenters its "work and power (*werck und crafft*)."[72] Faith relies on the strength (*sterksten*) of baptism,[73] to the end of driving out (*ausz zu treiben*) sin from the earthly person (the same sin that is already forgiven). The grace and power (*mechtig*) of God slay sin and death through the death signified in baptism.[74] Baptism announces a heavenly salvation, upon which the earthly sinner can rely as a defense. Whatever similarities Luther's theology of the Lord's Supper had with his theology of baptism in 1519, it did not emphasize this connection between the two realms of heaven and earth. To be sure, communicants relied on the strength of Christ and the saints; it was made their own, but the precise object of their strength was something of a potpourri, a series of weaknesses to be combatted. It was hard to discover an underlying principle of the shortcomings Christ's strength was supposed to overcome, a vagueness largely the result of the opacity surrounding the essence of the Supper.

Once the foundational character of the Eucharist as promise is specified, the content of the strength received through participation in Christ's body is also clarified. The communication of properties that occurs between Christ

---

[67] Luther, *Reception of the Sacrament*, 231 (WA 12:486).

[68] Luther, *Confession and the Lord's Supper*, 214 (WA 15:504).

[69] Ibid., 213 (WA 15:503).

[70] Luther also backs away from references to the "saints," especially the dead saints to whom he referred in 1519. The reason for this is his increasing suspicion that reliance on the mediation of the saints is an affront to the exclusive mediation of Christ ordained by God. On this point see *Abomination of the Secret Mass*, 317, 322 (WA 18:27, 31).

[71] Luther, *Holy and Blessed Sacrament of Baptism*, 36–37 (WA 2:732–33).

[72] Ibid., 37 (translation modified; WA 2:733).

[73] WA 2:733.

[74] Luther, *Holy and Blessed Sacrament of Baptism*, 38–39 (WA 2:734).

and the communicant,[75] the gift of righteousness to us and Christ's assumption of our sin, is the result of the promise of forgiveness of sins (and therefore, the promise of eternal life) in the words of institution.[76] Because Christ has already conquered the enemies of sin, death, and the devil for us, our eternal fate is guaranteed. The promise communicates and ensures the final result. This assurance in turn alters the actual, empirical person who communes, making love possible.[77] The order of the sacrament and its relation to power are shown dramatically in a sermon of 1523. Immediately preceding a discussion of the fruit of the sacrament in love, Luther says:

> Therefore I am fully assured and conscious that Christ, my Lord, bestows upon me all the treasures he has, and all his strength (*krafft*) and authority (*macht*) . . . Christ is a person who gives himself for you, so that it is impossible for sin, death, hell, and Satan to stand before him, not to mention that they should gain a victory over the Divine Majesty. Now where his flesh and blood are, there he will always without a doubt have his eyes open and never permit them to be trodden under foot; you have all power (*gewalt*) that God has; that is, we become one bread, one cake, with Christ, our Lord, so that we enter into the fellowship (*gemeynschafft*) of his treasures and he into the fellowship of our misfortune. For here his innocence and my sins, my weakness and his strength (*stercke*) are thrust together, and thus all become one. This is high, inexpressible grace (*genad*), because of which the heart must be happy and of good courage. If you are now one cake, as it were, with Christ, what more do you wish? You have all in superabundance, whatever your heart desires, and you are now sitting in paradise.[78]

The power of the Supper is based on the declaration that the believer already has the purity of Christ; the Christian already sits in heaven. With this assurance, the actual transformation of the person, in faith and love, can begin and continue.

---

[75] Luther, *Reception of the Sacrament*, 231, 233 (WA 12:486–87, 489) are examples, although the entire sermon is filled with such language.

[76] This notion of the communication of properties between Christ and the sinner is based more fundamentally in the salvific exchange of our sin and Christ's righteousness. See Martin Luther, *Against Latomus*, in *Luther's Works*, vol. 32, *Career of the Reformer II*, trans. George Lindbeck, ed. George W. Forell (Philadelphia: Fortress Press, 1958), 206 (WA 8:91); and chapter 3 below. While the mystical imagery of the heavenly marriage of Christ the bridegroom and the Christian bride may or may not be the source of Luther's understanding of this exchange, it does fit it very well, and Luther uses it on several occasions. For examples, see *The Two Kinds of Righteousness*, in *Luther's Works*, vol. 31, *Career of the Reformer I*, trans. Lowell J. Satre, ed. Harold J. Grimm (Philadelphia: Fortress Press, 1957), 297 (WA 2:145); *The Freedom of a Christian*, in *Luther's Works*, vol. 31, *Career of the Reformer I*, rev. and ed. Grimm, 351–52, 357 (WA 7 Band [1897], 54–55, 59); and *The Judgment of Martin Luther on Monastic Vows*, in *Luther's Works*, vol. 44, *The Christian in Society I*, trans. and ed. James Atkinson (Philadelphia: Fortress Press, 1966), 301–4 (WA 8:608–10).

[77] On the *telos* of the sacrament to actual transformation, see *Confession and the Lord's Supper*, 214 (WA 15:504).

[78] Luther, *Reception of the Sacrament*, 232 (translation slightly modified; WA 12:487).

The sacrament of the altar is a gift or grace[79] of God which gives power. The production of power occurs in the encounter of the sacrament with faith, on the one hand, and in the encounter of faith with the neighbor, on the other. In the first case, the external sacrament drives inward to create power, and in the second, faith moves into the external world. Power appearing at the border of the inward and the external has a *telos* in both directions. The basis of sacramental power is, moreover, the sovereignty of God, who alone makes the promise effected in the Supper. Yet the external, dominating aspect of God's unimpeded discretion, although it is the condition for the power of the Lord's Supper, is not power itself. Rather, power is instantiated in the encounter and fulfilled in reaching its ends, the strengthening of the faith of the believer and the creation of the community of love.

Two alternative interpretations of the sacrament's power are rejected. On the one hand, Luther continues to oppose the notion that power is inherent in the sacrament and therefore purely external to the recipient, insisting instead that power emerges between the sacrament and faith. There is no necessarily helpful power in mere consumption of the elements, as if power were effected without the faith of the communicant. On the other hand, at least in principle, Luther already denies any pure internalization of sacramental efficacy, a position he will impute to his radical opponents. This would eliminate any power attaching to the sacrament and would rely on faith only. But Luther is quite clear: the *sacrament* feeds faith; the external is important in the strengthening of faith; and inward participation in Christ is possible because the external body and blood of Christ reach their end when we become of one bread with Christ and our neighbor. Opposition to an interpretation of power as purely inward is implied in Luther's work of 1520 to 1524. It will become more complete and virulent when he takes up the challenge of the radicals in earnest.

There is, however, an unsettled aspect of Luther's sacramental theology that seems to be not only compatible with the radical position but in support of it. One component of the dispute with Zwingli and others is a struggle around the power of the sign. Against the position of the radicals, which asserts that the sign is fundamentally powerless, Luther's second sacramental geography seems to offer little defense, if it does not in fact offer encouragement to an erasure of the sign.

To be sure, the sign is given a stronger foundation than it had been, a bolstering made necessary by the new question of the economy of the mass. But although the sign is no longer obscured by meaning and faith in front of it, its significance now seems obfuscated by the testament behind it. The

---

[79] "Gift" is the term in *Babylonian Captivity*, 54, 125 (WA 6:573); *Reception of the Sacrament*, 228 (WA 12:482–83), whereas "grace" is employed in *Reception of the Sacrament*, 232 (WA 12:487). Luther calls the sacrament both gift and grace at various times. For example, both terms are used in *Misuse of the Mass*, 169, 172 (WA 8:512, 515).

sign cannot be efficacious on its own; this would bring Luther dangerously close to Rome. That option excluded, Luther argues that the basis of sacramental power lies in the Word of promise made by the institution of Christ. The sacrament is "constituted and sanctified and consecrated through God's Word," and therefore "these words are a thousand times more important than the elements of the sacrament."[80] Indeed, Luther can say, "the sacrament would be nothing if there were no Word,"[81] repeating Augustine's formula, "Believe, and you have eaten."[82] If it is true that the whole effect of the sacrament resides in the words, why is the sign necessary at all? Even granting that the bread and wine contain the body and blood of Christ, there seems to be nothing which makes consumption of the elements important, to say nothing of its being necessary. Reinhold Seeberg is surely right: "Nothing is here made to depend upon the *eating* of the body."[83] The sign appears to be rendered powerless because of the overriding importance of the words of institution.[84]

Luther gives several answers to the question of why the elements are necessary. The first is an incipient doctrine of accommodation. How could we, he asks, "think of such faith, sacrifice, sacrament, and testament if it were not administered bodily in certain designated places and churches?"[85] Some external means is necessary for the reflection of faith; however, except for the fact that Luther does not consider hearing the Word to be bodily and material in the same way the reception of the sacrament is, there seems no reason why the Word itself, which is certainly external, cannot perform this function. Moreover, it is not at all clear why the specific bodily materiality of the sacrament is the necessary external medium for faith. A second answer is that, because we still live in the flesh, "we need actually to come together, by example, prayer, praise, and thanksgiving to enkindle in one another such a faith . . . and through the outward (*leyplich*) seeing and receiving of the

[80] Luther, *Receiving Both Kinds in the Sacrament*, 244, 254 (WA 10[II].19-20, 29). The importance of the words accounts for one of Luther's objections to the Roman mass: "they conceal the words and give only the elements. That is a horrible thing." Indeed, this practice means that, in truth, "the sacrament is not given to anybody" (*Receiving Both Kinds in the Sacrament*, 254; WA 10[II]:29).

[81] Luther, *Confession and the Lord's Supper*, 202 (WA 15:490).

[82] Luther, *Babylonian Captivity*, 44 (WA 6:518).

[83] Seeberg, *Text-Book of the History of Doctrines* 2:288. See also Ralph W. Quere, "Changes and Constants: Structure in Luther's Understanding of the Real Presence in the 1520's," *The Sixteenth Century Journal* 16, no. 1 (Spring 1985): 63. Quere's article gives an extended treatment of Luther's shifting understanding of the sign throughout his career.

[84] The American edition of *Sermon on the New Testament*, 86, seems to give power to the sign specifically: "Christ . . . has affixed to the words a powerful and most precious seal and sign." The Weimar text (WA 6:359), however, contains no reference to power.

[85] Luther, *Treatise on the New Testament*, 104 (translation slightly modified; WA 6:372 reads: "solcher glauben, opffer, sacrament und testament gedencken, wen es nit in ettlichen bernantten örttern und kirchen leyplich gehandelt wurd?"). Alternatively, Luther suggests that a promise is confirmed by a sign (*Misuse of the Mass*, 174; WA 8:516), but it is unclear why the promise cannot be its own confirmation.

sacrament and testament to move each other to the increase of this faith."[86] Again, however, it is far from obvious why all this is not possible through the Word alone, without any requirement to partake of the sacramental sign. Finally, Luther suggests that in the sacrament, as in confession, "the Word is applied to your person alone. For in preaching it flies out into the whole congregation, and although it strikes you also, yet you are not so sure of it; but here it does not apply to anyone except to you."[87] If this assertion means only that one attends to the "for you" in the words of institution, as Luther's linking it with confession would indicate, it is in no way evident why the intensely interpersonal character of Luther's preaching, with its constant proclamation that the promises of God apply "to you," cannot fulfill the same function.[88]

Luther himself apparently finds none of these reasons pivotal. The principal reason for the bodily mass is the institution of God. The institution of the mass by Christ is also a command. Without any other reason to perform the mass, "then this is reason enough, that God so instituted (eyngesezt) and wills it."[89] God's commandment, "Do this," is sufficient to demand our obedience.[90] The importance of this command is reflected in Luther's resolution of the problem of receiving the sacrament in both kinds. His protest against the practice of withholding the cup is that it violates the practice of the original Supper, in which both bread and wine were distributed and ingested. It is tyranny that the Roman church takes away the "completeness" of the sacrament without any authority to do so.[91] The issue is conformity to the Supper of Christ and the usurpation of Christ's authority. What is not at issue is the power of the sign. Luther is impatient with both sides in the debate over both kinds.[92] On one side, the tenacity with which the practice of withholding the cup is maintained is incomprehensible to him:

[86] Luther, Treatise on the New Testament, 104–5 (WA 6:372–73).

[87] Luther, Confession and the Lord's Supper, 199 (WA 15:486).

[88] This may not be all Luther means, since he makes the same argument about the specificity of the sacrament in opposition to Karlstadt, Zwingli, and Oeclampadius. But its employment in those debates is rooted in an increased stress on the importance of the sign.

[89] Luther, Treatise on the New Testament, 104 (WA 6:372).

[90] Luther, Misuse of the Mass, 172 (WA 8:514). On occasion, Luther suggests that there is no absolute duty to partake of the sacrament (Receiving Both Kinds in the Sacrament, 256; WA 10[II]:30). Especially in the battle with the radicals, Luther insists on the duty to commune, as we will see, and even in the texts of the early 1520s, a duty to eat and drink is invoked. Although there is no resolution of the contradictory statement in Receiving Both Kinds about the command of communion, the reason Luther advises some people to stay away from it is its double efficacy — the sacrament is harmful to those who are uncertain whether they receive its benefits.

[91] Luther, Babylonian Captivity, 20–27 (WA 6:502–7).

[92] Karl Barth notes that Luther showed a "certain indifference" to this question, "which so exercised his contemporaries" ("Luther's Doctrine of the Eucharist: Its Basis and Purpose," in Theology and Church: Shorter Writings, 1920–1928, trans. Louise Pettibone Smith [New York: Harper and Row, 1962], 76–77). Sasse has an excellent review of Luther's position on this issue (This Is My Body, 89–99).

> But now I ask, where is the necessity, where is the religious duty, where is the practical use of denying both kinds, that is, the visible sign, to the laity, when everyone concedes to them the significance of the sacrament without the sign? If they concede the significance, which is the greater, why not the sign, which is the lesser?"[93]

As little as he can discover a rationale for withholding the cup, so little does he understand the demand of the church at Wittenberg that both elements must be consumed. Because there is no "rigorous command" to commune in both kinds,[94] the reception in both kinds is among the "external" issues that are optional and should be treated much as Paul dealt with the problem of circumcision.[95] Without a clear and binding command of Christ, variability of practice is permissible because

> you have, after all, the words of the sacrament and these are the most important part of the sacrament. These words you can take and use (*uben*) just as well whether you receive one element or both elements, or even none at all. So you are in no danger whatever, and yet you do receive the real power (*krafft*) of the sacrament.[96]

The question of both kinds is resolved by the law of love, not through any consideration of the power of the elements.[97] The elements, body and blood contained under bread and wine, seem to be rendered impotent. Yet when Luther confronts his Protestant adversaries, he will insist on the necessity and importance of these elements.

Luther's position against the radicals is less a reversal of direction than a resolution of what had been unclear in 1519 and remains unclear in his second sacramental topography. It never occurred to Luther that the sacramental elements were utterly unimportant. They may be unnecessary on occasion, because God offers divine gifts through many means, but Luther consistently maintains that the sign is part of the sacrament. He moves freely between two alternative conceptions of the relation between sign and Word, for the occasion has not yet arisen that will make them appear as alternatives. On the one hand, Luther implies in the texts just reviewed that the Word of promise in

---

[93] Luther, *Babylonian Captivity*, 23 (translation slightly modified; WA 6:504 reads "rem," which is translated "significance," while the American edition translates it as "grace").

[94] Luther, *Babylonian Captivity*, 28 (WA 6:507).

[95] Luther, *Receiving Both Kinds in the Sacrament*, 239–53 (WA 10[II]:14–28).

[96] Ibid., 255 (WA 10[II]:30). This does not make the reception of the sacrament in one or both kinds entirely optional. The institution of Christ, in both kinds, makes our reception of cup and bread preferable, even "necessary" (Luther, *Eight Sermons at Wittenberg*, 90; WA 10[III]:45). See also the *Smalcald Articles* of 1537, which say: "administration in one form is not the whole order and institution as it was established and commanded by Christ" (Martin Luther, *The Smalcald Articles*, in *The Book of Concord: The Confessions of the Evangelical Lutheran Church*, trans. and ed. Theodore G. Tappert [Philadelphia: Fortress Press, 1959], 311). But, for the sake of love, it should not be made a "compulsory law," both because of the double efficacy of the sacrament and because, if the word is properly preached, the practice of reception in both kinds will develop of itself.

[97] Luther, *Receiving Both Kinds in the Sacrament*, 249–56 WA 10[II]:24–30).

the sacrament is independent and the sign is added as an incidental afterthought, without essential relation to the Word.

But a second option is present, and Luther supports it as well. It is possible that the sign incorporates the Word[98] such that the effects of the Word are concentrated into and transmitted through the sacramental sign, and thereby "through this single sacrament the Word of God and faith [are] fruitfully planted."[99] Luther asserts that the "real body of Christ is present by virtue of the words."[100] The sign still depends on the words to receive its content, but it nonetheless contains what the words themselves do not, namely, the body and blood of Christ. This argument comes to the forefront in Luther's vehement reaction to Zwingli and his allies.[101] In effect, perhaps, Luther's decision for this second alternative is made before the intra-Protestant dispute begins. It is difficult to see how the communication of properties between Christ and the communicant, a constant element of Luther's eucharistic theology, is possible in any way other than that the sign containing the body and blood of Christ is itself a medium of power. It may be such a medium only in dependence on the Word, which renders the body and blood present "for you," but body and blood themselves are already concrete means of Christ's help for earthly persons through the triumph of the resurrection:

> It is, of course, true that there is a distinction between Christ sitting on high in heaven, and being in the sacrament and in the hearts of believers. For certainly he ascended to heaven so that men should and must worship him there and confess him to be the Lord, mighty over all things, Phil. 2. But he is present in the sacrament and in the hearts of believers not really because he wants to be worshiped there, but because he wants there to work with us (*mit uns schaffen*) and help us.[102]

---

[98] It is worth noting that Luther does not, in general, consider the word to be a sign. An exception occurs in *Reception of the Sacrament*, 228 (WA 12:482).

[99] Luther, *Misuse of the Mass*, 191 (WA 8:531).

[100] Luther, *Babylonian Captivity*, 33 (WA 6:510). Quere occasionally periodizes Luther's understanding of the Lord's Supper too finely ("Changes and Constants"). Quere finds Luther introducing the possibility that the body is present in the Supper through the Word only in 1524 (pp. 57–64).

[101] In 1523, Luther shows just how peripheral the body and blood were to his sacramental theology, to say nothing of any specific efficacy that might be ascribed to them: "For if you do even believe that the Sacrament is the body and blood of Christ, how are you made better? To what end does that profit you? The devil believes that too; but what does it help him?" (*Reception of the Sacrament*, 226–27; WA 12:480). It became clear to Luther in the next two years that the devil did not believe it.

[102] Luther, *Adoration of the Sacrament*, 294 (WA 11:446). The translation of *mit uns schaffen* as "work with us" does not capture the link between Christ's sacramental presence and the "new creation."

Defense Against the Radicals

In the debates with the "fanatic"[103] Protestants, the sign, in which lies the body and blood, becomes a battleground because it is the only thing unique to the sacrament.[104] As is true of much in Luther's career, polemics force clarification of his position. In his first topography, Luther's eye was cast on what is subsequent to the sign; in the second, the foundation of the sign in the Word was the focus. In both cases, the point of reflection was to determine "how the heart should hold itself toward the external sacrament."[105] While this remains the most important part of the sacrament, theological emphasis must change with the times. The other part of the sacrament, what one should believe about it, its content "outside the heart and . . . presented to our eyes externally," has come under attack.[106]

"In Remembrance of Me"

What was at stake in the radical reformers' confrontation with Luther was largely this: Is the Eucharist merely a memorial, or does it have power of its own? This Protestant combat over the Eucharist was not about whether or not the sacrament is performed in memory of Christ. Luther's support of 1520

---

[103] Following Luther's disparaging terminology in reference to his opponents requires some explanation. This project is not concerned with the accuracy of Luther's arguments with respect to his many adversaries. Luther may have been unfair to many or all of them. However, an accurate historical treatment of the disputants is well beyond the scope of this effort, which seeks only to present Luther's position, whether fair or not. A lengthy argument that Luther in large part misunderstood Zwingli is found in Barclay, *Protestant Doctrine of the Lord's Supper*, 41–106. A good general discussion of the issues is Heinrich Bornkamm, *Luther in Mid-Career, 1521–1530*, trans. E. Theodore Bachmann, ed. Karin Bornkamm (Philadelphia: Fortress Press, 1983), 501–51, 638–52.

[104] Barth thinks that Luther's "unmoving axis" for interpreting the Lord's Supper had always been the real presence ("Luther's Doctrine of the Eucharist," 100). It is difficult to find evidence for this. It is true that Luther had always assumed the real presence of Christ in the Supper, but this assumption came to have specific consequences only after Luther met the assertion that there is no body of Christ in the Supper. As Seeberg argued earlier, eating itself had little significance before these debates over the real presence.

Seeberg introduces the disagreement with the radicals in 1522, when Luther learns of the alternative understanding of the Supper by some of the Bohemian Brethren (*Text-Book of the History of Doctrines* 2:288). We have placed Luther's sustained response to them in *Adoration of the Sacrament* in the previous section, antedating his defense against the fanatics, for two reasons: First, Luther appears to understand the Bohemian error as minor and correctable, and therefore his response lacks the violent tone of his later work. Second, his exposition of the sacrament does not introduce the new elements that will appear from 1525 on. Barclay (*Protestant Doctrine of the Lord's Supper*) and Sasse (*This Is My Body*) make the same division as this chapter.

[105] Luther, *Sacrament of the Body and Blood of Christ*, 335 (translation modified; WA 19:482 reads: "wie sich das hertz gegen dem eusserlichen Sacrament halten sol").

[106] Luther, *Sacrament of the Body and Blood of Christ*, 335 (WA 19:482–83).

for the duty of remembrance is unchanged.[107] There is no dispute about whether the Lord's Supper is a remembrance of Christ.[108] Remembrance is, after all, commanded by God[109] and obeyed through proclamation.[110] In fact, Luther continues to stress remembrance because it serves part of his own polemical purpose. Since memory refers to a past event for its content, the claim that the Supper is a remembrance is a bulwark against interpreting the sacrament as a sacrifice.[111] Long after the onset of the clash with the radical Protestants, Luther asserts:

> It is a blasphemous outrage to turn the Mass and Sacrament into a sacrifice which one performs for another, or which men sell to one another in order to merit further grace and help. It is to be a remembrance, which everyone is to do for himself, because of grace previously given and received. . . . The Mass has been perverted into a sacrifice, and Christ's remembrance has been suppressed.[112]

Against the repetition of the unique and unrepeatable sacrifice of Christ, Luther maintains the memorial function of the Eucharist this strongly: the sacrament is instituted "chiefly for the sake of this remembrance."[113]

The contest with the radicals is not about the memorial component in the Supper; it does concern the exclusivity of this element. The question is not whether the sacrament is a remembrance but whether it is only a remembrance. When the argument between Luther and his opponents is understood as a battle not between remembrance and its absence but between remembrance alone over against remembrance as one of the several effects of the sacrament,[114] the vista of much broader theological differences comes into view.

[107] Martin Luther, *Treatise on Good Works*, in *Luther's Works*, vol. 44, *The Christian in Society I*, rev. and ed. Atkinson, 55–57 (WA 6:230–31).

[108] Luther, *This Is My Body*, 30 (WA 23:89).

[109] Martin Luther, *Against the Heavenly Prophets in the Matter of Images and Sacraments*, in *Luther's Works*, vol. 40, *Church and Ministry II*, trans. Bernhard Erling and Conrad Bergendoff, ed. Conrad Bergendoff (Philadelphia: Fortress Press, 1958), 133 (WA 18:115).

[110] Luther, *Sacrament of the Body and Blood of Christ*, 349 (WA 19:505).

[111] This is especially clear in Martin Luther, *Admonition Concerning the Sacrament of the Body and Blood of Our Lord*, in *Luther's Works*, vol. 38, *Word and Sacrament IV*, trans. and ed. Lehmann, 102–24 (WA 30 Band [II] [1909], 599–615); see also Martin Luther, *The Private Mass and the Consecration of Priests*, in *Luther's Works*, vol. 38, *Word and Sacrament IV*, trans. and ed. Lehmann, 151 (WA 38 Band [1912], 199). In addition, *Abomination of the Secret Mass*, 27 (WA 18:317), is of interest, for it shows that, at just the time Luther is battling Karlstadt, he employs remembrance as a weapon against sacrifice.

[112] Martin Luther, *Psalm 111*, in *Luther's Works*, vol. 13, *Selected Psalms II*, trans. Daniel E. Poellot, ed. Jaroslav Pelikan (St. Louis: Concordia Publishing House, 1956), 371–72 (WA 31 Band [I] [1913], 411–12).

[113] Luther, *Admonition Concerning the Sacrament*, 111 (WA 30[II]:606).

[114] Jaroslav Pelikan frames Luther's position this way: "But because Christ had commanded the celebration of the Lord's Supper and had promised that his body and blood would be present, the remembrance of his words and deeds was an integral part of the total celebration: it was a means of grace and therefore a remembrance, not *vice versa*" (*Spirit versus Structure: Luther and the Institutions of the Church* [London: Collins, 1968], 124–25).

The nature of the sacramental sign, the presence of the body and blood of Christ in the Supper, and the power of the Eucharist are all in question along with the place of remembrance in the sacramental economy. The interlocking of these themes must be examined. Although the starting point here is the place of memorial, it would be possible to begin an exposition of Luther's position with any of these four issues. The length and virulence of Luther's debate with the radicals required him to construct an entire sacramental fortress. Many of the stones were already laid by Luther before 1525, but upon and around them he erects a more complete and imposing edifice.

Luther's opposition to reducing the sacrament to its use as a memorial is based initially in the suspicion that "mere remembrance" makes the Supper a human work rather than a work of God. Karlstadt "makes a pure commandment and law (gepot und gesetze) which accomplishes nothing more than to tell and bid us to remember and acknowledge [Christ]. Furthermore, he makes this acknowledgement nothing else than a work that we do."[115] According to Luther, the sacrament is supposed to strengthen faith through reception of the sovereign word of promise. It is just this promissory word which is ripped from the sacrament by reducing the meal to mere remembrance. Although Karlstadt proceeds in a way different from Rome, the result is identical—the promise is made into a command, and thereby what is supposed to be had in faith is produced in work, and finally Christ is made into nothing more than a lawgiver and an example.[116] In addition, because it denies the promise, reduction of the sacrament to nothing but a memorial is also a challenge to the sovereignty of God. Since Karlstadt in particular gives justifying power (macht) to the sacrament, the prerogative of justification is given to human inwardness in remembrance and is thus removed from the authority of God.[117]

It is not that Luther objects to the claim that there is a command to remembrance that must be obeyed; he says the same thing himself. But a mere command does not bring with it the ability to obey it, and the sinful human condition means that such demands, apart from the power of God, cannot be fulfilled.[118] As the next chapter demonstrates, the commands of God remain

---

[115] Luther, Against the Heavenly Prophets, 206 (WA 18:196). An excellent discussion of Luther's earlier dealings with Karlstadt, as well as an argument that Luther was not the only, or even historically the most significant, influence in early Reformation thought, is provided by Alister E. McGrath, Iustitia Dei: A History of the Christian Doctrine of Justification, vol. 2, From 1500 to the Present Day (Cambridge: Cambridge University Press, 1986), 20–32.

[116] Luther, Against the Heavenly Prophets, 207 (WA 18:196). Pelikan notes: "Despite their obvious differences, both views [Rome's and the radicals'] seemed to [Luther] to emphasize human initiative and responsibility in the sacrament at the cost of the priority of divine grace" (Spirit versus Structure, 123–24).

[117] Luther, Against the Heavenly Prophets, 207 (WA 18:197); see also Pelikan, Spirit versus Structure, 122.

[118] In 1528, Luther makes the same claim in reference to the Anabaptist doctrine of baptism. If baptism is made to depend on faith, it becomes a mere work. But its Kraft derives only from

in force for the Christian, but Christians are given the capacity of obedience through the gifts of God. What Luther thinks damnable about Karlstadt's understanding of the sacrament is that "only" the command is given; the sacrament accomplishes "nothing more" than state a law, becomes "nothing else" than a work, and so on. The comforting promise of God in the almighty Word, the condition for any possible obedience, is erased.

Moreover, Luther believes that Karlstadt, and later a bevy of others, fundamentally misunderstand the character of remembrance itself. Remembrance is not, as they believe, an inner work of thought, but a duty of external proclamation of God after reception of the Supper.[119] It is therefore not even true that Luther sees no benefit to the duty of remembrance:

> if you had no other reason or benefit (*nutz*) in this sacrament than such remembrance alone, should you not be satisfied with such urging and enticement? Should not your heart say to you: Although I receive no other benefit from it, I still want to be present to the praise and glory of my God; I want to help in upholding his divine glory and also have a share in making him into a true God? . . . I still desire to receive the sacrament for this reason, that by such reception I might confess and bear witness that I also am one who would praise and thank God, and therefore desire to receive the sacrament to the glory of God. Such reception shall be my remembrance with which I think of and thank him for his grace shown me in Christ.[120]

The efficacy of remembrance is not inward but outward; it is the public proclamation that breaks the power (*gewalt*) of the devil.[121] This difference with Luther's opponents, that what Luther insists is external they conceive as inward, discloses a basic conflict over the understanding of God's activity. Luther's assertion that the fanatics have confused the inner and outer realms of life is not limited to the instance of remembrance. This error infects their entire treatment of the Supper. It is especially evident in their understanding of the sign and the real presence of the body and blood of Christ.

Luther's earlier vagueness with respect to the importance of the sign has been noted. Under the attack of fellow Protestants, Luther declares himself. He distinguishes his opponents' position from his own by resorting to a distinction between a "mere sign" and the sacramental "sign."[122] He defends the

---

the ordinance of God. Baptism must be the cornerstone of faith, not the reverse (Martin Luther, *Concerning Rebaptism*, in *Luther's Works*, vol. 40, *Church and Ministry II*, trans. and ed. Bergendoff, 248–49; WA 26:161–62).

[119] Luther, *Against the Heavenly Prophets*, 207 (WA 18:197); *Psalm 111*, 377–78 (WA 31[I]:418).

[120] Luther, *Admonition Concerning the Sacrament*, 108–9 (WA 30[II]:604).

[121] Luther, *Psalm 111*, 377 (WA 31[I]:418). There are also personal benefits associated with fulfillment of the duty of remembrance, noted in *Admonition Concerning the Sacrament*, 125–26 (WA 30[II]:616–17). These too finally issue in external works and proclamation.

[122] Luther, *Sacrament of the Body and Blood of Christ*, 351 (WA 19:508); *The Marburg Colloquy and the Marburg Articles*, in *Luther's Works*, vol. 38, *Word and Sacrament IV*, trans. and ed. Lehmann, 34–35.

second; his opponents the first. What distinguishes the two is the sign's mode of being. A sign can mark something absent or be the signature of something present within the sign itself.[123] Luther's enemies attribute the first type of being to the sacramental sign; it signifies the body and blood of Christ, which are actually at the right hand of God but not in the Supper.

Luther's vociferous denial that the sacramental sign has this mode of being is more subtle than it first appears. He does not deny that a sign of this first type is devoid of value, even religious value. It was, ironically, precisely the recognition that images in churches are just such "memorial signs" that aided his opposition to Karlstadt's iconoclasm. Images may be retained because their lack of intrinsic sacredness does not destroy their usefulness for "witness."[124] On the other hand, it is absolutely unacceptable to argue that the sacramental signs simply point to something they do not contain, namely, the body and blood of Christ. Luther is adamant; if the sign only indicates the body of Christ, which is elsewhere, the sacrament has no special value.

Luther's denial of the analogy between the elements of the sacrament and their work should be placed in this context of the distinction between the two species of sign. Bread and wine have no similarity with the suffering of Christ or the shedding of blood. In addition, there are more adequate signs that could have been employed were bread and wine mere figures of Christ's suffering and redemptive work.[125] The metaphorical interpretation of the Supper "can be neither grammatical nor theological nor natural."[126] These objections to the adequacy of the analogy are not really the chief point. The foundation of Luther's objection is that the analogical understanding of the Supper does faith no good. Not only could the devil discover such natural analogies (if the sacrament contained them), but there would be no need for scripture to announce the presence of the body of Christ. Christians could discover the analogical meaning of bread and wine without the text, and since the fanatics claim this work of "reminding" is the only purpose of the Supper, the words of Christ would be superfluous.[127]

There is another reason to reject the analogical interpretation of the Supper. The separation of sign and what is signified requires an analogical work

---

[123] Luther, *This Is My Body,* 104–5 (WA 23:209). A fascinating comparison is suggested between this theory of the sign and Tillich's notion of the symbol, which "participates" in that to which it points. Tillich's "symbol" seems to be midway between Luther's two modes of being of the sign.

[124] Luther, *Against the Heavenly Prophets,* 91, 96 (WA 18:74, 80). Indeed, Luther thinks that to be a consistent iconoclast is impossible, for one must have images of things in the heart anyway. What harm is there, he asks, in also having images before the eyes (*Against the Heavenly Prophets,* 99–100; WA 18:83)?

[125] Luther, *Confession Concerning Christ's Supper,* 261–68 (WA 26:389–99), is Luther's most sustained attack on the adequacy of the supposed analogy in the sacrament.

[126] Luther, *Confession Concerning Christ's Supper,* 267 (WA 26:398).

[127] Ibid., 261–62 (WA 26:389–91).

to connect the two distinct entities. But this is the work of thought.[128] The recipient of the bread and wine performs the act of signification, connecting the signs to what they suggest, the body and blood of Christ. The material of the sacrament becomes a "memorial sign or thought sign."[129] On the basis of the sovereignty of God, it is clear that Luther must reject this understanding of the sacramental sign. The testament of Christ promises and actually delivers forgiveness; that is its meaning and benefit. Moreover, forgiveness must be granted by God and God alone. However, if the eucharistic work is not connected intrinsically to the sign but requires an act of human thought to make the tie actual, God is no longer the only ground of forgiveness, because, strictly speaking, God no longer constructs the sacrament. This is why Luther accuses Karlstadt not just of making the sacrament into a work but of making it into a work of justification.

Luther's opposition to human activity as in any way constitutive of the Supper explains both the intimate connection he draws between the thought-sign and the erasure of sacramental power, and the importance he attaches to the nature of the sign:

> [The fanatics] deprive us of [the body and blood] also, and in so cruel a manner that I believe the devil is trying his utmost and that the day of judgment is not far off. I should rather be dead than hear Christ so scorned and abused by them. They say that it is only a sign by which one may recognize Christians and judge them, so that we have nothing more of it than the mere shell. So they come together, and eat and drink, so that they may commemorate his death. All the power (*krafft*) is said to be in the commemoration (*bedencken*), the bread and wine are no more than a memorial sign (*malzeichen*) and a color by which one may recognize that we are Christians.[130]

The effect is that "the appearance and shell" of the Supper remain, "but the kernel and the power (*krafft*)" are removed.[131] The efficacy of the sacrament depends on the recipient's relation to it. The meal communicates mercy to the believer in order that faith may be strengthened, but it is poison to the unbeliever. In either case, the sacrament itself is constituted independently of the communicant, a point especially clear after Luther removed faith from the sacrament proper. Only the ordinance of God makes the Supper what it is. Against Rome, this preserved the sovereignty of God over against the appropriation of mediating power by an officiating priest. In the case of Zwingli and his allies, however, the believer becomes her or his own mediator. Faith not only determines one's relation to the sacrament but makes the

[128] Seeberg, *Text-Book of the History of Doctrines* 2:327.

[129] Luther, *This Is My Body*, 18, translates this as "symbol or memorial sign"; WA 23:71 reads instead, "malzeichen odder denckzeichen."

[130] Luther, *Sacrament of the Body and Blood of Christ*, 348 (translation slightly modified; WA 19:503–4).

[131] Luther, *Admonition Concerning the Sacrament*, 101 (WA 30[II]:598).

sacrament into a sacrament in the first place. The sovereign promise of God, as well as God's privilege of making the sacrament, is usurped.

To reduce the sacrament's effect and very existence to the human work of remembrance is, in fact, an obliteration of its power. Reminiscent of his famous saying "The God you believe, you shall have," Luther maintains that since the fanatics believe only bread and wine is present in the Supper, so it is—for them.[132] The power of the sacrament is utterly eliminated, and the sacrament works only injury upon them. It is important to notice that the emasculation of the sacrament occurs because Zwingli and his allies constitute the Supper inwardly, in the subjectivity of thought. The external sign does not do anything. Luther's rejection of this position implies, first, that the outer sign is a necessary component of sacramental power and, second, that purely inward power is a chimera. A defense of these two theses requires discussion of the second mode of being of a sign, proper to the Lord's Supper.

Against the claim that the sign of the Supper simply points to what is apart from it, Luther argues that the sacramental sign contains the reality of which it is the signature. The division is between the signified being "represented by" and being "in" the sign or, alternatively, between saying the sign "points to" the body and blood, and saying it "is" the body and blood.[133] The pivotal words of Christ, "This is my body," are Luther's bastion against any suggestion that Christ's body is absent from the sacrament. The path to conceiving of this second type of a sign's being was prepared by his earlier assertion that the Word makes the body and blood present in the elements of the Eucharist. When confronted by his Protestant detractors, he repeats: "For as soon as Christ says: 'This is my body,' his body is present through the Word and the power (krafft) of the Holy Spirit. If the Word is not there, it is mere bread; but as soon as the words are added they bring that of which they speak."[134] God's word is "certainly not an afterword (nachwort), but a power-word (machtwort) which creates (schaffet) what it says."[135] The Word of power

---

[132] Luther, *This Is My Body*, 131–32 (WA 23:255).

[133] Ibid., 34–39 (WA 23:97–103).

[134] Luther, *Sacrament of the Body and Blood of Christ*, 341 (WA 19:491); see also *Against the Heavenly Prophets*, 209–10 (WA 18:199); and *This Is My Body*, 104–6 (WA 23:209–13).

[135] Luther, *Confession Concerning Christ's Supper*, 181 (translation modified; WA 26:283); see also *Marburg Colloquy and Marburg Articles*, 27, where Luther identifies the power-word as the distinctive feature of God's Word compared with our words, which are "mere sounds." See also ibid., 41–42, 56–57. For Luther, this is the way to avoid the Donatist position he believes Zwingli must finally be driven to affirm.

Luther does, however, find some analogies to this intrasignificatory sign in ordinary language. Although they are never determinative for his theological understanding, they still illuminate the point he is trying to make. For example, a woodcut of a rose is really a rose in addition to signifying a "real" rose. The reason for this is that "is" refers to the essence of a thing, preeminently to its meaning. The "essence" of the thing is therefore uncoupled in Luther's thought from a simple naturalism and includes a more phenomenological emphasis on the meaning of the thing. For Luther, Rome's doctrine of transubstantiation and the radicals' obliteration of the body from the

grounds Luther's understanding of the second mode of being of the sign. If the sign points at all, it points to what it contains. Aside from being a dangerous exercise in thought, positing an analogy between the elements and the body of Christ is unnecessary. The Word brings body into bread irrespective of any similarity that may or may not exist between them.

The debate over the role of remembrance in the Lord's Supper and the nature of the sign was a vicious one. From Luther's perspective, its acrimony was justified by the size of the stakes. The contest was about nothing less than the power of God, in two ways. Luther's belief that the sovereignty of God's establishment of the sacrament had been attacked has been discussed. But there is another point in question, the character and operation of power itself.

Inward and External Power

There were many objections to Luther's assertion of the real presence of the body of Christ in the Lord's Supper. The one Luther treated most seriously (and contemptuously) was that Christ's body cannot be in two places at the same time. Since Scripture maintains that Christ ascended into heaven and is seated at the right hand of God, Christ's presence in the Supper is impossible.[136] Part of Luther's answer to this objection is that Christ is not "locally" present in the sacrament, "like meat from a butcher shop." The significance of the alternative modes of presence Luther delineates for a theory of power is analyzed later. For the moment, concentration is upon Luther's understanding of the "right hand of God." God's right hand is not, as the fanatics imagine, a "seat at a special, single location, like a bird in its bower."[137] That is a fleshly idea.[138] Indeed, the right hand is not a place at all, but the almighty power (*almechtige gewalt*) of God,[139] through which the Godhead rules all things.

Once the right hand is identified with God's power, Luther takes a crucial step. He immediately links God's omnipotence and omnipresence.[140] The basis for his argument is twofold. First, Luther is convinced that power is fundamental to the very notion of God. Power is God's self; it is not "an axe, hatchet, saw, or file with which he works, but is himself."[141] Second, God's power is transcendent, which explains why the activity of God cannot be submitted

---

Supper are both slaves of such naturalistic reason, although in opposite directions (see esp. *Confession Concerning Christ's Supper,* 255–58, 295; WA 26:383–84, 439).

[136] See, e.g., Luther, *Confession Concerning Christ's Supper,* 195 (WA 26:299–300).

[137] Luther, *This Is My Body,* 96, 73 (WA 23:197, 159). Luther seems to have a preference for bird metaphors on this point. See also *Confession Concerning Christ's Supper,* 281 (WA 26:422). They are cited here, fearlessly in the face of the obvious comic opening.

[138] Luther, *This Is My Body,* 55 (WA 23:131); see also *Sacrament of the Body and Blood of Christ,* 342 (WA 19:492); *Confession Concerning Christ's Supper,* 202–3 (WA 26:312–13).

[139] Luther, *This Is My Body,* 57 (WA 23:133).

[140] Sasse notes "where Luther speaks of the omnipotence of God or of the Lord of the Universe, the idea that this Lord is everywhere is expressed for the first time" (*This Is My Body,* 107–8).

[141] Luther, *This Is My Body,* 61 (WA 23:139).

to the standards of reason; reason cannot capture the power of God within its narrow confines.[142] It is exactly this transcendence of power which supports the possibility of God's ubiquitous immanence. Because God transcends any place, Christ can be present in all places:

> The Scriptures teach us, however, that the right hand of God is not a specific place in which a body must or may be, such as on a golden throne, but is the almighty power of God, which at one and the same time can be nowhere and yet must be everywhere. It cannot be at any one place, I say. For if it were at some specific place, it would have to be there in a circumscribed and determinate manner, as everything which is at one place must be at that place determinately and measurably, so that it cannot be meanwhile at any other place. But the power of God cannot be so determined and measured, for it is uncircumscribed and immeasurable, beyond and above all that is or may be.[143]

From this perspective, omnipresence occurs through omnipotence. But just as presence requires power, so conversely, power operates only through God's presence to creatures. If "God creates, effects, and preserves all things through his almighty power and right hand," this means "he *must* be present and must make and preserve his creation both in its innermost and outermost aspects" (emphasis added). Omnipotence directly implies God's essential presence in all places, to the point that "nothing can be more truly present and within all creatures than God himself with his power."[144] Power and presence are mutually implicating correlates to such an extent that one cannot be without the other. There is no temporal question of which comes first, power or presence. The power of God transcends all special places, so that God may be present everywhere, while God's presence makes the appearance of power

---

[142] See, e.g., Luther, *This Is My Body*, 59 (WA 23:137); *Marburg Colloquy and Marburg Articles*, 75.

[143] Luther, *This Is My Body*, 57 (WA 23:133); see also *Confession Concerning Christ's Supper*, 207 (WA 26:317–18); *Marburg Colloquy and Marburg Articles*, 66.

[144] Luther, *This Is My Body*, 57–58 (emphasis added), 58 (WA 23:133–35, 135); see also *This Is My Body*, 61 (WA 23:139). The frequent reversibility of priority of omnipresence and omnipotence in Luther is noted by Barclay, *Protestant Doctrine of the Lord's Supper*, 78.

In *This Is My Body*, Luther uses several different terms for "presence." In the passages quoted in this paragraph, Luther ranges from "God must be in all places (*an allen orten sein mus*)," to the claim that God must be "in" all things, as well as "in, . . . on all sides, through and through, below and above, before and behind" all things, to the interesting statement that God must be in all places essentially and presently (*gegenwartig*)," with the latter's connotations of temporal presence tied up with the assertion of spatial presence. All of these are accurately translated by "presence," but the English is more ambiguous since it collapses several German terms into one word.

The variety of prepositions used means that "in" should not be taken in a "physical" sense but is "equivalent to 'above,' 'beyond,' 'beneath,' 'through and through,' and 'everywhere'" (*Confession Concerning Christ's Supper*, 230 (WA 26:341). Luther finds support for this expansive meaning of "in" in the Hebrew Scriptures (*Confession Concerning Christ's Supper*, 320–21; WA 26:464–65). This is absolutely central to understanding Luther's persistent claim that he was misinterpreted by the radicals.

possible. There is a coexistence of power and presence on one hand, and transcendence and immanence on the other.

The correlation of power and presence is the foundation for Luther's explanation of the real presence of Christ in the Supper. Indeed, once power and presence demand each other, the question of Christ's presence becomes trivial — if Christ is present everywhere, surely the divine presence includes the Supper as an instance of this universal presence.[145] But does this presence have to be bodily? Luther does not limit himself to asserting a general divine omnipresence but adds that Christ "must be, orally and bodily, in places and localities."[146] It was not his assertion of the omnipresence of God that made Luther's opponents scratch their heads in astonishment, but the unyielding declaration that such presence is bodily.[147] Luther puts the attack of his opponents against him in several different ways. They argue that the presence of Christ occurs only through the faith of the recipient, that Christ's presence is, therefore, inward and spiritual rather than external and bodily. Alternatively, Oeclampadius claims that while God's truth is everywhere, truth does not entail bodily presence.[148] Especially in the latter form, it is clear that Luther's assurance that the presence of Christ in the Supper must be bodily opposes any idealist notion of presence or power. The presence through which power appears is a material, bodily one. It is inward and spiritual also (although these two are not the same), but neither presence nor power can be only inward. This claim contains momentous implications for how power is conceived.

It is useful to pause and note the choices available for a theology of power at this point. Since the purpose is to construct a theory of power that avoids the identification of power and external sovereignty, the easiest solution is to adopt the spiritual interpretation of the sacrament Luther so vehemently rejects. The radical reformers comprehend the power of the sacrament as purely inward. Luther believes, on the other hand, that a purely inward power is no power at all. He is in fundamental agreement with sovereignty theory on the external origin of power. Power not only has an external component, but the sacrament itself, which has to be the source of sacramental power, is constituted purely externally.[149] Why, then, follow Luther's lead rather than his opponents'?

---

[145] Luther, *This Is My Body,* 57, 63–64 (WA 23:137, 143).

[146] Luther, *Against the Heavenly Prophets,* 221 (WA 18:211).

[147] See, e.g., *Marburg Colloquy and Marburg Articles,* 29, in which Oeclampadius admits the presence of Christ according to Christ's (nonbodily) divinity, but not according to Christ's humanity. Luther refuses to sever the "two natures" in this way.

[148] Luther, *This Is My Body,* 55 (WA 23:131).

[149] See Barclay, *Protestant Doctrine of the Lord's Supper,* 6–7. Barclay is certainly right that Luther believes that faith is not the source of sacramental power; however, when he goes further and asserts that the sacrament has an "inherent" power in Luther which, moreover, reverses Luther's position of 1520, the argument becomes confusing. It does not make sense to say, as Barclay does, that the sacrament has an inherent power that only takes effect when it is appropriated by faith. The problem is that Barclay confuses "source" with "inherency." The argument he is

The arguments Luther makes in his own behalf will be examined; however, there is no need to be limited by the grounds he provides for rejecting the spiritualist position. The intuitive basis for lending a serious ear to Luther's position against the spiritualists is that a purely inward understanding of power comes very close to a complete transvaluation of power, in which real power is powerlessness, real strength is weakness, and so on.[150] A deep suspicion regarding the value and plausibility of this approach was expressed at the beginning. A frequent companion of this transvaluing tendency, the division of "good, spiritual" power from undesirable "natural" power, is examined in the final two chapters. If one opts for a pure transvaluation of power, Luther's opponents have more to say than Luther.[151] On the other hand, if a transvaluation of power collapses in contradiction, Luther's sacramental theology offers a productive alternative.

Sacramental power has a source external to the communicant. This is established prior to the controversy with the radicals. The arbitrariness Luther saw in the Roman interpretation of the meaning of the sacrament convinced him that the Word had to be the criterion of sacramental meaning. The promise is external, made by God alone. In the dispute with the radicals, Luther's application of the requirement for external power in the Supper means that the sacrament is not efficacious only through remembrance. The emphasis on the power and strength of the Word of promise is maintained throughout.[152]

Luther is presented with an additional problem, however, one not entirely solved by stressing "Word" without qualification. The spiritualists' claim that the content of sacramental meaning is inward and spiritual opens the possibility that one might receive the "inner Word" without the outer Word. In opposing a notion of any purely inward spirit or Word, Luther makes two decisions.

---

making is better expressed by saying that, according to Luther, the sacrament's power has an external source, without equating origin with inherent power

[150] It is perhaps no accident that Continental pacifist Christian traditions tend to have their roots in the radical Reformation rather than in Lutheranism or Calvinism.

[151] It is true that Luther sometimes performs his own transvaluation of power. This is especially true in his contrast between the "revealed" and "hidden" Christ. In the passion, for example, Christ's power is hidden under weakness. Moreover, he is not averse to employing Paul's formula of "power (krafft) will be perfect through weakness (unkrafft)" (Martin Luther, Admonition to Peace, a Reply to the Twelve Articles of the Peasants in Swabia, in Luther's Works, vol. 46, The Christian in Society III, trans. Charles M. Jacobs, rev. and ed. Robert C. Schultz (Philadelphia: Fortress Press, 1967), 32 (WA 18:315, for example). In The Freedom of a Christian, 355 (WA 7:57), this transvaluation of power is part of the definition of spiritual power (potentia), which can be powerful even when subject to domination (dominatur). Again, the fact that Luther never sets out to develop a theology of power means that several such theologies are present in his work, even if they coexist uneasily or not at all. The christological problem is, on its face, the most likely to invalidate the theology of power we are attempting to develop. The motif of "conquest through service" in Two Kinds of Righteousness, 301–2 (WA 2:148), vacillates between maintaining that this is true power and holding that it is the resignation of power. Attention is given to this issue in chapter 6.

[152] Luther, Against the Heavenly Prophets, 212 (WA 18:202); This Is My Body, 61, 132 (WA 23:139, 255–57).

First, "inner spirit," if it is from God, neither does nor can teach anything different from the external Word. In God's ordering of the world, the external must precede the inward.[153] Therefore, the external Word is necessarily prior to the inner Spirit, and this order cannot be reversed.[154] Absent agreement with the external ordinances of God, the affirmation that one has the "Holy Spirit with all [its] feathers and eggs"[155] is seditious nonsense. Whatever gifts of the Spirit one has are given only through God's Word and signs, the power (*krafft*) of God for salvation.[156] In short, God gives no Word or command without also giving something material.[157]

Luther is concerned that positing an inner Word independent of the external Word creates the same arbitrariness the sacramental theology of Rome produced by ignoring the words of institution. The radicals reverse the direction of error, of course—whereas the pope made inward matters external, Luther's Protestant opponents make properly external matters inward. The result, however, is the same: the Word of God is overthrown, and "whatever ideas occurred to some fool" are called "an inspiration of the Holy Spirit."[158] Luther is not shy about identifying the source of the radical interpretation. Against Schwenkfeld, Luther writes:

> The devil stalks about boldly and without disguise and teaches us to openly disregard Scripture, just as Münzer and Karlstadt did, who developed their wisdom out of the witness of their "inwardness," and needed the Holy Scriptures not for themselves but only for the instruction of others, as an external witness to the witness in their inwardness. Whoever believes such a manifest devil, however, will willingly go into the fire of hell.[159]

It is through these spirits of pure inwardness that the devil's ultimate goal of doing away with the sacrament and all outer ordinances of God can be accomplished.[160] In some sense, pure inwardness is not merely the devil's purpose, but the devil's self: "[the fanatics] want nothing but spirit; and indeed, this is what they do have: the devil, who has neither flesh nor bone."[161]

The interdependence of external and inward Word and the corresponding denial that a purely inward relation to God is possible have two implications. First, an outward, bodily component must be present as a condition of faith and any inward relation to the Spirit of God. This point is explored

[153] Luther, *Against the Heavenly Prophets*, 146 (WA 18:136); see also Sasse, *This Is My Body*, 145.

[154] Luther, *Against the Heavenly Prophets*, 195 (WA 18:185).

[155] Ibid., 162 (WA 18:152).

[156] Ibid., 146 (WA 18:136).

[157] Luther, *This Is My Body*, 135–36 (WA 23:261).

[158] Martin Luther, *Sermons on the Gospel of St. John, Chapters 6–8*, in *Luther's Works*, vol. 23, *Sermons on the Gospel of St. John, Chapters 6–8*, trans. Martin H. Bertram, ed. Jaroslav Pelikan (St. Louis: Concordia Publishing House, 1959), 174 (WA 33 Band [1907], 274).

[159] Luther, *Confession Concerning Christ's Supper*, 202–3 (WA 26:434).

[160] Luther, *Against the Heavenly Prophets*, 195 (WA 18:181).

[161] Luther, *This Is My Body*, 136 (WA 23:261).

in greater depth in a moment, in connection with Luther's distinction between the spiritual and the inward. Second, the external Word becomes the criterion of inward spiritual health. The external Word, moreover, is a public Word. To the extent that "inner power" is an operative concept in Luther, this cannot be interpreted in a privatistic manner. Rather, inner power is submitted to the public criterion of the Word. An analysis of this thesis is especially important in relation to the significance of the external law, a topic reserved for the next chapter.

Luther's refusal to sever the content of the external and inner word is not the most dramatic choice he makes in opposing the theology of inwardness. That honor is accorded his breaking of the equation of the inward and the spiritual, on one hand, and the external and fleshly, on the other.[162] This allows Luther to affirm, as he has from the beginning, that the Supper must be eaten spiritually. But his denial of the assumption that what is spiritual is inward, and what is bodily is fleshly, means that spiritual consumption does not exclude bodily and external eating. Only fleshly, not bodily, partaking, is an abuse of the sacrament. "Spirit" and "flesh" do not distinguish the anthropological areas of human inwardness and externality; rather, they are both inward determining principles.[163] What is spiritual is whatever is done through the Spirit and faith, including what is done outwardly with the body.[164] In fact, "spirit" must be given a breadth of meaning that encompasses what is outward and bodily, for two reasons. To begin with, all external acts would be thoroughly worthless if the body were per se condemned, for the soul requires the body in order to act outwardly. It is clear, also, that the body must act, for without the organs of the body there can be neither works of love nor proclamation of the Word. Under the reign of the Spirit, external action is spiritual.[165] In the second place, the body, no less than the soul, is part of God's creation. This means both that "flesh, bone, skin, and hair . . . are all good creatures of God," and that God's promise to redeem the whole of creation must include the body.[166]

Just as spirit is, first, an inward principle and secondarily affects outward activity, so it is with "flesh." This is true at least when Scripture refers to "flesh" unadorned, as it does in the second part of the disputed text of John 6:63: "It is the spirit that gives life, the flesh is of no avail; the words that I have spoken to you are spirit and life."[167] The text does not refer to the body of

---

[162] This is discussed by Barth, *Luther's Doctrine of the Eucharist*, 75–76. Luther's choice, at least, clarified an ambiguity in his thought. In the *Blessed Sacrament of the Body*, we saw, he did equate the fleshly with the external, the spiritual with the inward.

[163] Luther, *Confession Concerning Christ's Supper*, 287 (WA 26:432).

[164] Luther, *This Is My Body*, 92, 99 (WA 23:189, 203).

[165] Ibid., 92–93 (WA 23:189).

[166] Luther, *Confession Concerning Christ's Supper*, 237 (WA 26:351).

[167] All of the themes discussed in relation to this text are summarized in Luther's 1531 sermon on John 6:63 (*Sermons on John, Chapters 6–8*, 165–76; WA 33:259–78). The exegetical methods

Christ present in the sacrament, because it does not say "my [Christ's] flesh."[168] In 1520, Luther had also denied the applicability of John 6:63 to the sacrament, but on the basis of the parts of the text referring to spirit: "For the sacramental eating does not give life, since many eat unworthily. Hence Christ cannot be understood in this passage to be speaking about the sacrament."[169] The requirement of faith for the sacrament's proper efficacy, unmentioned in this verse, ruled out a sacramental referent. In the case at hand, his opponents' rejection of the benefit of Christ's flesh in the Eucharist becomes Luther's focus.[170]

"Flesh" is not the body, but the old Adam, which "has power (*vermag*) only to seek its own from everyone else."[171] It is whatever "is devoid of spirit, existing in its own power (*krafft*), work, use, wisdom, will, and ability."[172] The body may be the home of the "coarser sins," but the most dangerous sins are inward.[173] Flesh includes, Luther maintains, the "best faculties" of the natural person, "the intellect, senses, will, heart, and mind." The whole of the flesh, "all its actions and its powers are of no avail (*vermügen kein nütze*)."[174] John 6:63, so interpreted, is in keeping with the doctrine of justification by grace alone, since only God can effect the transition from the "old Adam" to the "new creation."[175] This rendering of "flesh" also means that the work of mortification, of putting the old, natural person to death, is no longer simply asceticism practiced in relation to the body, by donning the "grey coat" of self-abnegation, as Karlstadt did with all fleshly pride of heart. Rather, mortification is to be practiced on the entire flesh, both inward and external.

---

and conclusions of the combatants in these disputes, which were a crucial part of their differences, have been ignored for the most part. A superb analysis of Luther's methods is contained in Jaroslav Pelikan, *Luther the Expositor: Introduction to the Reformer's Exegetical Writings,* Luther's Works Companion Volume (St. Louis: Concordia Publishing House, 1959).

[168] Luther, *Against the Heavenly Prophets*, 203 (WA 18:193); *Confession Concerning Christ's Supper,* 249–52 (WA 26:374–78).

[169] Luther, *Babylonian Captivity,* 19 (WA 6:502).

[170] Luther believed that he eventually convinced Zwingli of the inapplicability of John 6:63 (*Brief Confession Concerning the Holy Sacrament,* 299–300; WA 54:152).

[171] Luther, *Confession Concerning Christ's Supper,* 201 (WA 26:310–11); see also ibid., 249–50 (WA 26:374–75); and *This Is My Body,* 95–96 (WA 23:195–97).

[172] Luther, *Confession Concerning Christ's Supper,* 237 (translation modified; WA 26:352).

[173] Luther, *Judgment on Monastic Vows,* 277 (WA 8:593); see also Martin Luther, *The Bondage of the Will,* in *Luther's Works,* vol. 33, *Career of the Reformer III,* trans. and ed. Philip S. Watson (Philadelphia: Fortress Press, 1972), 227–28 (WA 18:744), in which he says that to identify body with flesh also cheapens the grace of Christ. What kind of Redeemer is it, he asks, who is only capable of saving us from the basest part of ourselves, while we ourselves are able to care for what is greatest in us adequately?

[174] Luther, *This Is My Body,* 96 (WA 23:195–97). A sustained exposition is contained in *Bondage of the Will,* 222–29 (WA 18:740–45); see also *Treatise on Good Works,* 43–45 (WA 6:220–22); *Against Latomus,* 179 (WA 8:71); WA 18:719; *Against the Heavenly Prophets,* 203 (WA 18:193); *Lectures on Galatians, 1535, Chapters 1–4,* 40–41 (WA 40[I]:95–96).

[175] See esp. *Confession Concerning Christ's Supper,* 200–203 (WA 26:308–13).

The overarching definition of "flesh" must be distinguished from Christ's flesh, which does mean Christ's body.[176] The radicals' failure to distinguish these two meanings of flesh leads them to make Christ's body unprofitable (*unnütze*).[177] But, Luther maintains, since "spiritual" means anything having its source in the Spirit, including physical things, Christ's flesh is compatible with the Spirit;[178] born of the power (*krafft*) and work of the Holy Spirit, Christ's flesh is pure spirit, the Spirit's bodily dwelling place.[179] Luther goes further. This flesh, Christ's flesh, must be beneficial to Christians. The spiritual, idealist position of the fanatics really denies the efficacy of Christ, not only in the sacrament but in our salvation as a whole. If there is no benefit to Christ's body in the Supper, then neither can the body of Christ have helped us anywhere, even on the cross. On the other hand, if Christ's body is efficacious for us there, as it must be if the ancient heresies are to be avoided, then it can and does benefit us in the Supper also.[180]

The efficacy of the sacrament, then, is conditioned by a double externality. In the first place, the outer, public Word makes the body and blood of Christ present in the sacrament. At the intersection of Word and the visible elements of bread and wine, the power of the Word renders the body and blood present. In turn, the bodily presence of Christ in the Supper, dependent on the Word, conditions the benefits for the communicant. A subtle shift in Luther's emphasis can be detected. The power of the Word takes on a slightly different function than it had earlier in his career. While it had been unclear, previously, whether the body and blood actually served a purpose, even if they were present in the Supper, Luther now pronounces that the body and blood of Christ themselves, invisibly contained in the sign, are beneficial to the believer. Luther describes the relation of the components of the sacrament this way:

> See, then, what a beautiful, great, marvelous thing this is, how everything meshes together in one sacramental reality. The words are the first thing, for without the word the cup and the bread would be nothing. Further,

---

[176] The exegetical basis of Luther's distinction between a "flesh" that is not identical with the body and the flesh of Christ, which does refer to the body, is explained in *Bondage of the Will*, 215 (WA 18:735–36): "the Hebrew language has only the one word 'flesh' for what we express by the two words 'flesh' and 'body,' and I wish this distinction of terms had been observed in translation throughout the whole canon of Scripture."

[177] Luther, *This Is My Body*, 99 (WA 23:203).

[178] Luther insists on the compatibility of bodily and spiritual eating several times in the reports in *Marburg Colloquy and Marburg Articles*, 17, 39–40.

[179] Luther, *Confession Concerning Christ's Supper*, 237 (WA 26:352); *This Is My Body*, 95 (WA 23:195).

[180] Luther, *This Is My Body*, 82–85, 99 (WA 23:173–77, 201–3); see also *Confession Concerning Christ's Supper*, 246–47, 292 (WA 26:369–70, 436). Luther detects undertones of these heresies in the position of his opponents. He thinks they must finally be driven to a Marcionite denial that Christ had a body at all, since Christ's possession of a body could only have interfered with the salvific work.

> without bread and cup, the body and blood of Christ would not be there. Without the body and blood of Christ, the new testament would not be there. Without the new testament, forgiveness of sins would not be there, Without forgiveness of sins, life and salvation would not be there. Thus the word first connects the bread and cup to the sacrament; bread and cup embrace the body and blood of Christ; body and blood of Christ embrace the new testament; the new testament embraces the forgiveness of sins; forgiveness of sins embraces eternal life and salvation.[181]

The efficacy of the Word is now mediated by the sign and the body of Christ lying under it.

Although this twofold externality of Word and sign conditions sacramental benefit, it is not sufficient. Luther could not, of course, maintain that Word and sign guarantee the intended efficacy of the Supper without backing into the Roman position that the sacrament is efficacious irrespective of the inward faith of the recipient. The Lord's Supper is, of course, instituted for the spiritual benefit of the recipient, but the actual occurrence of this help depends on a three-way confluence of Word of promise, body and blood of Christ present in the bread and wine through the Word, and the Spirit of faith which both hears and believes the Word, and receives the elements containing Christ's body. The radicals' emphasis on spiritual eating is not in question.[182] Luther's objection is rather that they defeat their own intention; they cannot eat spiritually because they will not eat physically. An exclusive focus on inward remembrance is ultimately powerless at just the point it intends to be effective, that is, spiritually, for it makes the body of Christ into mere flesh.

In regard to the specific power and benefits of the Eucharist, much of what Luther says in the dispute with the radicals repeats what he said previously. The Supper's benefit for the heart is not now, as it had been earlier, the focus of the argument. The new element is that sacramental benefits are directly tied to the actual, physical eating of the sacrament; that communicates the power of the Word. The sign, while dependent on the Word, has a specific power that had not been clear earlier. The distinctive mark of Luther's writings against the Protestants is not in his exposition of the benefits of the Supper, but his account of the way they are communicated to the recipient.

The Supper retains its double efficacy. Luther preserves the distinction between the nature of the sacrament and its use.[183] All effects of the sacrament, whether flowing from its proper use or its abuse in unbelief, are effects of power:

> If a fornicator comes [to the table], he receives the true sacrament, because it does not lose power on account of his impiety and infidelity. Our unbelief does not alter God's Word. This I have often said. . . . Misuse does not change

---

[181] Luther, *Confession Concerning Christ's Supper,* 338 (WA 26:478–79).
[182] Luther, *This Is My Body,* 30 (WA 23:89); *Confession Concerning Christ's Supper,* 191 (WA 26:292).
[183] See, e.g., Luther, *Sacrament of the Body and Blood of Christ,* 346 (WA 19:501).

God's Word. A robber abuses the light of day, the sun, and yet it remains the sun."[184]

These two powers of the sacrament do not have equivalent standing. The proper intention of the sacrament, that for which it is instituted, is forgiveness of sin. It is instituted for the aid of spirit and heart. The condemning power of the Eucharist, on the other hand, occurs when the proper power of the sacrament does not attain this spiritual end, when there is no faith for it to confront and strengthen. If the sacrament meets unbelief, the communicant abuses the Supper.[185] This abuse of the sacrament, preventing it from reaching its inward destination of faith, takes its revenge on the unbelieving communicant. The loss of Christ's sacraments is the same as the total loss of Christ.[186]

To this point, Luther's understanding of the alien, condemning efficacy of the sacrament does not seem to differ much from the position he took between 1520 and 1524. He even returns to the argument that the specific power of the sacrament, both proper and distorted, occurs because the sacrament is given to the person individually, while the Word is spoken generally and without individual reference.[187] Luther's language is the same as in 1524. However, the meaning of the words is different. The personalism of the Supper now emerges from the mediation of the Word by the body and blood of Christ. The benefit of the sacrament no longer has its sole ground in hearing the Word connected to the Supper, but also in the peculiar efficacy of the body and blood. Guilt, sin, and the poisonous effect of the Supper are incurred in relation to the body of Christ, because the unbelieving communicant does not discern its presence. Here, too, the fanatics confuse spirit and flesh, for they make the communion (*gemeynschafft*) purely spiritual. They eat judgment upon themselves because of their external guilt in regard to the sacramental food.[188] Since body and blood mediate the powerful Word of the sacrament, guilty abuse of the Supper pertains to the body of Christ as well as the Word. Just as the proper spiritual effect of the sacrament occurs through the bodily consump-

---

[184] Martin Luther, *Ten Sermons on the Catechism*, in *Luther's Works*, vol. 51, *Sermons I*, trans. and ed. Doberstein, 189 (WA 30 Band [I] [1910], 118); see also *Against the Heavenly Prophets*, 205 (WA 18:194–95). An alternative expression of Luther's point is found in *Private Mass and the Consecration of Priests*, 193–94 (WA 38:235): "Abuse does not abolish the essence, but the essence endures the abuse."

[185] Luther, *Ten Sermons on the Catechism*, 189 (WA 30[I]:118).

[186] Luther, *Concerning Rebaptism*, 231–33 (WA 26:146–49).

[187] Luther, *Sacrament of the Body and Blood of Christ*, 348–50 (WA 19:504–7).

[188] Luther, *Against the Heavenly Prophets*, 179–86 (WA 18:169–77). Luther also attacks Rome on this new ground. The presence of the body and blood of Christ means that those who perform private masses "are the greatest thieves of God and robbers of the church," for they no longer give the body of Christ as a communion and common meal to strengthen and comfort [Christians] in their faith" (*Private Mass and the Consecration of Priests*, 159; WA 38:206–7).

tion of it,[189] so its spiritual misuse derives from failure to recognize this physical element.

A similar magnification of the special role of the body and blood in sacramental power is evident in relation to the spiritual *telos* of the Supper. Certainly, even the unbeliever may obtain the physical benefits of bread and wine in communing; however, this purely natural efficacy, since it is not the purpose of the sacrament, does not alter the spiritual hemlock the unbeliever consumes. Body and blood themselves become poison. The Supper would be simply unprofitable, but not injurious, if Christ were not present. The damage incurred by the unbeliever "proves that [Christ] is there. If he were not there, the physical eating would be harmless and useful; but now since it is of no avail (*kein nütze*) and even harmful, [Christ's body] must surely be present and be eaten."[190] The purpose of the sacrament determines its benefits and power, as before, but the *telos* declared in the Word is now either effected or corrupted through the interaction of faith and the body of Christ under the sign.

Distorted sacramental power has substantial affinities with the model of dominating power outlined in the first chapter. It is applied upon the communicant from outside and never becomes inner power. It is dominating and

---

[189] Luther, *This Is My Body,* 95 (WA 23:193). This is why Luther can deny the argument that if spiritual eating is sufficient, bodily eating is not necessary (*Marburg Colloquy and Marburg Articles,* 80).

[190] Luther, *This Is My Body,* 87 (WA 23:181); see also *Confession Concerning Christ's Supper,* 341–48 (WA 26:481–87), where Luther gives sustained attention to 1 Cor. 11:27–29, and *Marburg Colloquy and Marburg Articles,* 42–43.

Barclay dismisses this mediation of the Word through the materiality of the sacrament and continues to insist that the body of Christ really has very little function in Luther's sacramental theology (*Protestant Doctrine of the Lord's Supper,* 238–50). For example, Barclay says, "Luther also makes the body of Christ the substance of the Lord's Supper, but he denies to it this quickening energy ascribed to it by Calvin. Luther could not do otherwise, since he grants the substance of the Sacrament also to the unworthy" (p. 247). To begin with, to deny that the sacrament quickens faith in Luther is preposterous, for this is its purpose. In addition, Barclay neglects the double efficacy of the sacrament. It communicates power to the believer, condemnation to the unbeliever, exactly because the substance of the Supper, Christ's body, is given to all. It is true that the power of the sacrament is not independent of the believer, but occurs between faith and the Supper. But this is only to say: (1) power is not a substance or possession in Luther, which dominates the believer from outside, and (2) sacramental power has an external origin. In no way can Luther be taken to say that the Supper does not have an enlivening effect; rather, the effect it has is due to the twin factors of external origin of power and a nonsubstantialist understanding of power.

A similar error leads Barclay to see a contradiction between Luther's claims that the unworthy really receive the body and blood and that this reception is injurious. Barclay argues that if the body and blood are beneficial, then they must also benefit those without faith (p. 252). Again, Barclay attributes a substantialist interpretation of power to Luther which Luther rejects. Power is a process in Luther rather than a possession, and although the body and blood of Christ are intended for life, provided they reach their inward *telos* of faith, they are efficacious for damnation in unbelievers because their power remains external and dominating. Power occurs at the boundary of the sacrament and faith, even though its condition is the confluence of Word and element.

negative, working only injury. It is power one should fear. But, as the sun is a good thing that may be defiled, this is corrupted power, not power proper. It dominates and poisons the unbeliever because it is prevented from reaching the intended end of its appropriation in faith.[191] Although both fulfilled and degenerate power contain an element of domination in that God's sovereign will, and not the recipient, determines the means and meaning of the Supper, they are radically different. In its perverted form, the action of the Supper terminates in mere domination. The intention of the sacrament, on the contrary, is to help the recipient, and this help comes precisely through the sovereign domination of God. Domination, though, is not the end or purpose of the sacrament, only its condition.

The proper efficacy of the Lord's Supper is proclaimed by the words of institution; it is directed to spiritual life. Again, the alteration in Luther's sacramental theology is that the body and blood of Christ, under the sign, are given a specific effect they did not possess before. If the Word proclaims that the cup is the new testament, the cup is truly a new promise, not by virtue of the nature of the cup, but through the blood contained therein.[192] Indeed, the presence of the body of Christ guarantees the efficacy of the Supper, for it cannot be present in vain. Rather, "there is a secret power and benefit (*krafft und nutz*) which flows from the body of Christ into our body, for it must be useful (*nütze*)."[193] The radicals' position, in contrast, makes the body of Christ useless, insignificant for spiritual purposes, like any other flesh.[194]

It is not that the benefit communicated in the Lord's Supper is unique to the Eucharist, unattainable elsewhere in God's economy.[195] One is not necessarily condemned without the sacrament,[196] and Luther continues to advise abstention for those in error concerning the doctrine of the Supper so that they may avoid its injurious effects.[197] To ask for a unique benefit to the

---

[191] Luther, *Psalm 111*, 373–74 (WA 31[I]:414–15), repeats, in 1530, that "Christ did not institute His remembrance or Sacrament out of anger or displeasure. It is not to be a poison for you." Its misuse makes it an abomination.

[192] Luther, *Against the Heavenly Prophets*, 218 (WA 18:208).

[193] Luther, *This Is My Body*, 134 (WA 23:259). Luther does not mean "secret" in the sense that power is private and hidden after it is received. His meaning is closer to "invisible."

[194] Luther, *This Is My Body*, 49, 125 (WA 23:119, 245).

[195] Barth thinks that Luther must and does defend the uniqueness of the Supper (*Luther's Doctrine of the Eucharist*, 89, 93). But Barth confuses two senses of "uniqueness." Although Luther thinks that the Eucharist is a special gift of God that provides certain benefits, he does not claim, nor does he need to, that the benefits or fruits themselves are available only in the Lord's Supper. Barclay (*Protestant Doctrine of the Lord's Supper*, 233) and Sasse (*This Is My Body*, 180–81) are more accurate on this issue.

[196] Luther, *Against the Heavenly Prophets*, 145 (WA 18:135).

[197] Luther, *Sacrament of the Body and Blood of Christ*, 335 (WA 19:483). Abstention is, however, a dangerous procedure, because "when a person abstains from the sacrament and does not use it, then harm has to follow and it cannot but happen that his faith daily becomes increasingly weak and cold; and as a result, then, it must furthermore follow that he becomes lazy and cold in his love for the neighbor, sluggish and averse to doing good works, unfit and unwilling to

Supper surely demands too much, for "God means to fill the world and give himself to us in many different ways."[198] Yet the absence of a unique benefit does not imply that the Supper fails to communicate any benefit. Moreover, the Supper's work is effected in the meeting between the Word, faith, and the body and blood of Christ, rather than only between faith and Word.

Still, the duplication of effects of the "means of grace" goes only so far. It extends only to those things that are attached to the Word. It is especially important that Luther clarify what can and cannot bring spiritual benefit in his treatment of the Supper, because he has apparently endangered the special status of the sacrament by exactly the argument that assured him of Christ's presence in the Supper—the ubiquity of Christ. For if Christ is present everywhere, and if presence is tied closely to power in Luther's theology, why should the signs of the Supper have a place more exalted than any other sign? If, for example, Christ is present in all bread, is not all bread a means of spiritual grace, and not only the bread of the altar? In order to prevent an affirmative answer to this question, Luther invokes a distinction between "mere" presence and presence "for you."

To be sure, bread and wine are universally efficacious in the natural sense of nourishment for the body. The power of the Supper, however, is a spiritual one, and for this mere presence is not enough. If the body and blood mediate and actualize what is promised in the Word, they cannot have a spiritual effect independent of the Word. The Word does not as much make the body and blood present in the sacrament (for the ubiquity of Christ guarantees a universal presence) as it makes the body present for the spiritual efficacy of the Eucharist. God does not want to be sought elsewhere than in the Word, Luther maintains, even if God is present everywhere. To seek God elsewhere than the Word ordains and commands is idolatry.[199] There is a difference between presence and availability, between mere presence and presence for you.[200]

The importance of this delineation is this: however closely power and presence are associated in Luther's sacramental theology, they are never identical. To be sure, power requires presence, but the converse is not strictly true. There are relatively powerless presences.[201] If the mere presence of God still produces natural power, it does not always produce spiritual power. The simple assertion of presence is not enough to guarantee power. Moreover, the

resist evil" (*Admonition Concerning the Sacrament,* 126; WA 30[II]:617). This danger appears to become more acute the longer one does not commune.

[198] Luther, *This Is My Body,* 141 (WA 23:269). Luther repeats the same claim in *Marburg Colloquy and Marburg Articles,* 43, 81; see also *Private Mass and the Consecration of Priests,* 189 (WA 38:231), in which he argues that while the sacraments cannot exist without the Word, the Word can exist without the sacraments. However, Luther does appear to give the Supper a unique efficacy in regard to the body of its recipient. This is explored below.

[199] Luther, *Sacrament of the Body and Blood of Christ,* 342 (WA 19:492).

[200] Luther, *This Is My Body,* 68–69 (WA 23:149–51).

[201] See, e.g., *Marburg Colloquy and Marburg Articles,* 27, 39, 65.

distinction between mere presence and presence for you shows that presence is also teleological. It is not its own end. Attributing a sufficiency to mere presence would draw precariously near to the inefficacious memorial sign:

> [In the sacrament], Christ has given himself to us completely, and wishes to be and remain with us until the last day, not merely so that he may be there, as the papists have him and carry him about without fruit, nor as the others say, *ut signum*, that is, as only a password (*losung*), which would bring us no improvement nor fruit. Should Christ institute (*einsetzen*) so great a thing in vain, without any benefit (*nutz*) or good? On the contrary, this should be the fruit, that you strengthen (*sterckest*) your faith and make your conscience secure, so that afterwards you may also be able to preach. So they say, it is only an unprofitable thought (*unnutz bedencken*) which benefits (*nutz*) neither you nor anyone else.[202]

The sacrament aims to effect an actual betterment of the believer. The Word announces the places where the presence of God is to be effective spiritually.

Indeed, once the presence of Christ is announced for you, this carries with it the assurance that the sacrament is necessarily beneficial. If the cup is the new testament, Luther says, it must be effectual (*gellte*). The benefits communicated, in other words, define the specific power of the sacrament. Luther goes so far as to say to Karlstadt, "If it is not of any benefit (*nütze*), then there is no sacrament in the Supper, and no one receives anything."[203] Without the profit of the Supper, Christ is not there for us, for Christ's presence must have a purpose.[204] When received in faith, the Supper is powerful (*mechtig*) and beneficial (*nütze*); the power and force (*krafft und macht*) of Christ's suffering have been placed in the Eucharist.[205] The spiritual eating in faith that discerns this receives God's benefits.[206]

The benefits are severalfold. In conformity with Luther's second outline of the sacrament, the principal benefit, that for which the sacrament was instituted, is forgiveness of sins.[207] Confidence that this deliverance is accomplished in the Supper is the spiritual eating of the sacrament.[208] Again, the personal character of the Supper is important, given new meaning through the increased concentration upon the body of Christ. The Lord's Supper applies forgiveness to the recipient. There is a difference between the forgiveness won once for all on the cross, and the distribution of forgiveness:

---

[202] Luther, *Sacrament of the Body and Blood of Christ*, 351 (translation modified; WA 19:508).

[203] Luther, *Against the Heavenly Prophets*, 217, 203 (WA 18:208, 192); see also Luther's statement in *Marburg Colloquy and Marburg Articles*, 23.

[204] Luther, *This Is My Body*, 88 (WA 23:183).

[205] Luther, *Against the Heavenly Prophets*, 204, 210 (WA 18:193, 200).

[206] See, e.g., Luther, *This Is My Body*, 85 (WA 23:179).

[207] Luther, *Against the Heavenly Prophets*, 210, 217 (WA 18:200, 207); *This Is My Body*, 102 (WA 23:207).

[208] Luther, *This Is My Body*, 85 (WA 23:179).

The blind fool [Zwingli] does not know that the merit of Christ and the distribution of merit are two different things. And he confuses them like a filthy sow. Christ at one time earned and acquired for us the forgiveness of sins on the cross; but this forgiveness he shares (teylet) wherever he is, at all times and in all places, as Luke writes.[209]

The application is necessary because "all they who are forgiven still have sins."[210] The appropriation of forgiveness thereby serves to strengthen (gestercket) the heart.[211] Recalling the earlier language of the hungry soul, Luther says that one comes to the sacrament because of the feeling of infirmity and weakness of faith, so that its fire can ignite the heart against the variety of temptations attacking the flesh and especially against despair of God's grace[212] and one's worthiness to receive the Supper.[213] The forgiveness won by Christ on the cross would benefit no one if it were not distributed and put to use.[214] The inward telos of the Supper consists primarily in Christ's mercy being given to us in unceasing forgiveness[215] and, second, in the strengthening of faith through the knowledge that forgiveness is applied to you.

As Luther made clear before, the inward drive of the external sacrament does not complete the sacramental action. The transition from the inward power effected by the external sacrament to external love is accomplished by the bridge of communion in the body of Christ. The faithful reception of the body of Christ is participation in it and is at the same time communion, which is the body of Christ itself:

> The broken bread, with its pieces distributed, is communion (gemeynschafft) in the body of Christ. It is, it is, it is, [Paul] says, the communion of Christ's body. What is communion but the body of Christ? It can be nothing other than that as each takes a piece of the broken bread, they take the body of Christ. This community is to be really participation (teylhafftig), so that one's own along with what is another's is commended to the common (gemeynen) body of Christ, as Paul himself said, "We are all one body, for we partake (teylhafftig) of one bread."[216]

---

[209] Luther, *Confession Concerning Christ's Supper*, 192 (translation modified; WA 26:294); see also Quere, "Changes and Constants," 65.

[210] Luther, *Against the Heavenly Prophets*, 215 (WA 18:205).

[211] Luther, *Sacrament of the Body and Blood of Christ*, 350 (WA 19:507); see also *This Is My Body*, 102 (WA 23:207). In *Private Mass and Consecration of Priests*, 180–81 (WA 38:224), Luther maintains that the sacrament strengthens both faith and knowledge, though he does not specify what he means by "knowledge" in this context or how the sacrament does this.

[212] This is especially clear in *Admonition Concerning the Sacrament*, 127–33 (WA 30[II]:618–22). There, Luther also identifies this protection and strengthening as the powerfulness (krefftig) of the Supper (*Admonition Concerning the Sacrament*, 127; WA 30[II]:618).

[213] Luther, *Psalm 111*, 374–76 (WA 31[I]:414–16).

[214] Luther, *Confession Concerning Christ's Supper*, 193 (WA 26:296).

[215] Luther, *Psalm 111*, 375 (WA 31[I]:415).

[216] Luther, *Against the Heavenly Prophets*, 178 (translation modified; WA 18:168).

The sacrament is not simply consumption of the body of Christ, but communion in it.[217] The community of the body is participation.

Participation can be of a bodily or a spiritual nature.[218] In contrast to his opponents, Luther holds that spiritual participation occurs by means of bodily participation. The communicant becomes a member of the body of Christ when fed spiritually through physical eating and drinking.[219] At this point, Luther adds a benefit to the Supper. The physical precondition of spiritual eating also permits the sacrament to raise the body to eternal life, to make the body spiritual. Because Christ's flesh is born of the Spirit, it is spiritual flesh. The consumption of such flesh has an effect opposite to what happens in the eating of mere flesh. Instead of the body transforming its food into it, the spiritual flesh of Christ transforms our flesh. Our flesh becomes what Christ's flesh is, namely, a spiritual body; you are who you eat. This is a strength and power (*stark*) of the food, to give life to body and soul, so that the body also can experience resurrection on the last day.[220] This would be impossible if, as the radicals believe, the effect of the sacrament consists in mere thanksgiving, for then the sacramental bread would be the same as any other bread, and Christ would have been "an exceedingly great fool to institute a special Supper when the world is already filled to capacity with suppers which take place daily."[221] Instead, Luther maintains, only the bread attached to the Word can strengthen the body for eternal life.[222]

The sacrament is thus made to consist of two *teloi*. First, the physical consumption of the bread has its end inwardly, strengthening the faith of the recipient in forgiveness. This spiritual effect then strengthens the body for eternal life, making it a spiritual body:

> our body is fed with the body of Christ, in order that our faith and hope may abide and that our body may live eternally from the same eternal food of the body of Christ which it eats physically. This is a bodily benefit, nevertheless an extraordinarily great one, and it follows from the spiritual benefit.[223]

The controlling principle in this second transmission of sacramental benefit is the heart consumed by Spirit, such that "If the heart is filled, then also eyes

---

[217] Luther, *Against the Heavenly Prophets,* 181 (WA 18:171).

[218] Ibid., 181–82 (WA 18:172).

[219] Luther, *This Is My Body,* 119 (WA 23:235–37).

[220] Ibid., 99–101, 124–25 (WA 23:203–5, 243–45). On the notion of the mingling of Christ's flesh with ours, so that our bodies may be nourished for eternity and saved, see also *This Is My Body,* 115–16, 118 (WA 23:229, 233), and *Marburg Colloquy and Marburg Articles,* 57.

[221] Luther, *Brief Confession Concerning the Holy Sacrament,* 299 (WA 54:151).

[222] Luther, *This Is My Body,* 116–17 (WA 23:231–33).

[223] Ibid., 132 (WA 23:255). It may appear that the physical effect of the Supper is a benefit available in no way other than through the Supper, since Luther is so specific in accounting for the process. He does not, however, so far as I am aware, suggest that the resurrection of the body is dependent exclusively on the Eucharist. See Seeberg, *Text-Book of the History of Doctrines* 2:329.

and ears, mouth and nose, body and soul, and all members must be filled. For the way the heart behaves, so all the members behave and act, and each and every thing you do is nothing but an expression of the praise and thanks to God."[224]

Part of the reason this physical benefit is extraordinarily great is Luther's opposition to any reliance on pure inwardness. He attacks it because the inner person cannot effect acts of love, and needs the organ of the body. The possibility of a body under the sway of the Spirit is required by the necessity of external acts of love, as well as for the external proclamation of the Word.[225] The spiritualists' disdain of the bodily and the earthly, Luther maintains, ends in denial of the duty of love of the neighbor, who is always on earth. There is no choice but to live "in the flesh," even though we must not live "according" to it.[226] The community of the body of Christ has an external *telos* of love, symbolized in the many grains becoming one bread, the many grapes becoming one wine.[227] The fruit of the Supper, here as before, is love, "the unity of Christians in one spiritual body of Christ through one spirit, faith, love, and the cross."[228]

The Face of Sacramental Power

It is not easy to categorize Luther's theology of the Lord's Supper over the years in terms of continuity or fundamental change. Even when Luther's language remains the same, his meaning frequently varies. Yet this much can be said: The theology of power stated and implied in his sacramental thought undergoes, at the very least, considerable specification during the short time from 1519 to 1525 and remains substantially the same thereafter. That Luther should develop a richer theology of power in the face of challenges by Karlstadt, Zwingli, Oeclampadius, and others, is to be expected, for it is they who ask whether the sacrament communicates any power.

The basic features of Luther's mature Eucharistic theology that are relevant for understanding power are these. To begin with, in agreement with sovereignty theory, sacramental power is conditioned externally. The powerful Word of God makes the promise of the new testament available to faith. This same Word also places the body and blood in the sign. The Word, in short, presents the power and strength of God.[229] The double role of the Word,

---

[224] Luther, *Admonition Concerning the Sacrament,* 107 (WA 30[II]:603).

[225] Luther, *Private Mass and the Consecration of Priests,* 152 (WA 38:199).

[226] Luther, *Confession Concerning Christ's Supper,* 198–201 (WA 26:305–11).

[227] Luther, *Sacrament of the Body and Blood of Christ,* 352–53 (WA 19:511).

[228] Luther, *Confession Concerning Christ's Supper,* 275 (WA 26:411). Barclay is incorrect to say that Luther utterly abandoned the mystical union with Christ as a fruit of the Supper after 1520 (*Protestant Doctrine of the Lord's Supper,* 248).

[229] Luther, *This Is My Body,* 132 (WA 23:255–57).

to proclaim the promise and to effect the presence of the body and blood of Christ "for you," does not have quite the same relation to the believer. The content of the promise contained in the new testament is communicated in a direct encounter between Word and believer. Thus does the recipient know to what end the Lord's Supper is received.

The actual communication of these benefits, however, occurs through the mediation of the sign. This major shift in Luther's later sacramental theology is the source of the other alterations. Prior to his defense against the radicals, it had never been clear what role, if any, the sign played in producing the benefits of the sacrament. In the first topography, the sign lacked import because of the magnitude of what stood in front of it, meaning and faith. When this system became untenable because of the problem of the economy of the mass, it was at least an open question whether the sign was erased by its own foundation in the Word. When the radicals resolved this ambiguity by denying any importance to the sign and rejecting the real presence of Christ in the sign, Luther took his stand. The Word, after making the body and blood present in the elements, is then mediated by the body of Christ. Bodily presence itself produces power in the sacrament.

The power of the sacrament begins externally, both in regard to the Word and the body of Christ. Any attempt to remove either or both of these externalities is a direct challenge to God's sovereignty. Luther thus incorporates an element of domination, indeed he demands it, at the origin of the sacramental process. To this point, he is in agreement with sovereignty theory. But here sovereignty theory stops, and it therefore identifies power with this external dominating element. Luther, on the contrary, understands this external dominion as the conceptual beginning of power rather than the whole of power. At the meeting point of the external elements of Word and sacramental material, and the inward faith or unbelief of the recipient, sacramental power is created. If the recipient is without faith, the sacrament remains pure domination, an external, negative, and condemning power. Whereas for sovereignty theory this dominating and negative power is power itself, for Luther it is a corrupt power, founded on the misuse of the sacrament.

Luther's sacramental thought involves a theology of power that avoids an immediate involvement with political theories of power and therefore can escape their difficulties, one of which is that power is inevitably confined to what is external. Sacramental power, however, is directed to the heart, the inner life of the believer. If the external components of power meet faith, the real power of the Eucharist appears. The Supper was instituted for comfort and strength, not for poison. Its harmful effects are a distortion of its power. When the double externalities of Word and sign containing the body of Christ touch the boundary line of faith, it becomes clear that, although power has an external source, it does not remain external to the recipient. Sacramental power is defined in its content by its benefits to the believer. Power has an intrinsic entelechy. What begins externally has the inward aim of strengthening the weak faith of the believer through the promise and accomplishment of the forgiveness of sin. The power of God in the sacrament is directed not toward the domination of exclusive power but to the gift of power, the increase of the power for the believer. The divine glory, Luther says, is the glorification of creatures.[230] Sovereignty becomes power when it gives power.

What is true of the gift of power from God to the believer in the sacrament is also true of the power the believer receives. The work of the Supper is not fulfilled in the reception of the gifts of God, but expresses itself in love for the neighbor. Just as the external sacrament drives inward to produce power, so inward gifts drive outward for their completion. It is even deceptive to speak of the power of the believer, if this is taken to mean that the believer possesses it. God's power is perpetually active; only the raving fanatics think that "Christ has no other glory than to sit at the right hand of God on a velvet cushion and let the angels sing and fiddle and ring bells and play before him."[231] Similarly, faith is of its nature active externally, in love:

> Where such faith is continually refreshed and renewed, there the heart is at the same time refreshed anew in its love of the neighbor and is made strong and equipped to do all good works and to resist sin and all the temptations of the devil. Since faith cannot be idle, it must demonstrate the fruits of love by doing good and avoiding evil.[232]

Power directed to the heart is fulfilled externally.

Luther will not permit an either/or answer to the dimensions of externality and inwardness in relation to the Supper. He opposes the purely external interpretation of Rome and the purely inward one of the radicals. Finally, in both *teloi* of the sacrament, Luther demands the involvement of the body and asserts its spiritual possibilities. In so doing, he opposes an idealist conception of power and an exclusively inward one. He complies with the bodily criterion of power established by Foucault.

The presentation of Luther's sacramental theology is not quite complete, but it is at least clear in what ways Luther retains and departs from the usual political model of power. Yet Luther has his own political theology and, within it, an understanding of power that seems to identify domination and power, the notion from which we hoped to escape, and which his own sacramental theology did avoid.

---

[230] Ibid., 71 (WA 23:157).

[231] Ibid., 70 (WA 23:155).

[232] Luther, *Admonition Concerning the Sacrament,* 126 (WA 30[II]:617). There is a substantial ambiguity in Luther's position here. On the one hand, neither God nor the believer could, it appears, be said to be "powerful" in the sense that power is possessed, since power is active. On the other hand, Luther frequently resorts to formulas which do indicate that power is possessed, as a potentiality that is exercised and becomes actual subsequently. Both positions are included in this quotation. This problematic will be explored principally in the conflict between two versions of the proper relation between faith and works—whether faith without works is an undeveloped, "fruitless" faith or a "false" faith.

Politics and Power

The primary purpose of the presentation of Luther's political thought here is to highlight the differences between Luther's political and sacramental theologies. The dichotomy between them is not quite as sharp as it will appear, but the issues raised are significant enough to require the next chapter to detour into Luther's broader theology, temporarily abandoning an exclusive focus on the more limited question of power. As far as possible, the varied elements of Luther's theology must be formed into a unified architecture of thought. In this way, the foundation can be laid for a resolution of some of the apparent contradictions in his concept of power, although there remains a fundamental difference between Luther's sacramental and political conceptions of power.

Worldly Government

Luther's political thought takes shape within his conception of the worldly estates, which is an expression of the doctrine of the two governments.[233] In turn, the two governments are grounded in the two realms (*reyche*),[234] the realm of God under Christ and the worldly realm.[235] The distinction between these realms correlates with the two kinds of people in the world. On the one side are those who belong to the heavenly realm of God, and on the other, those who do not, being merely citizens of the world.[236] The two "children of Adam" require different modes of government that have different purposes. The realm

---

[233] Since the concern is with Luther's theory of government, there is no need to analyze the proper authority and operation of each earthly estate. It is sufficient to discuss political government, since it has the broadest authority to command.

[234] *Reich* has not been translated as "kingdom," except in direct quotations of a translation. In general, it has been translated as "realm." This has the disadvantage of not communicating the awe, majesty, and authority Luther associates with *Reich*. The other obvious alternative would be "empire," but this is perhaps even less satisfactory. Luther does not refer to God as emperor, but frequently calls God and Christ "king." Where "realm," "sphere," "arena," and similar terms would be plainly inappropriate or insufficient to communicate the intended meaning, the rather pretentious practice of using the German term alone has been adopted.

[235] Martin Luther, *Temporal Authority: To What Extent it Should be Obeyed*, in *Luther's Works*, vol. 45, *The Christian in Society II*, trans. W. A. Lambert, rev. and ed. Walther I. Brandt (Philadelphia: Fortress Press, 1962), 105 (WA 11:262). The English translation of the title of this essay is misleading. The title is *Von welltlicher Uberkeytt, wie weyt man yhr gehorsam schuldig sey*, which is more accurately rendered, "On Worldly Authority: To What Extent One Is Sinful to Obey It." Moreover, in none of his essays on government does Luther use "temporal" frequently as an adjectival description of political government. He usually prefers "worldly" or "earthly."

[236] Luther, *Temporal Authority*, 88 (WA 11:249); see also Martin Luther, *Sermons on the First Epistle of St. Peter* (hereafter cited as *Sermons on First Peter*), in *Luther's Works*, vol. 30, *The Catholic Epistles*, trans Martin H. Bertram, ed. Jaroslav Pelikan (St. Louis: Concordia Publishing House, 1967), 76 (WA 12:330).

of God is governed by the Holy Spirit and is intended to produce Christians and Christian righteousness. The worldly realm, in contrast, is governed by earthly authority in order that non-Christians may be restrained from evil-doing and that worldly peace may be maintained.[237]

To this point, the division between the two realms and their correlative two governments seems simple and straightforward. The water does not remain clear because the citizens of the heavenly realm still live in the earthly sphere. This is already evident from the discussion of Luther's sacramental theology and will become especially important in the next chapter, but it impinges on Luther's political theology also. The Christian is involved with both governments. To be sure, one's real citizenship is in heaven, but one must still live as a pilgrim or guest on earth.[238] This dual involvement creates a problem of determining the proper jurisdictions of the two governments and the Christian's role, if any, in earthly rule. Citizens of God's *Reich* on earth are placed in the interesting and rather uncomfortable position of having to be in the world without being a mere part of the world.[239]

This doubling of the fields the Christian must till leads Luther to a series of decisions with regard to worldly authority. To begin with, the "spiritual estate" is not defined by the official position one holds. Instead, all Christians are equal members of the spiritual estate.[240] Differences among Christians are in regard to their earthly, not their heavenly, status. Certainly, Christians do different things in the world, and greater or lesser honor is accorded these endeavors; however, these worldly distinctions have nothing to do with one's status or membership in the realm of God. The spiritual estate is not coextensive with the offices of the church. This is one of the reasons Luther can appeal to the Christian nobility, who are duly constituted authorities, to assist in the reform of the church. As members of the spiritual estate, their exercise of earthly power (*hirschafft*) is part of the Christian body, a spiritual estate, even if its work is bodily. These members of the spiritual estate have a responsibility to use their office for the improvement of the church.[241]

---

[237] Luther, *Temporal Authority*, 90, 92 (WA 11:251–52).

[238] Luther, *Against Latomus*, 159 (WA 8:58).

[239] Luther, *Temporal Authority*, 88 (WA 11:249).

[240] Martin Luther, *To the Christian Nobility of the German Nation Concerning the Reform of the Christian Estate* (hereafter cited as *Christian Nobility*), in *Luther's Works*, vol. 44, *The Christian in Society I*, rev. and ed. Atkinson, 127 (WA 6:407).

[241] Luther, *Christian Nobility*, 127–32 (WA 6:407–10). Luther's argument in *Christian Nobility* has a considerably stronger tone than his *Treatise on Good Works*, 90 (WA 6:258), written just a few months earlier. There he asserted that the nobility must deal with the spiritual estate of the church as a good child must deal with insane parents. In *Christian Nobility*, this image of sub-ordination is eliminated. The significance of the question of authority in the church is the focus of Bagchi, *Luther's Earliest Opponents*. Bagchi makes the interesting claim that the dispute over the nature of authority between Luther and Rome had extensive implications for the spread of the Reformation, since the Roman view of authority also handcuffed its own defenders.

There are other collateral effects of the decoupling of earthly office and status in God's sight. On the one hand, membership in the spiritual estate does not preclude possession of a worldly office. This is especially true of government. Since the offices of worldly government are instituted by God, office-holding is a great Christian calling and also makes honorable those occupations which support government.[242] But, on the other hand, the exercise of worldly authority is spiritual by virtue of the person exercising the office, not through the office itself. Offices of worldly government are just that—worldly. They exist in and for the worldly, not the heavenly, realm. There is nothing inherently spiritual about government. As a strictly earthly task, government is based on the principles of natural law and reason. Two consequences follow from this. First, although Christians are permitted and encouraged to follow a calling into worldly government, effective government does not require a Christian officeholder. Second, reason and natural law, aside from being the criterion of good government, also exclude an alternative, namely, that government should be conducted according to principles of the gospel. These principles are binding only on those who wish to call themselves Christian, because they are the standard of citizens of the heavenly realm. The gospel cannot and should not attempt to determine the conduct of worldly government.

Closer analysis of some of the effects of Luther's loosening the tie between the worldly and spiritual positions of the Christian will clarify the character of power in his theory of worldly government. Earthly government, legitimated through God's will and ordinance (*ordnung*), has existed from the beginning of the world. As God's institution, law (*recht*), and command (*gepott*),[243] officeholding and execution of the duties of government are required of human beings. Fulfillment of these duties involves both ruler and subjects. Rulers must govern, and their use of the authority given by God lays an obligation of obedience upon those subject to it. Obedience is owed to government not for its own sake but because submission to it is God's will.[244]

Luther's scriptural bases for the prerogatives of government and the demand of obedience are primarily Romans 13; 1 Peter 2:13-15; 2 Peter 2:1;[245] and the pronouncement "Render to Caesar the things that are Caesar's," drawn

---

[242] Luther, *Temporal Authority*, 96-103 (WA 11:255-60).

[243] Ibid., 85-86 (WA 11:247-48); see also *Christian Nobility*, 130 (WA 6:409). The assertion that the law of the sword has existed since the beginning of the world is unclear. Heinrich Bornkamm is correct to modify this statement of Luther to mean that government has existed since the Fall, if one conceives of the Fall as a historical event, as Luther does (*Luther's Doctrine of the Two Kingdoms in the Context of his Theology*, trans. Karl H. Hertz, Social Ethics Series 14 [Philadelphia: Fortress Press, Facet Books, 1966], 34-35). Since the purposes of government are negative and coercive, government was unnecessary before the Fall. Despite the statement "since the beginning of the world," in fact Luther provides no discussion of any government prior to the Fall.

[244] Luther, *Sermons on First Peter*, 74 (WA 12:329).

[245] See, e.g., *Christian Nobility*, 131 (WA 6:409-10).

from Luke 20:25 and Matthew 22:21.[246] The use of Romans and First Peter are worth special mention. Luther's translation of Rom. 13:1–2 leaves little doubt that he understands the demand of obedience to be a question of power: "Let every soul be subject (*unterthan*) to power (*gewallt*) and authority (*uberkeyt*), for there is no power except from God; the power which is everywhere (*allenthalben*) is ordained (*verordnet*) of God. Whoever resists power, resists God's order (*ordnung*); whoever resists God's order will achieve damnation."[247]

Luther's sermons on First Peter are even more interesting; there he unites the concepts of command and creativity. Luther divides the two governments by distinguishing the order (*ordnung*) of what "God creates (*schaffet*), commands (*gebeut*), and wills,"[248] that is, faith, from the analogous creativity of the ruler: "Now there is also a human and worldly creation, namely, that which is drawn up with commands as to how outward government should be."[249] Luther goes so far as to make the startling claim (to our ears, at least) that "to create" (*schaffen*) means "to command" (*gebieten*). One must obey the human orders as well as the divine, and since these orders are constituted by laws (*gesetze*), what the prince creates by means of the law must be done.[250] The power (*gewallt*) God gives to humans for government of the temporal and earthly realm[251] is a grant of creative authority.

God's commands of worldly authority and obedience are sufficient warrant for Luther to insist on the worth of government and the necessity of Christian obedience to it. Positively, honor of and obedience to authority (*uberkeit*) are the finest works of love of the neighbor; they include within themselves, Luther maintains, all virtue and good works. Negatively, disobedience is worse than all other outward sins, including murder, unchastity, and theft.[252] The commands of God require observance, and the force of God's

---

[246] Luther, *Temporal Authority,* 111 (WA 11:266); Martin Luther, *Against the Robbing and Murdering Hordes of Peasants,* in *Luther's Works,* vol. 46, *The Christian in Society III,* rev. and ed. Schultz, 51 (WA 18:358); Luther, *Dr. Martin Luther's Warning to his Dear German People* (hereafter cited as *Luther's Warning*), in *Luther's Works,* vol. 47, *The Christian in Society IV,* trans. Martin H. Bertram, ed. Franklin Sherman (Philadelphia: Fortress Press, 1971), 19 (WA 30 Band [III] [1910], 282). Hubert Kirchner adds Deut. 32:35 and omits Matthew and Luke (*Luther and the Peasants' War,* trans. Darrell Jodock, Historical Series 22 [Reformation] [Philadelphia: Fortress Press, Facet Books, 1972], 16). The inclusion of Deuteronomy is subject to the qualification that it is part of Old Testament law and is therefore valid only insofar as it accords with natural law. This point will be clarified in chapter 3.

[247] Luther, *Temporal Authority,* 85–86 (translation modified; WA 11:247).

[248] Luther, *Sermons on First Peter,* 73 (translation modified; WA 12:328).

[249] Ibid., 73–74 (translation modified; WA 12:328 reads: "Nu ist auch eyn menschlich und welltlich schaffen, nemlich, die da verfasset ist mit gepotten, wie das eusserliche regiment seyn soll").

[250] Luther, *Sermons on First Peter,* 73 (WA 12:328).

[251] Luther, *Temporal Authority,* 111 (WA 11:266).

[252] Luther, *Treatise on Good Works,* 80–82 (WA 6:250–52). This priority of obedience is based in Luther's claim that the Ten Commandments are laid out so well as to give an order of seriousness of offense against them. Honor of authority appears in the Fourth Commandment, which is also

law remains in effect for the Christian. If the fact that God commands something is enough reason to do it, this does not mean that Luther ceases his defense of the commands with this declaration. In the controversy over the Lord's Supper, Luther makes the rather embarrassing pronouncement, "If [God] should command me to eat dung, I would do it. The servant should not inquire about the will of the master. We ought to close our eyes,"[253] and would certainly prefer to in this case. Such a pungent statement did not, however, preclude Luther from producing secondary defenses of the biblical commands. These arguments were dependent on the content of the scriptural injunctions, which are necessarily valid because they are God's word, but supplemented the bare command by enumerating the benefits of obedience. The same effort is put forth by Luther with reference to the functions of worldly government.

The primary justification of government is a negative one. True, Luther argues that power exercised in the world, in any station of life, is not to be used arbitrarily, but as a service, for the benefit of those one is supposed to govern.[254] Power is exercised for the purpose of improving the world. Yet what Luther means by "improvement" is considerably less joyous than one might expect. Government's primary task is to exercise the "sword," so that worldly peace may be forced upon an unwilling, sinful world. It is God's will that the wicked be punished and the pious protected, so the world can be sustained.[255] The realm of God is one of mercy, but the earthly realm is wrath and severity.[256] Government restrains; it is the only way to prevent utter chaos.[257]

To say that government's purpose and operation are exclusively restrictive is not an overstatement. Luther concedes that if there were no evil, there would be no need of worldly authority.[258] Since the righteous do more than the law or right demands, a world of righteous people would render the sword and government unnecessary and unhelpful.[259] At times, Luther maintains that the sword is ordained by God because of unbelievers. This is somewhat deceptive; although Luther admits that if all Christians followed the gospel the offices of government would be without purpose,[260] he also knows that such a pleasant portrait, even of Christians, is not realistic. Government governs a fallen world,

---

the first commandment having to do with conduct toward the neighbor (the second table of the Commandments). Since it is first, it is also the most important.

[253] Luther, *Marburg Colloquy and Marburg Articles*, 19.

[254] Luther, *Sermons on First Peter*, 92 (WA 12:346). The English translation uses "authority," whereas the Weimar edition uses "*gewallt*."

[255] For these arguments, see *Sermons on First Peter*, 74–80 (WA 12:329–35); *Temporal Authority*, 86 (WA 11:248).

[256] Martin Luther, *An Open Letter on the Harsh Book Against the Peasants*, in *Luther's Works*, vol. 46, *The Christian in Society III*, rev. and ed. Schultz, 69 (WA 18:389).

[257] Luther, *Temporal Authority*, 90 (WA 11:251).

[258] Luther, *Sermons on First Peter*, 74 (WA 12:329).

[259] Luther, *Temporal Authority*, 89 (WA 11:249–50).

[260] Luther, *Sermons on First Peter*, 75–76 (WA 12:330–31).

and original sin infects Christians and non–Christians alike. Christians too require the law, for neither are they righteous by nature:

> You ask: Why, then, did God give so many laws (*gesetz*) to all humanity, and why does Christ prescribe in the gospel so many things for us to do? . . . To put it as briefly as possible, Paul says that the law has been laid down for the sake of the lawless [1 Tim. 1:9], that is, so that those who are not Christians may through the law be restrained outwardly from evil deeds, as we shall hear later. *Now since no one is by nature Christian or righteous, but altogether sinful and wicked, God through the law puts them all under restraint so they dare not willfully implement their wickedness in actual deeds.* In addition, Paul ascribes to the law another function in Romans 7 and Galatians 2, that of teaching men to recognize sin in order that it may make them humble unto grace and unto faith in Christ.[261]

This explains why, even in a culture predominantly composed of baptized Christians, Luther maintains the need for two governments ordained by God, rather than simply prescribing government according to the principles of the gospel:

> If anyone attempted to rule (*regirn*) the world by the gospel and to abolish all worldly law (*recht*) and sword on the plea that all are baptized and Christian, and that, according to the gospel, there shall be among them no law or sword — or need for either — pray tell me, friend, what would he be doing? He would be loosing the ropes and chains of the savage wild beasts and letting them bite and mangle everyone, meanwhile insisting that they were harmless, tame, and gentle creatures; but I would have the proof in my wounds.[262]

The purpose of government is quite narrow. It has, in Foucault's terminology, only a negative, prohibitory function, enforced by sovereignty. The means of its power are domination and command. Government has only the restricted task of controlling sin. The world that would permit government by the gospel is not our world, and it would render earthly government unnecessary anyway. Government is instituted to prevent the world from going from bad to worse. Certainly, it attempts to preserve worldly justice and to keep the peace, but these are less positive functions than disaster prevention. Moreover, these labors of government, which attempt to hold on by the fingernails to an endangered order, are exercised by "the sword," that is, by negative and prohibitive commands.

There is an obvious and substantial variance from the theology of power developed in Luther's sacramental thought. Even so, Luther's political theory might be easier to square with his theology of the Eucharist if the world ran

---

[261] Luther, *Temporal Authority*, 89–90 (emphasis added, translation modified; WA 11:250). This passage is also interesting because it places what is usually called the "first function of the law," its usefulness for the recognition of sin, in second place. In addition, it is clear that the law is relevant to Christian life after one is made aware of one's sinfulness.

[262] Luther, *Temporal Authority*, 91 (WA 11:251).

smoothly under God's ordinance of earthly government. Were government exercised in accord with Luther's demands on it, namely, the preservation of justice and peace for the betterment of the world, Luther's thought might be less problematic than it is. If worldly rulers were responsible in exercising their proper function, there could be little protest against Luther's exhortation to obey them. But he recognizes that although "the offices of princes and officials are divine and right, . . . those who are in them and use them are usually of the devil."[263] Since rulers "are generally the biggest fools or the worst scoundrels on earth," and "one must constantly expect the worst from them and look for little good,"[264] why does Luther still insist that it is the duty of the governed to obey?

It is not that Luther's reading of the biblical demand to obedience is unconditional. He is more than willing to write and speak against whatever misuses of governmental authority come to his attention. He also recognizes a right to refuse obedience to government whenever it seeks to compel something clearly contrary to a command of God.[265] For example, since the government has no authority to meddle in the things of God, Luther prohibits following edicts of princes that order subjects to turn in copies of the New Testament, "on pain of losing their salvation."[266] Luther does not, therefore, assent to Hobbes's radical separation of divine and earthly, such that even the idea "justice"—not to mention its content—is determined solely by the sovereign's will. Luther recognizes earthly standards of justice, derivable from God's will but available to reflection and transcendent of the ruler and law of the land. Hobbes's solution may be simpler, but it is also less profound—besides, we would still have against it "proof in our wounds."

All forms of disobedience are not forbidden, but attempts to overturn the authority of worldly government certainly are. For those without official authority, only "passive disobedience" is allowed. Although one is not required to turn in one's New Testament, one is not allowed to stop the authorities from taking it.[267] Luther's own range of action, as a doctor of the church, was somewhat broader. He allowed himself nothing like armed resistance, of course, but doctors of the church were permitted to teach, and part of this task included rebuke of official misconduct. This was hardly, from Luther's viewpoint, passive disobedience. It was neither passive nor disobedient. Luther believed that the preaching of the Word was so far from passive as to be able to bring down the papacy.[268] However, the protest lodged in the name of the Word

263 Martin Luther, *Psalm 101*, in *Luther's Works*, vol. 13, *Selected Psalms II*, ed. Pelikan, 212 (WA 51 Band [1914], 254).

264 Luther, *Temporal Authority*, 113 (WA 11:267–68).

265 Ibid., 125–26 (WA 11:277–78).

266 Ibid., 112 (WA 11:267).

267 Ibid.

268 Martin Luther, *A Sincere Admonition by Martin Luther to all Christians to Guard Against*

was not an authority one had by virtue of being a Christian. Luther felt justified in his activity because he was duly constituted

> a Doctor of Holy Scripture against my will. . . . Once in this position, I had to stay in it, and I cannot give it up or leave it yet with a good conscience, even though both pope and emperor were to put me under the ban for not doing so. For what I began as a Doctor, made and called at their command (*befelh*), I must truly confess to the end of my life.[269]

The difference between rebellious rabblerousers and obedient Christians lies not in their actions but in their office, which gives authority to act in certain ways and circumstances. All rebuke of rulers cannot, therefore, be called sedition. Princes, charged with the protection of their territory and subjects, had the greatest mandate of resistance. In his *Warning* to the German people, Luther maintains that self-defense is not rebellion, but the right of princes. If attacked, they can defend, especially if such an attack is begun contrary to divine command as well as natural and imperial law.[270]

Commoners have no such recourse against injustice. No matter what the abuses of authority, they must abstain "from the words and even the passions which lead to insurrection, and do nothing in the matter apart from a command (*befelh*) of the authorities (*ubirkeyt*) or an act of the powers (*gewalt*)."[271] God has ordained the offices of government not merely to rule, but to rule exclusively. They alone have the charge to punish.[272] Indeed, the principle of authority is based on an inequality of power. If, Luther maintains, all have the same

---

Insurrection and Rebellion, in *Luther's Works*, vol. 45, *The Christian in Society II*, rev. and ed. Brandt, 60 (WA 8:678).

[269] Martin Luther, *Psalm 82*, in *Luther's Works*, vol. 13, *Selected Psalms II*, ed. Pelikan, 66 (WA 31[I]:212); see also *Psalm 82*, 43, 50 (WA 31[I]:190, 197–98); and *Against Latomus*, 147–48 (WA 8:50).

[270] *Luther's Warning*, 20–21 (WA 30[III]:283–84). The introduction to this treatise in *Luther's Works*, 47:6–9, sees a substantial shift from Luther's earlier position forbidding armed resistance to government. In fact, however, there is no "important modification." Nowhere does Luther find a general right to armed resistance; he grants it only to those who rule, so that they may defend themselves and their subjects against attack. Further, Luther's assertion of a right to resist is based largely on the fact that he has discovered such a right in imperial law (*Luther's Works* 47:8). Presumably, had the emperor been more clever or strong enough to leave this provision out of the law, any armed resistance would have been considered rebellion rather than self-defense. Finally, Karl Holl (*The Reconstruction of Morality*, trans. Fred W. Meuser and Walter R. Wietzke, ed. James Luther Adams and Walter F. Bense [Minneapolis: Augsburg Publishing House, 1979], 154) notes Luther's ambivalence in accepting any right of resistance: "the prince is a 'political personage' and according to the prevailing law of the Empire has a *right* to offer resistance. But for Luther, this is very far from implying that he *ought* to do so."

[271] Luther, *Sincere Admonition*, 62 (WA 8:679). Luther does grant some recourse. For example, he suggests that the peasants employ territorial courts; however, Kirchner notes that this "had truly only a *pro forma* value. Practically speaking, this way was not accessible to the subjects" (*Luther and the Peasants' War*, 27).

[272] Luther, *Sincere Admonition*, 62 (WA 8:680).

power or right, there can be no authority.[273] Governmental power, therefore, is constituted as a zero-sum; it is a problem of balances of power in which the power of wickedness must be lessened by authoritative and potent rule.[274] If one of the parties in such a confrontation has more power, the other must necessarily have less.

Luther was certainly aware that the unjust ruler rains down suffering upon subjects. Still, he is adamant that there is a duty to obey such rulers, and the consequences of his vehemence were revealed brutally in the aftermath of his treatises on the Peasants' War.[275] It is not that he thought the rulers were in the right so far as many of the peasants' demands were concerned. On many points, he agreed with the justice of the content of the peasants' position.[276] What he could not condone was any effort on their part to attain their goals if the nobility refused to concede them in negotiations.[277] Luther had announced as early as 1522, "I am and always will be on the side of those against whom insurrection is directed, no matter how unjust their cause; I am opposed to those who rise in insurrection, no matter how just their cause, because there can be no insurrection without hurting the innocent and shedding their blood."[278] When revolt came, Luther's position did not soften. The peasants had sworn loyalty to the prince and were now breaking this oath. They were outlaws before God and emperor, meriting death in body and soul for their disobedience. Indeed, princes who did not strike the rebels down, thereby failing to fulfill the duty of their office, forfeited God's grace and became guilty of whatever subsequent atrocities were committed by those they

[273] Luther, *Temporal Authority*, 117 (WA 11:271).

[274] Luther, *Sermons on First Peter*, 76 (WA 12:330).

[275] There is no effort to trace the events of 1525 here. A wonderful essay on these events and their context, as well as an interesting interpretation of the theology of the "Gospel of Social Unrest," is contained in Heiko Oberman, *The Dawn of the Reformation: Essays in Late Medieval and Early Reformation Thought* (Edinburgh: T & T Clark, 1986), 154–78.

[276] Luther, *Admonition to Peace*, 46:22–23 (WA 18:298–99).

[277] Kirchner notes Luther's extremely favorable reaction to the negotiated Weingarten treaty (*Luther and the Peasants' War*, 8–9).

[278] Luther, *Sincere Admonition*, 63 (WA 8:680). This statement should at least temper accusations of Luther's duplicity or self-seeking when the events of 1525 actually occurred. We are in agreement with Kirchner's effort to understand Luther's arguments on the basis of his theology rather than sociologically or psychologically (*Luther and the Peasants' War*, 15–18). In contrast, see James S. Preus, "The Political Function of Luther's *Doctrina*," *Concordia Theological Monthly* 43, no. 9 (October 1972): 591–99. Preus claims that Luther formulated the political doctrine of the two realms only in reaction to the events of 1525, that he was "trapped," a position that ignores both Luther's Scriptural/theological arguments that obedience is a command of God and the fact that Luther had taken the same stand at least as early as 1522 and laid most of the necessary argumentative groundwork well prior to 1525. H. Oberman argues persuasively against the implication that Luther was an opportunist (*Luther: Man Between God and the Devil*, trans. Eileen Walliser-Schwarzbart [New York: Doubleday, Image Books, 1989], 18–20).

failed to punish.[279] This duty too was based in the command of God.[280]

In view of his earlier pronouncements, Luther's vehement position with respect to the uprising of the peasants is not surprising. It is still shocking. Several aspects of it deserve examination. The constitution of worldly authority is an ordinance of God, and the power of the sovereign thus instituted is the sole legitimate power. The hand and sword are their jurisdiction and theirs alone, and whatever is done through this ordained power is not rebellion.[281] The land princes govern belongs to them, not to their inhabitants, and princes therefore possess the power and right (gewalt und recht) to administer what belongs to them as they see fit.[282]

Once again, Luther embarks on a double defense of the command to obedience. Fundamentally, the Christian is to be obedient to authority because God has commanded it in the New Testament. But, as we have seen before, Luther is not averse to showing the necessity and benefit of such commands, in order to illustrate that God is not arbitrary, but wise. In the absence of the sovereign's control of evil, the world would be one of anarchic chaos. Revolt is forbidden by God because it is

> an unprofitable (keyn nutz) method of procedure. It never brings about the desired improvement. For insurrection lacks discernment; it generally harms the innocent more than the guilty. Hence no insurrection is ever right, no matter how right the cause it seeks to promote. It always results in more damage than improvement, and verifies the saying, "Things go from bad to worse." For this reason authority (ubirkeyt) and the sword have been instituted (eyngesetzt) to punish the wicked and protect the upright, that insurrection may be prevented, as St. Paul says in Romans 13 and as we read in 1 Peter 2. But when Sir Mob breaks loose he cannot tell the wicked from the upright, or keep them apart; he lays about him at random, and great and horrible injustice is inevitable.[283]

Luther really only reverses what Hobbes says later. Hobbes posits an anarchic condition of war from which people are sensible enough to escape because it is a perpetual state of war of all against all, in which life is "solitary, poore,

---

[279] Luther, *Against the Robbing and Murdering Hordes of Peasants,* 49–53 (WA 18:357–60). Kirchner does not emphasize this document because of its unusually vitriolic tone and the fact that it is a direct response to Luther's negative experiences with the peasants in and around Eisleben (*Luther and the Peasants' War,* 10, 14). It is not the most frequently used document in our presentation, either, but this is not due to any similar theological scruples. If one were to eliminate all Luther's rather bitter writings from consideration, there is a serious question how much of his work would remain. In any case, the judgments about the peasants cited from this treatise are never retracted by Luther, and in most cases, are repeated elsewhere.

[280] Luther, *An Open Letter on the Harsh Book Against the Peasants,* 66 (WA 18:386).

[281] Luther, *Sincere Admonition,* 61 (WA 8:679).

[282] Luther, *Against the Heavenly Prophets,* 116–17 (WA 18:100–101).

[283] Luther, *Sincere Admonition,* 62–63 (translation slightly modified; WA 8:680).

nasty, brutish, and short."[284] Luther, on the other hand, believes that God was wise enough to see this universal war coming and established government to avoid it. What concerned Luther about the Peasants' War was that he saw a Hobbesian state of war on the horizon, not in the past.[285] The act of rebellion is itself anarchic, for it attempts to arrogate power to oneself by violence. It is not just that rebellion foments anarchy. It is anarchy, as are even the "passions" of rebellion, because it seeks to take the authority and power of princes from them, making rebels judges of their own case. To make oneself one's own judge is contrary to Christian law (recht) and the gospel as well as natural law and all principles of equity. If all this stands in opposition to one, a special command of God must be produced to legitimate such activity. This the peasants could not do to Luther's satisfaction, and therefore their rebellion merited eternal condemnation.[286] To put the point as strongly as possible, no matter what a ruler steals from subjects, the subjects do a greater wrong if they revolt, for they invade God's power and law, putting themselves above God and the instituted order of worldly government. Were the peasants' theory of government upheld, "in this way would anyone become judge over another, and no power nor authority, order nor right would remain in the world, but only murder and bloodshed."[287] The prevention of such a condition is why God forbids rebellion and why any effort to be the judge in one's own case is a suggestion of the devil.[288]

Luther views the danger of anarchy as invariably more severe than that of governmental terror because of his conception of the relation between office and person. Possession of a particular office does not change the status of a person in the sight of God, but it does establish earthly authority. The officeholder has power not because of intrinsic merit but because the office

---

[284] Thomas Hobbes, *Leviathan*, ed. C. B. Macpherson (Harmondsworth, England: Penguin, Penguin English Library, 1968), 186.

[285] Luther, *An Open Letter on the Harsh Book Against the Peasants*, 75 (WA 18:393–94); Holl is incorrect to assert that Luther, like Hobbes, sees a "state of nature" before government (*Reconstruction of Morality*, 109). In fact, at least since the Fall, government has always existed, and Holl provides no evidence that Luther made any reference to a state of nature in the past.

[286] Luther, *Admonition to Peace*, 25–26 (WA 18:302–6). On judging one's own case, see also *An Open Letter on the Harsh Book Against the Peasants*, 71–72 (WA 18:391). The same principle is applied in the theological dispute with Louvain: "the foolish Luther believes that it is the task of the judge, and not of the disputants, to determine the truth" (*Against Latomus*, 149; WA 8:51).

The most obvious biblical counterexamples to Luther's position are the prophets. However, they did have a direct commission from God, both in command (*befelh*) and office (*ampts*) (*Psalm 101*, 202; WA 51:245). With respect to the implicit rebellion of uncalled preachers, the apostles also had such a direct commission (*Psalm 82*, 64–65; WA 31[I]:210–11). Presumably, so did John the Baptist, and Jesus, being God, did not need one, although in all these cases, it is curious that God did not employ the call process Luther is certain God ordained.

[287] Luther, *Admonition to Peace*, 27 (translation modified; WA 18:306 reads: "So würde eyn iglicher widder den andern richter werden und keyne gewallt noch oberkeyt, ordnung noch recht bleyben ynn der wellt, sondern eytel mord und blutvergiessen").

[288] Luther, *Sincere Admonition*, 63–64 (WA 8:680–81).

has been given to the official.[289] A person possesses power by virtue of the office. Formally, it is the offices and the system of worldly government that have been ordained by God. To be sure, God places individuals in those offices as well, but the power they will exercise is waiting for them there. In fact, this is the ground for Luther's criticism of officials. Because God ordained offices with special responsibilities, Luther can scold officials when they overreach their proper domain.[290] To do more than one has been commanded is a misuse of power (*gewalt*).[291] By the same token, the residence of power within the office establishes some semblance of social order, and this is the order rebellion tries to destroy by making one a judge in one's own dispute rather than allowing those entrusted with the office of judge to perform their task:

> As soon as anyone saw that someone was wronging him, he would begin to judge and punish him. Now if that is unjust and intolerable when done by an individual, we cannot allow a mob or crowd to do it. For in both cases, the cause is the same, that is, an injustice. . . . Would you not say that he must let others, whom you appointed, do the judging and avenging? What do you expect God and the world to think when you pass judgment and avenge yourselves on those who have injured you and even upon your rulers, whom God has appointed?[292]

Punishment of the wicked "is not the responsibility of everyone, but of the worldly rulers (*oberkeyt*) who bear the sword."[293] The proper question is not whether the master is unjust, but whether God has commanded obedience.[294] It is not enough that one suffers injustice or that one's cause is right; to seek redress by force requires also that one have the right and power (*macht*) of the sword.[295]

The basis of rule in the office—rather than in the facilities of the office-holder, and in opposition to any intrinsic ability of those without an office to perform an official function—has one more aspect particularly relevant to Luther's understanding of power. Rule (*regirn*) and government (*regiment*) are

---

[289] Luther, *Psalm 82*, 51 (WA 31[I]:198). The interesting distinction between *potestas* as *Oberkeit* or "authority," present in the office and a condition for *virtutes* as *Gewalt* or "power" is illustrative. Both are underlain by *principatum* as *Herrschaft* or "rule" (*Commentary on 1 Corinthians 15*, 127; WA 36:573). These distinctions are not employed with utter consistency by Luther, but the point remains—power depends on jurisdiction and office and becomes personal only at the last.

[290] See, e.g., *Temporal Authority*, 109–12 (WA 11:265–67), where Luther criticizes both the church of Rome and the worldly governments for illegitimately trading responsibilities with each other.

[291] Luther, *Treatise on Good Works*, 89 (WA 6:256).

[292] Luther, *Admonition to Peace*, 27 (WA 18:306).

[293] Ibid., 25 (WA 18:303). The official character of power explains why rebellion is worse than even murder. The common murderer does not attack the head of government, but only the person and property of the members of the social body. In contrast, the rebel attacks the office itself (*An Open Letter on the Harsh Book Against the Peasants*, 80; WA 18:397).

[294] Luther, *Sermons on First Peter*, 83 (WA 12:338).

[295] Luther, *Admonition to Peace*, 30 (WA 18:311).

a segment of power, but they are not power's whole. In Luther's discussion of the spiritual estate and the offices of the church, he argues:

> Therefore, when a bishop consecrates it is nothing else than that in the place and stead of the whole community, all of whom have like power (*gleiche gewalt*), he takes a person and charges him to exercise this power on behalf of the others. It is like ten brothers, all king's sons and equal heirs, choosing one of themselves to rule the inheritance in the interests of all. In one sense they are all kings and of equal power, and yet one of them is charged with the responsibility of ruling (*zuregieren*).[296]

Rule is a subspecies of power. This has two implications. The most obvious is that sovereign rule establishes a variety of power not universally accessible. It is therefore the exclusive prerogative of the officeholder, since such power is contained in the office. But the fact that rule is not coextensive with power also means that one's lack of a particular office of authority is not the same as saying one is powerless. Even Luther's political theology admits the possibility of extrapolitical power. This opening takes on considerable importance later, when our concern will be to fit Luther's political and sacramental thought into a coherent framework of power.

The Rigors of Christian Obedience

Before the examination of Luther's political thought can be concluded, a final element requires notice. Apart from the division of people into the children of God and the children of the world, no attention has been paid to any uniquely Christian obligation toward the political community. Even the distinction of two kinds of people refers more to the government of the realm of God than it does earthly government. Worldly government would be necessary even if there were no salvation beyond it. Furthermore, Luther's positing of two governments was designed to prevent any effort to administer the worldly realm on the basis of the gospel. The clearing of the gospel established a relative autonomy for government. Of course, the principles by which government performs its work are found in Scripture, but not only there. One need not be a Christian to be a competent ruler, and Luther is willing to look to non-Christians for guidance in the art of government.[297] This is because the principles of government are those of reason and natural law.[298] Reason, not the gospel, is the instructor of princes. Because of this, revolt is opposed not only to Christian law but also to natural law, and rebels have earned death both eternally and on earth. There is a "common, divine, and

---

[296] Luther, *Christian Nobility*, 128 (WA 6:407).
[297] Luther, *Psalm 101*, 198–200 (WA 51:242–44).
[298] Luther, *Temporal Authority*, 128–29 (WA 11:279–80).

natural law which even the heathen, Turks, and Jews have to keep if there is to be any peace or order in the world."[299]

Conformity with natural law, of which God is the author, is a minimum standard as far as Christians are concerned. They must obey it, but that is not enough. Luther divides his *Admonition to Peace* on the basis of two laws, natural and Christian, and announces that mere satisfaction of the requirements of natural law does not suffice: "For no one is a Christian merely because he does not undertake to function as his own judge and avenger but leaves this to the powers (*gewallt*) and authorities (*oberkeyt*)." The law of Christ and the gospel go beyond this. It "is not binding on the heathen, as the other law is." But "if you claim that you are Christians, . . . then you must also allow your law (*recht*) to be held up before you rightly. Listen, then, dear Christians, to your Christian law!"[300] Luther's central complaint against the peasants is their appeal to the gospel for support.[301] A Christian must do more than obey natural law, or rather a Christian must do less. The Christian law is drawn largely from the commands of the Sermon on the Mount. Luther will not allow the stringent demands of Matthew to be reduced to mere "counsels" or "precepts" for those who would become perfect. Rather, they apply to all Christians.[302] The Sermon's paradigmatic command is, "Resist not evil." Yet Luther has asserted also that the obligation of the civil authorities is not only to resist evil but to do so firmly. There is at least the appearance of a contradiction between the universally binding commands of the Sermon on the Mount and Luther's claim that Christians not only can but should participate in earthly government, whose task it is to strike evil down through the sword.

As early as 1519, Luther attempted to distinguish the obligation of a Christian under the injunctions of the Sermon on the Mount and the public obligations of Christian officials.[303] Two possible alternatives, if not closed entirely

---

[299] Luther, *Admonition to Peace*, 27 (WA 18:307).

[300] Ibid., 27 (translation modified), 28 (WA 18:307, 308–9). The same division is employed in *Luther's Warning*, 13 (WA 30[III]:277); in the first part, he speaks "as in a dream, as if there were no God."

[301] Kirchner, *Luther and the Peasants' War*, 13.

[302] Luther, *Temporal Authority*, 92–93 (WA 11:252); see also Martin Luther, *The Sermon on the Mount*, in *Luther's Works*, vol. 21, *The Sermon on the Mount (Sermons) and The Magnificat*, trans. and ed. Jaroslav Pelikan (St. Louis: Concordia Publishing House, 1956), 3–294 (WA 32 Band [1906], 299–544) and *Judgment on Monastic Vows*, 256–60 (WA 8:580–83). Holl resists using *The Sermon on the Mount* because it did not proceed from Luther's hand, but from sermons, the transcriber of which is unknown (*Reconstruction of Morality*, 150). At the very least, however, when confirmed from other sources, there is no reason to suspect the inaccuracy of the sermons. At this point, they are used only to show that Luther did not change his mind about the general applicability of the Sermon on the Mount. This point is repeated so frequently in the sermons that it would be unreasonable not to attribute the claim and its importance to Luther. In contrast to Holl, H. Bornkamm concentrates almost exclusively on Luther's understanding of the Sermon on the Mount, and includes these sermons extensively (*Luther's Doctrine of the Two Kingdoms*).

[303] Luther, *Two Kinds of Righteousness*, 304–6 (WA 2:151–52).

in 1519, would be shut off soon. He rejects the reduction of the applicable range of these commands to an elite few Christians, and he will not allow that, in view of their being addressed to all Christians, the sword cannot be wielded by a Christian. Instead, he distinguishes two interests of the Christian, self-interest and the interest of one's neighbor. These correspond to two types of Christian conduct. Public officials receive an office in order to use its power for the best interest of those subject to it. For the prince, this means simply that the welfare of the public, not the prince himself, should be the central concern.[304] The functions of the sword have been examined. There is a clear public interest in preservation of peace, protection of good people, and punishment of the wicked. Consequently, "in what concerns the person or property of others, you govern yourself according to love and tolerate no injustice toward your neighbor. The gospel does not forbid this; in fact, in other places, it actually commands it. From the beginning of the world all the saints have wielded the sword in this way."[305] Rule is a heavy responsibility and service, not an excuse for indulgence of private appetite. Whether government is administered for self-interest or love of the neighbor is an eternally serious matter—the prince who acts "toward the pleasure, benefit, honor, comfort, and salvation of self" is damned, just as "cursed and condemned is every sort of life lived and sought for the benefit and good of self."[306] For a public official, to love the neighbor requires maintaining an orderly, peaceful society and employing force when injustice is done. God institutes two governments because application of the principle "Resist not evil" in the worldly realm would be impossible and disastrous.[307]

Still, all Christians are commanded to suffer evil and injustice. The command binds them as private Christians, when their own interests are at stake. Entry into the *Reich* of God depends on destroying the passion for one's own

---

[304] Luther, *Sermons on First Peter*, 76 (WA 12:330); *Temporal Authority*, 100 (WA 11:257).

[305] Luther, *Temporal Authority*, 96 (WA 11:255). Christ did not wield the sword, but this does not constitute a prohibition against followers of Christ doing so. To begin with, worldly authority and the variety of estates are creations of God and therefore are good. In addition, the reason Christ did not assume a position of worldly authority or do many other things was to prevent Christians from believing one could not be Christian without also doing those things. Christ was economical, appearing "wholly in connection with that estate and calling which alone served his kingdom (*reych*)," which "exists only by God's Word and Spirit" (*Temporal Authority*, 101; WA 11:258).

[306] Luther, *Temporal Authority*, 118 (WA 11:272). This leads Luther into one of his transvaluations of power (*Temporal Authority*, 120; WA 11:273). Consistent with most of his political theology, and at least present elsewhere, Luther here assumes that power is a possession through which one has the ability to dominate others. Therefore, he urges leaders to empty themselves of power. The problem is really one of the geography of power, whether power is inward, external, or neither. This will be considered in chapter 4 in reference to faith.

[307] Luther, *An Open Letter on the Harsh Book Against the Peasants*, 68 (WA 18:388).

advantage,[308] while condemnation is assured if one seeks benefit for the self. A Christian is allowed to resist evil for the sake of others, but not for one's own sake.[309] Scripture is so clear that "even a child can understand that the Christian law tells us not to strive against injustice, not to grasp the sword, not to protect ourselves, not to avenge ourselves, but to give up life and property, and let whoever takes it have it."[310] There is no use appealing to natural law, for it is not at issue here. Nothing is changed if Christian freedom is invoked, for "there stands our Master, Christ, and subjects us, along with our bodies and our property, to the emperor and the law of this world, when he says, 'Render unto Caesar the things that are Caesar's.' . . . [B]aptism does not make men free in body and property, but in soul; and the gospel does not make all goods common."[311]

The consequences Luther draws from this Christian law are startling. Not only does he oppose the peasants' right to seek redress for their grievances through force, but he also disputes their right to complain of unjust treatment. Even if they are correct in their assessment of the situation, and in general they are, "Nevertheless, almost all of the articles are framed for their own benefit (nutz) and for their own good, though not for their best good."[312] They may protest if they please, but not while calling themselves Christians. To press for fair treatment in accord with natural law is their privilege, but to invoke Christ and Christianity in support of such action is a blasphemy that assures Luther's prayer against them.[313]

A vast chasm has opened between Christians' citizenship in heaven and their pilgrimage on earth. To be in the world without being "of" it comes to mean that what others may demand for themselves, Christians may not.

---

[308] Luther, *Two Kinds of Righteousness*, 306 (WA 2:152). The three classes of people Luther designates in this treatise and the exception to the general rule of renunciation of one's own interest, found both here and in *Temporal Authority*, 103, are not relevant here. They are, however, important to Luther's thought because they are tied closely to the question of whether Luther's ethics ends in a schizophrenic split of personal and public morality. Holl makes a valiant and fairly persuasive effort to defend Luther against the charge of having supported two utterly contradictory moralities (*Reconstruction of Morality*, 98–138); however, Holl does not consider a potentially more serious problem — namely, that Luther's ethic depends on a clean distinction of functions that are all supposed to be performed by the same person. Especially in *The Sermon on the Mount*, it is quite clear that one individual often occupies a variety of estates. Luther seems to assume that it is possible to change roles in the same way that one changes clothes, and he does not consider the possibility that one may be placed in a position of being in two or more "estates" simultaneously. He does not, in short, allow the same tension to develop, nor does he achieve the same ultimate unity, as in the distinction between the heavenly and earthly person who is totally sinner and totally righteous *at the same time*.

[309] Luther, *Sermons on First Peter*, 75 (WA 12:330). Here also, Luther refers to Matthew 5, which provides the initial problematic of *Temporal Authority* (81–84; WA 245–47).

[310] Luther, *Admonition to Peace*, 29 (WA 18:310); see also *Temporal Authority*, 95 (WA 11:254).

[311] Luther, *Against the Robbing and Murdering Hordes of Peasants*, 51 (WA 18:358–59).

[312] Luther, *Admonition to Peace*, 22 (translation modified; WA 18:298).

[313] Ibid., 31–33 (WA 18:314–17).

The only interest they may uphold, insofar as they are Christian, is the neighbor's. The reason is that citizenship in heaven carries with it the consequence that the world has nothing to give a Christian. The government of the world is merely external and is not germane to Christian righteousness. This position initially supplied Luther with support in his attack against the worldly pretensions of the papacy. Since worldly rule and the various offices and estates in the world are external matters, they do not bind the conscience (*gewissen*); therefore, they cannot affect one's inward relation to God. Government of the world pertains only to outer and bodily things.[314] Christians must obey such government even if it is tyrannical. But if, through its worldly rule, the papacy and any other government

> want to encroach on the spiritual government and want to take our conscience captive where God alone must sit and rule, one must by no means obey them and should sooner let them have one's life. Worldly commands and government do not extend beyond outward and bodily things. . . . Therefore they have no power to interfere in God's order and to give commands concerning faith.[315]

The distinction of jurisdictions for rulers holds also for other Christians. Obedience to worldly government is external, pertaining not to the spirit but to the body.[316] If worldly government is properly confined to concerns of life, property, and external affairs, while only God rules the soul,[317] loss or gain of these external goods becomes a matter of indifference for the Christian. The *Reich* of God is not of this world, and it does not promise us things in this world. This is the basis of Luther's claim that Christian freedom is misunderstood if it is applied to physical life. In the world, the Christian is to be subject to all, for the gospel has nothing to do with the things of the world. A striking summary of his position is his rebuke to the peasants:

> Furthermore, your declaration that you teach and live according to the gospel is not true. Not one of the articles teaches anything of the gospel. Rather, everything is aimed at obtaining freedom for your person and property. To sum it up, everything is concerned with worldly and temporal matters. You want power and wealth so that you will not suffer injustice. The gospel, however, does not become involved in affairs of this world and external life, but speaks of our life in the world in terms of suffering, injustice, the cross,

---

[314] Luther, *Sermons on First Peter*, 76–80 (WA 12:331–35); *Temporal Authority*, 110 (WA 11:265–66).

[315] Luther, *Sermons on First Peter*, 80–81 (translation modified; WA 12:334–35 reads: "Aber wenn sie ynn das geystlich regiment greyssen wollen und das gewissen fangen, darynn Gott alleyn sitzen und regiren muss, soll man yhm gar nicht gehorchen und auch ehr den halfs drüber lassen. Welltlich gepiet und regiment strecket sich nicht weytter, denn auff eusserlich und leyblich ding").

One of the reasons Luther felt so free to criticize the institutions of Rome was his conviction that although worldly authority had been instituted by God, the prevailing ecclesiastical authorities had no specific scriptural basis (*Against Latomus*, 146; WA 8:49).

[316] Luther, *Sermons on First Peter*, 88 (WA 12:342).

[317] Luther, *Temporal Authority*, 105 (WA 11:262).

patience, and contempt for this life and temporal wealth. . . . If you want to be Christians and use the name Christian, then stop what you are doing and decide to suffer these injustices.[318]

To seek redress on one's own, against the commands of God, for things irrelevant to spiritual life, demonstrates a lack of confidence and faith in God, a defiance of divine will. This can lead only to the peasants' eternal and temporal destruction.[319] The peasants ignore the true character of Christian life: suffering and the cross.

In Luther's political writing, Christian suffering generally refers to endurance of injustice. Endurance of punishment deserved may be painful, but it is not suffering.[320] The injunction against pressing a just claim guarantees that the Christian will suffer. After all, the world is God's enemy;[321] the devil its powerful prince.[322] As Christ suffered at the hands of the world, so must every Christian expect a share of the same. Christians must not only be willing to suffer wrong; they are commanded to do it: "Suffering! Suffering! Cross! Cross! This and nothing else is the Christian law."[323] In addition to the assertion that the pillage of external goods does not concern the Christian, Luther poses the consideration that Christian existence is martyrdom on earth.[324] Not only the inevitability of suffering is affirmed, but its therapeutic value: "He who is a Christian must also bear a cross. And the more you are wronged, the better it is for you. Therefore you must accept such a cross willingly from God and thank Him."[325]

A Contrast of Power

It is clear that there is a considerable distance between Luther's political theory, with its strong emphasis on sovereignty and suffering, and the perspective on power developed in his sacramental theology. It is useful here to summarize these differences and certain similarities between the two theologies. Both are based in the theory of the two realms, and the next chapter begins from this common ground. Further, both the theology of the Lord's Supper and Luther's theory of government contain an external aspect to their power,

---

[318] Luther, *Admonition to Peace,* 35–36 (translation modified — the English translation omits "and external life"—WA 18:321–22).

[319] Luther, *Admonition to Peace,* 33–34 (WA 18:317–19).

[320] Luther, *Sermons on First Peter,* 84 (WA 12:338).

[321] Luther, *Temporal Authority,* 113 (WA 11:257); *Psalm 101,* 221 (WA 51:261).

[322] Luther, *Against the Robbing and Murdering Hordes of Peasants,* 51 (WA 18:358); Luther, *Against the Antinomians,* in *Luther's Works,* vol. 47, *The Christian in Society IV,* ed. Sherman, 113–14 (WA 50 Band [1914], 473).

[323] Luther, *Admonition to Peace,* 29 (WA 18:310).

[324] Ibid., 40 (WA 18:328).

[325] Luther, *Sermons on First Peter,* 84 (WA 12:338).

but the two conceptions of power share little else. Sacramental power had an external source, but this component was not the whole of power. The appearance of power required that the external Word and elements extend themselves toward the inwardness of the recipient, meeting either faith or unbelief. Power emerged in this meeting, either in its fulfilled or distorted sense. This power was not yet complete; the drive from externality to inwardness was itself fulfilled only in another external contact, the neighbor. Political power, on the other hand, not only begins externally, it remains external. In fact, political power is possible only if it is intractably external. Power is contained in and possessed by an office external to both its subjects and its occupant. Power's existence in an office does not depend at all on the worth of the official, nor are those of equal or superior ability permitted to perform the functions reserved for particular office if such position has not been granted them. The office is the reservoir of political power, and its existence is fundamentally external to all people. Any personal referent of power is purely accidental; it is not essential to the constitution of power itself. Power lacks the teleological, processual nature that characterized Luther's sacramental theology. Power has nothing other than an external face, and it is therefore incapable of affecting the inner person.

The consequences of the wall constructed between inwardness and power are considerable. First, since power cannot be referred to any personal center, neither can the marks of power. Power has an intrinsic connection only to the office, where it resides as a potentiality that the occupant makes actual. The official becomes powerful by calling upon this warehouse of potentiality. Power, therefore, through an office, is the possession of the powerful, a thing they use with more or less frequency. Power is legible and actual only in a contest between powers. Rebellion, for example, attempts to take the power of government for itself. If successful, it robs rulers of the best thing they have, their power.[326] If a failure, it is only because the greater power activated by rulers overcame the rebels' power. Power has been returned to a zero-sum framework, a thing to be owned. It requires, for every winner, one or many losers. If one party in an encounter of power has or gains power, all other parties lack or lose power in precisely the same proportion. The disequilibrium of possessed power is the only basis for authority; if all had the same power, authority would be impossible. In Luther's political theory, power is synonymous with sovereignty and domination. While sacramental power intends universal power, political power, at its limit, is exclusive; it is the only power — and therefore, in its particular official functions, all power.

Second, political power operates only negatively. Preeminently it is the power of the sword, which tames those who attempt to arrogate power unto themselves. Without the Fall, power would be unnecessary. It exists only to control other assertions of power. This is related to a third effect of the

---

[326] Luther, *Admonition to Peace,* 26 (WA 18:305).

confinement of power to externality. In opposition to the omnipresence of power that Luther asserted in his sacramental thought, political power reverts back to being occasional and relatively infrequent in appearance. It is exercised only upon those against whom the ruler wants to employ it, and then only coercively. In the Lord's Supper, the body and blood of Christ were consumed by the worthy and the unworthy alike. It was inevitable, under these circumstances, that power of some variety emerged from the meal, either the deformed power that resulted from faithless eating or the true power that appeared in the confluence of Word, elements, and faith. In addition, the presence of the body and blood in the sacrament were underlain by a close association between the omnipresence and omnipotence of God. The best government, in contrast, exercises its power only upon the wicked. The pious feel the effects of power at most indirectly, as safety procured by power's coercion of the unjust. In the worst government, the good may be terrorized, but this has nothing to do with the inevitability or inescapability of power itself. It depends instead on the will of the one who exercises power. In its essence, power is occasional, appearing only at certain times, subject to the will of its possessor.

The occasional, discretionary nature of power is related to the teleological question discussed earlier. The power of the ruler can be turned in any direction, used toward any end. It is purely formal, its form being rule, sovereignty, domination. In Luther's sacramental theology, this was not the case. In addition to its formal characteristics, which included a moment of sovereignty, power contained within itself a criterion of content, related to whether it reached its fruition. Power was defined by its benefit and help, while distorted power was deformed precisely because it did not reach this aim but remained mere external domination. This criterion of power's content tends to disappear in Luther's political thought. It is true that it is not entirely absent. Luther maintains that power is designed for the world's benefit, to preserve the peace and uphold justice. In addition, if one had to suffer under a tyrannical government, this too was not only the Christian law, but was also a benefit.

There is reason to wonder, though, whether "benefit" means the same thing, or is argued with the same closeness, in Luther's political thought as in the theology of the sacraments. The notion of power as a positive help is utterly lost in his understanding of political power. Government works almost exclusively through coercion, and responsible government coerces only because there is evil. It prevents disaster, but that is all. The positive efficacy of government depends on the presence of the negative — evil and injustice; it is only activated in their presence. In the case of irresponsible government, which neglects its duty and practices the evils it is supposed to prevent, there is a second point. The worst abuse of government does not affect its power. Power which is exercised badly is just as much power as that which is employed properly. Luther does assure us that rulers will pay for their wickedness eternally, but this punishment is visited upon the person who exercises power. It does not alter the power of the office which made the evil possible, nor does it change rulers' power so long as they remain in their office. Power is the formal capacity for, and exercise of, domination, for its aim is not part of its constitution. It does not contain an inherent reference to its purpose.

Even in the case of tyrannical government, when the benefits Luther attributes to political power are tenuous, he forbids resistance. His primary ground for this prohibition is the command of God. In defense of it, he adds two other reasons for enjoining revolt. The first is that, however bad the government is, rebellion is inevitably worse because it is the incarnation of anarchy. This is an extremely broad judgment, and we return to it in chapter 4. For now, it is enough to note that this evaluation depends on conceiving power as finite, occasional, and involved in a zero-sum exchange. The worst imaginable government is superior to anarchy because, in an anarchic state, everyone would have power. But the small quantity of power each would possess would be threatened by everyone else's power, and peaceful life would be impossible.[327]

For the Christian, there is another reason to endure whatever abuse is received from the hand of government: the call to suffer. The Christian not only has a share of the good accomplished by Christ but also of the suffering endured. Typically, Luther attempts to discern a benefit to this suffering as a supplement to the simple command. In contrast to the depth of his arguments concerning the benefits of the sacrament, his advocacy of the value of suffering, as he presents it in his political writings, is strained. He makes the simple statement that the more one suffers, the better it is. The evidence he brings to bear to support this claim is based in the desirability of imitating Christ: "Therefore you must tread justice underfoot and say: 'Thank God, I have been called to suffer injustice. For why should I complain when my Lord did not complain?'"[328] Aside from the fact that Luther maintained that the imitation of Christ is the least important part of the New Testament witness,[329] since it teaches only works,[330] there is an additional problem. Luther's entire Christology, and especially his theology of atonement, is dedicated to demonstrating the benefits Christ's suffering communicated. His paraphrase of First Peter includes, "He suffered for our benefit (*gutt*)."[331] Luther makes no effort to apply this to the Christian. If Christ suffered for our good, for whose good do the oppressed suffer? Luther does not say. Luther's exposition of the command

---

[327] See also Hobbes, *Leviathan*, 185.

[328] Luther, *Sermons on First Peter*, 85 (WA 12:339).

[329] Martin Luther, *Letter to the Christians at Strassburg in Opposition to the Fanatic Spirit*, in *Luther's Works*, vol. 40, *Church and Ministry II*, trans. and ed. Bergendoff, 70 (WA 15:396).

[330] Luther, *Against the Heavenly Prophets*, 131–33, 207 (WA 18:114–15, 196–97). Regin Prenter gives an excellent treatment of the "imitation" of Christ over against "conformity to Christ" (*Spiritus Creator*, trans. John M. Jensen [Philadelphia: Muhlenberg Press, 1953], 10–29). Although Luther's terminology is less precise, Prenter's clarification is helpful and faithful to Luther's message.

[331] Luther, *Sermons on First Peter*, 86 (WA 12:340).

to suffer does not follow his usual procedure of supplementing command with benefit. In this case, the benefit remains merely asserted.

It would be difficult, in any case, for Luther to provide content for the benefits of suffering within the context of his political thought. Suffering in body, property, and life, cannot have any more intrinsic meaning than loss of such external things. This exposes the most striking difference between Luther's sacramental and political thought. External things are given a wildly different value in each case. In the Lord's Supper, Word and the elements that contained the body and blood of Christ constituted a double externality that mediated spiritual power. In response to the radicals' understanding of spirituality, Luther went further, asserting that these externals were spiritual because they arose from the Spirit. This claim was applied especially to the body of Christ. The effect of realigning the relation between the spiritual and external meant that all means of the Spirit became spiritual, and this had to include external means, since the external always precedes what is inward. The process of sacramental power was determined by this argument. The efficacy of the sacrament began externally, reached inwardly, and was completed in a return to the external world.

In Luther's political theology, the second movement remains. A ruler, for example, can be a member of the spiritual estate, and such a prince acts spiri- tually. Luther made this plausible by disentangling the spiritual estate from offices of the church. The reference of "spiritual," in this case, applies to the person of the ruler. But when Luther makes the focus of worldly power the office rather than the person, the first segment of the sacramental process, the movement from the external world to the inner person, ceases. Luther does make a partial exception for Scripture—one must not surrender one's New Testament, for it is spiritual. But government itself, as distinct from the per- son who governs, has no relation to spirit. The contrast abandoned in eucha- ristic theology, between spirit and what is external and bodily, is reintroduced in politics. Since government is merely external, it can have nothing to do with spirit or Spirit. External conditions mediate nothing spiritual. This is why Luther can admit the value of non-Christian government. This is hardly symptomatic of any broad-mindedness on his part, but just the reverse. Governors could be heathen because government and its action had nothing to do with spiritual life. The external world, whose importance Luther had defended so strongly in his sacramental thought, seems reduced to irrelevance in his political theory.

The contrast is more striking because the two evaluations of the world were developed, in large part, contemporaneously. It is tempting to call Luther's two approaches to the world contradictory, but our assumptions are different from Luther's. Luther was consistent on his criterion: his interpretation of Scripture.[332] Moreover, there are elements of his sacramental and political

---

[332] This is frequently neglected in discussions of Luther; an exception is Gerhard Ebeling, *Luther: An Introduction to his Thought,* trans. R. A. Wilson (Philadelphia: Fortress Press, 1970), 43–58.

theologies that tend to reduce the difference between them. On the side of the sacrament, the powerful presence of the body and blood depends on their attachment to the Word. The Word brings that of which it speaks. Not only that, but the connection to the Word makes the body of Christ powerfully present—or available, rather than merely present. In effect, the claim he makes with respect to government is that there is no Word of God that makes government spiritually effective. God may be present there, without being available. It is certainly less clear to our world that the words of Scripture are the sole means by which the Spirit or Word of God is made available.

There is also a part of Luther's political thought that tends to bring it into closer contact with the theology of the sacraments. He concedes that rule is only a part of power, not its entirety. Luther departs from political theory here, admitting the existence of power beyond political, governmental power. We have already implied agreement with Luther's (and Foucault's) position on this point, although we will not agree with Luther that rule is identical with power even in the case of political power. A definition of power must be able to subsume both the aspect of sovereignty stressed in Luther's political and sacramental thought and his emphasis on the process and production of power contained only in his sacramental theory. The latter element is not only left out of Luther's political theology but stands in opposition to it. Sacramental power is kin to the new creation, while political power is merely a desperate answer to the Fall. If there is no unavoidable conflict between the Lord's Supper and politics on the criterion of Luther's interpretation of the Word, there is a sharp opposition with regard to power.

If, on Luther's own principles, sacramental and political theology can be made consistent, even though this may involve a conflict in his understanding of power, there is an issue raised by his theory of government that Luther does not resolve in a satisfactory manner. It was put to him in various forms during his lifetime. If the things of the world are irrelevant to the Christian, why is it that Luther himself is so concerned with the world? Suffering at the hands of tyrants is tolerable because, thankfully, their authority does not extend to the inwardness of the person. They can compel nothing to a conscience. Why, then, is Luther so concerned that justice be upheld for the neighbor? If suffering is inflicted, that is all the better for Christians. Luther does not seem especially concerned about the suffering of the heathen, and in any case, their worldly suffering is assuredly less than the eternal suffering God has in store for them. True, the commands of God declare that one should be concerned with worldly justice. Why, if the world has no significance? Why, in fact, does God care for the world in such a way that the commands of God concern action in the world? Why is Karlstadt's "inner faith" not sufficient for Luther? If the world is truly of no concern, either to the gospel or to theology, why, in sum, does Luther's theology, which he claims is determined by the gospel alone, spend so much time and paper on "worldly" questions?[333] Why, after he asserts that worldly matters are trifles in the sight of God, and therefore obedience even to the unjust is not burdensome, does he claim in the next breath that evil rulers are "the greatest of plagues" and follow this with extensive advice on the conduct of government?[334] The rather circuitous route of the next chapter attempts to answer such questions and, through those answers, to return to the topic of power in the fourth chapter.

[333] This question is left open in George Wolfgang Forell, *Faith Active in Love* (Minneapolis: Augsburg, 1954), 158–59. Forell claims that Luther's apocalyptic tendency made him "see in all attempts to reform society merely efforts to repair a social order destined to collapse very soon." But if the issues at stake were "merely" these, why did Luther suggest and oppose reforms, and how is it consistent for Forell to say that "Luther felt that this mending and repairing was important"?

[334] Luther, *Treatise on Good Works*, 91–97 (WA 6:258–63).

CHAPTER 3.

THREE DUALITIES
OF JUSTIFICATION

The conflict between Luther's political and sacramental theologies, and the attitude of each toward the world, cannot be evaded by asserting that Luther was momentarily careless. The problem exemplifies a tension running through the heart of his theology. The question is the proper description of the difference in Luther's viewpoint. Does Luther's theology finally collapse in irresolvable conflict between the value ascribed to the world in his sacramental thought and his attitude toward the world in his political theology, the latter of which seems to oscillate between disregard and demand for action? Or is there a fundamental unity between his two valuations? Were this simply an argument between sacramental and political thought, or even one within Luther's political theology, there would be less need to decide between unity and contradiction. One could merely sever either or both of these two theologies from the body of Luther's work, without great cost to the whole. If, on the other hand, the difficulty simply expresses in especially clear terms two currents etched deeply in the formation of Luther's entire theology, such limited options are no longer available. The alternative that is chosen, whether contradiction or compatibility, becomes a more sweeping judgment, not only upon Luther's worth for a theology of power but upon his value for Christian thought more generally.

There are several tasks to accomplish. First, evidence must be brought forth to support the thesis that a duality in Luther's evaluation of the world is present throughout his theology. Second, the complementary character of these two theological movements requires clarification. The theological linchpin of Luther's work, the doctrine of justification, acquires his peculiar and original stamp from his distinction between grace and gift. Luther's discussion of the law cannot be isolated from this duality; it is, in fact, contained within the broader notion of "gift." Finally, the basic differentiation of grace and gift carries with it a "geographical" distinction between them with respect to their inwardness and externality.

131

Grace, Gifts, and the Two Realms

Before approaching the body of the chapter, a terminological problem in Luther's work should be noted. Luther uses the terms "grace" and "gift" often without a great deal of technical precision. Sometimes there is a systematic reason for this, which will be explored later, but frequently gift and grace are interchangeable. The Supper, for example, was sometimes called a grace, although not "grace" as a whole, and sometimes a gift. This substitutability is especially prevalent in Luther's nonacademic work. There is certainly a close connection between grace and gift. What grace God gives, to state the obvious, is given; that is, grace is from one perspective a gift.[1] Moreover, all gifts are given freely, out of God's gracious will, and are therefore manifestations of grace. Luther's technical use of these two terms differentiates them, but he does not feel the need to make the distinction terminologically rigorous. These linguistic variations are not especially troubling, except perhaps for academics who demand that everyone speak with academic precision. Once Luther's technical employment of the terms "grace" and "gift" is understood, their theological meaning can be found throughout his work, sometimes under one heading, sometimes under the other, or both. The meaning of the terms is what demands elucidation; the words themselves are relatively unimportant. As Luther himself comments, "even in the eyes of the world it is disgraceful . . . to be in agreement in substance and yet to quarrel about words."[2]

Grace from Heaven

The specific meaning of grace and gift clarifies the two aspects of Luther's understanding of justification.[3] On one hand, the justified person is righteous according to the forensic judgment of God and with respect to the heavenly realm. This forensic, declared justification describes one's true citizenship and ultimate state. Distinct from the static character of forensic justification, but dependent on it, is the process of being made actually righteous in the world.

---

[1] Even when Luther is interested in distinguishing grace and gift, he still speaks of forgiveness, for example, as a "gift of grace" with little difficulty (*Against Latomus*, 232; WA 8:109); see also *Lectures on Galatians, 1535, Chapters 1–4*, 104 (WA 40[I]:188–89).

[2] Luther, *Against the Heavenly Prophets*, 119 (WA 18:103).

[3] A good deal of the discussion of grace and gift follows the excellent work of F. Edward Cranz, *An Essay on the Development of Luther's Thought on Justice, Law, and Society*, Harvard Theological Studies 19 (Cambridge, Mass.: Harvard University Press, 1959), except that we are interested less in the genesis of Luther's development of this position than in the Luther of 1525 and after. In addition, Cranz is not concerned at all with the implications of Luther's position for an understanding of power, nor does he take up the problematic of the inward and the external in Luther in much detail. This latter omission tends to separate the two realms somewhat more than Luther does, for Cranz does not pay much attention to the mechanics of mediation between the realms.

This processual aspect of justification refers to the earthly realm and to the actual, living believer in the world. Luther's use of the distinction between grace and gift is most clearly and forcefully expressed in his masterful response to Louvain, *Against Latomus*. This essay of 1521 is the paradigmatic example of the execution of Luther's theological project.[4]

The law of God is the cornerstone of Luther's thought concerning the justice or righteousness (*iustitia*) of God and humanity. Sin is understood in terms of the law. In its basic meaning, sin is simply violation of God's law (*legem*). Righteousness requires nothing more nor less than fulfillment of the law. But original sin has made obedience to God's law impossible for fallen humanity. Latomus's charge that Luther's position means that God commands the impossible—that is, fulfillment of the law—is accepted by Luther with enthusiasm. All have been consigned to disobedience of God. Free will cannot satisfy the law of God;[5] it "is nothing and neither does nor can do good in the absence of grace—unless you wish to give 'efficacy' a new meaning."[6] Free choice, Luther never tires of pointing out, has no "power,"[7] or rather, "has no power (*vis*) while Satan rules over it but to spurn grace."[8] Reason thinks this preposterous; what is commanded must be possible. "Should" implies "can." But the ways of God mock reason, for the

> words of the law are spoken, therefore, not to affirm the power (*vim*) of the will, but to enlighten blind reason and make it see that its own light is no light and that the virtue of the will is no virtue. . . . [I]t is not to reveal or confer any power (*virtute*). For this knowledge is not power, nor does it confer power, but it instructs and shows there is no power there, and how great a weakness there is.[9]

This incapacity does not refer merely to the outward performance of the law's demands. Outward violation of God's law is merely the consequence or fruit of the sin residing in us. Primordially, sin is an inward matter, and it is this aspect of sin that Luther regards as most important, because it determines the outward face of sin. Luther's exposition of the Ten Commandments is instructive. The first table of the commandments (1–3), and especially the first commandment,[10] has an inward reference. The first commandment

---

[4] A good exposition of this treatise from a somewhat different vantage point is H. Bornkamm, *Luther in Mid-Career 1521–1530*, trans. E. Theodore Bachmann, ed. Karin Bornkamm (Philadelphia: Fortress Press, 1983), 183–97.

[5] Luther, *Against Latomus*, 151–95 (WA 8:53–83); see also *Freedom of a Christian*, 349 (WA 7:53).

[6] Luther, *Bondage of the Will*, 68 (WA 18:636).

[7] See esp. *Bondage of the Will*, 64–87, 171–74 (WA 18:634–51, 706–8).

[8] Ibid., 158 (WA 18:698). That "no power but to spurn grace" and "no power at all" are in fact equivalent expressions is shown in *Bondage of the Will*, 286 (WA 18:781).

[9] Luther, *Bondage of the Will*, 126–27 (WA 18:677).

[10] The second and third commandments do nothing but keep the first (*Treatise on Good Works*, 60; WA 6:233–34); see also *Treatise on Good Works*, 39–54 (WA 6:217–29); *Ten Sermons on the Catechism*, 141–45 (WA 30[I]:61–66).

requires one to honor God, which includes both fear of God and inward trust in God's loving will but not external works, at least initially.[11] Inward trust provides the confidence to accept and act in all external circumstances. Moreover, external good works proceed only from the prior fulfillment of this command; if the first commandment is satisfied, no difficulty is involved in performing good works externally.[12]

In crossing the boundary of inwardness, Luther simultaneously passes into specifically Christian knowledge of the law. One of the ways he interprets Paul's claim that the law increases sin is that the revelation of the law unveils sin's inward nature. The law deals with sin only in order to reveal it, disclosing a different quality and geography of sin. Sin, aside from originally making it impossible to fulfill the law, and actually transgressing it, also produces ignorance of the law. After original sin and in the absence of God's revelation, we are left with only natural knowledge of sin — and nature regards only outward acts of transgression as sin. It does not call perverse inner desire "sin." The law does. Inner rebellion against God is the root of sin. Sin does not remain hidden, and it does produce external wrongs; but the elemental character of sin is inward.[13]

Sin, then, is a "substance" of the soul, and this substantial character of sin, which means that people are sin before they commit sin, is the primary offense against God.[14] Luther's argument involves a curious reversal of Latomus's position. While Latomus argues that grace is a quality of the soul and sin is an external act, Luther claims the opposite; sin is a quality of the soul and grace is not. Asserting the substantial possession of grace, as Latomus does, has the effect of making the person capable, in part, of self-justification, making an idol of the self. For Luther, however, one's substantial constitution in original sin predates any works;[15] just as he will say that grace is not achieved by means of any works on our part, so sin fundamentally is also independent of individual human works. Luther can say with such confidence that "every good work of the saints while pilgrims in this world is sin,"[16] because they, like everyone else, are sin, and this possession guarantees their commission of sins. The ability to fulfill the commands of God is utterly lost, inwardly as well as externally, both in original and in actual sin.

Indeed, Luther is willing to grant that, were the obligations of the law met completely, the mercy of God would be unnecessary. It would be possible, in that case, to stand before God and ask that one's righteous and just

---

[11] Luther, *Ten Sermons on the Catechism,* 137–41 (WA 30[I]:57–61); see also *Treatise on Good Works,* 33 (WA 6:212).

[12] Luther, *Freedom of a Christian,* 353 (WA 7:55–56).

[13] Luther, *Against Latomus,* 195–224 (WA 8:83–104).

[14] Ibid., 201 (WA 8:88).

[15] Luther, *Two Kinds of Righteousness,* 299 (WA 2:146); *Commentary on 1 Corinthians 15,* 114 (WA 36:553).

[16] Luther, *Against Latomus,* 159 (WA 8:58).

work be crowned with glory according to God's righteousness and justice.[17] He goes so far as to say that even one sinless work would be sufficient armor with which to present oneself before God: "You cannot hold at one and the same time that, 'I have a work without sin' and 'I am not justified (*iustificatus*) in this.' Do not make God unjust so that he would not acquit a good work without sin. What would he condemn in it?" If Latomus has a work upon which he can surely rely, Luther urges him to present it to God and ask for God's justice, but adds, "Latomus, doesn't this make you shudder and sweat?"[18] If Latomus does not perspire, he should, and will assuredly sweat profusely in the fires of hell if he dares press his bluff. No work, no righteous deed is unpolluted by sin, and none has anything good enough about it to cause God to withhold an angry judgment.[19]

The crippling of all ability to meet the demands of the law involves a series of power relations. In the first place, humanity's natural powers (*viribus*) are no longer effective (*effici posse*) for obedience to God's law.[20] Nor is the law any help. Law is imposed externally; it may tell us what to do, but it does not give power (*virtutem*) to meet its demands.[21] This is the principal reason justification is impossible through the law. What was originally given as a help for us has now become a hindrance. The law, like the sacraments, has a double efficacy: it is a positive good if it is observed, but "also it is death, wrath, and no good to you if you do not observe it—that is, if you do not have faith." By nature, obedience is impossible, so the law is wrath to the natural person; "no one can withstand the power (*vim*) of the law."[22] In light of two considerations, natural powerlessness and the conviction that our destiny need not be the final and ultimate weakness of damnation, a different power must arise to save us. Existentially, corruption cries out for the power of God to make us just; theologically, it calls for a doctrine of justification.[23]

---

[17] Ibid., 190 (WA 8:79); Martin Luther, *Disputation Concerning Justification,* in *Luther's Works,* vol. 34, *Career of the Reformer IV,* trans. and ed. Lewis W. Spitz (Philadelphia: Muhlenberg Press, 1960), 187 (WA 39 Band [I] [Weimar: Hermann Böhlaus Nachfolger, 1926], 118). In *Against Latomus,* at least, Luther does grant the theoretical possibility that in grace the commandments (*mandata*) of God may be fulfilled in this life. Luther believes this was true of Mary. But in opening this conceptual possibility, Luther denies that this actually occurs, except in the cases of Mary and Jesus (*Against Latomus,* 156–57; WA 8:56).

[18] Luther, *Against Latomus,* 191, 190 (WA 8:80, 79).

[19] Ibid., 169 (WA 8:65).

[20] Ibid., 153–54 (WA 8:54).

[21] Luther, *Freedom of a Christian,* 348 (WA 7:52); see also David C. Steinmetz, *Luther in Context* (Bloomington: Indiana University Press, 1986), 116.

[22] Luther, *Against Latomus,* 178, 177 (WA 8:71, 70); see also *Lectures on Hebrews,* 212 (WA 57[III]:210–11).

[23] See Luther, *Bondage of the Will,* 244, 248 (WA 18:754–55, 757–58), in which this problem and its solution are cast specifically in the language of impotence and power. The same is true of *Disputation Concerning Justification,* 176 (WA 39[I]:97).

To be justified is to be just or righteous. Luther's doctrine of justification, however, is not univocal, but contains an inner duality, revealing a double modality of God's power expressed in the conceptual distinction of grace and gift. Isolated from its complementary notion of gift, Luther's theology of grace understands justification as God's forensic declaration of righteousness, which produces and announces one's ultimate salvation in eternal life. To be sure, Luther's understanding of justification is not only forensic (but it is forensic also, whatever else it may be), and this segment of Luther's conception should be given discrete analysis before it is fitted with other aspects of Luther's theology.[24] The forensic, declarative, and effective character of grace creates a structure of power with considerable affinity to Luther's political theology.

An initial hint that the type of power involved in grace and politics might be similar is Luther's frequent use of the same terms to describe God and the political authorities. Both are lords and princes.[25] The resemblance is in fact much more precise than this suggestive language. To begin with, grace is a purely external process of God's imputation. Imputed grace has two aspects. In the first place, our sin is imputed to Christ, who assumed it for us. This changes neither the nature nor the inward inherency of sin, but it does alter sin's ascription. Instead of being charged to the sinner, it is charged to the guiltless Christ.[26] Sin is truly removed from us, not in its substance but only by standing under and within the mercy of God. The key point is not the nature of the object under consideration, sin, but the personal relation between God and the sinner:

> What then, are we sinners? No, rather we are justified (*iustificati*), but by grace. Righteousness (*Iustitia*) is not situated in those qualitative forms, but in the mercy of God. In fact, if you remove mercy from the godly, they are sinners and really have sin, but it is not imputed (*imputatur*) to them because they believe and live under the reign of mercy, and because sin is condemned and continually put to death in them.[27]

In its "proper sense," grace is not a quality of the soul, but merely the good favor of God which cancels God's wrath toward sin.[28]

---

[24] The literature on Luther's doctrine of justification is immense. Much of it deals with exactly this issue, whether justification involves *merely* imputation, or whether it also includes impartation. H. Oberman is surely right that it is inadmissible to claim that Luther says righteousness is "'only' imputed" (*The Dawn of the Reformation: Essays in Late Medieval and Early Reformation Thought* [Edinburgh: T & T Clark, 1986], 121). In saying this, however, this essay makes it seem as if there is no imputation at all. On the second aspect of justification, developed in Luther's theology of the gift, Oberman's essay is excellent.

[25] Among countless examples, see *Lectures on Hebrews,* 118, 141 (WA 57[III]:108–9, 135); *Against Latomus,* 174 (WA 8:68); *Receiving Both Kinds in the Sacrament,* 246 (WA 10[II]:21). In *Freedom of a Christian,* 355 (WA 7:57), believers are also participants in God's "royal power."

[26] Luther, *Against Latomus,* 208 (WA 8:92–93).

[27] Ibid., 208 (WA 8:92).

[28] Ibid., 227 (WA 8:106).

If grace is not a quality of the soul, several consequences follow. First, nonimputation of sin, and the corresponding imputation of righteousness, has no direct effect on the actual worldly being of the one favored by God. Therefore,

> although forgiveness has been imputed and thus sin is removed so that it is not imputed, nevertheless, it is not substantially or essentially destroyed except in the conflagration of fire by which the whole world and our bodies will be completely purified on the last day. . . . In the meantime, while we live, original sin also lives. . . . Therefore, sin is only remitted by imputation, but when we die, it is destroyed essentially.[29]

Grace is an exclusively outward good.[30] Only if grace is removed from the actual being of its recipient completely is it possible to avoid a partial dependence on works for attaining of eternal life.

In addition, the externality of grace implies its totality: grace describes a condition or state into which the person is either placed or not, not something one may have in relative degrees. A worldly judge cannot put only part of the criminal behind bars or free only part of the person declared innocent; similarly, grace and wrath are judgments upon the whole person:

> Now it follows that these two, wrath and grace, are so related — since they are outside us — that they are poured out upon the whole, so that he who is under wrath is wholly under the whole of wrath, while he who is under grace is wholly under the whole of grace, because wrath and grace have to do with persons. . . . [God] does not divide this grace as gifts are divided.[31]

It is senseless to speak of degrees of grace. It is granted totally or not at all. Despite the persistence of the substance of sin which infects being and act, the external nonimputation of sin means that the same person, from another angle, is righteous and just. One to whom grace is promised is not only both sinner and righteous at the same time but also totally sinful and totally righteous at the same time.[32] Totally righteous, because this is the declaration of God,

---

[29] Luther, *Disputation Concerning Justification,* 164 (WA 39[I]:95). The entire disputation is particularly strong in its emphasis on imputation. At the same time, it makes clear that imputation cannot be separated from the gifts of God, especially faith.

[30] Luther, *Against Latomus,* 227 (WA 8:106).

[31] Ibid., 228–29 (WA 8:106–7). Such a total conception of worldly judgment and the forensic authority of God obviously predates what Foucault called the microscopic mechanisms of power. It belongs to an era of contest between sovereign and subject. Judgment in all walks of life has become more specialized, and the variety of social judges do attempt to judge only particular areas of life instead of the entire person. Whether such specialized judgment is finally possible without a corresponding total judgment is still questionable. For Luther, all partial judgments, which belong to the theology of gift, depend on the initial total judgment of the entire person by grace or wrath.

[32] Cranz identifies this totalistic viewpoint as an important difference from the early Luther (*Development of Luther's Thought,* 48).

and totally sinful in one's actual being.[33] The righteousness contained in grace is an "alien righteousness."[34] From the viewpoint of the forensic decision of God, the difference between the Christian and the non–Christian does not lie in their sinfulness; pithily put, "Just as the latter are damnable hypocrites, so the former . . . are saved hypocrites."[35]

The externality of grace in relation to its object is not the only similarity with political power. The bestowal of grace is also the exclusive privilege of the sovereign God. Luther's vehement attack on attempts to establish righteousness by human action is motivated in large part by concern to maintain the exclusive sovereignty of God. Those who try to reserve even a little bit of their salvation to their own efforts deserve only contempt. What makes works and the person who performs them damnable is the use of them to contribute to salvation through such deeds.[36] If Christ, grace, and the Spirit are not needed for the whole of one's salvation, they are not needed at all.[37] Either grace is completely the work of God, and none of ours, or it is not grace. Free choice with respect to salvation is a power (virtutis) of God alone.[38] One power, and only one, can decide salvation.

A third feature of grace is that it is occasional rather than omnipresent. This is true in two respects. First, only some are granted grace. Second, although forgiveness is a daily event, it is for the sake of the justified, that is, the already forgiven.[39] There are two types of forgiveness, one related primarily to forensic justification and a second, daily forgiveness, which is

---

[33] On the latter, see *Freedom of a Christian*, 346–47 (WA 7:51).

[34] Luther, *Two Kinds of Righteousness*, 298–99 (WA 2:146). Despite the descriptive force of "alien righteousness," the conception of the two kinds of righteousness Luther had in 1519 is appreciably changed by the time he writes in opposition to Latomus in 1521. An important difference is that in 1519 Luther holds that alien righteousness is infused, becoming part of one who receives it. This accounts for a confusion about which form of righteousness, alien or proper, is assigned to drive out the old fleshly person, and it explains why Luther can say that alien righteousness, like its proper counterpart, admits of degrees and gradations.

[35] Luther, *Against Latomus*, 256 (WA 8:125–26).

[36] Luther, *Freedom of a Christian*, 349, 363 (WA 7:53, 63).

[37] Luther, *Bondage of the Will*, 109, 113, 125 (WA 18:665, 667, 676). This exclusivity is also Luther's answer to congruous merit, which he thinks inevitably becomes condign (*Lectures on Galatians, 1535, Chapters 1–4*, 124–27 (WA 40[I]:220–24). In Martin Luther, *The Disputation Concerning the Passage: "The Word Was Made Flesh" (John 1:14)*, in *Luther's Works*, vol. 38, *Word and Sacrament IV*, trans. and ed. Lehmann, 248 (WA 39 Band [II] [Weimar: Hermann Böhlaus Nachfolger, 1932], 13–14), this principle of exclusivity implies Luther's critique of reason and philosophy. If human reason, unchanged by the Spirit, is able to reach the central theological truths by deduction, there is no room left for the Christ-*event*, which is underivable because accomplished in God's sovereign and free omnipotence. Justification and forgiveness cannot be inferred from the structure of the world.

[38] Luther, *Bondage of the Will*, 107, 280 (WA 18:664, 778); see also *Against Latomus*, 182 (WA 8:74).

[39] Continual forgiveness is a constant instantiation and repetition of the overarching decree of eternal life, and has the total forgiveness granted by grace as its end. See Luther, *Disputation Concerning Justification*, 164 (WA 39[I]:94–95).

logically dependent on the initial forensic declaration. Forgiveness promised and delivered to the faithful in the Supper, for example, lies in this second category. It cannot and does not apply to those whom God has not fore-ordained for salvation; for them, the Eucharist is but another lick in the flames of hell. The power (*krafft und macht*) of Christ's suffering is contained in the Supper so the recipient can lay hold of it for redemption from sin.[40] The forgiveness won on the cross is distributed in sacrament and Word continuously, as it must be because those who are forgiven still are sinners:

> Since now all they who are forgiven still have sins, the body and blood of Christ are necessary for them. Thus it is still true that he is given for them. For while the act [the unrepeatable sacrifice] has taken place, as long as I have not appropriated it, it is as if it had not taken place for me. . . . When it is given for me and to me, it is shed for me. That which is shed for me, does and must take place daily.[41]

Daily, constant forgiveness depends for its efficacy on the prior complete forgiveness of grace.

Grace is an act of sovereign power. As in Luther's political theology, the issue is what reigns over the subject. The possibilities are grace or wrath; God's reign is "over," not "in." The conquest of sin, its domination by grace, is accomplished purely by the sovereign mercy of God. If works that are considered good in the view of humanity are not good in their substance because infected with the disease of sin, "It follows, therefore, that our good works are not good unless His forgiving mercy reigns (*regnante*) over us."[42] Rescue from the law of sin and death does not mean freedom from sin and death themselves —"Sin is indeed present, but having lost its tyrannic power (*possit*), it can do nothing." Grace conquers sin ultimately, even if it remains present. Sin becomes like a condemned criminal upon whom final sentence has been pronounced, one existent and present but without power:

> That man is indeed condemned whose robberies and wicked crimes are not simply forbidden [as the law does with sin], who is not simply arrested and imprisoned, but upon whom the verdict is pronounced and who, bearing the sentence of death, is led to execution so that, even though he has not yet suffered, nothing can happen to him except to be taken away. Where then is the power (*virtus*) of such a robber?
>
> So also through baptism, sin in us is arrested, judged, and wholly incapacitated so that it can do nothing, and is appointed to complete annihilation.

The notion of a powerless presence employed in Luther's dispute with the radical sacramentarians had already appeared in the construction of his theology

---

[40] Luther, *Against the Heavenly Prophets*, 210 (WA 18:200).
[41] Ibid., 215–16 (WA 18:205).
[42] Luther, *Against Latomus*, 172 (WA 8:66).

of grace. Sin is present, but it "no longer reigns (*regnet*); while outside of grace, sin prevails, under grace the same sin has "no dominion (*potest*)."[43]

The characteristics of the power of grace, its sovereignty, exclusivity, and externality, are not accidental. If Luther's two assumptions are granted, that no human work can be without sin and that one must be certain of God's salvific promise, grace's power has these three features because it must. Only if grace is reserved to sovereign and external dominion can salvation be utterly delivered from our hands and into the bosom of God. Only because our salvation has nothing to do with our intrinsic worth can we be confident of it, for the Word of promise alone is that against which nothing can prevail, and that upon which we may rely with a sure and certain heart.[44] Luther maintains that "sin is a very cruel and powerful (*potentissimus*) tyrant over all men throughout the world, a tyrant who cannot be overthrown and expelled by the power (*potentia*) of any creatures, whether angels or men, but only by the infinite and sovereign power of Jesus Christ, the Son of God, who was given for it."[45] Salvation is no longer a question of activity or even spiritual health, but of a status which, like a worldly estate, is one into which we are beckoned, not into which we force ourselves. The operation of grace shares all these characteristics with political power: it is external, occasional, exclusive, a sovereign domination both of its enemies and those whom it protects.

The principal difference between politics and grace is obvious: they operate in different realms.[46] Whereas political authority is limited to worldly affairs, grace has nothing to do with the world. It changes nothing in the world directly. It does not remove sin from the believer; indeed, it has no effect on its recipient. Luther's understanding of grace depends on a nonpolitical doctrine of the two realms or, rather, the political use of this doctrine is indebted to the fundamental distinction between the two realms in the marrow of his theology of justification. The person standing within the reign of grace is at the same time, and totally, righteous and sinner. This is possible because the predicates "righteous" and "sinner" are viewed from two perspectives. Since natural reason has only an external perspective, while God's viewpoint includes the root of sin, what is good before the world is not good before God. God alone makes good before God; works that appear good to the human eye are worthy of divine praise only if blanketed by God's pure forgiving mercy.[47]

Grace, in short, has nothing to do with worldly being. If it did, it would deal with works and would shatter the confidence in the mercy of God that Luther is at pains to assure. Moreover, not all would depend on Christ, but

---

[43] Ibid., 207, 206, 204, 211 (WA 8:92, 91, 89, 94); see also *Bondage of the Will*, 64–69 (WA 18:634–39).

[44] Luther, *Against Latomus*, 192–93 (WA 8:82).

[45] Luther, *Lectures on Galatians, 1535, Chapters 1–4*, 33 (WA 40[I]:84–85).

[46] An effect of this difference is that God's sovereignty is characterized more by promises than the worldly sovereignty of the prince (*Treatise on Good Works*, 67–68; WA 6:240).

[47] Luther, *Against Latomus*, 172–75, 185–86, 246 (WA 8:67–69, 76, 119).

a part of salvation would be reserved for pious athleticism by the faithful. The division between heavenly grace and the earthly realm goes a long way to explaining Luther's attitude toward the world in his political thought. Exactly because the one living under grace has a heavenly home, the things of the world are of such little moment, and suffering can be endured. Refusal to suffer expresses insufficient confidence in God's promise of eternal deliverance.

For our purposes, the significance of the doctrine of grace is twofold. First, it shows that a theology of the two realms is contained in the central article of justification by grace. If, to avoid the more unpalatable aspects of Luther's political theology, one eliminates the doctrine of the two realms, not only is Luther's political theology obliterated, but the entire doctrine of justification by grace is also erased.[48] Second, although political theology and justification concern different realms, both express the same attitude toward the world, and both operate with a similar mode of power. Because the justified person is secure eternally, suffering can be tolerated in the world, and the world can be understood as of merely secondary, and perhaps no, significance. If the doctrine of justification, with its nearness to his political thought, were the beginning and the end of Luther's theology of power, it would be difficult to understand why the world occupies such a large place in his work.

Gifts on Earth

Despite the sovereign decree of grace, Luther admits his own flagging confidence in its promise and concedes he must daily battle against the desperate feeling of being deserted by God,[49] a terror "not that the devil is his enemy but that God might be."[50] Conquest of this fear through confidence or faith in God's promises introduces an element beyond the bare theology of grace. For faith is an inner attitude, a certainty of inclusion in eternal life, a trust in God and God's promise of salvation.[51] Faith is not merely one virtue beside others, but the animating principle of all virtue, for it alone has the power (*virtutis*) to provide courage for all one's work.[52] But why is it necessary?

---

[48] The fundamentally extrapolitical nature of the notion of the two realms is discussed by Cranz (*Development of Luther's Thought,* 41–71). It is also noted, albeit quite unsympathetically, by Juan Luis Segundo, *The Liberation of Theology,* trans. John Drury (Maryknoll, N.Y.: Orbis Books, 1976), 143. Segundo advocates a return to a theology of merit as constitutive of justification, a possibility Luther rejects as ultimately self-defeating. Segundo opposes the notion of two realms on the ground that it eliminates any significance to the world. If this is true of some of Luther's followers, it is not true of Luther.

[49] Luther, *Lectures on Galatians, 1535, Chapters 1–4,* 36 (WA 40[I]:89).

[50] Steinmetz, *Luther in Context,* 31.

[51] This notion is especially prominent in the *Treatise on Good Works.*

[52] Luther, *Freedom of a Christian,* 343–44 (WA 7:49). This is why the notion of certainty looms so large in Luther's thought, and why it implies a doctrinal certainty as well. Uncertainty of any kind, and especially regarding doctrine, throws the promises of God into doubt and destroys Christian confidence.

The sovereign God gives grace without reference to the worth of the person affected. It is not obvious why such a decision needs public proclamation in Word and sacrament, or personal appropriation in faith. Just as easily, God could throw a surprise party for the lucky on the day of judgment when, unexpectedly and joyously, the redeemed would discover their good fortune. It is more than significant that Luther never considers even the possibility of such secret, unpublicized decision making. God decides and proclaims.

The proclamatory supplement to the decision of God indicates that the point of Luther's distinction between the two realms is not their utter disjunction. The association between these two moments, earthly announcement and heavenly decision, must be clarified. One of the pivotal questions in Luther's dispute with Latomus revolved around what was and was not accomplished in baptism. After baptism, can the work of a Christian be both sinful and not sinful? Luther's answer is that it can and must.[53] Baptism, we have seen, signifies the actual granting of grace and the promise of salvation. The consequences Luther will draw from this are prefigured in his 1519 treatise on baptism: "With respect to the sacrament, then, it is true that [the recipient] is without sin and guilt. Yet because not all is completed and he still lives in sinful flesh, he is not without sin. But although not pure in all things, he has begun to grow in purity and innocence."[54] The meaning of baptism, which outlasts the sacramental act, is that it is both the actual beginning and the purpose of Christian life. On the last day, the work of baptism is completed. This basic structure is developed further in Luther's argument with Latomus. The imputation of righteousness in grace means that the one who is declared just by the heavenly decree of God performs just and righteous works from the forensic standpoint of on high, which is a judgment on the entire person rather than a question of that person's acts or inward condition. Baptism does not change the heart of the recipient directly. Instead, it is a declaration of that person's true character, which shall be made actual only in the final purification. Such a conception of the forensic activity of the heavenly realm depends on a doctrine of the two realms that is not political.

In essence, Luther's argument is that to be called just is not the same as actually being just. Thus, "a man who is justified (*Iustificari*) is not yet a righteous (*iustum*) man, but is in the very movement or journey to righteousness (*iustitiam*). Therefore, whoever is justified is still a sinner; and yet he is considered fully and perfectly righteous by God who pardons and is merciful."[55] Moreover, the declaration comes before the fact; God does not confirm what is already the case, but promises what shall be. Between the act of baptism and the future promised by God stretches the entirety of actual earthly life. It is in relation

---

[53] Luther repeats this argument in *Disputation Concerning Justification*, 179–83 (WA 39[I]:110–12), fifteen years after his response to Latomus.

[54] Luther, *Holy and Blessed Sacrament of Baptism*, 33 (WA 2:729).

[55] Luther, *Disputation Concerning Justification*, 152–53 (WA 39[I]:83).

to life that Luther develops his second theology of justification and a second theology of power. Any justice or righteousness of the believer's actual, earthly life does not convey or produce eternal salvation, for then salvation would depend on what the person does, that is, on works. Rather, actual righteousness is a developing and progressive justness that depends on the divine decree of eternal salvation.

The mechanism of sanctification, or actual *iustitia,* is the spiritual gifts of God. The gifts of God fall into two classes. The first may be termed "common gifts." These include not only the outward things of nature but also "whatever natural, moral, and impressive goods there are," all inner faculties of the natural person, including reason and will. As "gifts (*dona*) of God," all these things are truly good and are rewarded by God "with temporal benefits, such as rule, wealth, glory, fame, honor, enjoyment, and the like." Moreover, these are gifts "freely distributed among the evil more often than among the good."[56] As means of preserving and improving the world, they show God's "motherly care" for the things of creation.[57] Worldly government lies within this framework of common gift.

Luther's expansive understanding of what is included in common and natural gifts has several effects. It accounts for his opposition to the anthropological dualism of flesh and spirit encountered in his sacramental thought. To segment the person such that one part is flesh and another spirit had at least two heretical consequences. It implicitly denied the Christian affirmation of the resurrection of the body and, conversely, made the work accomplished in the incarnation impossible. In addition, the refusal to exclude the body from the impact of spirit alters Luther's understanding of the mortification of old Adam. It does not and cannot be identical with mortification of the body. Asceticism cannot include what is ruinous to the body, for the body too is a gift of God and is therefore good.[58]

The whole person and all faculties are included in the category of flesh. This provides Luther the latitude to draw a sharp line between flesh and spirit. Flesh, being in the first instance inward rather than external, means that the good common gifts of God are subject to distortion by the "spirit" of flesh. Indeed, it is largely because of their very goodness that God's natural gifts become evil.[59] Luther's understanding of the distortion of sacramental and natural gifts has been noted. Just as the question of sin and grace is not resolved by the nature of sin but by the personal relation between God and the sinner, Luther also distinguishes between the nature or substance of the gifts and their relation to the user. The good gifts of God are abused by the sinner; and abuse,

---

[56] Luther, *Against Latomus,* 226, 225, 226 (WA 8:105).

[57] Luther, *Lectures on Hebrews,* 112 (WA 57[III]:101).

[58] See, e.g., Luther, *Eight Sermons at Wittenberg,* 86 (WA 10[III]:36–37).

[59] In twentieth-century theology, this insight was appropriated with special clarity by Reinhold Niebuhr's reflections on *hubris.*

recalling the Augustinian distinction, consists in their being enjoyed in lieu of God: "that deeply hidden root of sin . . . is the cause of men being pleased with, relying, and glorying in these things which are not felt to be evil. This is now and always the innermost evil of sin, for trust, pleasure, and glorying must be in God alone."[60]

"Natural blindness" that does not know God, the true good, makes subordinate goods into its true good, "confidently and stubbornly" maintaining that they are ultimate goods. But all of them, because their use is infected by sin, "fall under wrath and the curse, nor do they profit anyone, nor indeed, prepare a 'congruence to grace,' but rather fatten the heart so that it neither desires nor sees the necessity of grace."[61] This is the root of Luther's polemic against reason, for natural reason, interested only in the substance or nature of things, cannot comprehend that these good gifts become evil by virtue of use apart from God. Reason also is part of the flesh, instrumental in corrupting the subordinate good natural gifts of God into evils by relying on them. The law is required to set us straight, and in the knowledge of sin it communicates, it becomes clear "how incomparably the law transcends natural reason." The fair warning of God is "not to follow [one's] own understanding but to listen to his voice."[62] It is not, then, reason that is the object of Luther's ire but fleshly reason, that is, reason which attempts to exempt itself from flesh and thereby claims to give access to God naturally and without faith. Used this way, "there is nothing more dangerous in us than our reason and will."[63] The natural gifts of God are good, but, subjected to spiritual evil and sin, they are not only incapable of making one just and righteous but actually contribute to perdition.

The major formal difference between "grace" and "gift" is already implied. The gifts of God are owned, possessed, and used by their owner. If they are external, they are "ours" in the sense that they may be used outwardly in accord with such ownership. If they are inward possessions—for example, reason or will—they are part of the actual, worldly person. Ownership and usefulness distinguish grace and gift. Grace is not only external; it is also not possessed. Favor cannot be owned; it can only be granted and received. This is why there can be no question of our part in it or cooperation with it. It is favor and a favor; it cannot rightly be made into a demand.

Common gifts cannot make one actually just. Strictly speaking, they do not contribute to personal righteousness, for there is no such gift that cannot

---

[60] Luther, *Against Latomus*, 226 (WA 8:105); see also the fascinating distinction between God and God's masks in *Lectures on Galatians, 1535, Chapters 1–4*, 95 (WA 40[I]:174). In the earlier *Lectures on Hebrews,* Luther claims that "flesh" too has both a substantial component and an object, designating both what "a man is called and what he loves" (*Lectures on Hebrews,* 134; WA 57[III]:127). This explains why all things are things of the flesh, despite their being intrinsically good; subjected to flesh, they become objects of fleshly love.

[61] Luther, *Against Latomus,* 225, 226 (WA 8:105).

[62] Ibid., 226, 225 (WA 8:105).

[63] Luther, *Treatise on Good Works,* 74 (WA 6:245).

be abused, turned from its good nature to evil use. Luther is suspicious of religious, social, and political movements for this reason: whatever good they may accomplish in the realm of worldly justice, they cannot produce any direct spiritual improvement for their advocates or beneficiaries. In order to be made actually righteous (the second aspect of justification), a second class of gifts is required, spiritual gifts. One such gift is the Lord's Supper. The activation of the proper power of the Supper depends on its linkage to the external Word on one side and faith on the other, both of which are also gifts of God. The meaning and place of faith has up to now entered the discussion of Luther peripherally. It must now take center stage.

Faith is a precondition of actual righteousness, the process of actually being made just during our life on earth. The power of sin, definitively broken and dominated by grace, remains to be expelled from the person under grace. Luther never questions the need for the earthly contest against sin, as if the forensic justifying decision of God removed the need for the drama of life. Similarly, it never crossed Luther's mind that God would simply make the justifying decision without publicizing it in the Word. The forensic, salvific decision of God belongs to the heavenly realm, but it is intended to have effects in the earthly realm, and this is why the world and its problems occupy so much of Luther's time. The progressive eradication of sin throughout the believer's earthly life is, to be sure, never completed, for some substance of sin clings until it is removed in the resurrection. In anticipation of this final deliverance and purification, the believer gains confidence to combat the sin which remains. Because the outcome of the war is decided, the heart is encouraged to fight the remaining battles in a sort of spiritual mop-up operation. Demonstration of these assertions requires an examination of Luther's understanding of faith.

The function of God's gifts is to heal the person who is already forgiven forensically. The righteous person always has both grace and gift.[64] This must be the case, since grace and gift refer to two different realms of righteousness. Gifts of God are designed for earthly righteousness. Corruption's healing is accomplished "by the true righteousness which is the gift of God, namely, faith in Christ."[65] This is Luther's interpretation of Paul's "justified by faith." To make this actual recovery a function of the gift assumes a particular ordered association of grace and gift. This order is not a temporal one, for the righteous person stands under the grace of God and has gifts of the Spirit. But Luther posits a necessary conceptual and logical order, as well as an order of meaning:

> For [God] begins in reality to cleanse. For he first purifies by imputation, then he gives the Holy Spirit, through whom he purifies even in substance. Faith cleanses through the remission of sins, the Holy Spirit cleanses through the effect. This is the divine cleansing and purification which is let down

---

[64] Luther, *Against Latomus*, 227–29 (WA 8:106–7).
[65] Ibid., 227 (WA 8:106).

from heaven, by faith and the Holy Spirit. This is spiritual theology, which philosophers do not understand since they call righteousness a quality.[66]

"As was said, grace must be sharply distinguished from gifts, for only grace is life eternal (Rom. 6[:23]), and only wrath is eternal death." The reservation of eternal life to grace is necessary for two reasons. First, only grace is total and poured out upon the whole person. Second, this totality is possible on the twin conditions that grace is external to its recipient and the world, and that it therefore is not affected by worldly decisions and actions. Grace's transcendence of the world does not imply indifference to it. The total forgiveness of grace is publicized by the gifts of God, preeminently the Word and faith. In reference to faith, "the glory of the Spirit is that revelation, or knowledge, of grace which is faith."[67] The Word publishes the edict of grace; faith reads and understands it. Faith is, therefore, at the midpoint of the two realms, the knowledge of the passive righteousness of grace imputed from heaven;[68] it is the medium through which the two realms communicate, the pivot by which one is turned to the other. While faith is a gift of God present to believers in their earthly sojourn, its object is God's heavenly declaration of safety and salvation. The gift of faith does not produce the grace of God, but it does communicate the proclamation of grace. Thus, faith is given "*in* justification," but "Luther avoids any suggestion that man is justified *on account of* his faith."[69]

Faith's relay function between the two realms explains why it is credited with "healing from corruption" and why God's gifts, which depend on faith for their proper efficacy, heal the believer from "corruption of body and soul."[70] Confident knowledge of heavenly possession of the promise of total forgiveness, the knowledge of faith, is essential for actual purging of sin. Faith is confidence in one's inclusion in the promises of Christ; it is, therefore, "for you." Faith cannot be a general knowledge of God, which would leave one's own status in doubt.[71] The believer is defined by trust of personal inclusion in these promises. A general knowledge of God does not imply God's activity in or for us. Certainty of God's favor, on the other hand, must live and act within

---

[66] Luther, *Disputation Concerning Justification,* 168–69 (WA 39[I]:99).

[67] Luther, *Against Latomus,* 229, 177 (WA 8:197, 70).

[68] Luther, *Lectures on Galatians, 1535, Chapters 1–4,* 4–12 (WA 40[I]:40–51); see also *Judgment on Monastic Vows,* 286 (WA 8:599).

[69] Alister E. McGrath, *Iustitia Dei: A History of the Christian Doctrine of Justification* (Cambridge: Cambridge University Press, 1986) 2:14; see also Cranz, *Development of Luther's Thought,* 53. *Against Latomus,* 227 (WA 8:106), appears to indicate the contrary: "we would not highly esteem God's gift, if . . . it did not gain for us the grace of God." However, Luther is here speaking of the subjective knowledge of grace in faith, so that he continues, "This grace truly produces peace of heart until finally a man is healed from his corruption and *feels* he has a gracious God" (emphasis added). I thank Lynn Sawlivich for his help with this text.

[70] Luther, *Against Latomus,* 227, 229 (WA 8:106, 107).

[71] Luther, *Lectures on Galatians, 1535, Chapters 1–4,* 34 (WA 40[I]:86).

the believer,[72] and this is possible only if one is certain of being a participant in the promise of salvation. For example, it is "not enough or in any sense Christian to preach the works, life, and words of Christ as historical facts, as if the knowledge of these would suffice for the conduct of life," for this teaches only about Christ, but not "Christ for you and me, [so] that what is said of him and is denoted in his name may be effectual (*operetur*) in us."[73] The peace produced by the complete remission of sin in the forensic declaration of God,[74] provided it is published in the Word and appropriated in faith, is the necessary condition of actual righteousness. Only a certainty of forgiveness can save one from the twin evils of despair and self-righteousness. Moreover, with the external security of God's grace in place and certain, it is finally possible for the believer to turn attention to the inner disease of sin.

Faith is "possessed"; believers have and "own" it as part of their actual earthly being. It is a component of "proper righteousness." Faith exists, temporally, between the promise of God made in baptism and God's delivery on the promise in eternal life. Luther's language often is imprecise in its use of "grace" and "gift" because a rigorous distinction is seldom necessary. The spiritual gifts of God are always wrapped in grace and are therefore manifestations of grace. The gifts of the Spirit cannot in any way be beyond or outside of grace, for three reasons. First, logically, faith (and the proper efficacy of the sacrament, which depends on faith) is given by the Spirit only when the forensic decision to forgive and save is already made, since faith is the means by which that decree is made known. Second, christologically, faith is "the gift in the grace of one man, for it is given to us through the grace of Christ, because he alone among all men is beloved and accepted and has a kind and gentle God so that he might merit for us this gift and even this grace."[75]

Third, existentially, the gift must be consequent to, and dependent on, grace, because the peace faith appropriates and makes one's own is total grace, and faith's knowledge that the entire person is saved in spite of sin is the condition for acceptance and acknowledgment of sin without conceited self-righteousness or utter and complete despair. Because faith knows that "for grace there is no sin because the whole person pleases," it is free to recognize sin: "for the gift there is sin which it purges away and overcomes."[76] The denial that there is real sin remaining after the bestowal of grace is the foundation of attempts to make oneself righteous by self-exertion. Arrogant self-righteousness and despair have a common root, though their manifestations are polar opposites. Both are based in the belief that "God hears no one who is in sin," and therefore neither is able to begin "with faith and trust in God's

---

72 Luther, *Treatise on Good Works*, 105 (WA 6:270).
73 Luther, *Freedom of a Christian*, 357 (WA 7:58).
74 Luther, *Against Latomus*, 227 (WA 8:106).
75 Ibid., 228 (WA 8:106).
76 Ibid., 229 (WA 8:107).

favor (*hulden*), but [begin] with their own works."[77] The difference is that self-righteousness does not recognize its own disease and inability to be just on its own, while despair recognizes its own impotence all too well. With this initial misstep, the actual healing of the person by means of God, the spiritual physician, becomes impossible, for one is not placed in God's care. The refusal to accept sin as sin is to blaspheme the gift of God, to give it nothing to do, since all is assumed to be well.[78] The pomposity of self-righteousness arises from the denial that one is simultaneously and totally sinful and just. This accounts for Luther's theological location of repentance. Repentance does not precede grace and faith but follows them. As grace is prior to faith, so faith is prior to repentance.[79] Repentance "is the transformation of corruption and the continual renewal from sin which is effected by faith, the gift of God."[80] Believers' confidence of acceptance in spite of themselves makes all attempts to deny their unrighteousness unnecessary. The closet of the heart in which sin is hidden is opened by faith, that its disastrous condition might be recognized and the labor of cleaning it begin.

The antithesis of concealment of unrighteousness is recognition of the depths of sin without the security of the promise of forgiveness understood in faith. This was, in fact, the problem Luther himself faced. Recognition of guilt, combined with an inability to see any escape from it, is despair, imprisonment within one's own corruption. Despair is, for Luther, the most profound opponent of faith, for it understands the human condition without comprehending a remedy. Despair believes that God has deserted the afflicted person and has become the enemy, for the bedrock of works, upon which that person attempted to stand, confident of salvation, has proved to be quicksand. One of the great barriers to sacramental power, that the communicant feels unworthy to ask anything of the majesty of God, is a general feature of a life of despair.[81] The work of inducing despair is the "evil spirit's."[82] But to bring one to the brink of despair is also God's work, because despair is the profound opponent of faith and is therefore "near to grace,"[83] exactly because it is faith's diametrical opposite. God brings one to the precipice of despair through the law, "since the law must be fulfilled so that not a jot or tittle shall be lost," and yet the truthful consciousness knows this obedience is impossible

---

[77] Luther, *Treatise on Good Works*, 64 (WA 6:237).

[78] Luther, *Against Latomus*, 230 (WA 8:108).

[79] It also follows that grace and forgiveness are prior to repentance, which sharply opposes the order in which these events are usually placed, namely, one repents and then is forgiven. This consequence is drawn only sporadically by Luther; see, e.g., *Disputation Concerning Justification*, 176 (WA 39[I]:107). It is somewhat clearer, but not entirely so, in John Calvin, *Institutes of the Christian Religion*, vol. 2, trans. Ford Lewis Battles, ed. John T. McNeill, The Library of Christian Classics, vol. 21 (Philadelphia: Westminster Press, 1960), 3.3, pp. 592–621.

[80] Luther, *Against Latomus*, 232 (WA 8:109).

[81] Luther, *Treatise on Good Works*, 28–63 (WA 6:208–36).

[82] Ibid., 62 (WA 6:235).

[83] Luther, *Bondage of the Will*, 190 (WA 18:719).

through one's own efforts. One in despair has properly given up on the self, but improperly assumes that there is no rescue in spite of the self.[84] The cure is faith which looks to grace, relying only on the promises of God.[85] The dividing line between despair and faith is a razor's edge, for the "word of grace does not come except to those who feel their sin and are troubled and tempted to despair."[86] Faith's reliance on grace avoids despair, for grace, being utterly unrelated to our actual worth, is the sole haven in which nothing can accuse us, because the "works of Christ are more powerful (*Potentiora*) to save us and to give us peace than are our works to capture and terrify."[87] God has already accused believers and acquitted them despite their substantial and active guilt. The faithful are certain that their sins are covered by the merit of Christ; in Christ alone a believer may trust in the knowledge that God has made "you a chick, and Christ a hen."[88] Despair, on the other hand, lacks the assurance that God's promise is a mighty fortress.

The Fabric of the Two Realms

The relation between gift and grace is therefore one of dependence and complement. Spiritual gifts rely on grace, but they also do what grace in its strict forensic sense cannot, since the gift is required in order to communicate the justifying decision of grace. Indeed, the publication of grace is the *telos* of the forensic decree of salvation; the combination of decision and proclamation makes the growth of actual righteousness possible, and the change in earthly life resulting from this complementary relation is one of the purposes of God:

> What is this except to change one's life, as is done by faith in purging away sin, and to be under the rule of God, as is accomplished by forgiving grace? John calls this a worthy fruit [Matt. 3:8] if sin is purged and outward works not feigned . . . . The parable of the man half-dead cured by the Samaritan [Luke 10:30ff.] also pertains completely and first of all to this matter. This man was not healed all at once, but *was raised up all at once in order to be cured.* The Levite and the priest, ministers of the law, saw him, but did not help. So as I said, the law makes sin known, but it is Christ who *heals through faith and rescues through God's grace* [emphasis added].

Luther establishes an order of power. On the one hand, faith cannot endure unless it is faith within grace. Believers "are safe in [Christ's] grace, not because they believe or possess faith and the gift, but because it is in Christ's grace

---

[84] Ibid., 61–62 (WA 18:632–33).

[85] Luther, *Freedom of a Christian*, 348–49 (WA 7:52–53); *Lectures on Galatians, 1535, Chapters 1–4*, 5–6 (WA 40[I]:42–43).

[86] Luther, *Bondage of the Will*, 137 (WA 18:684). This point is emphasized by Paul Althaus, *The Theology of Martin Luther*, trans. Robert C. Schultz (Philadelphia: Fortress Press, 1966), 59.

[87] Luther, *Judgment on Monastic Vows*, 299 (WA 8:607); see also *Against Latomus*, 230 (WA 8:108).

[88] Luther, *Against Latomus*, 236 (WA 8:112).

that they have these things." The "power (*virtus*) of faith"[89] relies on the greater strength (*robitissimum*) and power (*virtute*) of grace.[90] Faith's efficacy is through grace's power, in the discovery that "the work of God accomplished for you in Christ is boundless, in that he has foreordained such powerful (*potentam*) grace for you in Christ." On the other hand, the very existence of gifts-power shows that the power of grace is not its own end. If it were, there would be no need for the gifts of God or the publication of grace. The forensic declaration of justification also has its purpose in the actual, worldly justification of the believer. Grace does not have its only end in eternal life, but also intends to alter actual life, to make the kingdom of God "at hand."[91] Grace is designed to allow acceptance of God's gifts to cleanse the earthly person. Salvific, forensic justification is the primary condition for the actual righteousness and justification toward which it is directed: God's will is that our sinful nature be healed and that we be sanctified from sin.[92] Thus, the time of mercy, in which the Christian lives, is one "wherein we are not only acceptable and assured of God's favor and good will toward us, but we experience even as we have been assured — that God really does help us."[93]

The *telos* of grace to sanctification, or earthly righteousness, implies that grace, properly understood, does not lead to contentment or security in the saved.[94] Listlessness of life on the assumption that one has grace and that therefore everything is secure misunderstands the nature of grace, claiming that it has no other end than itself, that is, heavenly justification. Rather, grace comprehended in faith is supposed to provide the confidence and strength of heart and spirit to begin the process of real elimination of the substance of sin in the faithful. As Heiko Oberman says, "The characteristic of Luther's doctrine of justification can therefore be designated as the reunification of the righteousness of Christ and the justice of God by which the sinner is justified 'coram deo,' which forms the stable *basis* and not the uncertain *goal* of the life of sanctification, of the true Christian life."[95] An indifferent attitude toward the actual condition of believer and world is ruled out from the beginning because faith is a part of life, and what is alive is active. Just as the living God's glory is not to sit on high in heaven, so a living faith cannot but be an active

---

[89] Ibid., 232 (emphasis added), 239, 245 (WA 8:109, 114, 118).

[90] Ibid., 239 (WA 8:114).

[91] Ibid., 240, 232 (WA 8:115, 109).

[92] Ibid., 254 (WA 8:124); see also Karl Holl, *The Reconstruction of Morality*, trans. Fred W. Meuser and Walter R. Wietzke, ed. James Luther Adams and Walter F. Bense (Minneapolis: Augsburg Publishing House, 1979), 82–87.

[93] Martin Luther, *The Epistle of the First Sunday in Lent: 2 Corinthians 6*, in *The Sermons of Martin Luther*, vol. 7, *Sermons on Epistle Texts for Epiphany, Easter, and Pentecost*, trans. John Nicholas Lenker and others, ed. John Nicholas Lenker (Minneapolis: The Luther Press, 1909; reprint, Grand Rapids, Mich: Baker Book House, 1988), 136 (page references are to reprint edition); Martin Luther, *Luthers Werke*, 17 Band (II) (Weimar: Hermann Böhlaus Nachfolger, 1927), 181.

[94] Luther, *Against Latomus*, 235 (WA 8:111).

[95] Oberman, *Dawn of the Reformation*, 124; see also Cranz, *Development of Luther's Thought*, 57.

one. Moreover, sin and flesh, which faith is supposed to oppose, are themselves living and active and can be defeated only by a moving and dynamic faith. It is "impossible" that sin be dormant, "for sin is a living thing in constant movement, changing as its objects change."[96] Nothing static exists in humanity, for human nature itself is dynamic:

> Now since the being and nature of man cannot exist for an instant unless it is doing or not doing something, putting up with or running away from something (for as we know, life never stands still), well then, let him who wants to be holy and full of good works begin to exercise himself at all times in this faith in all his life and works.[97]

It is, therefore, "through active faith that the feet, that is, the remaining sins, are cleansed."[98] Contentment in the heavenly grace of God indicates, in fact, that one has not been granted it, for such an attitude ignores its purpose, which is to be a weapon of the Spirit for the purging of sin.

The *telos* of grace to sanctification is complemented by a direction of the gifts of God to heavenly righteousness. The spiritual gifts of God are aimed at destroying "sin itself. This is done through the gift of faith, which kills and crucifies what Paul calls the old man of sin." The destruction of the corrupted old creation is simultaneously a transformation into a "new creation."

> [God] does not want us to halt in what has been received, but rather to draw near from day to day so that we may be fully transformed into Christ.
>
> His righteousness is perpetual and sure; there is no change, there is no lack, for he himself is the Lord of all. Therefore whenever Paul preached faith in Christ, he did so with the utmost care to proclaim that righteousness is not only through him or from him, but even that it is in him. He therefore draws us into himself and transforms us.[99]

God's forensic decree has determined that Christ's righteousness is ours. All spiritual gifts of God have their end in the work of conforming the earthly person to the heavenly person, the heavenly person having already been declared to be the believer's true character,[100] although this character will not actually be possessed until death.[101] The heavenly realm is alternatively

---

[96] Luther, *Against Latomus,* 253 (WA 8:124).

[97] Luther, *Treatise on Good Works,* 34 (WA 6:212).

[98] Luther, *Against Latomus,* 232 (WA 8:109).

[99] Ibid., 233, 235 (WA 8:110, 111).

[100] See, e.g., Martin Luther, *The Disputation Concerning Man,* in *Luther's Works,* vol. 34, *Career of the Reformer IV,* trans. and ed. Spitz, 140 (WA 39[I]:177).

[101] This double relation of the heavenly to the earthly explains the statement "Christian righteousness (*iustitia*) consists in two things: first, in faith, which attributes glory to God; secondly, in God's imputation. For because faith is weak, as I have said, therefore God's imputation has to be added" (*Lectures on Galatians, 1535, Chapters 1–4,* 232; WA 40[I]:368). This appears to reverse the order we have posited between God's declaratory forgiveness and faith. In fact, the difference is one of perspective. For *actual* being, faith is the first righteousness, for the declaration of grace has no direct empirical effect in this life. The imputation of righteousness and nonimputation

condition and end of the spiritual gifts of God. The work of the faithful on earth is to become their truth.

This work of conformity is a progressive one, a labor that is "day by day." This implies a substantial difference between the pairs of sin and gift, and wrath and grace. Whereas grace and wrath could not both be simultaneously bestowed upon the recipient, sin and the gift are both present to the believer. They battle with each other, fighting in such a way that "one dominates the other."[102] Of course, the status of sin is altered by the gift of God. The sin that remains is consigned to the inferior status of being a rebel, since the Spirit of faith complains against it, even if the person occasionally submits to sin. These battles will be concluded on the last day; until then the drama of earthly life is the conflict between flesh and spirit, sin and faith.[103]

The coexistence of spirit and flesh in the actual person is a consequence of their being anthropological properties. In distinction from grace, which only establishes believers' position without reference to personal worth, faith and God's gifts are actually ours when given to us, and sin and flesh are also ours by nature. The conflict between them occurs in life, since both sin and spirit are predicates of living human beings. This is why Luther can speak of degrees of faith, greater and lesser. The life of faith navigates in the narrow channel between despair and self-righteousness, the rocks that can scuttle the craft on either side never far away. A strong faith stays close to the middle of this passage, and on either side lie infinite increments of the person's strength and weakness of faith, one's confidence in the grace of God, and the progress of actual justification. The efficacy of the sacraments for strengthening faith presupposes that faith within the person has varying degrees of dominance over the flesh, that is, that the promises of God are not believed with "unshaken faith";[104] if faith were complete in the faithful, the sacraments would cease. The same presupposition is reflected in Luther's counsels to be considerate of the "weak in faith."[105] Grace is an all-or-nothing declaration, but just as it makes sense to speak of more and less in connection with common gifts, so it is sensible when treating gifts of the Spirit. Faith can be strengthened, increased, weakened, or decreased because the earthly person, unlike the

---

of sin will have a direct effect on human beings only after death, which is why Luther makes imputation the second part of justification in this passage. Still, faith's object is God's mercy, which faith is confident of receiving both in the present and in the future. Moreover, faith cannot be without a merciful decision of God having already been made. The two orders are really the same events from different perspectives; the whole is captured by the formulation that the heavenly realm is both condition and end of God's spiritual gifts.

[102] Luther, *Against Latomus,* 246 (WA 8:119).

[103] Ibid., 207–51 (WA 8:92–122).

[104] Luther, *Babylonian Captivity,* 40–41 (WA 6:515).

[105] See, e.g., Luther, *Freedom of a Christian,* 373–74 (WA 7:71); *Receiving Both Kinds in the Sacrament* (WA 10[II]:11–41); *Eight Sermons at Wittenberg* (WA 10[III]:1–64). When Luther became impatient, which was often, and especially toward theologians as opposed to average parishioners, he simply consigned his opponents to the category of "no faith" rather than "weak faith."

heavenly one, remains in the changeable and historical world. Luther does not abide a removal of the worldly person from the world, even in the case of the inner life of the believer. Our life is not heavenly life, either inwardly or outwardly. The Spirit's gifts are worldly gifts; their performance and effect occur in the worldly realm.

The power of grace and the power of gift, properly understood, are each defined by their profit to the believer, both on earth and in heaven. These are not unrelated functions. The grace that operates in the heavenly realm has an intrinsic teleology toward the earthly realm, while the power of the gift is defined by its entelechy of conformity of the earthly to the heavenly person, the new creation in Christ. The worldliness of the gifts of the Spirit substantially changes the character of power. There is certainly a moment in Luther's theology of justification that is characterized by sovereignty and domination. The heavenly, sovereign decision of God is the entire basis of justification and grounds the sovereign moment of the Spirit, which blows where it wills,[106] determining who receives faith and the proper efficacy of the sacraments. In this moment, power remains external in its origin, sovereign in its decision. But the power of grace is not power completed, nor is it the proper power of the Spirit at all. Spiritual power is defined by its effecting change in the believer's heart, and this change is gradual. It does not obliterate the earthly person but begins to transform its recipient. The powers of grace and Spirit are completed by the progressive strengthening of faith, which in its turn has its end in the labor of conforming and approximating earthly nature to heavenly declaration.

Luther understands this order of power of grace and gift as unalterable. If changed, it is destroyed. He is convinced that Rome, and many of his Protestant opponents, inverted and therefore wrecked the proper theological order, making grace dependent on sanctification, heavenly righteousness consequent to earthly righteousness. The contours of these debates will be analyzed in relation to works and the law later. Now, it is sufficient to reemphasize that the order of grace and gift is unchangeable because grace is the condition of God's spiritual gifts, and these gifts are the means by which heavenly grace can have a worldly effect. Faith "is the gift of God, which the grace of God obtains for us."[107] This order is required by the differentiation of the two realms:

> We set forth two worlds, as it were, one of them heavenly and the other earthly. Into these we place two kinds of righteousness, which are distinct and separated from each other. The righteousness of the Law is earthly and deals with earthly things; by it we perform good works. But as the earth does not bring forth fruit unless it has first been watered and made fruitful from above—for the earth cannot judge, renew, and rule the heavens, but

---

[106] Luther, *Bondage of the Will,* 18 (WA 18:602); *Disputation Concerning Justification,* 171 (WA 39[I]:103).
[107] Luther, *Against Latomus,* 236 (WA 8:112).

the heavens judge, renew, and fructify the earth. so that it may do what the Lord has commanded — so also by the righteousness of the Law we do nothing even when we do much; we do not fulfill the Law even when we fulfill it. Without any merit or work of our own, we must first be justified by Christian righteousness, which has nothing to do with the righteousness of the Law or with earthly and active righteousness. But this righteousness is heavenly and passive. We do not have it of ourselves; we receive it from heaven. We do not perform it; we accept it by faith, through which we ascend beyond all laws and works. "As, therefore, we have borne the image of the earthly Adam," as Paul says, "let us bear the image of the heavenly one" (1 Cor. 1:49), who is a new man in a new world, where there is no law, no sin, no conscience, no death, but perfect joy, righteousness, grace, peace, life, salvation, and glory.

If given heavenly righteousness, "I descend from heaven like the rain that makes the earth fertile. That is, I come forth into another kingdom."[108]

The complementary and mutually fulfilling relation between grace and gift has effects on their geography. Faith is the inner correlate of external grace, the "gift and inward good which purges the sin to which it is opposed."[109] It comes from the infusion of God's power (*infusam virtutem dei*) accompanying baptism.[110] In contrast to the imputation of heavenly righteousness, earthly righteousness is accomplished through the giving or impartation of the gifts of God. The inward location of faith is subject to misinterpretation. It does not imply faith's privatization. In fact, Luther's understanding of inwardness is so far removed from such a conception that even the basic assertion that faith is inward becomes ambiguous, as the next chapter suggests. In any case, there is no sense in which the inwardness of faith can be taken to involve unrelatedness to what is outside it. Faith's constitution depends on what is external, both vertically and horizontally.[111] Vertically, just as in the sacrament, faith originates externally and from above, through the media of Word and Spirit. This is a central point of dispute with Karlstadt's legalistic spiritualism. In addition, faith must have an external object — the form of faith as trust and confidence does not permit its object to be faith itself without becoming self-righteousness. Faith's object must be the grace of Christ; mere faith is not sufficient. In other words, faith is not a quality of the soul any more than grace is; despite faith's being truly ours, its value depends on its object, its relation with Christ: "faith is not enough, but only the faith which hides under the wings of Christ and glories in his righteousness."[112] Without an object worthy of trust, faith is worthless.[113] This means, further, that one cannot rely on a

[108] Luther, *Lectures on Galatians, 1535, Chapters 1–4*, 8, 11 (WA 40[I]:46–47, 51).

[109] Luther, *Against Latomus*, 227 (WA 8:106).

[110] Ibid., 202 (WA 8:88).

[111] See also Donald C. Ziemke, *Love for the Neighbor in Luther's Theology: The Development of His Thought, 1512–1529* (Minneapolis: Augsburg Publishing House, 1963), 61–64.

[112] Luther, *Against Latomus*, 235–36 (WA 8:111–12); see also *Against Latomus*, 239 (WA 8:114).

[113] Luther, *Lectures on Galatians, 1535, Chapters 1–4*, 88–89 (WA 40[I]:163–65).

static, "past" faith as a possession. Here, Luther is concerned with refuting an interpretation of faith as principally a possession of cognitive knowledge or "articles of faith." Faith is cleaving[114] and trust, and such reliance is always an act in the present.

Faith's dynamism is not exhausted in this vertical external relation. There are also two horizontal relations of faith. First, faith and the Spirit within are engaged in battle with flesh and sin constantly. The Spirit of faith is not compartmentalized within the person as a separate faculty any more than flesh is. Since sin's activity changes the inner and external objects it attempts to conquer, faith must fight at every turn, in order to keep sin imprisoned and daily remove and expel the substance of sin "so that it may be utterly destroyed" in the end.[115] Second, faith must be active.

The two contests of faith and the Spirit are not existentially separable. To begin with, the Spirit's work alters the relation between the person and the common gifts of God. As all good gifts of God are corrupted by the sinner under the dominance of flesh, all are properly used by faith. In other words, the person is reconstituted in such a way that use of God's common gifts now conforms to their substantial goodness. Gifts of Spirit do not create a separate compartment or "faculty" within the receiver. Luther's opposition to the segmentation of the individual according to "flesh" and "spirit" has made this clear. These principles underlie and animate any special faculties. Therefore, spiritual gifts transform the "natural" person into a "spiritual" one. Under the tutelage of the Spirit, what was once despised as "flesh," because used and dominated by flesh, is transformed into "spirit." We now labor under the "law of the Spirit" rather than the law of the flesh.[116] The components of nature or flesh are in no way eradicated, but their meaning and operation are revolutionized because the instruments of flesh are not themselves irredeemably fleshly. Through the power of the Spirit, all that was natural is made spiritual. This is why, as one example, Luther can both attack reason as the greatest evil of flesh and defend its usefulness within theology,[117] extolling it as God's greatest gift to humanity.[118] Reason is evil and fleshly if it is not employed

---

[114] Luther, *Against Latomus*, 236 (WA 8:112).

[115] Ibid., 208–9 (WA 8:93).

[116] Ibid., 207 (WA 8:91–92).

[117] While attacking his sacramental opponents for their reliance on reason as lord of faith, Luther also castigates them for poor logic, convoluted reasoning, and a destruction of the natural sense of language. Similarly, Luther's disdain for Karlstadt's attempt to determine theology through reason does not exclude his claiming that Karlstadt's illogical arguments show that he has lost all reason and understanding. In addition, Luther takes Karlstadt's linguistic analysis to task, on grounds of both scholarly linguistics and an exposition of common usage (*Against the Heavenly Prophets*, 137, 162–68 (WA 18:119, 152–58). In *Judgment on Monastic Vows*, 336 (WA 8:629), Luther maintains that reason cannot make affirmative statements about God, that is, cannot tell us what God is, but does have negative jurisdiction; that is, reason is a criterion in determining what God is not.

[118] Luther, *Disputation Concerning Man*, 137 (WA 39[I]:175).

in obedience to the Word of God, that is, if it is given authority over the content of faith.[119] But if nature can serve spirit, reason can serve faith. The instruments of learning, the arguments of logic, and all else are useful and necessary as long as they are kept in their proper place and order. Human nature is transformed by the Spirit, so that its nature, the new creation, becomes spiritual.[120] The world of the self is reconstituted in its significance for the believer.

There is a second horizontal relation of faith. Faith must be active to be faith, and this includes not only the primarily inward battle of the Spirit (or Christ in us) against the substance of sin but also an external activity.[121] Faith desires to do good in the world and cannot, therefore, be restricted to a private, self-contained inwardness. As in the sacrament, inward strengthening of faith is not its own end but contains an outward motion in works of love. The world that was despised in Luther's theology of justification regains significance for the believer who has received the gifts of the Spirit. What is given by God is not to be destroyed; only the perversion of God's gifts is to be eradicated. Indeed, the world must be reinvested with meaning and value. In the first place, the world is the only stage on which the drama of sanctification can be played. Second, the world is the realm of the common gifts of God, and these gifts are given because of God's determination to change and renew the world. Moreover, the gifts of God are good. If the world is the "kingdom of Satan," this does not imply that all things to be found in the world are part of that kingdom, but only those things which remain worldly and refuse transformation by the Spirit.[122]

Gifts, Works, Laws, and Christians

It is on the stage of the world and within his conception of gifts that Luther's theologies of works and law appear. His understandings of law and works are obviously closely related. When Luther speaks about "works," he frequently means works of the law. The difference between works in general

[119] If reason is the criterion of Scripture, rather than the other way around, reason can turn the Scriptures in any direction it pleases (*Bondage of the Will,* 120–21; WA 18:673).

[120] Even that which is not a "good gift," the devil, works toward good in believers (*Against Latomus,* 241; WA 8:116); see also *Babylonian Captivity,* 72 (WA 6:537), in which Luther cites Rom. 8:28 in support of this claim, and *Freedom of a Christian,* 354–55 (WA 7:57–58), where Luther maintains that this capacity to use all things for good is part of the omnipotence (*omnia potest*) of faith. Conversely, those who do not believe are ultimately impotent because they cannot be helped by anything.

[121] Luther, *Treatise on Good Works,* 73 (WA 6:244). A superb account of this horizontal direction of Luther's thought, and the resulting significance given to the word in the theology of the gift, is Oberman, *Luther,* 179–206. Oberman's line of argument is presented also in Walter Altmann, *Luther and Liberation: A Latin American Perspective* (Minneapolis: Fortress Press, 1992), 37–39.

[122] Luther, *Bondage of the Will,* 21, 277 (WA 18:626, 776).

and works of the law is that the latter is a narrower category than the former—
there are works that are not works of the law. Still, what Luther says about
works of the law usually applies as well to the broader category of works,
and vice versa. The exception to this equivalence is the complaint against self-
contrived works, that is, works called "good" but not commanded by God
in written or natural law. When such nonmandatory works are demanded,
Luther inveighs against them as violations of Christian freedom. The status
of these humanly invented works in comparison with those commanded by
God becomes a focal concern later. For the moment, the difference between
the wide category of "works" and "works of the law" is not important, and
they are interchangeable terms.

Luther's polemic against "legalist" theology is well known, and some of
its features were examined earlier. Anyone who fulfilled God's commands
would, by that fact alone, be justified before God, acquitted of all guilt;
however, the Fall and the introduction of original sin made fulfillment of God's
law impossible. Thus, the Fall materially changes the effect of the law. Although
in its original purpose, the law was designed as an aid for salvation, now it
is efficacious only for damnation, like all gifts of God not dominated by Spirit.
The relation between law and the heavenly realm is a purely negative one.
However good works of the law may appear before human eyes, they are incapable of justifying the doer before God, for they always contain guilt. For
a theology of power, this means that the power of the law, after the Fall, is
purely dominating. It makes demands on the earthly person, but because it
is purely external, it provides no help toward its fulfillment and becomes effective for condemnation. Luther evades the consequence of universal condemnation by shifting the externality of power from the earthly to the heavenly
realm. Jesus' earthly life perfectly fulfilled the commands of God, and now
that accomplishment is transferred to those upon whom God bestows grace.
God's commands are fulfilled, but by heavenly, forgiving mercy rather than
by earthly works.[123] The gracious judgment of God declares the character of
the believer's true person in advance of its actuality and, through both the
gospel's publication of the decree of grace and the granting of spiritual gifts,
helps the faithful to advance toward their true persons.

It is important to recognize what is not a necessary conclusion of this
critique of the law. To say that the law is worthless and counterproductive
for obtaining a favorable forensic judgment from God, that in this heavenly
arena the law functions only to demonstrate our sin, is not at all the same
as outright and total exclusion of positive possibilities for works and the law.
Just as all gifts of God, once captured by the Spirit and faith, are made weapons
of the Spirit, so it may be with works performed by means of God's gifts,
as well as with works of the law, the law being a gift of God. Just as no gift
of God is sufficient to compel or induce God to declare one's righteousness,

---

[123] Luther, *Against Latomus*, 209 (WA 8:93).

but all are useful and productive for those who are granted grace, it may be even more true that the content of the law, when employed by the Spirit, is instrumental and indispensable for the sanctification of believers and directing action in the world. To claim that no gift is sufficient for grace does not imply that any gift is inadequate for its purpose but only that if its purpose is not specified strictly, the economy of forensic and earthly justification is turned upside-down and is therefore destroyed. To say that carrying a refrigerator prevents one from swimming does not impugn the worth of refrigerators; nor are "Law, circumcision, worship, etc., . . . condemned for their inability to justify."[124] The fruitlessness of the law as a means to heavenly, forensic justification has already been examined. The law's relevance and limits in the earthly realm, the theater of sanctification, must now be shown.

The conclusion of our analysis of works and the law in Luther's theology is this: His argument with theological alternatives was never about whether work in the world was important, nor about whether the world mattered. Instead, as in the argument with the Zwinglians regarding the place of memorial in the sacrament, Luther complains that his opponents reversed the proper theological order of event and meaning. A theology of works is a crucial part of Luther's theology; what is at issue is its place in the order of things. Evidence for this pronouncement requires that certain elements of Luther's theology be set in place. This creates the deceptive but unavoidable impression of separation between these components. The crucial aspect of Luther's thought, however, is not the elements of his theology but the relation between them. Our recourse to the order of things expresses this. For the sake of clarity, however, it may help to lay some of the clothing on the dresser before discussing how it is worn.

Works belong to the righteousness of one's actual life, that is, to proper righteousness. Faith is the foundation of actual justice, and works follow from it.[125] Works are part of proper righteousness because our works are ours. We do them. Good works are, certainly, impossible without grace, but works have in common with all gifts of God that they are owned. Luther protests that Erasmus is wrong to claim Luther denies that good works can be ours. Good works are indeed our good works because gifts, once given, are owned by the recipient, and good works are accomplished by these gifts, just as what is done through our body is truly ours, even though a body is given and not self-produced.[126] The performance of good works through the owned gifts of God is what enables them to be ours.

"Ownership" is perhaps not the most fortunate term, for it tends to imply

---

[124] Luther, *Lectures on Galatians, 1535, Chapters 1–4*, 122 (WA 40[I]:217).

[125] Again, *Two Kinds of Righteousness* presents a somewhat deceptive, because incomplete, impression of Luther's theological order. In that essay, Luther moves directly from the alien righteousness of grace to works without including faith as the link connecting the two realms.

[126] Luther, *Bondage of the Will*, 156 (WA 18:696).

that the gifts of God are possessed in a static way, held and kept for private use. The introduction of works into the notion of ownership corrects that impression. Good works are "ours" and yet cannot be ours in the sense of being kept and stored because they are by definition active, with an object external to the worker. The same characteristic of being ours without being really possessed applies to all gifts of God, if conquered by the Spirit. Luther's notion of ownership means to stress only that gifts and their use are matters of earthly being, rather than remaining in the heavenly realm.

Gifts of God are, by their nature, alive and active. The characteristic of life applies not only to the more inward object of the battle with flesh but also to the external aim of faith. In both cases, gifts have a *telos*. It is true that the gifts of God are part of earthly being, and in this sense are "owned," but the very possession of them is constituted in and by their external use. Use and possession, in virtue of the liveliness of the gift, are simultaneous, and only by use can one be said to possess. The power of sacramental gift was constituted in its external fulfillment in love for the neighbor. The same is true of the other gifts of God:

> Through the figure of the members of the body Paul teaches in Rom. 12[:4–5] and 1 Cor. 12[:12–27] how the strong (*robusta*), honorable, healthy members do not glory over those that are weak, less honorable, and sick as if they were their masters (*dominentur*) and gods; but on the contrary they serve them the more, forgetting their own honor, health, and power (*potentiae*). For thus no member of the body serves itself; nor does it seek its own welfare but that of the other.

Gifts of the Spirit do not intend to be hoarded; such attempts prove those gifts have not, in fact, been given. The *telos* of spiritual gifts is not inward possession but external sharing. Power is not domination but a communication. It is directed not at exclusivity but at universality:

> In like manner [God] will treat all of us whenever we, on the ground of our righteousness, wisdom, or power (*potestate*), are haughty or angry with those who are unrighteous, foolish, or less powerful than we. For when we act thus — and this is the greatest perversion — righteousness works against righteousness, wisdom against wisdom, power against power. For you are powerful, not that you may make the weak (*impotentes*) weaker through oppression, but that you may make them powerful by raising them up and defending them. . . . But the nature of man violently rebels. . . . This perversity is wholly evil, contrary to love, which does not seek its own good, but that of another.[127]

When exclusivity is sought, righteousness is no longer righteousness, but injustice; wisdom is no longer wisdom, but foolishness; power is no longer power, but oppression. The quest to be the most just, wise, and powerful, the final aim of which must be to become the only just, wise, powerful one,

---

[127] Luther, *Two Kinds of Righteousness*, 302–3, 303–4 (WA 2:149, 150).

is not virtue, but its perversion. Virtue has an external aim. God's gifts are intrinsically teleological. If they fail to reach their end, it is the fault of human corruption. The nature of virtue apart from its use is impossible to determine, for nature involves use. Vertically, gifts are given by God to the believer; horizontally, they are given by the recipient to others. This dynamic defines the true character of gifts. Good works are defined by their benefit for the neighbor.[128] As participants in Christ's righteousness, the Christian must attend to the fact that Christ "did not count equality with God as a thing to be grasped," but to be shared in its benefits.[129] The world is an essential theater for Christians, not in the doctrine of forensic justification but still through it.

Indeed, not only a revaluation, but the attribution of any independent value to the world, must be accomplished through the heavenly declaration of righteousness and its publication in the gospel. When the importance of God's gracious forgiveness of the sinner for the purpose of the primarily inward battle of flesh and spirit was discussed, we noted that this context had an intrinsic *telos* toward the external world, that is, toward works. This already meant, as the discussion of outward love of the neighbor as a part of the power of the Supper had also, that action in works was far from being an irrelevant afterthought to Luther. It is now time to examine the relation between forensic justification and external activity more closely. As a preface, this much can be said. External action is an essential part of the battle against sin, provided that works are done from within the relation of grace. Indeed, it will become clear that *good* works can only be done from within the framework of grace. Because "we believe that the remission of all sins has been without doubt accomplished," it is possible and demanded that "we daily act in the expectation of the total removal and annihilation of all sin."[130] Good works are a thanksgiving to God and flow from a desire to please a friend, God.[131] This labor has inward significance as the battle of spirit against flesh. But action is primarily external. Of course, the inward and external fields of activity are inseparable. The progression of actual righteousness to and for sanctification is the point at which Christian adherence to the example of Christ enters the theological picture. In forensic justification, the believer's sin becomes Christ's and Christ's righteousness is given to the believer; Christ is declared ours. Conversely, however, the marriage of Christ and the faithful requires the latter to declare they are Christ's. The effect of both movements, in their proper arrangement, is to transform the believer into the image and likeness of Christ, and this further implies the imitation of Christ's love.[132] This is the external, horizontal *telos* of forensic forgiveness and the reception of the gifts of God.

---

[128] Luther, *Eight Sermons at Wittenberg*, 74 (WA 10[III]:11).
[129] Luther, *Freedom of a Christian*, 366 (WA 7:65).
[130] Luther, *Against Latomus*, 213 (WA 8:96).
[131] Luther, *Against the Heavenly Prophets*, 122 (WA 18:105); *Treatise on Good Works*, 27 (WA 6:207).
[132] Luther, *Two Kinds of Righteousness*, 300 (WA 2:147).

The necessary condition for reaching the external end of outward grace and inward gift is that the beloved of God "no longer seeks to be righteous (*iusta*) in and for itself, but it has Christ as its righteousness (*iustitiam*) and therefore seeks only the welfare of others."[133] If confidence in God's promises were complete, if faith were absolute, the believer would lack nothing and, just as important, would know there is nothing to gain for oneself from external good works. Eternal life and meaning are assured, so there can be no incentive to act toward that end. Believers are free to act for the sake of others, and only for their sake. Luther believes his reordering of grace and gift, which makes God's forgiving judgment of righteousness proleptic rather than a confirmation of what the person is (in which case there could be no salvation), establishes the possibility of truly ethical action. This is a basic reason for Luther's disgust at the peasants' program. In his view, they sought only their own advantage, proving their lack of confidence in the heavenly promises of God.

The central components of Luther's theology of works and the law are in place. It remains to be seen how they play themselves out. Two of his polemical targets are important—those Luther accused of being legalists and those against whom he made the charge of antinomianism. To omit Luther's response to one or the other of these extremes invites distortion of his thought.

Ethical Order:
Luther, Legalists, and Antinomians

Luther maintains that the legalist theology of Rome and others had the effect of creating an equality between works and God's grace. Aside from the affront to God's sovereignty produced by such theology, and distinct from the final condemnation it visits upon its adherents, Luther adds another reason to oppose this theological construction, an objection specific to its worldly implications. If one is convinced of the justifying power of works in general, including works of the law, earthly ethics are utterly shattered. The ethical act becomes a functional impossibility. The reason is simple. A truly good work has external objects—vertically, praise of and thanks to God; horizontally, the neighbor. But a theological claim that good works have something to do with one's own eternal fate acts as a mirror upon the light of good works, reflecting their benefit back upon the person who acts. Even the world's best people love themselves more than their neighbor,[134] and any works performed with the end of personal salvation in mind are in fact works of self-love, a charity that begins and ends at home. That is to say, they are not good works any longer, because their purpose is self-enhancement rather than praise of God and love of neighbor.

---

133 Ibid., 300 (WA 2:147).
134 Luther, *Lectures on Hebrews*, 118–19 (WA 57[III]:108–9).

A good work cannot be performed with an inner motive of self-profit.[135] To add any personal salvific efficacy to the theology of good works vitiates by addition:

> If works are sought after as a means to righteousness, are burdened with this perverse leviathan, and are done under the false impression that through them one is justified, they are made necessary and freedom and faith are destroyed; and this addition to them makes them no longer good but truly damnable works. They are not free, and they blaspheme the grace of God since to justify and to save by faith belongs to the grace of God alone.[136]

Luther goes so far as to say that the good work requires one to forget its salvific implications altogether, desiring the good even if there were no hell or salvation:

> a kingdom awaits the godly, even though they themselves neither seek it nor think of it. . . . What is more, if they did good works for the sake of obtaining the Kingdom, they would never obtain it, but would rather belong among the ungodly who with an evil and mercenary eye "seek their own" even in God. But the children of God do good with a will that is disinterested, not seeking any reward, but only the glory and will of God, and being ready to do good even if—an impossible supposition—there were neither a kingdom nor a hell.[137]

What may conform to the outer content of right action no longer conforms to the inner attitude necessary to make works good. Luther's basic intuition is this: no one is good enough to erase benefit to themselves from consciousness. Only if, objectively and because of the grace of God, all self-benefit of good works has already been removed, can works be made truly good, for the aid of the neighbor and praise of God. No human doctrine, no doctrine other than the doctrine of the Christ, can remove love of self as a basis for action,[138] and "morality . . . no less than religion, requires emancipation from the self-centeredness that confuses a good deed with a merit."[139]

Two additional points are worth mention in connection with the impossibility of ethics in a doctrine of good works that does not cede the grace of God absolute sovereignty in the matter of eternal life. First, Luther does not deny that self-motivated works may have beneficial external effects. This is

---

[135] Luther, *Freedom of a Christian*, 370 (WA 7:68).

[136] Ibid., 363 (WA 7:63). Peter's error, in his dispute with Paul, was exactly this: to seek to justify by Law and Gospel rather than simply by Gospel (*Lectures on Galatians, 1535, Chapters 1–4*, 116–17; WA 40[I]:208–9).

[137] Luther, *Bondage of the Will*, 152–53 (WA 18:694). John Calvin, *Institutes of the Christian Religion*, vol. 1, trans. Ford Lewis Battles, ed. John T. McNeill, The Library of Christian Classics, vol. 20 (Philadelphia: Westminster Press, 1960), 3.2.26, p. 572, takes the same position.

[138] Luther, *Lectures on Hebrews*, 118–19 (WA 57[III]:108–9).

[139] B. A. Gerrish, *The Old Protestantism and the New: Essays on the Reformation Heritage* (Chicago: University of Chicago Press, 1982), 89.

why, for example, there is no necessity that Christians control earthly governments. But external desirability of the work does not change the evaluation of the worker. At best, it is evidence of "good behavior, while man remains as he has been of old."[140] God may turn evil to good externally, but it is still evil inwardly. Second, the basic problem Luther confronts here is not a matter of the self's place in the heavenly realm but of the neighbor's place in the earthly realm. A key issue is that the personhood of the neighbor is denied by a legalist doctrine of good works. Without confidence in the salvific accomplishment of God, the basis of works is self-doubt and one's own anxiety; action is performed in labor and sorrow, with the needs of the actor the uppermost consideration.[141] The other becomes nothing more than a means to my end, a convenient stepping-stone. Even though such works may help others, they are not for them. The reflecting mirror of the self prevents recognition of the humanity and needs of the neighbor, which have a claim independent of the self. Whether or not works have an egoistic basis is resolved theologically in this question: Does the worker attempt to become a Christian by their means?[142] If the answer is affirmative, what is done is for the sake of the doer, not the other. The issue is not about the elements of Christian life, whether works can be dispensed with, but involves the order of Christian existence. Any effort to become a Christian by good works is a contradiction in terms, for the adjective "good" is removed in the very attempt. Rather, "they must first be justified (*rechtfertig*) who would preach, proclaim, and practice the outward remembrance of Christ."[143] The Christian acts; acts do not make the person Christian.

Luther's conclusion about the proper order of the declaration of righteousness and works is not logically necessary. In fact, agreement with Luther about the valuelessness of works with respect to the forgiving decision of God promptly creates a fork in the road. If Christian freedom is freedom from law and works, this implies either that works are thereby rendered utterly purposeless or that they lack positive significance only so far as the declaration of righteousness by God is concerned. The first alternative is the antinomian interpretation of works and law. Luther's opposition to it is vehement. Lazy indifference to the world is not the proper implication to be drawn from Christian freedom, but a monstrous perversion of it.[144] In essence, the claim of

---

140 Luther, *Lectures on Hebrews*, 118 (WA 57[III]:109).

141 Luther, *Treatise on Good Works*, 27–28 (WA 6:207–8).

142 Luther, *Against the Heavenly Prophets*, 81 (WA 18:64).

143 Ibid., 208 (WA 18:198).

144 See, e.g., *Treatise on Good Works*, 76 (WA 6:247). It is not possible to maintain that Luther was in any sense a "Quietist," as asserted by Ernst Troeltsch, *The Social Teaching of the Christian Churches*, vol. 2, trans. Olive Wyon (London: George Allen & Unwin; New York: Macmillan, 1931; reprint, Chicago: University of Chicago Press, 1981), 497 (page references are to reprint edition). This may be true of parts of the Lutheran tradition, but it is not so with Luther, for

Protestant antinomianism was this: works in the world, and therefore the world itself, are unimportant because the declaration of God, and its publication in the Word, assures the heavenly destiny of the forgiven, and this is the only thing of value. Luther's disgust for this conclusion implies a quite different attitude toward the worldly realm and Christian activity in it.

Luther's own reordering of works and forensic justification is an instance of interrelation and difference between grace and gift. The futility of works as means to receive grace in no way implies their fruitlessness with reference to the earthly realm, the arena in which the gifts of God are deployed. That the gifts of God concern the world and actual earthly persons suggests that, far from being a disposable appendix to the divine economy, the world and activity with it are significant, not in order to bring salvation but for themselves.[145] Neighbor, sanctification, worldly activity, all are prevented from becoming merely means to an end. To be sure, sanctification is a work of conforming the earthly to the heavenly person, but it can no longer be directed toward gaining an advantage for one in heaven. Rather, the forensic declaration of God frees sinners for the work of actual righteousness for the sake of the neighbor and the glory of God. Anyone in whom "only God Himself dwells"

> reaches such a pitch of peace and poise that he is no longer upset whether things go well or ill with him, whether he dies or lives, whether he is honored or dishonored. . . . This is what it means to observe the day of rest and keep it holy. It is then that a man ceases to rule his own life, then that he desires nothing for himself, then that nothing disturbs him: God himself leads him. It is then that there is nothing but godly happiness, joy, and peace, and all other works and virtues as well.[146]

"And all other virtues and works as well." Sanctification is valuable insofar as it makes the neighbor and the world ends in themselves; eternal life for oneself is no longer an end at all—what is good is good for earth, "not on account of a halo in heaven."[147] Because the heavenly fate of Christians is

---

heavenly justification was not the only end of the doctrine of justification. Justification by grace invests the world with a new significance.

[145] It belongs to Max Weber (*The Protestant Ethic and the Spirit of Capitalism,* trans. Talcott Parsons [New York: Charles Scribner's Sons, 1958) to have noticed the overriding importance of this basic Protestant understanding of the world for the later development of Western society. It is not the case, certainly, that Luther's reinvestment of the world was itself desacralized, for the world constantly had to be referred to creation and providence. For Luther, all reality was sacralized, as his expansion of the Sabbath to every day and place of life shows (*Treatise on Good Works,* 71–80; WA 6:243–50). But Luther's stress on totality (nothing is profane for the Christian) is double-edged, for if the theological meaning of the world is broken at one point, it is more susceptible to being broken at all points simultaneously. This is, according to Weber, exactly what happened in Western society, albeit quite against the Reformers' intentions. Cranz is interesting on the issue also (*Development of Luther's Thought,* 177).

[146] Luther, *Treatise on Good Works,* 77, 77–78 (WA 6:248).

[147] Luther, *Judgment on Monastic Vows,* 264 (WA 8:585).

assured, and because faith, through the proclamation of the gospel, is aware of that assurance and keeps it in constant view, the Christian is free to act for the neighbor alone. In opposition to "self-imposed" works, the commands of God drive us to the need of the neighbor rather than to our own profit.[148] A true Christian acts without thought of personal gain, seeking "neither benefit nor salvation since he already abounds in all things and is saved through the grace of God because in his faith he now seeks only to please God."[149] The proper end of works, service to neighbor and God, and them alone, can now be reached. The vertical relation between God and the one declared righteous, known through faith, conditions the new horizontal relation between believer and neighbor: "We conclude, therefore, that a Christian lives not in himself, but in Christ and his neighbor. Otherwise he is not a Christian. He lives in Christ through faith, in his neighbor through love. By faith he is caught up beyond himself into God. By love he descends beneath himself into his neighbor."[150] Underneath this argument, one cannot help but recognize Luke 9:24–25: "For whoever would save his life will lose it; and whoever loses his life for my sake, he will save it. For what does it profit a man if he gains the whole world and loses or forfeits himself?" It is possible to contemplate only the advantage of the neighbor because Christ considered only our advantage and benefit, and "Surely we are named after Christ, not because he is absent from us, but because he dwells in us, that is, because we believe in him and are Christs to one another."[151] Divine power, and therefore also human power, aims to make others powerful.

The teleological character of power, its inability to be purely inward and remain undistorted, locates the difference between Luther and the antinomians. To draw antinomian implications from Luther's doctrine of Christian freedom proves that the self is still the primary concern. The antinomian lives in self and for self, proving indubitably that the grace and Spirit of God, whose purpose is communication of benefit to the other, are absent. Although the actions of those who expect eternal reward for their works and the libertines are opposite, they are equally condemned, because "neither party acts toward the other according to the love that edifies."[152] Luther's two principles—"A Christian is a perfectly free lord of all, subject to none. A Christian is a perfectly dutiful servant of all, subject to all"[153]— can be translated as "freedom from

---

[148] Luther, *Treatise on Good Works,* 71 (WA 6:242).

[149] Luther, *Freedom of a Christian,* 361–62 (WA 7:62).

[150] Ibid., 371 (WA 7:69). "Descent" is metaphorical. Usually the neighbor is discussed as equal; see, e.g., *Ten Sermons on the Catechism,* 152 (WA 30[I]:74): "The following commandments [5–10] refer to our neighbor, who is our equal (*der uns gleich ist*). The first four refer to those who are over us."

[151] Luther, *Freedom of a Christian,* 368 (WA 7:66).

[152] Ibid., 372 (WA 7:70).

[153] Ibid., 344 (WA 7:49).

the world for the world,"[154] or, conversely, "Whoever loses the world finds it." Christian freedom is freedom from the world, the law, and works, to be certain; but it is freedom from the world in order that the world be served. The world, despised in Luther's conception of grace, takes on considerable — and relatively independent — value in his theology of God's gifts, and the conviction that God intends the preservation and betterment of the world. But this reinvestment of world, works, and law is possible only through the initial triumph over the world in the doctrine of grace and forensic justification. The world matters, both before and after God's decree of salvation — Luther cannot abide the antinomian solution. This is why Luther emphasizes that works are necessary, not as a cause of salvation but as an accompaniment to or evidence of it.[155] But because the decision of eternal life has been taken entirely from human hands, the world now matters rightly, that is, for its own sake and not as a means to a selfish end.

There is, therefore, a specific order to earthly life. First, the law of God must be preached and heard, so that, beyond the merely external interpretation of law in natural reason, sin might be truly recognized in both its external and inward character. Second, "when now sin is recognized and the law is so preached that the conscience is alarmed and humbled before God's wrath, we are then to preach the comforting word of the gospel and the forgiveness of sins, so that the conscience again may be comforted and established in the grace of God." We have called this preaching of the gospel the publication of God's decree of forgiveness. Third, and not before, "is judgment, the putting to death of the old" person, which involves works and such self-discipline as may be necessary. Closely related to the third, distinguished from it conceptually but not actually, is that "such works of love toward the neighbor should flow forth in meekness, patience, kindness, teaching, aid, and counsel, spiritually and bodily, free and for nothing, as Christ has dealt with us." Finally, the law must again be proclaimed,

> not for the Christians, but for the crude and unbelieving. For among Christians we must use the law spiritually, as is said above, to reveal sin. But among the crude masses, for Mr. Everyman (*fur er Omnes*), we must use it bodily and roughly, so that they may know what works of the law they are to do and what works ought to be left undone. Thus they are compelled by sword and law to be outwardly pious, much in the manner in which we control wild animals with chains and pens, so that external peace will exist among the people. To this end worldly authority (*welltliche öberkeyt*) is ordained, which God would have us honor and fear, Rom. 13, 1 Pet. 3 [1 Pet. 2:13, 17].[156]

---

[154] For the second formula's applicability to Luther, I thank David Tracy.

[155] Luther, *Disputation Concerning Justification,* 165 (WA 39[I]:96). Luther's distinction is between "cause" and "necessity." While outward works, contrition, and so on are necessary for salvation, they are not the cause of it.

[156] Luther, *Against the Heavenly Prophets,* 82, 83, 83, 83 (translation of last quotation modified; WA 18:65, 65, 65–66, 66).

This order is not a matter of whim. Any modification of it is disastrous. On one hand, the antinomian problem arises because "they reverse the order of things and teach the law after they teach the gospel, and wrath after grace." The effect is twofold. First, grace is cheapened because nothing is overcome by it. The conquest of sin by grace is ignored. Second, preaching the law loses purpose; reliance on God's grace through Christ is helpful only for those who understand their actual sinful condition. Only they can rely constantly upon grace. The central mistake of the antinomians is their assumption that grace and gift are identical, that is, that God's declaration of one's righteousness corresponds to actual righteousness and that, therefore, "all who are listening to the message are pure Christians, without sin—though in reality they are dejected and downcast hearts who feel their sin and fear God and who therefore must be comforted."[157] The antinomians have never been brought to the edge of despair. The antinomian reversal is no more or less serious than the legalist. If libertinism effectively removes the law altogether, identifying grace and gift at the beginning, legalism misplaces the third and fourth parts of the Christian life (the mortification of the old person and works for the neighbor) into first place. Thus, saving grace is subsequent to the new creation accomplished in sanctification. Sanctification and good works are rendered effectively impossible, since the reflection of the self is always placed in front of the neighbor. Luther admonishes:

> So, my brother, cling firmly to the order of God. According to it the putting to death of the old man, wherein we follow the example of Christ, as Peter says, does not come first, as the devil urges, but comes last. No one can mortify the flesh, bear the cross, and follow the example of Christ before he is a Christian and has Christ through faith in his heart as an eternal treasure.

The right order of the life of actual justification is, "At the beginning and first of all is faith in the heart, the righteousness of the spirit, then follows the mortification and death of the old nature (Rom. 8[:13]), 'For if by the Spirit you put to death the deeds of the body you will live.' By the Spirit, he says, which thus must be there." "Whoever," Luther says firmly, "does not teach according to this order certainly does not teach correctly." Karlstadt and legalism, by placing works first, teach but a "new monkery."[158]

Luther's major objection to the theological order of the legalists is that it employs the law improperly, making obedience to it at least partially effective for justification in the heavenly realm. No work of the law, much less any other work, can do this. Rather, Christians hear the law proclaimed and know, if law is understood as having both an external and inward referent, that obedience to it is impossible. The law, being purely external, does not

---

[157] Luther, *Against the Antinomians*, 114, 111 (WA 50:474, 471–72).

[158] Luther, *Against the Heavenly Prophets*, 149, 222, 83, 81 (WA 18:139, 212, 66, 64). See also Bornkamm, *Luther in Mid-Career*, 169–74.

give one the ability to fulfill its commands. It merely enjoins. The law cannot save, and therefore if salvation is possible, it must come through the divine decree of forgiveness.

The humbling effect of the law, driving the hearer toward a recognition of sin and reliance on the grace of God, involves the vertical relation of the person to the heavenly realm. The question that is answered negatively is whether the law can be effective for salvation. What is undetermined is if the law is of any use for earthly life, in horizontal, worldly relations — externally, in relations between people, or internally, in the conquest of flesh by Spirit. In our discussion of the proper ordering of life, it was clear that the law and God's commands given in the law had a significant role in controlling the external behavior of non-Christians. If the law cannot produce righteousness, it can at least recognize external evil and provide the blueprint for controlling it.

Moreover, Luther argued that the law should not be necessary for Christians. If inner faith is complete, it produces love, which teaches all the law does and more. This was Luther's interpretation of the first table of the Ten Commandments, and the first commandment above all. Faith is the inner motive of all truly good works.[159] If the Christian is truly one in whom "God alone dwells," that is, if the Christian is sanctified and actually just, there could be no need for the proclamation of the law, for everything the law could require would be done automatically by the Christian, out of faith expressed in love. This is the ground upon which Luther can say that the Christian is free from all law. To leave Luther's understanding of the law here, at the point of utter freedom from it after justification, conforms to a popular interpretation of him.[160] The validity of such an understanding, however, rests on one or both of two assumptions. The first is that "justification" has a univocal meaning that does not change at all depending on whether one speaks of the heavenly

---

[159] Luther, *Treatise on Good Works*, 39 (WA 6:217).

[160] The persistence of this absolute dualism between law and gospel is shown by the interpretation of William H. Lazareth, "Love and Law in Christian Life," in *Piety, Politics, and Ethics: Reformation Studies in Honor of George Wolfgang Forell*, ed. Carter Lindberg, Sixteenth Century Essays and Studies 3 (Kirksville, Mo.: The Sixteenth Century Journal Publishers, 1984), 103–17. Lazareth seems driven by the need to perish the thought that Luther and Calvin might have something in common. Most stunning is Lazareth's unwillingness to note the very dependence of the range of Christian freedom on the law, and his failure to recognize that the content of love in Luther is determined largely through reflection on the commands and law of God.

Steinmetz (*Luther in Context*, 120–25) makes an error similar to Lazareth's, accusing Luther of a Pollyannish streak in asserting that the Christian needs no law. Steinmetz is thankful Calvin made clear that even the saint needs direction. But the charge against Luther depends on the assumption that faith and the Christian with faith are the same, that is, that no battle of flesh and spirit occurs within the Christian who is justified by grace and has been given the gift of faith. It is clear that Luther did not think this. The best answer to both Lazareth's and Steinmetz's position in the literature, apart from Luther himself, is in Cranz, *Development of Luther's Thought*, 97–111.

or earthly realm. The second presupposition is that Luther's opposition to the law as a means of attaining of eternal life is equivalent to denigrating law and God's commands for all purposes. These, in their turn, can depend on or lead to a third contention, namely, that possession of faith and Spirit are not subject to degrees of greater and lesser, but rather that any faith is complete faith.

None of these assumptions is correct. The difference in the meaning of justification in the earthly and heavenly realms was examined earlier. In itself, this distinction gives good reasons for questioning the supposition that God's commands are utterly unimportant for Christian life. There are other reasons for suspecting that a complete elimination of the significance of the law is an overly simple understanding of Luther. To begin with, the law is a gift of God, "the best of all things in the world."[161] The law is among the benefits offered to us in the gospel.[162] It is reasonable to expect, therefore, that Luther's understanding of the law will conform to his treatment of the other gifts of God. This is especially true since the commands of God are placed in the category of natural gift. This is what allows Luther to employ the notion of "natural law," whose consummation is love. God's gifts are effective only for condemnation as long as they are under the domination of the flesh. On the other hand, in the faithful, the Spirit progressively drives out the substance of sin and reconstitutes the gifts of God, making them spiritual rather than fleshly. The gifts of God are turned from tools of the flesh to weapons of the Spirit, made spiritual under the sovereign rule of the Spirit. If one denies that the same reinvestment is possible in relation to God's commands, the law is made an utterly unique gift of God. Indeed, it becomes so different from the rest of God's gifts, it is hard to understand how the law can still be termed a "gift" at all.

In the second place, to deny the law any value for the Christian makes many, perhaps even most, of Luther's writings incomprehensible. It is difficult to read any twenty consecutive pages of Luther without being confronted with a position something like, "A Christian must do this because God commands it," or "One who claims to be a Christian must do this because this is the law of God." It is impossible to account for Luther's use of such arguments, much less his incessant use of them, if one claims he thinks the law is without any value for Christians, even in the earthly realm. One does not become a Christian by works of the law, but a Christian nonetheless performs works of the law. And if, by definition, a Christian has sufficient faith to perform good works of the law by means of faith alone, it is impossible to explain why Luther so persistently keeps the law before Christians.

---

[161] Luther, *Lectures on Galatians, 1535, Chapters 1–4*, 5 (WA 40[I]:42).
[162] Luther, *Judgment on Monastic Vows*, 256 (WA 8:580).

Law and Life

Until now, the point of concentration in Luther's theology of the law has been the necessity of the proper inward motivation for good works. The reason the law is ineffective for salvation is because the possibility of obedience to it, the gift of the Spirit, is not given in and with the law itself. The law, in short, is purely external, written upon "stone tables" which "preserve only written letters but achieve nothing";[163] law is "designated 'letter' because it does not give that which it signifies. . . . The law may well be called spiritual in so far as it *characterizes* the Spirit. But it must be satisfied to characterize; it cannot give the Spirit."[164] Thus, it becomes a "heavy burden" because it is capable only of sanctifying one externally. Merely external obedience comes from fear of external punishment for violation of the law, not from intrinsic respect for its prescriptions.[165] The requirement of inward regard for and obedience to the law is ignored, and this becomes the target of Luther's polemic.

But if inner obedience cannot be produced by the law, it is still indicated and commanded by it. Faith is the fundamental demand of the first commandment.[166] In Luther's thought, there is no simple opposition between faith and law, as if one excludes the other. The nature and content of faith are discovered in the law. The law does characterize the Spirit. Faith is necessary; it is part of actual justification, exactly because it is commanded by God. And if the law is indispensable insofar as through it the demand of faith is given, there is no reason to assume the remainder of the law does not assume a similar function. Luther asserts that obedience to the first table of the Ten Commandments, which refers to one's inward relation to God, automatically fulfills the second table also, which refers to action toward the neighbor. Conversely, sin obscures the first table; natural reason cannot recognize the inward character of sin. This is why the law must be proclaimed, so that sin can be recognized beyond the pale of the capacities of natural reason. It is important to notice that the ability of natural reason to understand sin is not coextensive with Luther's understanding of natural law.[167] We shall see shortly that the entirety of the Ten Commandments, including their first table, is but a concise expression of natural law. The law conforms to the order of the world because it

---

[163] Martin Luther, *Lectures on Deuteronomy*, in *Luther's Works*, vol. 9, *Lectures on Deuteronomy*, trans. Richard R. Caemmerer, ed. Jaroslav Pelikan (St. Louis: Concordia Publishing House, 1960), 108 (WA 14 Band [Weimar: Hermann Böhlaus Nachfolger, 1895], 637).

[164] Regin Prenter, *Spiritus Creator*, trans. John M. Jensen (Philadelphia: Muhlenberg Press, 1953), 58.

[165] Luther, *Lectures on Hebrews*, 206, 122–23 (WA 57[III]:205, 113).

[166] Luther, *Treatise on Good Works*, 23–39, 60 (WA 6:204–16, 233–34).

[167] The identification of the two causes some confusion in the discussion by Holl (*Reconstruction of Morality*, 98–107).

is but the expression of the order of creation. But natural reason does not comprehend natural law, and if reason is fallible in its failure to recognize an inward component of sin, can it not also mistake what does and does not constitute the external goodness and evil of works perpetrated on the neighbor? The second table of the law may aid one in recognizing the content of external sin, in the same way that the first table revealed the inward aspect of sin.

None of this shows that the external law has continuing relevance for Christians. Non-Christians must be restrained by the law, but it is not yet clear whether Christians can be guided by it. The love given through the Spirit in faith[168] should make the externally posited law unnecessary for the Christian, for "if every man had faith we would need no more laws. Everyone would of himself do good works all the time, as his faith shows him."[169] Obedience to the first commandment is, it was noted earlier, sufficient guarantee of obedience to the remaining commands.

Flesh of the Faithful

The actual situation is not so simple, for there is a battle between Spirit and flesh in the Christian. There are, therefore, in principle four kinds of people: first, the Christian for whom no law is needed; second, the antinomian who takes liberty as an excuse for license; third, the wicked, "who are always ready to sin"; and finally, the weak in faith. Law is unnecessary for the first group, and for them alone. Moreover, it is only for the third group, the wicked, that law is exclusively a matter of restraint. Libertines are an ambiguous case. Later in his career, especially if one taught antinomianism, such a person showed clearly that they were entirely without God's Spirit; that is, advocates of utter license were subsumed in the category of the wicked. Earlier, however, Luther maintained that, unlike the thoroughly wicked, who "must be restrained like wild horses and dogs by spiritual and temporal (*weltlich*) laws," those who use liberty as an occasion for a fleshly life "must be urged by laws and safeguarded by teaching and warning." The significance of this claim should not be overlooked. At just this point, the "safeguarding" of Christians, a simple opposition between unbelievers in need of external restraint of the law, and Christians without any need for the external law because of the victory of faith, breaks down. A third category of relation to and usefulness of the law is introduced — the Christian who is to be protected and urged on by the law. The continuing membership of libertinism within this third relation to the law is in doubt in Luther's later theology. But the existence of such a relation is not. The final group of people, those weak in faith, those "lusty and childish

---

[168] Luther, *Babylonian Captivity*, 40 (WA 6:515) reads "charitas, per spiritum sanctum in fide Christi donata."

[169] Luther, *Treatise on Good Works*, 34–35 (WA 6:213).

in their understanding of such faith and the spiritual life"[170] always have such a connection to the law.

Two things must be kept in mind before we proceed further. First, the contest between spirit and flesh in the believer occurs within the worldly realm and concerns the empirical being of the person. Second, there is a difference between faith and the person who has faith as a gift of God. The contest within the person is between flesh and spirit, both of which traverse, at various times, the whole person. Spirit battles flesh at every turn in its attempt to reduce and drive out the substance of sin. When, therefore, Luther maintains that faith requires no law, this does not mean—in fact it cannot mean—that the person who has faith needs no guidance of the law. This would imply that the movement of sanctification, the progressive and daily battle against sin, is already completed, that one is not only faithful, but *nothing but* faithful, with no admixture of flesh.[171] But this "shall be only at the last day, the day of the resurrection of the dead. As long as we live in the flesh we only begin to make some progress in that which shall be perfected in the future life."[172] Faith and the person who has faith are not subject to the same theological description. The same distinction is valid in Luther's discussions of the relation of faith and works. In his *Treatise on Good Works,* Luther cautions:

> since we have undertaken in this discourse to teach what good works rightly are, and are now speaking of the highest work [faith], it is clear that we do not speak of the second, third, or fourth class of men [the libertine, wicked, or weak in faith] but of the first [the righteous who need no law], like whom all the others should become.[173]

Utter freedom from the law is implied for those who "do freely what they know and can, because they are distinguished for their firm confidence that God's pleasure and favor rests upon them in all things."[174] But this applies to no one else. Only those who not only have faith but really are faith need pay no heed to the law, for their faith is sufficient to do what the law requires anyway.

In principle, there are four kinds of people, with three possible relations to the external law. In fact, however, there are only three kinds of people—the

---

[170] All quotations in this paragraph are to be found in *Treatise on Good Works,* 35 (WA 6:213, 214).

[171] The persistence of flesh in the justified is largely ignored in the otherwise excellent work of Gerhard Ebeling (*Luther: An Introduction to his Thought,* trans. R. A. Wilson [Philadelphia: Fortress Press, 1970], 159–74), and therefore the distinction between faith and the faithful person does not appear clearly. Ebeling occasionally makes it appear as if the person with faith is utterly pure. This is not Ebeling's intention, but it indicates the result of not keeping the distinction in mind between the essence of faith and the existential presence of faith in opposition to flesh.

[172] Luther, *Freedom of a Christian,* 358 (WA 7:59).

[173] Luther, *Treatise on Good Works,* 36 (WA 6:214).

[174] Ibid., 35 (translation modified; WA 6:213 reads "thunn freiwillig, was sie wissen und mugen, allein angesehen in fester zuvorsicht, das gottis gefallen und huld uber sie schwebt in allen dingen").

one who is perfectly faithful does not exist. Not only can one "never do all the good works he is commanded to do externally," but there is no one, "not a man living who does not have a full share in breaking the first and greatest commandment, i.e., the commandment to believe."[175] Inwardly, "we do not really want to be righteous; we only pretend because we are afraid of being punished and disgraced, or because we seek our own ends and pleasure in these works."[176] The difference between faith and the faithful person is clear. Faith is a sufficient guarantee of the propriety of one's external works only if one is perfectly faithful, if resurrection day is already come, if one possesses the heavenly righteousness which is only promised. Indeed, those who maintain that they are members of the first possible group of people, those for whom faith and Spirit have utterly expelled flesh from them, are not Christians at all:

> these [antinomian] spirits themselves are not such [pure] Christians, for they are so secure and confident. Neither are their listeners, who are also secure and happy. . . . If the Magnificat speaks the truth, then God must be the foe of the secure spirits who are unafraid, as such spirits who do away with law and sin are sure to be.[177]

Faith may be able to consider the law superfluous; one who is faithful cannot.

Because the Christian is, in varying degree and at various times, dominated by faith or flesh, Luther must maintain two things: (1) that faith has no need of law; and (2) that the law has enduring significance in the earthly realm, and for Christians within that realm.[178] The Ten Commandments, for example, are the best possible "mirror in which to see your own need"; in them, "you will find what you lack and what you should seek," for there is "no one who has not sinned." The law's necessity for pointing to what is required of us inwardly in view of the ignorance of natural reason is complemented by its necessity for pointing to what is required of us externally. Since these external virtues, too, have been "lost among Christians," it is necessary for the believer to keep the commands of God "constantly before the eyes of his heart as an exercise whereby he may curb his spirit."[179] The perfect Christian, after the Christ, exists but in principle. The rest, which is to say everyone, are caught up in the struggle of flesh and spirit within, and "in a Christian the Law must

---

[175] Luther, *Treatise on Good Works*, 113, 60 (WA 6:276, 234).

[176] Martin Luther, *A Sermon on the Three Kinds of Good Life for the Instruction of Consciences*, in *Luther's Works*, vol. 44, *The Christian in Society I*, trans. and ed. Atkinson, 241 (WA 7:800).

[177] Luther, *Against the Antinomians*, 111 (WA 50:471–72).

[178] The opening argument in *Lectures on Galatians, 1535, Chapters 1–4*, 7–9 (WA 40[I]:45–48), is especially clear on this.

[179] Luther, *Treatise on Good Works*, 63, 102–3 (WA 6:236, 266–67). The latter quotation is drawn from Luther's reflections on the fifth commandment, but the principle applies to all the commands of the second table, as Paul Althaus points out (*The Ethics of Martin Luther*, trans. Robert C. Schultz [Philadelphia: Fortress Press, 1972], 30–32).

not exceed its limits but should have dominion only over the flesh, which is subjected to it and remains under it. When this is the case, the Law remains within its limits."[180]

The question, then, is not whether God's law and commands are binding upon the Christian, nor whether the actually faithful Christian can dispense with the law as a guide, but rather, as in the case of all gifts of God, whether the commands of God are to be a weapon of Spirit or an instrument of flesh. The argument is not about the law's validity or its commands but about its place in the divine order. The choice is not law or no law, but relates to the place of the law. God's commands make no contribution toward heavenly righteousness, but they are indispensable in the earthly realm, the arena of sanctification and action. So important are they that "we should indeed give up our property and honor, our life and limb, so that God's commandments remain."[181] We have already seen why this is so. The commands of God accord with the proper order of the world. Luther's secondary justification of commands to obedience was a worldly one, for nothing "is more necessary in the world than the Law and its works."[182] Violation of God's commands creates worldly disaster, and it is the Christian's job to prevent the degeneration of the world. The Christian lives under the "law of the Spirit."

If the law could be considered a disposable accessory for the Christian, of no enduring significance for the believer's actual being or life in the world, Luther's polemics against the "spiritualists" and the antinomians would be incomprehensible. Despite the variant ethics they advocate, both make the same fundamental error: they assume that the law has no meaning for them because faith and Spirit possess them. Both eradicate the significance of divine commands on the ground that they are among the first group of Christians, in whom "God alone dwells," a group with no current members. Both overturn the law of God because they possess the Spirit, and neither recognizes the difference between pure faith and the actual person who has faith.

Law of Freedom, Telos of Grace

The antinomian problem has been examined, but it is worth returning here to Luther's argument with Karlstadt. If Luther simply abrogates the law once the inward gifts of the Spirit are received, then his battle with Karlstadt and the spiritualists, as with the antinomians, can only be a battle against himself, the self-criticism of one very confused about what he said. But it is not, and the significance of the law becomes clear in his skirmish with Karlstadt. Luther's objection to Karlstadt's spiritualism, we have seen, was that Karlstadt's claim to "have the Spirit" overturned the law of God. In distinction from any

---

180 Luther, *Lectures on Galatians, 1535, Chapters 1–4*, 11 (WA 40[I]:50).
181 Luther, *Treatise on Good Works*, 100 (WA 6:265); see also *Bondage of the Will*, 53 (WA 18:627).
182 Luther, *Lectures on Galatians, 1535, Chapters 1–4*, 112 (WA 40[I]:202).

antinomianism, Karlstadt replaces the law of God with a law of his own, on the ground (according to Luther) of "the boast of daily speaking with God!"[183] Karlstadt has the worst of both worlds. On the one hand, he lives under a law not commanded by God. The Old Testament prohibition of images, which Karlstadt makes compulsory, is with the coming of Christ no longer in force. Moreover, Karlstadt brings justification under the tutelage of petty works yet again; the serious issue of Karlstadt's iconoclasm is grouped with his emphasis on dress and appearance. The latter frustrates Luther because it makes salvation depend on pure silliness. Karlstadt's other hand is perverse as well, for he does not live according to laws commanded by God. He preaches in disobedience to the princes and foments rebellion. God does command, but what is commanded is discovered only in Scripture. To mandate what God does not, and to make optional what God commands, is a misuse of power (gewalt).[184]

Luther's presupposition in his argument with Karlstadt is that the law of God is the criterion for good works; that is, the content of good works coincides with what God has commanded (gebotten). Therefore, at least on its external face, a good work can be recognized from its correspondence to God's ordinances. Works in accord with the law are good, and even their level of goodness, as in the case of the Decalogue, is established by the order in which they are given.[185] Luther thus provides additional support for his claim that disobedience to authority is the most grievous external sin, for he expands the fourth commandment (the first command of the Second Table) to include obedience to all authority. The works God commands, in short, must be performed because they are commanded.

On the other hand, the ordinances of God also provide a negative criterion of what constitutes a good work. Everything outside the law is optional, at the discretion of Christian freedom. The devilish laws of the pope and Karlstadt are, on this reading, simply inverse methods of decimating the freedom of Christians:

> Christian freedom perishes in either case. The pope destroys freedom in commanding outright that the sacrament is to be elevated, and would have it a statute and a law. He who refrains from keeping his law sins. The factious spirit [Karlstadt] destroys freedom in forbidding outright that the sacrament be elevated, and would have it a prohibition, a statute, and a law. He who does not act in accordance with this law sins. Here Christ is driven away by both parties.[186]

A considerable portion of Luther's anti-Roman writings (particularly the *Treatise on Good Works* and the *Judgment on Monastic Vows*) centers on the contention that the Romans busy themselves with doing works not commanded

---

[183] Luther, *Against the Heavenly Prophets*, 133 (WA 18:115).
[184] Luther, *Treatise on Good Works*, 89 (WA 6:256–57).
[185] Ibid., 23, 81 (WA 6:204, 250).
[186] Luther, *Against the Heavenly Prophets*, 128–29 (WA 18:111–12).

by God, while neglecting those that are. In Karlstadt he confronts the opposite problem of one who prohibits what God does not. But it is shameful, Luther contends, for a free Christian to be subject to any but heavenly ordinances.[187] Only God's sovereign power (*macht*) can command and forbid, and where God "has taught, commanded, and forbidden nothing, there we should permit free choice as God himself has done."[188]

Christian freedom is established between the poles of God's prescription and proscription. It is impossible to emphasize this too strongly: to interpret Luther as opposing Christian freedom and the divine command is a gross misreading of what Luther says. Far from saying that Christian freedom dispenses with the law altogether, Luther in fact asserts that the range of Christian freedom is established precisely by means of God's ordinances. Karlstadt, for his part, sets up a law (*gesetz*) compelling the conscience; only God has the right and authority to do this.[189] It is the very definition of tyranny that it seeks to rob Christians of their proper sphere of freedom, whether such a deprivation is in the form of excessive demands or excessive prohibition.[190] Works neither specifically ordained nor forbidden may be done or not done, as the situation requires, and the sacrifice of this Christian liberty is so disgraceful it signifies the loss of salvation. Conscience becomes trapped in laws it believes necessary for its salvation, and this is death to the soul.[191] *Nothing could be more deceptive than to say that Christian freedom dispenses with the law, for it is first established by the law.* Christian freedom exists only because there is no divine command in the first place; it arises in the law's void, empty space created by the law itself. Freedom is, therefore, an outgrowth of God's ordinances, occupying the territory bounded by what God demands we do, on the one side, and what God prohibits, on the other. The content of Christian freedom, what remains optional, is determined by the law's self-differentiation of freedom and command, establishing liberty and choice only in relation to "human traditions and laws."[192] Thus, "freedom comes from divine authority. God ordained it. He will never revoke it."[193]

Obedience is due to scriptural ordinances, and to them alone. Compliance is required because God's prescriptions lie within the Word and are given to be followed;[194] the commands "are not mere idle talk, but commandments; therefore observe them!"[195] On the other hand, what is not commanded in

[187] Luther, *Babylonian Captivity*, 111 (WA 6:563); *Bondage of the Will*, 49 (WA 18:624).
[188] Luther, *Against the Heavenly Prophets*, 129 (WA 18:112).
[189] Ibid., 129 (WA 18:112).
[190] Luther, *Babylonian Captivity*, 103 (WA 6:558).
[191] Luther, *Against the Heavenly Prophets*, 134, 91 (WA 18:116, 73).
[192] Luther, *Bondage of the Will*, 54 (WA 18:627).
[193] Luther, *Judgment on Monastic Vows*, 309 (WA 8:613).
[194] Luther, *Against the Heavenly Prophets*, 135 (WA 18:117).
[195] Luther, *Ten Sermons on the Catechism*, 145 (WA 30[I]:67); see also *Judgment on Monastic Vows*, 298 (WA 8:606).

Scripture is not compulsory, but free. There are two important specifications regarding what constitutes a command. Not everything in Scripture demands Christian obedience. The first qualification refers specifically to what is done in the New Testament generally and, more particularly, to the example of Christ. To follow the Word of God has an exclusive as well as an inclusive aspect. Luther distinguishes mere works not connected with a command from works attached to an ordaining word. The former are not demanded, even if they are acts of Christ, whereas the latter are compulsory. Luther puts the distinction this way:

> For after [Karlstadt] has seen how we will pay no attention to human words and works, be they ever so holy or ancient, etc., and would have Christ alone as our master, the rogue divides Christ into two parts. Namely, how Christ, on the one hand, without words refrains from doing certain works, and, on the other hand, how with words he refrains from doing works. Dr. Karlstadt is so knavish that he presents Christ alone as he does and refrains from doing without words, wherein he is not to be followed by us, and is silent where Christ does and refrains from doing with words, wherein we are to follow him.
>
> Do you see here the devil who before has misled us through saints? He would now mislead us through Christ himself. Beware where you do not hear God's word commanding or forbidding you so that you may not be led astray and pay no attention to it, even if Christ himself did it. . . . The Word, the Word is to be followed, don't you hear? When one holds before you how Christ has done it, speak up briskly: Very well, he has done it. Has he also taught and commanded it to be done? Also if one holds before you, this Christ has not done, then speak up briskly: Has he also forbidden it? And if they cannot point to his Word, then say: Put it aside, let it be. That doesn't apply to me. Nor is it an example, it is his work, done for his own part. If they say: All of Christ's doing is for our instruction, let them say it. But note carefully what is meant with instruction. A man has said it. He has as much authority as you yourself.[196]

The variety of acts in the New Testament, as well as all that which is not done there, has prescriptive or proscriptive force when a general command is given with it. The relative and occasional nature of act and inaction in the canonical documents is applicable beyond that limited context only if the New Testament says it is.

This first qualification on what constitutes a command valid for us is the ground upon which Luther's constant emphasis on the ordinances of God in his sacramental and political writings makes sense. It is incomprehensible if the law is irrelevant to Christians. Luther is so strident with regard to his theology of the Lord's Supper because there is a command to "Do this in remembrance of me." His opponents ignore this command by altering its meaning irresponsibly. In fact, the entire definition of the sacrament is based on the words of Christ. What is not instituted by Christ is not a sacrament and

---

[196] Luther, *Against the Heavenly Prophets*, 134–35 (WA 18:116–17).

cannot be given that status. On the other hand, institution is also command; if Christ instituted it, it must be done, we must "speak the divine, almighty, heavenly, and holy words which Christ himself spoke at the Supper with his holy lips and commanded (*befalh*) us to speak."[197] The same is true of the injunction against resistance to political authority. It is because of the continued binding force of Paul, First Peter, and Jesus' saying "Give to Caesar what is Caesar's" that obedience is demanded and that Luther is so concerned to discover secondary, worldly reasons to obey, no matter how unjust a prince's conduct. These are commands that bind Christians for all time, because the scriptural account includes not just an action of Christ or the apostles but also a demand to follow their example.

The second differentiation between what Scripture dictates and what is imposed on the Christian is an intertestamental one. The law of the Old Testament, moral as well as ceremonial, is utterly abrogated with the advent of Christ. This is the centerpiece of Luther's opposition to Karlstadt's iconoclasm: "I now speak as a Christian for Christians. For Moses is given to the Jewish people alone and does not concern us Gentiles and Christians. We have our gospel and New Testament. If they can prove from them that images must be put away, we will gladly follow them. If they, however, through Moses would make us Jews, we will not endure it."[198] Two points should be emphasized. First, the Mosaic law has no intrinsic force for Christians. Second, were Karlstadt able to support his iconoclastic demand with a New Testament injunction, Luther would become his eager advocate. The eradication of the significance of the Mosaic law does not concern the ceremonial law alone, but the entire law, including even the Decalogue. For the Christian, "the whole of Moses with all his laws" has no status as command, and the distinction between the ceremonial law and the decalogue, while "an old and common distinction . . . is not an intelligent one."[199]

Yet Luther returns to the substance of the Decalogue frequently, employing it as a criterion of what constitutes a good work as opposed to an unnecessary or optional one. He recoils at the suggestion that he is antinomian and is especially offended when the antinomians, notably Agricola, claim the spirit of the young Luther in support of their position. He rejects the "favor [Agricola] did me and my spirit in this — a spirit for which I also, by the way, have some regard." Luther expresses utter disbelief

> that anyone can claim that I reject the law or the Ten Commandments, since there is available, in more than one edition, my exposition of the Ten Commandments, which furthermore are daily preached and practiced in our churches. . . . I know of no manner in which we do not use them, unless

---

[197] Ibid., 212 (WA 18:202).
[198] Ibid., 92 (WA 18:76).
[199] Ibid., 92, 92–93 (WA 18:76, 76–77).

it be that we unfortunately do not practice and paint them with our deeds and our life as we should. I myself, as old and learned as I am, recite the commandments daily word for word like a child.[200]

It is possible for Luther to assert both that the Decalogue is not binding on the Christian and that its substance is still commanded because "the natural laws were never so orderly and well written as by Moses." As far as Mosaic law, or for that matter any law, conforms to natural law established in creation, Christian obedience is required. Indeed, there is nothing specifically scriptural about even the law of love: this "also the natural law teaches." The prescriptions of natural law are not significant simply because they are scriptural (in the case of Old Testament law, their scriptural status has no significance), but because they are "the natural law (gesetz) written in each man's heart." With this coincidence between natural and Old Testament law, "there the law (gesetze) remains and is not abrogated externally, but only through faith spiritually, which is nothing else than a fulfilling of the law (Rom. 3[:31])." The demand to obey natural law is, moreover, also a demand for conformity with natural reason, through which natural law can be known. Thus, for example, "It is not necessary to observe the sabbath or Sunday because of Moses' commandment. Nature also shows and teaches that one must now and then rest a day, so that man and beast may be refreshed. This natural reason (ursache) Moses also recognized in his sabbath law, for he places the sabbath under man, as also Christ does." Outside its conformity with natural law, "Moses' legislation . . . is free, null, and void, and is specifically given to the Jewish people alone. It is as when an emperor or king makes special laws and ordinances in his territory, . . . and yet common and natural laws such as to honor parents, not to kill, not to commit adultery, to serve God, etc., prevail and remain in all lands."[201] The connection with natural law is important. As with Luther's political theology, which found justifications for the ordinance of God within the proper ordering of the world, the Ten Commandments are not arbitrary injunctions of an irresponsible God. Rather, they are instituted because conformity with the order of things is beneficial for all.[202] Obedience to the law is good because it produces good.

Beyond natural law, the commands that Christians are obliged to obey are these: demands, institutions, and prohibitions given in the words of the New Testament. There should be no mistake; injunctions and prescriptions meeting this criterion are compulsory: "There is to be freedom of choice in everything that God has not clearly taught in the New Testament,"[203] but

---

[200] Luther, Against the Antinomians, 108, 109 (WA 50:469, 470).

[201] The previous series of quotations is from Against the Heavenly Prophets, 97–98 (WA 18:80–82).

[202] Luther, Ten Sermons on the Catechism, 150 (WA 30[I]:71).

[203] Luther, Against the Heavenly Prophets, 127 (WA 18:110). Obedience to the commands of the New Testament is demanded, irrespective of any proof of conformity with natural law. Troeltsch tends to collapse the New Testament demands into those of the natural law (Social Teaching of

freedom does not extend beyond this. Luther assures us that well prior to the dispute with Karlstadt his position was firm.[204] Indeed it was! Contemporaneous with his treatise on Christian liberty from the law, Luther claims in *The Babylonian Captivity,* "a Christian is subject to no law but the law (*legis*) of God." What is commanded (*praecepta*) by God is not optional for the Christian, but must stand despite any and all other considerations "because it is commanded by God." What is given for the church universal in Scripture may not be abandoned or weakened by "one jot or tittle."[205] An assertion that the New Testament commands need not be obeyed by the Christian, or that obedience and being Christian are synonymous, both of which mean that the external law is of no significance for the Christian, cannot be defended. That the prescripts of the New Testament are to be followed is clear. But this is not all. Luther continually keeps them in view of the Christian; he does not allow faith to make their content invisible, as if with the coming of faith all is well, for if it is true that faith fulfills all commands, it is also true that the empirical being of the Christian is not all faith. Luther is definitive: "Those who have received the Spirit are they from whom obedience is due. . . . The trouble is, we are in danger of becoming indolent and negligent, forgetful and ungrateful—vices menacing and great, and which, alas, are altogether too frequent."[206]

To claim that it is a misinterpretation of Luther's thought to suggest that he simply abandons the exposition of the law as pointless for Christians after they are in a relation of faith with God appears to have been evidenced by the opposite distortion, namely, by discounting Luther's many statements that the law is abrogated and overcome by faith, that it no longer binds Christians, and so on. How can Luther argue both that God demands Christian obedience and that the law is overcome for Christians? Two results of our examination up to now must be recalled. First, faith itself, as opposed to the believer who is both flesh and spirit, has no intrinsic need of the law. Spirit obeys the law and more. Indeed, the law is a manifestation of the Spirit. Second, the question with respect to the value of the gifts of God is not their inner structure but their dominating principle. If flesh dominates one's faculties, desires, and actions, all gifts of God are efficacious only for damnation, irrespective of their possibly desirable effects. On the other hand, these same

---

the Christian Churches 2:471–501). Holl was correct to criticize Troeltsch's overly expansive use of natural law in interpreting Luther. Although Luther is not opposed to such an enterprise and attempts it with respect to some New Testament commands, it is not necessary and in some cases is mistaken, notably in the sacrament and in that obedience which is beyond the requirements of natural law.

204 Luther, *Against the Heavenly Prophets,* 127 (WA 18:110).

205 Luther, *Babylonian Captivity,* 76, 101, 25 (WA 6:540, 557, 505–6).

206 Martin Luther, *The Epistle of the Second Sunday in Lent: 1 Thess. 4,* in *The Sermons of Martin Luther,* vol. 7, *Sermons on Epistle Texts for Epiphany, Easter, and Pentecost,* ed. Lenker, 145–46 (WA 17:197–98).

gifts, brought under the dominion of Spirit, are animated by the end of pleasing God and loving the neighbor. They are of no assistance in cajoling God toward a more favorable verdict in the question of eternal life, but for that very reason, they are crucial for the actual justness of the believer.

The revolution undergone by the law prior to and subsequent to the reception of the gospel promises in faith follows the same structure. Obliteration of the law's heavenly efficacy is the condition for the constitution of the value of the divine commands for the world, under the Spirit's sovereignty. Properly understood, the commands of God concern life,[207] and life must be lived even after God's decree of grace becomes known in faith through the gospel. To assert the opposite would bring one to the precipice of antinomianism. The vast difference between the devil's more libertine moments and the true God is that "the devil, or man, . . . commands nothing and compels nothing, but only bids fair and makes promises," whereas God "gives the promises, constrains, and commands us."[208] Put simply, the law is abrogated as far as its heavenly efficacy is concerned but in no way superseded in its earthly worth. The commands of God have changed their allegiance. Prior to the gospel's publication of grace, the law, despite its being a good gift of God, was a weapon of the devil because it was set against us as external domination. When captured by the Spirit, the commands become weapons of the Spirit, guiding action and one's progress in sanctification.

If the Spirit's appropriation of the law does not change the content of the law, it does change the believer's relation to it.[209] The law itself does not change. It is, as it has always been, a gift of God, "holy, righteous, and good."[210] But it is no longer understood as cowing the believer before its impossible demands. Faith is the spiritual fulfillment of the law, and this means that the law's content has been taken up into faith and the operation of the Spirit. Grace frees one not from the law but from *life under the law,* or "the 'spirit of slavery' (Rom. 8.15), which always makes men worse, because it leads them to a greater hatred of the Law and righteousness." In contrast to this servile attitude, the Christian is "freed from the Law by the Spirit, not so that the Law does not exist, but so that the Law is not feared." The person's relation to the law, and the law's relation to the Spirit, is shifted: the law is used properly when employed not for heavenly justification but for actual, worldly justice and sanctification. One is truly outside the law completely insofar as one is actually righteous. But this would mean not that the law is ignored but that it had become submerged into faith to such an extent that the Christian "keeps the Law, and his life is the Law itself, living and fulfilled."[211] This is nothing else

---

207 Luther, *Against the Heavenly Prophets,* 94 (WA 18:78).
208 Luther, *Treatise on Good Works,* 48 (WA 6:224).
209 Ziemke, *Love for the Neighbor,* 73.
210 Luther, *Lectures on Galatians, 1535, Chapters 1–4,* 123 (WA 40[I]:218).
211 Luther, *Lectures on Hebrews,* 141, 141, 193–94 (WA 57[III]:135, 135, 192).

than to say that the commands of God are now obeyed for their own sake, for their original purposes of thanksgiving and love, and without an ulterior motive of self-benefit; we "learn to do right for the sake of God's command-ments (*gebots*)."[212] Luther too teaches the law, but "after the doctrine of faith."[213]

This changed relationship to the commands of God is not visible from the outside. What is open to external view is only whether the law is obeyed outwardly or not. If, for the moment, external obedience is assumed, it is impossible to tell whether any person stands under the principle of Spirit or flesh at any particular time from external examination of the evidence. The reason for this is that the capture of the commands by Spirit transposes the meaning of one's external activities but does not necessarily change the activities themselves: "Christianity," notes Cranz, "affects the nature of the Christian's commitment; it does not affect that to which he is committed."[214] It must be reemphasized that external obedience to the commands of God is not "suffi-cient in itself. It must be done in confidence of God's favor (*huld*). A man must have no doubt that he is well pleasing to God in what he is doing, and he should let work of this kind be nothing but an expression and exercise of this faith. He should trust in God and look to him for blessings and a gracious will (*gnedigen willen*)."[215] A real love of righteousness implies, of itself, a hatred of lawlessness.[216] Commands begin to become not a burden but a pleasure. They remain burdensome only to the flesh, the rebel that the heart, being dominated by the Spirit, desires to conquer. Works start to be done with an inner attitude that is joyful, out of thanksgiving and glorification of God.[217] Such an attitude of the heart cannot be proved from any external viewpoint nor demonstrated conclusively by any outward evidence. This opacity of motives for obedience does not mean that God's law is dispensable for earthly life, but only that faith no longer feels it as oppressive law. There is no necessary conflict between the demands of the law and the inner desire of the person.[218]

This inner attitude is not established once and for all, for flesh and spirit are engaged in battle and the process of earthly life is not a constant advance from glory to glory but includes setbacks as well. The person under grace is always composed of Spirit and flesh, and their relative dominance at any

---

[212] Luther, *Treatise on Good Works*, 44 (WA 6:221).

[213] Luther, *Lectures on Galatians, 1535, Chapters 1-4*, 4 (WA 40[I]:40).

[214] Cranz, *Development of Luther's Thought*, 145. Moreover, there are, on occasion, good reasons to violate the commands, even those that are also natural law. The circumstances say a good deal about the acceptability of a course of action: the law that is inviolable is love (*Judgment on Monastic Vows*, 390–93; WA 8:662–64).

[215] Luther, *Treatise on Good Works*, 87 (WA 6:255).

[216] Luther, *Lectures on Hebrews*, 119–20 (WA 57[III]:110).

[217] Luther, *Freedom of a Christian*, 350–59 (WA 7:54–60).

[218] Holl is especially persuasive on this point (*Reconstruction of Morality*, 114–15).

particular time is variable.[219] Faithful confidence in God's grace always operates in the fissure between despair and arrogance. In his summary discussion of the last two commandments, Luther enunciates a principle that applies to all God's ordinances, because paradigmatically it refers to the demand to believe:

> These two commandments are set as a goal which we do not attain, and we reach out to them only in thought right up till death. For nobody has ever been so holy that he never felt some evil inclination within himself, especially when occasion and temptation were present together. For original sin is born in us by nature: it may be checked, but it cannot be entirely uprooted except through death.[220]

Earthly life, beginning the new creation, attempts to contain sin within narrower and narrower confines; only fulfillment of this new creation promised by grace through faith, to which actual life tries to conform with varying degrees of success, eradicates sin altogether.

One part of the sanctifying relation between law and Spirit is that the law's content becomes an instrument of the Spirit rather than the flesh. Another is that the new synergism between them means that obedience to the commands is also increased as the Spirit becomes dominant in the heart. The inward character of the commands, we have already seen, cannot be even understood without the Spirit's inward teaching. Moreover, Spirit, which is responsible for sanctification of the faithful, teaches one how the commands might be fulfilled in the most desirable way.[221] The "law of the Spirit," therefore, is not a law that eradicates law but instead puts the commands of God under the Spirit so that they might be fulfilled, although "at this point you will discover how hard it is to do the good works God commands, how the natural man turns up his nose at them, wriggles out of them, and turns away from them, but yet does the good works of his own choosing easily and gladly."[222] Spirit, in short, turns the law which had been against us into commands for us, and turns the faithful, who had been against the law, toward it, so that it is possible to say that faith and confidence in God increase through obedience to the commands.[223]

The Christian's relation to the law, which ranges from the law's counterproductivity as a means of salvation to its inclusion in the process of slaying sin in the advent of proper righteousness, to one's inability to fulfill it even then (requiring a return to confidence in the grace of God, which itself always waxes and wanes), is demonstrated clearly and concisely in Luther's sermon

---

[219] Prenter (*Spiritus Creator*) is correct to object to the externally verifiable, unambiguously progressivist understanding of sanctification he finds in Holl and others, although it is not entirely clear that Holl ignores the tensive aspect of sanctification Prenter defends.

[220] Luther, *Treatise on Good Works*, 114 (WA 6:276).

[221] Luther, *Babylonian Captivity*, 115 (WA 6:566); *Treatise on Good Works*, 105–6 (WA 6:270); *Bondage of the Will*, 19, 259–60 (WA 18:602, 765).

[222] Luther, *Treatise on Good Works*, 109 (WA 6:272–73).

[223] Ibid., 46–47 (WA 6:223).

on Colossians 3 in the 1525 Lenten Postil. The law (*recht*), Luther maintains, is abolished for all Christians.[224] Law (*gesetz*) is suspended by God, as it must be for any salvation to remain, for "Were God to deal with us according to the rigor of his laws (*gesetze*), we should all be lost." But mercy is not its own aim; it is directed outside itself, toward the production of power, which is possible only if mercy has already been shown. Mercy is directed toward actual reformation of its recipient, and this divine model applies also to human mercy:

> they who are mercifully tolerated must not imagine that because they escape censure and force, their beliefs and practices are right. They must not construe such mercy as encouragement to become indolent and negligent, and to continue in their error. *Mercy is not extended to them with any such design. The object is to give them opportunity to recover zeal and strength (stark).* But if they be disposed to remain as they are, very well; let them alone. They will not long continue thus; the devil will lead them farther astray, until finally they completely apostatize, even becoming enemies to the Gospel.[225]

It is at this point that the law reenters the Christian life, invigorated for the first time by the mercy proclaimed in the gospel and accepted in faith and Spirit, a principle of life rather than death.

The face of the law is changed from "law" to "admonition."[226] The difference is that, if one teaches the law, one must "command, urge, [and] threaten," while an admonition teaches "what manner of fruit properly results from faith," and "persuades with loving words *in view of the blessing and grace of God received,* and in the light of Christ's own example. Christians should act with readiness and cheerfulness, being moved neither by fear of punishment nor desire of reward, as frequently before stated" (emphasis added). What one does is a matter of feeling the power of God's declaration that one is elect, of feeling the certainty that "such God chooses, and has chosen from eternity" over against any efforts to elect and love ourselves. Paul

> does not drive us with laws, but persuades us by reminding us of the ineffable grace of God; for he terms us the "elect of God," and "holy" and "beloved." He would call forth the fruits of faith, desiring them to be yielded in a willing, cheerful and happy spirit. The individual who sincerely believes and trusts before God that he is beloved, holy and elect, will consider how to sustain his honors and titles, how to conduct himself worthily of them; more, he will love God with a fervor enabling him to do or omit, or to suffer,

---

[224] Martin Luther, *The Epistle of St. Paul to the Colossians on the Fifth Sunday after Epiphany* (hereafter cited as *Sermon on Colossians 3*), in *The Sermons of Martin Luther,* vol. 7, *Sermons on Epistle Texts for Epiphany, Easter, and Pentecost,* ed. Lenker, 83 (WA 17:115). "Recht" is here meant in two senses: it designates (1) law and (2) the right of Christians. The abolition of law includes both elements of *Freedom of a Christian* — namely, that one is lord of all and subject to all. In the same way, Luther opposed the peasants' demands for their rights.

[225] Luther, *Sermon on Colossians 3,* 79, 80 (emphasis added; WA 17[II]:112, 113).

[226] The whole of the epistolary segment of the Lenten Postil is concerned with this notion of admonition.

all things cheerfully, and will never know how to do enough. But he who doubts such an attitude of God toward himself will not recognize the force of these words. He will not feel the power (*erwelet*) of the statement that we are holy, beloved, and elect in the sight of God.[227]

The elements analyzed earlier are all present here: change of the object toward which works are directed (from benefit or harm of self to the praise and thanksgiving of God), dependence of action on the publication of grace in the gift of faithful confidence, and finally, a new attitude toward the commands—admonition instead of law. What does not change is the content of what is commanded; the admonition is identical to the dominating law. The difference between law and admonition is not the command or its imperative structure. "Law" and "admonition" differ only insofar as their presentation is concerned, and this in turn depends on the gift of faith in the hearer of the message.

Another significant element of this sermon is that there is no possibility of the Christian's fulfilling the commands of God in this life. If there is "one requiring absolute perfection in Christians—know that such a one is merely an enforcer of the Law, a base hypocrite, a merciless jailer, with no true knowledge of Christ." This must be understood: "Christians are not perfectly holy. They have begun to be holy and are in a state of progression. There are to be found among them anger, evil desire, unholy love, worldly care and other deplorable infirmities, remains of the old Adam." Once again, in this battle between flesh and Spirit, the law is turned against its former co-conspirator, the old creation of flesh:

> But whoso recognizes Christianity as a progressive order yet in its begin-
> ning, will not be offended at the occasional manifestation of ungentleness
> and impatience on the part of a Christian; for he remembers that Christians
> are commanded (*heysst*) to bear one another's burdens and infirmities. He
> knows that the enumeration of the fruits of the Spirit is not a record of laws
> the observance of which is imperative or Christ will be denied. He is aware
> that the passage is to be interpreted as meaning that Christians are to strive
> to be kind; *that is the mark at which they aim. However, even though they have
> made a beginning and some progress in this virtue, they are often unkind and bear
> fruits directly the opposite of the fruits of the Spirit. True, the text quoted says we
> should be kind, but it does not say we are kind. We are tending toward it, we are
> in a state of progression; but during the progress much of the old and as yet untransformed
> nature is intermingled.*[228]

What dominates the heart, Spirit or flesh, cannot be seen from the outside as if there were an absolute and inviolable correlation between these two spheres. The search for certain evidence of another's overall spiritual condition

---

[227] Luther, *Sermon on Colossians 3*, 76, 80, 77 (WA 17[II]:110, 111, 110–11).

[228] Ibid., 79, 83, 84 (emphasis added; WA 17[II]:112, 115–16, 116). The reference of at least the first quotation appears to be to the spiritualists, since Luther here calls such people by the term "*schwermer*."

is bound to fail. Obedience to the external aspect of God's commands can mask an inner contempt of God and neighbor, those who are supposed to be served through such acts. On the other hand, while disobedience does announce a victory for the flesh, it does not necessarily indicate the flesh's triumph over the whole person, nor does it indicate that the conquest is forever.

The gap opened, at least slightly, between the gifts of the Spirit and the external fulfillment of God's commands is closed where disobedience clearly and invariably shows the absence of the Spirit within, and grace without. Love is to be shown to those with weakness of works, that they may triumph over it, "But the liberality of kindness is not to be extended to false doctrine. Only relative to conduct and works is love to be exercised." Luther goes on:

> Love will be, even must be, kind even to the enemy so long as he assails not doctrine and faith (lere und glauben). But it will not, it cannot, tolerate the individual who does, be it father, mother or dearest friend. Deut. 8 [Deut. 13:6–8]. Love, then, must be exercised, not in relation to the doctrine and faith of our neighbor, but relative to his life and works. Faith, on the contrary, has to do, not with works and life, but with his doctrine and belief.[229]

The presupposition of love is unity in teaching and faith. This explains why Luther, particularly in his anti-Roman polemic, so often stresses that what is at issue is not the faulty life of his opponents (although he is willing to point this out also, if the occasion arises) but their false doctrine.[230] This, as much as anything else, distinguishes Luther from Erasmus, who, Luther claimed, was willing to keep external peace at the expense of true doctrine, treating "Christian dogmas as no better than philosophical and human opinions."[231] The difference between the rancorless firmness of the *Admonition to Peace* and the vitriol of *Against the Robbing and Murdering Hordes of Peasants* consists primarily in this: When rebellion broke out, the peasants showed not only disobedience to authorities but, more important, defended their violation of the divine commandments as the way of God even after Luther had shown them the error of their ways. He begins the latter treatise by referring to the *Admonition*:

> In my earlier book on this matter, I did not venture to judge the peasants, since they had offered to be corrected and instructed; and Christ in Matthew 7[:1] commands us not to judge. But before I could even inspect the situation, they forgot their promise and violently took matters into their own hands and are robbing and raging like mad dogs. All this now makes it clear that they were trying to deceive us and that the assertions they made in the their *Twelve Articles* were nothing but lies presented under the name of the gospel.[232]

---

229 Ibid., 81 (translation modified; WA 17[II]:114).
230 See, e.g., *Freedom of a Christian*, 335 (WA 7:43–44).
231 Luther, *Bondage of the Will*, 23 (WA 18:605); see also *Bondage of the Will*, 50 (WA 18:625).
232 Luther, *Against the Robbing and Murdering Hordes*, 49 (WA 18:357).

The betrayal which cannot under any circumstances be condoned is a doctrinal one. The call for humility and love in works does not extend to doctrines.
Love must yield; faith may not.[233]

With this assertion, the sermon on Colossians has brought us full circle
in regard to a geography of faith and the Spirit. The inability to read others'
faith and spirit from the marks inscribed by their works implies no similar
noncorrespondence between faith and doctrinal profession. The apparent
inward location of the Spirit does not, in the case of doctrine, prevent its
external recognition. If not all those who profess to be Christian are indeed
Christian, at least Luther is certain that those whose professions are un-
Christian are not Christians. Agreement with "the faith" does not guarantee
"faith," but there is certainly "unbelief" wherever "the faith" is denied. At least
negatively, correspondence between external doctrine and inward unbelief is
certain.

This doctrinaire tendency in Luther should trouble any use of Luther in
the present. For Tillich, this problem was overcome only by the revelatory
claim of Martin Kähler that justification by grace is given in spite of not only
moral corruption but intellectual error as well.[234] Because we employ Luther
for a contemporary theology of power, and because the question of power's
location is important for this endeavor, it would be irresponsible to pass over
Luther's assertion of this external mark of the Spirit without comment. It calls
for a brief diversion from an analysis of the Spirit's locale in Luther.

Luther's position is the product of three assumptions. The first is that the
Word is not simply a means by which one receives the Spirit but the *only* means.
Second, the disagreement with the commands of Scripture demonstrated in
any attempt to weaken or circumvent them implies one's conviction, Luther
says so frequently, that "God is a liar."[235] A liar once, a liar always — and particularly with respect to the promise of salvation. If one disbelieves God in
a single instance, it is impossible to have adequate trust in God's greatest feat,
one's salvation through Christ. But "faith" and "the faith" are not yet locked
together absolutely without the addition of a third assumption, namely, that
intellectual affirmation is a necessary, although not sufficient, condition for
any life in accord with such affirmation. The 1559 edition of Calvin's *Institutes*
is concise: "It now remains to pour into the heart itself what the mind has
absorbed."[236] Luther did not give such a condensed phrase, but the sentiment

---

[233] Luther, *Lectures on Galatians, 1535, Chapters 1–4,* 99–100 (WA 40[I]:182). An outstanding
and much more nuanced account of the importance of doctrine is given by Ebeling (*Luther,* 59–75).

[234] Paul Tillich, "Author's Introduction," in Tillich, *The Protestant Era,* abridged edition, trans.
James Luther Adams (Chicago: University of Chicago Press, 1957), ix–xi. A similar point is made
by B. A. Gerrish, "The Chief Article—Then and Now," *Journal of Religion* 63, no. 4 (October 1983):
373–74.

[235] See, e.g., Luther, *Holy and Blessed Sacrament of Baptism,* 37 (WA 2:733); *Adoration of the Sacrament,* 279–80 (WA 11:434).

[236] Calvin, *Institutes,* 3.2.36, p. 583.

is his as well, expressed in such statements against Erasmus as, "it is not the mark of a Christian mind to take no delight in assertion; on the contrary, a man must delight in assertions or he will be no Christian"; and "take away assertions and you take away Christianity. Why, the Holy Spirit is given them from heaven that he may glorify Christ and confess him even unto death — unless it is not asserting when one dies for one's confession and assertion."[237] While faith is finally and chiefly a matter of the heart for both Luther and Calvin, the way to the heart is through understanding. Certainty of faith depends on certainty about the doctrines of the faith.[238] It is not a modern turn to practice that makes the Reformers' claim doubtful to us — they too emphasized practice — than that we neither accept the assumption that it is possible to ground doctrine and "the faith" absolutely or finally, beyond the vagaries of history, society, and culture, nor do we take for granted the primacy of discursive understanding in relation to practice. With respect to the latter, the self-evidence of the assertion that one must first understand linguistically in order to act in accord with the content of such understanding has been shattered; the extent to which it has been broken is expressed in and furthered by such notions as ideology, the unconscious, implicit faith, and others. Even attempts to overcome such concepts in modern thought, as in Foucault's work, are hardly a return to Luther's understanding.

Luther presupposes that to believe in Christ requires belief in what God has declared in Scripture and, furthermore, that one must be capable of saying one believes it if one actually does. This is the difference between doctrine and life. The life of works does tend to confirm the presence or absence of the Spirit, but not with certainty. Works are not an utterly transparent expression of the heart, but words are a transparent mark of the intellect, and the proper cognitive understanding of doctrine is a precondition for faith's presence to the heart. Luther can therefore be absolutely certain when speaking of the parts of the Catechism that "one who does not know them should not be counted among the number of Christians. For when a person does not know this, it is a sign that he has no regard for God and Christ." Such a person "belongs body and soul to the devil, and it will never go well with him here and hereafter."[239] A dissolute life must be tolerated, at least to a point, because the best must be assumed; doctrinal disobedience cannot be tolerated, because there is only one conclusion to draw.

---

[237] Luther, *Bondage of the Will*, 19–20, 21 (WA 18:603, 603).

[238] Ibid., 21–23 (WA 18:604–5). Occasionally, Luther draws back from this conclusion, particularly when he opposes the doctrine of a person he admires. See his treatment of Francis of Assisi and Bernard of Clairvaux in *Judgment on Monastic Vows*, 268, 289–90 (WA 8:587–88, 600–601). Bernard, according to Luther, realized his error "when he was at the point of death" and was thus saved. Francis's case is not explicitly resolved.

[239] Luther, *Ten Sermons on the Catechism*, 137, 138 (WA 30[I]:57, 58).

The Teloi *of Spirit*

The defensibility of Luther's position is not the primary issue at this point. But even if one accepts Luther's own assumptions, a question arises. On the one hand, Luther asserts that the gifts of the Spirit are inward. On the other, he maintains that disobedience to external commands, and especially any attempt to defend one's disobedience, proves the Spirit's absence. The inner presence or absence of the Spirit can, at this point, be judged by external criteria. This is one suggestion that the Spirit cannot be, for Luther, related merely to inwardness.

There are others. There is a basic difference between faith, the chief gift of the Spirit, and its confirmatory evidence. If obedience to God's commands is not a *de facto* sign of faith and Spirit, and therefore of grace, this does not imply that faith itself is a purely inward event. Rather, it means just the opposite. The very definition of faith included a *telos* and object external to the person. Its vertical referent was Christ and God's promises; horizontally it reached its objective in love for the neighbor. Faith cannot have the self in view.

Even the inward conquest of flesh by Spirit is conquest, instead of submission to flesh, only if the person in whom the Spirit is driving out sin progressively does not have the self in view during his or her activity. If the objective of one's acts in the world is to become righteous, to improve the self for the self, it is the way of flesh rather than Spirit. To speak of the *telos* of God's declaration of righteousness toward sanctification, or actual righteousness, although accurate, is deceptive. This sanctification is not its own end either; that would involve a return of self-righteousness into the lifeblood of Luther's theology and into the Christian heart. Rather, sanctification is qualified by an end beyond itself, in one of two ways. First, if one seeks to slay sin more and more, this must be accomplished with the ends of love of neighbor and praise of God in mind. It cannot be sought for its own sake without again stretching one upon the rack of despair and the righteousness of works. Faith will have failed in its purpose, which is an external one. Second, it is possible that actual righteousness is not sought at all by the Christian, but is rather an effect of thanksgiving and love, an effect of which one is aware only after loving and obedient action. In this latter possibility, we arrive once again at the principle of recognition of the other and its close link to Luke 9:24: "For whoever would save his life will lose it; and whoever loses his life for my sake will save it." Luther's theology of sanctification is not a theology of self-help, which could not be "theo-"logy at all. It is rather a theology of recognition first of the other and then and only then of the self who, through the Spirit, has slain sin more and more. And the reason Luther defends this order is that he is convinced that it alone can recognize the neighbor's real needs and God as others worthy of recognition and worship.

The gifts of the Spirit are inward gifts; nevertheless, obedience to the external commands of God's Word is still required. How does Luther reconcile this seemingly incongruous pair of assertions? To this point, concentration has been focused on the external end of the Spirit's gifts. They are not purely inward. In fact, they are inward neither in end nor beginning; their relation to inwardness is a mediate stage between the double externality of end and origin. Moreover, the original externality of the Spirit is what allows Luther to assert the external *telos* of the Spirit and faith.

Luther's assertion of the necessity of an external origin of the Spirit is seen most clearly in his reaction to Karlstadt. Karlstadt, like Luther, maintained that the Spirit was inward. The difference was that Karlstadt asserted the inward *reception* of the Spirit in addition to its effecting inner change, whereas Luther is adamant in maintaining that the Spirit must be received externally. Karlstadt's position, Luther argues, is a blasphemous and pompous reversal of divine order. If theology begins inwardly, rather than externally, the result is to tear down all means by which the Spirit might come to a person. The effect is that Karlstadt teaches not how the Spirit might come to people but how they might arrive at the Spirit, that is, a more subtle and dangerous form of active righteousness as the way to salvation.[240] By dispensing with the media of the Spirit's activity and concentrating on one's own actions, the Word is overturned. Luther ridicules Karlstadt: "If Scripture will not help, my big head will, for it is full of spirit."[241] Because Karlstadt thinks he has swallowed the Spirit "feathers and eggs," his own spirit pays no attention to the external Word.[242]

Luther, on the other hand, maintains that the inviolable order of God is to move from the external to the inward:

> Now when God sends forth his holy gospel he deals with us in a twofold manner, first outwardly, then inwardly. Outwardly he deals with us through the outer word of the gospel and through material signs, that is, baptism and the sacrament of the altar. Inwardly he deals with us through the Holy Spirit, faith, and other gifts. But whatever their measure or order the outward factors should and must precede. The inward experience follows and is effected by the outward. God has determined to give the inward to no one except through the outward. For he wants to give no one the Spirit or faith outside of the outward Word and sign instituted by him, as he says in Luke 16[:29], "Let them hear Moses and the prophets."[243]

"Spirit" must have scriptural authority to prove it is the Spirit of God and not the devil. Without the Word, all understanding of God is merely a product of fictive imagination.[244] If it is true that "the letter by itself does not impart

---

240 Luther, *Against the Heavenly Prophets*, 147 (WA 18:136–37).
241 Ibid., 179 (WA 18:169).
242 Ibid., 162, 177 (WA 18:152, 166).
243 Ibid., 146 (WA 18:136); see also *Lectures on Galatians, 1535, Chapters 1–4*, 73 (WA 40[I]:142).
244 Luther, *Against the Heavenly Prophets*, 160–70 (WA 18:150–60).

life, yet it must be present, and it must be heard or received. And the Holy Spirit must work through this in the heart, and the heart must be preserved in the faith through and in the Word against the devil and every trial."[245] Karlstadt's devil seeks, in short, to destroy the authority of the external Word and, thereby, the order of God.[246]

Luther's argument is based firmly in his theology of the gifts of God. The gospel is a gift of God,[247] and it is an external gift. The "preached gospel [is] a power of God (*krafft Gottes*)." Karlstadt is chastised for suggesting that "the bodily voice cannot be the power of God. So St. Paul is lying when he speaks of a bodily vocal sound as the power of God."[248] The power-Word is externally originating. Moreover, it is inherently teleological, for inward experience is effected by the external. Luther links, for example, "spirit" to the "right skill" in interpreting Scripture.[249] This movement is precisely the same as the process of sanctification. Just as individuals cannot act spiritually or in faith except insofar as they recognize themselves through the neighbor and God—and not the other way around—so they cannot receive the Spirit except if the walls surrounding the self are overcome initially by the external Word. The Spirit refers inwardly, but it is received only externally, in the beginning through the Word and subsequently through God and the neighbor.

The dynamic through which the Spirit is originally present to its recipient permits two conclusions. On the one hand, there can be no reception of Spirit without external preaching of the Word. If the gospel is defeated, so is any possibility of faith.[250] The Word is necessary for "Christian life, righteousness, and freedom." Conversely, there is no greater indication of God's wrath than the deprivation of the Word, for "to preach Christ means to feed the soul, make it righteous, set it free, and save it, provided it believes the preaching. Faith alone is the saving and efficacious use of the Word."[251] "Provided it believes the preaching." The Word cannot be used properly unless it is also taught inwardly, by the Spirit or presence of Christ, which teaches the proper use of the Word, not merely the knowledge of it.[252] Without inward instruction by the Spirit, "one would not be helped if a thousand preachers stood around his ears and shouted themselves into a frenzy with such words."[253] The condition of any possible reception of the Spirit is external preaching of the Word, but that is not enough: it "requires also the Spirit of God to give

---

[245] Luther, *Commentary on 1 Corinthians 15,* 77 (WA 36:500–501).

[246] Luther, *Against the Heavenly Prophets,* 214 (WA 18:204).

[247] Ibid., 146, 213 (WA 18:135, 203). In these two citations, Luther alternatively uses *gabe* and *geschenke,* which have been translated as "gift."

[248] Ibid., 198 (WA 18:187, 188).

[249] Ibid., 167 (WA 18:157); see also *Bondage of the Will,* 17–19 (WA 18:601–2).

[250] Luther, *Treatise on Good Works,* 111–12 (WA 6:274).

[251] Luther, *Freedom of a Christian,* 345, 346 (WA 7:50, 51).

[252] Luther, *Against the Heavenly Prophets,* 208 (WA 18:198).

[253] Ibid., 142 (WA 18:124).

the growth and to be a living teacher of living things inwardly."[254] What remains external cannot be efficacious; the external Word contains within itself an inward drive.

This drift from the external to the inward is the broader principle on which the same dynamic of the Lord's Supper was based. The body and blood of Christ are everywhere, but not everywhere "for you." They become spiritually profitable where the Word promises the Spirit as an effect of their consumption. Moreover, the sacrament had no benefit and power without the body and blood. Only the body of Christ, proclaimed in the Word, which is also external, brought the Spirit. Luther's absolute and unqualified opposition to any theology of pure inwardness is clear: "I have often asserted that the ultimate goal of the devil is to do away with the entire sacrament and all outward ordinances of God. Then as these prophets teach, all that would count would be for the heart to stare inwardly at the spirit." But the heart would thereby contemplate a "lying spirit."[255]

The necessity of a bodily component for the inward operation of the Spirit permits Luther to turn over the argument. If the presence of the Spirit has outwardness as a condition, then the Spirit's presence or absence can be judged by those same criteria. In short, the inward presence of Spirit cannot and does not exist only inwardly. Rather, the Spirit's presence is judged by public criteria. What is done against the commands of God, or not done in accord with those commands, proves the absence of the Spirit in the believer's heart, particularly if such conduct is defended as the divine way against God's commands. Karlstadt's violation of the laws of God shows that he does not have the Spirit, since Spirit, although inward, has an external *telos:*

> For God does not change his old order for the new one unless the change is accompanied with great signs. Therefore one can believe no one who relies on his own spirit and inner feelings for authority and who outwardly storms against God's accustomed order, unless he therewith performs miraculous signs, as Moses indicates in Deut. 18[:22].[256]

As there is no purely inward reception of Spirit, so there is no purely inward possession of the Spirit after its reception. Luther's attacks on his opponents in the disputes discussed so far turn on this assumption of the publicity of the Spirit. Without it, his invectives against all his sacramental opponents—the peasants, the legalists, the antinomians, and the clandestine preachers—are nonsensical. The volley against secret preachers is especially instructive. Luther's attack is not based on these preachers' lack of theological knowledge or dissolute life (although these may be suspected, since these

---

[254] Luther, *Bondage of the Will,* 18 (WA 18:602).
[255] Luther, *Against the Heavenly Prophets,* 191, 173 (WA 18:181, 163).
[256] Ibid., 113 (WA 18:96–97).

individuals ignore God's ordinance of the call).[257] Their teaching does not require examination, for "it is the teaching of the devil no matter how it glistens."[258] The reason for this summary dismissal is that these preachers operate without a public call and attempt to perform the functions of the office of preaching without being granted possession of it. Therefore, they were "secret" despite their rather open preaching, because they claimed to receive a call inwardly, without public confirmation. Their presumption to have the Spirit is refuted because a call is necessarily public, received "not in some corner, as the sectarians boast, but through the mouth of a man who is carrying out his lawful right."[259] Luther attacks Agricola and Karlstadt also for their secrecy.[260] The difference between God's Spirit and the devil's lies in their public character:

> when God compels anyone to speak, such a one makes public proclamation, even if he is alone and no one follows him, as in the case of Jeremiah. I too can claim that this was my way. It is the way of the devil to glide around in secrecy and conspiracy, afterward making the excuse that at first his spirit was not strong enough. No, Sir Devil, the spirit that is of God makes no such excuse. I know you well.[261]

Publicity is a criterion of the Spirit, and refusal of public criteria is evidence of spiritual bankruptcy.[262] There can be no secret Spirit, no inward Spirit that either originates inwardly or remains inward upon its reception.

There are, then, two teleologies of the Spirit. First, Spirit is received only through what is outward; seen from this external point of view, Spirit has a *telos* to the believer's inner life. But from the point of view of inwardness, the Spirit's *telos* is external, toward obedience of God's commands, which has the dual purpose of benefitting the neighbor and honoring God. Within this second teleology, an ambiguity remains. We have noted that the criterion of judgment for the presence of the Spirit is a public one. Does this mean that the public manifestation of the Spirit is simply the "fruit of the tree" of the Spirit's gifts, or is it constitutive of the Spirit's presence and power? Put another way, does the Spirit operate in a kind of dialectical loop, first externally, then internally, and then again externally, as Luther's frequent use of the metaphor of the tree and its fruit implies? Or is it not even possible to assert any of these distinct presences properly? In the next chapter, two formulations of the relation

[257] Martin Luther, *Infiltrating and Clandestine Preachers*, in *Luther's Works*, vol. 40, *Church and Ministry II*, ed. Bergendoff, 385 (WA 30[III]:519).

[258] Ibid., 387 (WA 30[III]:521); see also *Lectures on Galatians, 1535, Chapters 1–4*, 19–20 (WA 40[I]:62).

[259] Luther, *Lectures on Galatians, 1535, Chapters 1–4*, 19 (WA 40[I]:61).

[260] On Agricola, see Luther, *Against the Antinomians*, 109 (WA 50:470). On Karlstadt, see Luther, *Against the Heavenly Prophets*, 110–11, 222 (WA 18:93–94, 213).

[261] Luther, *Against the Heavenly Prophets*, 144–45 (WA 18:134).

[262] Luther, *Lectures on Galatians, 1535, Chapters 1–4*, 18 (WA 40[I]:59–60).

between faith and works, both of which are used by Luther, will provide the point of entry through which this issue is decided.

A similar difficulty arises in the case of the law. The law is clearly external; it imposes obligations, prescriptions, and prohibitions with regard to what should be done. But it is also true that there is an inward component to the law. It concerns life in the earthly realm, but this refers not only to others' lives but also one's own. The law of the Old Testament, for example, is still in force, but not as a religious, spiritual injunction. The content of Old Testament law remains valid insofar as it conforms to natural law. But natural law is not merely external; it includes an inward component. It is a demand not simply of external being but of inward being:

> There is nothing but the law's (*Gesetzes*) perceptible preaching in man's conscience. The devil knows very well too that it is impossible to remove the law from the heart. In Romans 2, St. Paul teaches that the Gentiles who did not receive the law from Moses and thus have no law are nevertheless a law to themselves, being obliged to witness that what the law requires is written in their hearts, etc.[263]

God's commands are a mirror of our own need and the needs of the neighbor.[264] To eliminate the law is not simply to erase a page of unnecessary verbiage. It is to abandon laws of a good life. The law too is located ambiguously. It is external, but it is valid also because it is an internal law. The same is true of the commands of the New Testament, whose conformity with natural law need not be shown, although Luther frequently attempts such a defense. The consumption of the sacrament, for example, is commanded in a certain way because it strengthens inner life and love of the neighbor.

The antinomy of power and the conflicting valuation of the world which seemed to appear between Luther's sacramental and political theologies has been overcome, in part, by placing each of these theologies within his broader theological understanding. The apparent dualism in Luther's thought arises from his conception of the two realms. If the interpreter's viewpoint is restricted to finding simply the elements of Luther's theology, not only does he appear to develop a self-contradictory theology, but his arguments with his opponents turn out to be refutations of various aspects of his own thought. But Luther himself always elevates use over nature. His disputes concerned not the elemental components of his opponents' theologies but the order and relation to the whole in which the pieces were placed. The difficulties relevant for a theology of power that are not resolved by the prioritization of order and meaning over discrete components remain for the next chapter.

Several results of the examination of Luther's thought to this point are significant for a theory of power. First, the doctrine of the two realms is not

---

[263] Luther, *Against the Antinomians,* 111 (WA 50:471). Rom 7:22 is also important (*Sermons on First Peter,* 70; WA 12:324); see also *Against the Heavenly Prophets,* 97 (WA 18:80).

[264] Luther, *Treatise on Good Works,* 63 (WA 6:236).

primarily a political theory, but the center of Luther's entire theology. Second, the two realms are distinguished by their tasks and significance. To the heavenly realm belong the things of eternal life, and to the earthly realm the gifts of God. The introduction of God's gifts means that Luther's theology is not exhausted by constant repetition of the doctrine of justification by grace, but rather that the notion of grace must be explicated in its direction to the earthly realm and the theology of gift, whereas the latter must be analyzed in terms of its relation to the heavenly realm. A theology of the world remains an important component of Luther's theological effort. The value of all earthly things is reconstituted under the impact of the Spirit. Third, correlative to the second point, what is external and bodily is not merely a disposable container for the internal and spiritual but is inextricably bound to the very meaning of the latter. Finally, the exposition of this chapter has implied, and sometimes stated, a particular view of power contained in Luther's theology. It remains to concentrate these occasional expressions into a single definition.

CHAPTER 4

POWER AND COMMUNICATION
OF EFFICACY

Considerable attention has been paid to Luther's self-interpretation of the turning point of his early years. In the 1545 foreword to his Latin works, he gives this account:

> At last, by the mercy of God, meditating day and night, I gave heed to the context of the words, namely, "in it the righteousness of God is revealed, as it is written, 'He who through faith is righteous shall live.'" There I began to understand that the righteousness of God is that by which the righteous lives by a gift of God, namely by faith. And this is the meaning: the righteousness of God is revealed by the gospel, namely the passive righteousness with which merciful God justifies us by faith, as it is written, "He who through faith is righteous shall live." Here I felt that I was altogether born again and had entered paradise itself through open gates. There a totally other face of the entire Scripture showed itself to me.[1]

The autobiographical features of this experience — whether Luther describes an actual, sudden experience, when it occurred if it did, whether its language belongs more to Luther's early theology or more to the time at which he recalls it, and so on[2] — are not our concern. What is significant, and less often discussed, is that Luther continues, "Thereupon I ran through the Scriptures from memory. I also found in other terms an analogy, as, the work of God, that

---

[1] Martin Luther, *Preface to the Complete Edition of Luther's Latin Writings,* in *Luther's Works,* vol. 34, *Career of the Reformer IV,* ed. Spitz, 337 (WA 54:186).

[2] H. Oberman expresses considerable doubt about the usefulness of a literalistic interpretation of the "tower experience" (*The Dawn of the Reformation: Essays in Late Medieval and Early Reformation Thought* [Edinburgh: T & T Clark, 1986], 109–12). G. Ebeling doubts the suddenness of it (*Luther: An Introduction to his Thought,* trans. R. A. Wilson [Philadelphia: Fortress Press, 1970], 41–42), and B. A. Gerrish notes the impact interpreters' theological decisions make on their dating of this experience as well as the variety of difficulties involved in attempting to discover its date (*The Old Protestantism and the New: Essays on the Reformation Heritage* [Chicago: University of Chicago Press, 1982], 70–89). F. E. Cranz argues that it is almost by definition a distortion to try to establish what Luther's earlier thought really was solely on the basis of this autobiographical statement (*An Essay on the Development of Luther's Thought on Justice, Law, and Society,* Harvard Theological Studies 19 [Cambridge, Mass.: Harvard University Press, 1959], 42–43).

is, what God does in us, the power of God, by which he makes us powerful (*potentes*), the wisdom of God, with which he makes us wise, the strength (*fortitudo*) of God, the salvation of God, the glory of God."[3]

Power as Communication of Efficacy

The power of God is the power of God because it is used for us. This is the basis of Luther's analogous claim that human power is truly power, rather than its destructive distortion, when it produces power for others. To speak of God's attributes and essence is not the principal task of theology. Indeed, if taken as the theologian's primary work, the result is disastrous, because God's essential righteousness, justice, and power are terrible and fearful. God becomes loving when these predicates are no longer staid attributes but transactive, living communications to creatures. The God who remains self-contained is the God of judgment, the God Luther feared and was driven to hate. Luther has a special distaste for speculation on God's nature because it can discover nothing but the terrible divine majesty.[4] Instead, theology must begin with Christ and the Word. Such are the ways God's will toward us becomes clear, and it is in this relational character of will rather than in a comparison of human and divine essences that salvation and life are possible.[5] Salvation is, after all, an act of God upon us. To understand it as one's attempt to rise up toward the essential God is the problem rather than the solution. Human efforts to reach up to God cannot succeed because we always stand in sin; such efforts lead to over-confidence and false self-righteousness or the despair of condemnation. In either case, the promises and activity of Christ, which refer principally to will and not nature, are ignored.[6]

---

[3] Luther, *Preface to Luther's Latin Writings,* 337 (translation modified; WA 54.186); see also *Letter to the Christians at Strassburg,* 70 (WA 15:396). Luther sees this newfound understanding as principally Hebraic rather than Latin. God's righteousness, for example, "in Latin means the righteousness that God possesses, but a Hebrew would understand it as the righteousness that we have from God and in the sight of God" (*Bondage of the Will,* 265; WA 18:769).

[4] Luther, *Bondage of the Will,* 138–47 (WA 18:684–90); *Lectures on Galatians, 1535, Chapters 1–4,* 28–30, 42 (WA 40[I]:75–80, 98–99). Good discussions of this are found in John Dillenberger, *God Hidden and Revealed: The Interpretation of Luther's deus absconditus and its Significance for Religious Thought* (Philadelphia: Muhlenberg Press, 1953); Ebeling, *Luther,* 226–41; and David C. Steinmetz, *Luther in Context* (Bloomington: Indiana University Press, 1986), 23–31.

[5] In addition to scattered references in the last two chapters, see esp. Martin Luther, *Lectures on Genesis, Chapters 1–5,* in *Luther's Works,* vol. 1, *Lectures on Genesis, Chapters 1–5,* trans. George V. Schick, ed. Jaroslav Pelikan (St. Louis: Concordia Publishing House, 1958), 11–18 (WA 42 Band [Weimar: Hermann Böhlaus Nachfolger, 1911], 9–15). Almost all the important elements of his argument on the speculations of reason over against the knowledge of theology are present.

[6] Alister E. McGrath, *Iustitia Dei: A History of the Christian Doctrine of Justification* (Cambridge: Cambridge University Press, 1986) 2:7–8.

The Word of God is God's self, for it is the life and activity of God,[7] and it both is and promises the power (*virtute*) of God.[8] The essential divinity of the Christ is important as a guarantee of the theoretical possibility of atonement, but it is Christ's self-emptying of the "form" of God that defines God's will. In Christ and Word lie the possibilities of eternal life, heavenly righteousness, and earthly righteousness, the latter of which involves the communication of these forms of "wisdom, power (*virtus*), righteousness, goodness — and freedom too" to us. And if Christ did not stockpile virtue, which cannot be self-possessed without ceasing to be virtue, neither should Christians "wish to be like God, sufficient in themselves,"[9] for this creates wisdom that is no longer wisdom, justice that is unjust, and power that is powerless. The aseity of God does not, in fact, describe God well at all, for it leaves out of account the divine will toward creatures. Even less can it describe the meaning of human life, for the striving toward self-sufficiency is mere presumption. God's Word, concentrated in the promises and activity of Christ for our benefit, is living because "it gives life to those who believe," and it is powerful (*efficax*) "because it makes those who believe able to do everything (*quia facit omnia posse eos*)."[10] The life and power of God are constituted in the benefits they provide the faithful, that is, the power of believers, which in turn emerges in the profit and power provided for the neighbor. Power of this kind can be described as a "communication of efficacy."

Many of the structural characteristics of this notion of power as communication of efficacy have appeared already. The concentration of the previous investigation into a single description of power means that a turning point has been reached. This pivot requires both a backward and a forward glance: backward in order to show that the exposition of Luther's conception of power analyzed up to now is distilled appropriately as communication of efficacy, and forward in order to take us beyond mere repetition of Luther. The latter is necessary not only in view of the distance that separates the twentieth from the sixteenth century, but also because Luther made no explicit effort to develop a theology of power. The significance of this point is that Luther's thought regarding power is neither complete nor altogether consistent. It is suggestive, providing basic clues and the central definition of power developed in the balance of the project.

The retrospective toward the elements of Luther's thought in the last two chapters can, in light of the new unifying principle of communication of efficacy, be supplemented with a discussion of a fundamental example of divine omnipotence, the creation. In the theology of creation more than at any other

---

[7] Luther, *Lectures on Hebrews*, 153 (WA 57 [III]:148).

[8] Luther, *Lectures on Deuteronomy*, 22 (WA 14:557).

[9] Luther, *Two Kinds of Righteousness*, 301 (WA 2:148); see also *Judgment on Monastic Vows*, 301 (WA 8:608).

[10] Luther, *Lectures on Hebrews*, 185 (WA 57[III]:185).

point in Christian thought, the absolute sovereignty of God is most apparent. At first glance, therefore, it appears to constitute a serious challenge to a theology of power that pretends to escape identifying power and sovereignty. On the other hand, if Luther's theology of creation, presented most extensively in his *Lectures on Genesis*,[11] conforms to the notion of power as communication of efficacy, and if his account of creation follows the structure of power posited in his broader theology, the previous presentation of his understanding of power receives a weighty confirmation. More important, an analysis of Luther's understanding of creation-power provides a more complete theological picture. The preceding two chapters concentrated on Luther's theology of power in relation to redemption and God's activity in the fallen world. To omit God's activity in creation would limit the persuasiveness of a theory of power for Christian theology.

Nowhere could an identification of power and sovereignty be so much in evidence in Christian theology as in the doctrine of creation *ex nihilo*. What is created is a sovereign and exclusive decision of divine will. In the originating moment of creation, however that is understood, power must be purely external, because there is no creaturely "inwardness" in existence, and it must be exclusive because there is no other power. This is significant not only for our examination of the relation between power and creation but also because it indicates how far from the usual political understanding of power Christian thought that takes the doctrine of creation out of nothing seriously should be. In political theory, the logical aim of power, identified with external sovereignty, is an ever-increasing domination over one's opponents. Possibilities of increase in one's own power depend on corresponding decreases in power for all other participants in the power game. The quest for power is finally a quest for omnipotence. The striving to acquire more power has its logical completion in one's becoming the only power.

Theology's appropriation of this equation between power and domination, which implies the zero-sum character of power, should be limited, but frequently is not, by the notion of creation out of nothing. If nothing is except God, then by definition God has all power by virtue of being the only power.

---

[11] The use of Luther's lectures on Genesis has been the subject of some debate. After all, they include some fairly un-Lutherlike material, such as proofs for the existence of God. But the questionable nature of some of the material does not justify dispensing with the lectures altogether. We have waited to employ them largely out of deference to the skeptics; however, the principal way in which they are used here is as a doctrinal supplement to and confirmation of an understanding and structure of power that appears throughout Luther's work. There is no reason to doubt their accuracy in these respects, since they apply to the doctrine of creation positions that are unquestionably Luther's. Defenses of the usefulness of these lectures are contained in Pelikan's preface to the American edition of the *Lectures*, and in Steinmetz, *Luther in Context*, 98–99. H. Oberman points out that neglect of these lectures both derives from and contributes to a one-sided emphasis on the young Luther (*Luther: Man Between God and the Devil*, trans. Eileen Walliser-Schwarzbart [New York: Doubleday, Image Books, 1989], 166–67).

The objective that power seeks, if it is pure domination, was already God's possession "prior" to creation. Mythologically speaking, God already had absolute power. Yet God creates something other than God, beings not identical with God. This is at the same time creation of power not identical with God, even if such power stands under God. This is the antithesis of what is expected if one begins with the usual political identification of power and domination.

Three possible conclusions are suggested on the basis of this opposition between the purpose of power in sovereignty theory and the action of God in creation. First, any claim that God is omnipotent, in light of God's creation of something other than God, is senseless. At best, one could say God was or is potentially omnipotent, all-controlling, or all-dominating, but engages in a kind of self-limitation of divine power.[12] Second, it could be suggested that power requires an other in order to be exercised, that is, in order to show itself powerfully. This is true, and the sense in which our theology of power takes this claim is explored later. But if this assumption is coupled with an equation of power and control/domination/sovereignty, a basic and irresolvable ontological conflict is created. On the one hand, power as domination requires an other in order to dominate it. On the other, it must seek the destruction of that other, since the other is always a threat to domination because it constitutes a nonidentical center of power which robs and decreases one's own power. Domination seeks to create puppets, but the puppet is never utterly controlled by the puppeteer. If it were, the other would cease to be an other, being either destroyed or completely identical with the dominator, the latter of which is impossible. The subsumption of power within domination is self-defeating and self-contradictory, for if it reaches its own inner objective, it eradicates its own power in eliminating the power of all others. Foucault noted this problem of sovereignty theory in political thought; Georg Simmel in sociology.[13] The common recourse to "balances of power" as what can save us from this dangerous state of affairs conceals a similar insight, though frequently unexpressed.[14] The assumption of the ubiquity of power leads to

---

[12] This is the position of Langdon Gilkey, *Reaping the Whirlwind: A Christian Interpretation of History* (New York: Seabury Press, 1976), 248–50. If power is not essentially domination, however, God's creation of free beings is not an act of self-limitation but an act of power.

[13] Georg Simmel, *Domination and Freedom,* in *The Sociology of Georg Simmel,* trans. and ed. Kurt H. Wolff (New York: Macmillan, The Free Press, 1978; reprinted in *Power,* ed. Steven Lukes [New York: New York University Press, 1986]), 203 (page references are to reprint edition).

[14] Jean-Jacques Rousseau is more explicit than most (*The Social Contract,* in *The Social Contract and Discourses,* trans. G. D. H. Cole, rev. J. H. Brumfitt and John C. Hall [London: J. M. Dent & Sons, 1973], 209). If the arithmetic input and output of power between the people and the sovereign is not absolutely identical, "the State is dissolved and falls into despotism or anarchy." This mathematical formula has been transmuted into notions of balances of power between branches of government. The critique of this approach by G. W. F. Hegel (*Elements of the Philosophy of Right,* trans. H. B. Nisbet, ed. Allen W. Wood [Cambridge: Cambridge University Press, 1991]) is perhaps more pertinent today than in Hegel's own time: "the principle of the division of powers" receives

a different conclusion, namely, that the complex of power and control is the basic conceptual identification that must be broken. Otherwise God must finally be conceived of as our greatest enemy, perpetrating a vicious and meaningless hoax. The self-contradiction of tyrannical domination is not merely ontic, but ontological.

The identity of power and domination is shattered in Luther's theology of creation. Creation is a fundamental example of divine omnipotence, to be sure, but as an example, it shows how far Luther is from equating power and exclusive dominion. Rather, Luther describes the creation of heaven and earth out of nothing, through the Word, and then adds:

> Over these the Holy Spirit broods. As a hen broods [over] her eggs, keeping them warm in order to hatch her chicks, and, as it were, to bring them to life through heat, so Scripture says that the Holy Spirit brooded, as it were, on the waters to bring to life those substances which were to be quickened and adorned. For it is the office of the holy Spirit to make alive.

Divine Spirit gives life and efficacy to what is created. God's omnipotence is defined by production of power that is not God, rather than by God's sovereignty. This is clear in Luther's claim that creation is accomplished through the Word. The notion of the "powerful Word (*potens verbum*)" arises at the moment of origin. To be sure, the Word can be conceived of as existing before all creatures, since it is the means of their creation, but only when the Word is spoken does it become a power-Word. Even in the moment "before" creation, the Word is omnipotent because it is "uttered in the divine essence. No one heard it spoken except God Himself, that is, God the Father, God the Son, and God the Holy Spirit. And when it was spoken, light was brought into existence, not out of the matter of the Word or from the nature of Him who spoke but out of the darkness itself." The Word is spoken rather than silent; omnipotence first appears when the Word is spoken between the persons of the Trinity. Simultaneous with the immanent speaking of the Word, creation begins. Here, the Word is the "omnipotent Word (*omnipotens Verbum*)" because it is the "spoken Word, by which some command and order is given," a command directed externally, outside the Trinity, to bring into being an other. The effect is that God communicates to creation the divine "power and office (*potestatem et officium communicat*),"[15] a power constituted in the Word of creation with a *telos* to creatures. God's sovereignty is a necessary precondition for divine omnipotence, but it is not sufficient. Power arises in the divine

---

"the false determination of the *absolute self-sufficiency* of each power in relation to the others, and . . . one-sidedly interprets the relation of these powers to one another as negative, as one of mutual *limitation*. In this view, the reaction of each power to the others is one of hostility and fear" (sec. 272). Who can fail to hear America in the 1990s in Hegel's words?

[15] Luther, *Lectures on Genesis, Chapters 1–5*, 9, 17, 19, 18–19, 12 (WA 42:8, 14, 15, 15, 10). Note again the close link between creativity and command.

communication of efficacy to creatures. What applies to the event of creation applies also to God's preservation of the world. All things are upheld and preserved by the Word of power (*verbo potentiae*). Word becomes omnipotent Word because it gives strength (*firmat*) to all creation.[16] All gifts of God are intended for the life and power of creation;[17] power itself has the character of a gift, a sharing of blessing.[18]

Two aspects of power appear in Luther's discussion of creation and preservation through the natural gifts of God. The first is God's sovereignty; the second is what has been called a communication of efficacy. Can one of these modes of power be said to be more fundamental than the other? The answer is affirmative, but two senses of fundamental priority must be distinguished. There is, first of all, for Luther, a temporal priority. It is obvious that the exercise of God's sovereignty is temporally prior because there is nothing else (although the notion of "temporality" is qualified because creation is concurrent with the speaking of the Word). But Luther's notion of power is inherently teleological; that is, power becomes power in reaching its end. The temporal or logical priority of one moment of power does not coincide with the fundamental meaning of power, which is its *telos*. God adorns creation with gifts and gives it life. It is the life-giving office of the Spirit which, through the Word and prior to the Fall, accounts even for creatures' natural efficacy. The whole created world was aimed at our benefit.[19] God's creative act is designed to profit creatures; the creation is "for us." The things of creation "were created not only so far as their substance and their masses are concerned, but also as far as their blessing, that is, their effects (*effectus*), power (*vim*), and force (*vires*) are concerned."[20] Power emerges not in substances but in blessings; it is a gift that produces efficacy.[21]

The gifts given in creation and those through which the world is preserved, however, lack spiritual efficacy, and the disobedience in the garden destroys

---

[16] Luther, *Lectures on Genesis, Chapters 1–5*, 21–35 (WA 42:17–26).

[17] See esp. Luther's interpretation of Genesis 1:10–11 (*Lectures on Genesis, Chapters 1–5*, 35–40; WA 42:32–30). The latter verse begins to make the transition from the natural gifts of God to the spiritual gifts, which become necessary after the Fall.

[18] Luther, *Treatise on Good Works*, 52 (WA 6:227–28).

[19] Again, Gen. 1:10–11 (*Lectures on Genesis, Chapters 1–5*, 35–40) makes this aim of profit and benefit especially clear.

[20] Luther, *Lectures on Genesis, Chapters 1–5*, 40 (translation modified; WA 42:30).

[21] Luther is in agreement with Augustine's response to the question "What was God doing before he made heaven and earth?" (Saint Augustine, *Confessions*, trans. R. S. Pine-Coffin, Penguin Classics [Harmondsworth, England: Penguin Books, 1961], 11.12, p. 262). For Augustine, as for Luther, this is a non-question. On the basis of this theology of power, it becomes clear why. The power of God simply does not exist prior to its instantiation, because power is teleological. In fact, Luther maintains that philosophy's failure is that, in contrast to theology, it cannot recognize the efficient or final cause of existence, that is, it concentrates only on the nature of things and not their origin or purpose (Luther, *Disputation Concerning Man*, 138; WA 39[I]:175).

spiritual power for Adam and Eve and subsequent generations. There are, therefore, instances of power that do not communicate efficacy.[22] The paradigmatic instances of power that remains pure domination are the power of the devil and divine power which damns. Satan's power does not communicate any ultimate efficacy to the world but is exactly utter domination that causes the condemnation, that is, the ultimate powerlessness of those bound by the devil.[23] The Fall removed spiritual efficacy from our nature. The condemning judgment of God simply allows this dominion of the devil to play itself out. There can be no question, however, that the devil's power is distorted, tyrannical power,[24] and Luther never tires of emphasizing that God's purpose for the world is salvific. Condemnation is an alien work of God, whereas salvation is God's proper work.[25] Power, properly so called, is a communication of efficacy. The "power" of pure domination—domination without an end beyond itself—is distorted, partial power because it contains only one of power's moments. The law, for example, outside grace and the gift is purely external, condemning power, which must be overcome by the power of God, the powers of grace and gift.

Though purely external domination is distorted power, it is still power. Luther's understanding of power is truly profound. What opposes the fulfilled power of communications of efficacy, that which is finally and ultimately powerless, is not the opposite of power in terms of its constitution. Pure domination, with its ontological self-contradiction, is not nonpower but distorted, tyrannical, devilish power. It is power that does not reach power's

---

[22] The daring argument in *Bondage of the Will,* 175–84 (WA 18:709–14) that God is responsible for the motion of the will in evil is an example of this. God cannot but move the will of all, for this perpetual activity in all things is part of the definition of God's omnipotence and part of the definition of life itself. The motion itself is good, but the perverse instruments, Satan and Satan's subjects, turn this in the direction of wickedness. The sovereignty of God is the condition for the activity of an evil will, even if God does not make the will itself evil. The *telos* of power fulfilled is severed from power, resulting in a distortion of power; God's action is upon the will, not in the will. Some form of Luther's position on the relation of God to evil is absolutely necessary if God's omnipotence is to be preserved, if a cosmic and existential dualism of good and evil is to be avoided, and if, therefore, God is not to be reduced to the cuddly, petlike God of much contemporary Christianity, which eliminates the ultimacy of God and God's claim to be called "God."

[23] Luther, *Bondage of the Will,* 64–70 (WA 18:634–39). Luther's view here cannot be confused with determinism. He is quite clear that he is speaking only of freedom's inability to reach eternal life. He is more than willing to grant freedom of choice as far as action is concerned, but he will not grant that we are capable of investing these actions with salvific meaning.

[24] See, e.g., Luther, *Lectures on Galatians, 1535, Chapters 1–4,* 40 (WA 40[I]:94).

[25] Double predestination appears to present a serious difficulty for this thesis, particularly since it is necessary to Luther's theology. Double predestination is the inevitable result of Luther's claim that faith is a gift of God alone and not a human achievement. To anticipate the discussion in the final chapter, predestination's significance changes dramatically if it is recognized that the doctrine emerges from within the context of faith. The difficulties arise when it is viewed from outside that complex.

intrinsic aim of communicating efficacy and thereby becomes a perversion of power because it takes a moment of power, the moment of sovereignty and dominion, as the aim of power. Put another way, it is the use of what is potentially powerful, what might communicate efficacy, "not for building up — which is why God gave it . . . — but for destroying."[26] Domination is a moment of power as communication of efficacy, in fact the necessary original moment of it, but not the end of power.[27] The difference between power and its distortion lies less in their substance than in *telos* and use.

Spiritual powerlessness is to stand under the sovereignty of the devil, who seeks not to communicate efficacy but to dominate and bind for destruction. God's righteousness and power, which make the elect righteous and powerful, intervene to rescue from the devil's perverse power. It should come as no surprise that God's justification of the elect often comes clothed in the language of "new creation."[28] It is no accident that the metaphor of the hen and its chicks, applied to the Holy Spirit in creation, is applied to the security of faith in the recovery of righteousness after the fall. The "power to become children of God" (John 1:12), the transformation of the old person, is "power (*potestate*) divinely bestowed (*donata*) on us."[29] Again, the whole of this second creation is underlain by the exclusive sovereignty of God, visible in the distinction between the two realms and their operation. The ground of the new creation is found in the atoning work and merit of Christ,[30] while its possibility for any given person is determined by God's decree of election. Both are external to their recipient. Grace is the exclusive decision of God and has a direct effect only in and for a heavenly life that is not yet ours except in hope and faith. It does not have a direct effect on the actual being of the believer. Domination and sovereignty are the initial moment of power.

But the power of the one atoning sacrifice in the past and the divine decision of election do have their end in the actual earthly life of the believer. To

[26] Martin Luther, *That Parents Should Neither Compel nor Hinder the Marriage of their Children, and that Children Should Not Become Engaged without their Parents' Consent,* in *Luther's Works,* vol. 45, *The Christian in Society II,* ed. Brandt, 386 (WA 15:164). The English uses "authority," the German *gewallt.* Notice that this conception of power distinguishes power from potentiality as much as from actual domination.

[27] This relation between fulfilled power and mere domination precludes any simple transvaluation of power. Despite Luther's occasional lapses into such a transvaluation, the structure of power in his thought leaves little room for it. In fact, those elements that seem closest to "power is weakness," for example, that the Christian must be the servant of all, conform to the notion of power as communication of efficacy formally, for the purpose of these injunctions is to benefit the neighbor, and this requires a measure of sovereignty and control exactly in service. Luther's use of the Pauline formula sometimes conceals the difference between his thought and a more strictly transvaluing use of the same biblical language.

[28] See, among many examples, Luther, *Lectures on Hebrews,* 195 (WA 57 [III]:194); *Two Kinds of Righteousness,* 299–300 (WA 2:146–47); *Against Latomus,* 233 (WA 8:110).

[29] Luther, *Bondage of the Will,* 157 (WA 18:697).

[30] Luther, *Freedom of a Christian,* 347 (WA 7:51).

suggest otherwise would fall into the error of thinking of "both God and the devil as a long way off, and as if they were only observers,"[31] as if God were watching "from a distance." The difference between the ungodly and the godly lies largely in the process of power; for the former, God's sovereignty is mere external domination, whereas in the latter, sovereignty contacts the inwardness of the new creation:

> For what we assert and contend for is this, that when God operates without regard to the grace of the Spirit, he works all in all, even in the ungodly, inasmuch as he alone moves, actuates, and carries along by the motion of his omnipotence all things, even as he alone created them, and this motion creatures can neither avoid nor alter, but they necessarily follow and obey it, each according to his capacity as given it by God; and thus all things, even including the ungodly, cooperate with God. Then, when he acts by the Spirit of grace in those whom he has justified, that is, in his Kingdom, he actuates and moves them in a similar way, and they, inasmuch as they are his new creation, follow and cooperate, or rather, as Paul says, they are led.[32]

Without knowledge of one's own inclusion in Christ's promise of salvation, the promise itself is rendered powerless, despite its substantial character as promise remaining the same. Word, faith, and sacrament are necessary to assure us of our place in this promise. Moreover, the publication of the decree of election in the Word and through the Spirit's gifts shows that the heavenly decree has its end in the communication of efficacy to the believer's real, earthly life, "the start of a new creature [accompanying] faith and the battle against the sin of the flesh, which this same faith in Christ both pardons and conquers."[33] Luther does not consider the possibility that God would make a secret, hidden decision. The absolute sovereignty of the divine will with respect to eternal life is, in fact, the condition for earthly power. Without the sovereign moment, eternal life is not at the sole discretion of God, which implies that one's conduct on earth has some role in its attainment, and this is a recipe for destruction. It destroys persons because it holds them between the talons of self-righteousness and despair, and it destroys relations with others because the other becomes merely a means to one's own salvation, not another who must be respected and recognized in her or his own right. From the point of view of the external, heavenly realm, the aim of power is to communicate efficacy to the world and is the condition of power in the world. Power is a transmission; use has been elevated over substance to such a degree that it is possible to say that the "substance" of power is constituted only in its use. The new creation is a bringing forth in power.[34]

---

[31] Luther, *Bondage of the Will*, 237 (WA 18:750).
[32] Ibid., 242 (WA 18:753).
[33] Luther, *Disputation Concerning Justification*, 153 (WA 39[I]:83).
[34] Luther, *Bondage of the Will*, 243 (WA 18:754).

Grace drives toward the reconstitution of the world. It is communicated externally by the Word's promise and inwardly through the Spirit's gifts. The *telos* of external sovereignty is inward power, in the same way that, while the externalities of Word and element are required for sacramental power, the Supper produces no power unless it meets faith inwardly. What remains external is not power but mere domination. The gifts of God must originate externally, but their power appears in their efficacy for the earthly life of the believer. This is why the substance of all external gifts of God may be good, but their power or powerlessness depends on what they confront inwardly. If flesh is confronted, all is for damnation and domination. If the Spirit is met, God's external gifts, including the law, are once again made spiritual. Considering only the receiver of grace and gift, the gifts of God are given in order to drive out or imprison the substance of sin more and more, in short, to dominate sin and render it powerless, in anticipation of its complete eradication on the last day. As the power of heaven in grace has its *telos* in the giftful reconstitution of actual existence, so the gifts of God are efficacious because they are aware of the gracious promise of final purification.

If this transcendent *telos* of God's gifts is not kept in constant view, so that there is a life of faith (faith being the mediation between the two realms) as distinct from a static possession of faith, the result is the antinomian distortion of power, which understands the powers of faith and grace as things to be had and held, without external aim. Conversely, the legalist error derived from a self-conscious attempt to strengthen one's own faith and Spirit, the neighbor being made simply a conduit by which this work could be effected. Luther, on the contrary, holds that the attempt to possess faith proves that there is no faith but only a fleshly notion of faith. His understanding of the undistorted power of the gifts of God, as distinct from the person who has been given them, involves a necessary teleology toward the other. The inward gifts of Spirit are not self-sufficient. If they were, power would be a possession, exactly the opposite of divine power. Rather, sanctification is an indirect effect of the outward view and external end of faith. The conquest of Spirit over flesh inwardly depends on faith having external objects in view; vertically, its object is Christ, and it acts for the praise and thanksgiving of God, whereas horizontally, its object is the neighbor, for whom it acts in love. The inward conquest of sin is possible only through power being directed outwardly. *Power has a direction that is always elsewhere; its external moment is directed inwardly, its inner moments are directed externally. Power arises in the movement itself.* Power understood as purely inward or purely external is distorted power, derived from true power but amputating its teleological character. The constitution of power in the Lord's Supper is a typical example. The power present through the external element and Word in the Supper becomes power when it is transmitted to the inwardness of believers for their profit, which, in its turn, becomes power for the first time in efficacy for the neighbor. Divine power is truly power when it is "for us," and human power is truly power when it is "for you." Power is defined by its communication of efficacy.

The use of Luther's thought to establish a definition of power as the communication of efficacy is inadequate, both to Luther's theory of political power and to the range of a theology of power that hopes to establish power's ubiquity. Whether the conception of power as communication of efficacy is compatible with Luther's political theology and whether it is of any value to the more general realm of political thought about power remain to be seen. For now it is sufficient that the content of power has been delineated in a preliminary fashion. But the description of the incessant movement of power, from externality to inwardness, repeatedly back and forth, reintroduces the question of power's geography that was uncovered at the close of the previous chapter.

The Locus of Power

The problem of describing power's geography did not seem much of a problem initially, but Luther's persistent movements between the inward and outward regions became increasingly puzzling as the presentation went along. The efficacy of the Spirit, which appeared initially to be inward, nevertheless had an outward direction and was subject to external, public criteria of validity. Moreover, the law, which seemed to be the exemplar of all that was external, entered the human heart in the notion of natural law. The neat categorization of phenomena in terms of inwardness and externality broke down progressively. For a theology of power, and especially one that opposes the confinement of power to an external prison, this apparent disintegration raises a question of the locale of power. Can we speak meaningfully of inner or outer power, of both, or of neither? Of course, the mere fact that the site of power's appearance is unclear does not of itself demand further investigation of the matter. However, the geography of power bears directly on the possibility of conceiving of power as communication of efficacy.

Potentiality, Actuality, and Power

At least since Aristotle, Western discussions of power have been conducted almost universally in the language of potentiality and actuality. Aristotle employs both categories. In the *Metaphysics,* power is potentiality, whereas in the *Politics,* power is both potentiality and external actuality, actually possessed as potentially usable and exercised by the powerful out of their storehouse of potentiality.[35] The question of forms of government is a question of who

---

[35] Aristotle, *The Metaphysics, Books I–IX,* in *Aristotle,* vol. 17, *The Metaphysics, Books I–IX,* trans.

dominates the *polis*. Twentieth-century thought, despite considerable concern with developing new understandings of power, has not overcome these alternatives. On the one hand, the conception of power through a language of actuality is endorsed by influential thinkers such as Robert Dahl, who substitutes "control" of others' behavior for "power" without hesitation.[36] Steven Lukes, whose principal polemical target is Dahl, and despite his attempt to be "radical," is in agreement with Dahl's subsumption of power within the category of actuality: power is the actuality of effect of agent upon patient, contrary to the interests of the patient.[37] It is coercion, domination, and nothing more, as it is also for C. Wright Mills and Marilyn French.[38] Likewise, Bertrand Russell defines power as "the production of intended effects."[39]

Yet, if power is "getting what one wants,"[40] the question arises as to the prior resources possessed by one who is actually powerful, and this emphasis has accounted for the description of power in the language of potentiality. This alternative is defended by Max Weber, who frames much of the modern debate about power ("'Power' [*Macht*] is the probability that one actor within a social relationship will be in a position to carry out his own will despite resistance," or "the possibility of imposing one's own will upon the behavior of other persons"), Talcott Parsons (the "core" meaning of power refers to "the capacity of persons or collectivities 'to get things done' effectively, in particular when their goals are obstructed by some kind of human resistance or opposition"), the Aristotelian Hannah Arendt, the Marxist Nicos Poulantzas (power is "*the capacity of a social class to realize its specific objective interests*"), and the feminist Mary Daly ("active potency is the ability to effect change. It is power"), to name a few.[41] The result of tying the cart of power to the horses of potentiality

---

Hugh Tredennick, Loeb Classical Library (Cambridge, Mass.: Harvard University Press; London: William Heinemann, 1980), 428–73; idem, *The Metaphysics, Books X–XIV,* in *Aristotle,* vol. 18, *The Metaphysics, Books X–XIV, Oeconomica, Magna Moralia,* trans. Hugh Tredennick, Loeb Classical Library (Cambridge, Mass.: Harvard University Press; London: William Heinemann, 1977), 2–51; idem, *Politics,* in *Aristotle,* vol. 21, *Politics,* trans. H. Rackham, Loeb Classical Library (Cambridge, Mass.: Harvard University Press; London: William Heinemann, 1977).

[36] David L. Sills, ed., *International Encyclopedia of the Social Sciences,* vol. 12 (n.p.: Crowell Collier and Macmillan, 1968), s.v. "Power," by Robert Dahl (reprinted in *Power,* ed. Steven Lukes [New York: New York University Press, 1986]), 37–58 (page references are to reprint edition).

[37] Steven Lukes, *Power: A Radical View* (London: Macmillan, 1974), 34.

[38] C. Wright Mills, "The Structure of Power in American Society," in *Power, Politics, and People: The Collected Essays of C. Wright Mills,* ed. Irving Louis Horowitz (London: Oxford University Press, 1963), 23–38; Marilyn French, *Beyond Power: On Women, Men, and Morals* (New York: Ballantine Books, 1985), 18.

[39] Bertrand Russell, *Power: A New Social Analysis* (London: George Allen & Unwin, 1938), 35.

[40] Alvin I. Goldman, "Towards a Theory of Social Power," *Philosophical Studies* 23, no. 4 (1972) (reprinted in *Power,* ed. Lukes, 157 [page references are to reprint edition]).

[41] Max Weber, *Economy and Society: An Outline of Interpretive Sociology,* 2 vols., ed. Guenther Roth and Claus Wittich (Berkeley: University of California Press, 1978) 1:53, 2:942. It is interesting, and unique, that for Weber domination, as a subspecies of power, is also conceived through potentiality. This accounts in large part for his fascinating and multilayered conception of authority;

and actuality is to make power into a quantity that can be had and possessed, either as potentiality, actuality, or both. Even a more dialectical definition of power, such as Tillich's, is subject to the same tendency, as we will see.

To treat power as potentiality or actuality involves several difficulties. First, power is contained within a being or group of beings designated as "powerful." One being has more or less power than another, and a comparison of quantities of power compares the power of independent entities. Second, the categories of potentiality and actuality do not divide cleanly. One slips into the other. Potentiality, for example, is actual, perhaps below the level of expression, but actual nonetheless. This is why Aristotle is unable to hold consistently that power is pure potentiality with no admixture of actuality. Weber too feels compelled to add to the notion of power as possibility a proviso that "power of command does not exist unless the authority that is claimed by somebody is actually heeded to a socially relevant degree."[42] Perhaps the clearest expression of the alternating register of potentiality and actuality is Talcott Parsons's analogy between power as political resource and money as an economic one. It is true that money is the potential for economic effect, but money is also actual and palpable prior to its use. Money, as a possession of the wealthy, in the same way that power is a possession of the powerful, is both actual and potential in different respects. In all these cases, potential power comes to depend on its expression as actuality, precisely because it was always unexpressed actuality.[43]

More important than this conceptual morass, attempts to understand power as potentiality are fundamentally ahistorical. Nothing that appears can be really new, because everything can be referred back to some latent potentiality. The "new" is really just the old come out of hiding. In part, precisely these difficulties have been used in support of the identification of power and actual domination, although the restriction of power to actuality can only be maintained by an almost willful blindness to the conditions for domination

Talcott Parsons, "On the Concept of Political Power," *Proceedings of the American Philosophical Society* 107, no. 3 (June 1963): 94; Hannah Arendt, *The Human Condition* (Chicago: University of Chicago Press, 1958), 199–212; Nicos Poulantzas, *Political Power and Social Classes,* trans. and ed. Timothy O'Hagan (London: New Left Books; London: Sheed & Ward, 1973; reprinted in *Power,* ed. Lukes, 144 [page references are to reprint edition]); Mary Daly, *Pure Lust* (Boston: Beacon Press, 1984), 166. See also Letty M. Russell, *Household of Freedom: Authority in Feminist Theology* (Philadelphia: Westminster Press, 1987), 23; and Anthony Giddens, *A Contemporary Critique of Historical Materialism,* vol. 1, *Power, Property and the State* (Berkeley: University of California Press, 1981), 51.

[42] Weber, *Economy and Society* 2:948.

[43] A similar equivocation is evident in Louis Marin, *Food for Thought,* trans. Mette Hjort, Parallax Re-visions of Culture and Society (Baltimore: Johns Hopkins Press, 1989). Marin begins by defining power as "first and foremost a matter of being in a position to exert an action on something or someone; it does not necessarily reside in the performance of an action" (p. xvii). That is, power is first of all potentiality. Throughout the remainder of the book, however, Marin speaks of power as subjugating, annihilating force which serves only to effect one desire over another, competing desire.

which are "potential" prior to their use in the external controlling act.[44] In fact, most conceptions of power, no matter how rigorously they try to contain themselves within either power as potentiality or power as actuality, eventually require recourse to the other of these two notions.

These two points have an important implication for definitions of power based in potentiality and actuality. The exercise of power rather easily comes to be understood as external and sovereign, particularly when power is understood, as eventually it must be, as actuality. Power's exercise can be seen as a struggle of one intensity of power against another. The pure externality of the effects of power means that power can be, in its full sense, without having a *telos* beyond that externality. Alternatively, the end of external power can be viewed as an increase of individual power, which is to be held and stored as potential for use when necessary. Notions of "struggle" for control and "balances of power" to prevent domination are not far behind these conceptions.[45] In these formulas, moreover, are frequently contained ethical abhorrence

---

[44] The attempt not to be blinded in this way causes Lukes (*Power: A Radical View*, 43–44) to introduce the concept of "reputation for power," and Dahl to distinguish between "having and exercising" power, both of which introduce potentiality. In order to understand these concepts as actual power, however, Lukes and Dahl are compelled to contradict both the structure and the direction of power's exercise that they defended until then. Part of the problem, though by no means all of it, is that both authors refuse to consider the possibility of an exercise of power except by one party in a relationship, a conception refuted by Foucault. The remaining difficulty is the restriction of the analytic of power to actuality and potentiality.

[45] This is the major point of disagreement with Anna Case-Winters, *God's Power: Traditional Understandings and Contemporary Challenges* (Louisville, Ky.: Westminster/John Knox Press, 1990). Case-Winters understands God's omnipotence as "the capacity to be influenced by *all* and to influence *all*" (p. 211). God's power, she argues, must be limited at least by the freedom and power of creatures: "Power of influence is always power within limits" (p. 209). Thus, the framework of balances of power is retained because power is a possession and not a communication. A fear of power remains, despite Case-Winters's intention to overcome it—at all costs, power must not be unlimited. This anxiety about power remains precisely because power is confined to a framework of potentiality and actuality (p. 211).

Moreover, Case Winters's introduction of divine power as all-inclusive, unsurpassable, and the product of the subjective intentionality of God (all intended to preserve the divinity of God) appears to include serious conceptual difficulties. This difference between "influence" and "control" at their limits seems very slight indeed. If one has an unsurpassable influence, one approaches "control" asymptotically, and if one *intends* unsurpassable influence, the way to achieve such influence is by attempts to eliminate all competing influences—the result is control or eradication of the other. Case-Winters's attempt to establish a "metaphysical limit" on God's power by the fact of the existence of creatures is thus another statement of the ontological self-contradiction of domination. But if God "has" unsurpassable power, God is the ontological contradiction, since God's creation frustrates the very intention of divine power to become truly unsurpassable. When influence is confronted by opposing influence and if one influence seeks to become unsurpassable, it must seek to become determinative. Power understood as communication of efficacy, on the other hand, allows omnipotence to take a stronger form, that is, God is all power, but avoids the necessity of balances of power and the eventual impossibility of such balances when the power of a single God is introduced. God does not have power; rather, God is power. The significance of the question of power's geography cannot be overestimated.

of power. If power is a possession that dominates those without it when it becomes actual, there is little room to dispute the contention that "power is inimical to every form of freedom" or that freedom itself depends on a precarious, because intrinsically self-destructive, balance of power.[46]

There is a third point. Defining power as either potentiality or actuality, or as a dialectic between the two, ignores one of the most important characteristics of power. Power is power precisely in its exercise; it is dynamic in nature. A definition of power as potentiality, however, leaves open the possibility that power could remain forever latent, an unused capacity. Similarly, power defined as actuality is often qualified by the "exercise" of a power, which presumably was already possessed potentially. The addition of "exercise" to "power" is superfluous; "exercise of power" conceals an implicit assumption that power can be without being exercised. Few, if any, thinkers really believe that a power can be had which is not exercised, and this is why "power" is so often placed in phrases like "exercise of power" or "actualization of power." Power is fundamentally act, an exercise in and of itself. Only a definition of power in which something is seriously amiss need supplement "power" with "act." An adequate theory of power should at least include activity within the very definition of power, and this suggests that it should avoid "potentiality" and "actuality," not entirely but as constitutive of power.

Apart from Tillich, whose thought is examined later, the most persuasive contemporary interpreter of power who still takes potentiality and actuality as central to the notion of power is Hannah Arendt. Arendt is thus a challenge to the thesis that potentiality and actuality must be overcome in the construction of a better understanding of power. Following Aristotle's *Metaphysics,* she conceives of power as potentiality. For Arendt, however, potentiality is not an inner property, but the potentiality of the "space of appearance": "power is what keeps the public realm, the potential space of appearance between acting and speaking men, in existence."[47] Power is a condition for the public, external realm, but is not synonymous with domination because power cannot be actual.

The cost of this approach is to eliminate the possible ubiquity of power in order to save its productivity. Power is reduced to an ontic and occasional phenomenon because, in principle, power can not be. In the course of history, power has not been in fact, particularly in tyrannical governments. Arendt explains:

> But while violence can destroy power, it can never become a substitute for it. From this results the by no means infrequent political combination of

[46] Werner Kaegi, "Freedom and Power in History," in *The Responsibility of Power: Historical Essays in Honor of Hajo Holborn,* trans. Flora Kimmich, ed. Leonard Krieger and Fritz Stern (Garden City, N.Y.: Doubleday & Co., 1967), 224, 227.

[47] Arendt, *Human Condition,* 200.

force and powerlessness, an array of impotent forces that spend themselves, often spectacularly and vehemently but in utter futility, leaving behind neither monuments nor stories, hardly enough memory to enter into history at all. In historical experience and traditional theory, this combination, even if it is not recognized as such, is known as tyranny, and the time-honored fear of this form of government is not exclusively inspired by its cruelty, which — as the long series of benevolent tyrants and enlightened despots attests — is not among its inevitable features, but by the impotence and futility to which it condemns the rulers as well as the ruled.[48]

One thing power is not is necessary and unavoidable.

Power is restricted to ontic status on another ground as well; it is prohibited from any connection with inwardness. This challenges one of our basic tenets, namely, that it is possible to avoid equating power and domination if a connection between power and inwardness is posited. Arendt's argument is directed less against a notion of inward power than against the possibility of individual power. For our purposes, however, this makes little difference, because any association of power with inwardness assumes the legitimacy of a connection between power and individuality. The attribution of power to individuals, according to Arendt, misrepresents the nature of power. If power is viewed as the possession of an individual, confusion between "power" and "violence" or "force" ensues quickly.[49] In other words, individuation of the notion of power is responsible in large part for the conceptual identity of power and domination. Too easily, notions of personal power translate into images of political domination, raising the possibility of human omnipotence in the sense of exclusive possession of power.[50] For Arendt, *"Power* corresponds to the human ability not just to act but to act in concert. Power is never the property of an individual; it belongs to a group and remains in existence only so long as the group keeps together."[51] What can be possessed by an individual is strength and not power.[52] When ordinary language speaks of "a 'powerful man' or a 'powerful personality,' we already use the word 'power' metaphorically; what we refer to without metaphor is 'strength.'"[53] The division is a sharp one and corresponds to Arendt's equally sharp distinctions between public and private, individual and social.[54]

A first answer to this challenge must be to restate the definition of power as the communication of efficacy. If power is defined in this way, does it not retain a relation both to the inward qualities that give one "strength," as well as to the external realms of force and violence? The notion of power as

[48] Ibid., 202.

[49] See Arendt, *Human Condition,* 200–207; idem, *On Violence* (New York: Harcourt, Brace & World, 1970), 43–56.

[50] Arendt, *Human Condition,* 201.

[51] Arendt, *On Violence,* 44.

[52] Ibid.; idem, *Human Condition,* 199–207.

[53] Arendt, *On Violence,* 44.

[54] See esp. Arendt, *Human Condition,* 199–207.

communication of efficacy, in other words, connects the variety of ontic realms Arendt specifies as that through which those realities have their existence and can be related to each other.

Just this issue of the possible relation of strength, power, force, and violence constitutes the basis of a second answer to Arendt's position. The impermeable boundary between public and private, which issues in the erection of a similar wall between strength and power, is not satisfying. Arendt is unable to explain why the strong individual so frequently seizes or is entrusted with authority and the task of representing the power of the political body. In fact, she assumes just the opposite. The strength of the individual is overcome by the power of the group, which resists individual strength. In fact, the group seeks to "ruin strength"; this is the "nature of a group."[55] It is true that power (in Arendt's sense) has sometimes destroyed strength, but to assert this to be always the case, and to claim further that this demolition of individual strength is inherent in the notion of a group, goes too far. If strength can take or be given power, as it certainly has done, then it must be possible to posit a relationship between the two. Such a connection between individual strength and group power is precluded by Arendt's view that the two are contradictory. If, on the other hand, strength and power are related historically and therefore must be related conceptually also, the ground for excluding power from any relationship to the individual as individual is eliminated.

To endorse an association between power and inwardness does not, however, indicate the nature of that relation. If Arendt's total exclusion of a connection of power and individuality is unsatisfactory, the concern from which her argument arises remains important. She is correct that an equation of strength and power tends in the direction of a final identification of power and domination, for it implies that power can be stored and that its nature is to be possessed. If that is so, it is possible for power not to be communicated, and its inner aim is the possession of absolute, exclusive power, expressed politically in tyranny. All limits to an individual's power and strength, the plurality of the other, must be overcome. That the *telos* of power is destruction of plurality is, for Arendt, unacceptable and inaccurate as a description of the human and social world; earlier, we expressed the conviction that, for Christian theology, it is an equally unacceptable account of divine omnipotence.[56]

Our thesis is this: Power is a communication of efficacy that occurs at the borders of inwardness and externality. If this claim is made plausible, power retains a connection to both the inner and outer, but could not be spoken of as being located either "inside" or "outside" a being or group of beings. Instead,

---

[55] Arendt, *On Violence*, 44.

[56] See Arendt, *Human Condition*, 201–2. It is interesting to say the least that the model of exclusive power as a description of divine omnipotence is retained by Arendt, while she simultaneously struggles against this very notion as an accurate account of power in the world.

if something or someone is said to "have" power, this is not a literal reference. Power is an occurrence, an event, between inwardness and externality or, speaking metaphorically, at their border or at the border of any encounter of efficacy. In this way, it is possible to avoid the difficulties of a concept of power that vacillates between potentiality and actuality while at the same time maintaining power's ubiquity.

Moreover, the conception of power as communication of efficacy at the border of encounter allows us to overcome the pure formalism into which the identification of power with potentiality or actuality usually leads. Power as communication of efficacy contains both formal and material elements. Its formal characteristics consist principally in the notion of communication and its location as a border event. But unlike the pure formality of potentiality and actuality, as well as Foucault's notion of power as "unformed" in the sense of being a relatively random link between contents, the material *telos* of power restricts the range of the formal by saying that the formal character of power is not equally directed to any content but only toward content efficacious for its intended object. To make these conclusions hold good requires a more extensive examination of the problem of power's locale.

The Geography of Power in Luther

The interpretation of Luther up to this point shows that communication of efficacy is the central concept of power in his theology. There are also indications that power is situated at the border of the inner and outer. It is not that Luther actually makes this claim. Indeed, his failure to clarify the locale of power creates some confusion in his thought.

There are two hints of this border character of power worth noting.[57] The first returns us to Luther's theology of the Lord's Supper. Twice during his career, Luther dealt with the question of how the body of Christ could be present in the Supper. The basic answer he gives is that the power of God guarantees the possibility of Christ's presence. In response to how this power operates, however, Luther refuses to answer. From 1520 on, he rejects

---

[57] Ernst Troeltsch notes the fundamental abandonment of the categories of potentiality and actuality in Luther's understanding of grace, which operates so that "the idea of evolution has disappeared in its Catholic form of an ascent from Nature to Grace, which Catholicism had combined with the Aristotelian doctrine of the steady process of the development of latent potentialities into actualities, or of the whole process of Nature as a struggle toward perfection" (*The Social Teaching of the Christian Churches,* trans. Olive Wyon [London: George Allen & Unwin; New York: Macmillan, 1931; reprint, Chicago: University of Chicago Press, 1981] 2:475 [page reference to reprint edition]). It is too much to say, as Troeltsch does, that Luther leaves "no room" for evolutionary processes, however. Sanctification, for example, is precisely evolutionary, though underlain and completed by the revolutionary moment of heavenly justification. The categories of potentiality and actuality are not abandoned utterly by Luther, as we will see.

transubstantiation as an explanation of the process of God's power.[58] He provides no alternative, even when the radical reformers criticize him persistently for failing to specify the mechanism through which Christ's body and blood are present. He is willing to remain ignorant concerning this question.[59] It is, he says, of no importance how the body and blood of Christ are in the Supper.[60] It is enough to say that the presence of Christ is possible.[61]

Is Luther's failure to explain the mechanics of his interpretation of the Eucharist fatal to its persuasiveness? He does not think so. The presence of Christ is assured because God's Word affirms it. Any effort to go beyond the confirmation of the Word is merely an investigation of reason. It is not that appeal to reason is strictly forbidden by Luther; rather, one is forbidden to consult reason first, for this makes reason a "judge over God."[62] Scripture is the limit of reason, and intellect and reason must be held captive by Christ and the Word if one is to avoid heresy.[63] On the question of the mechanics of presence, failure to maintain the proper relation between faith and reason led to two errors. The first was Rome's doctrine of transubstantiation, which is both unnecessary (after all, the incarnation required no such transubstantiation) and a source of embarrassment to Christian doctrine in that it is asserts

---

[58] For a fuller discussion of the issues involved in the question of transubstantiation, see Alexander Barclay, *The Protestant Doctrine of the Lord's Supper: A Study of the Eucharistic Teaching of Luther, Zwingli, and Calvin* [Glasgow: Jackson, Wilie & Co., 1927), 29–31.

[59] See, e.g., Luther, *Babylonian Captivity*, 33 (WA 6:510); *Against the Heavenly Prophets*, 176, 210 (WA 18:166, 199); *Marburg Colloquy and Marburg Articles*, 16, 60. Luther claims disinterest also in the question of the mechanics of, for example, the doctrines of the Trinity and the humanity of Christ (*Bondage of the Will*, 28; WA 18:608–9).

[60] Luther, *Adoration of the Sacrament*, 297 (WA 11:449–50); *Marburg Colloquy and Marburg Articles*, 45. A good discussion of this issue is in Hermann Sasse, *This Is My Body: Luther's Contention for the Real Presence in the Sacrament of the Altar* (Minneapolis: Augsburg Publishing House, 1959), 99–106, 160–64.

[61] Luther does on occasion attempt to make the co-presence of the body of Christ and the material of bread and wine plausible through a metallurgic analogy. As fire and iron are two distinct substances but are copresent to each other in heated iron, so the body of Christ can be present in the bread (*Babylonian Captivity*, 32 [WA 6:510]; *Against the Heavenly Prophets*, 196 [WA 18:186]). Lest this be taken as a physical explanation, however, Luther quickly adds that we do not understand how this natural process occurs. His point is that it is inconsistent to so easily tolerate natural things we do not comprehend and yet be unwilling to accept the incomprehensible operations of God for our salvation.

[62] Luther, *Brief Confession Concerning the Holy Sacrament*, 306 (WA 54:157); see also Jaroslav Pelikan, *Luther the Expositor: Introduction to the Reformer's Exegetical Writings*, Luther's Works Companion Volume (St. Louis: Concordia Publishing House, 1959), 140–41.

[63] Sacramental memorialists, defenders of works righteousness, Arians, and other heretics all are led astray by allowing reason to reign in theology (*Against the Heavenly Prophets*, 80–81, 100, 197; WA 18:63, 83, 186–87). This is one of the reasons Scripture must provide its own rules for interpretation (*Against the Heavenly Prophets*, 153; WA 18:143). On the need for reason to be captive to Christ and Word, see *Lectures on Hebrews*, 29 (WA 57[III]:234); *Babylonian Captivity*, 34 (WA 6:511); *Confession Concerning Christ's Supper*, 296 (WA 26:439); *Commentary on 1 Corinthians 15*, 63–74 (WA 36:486–98).

what is visibly not true, that is, that the substance of bread and wine is supplanted and no longer remains in the Eucharist.[64] Transubstantiation is not the most malicious error. Once again the radicals earn this distinction, for they use reason to deny the presence of Christ in the Supper altogether, simply because they cannot account for its mechanics. The means of Christ's presence, however, is something we are not meant to know, and there is hazard in inquiring of such things.[65] When reason's inability to explain becomes grounds for overturning the Word of God, surely reason is the "devil's prostitute."[66] There is no need to account for the "how" of Christ's presence. There is only a need to believe it.

The accuracy of Luther's opinion regarding reason's means of financial support does not concern us. What is of interest is the effect of his refusal to debate the mechanics of sacramental power on his theology of power. Its unintended result is an abandonment of the categories of potentiality and actuality. Power does not reside in the sacramental material as a capacity that awaits a particular operation in order to become actual, as it seemed to in transubstantiation. Nor is it subject to natural mechanical chains of cause and effect, as the radicals demanded. Instead, power instantiates itself as a leap beyond all such preparations. Power is transcendent in relation to explanatory physical mechanics; it cannot be confined by them, as if it did not create them and could not escape them.

The leap of power occurs at the borders of inner and outer, but is contained in neither. Power is not a thing that can be had separately from its use: "By the omnipotence of God, however, I do not mean the potentiality by which he could do many things which he does not, but the active power by which he potently works all in all, which is the sense in which Scripture calls him omnipotent."[67] Similarly the elements of the sacraments, their "nature," is not a guarantee of power, but only a prelude to an appearance of power which remains in suspense until the sacrament touches faith inwardly. In the preceding chapter, the teleological character of power in Luther was noted in some detail. What first seemed inward became power in its external use, and what first appeared external acquired its power by its *telos* toward inwardness.

Of course, this teleological notion of power could be interpreted dialectically, as a power first existing externally and then internally, or vice versa, but as truly power prior to its teleological fulfillment. In fact, Luther hesitates at just this point of decision between a dialectical concept of power and power that appears at the border of encounter. An ambivalence develops in Luther's

---

[64] Luther, *Babylonian Captivity,* 29–35 (WA 6:508–12); *This Is My Body,* 64 (WA 23:145); *Private Mass and the Consecration of Priests,* 158 (WA 38:205–6).

[65] Luther, *This Is My Body,* 29 (WA 23:87); *Confession Concerning Christ's Supper,* 194 (WA 26:297–98).

[66] Luther, *Against the Heavenly Prophets,* 175 (WA 18:164).

[67] Luther, *Bondage of the Will,* 189 (WA 18:718).

theology; it can be seen clearly in his two formulations of the location of faith.[68] Luther oscillates between two treatments of the power of faith that are not altogether consistent. On the one hand, he produces a dialectical formulation of faith's power that understands it as centered in the inner life of the believer first, reaching out into the world only subsequently. At its root, this centered version of faith depends on the categories of potentiality and actuality. Especially under the pressure of the supposedly antinomian consequences of this first conception, Luther superimposes a second understanding of faith over it. There power is localized, or perhaps de-localized, at the border of inwardness and externality without being centered in either. The power of faith is constituted in this uncentered boundary. The two explanations of faith's power occur frequently in close proximity to each other, an indication that Luther did not sense the tension between them.

The first exposition of the relationship of inwardness and externality in regard to the power of faith is metaphorical. Consonant with certain passages of Scripture and parts of the Christian tradition, Luther argues that the tree of faith produces its fruit in good works.[69] The tree of faith, it would seem, could exist without the fruit. This metaphor leaves open the possibility that a real power of faith could be present that has the potency, although not the achievement, of good works. A tree can have potentiality for fruit without actually producing it. What is inwardly real and powerful could simply not yet have made its appearance outwardly. The teleological movement of power would, on this reading, not be complete but would be a possibility held in abeyance.

Luther's second account of faith removes this possibility. He vehemently denies that one can have faith without outward marks. Faith is not a matter of inwardness, and those who assert that they have faith in this way, without any outward alteration, are deceived. They do not have the faith they claim. Luther distinguishes between "true" and "false" faith on public criteria of works, and especially of doctrine. Faith not manifest is simply not faith. Purely inner faith is not a tree with unrealized potential for bearing fruit; it is not even a dying tree; it is not a tree of faith at all. An especially clear example of this

[68] It is not, however, restricted to faith. The same indecision is present in Luther's discussions of power more generally. There are times when God's power, for example, does seem to predate its use, in contrast to the exposition of Luther's understanding of creation, grace, and gift developed in the previous two chapters. Luther wavers between an understanding of power as communication of efficacy, and one still indebted primarily to potentiality and actuality. Obviously, we have followed the first line more than the second, but the latter train of thought is still present (see, e.g., *Bondage of the Will*, 191; WA 18:719).

[69] The examples are legion. A few are *Treatise on Good Works*, 113 (WA 6:275); *Freedom of a Christian*, 361 (WA 7:61–62); *Sermon on Colossians 3*, 76 (WA 17[II]:110); *Disputation Concerning Justification*, 161 (WA 39[I]:91–92); *Disputation on "The Word was Made Flesh,"* 250 (WA 39[II]:16–17). Holl understands Luther's thought almost entirely in terms of this metaphor (*The Reconstruction of Morality*, trans. Fred W. Meuser and Walter R. Wietzke, ed. James Luther Adams and Walter F. Bense [Minneapolis: Augsburg Publishing House, 1979], 83–84).

cancellation of the metaphor of the tree even during its employment is found
in *The Disputation Concerning Justification:*

> Works save outwardly, that is, they show evidence that we are righteous
> and that there is faith in a man which saves inwardly, as Paul says, "Man
> believes with his heart and so is justified, and he confesses with his lips and
> so is saved" [Rom. 10:10]. Outward salvation shows faith to be present, just
> as fruit shows a tree to be good.

Fruit shows the *goodness* of a tree, but while there can be a "bad" tree, it is
impossible for faith to be not good. Indeed, it is impossible for faith to be
inactive, and this means that "faith which lacks fruit is not an efficacious but
a feigned faith."[70] The goodness of the tree is transposed to the efficacy and
even the *presence* of faith, because God does not give inactive or impotent gifts
and because (as we saw in Luther's disputes with legalists and antinomians
alike) "it belongs to the nature of faith to exist outside of itself since faith overcomes the sinful tendency of the self to serve only itself."[71] But presence applies
to existence and is presupposed in any evaluation of its worth. In the absence
of fruit, there is no tree. The criterion of publicity employed in his dispute
with Karlstadt returns with a vengeance in the notion of true and false faith,
a notion that damages the integrity of the more usual language of the tree
and its fruit.

Luther seems never to feel the partial incompatibility of his two renderings of faith. Their frequent proximity to each other in his writing is not
approached as a problem requiring resolution.[72] The indications of the border
character of power in general, and the power of faith in particular, remain only
indications. They are not Luther's solution to the question of power's geography; for him, no question exists. To the extent that there is a solution in
Luther, he probably more often employs the language of tree and fruit than
true and false faith.[73] If, however, the placement of power within the categories

[70] Luther, *Disputation on Justification,* 165, 176 (WA 39[I]:96, 106); see also ibid., 183 (WA
39[I]:114).

[71] Donald C. Ziemke, *Love for the Neighbor in Luther's Theology: The Development of His Thought,
1512–1529* (Minneapolis: Augsburg Publishing House, 1963), 61.

[72] For the nearly simultaneous use of both accounts, see, e.g., Luther, *Against Latomus,* 230,
233 (WA 8:108, 109); *Sermons on First Peter,* 34 (WA 12:289–90); *The Epistle of the Third Sunday
in Lent: Ephesians 5,* in *The Sermons of Martin Luther,* vol. 7, *Sermons on Epistle Texts for Epiphany,
Easter, and Pentecost,* ed. Lenker, 157–59 (WA 17:210–12).

[73] The issue hinges, of course, on the distinction between "essence" and "manifestation." Luther
rarely discusses this principally philosophical problem but has a suggestive treatment of it in
his 1525 Lenten Postil, *The Epistle of Palm Sunday: Philippians 2,* in *The Sermons of Martin Luther,*
vol. 7, *Sermons on Epistle Texts for Epiphany, Easter, and Pentecost,* ed. Lenker, 171–72 (WA
17[II]):239–40). The treble possibilities of relating essence and manifestation allow one to understand both modes of the relation of faith and works discussed here, as well as the false mode
of relating the two to which Luther thought his opponents succumbed, for it is a "trick of the
devil," and apparently one of the devil's favorites, to give a "manifestation of divinity without
the essence." In general, this sermon is interesting and unique; Luther employs a variety of new
formulations of common issues in his thought.

of potentiality and actuality makes problematic an account of power as communication of efficacy by recovering the possibility of viewing power as a
stored possession that can be turned into a domination of pure strength, then
it is worthwhile to follow to its conclusion the alternative that power posits
itself at the border of encounter. We shall explore its implications through
the theologies of Luther and Tillich.

In Luther's work, what effect does the specification and partial cancellation of the metaphor of the tree and its fruit by means of the distinction between
true and false faith have for his view of power? Faith, while clearly relevant
to inner life, does not reside there. Nor is faith external to the believer. Instead,
faith's power instantiates itself between the inner and the outer and reverberates
toward each of these realms. There is no such thing as faith that can be held
and possessed; it is re-created in greater or lesser intensity at each moment
of life at the border of inwardness and externality. Faith cannot be stored; its
power cannot be held in reserve but is inherently active. Luther's insistence
on the incessant activity of faith is why faith and love, and faith and doctrine
even more, cannot be divided into independent entities, despite the opening
for just such a division provided in the metaphor of tree and fruit. Power is
created at a place that cannot be found or even defined except metaphorically,
at the intersection of inwardness and externality. It is visible at just the point
it vanishes instantly. In reality, the *telos* of power is not from inwardness to
externality or vice versa, but is a communication of efficacy from the border,
where it appears and vanishes, into the inward and external. The border
character of power is an additional reason to emphasize the definition of power
as a "communication," a term that stresses the in-between nature of power.
If it is still possible to speak of something "having" or "losing" power,
"increasing" or "decreasing" its power, this is not a literal reference, but an
assumption about that being's continuity in reception and communication
of efficacy.

Faith has been taken as a paradigmatic example of the instantiation of
power at the borders. The notion can be applied more broadly. It is evidently
applicable whenever faith is associated with a phenomenon, as in the sacrament. The efficacy of the body and blood of Christ depends on their presence
to faith. The communication of efficacy that occurs in the sacrament does not
occur only outwardly, independent of faith. Nor does it occur inwardly, since
this is not the residence of faith. Sacramental power, too, appears at the
borders — at the border between the sacramental elements and faith and, because
of the requirement of faith, at the border of the inner and outer. However
much Luther speaks of efficacy communicated inwardly to the heart, there
is not even a possibility of efficacy except on the twin prior conditions of the
public Word and the body and blood of Christ, on one side, and the heart's
external directedness to God and neighbor, on the other. As communication
of efficacy, in opposition to the distortions of power deriving from just such
efforts to hold faith inwardly, inwardness is not only hemmed in but does not

exist as power until it meets the external at the border of the two. What is external, for its part, has no power unless it meets inwardness at the same place. The sovereign decision of grace, for example, becomes truly powerful because the "inward" gifts of God are given at the same time. Heavenly justification is not an end in itself, but the condition for fulfilled spiritual life. It finds its end only where it is copresent with the spiritual gifts of God. In creation, God becomes omnipotent in the act itself. Power posits itself in creation, at the moment when it produces the new and a border upon which it can articulate itself. Power is posited in a leap.

The locale of power has been expressed as a phenomenon of the borders. Power is not a quantifiable capacity or possession of the powerful. Instead, it is more properly described as a leap for which all preparatory capacities are inadequate, a leap that cannot be predicted but only accomplished above and beyond any preparations. The self-positing of power at the borders of encounter evades the difficulties of defining power in the categories of potentiality and actuality.[74] Power can now be defined as the communication of efficacy which posits itself at the borders, at the borders between beings or between inwardness and externality, having a *telos* to everything that is articulated on the border.[75]

The metaphor of the border, which includes a *telos* toward what is articulated on it, has an advantage in addition to avoiding the difficulties of the categories of potentiality and actuality. It is a spatial concept that incorporates a temporal dimension because of its teleological nature. The border is a permeable one, a place that moves into metaphors of time. Power retains its spatial relation, as Foucault argues it must, but it also allows for change and the appearance of the new because history penetrates space and moves

[74] It is fascinating that Aristotle, despite the momentous significance of his conception of power through potentiality and actuality, is driven finally to a conclusion very close to the self-positing of power. When power is defined as potentiality in the *Metaphysics,* Aristotle finds himself in a serious difficulty. If power is purely potential, it can never "exist" in any sense. In book 10, he attempts to escape this problem by claiming, in a flat contradiction to book 9, that actual existence includes a process. Aristotle soon backs away from this assertion and substitutes the claim that the complete reality of potential existence is motion, not as itself but as movable. This maneuver has the effect, however, of collapsing any distinction between potentiality and actuality by mixing the two into something like an actual potentiality or a potential actuality.

Power is thus brought closer to being defined as the motion that creates this hybrid. Motion is defined as the complete reality of potential as potential, since actuality must remain a substance without potentiality. But then Aristotle reverses this definition of motion and asserts that motion *results from* the complete reality of the potential. What initially was identical with the complete reality of the potential (motion) now is the result of that reality. What else does this mean but that motion creates motion? Motion posits itself and is identical with the complete reality of the potential, which must also produce itself as a leap.

[75] Metaphors other than "border" could be used to express the same point. One could call power a phenomenon of an intersection, a point, or a plane. The latter two are particularly helpful because they, like a border, are spatial without having any definable spatial characteristics. The point and plane are spaces of appearance that vanish as soon as they appear.

between spaces. Power's self-positing at the borders includes a movement char-acteristic of time. Thus, it breaks the stranglehold of space, which saturates Foucault's historical investigations. His analyses of power were ultimately ahistorical, because they created enclosed, self-contained spaces that were analyzed as separated wholes. The notion of the permeable border, however, suggests that power is less within these spaces than between them. Foucault's reliance on hardened spatial categories is overcome, and a history of change once again becomes possible because change and the new can appear at the borders of his periodizations.

Political Power

The basic definition of power as a communication of efficacy developed outside the arena of political theory. It cannot be established adequately, however, without returning to politics. One of our objectives is to emphasize power's ubiquity. If power is omnipresent, it must also be present in politics. In addition, "power" is used most often in reference to politics; an effort to reconstruct the notion of power which does not take account of its most com-mon application is doomed to irrelevance.

Since the definition of power has been gleaned from Luther, to his political thought we must return. Luther's political theory takes shape within the con-text of a fallen world. It is important to remember, however, that the power of God's natural gifts remains even in this world. Earth is provided with means of sustenance and renewal. What is lost in the Fall is freedom of the will. Will is now bound by the devil. The Fall destroyed human spiritual power. The duality of power in the fallen world is this: natural power remains; spiritual power does not. Even natural power has been distorted through the original sin of Adam and Eve. The devil's corruption of the will has the effect of sub-jecting the good natural gifts of God to distorted spirit. This explains why, in the condemned, even natural gifts work only to damnation. They are good gifts in themselves but sustain and are subjected to spiritual bankruptcy. Natural power increases and supports the ultimate spiritual powerlessness of the unbeliever.

Luther's political theory is inserted into this complex of natural power and spiritual powerlessness. Because justice and peace remain worthy goals for the earthly realm, God instituted worldly government for their increase and preservation. Government's power is contained in the offices God in-stituted; it becomes the possession of those who occupy those offices and is theirs alone for as long as they are responsible for the functions for which their offices were created. Government exercises sovereign, exclusive, dominating power. The tools of its power are prohibition and coercive en-forcement. Luther's defense of the wisdom of God's establishment of worldly government is framed in predominantly negative language. Government is a worldly device to preserve an order that would be shattered were the sinful inclinations of human beings given free rein, a means necessary to preserve order, to prevent sin, injustice, and strife from making the world its carnival.

Such a theory of government does not of itself justify Luther's demand of obedience. The basic warrant for the demand of obedience is that the New Testament commands it. The distinctiveness of New Testament commands compared to Old Testament law is that the commands of the former have no need of any justification apart from the fact that they are present in the canonical New Testament. For Luther, they are legitimate commands regardless of their apparent propriety, for they are God's will. Still, Luther assumes that these commands are instituted for the good of the world. Therefore, he avails himself of the opportunity to justify their importance for the world's well-being, even though he says he need not do so because the will of God is sufficient reason to obey. The second, dependent justification for the New Testament commands is a worldly one. Luther is excessively frightened of anarchy; resistance has the fiendish desire for anarchy at its root, and the fact of anarchy is its being and result. Any unordained resistance to authority is a joyous occasion to the devil, who would love nothing more than the unrestricted play of sin throughout the world, untrammeled by any government. Even if earthly government is manifestly unjust, obedience is still demanded, provided it does not pretend to compel the conscience. Obedience, despite its costs, is tolerable because government neither seeks nor has the ability to extend its effects to the inwardness of the believer. Furthermore, it is advantageous because Christian law is the law of suffering.

Luther's definition of power, which we termed "communication of efficacy," emerged from his theology of the two realms. The doctrine of the two realms is not exclusively, or even primarily, a political theology. Eliminating Luther's political thought by disposing of the doctrine of the two realms eradicates at the same time Luther's theology as a whole and his concept of power. We are permitted, though, to inquire into his political doctrine from the standpoint of Luther's own broader theology of the two realms, and we are free to criticize it from beyond Luther's theology.

This question can be put to Luther: What is the propriety of the assertion that worldly authority has only a negative function? Luther's own answer has been given. Government is only an external force without relation to the inwardness of its subjects. It has the negative function of controlling outer evils, but because it is irrelevant to the inner human subject, it is not productive of anything positive. This establishes a radical disjunction between politics and other instances of worldly power. In the case of gifts of God, given out of sovereign power, external origin did not prevent inward effect. Indeed, their purpose was to effect inward change, to communicate efficacy to the receiver. It was quite clear, in addition, that there could be no inward effect without an external, bodily component. Against Karlstadt, Luther argued that the Spirit could not pierce the heart purely inwardly. Against the radical sacramentarians,

Luther's position was that spiritual eating, far from excluding bodily eating or making it irrelevant, required a bodily, external eating. Yet Luther holds that government is incapable of penetrating into the heart because of its externality to the human subject.

There is only one other category of gifts for which the same incapacity is assumed, namely, natural and common gifts of God, which have power only relative to the outer person. Surely it is implausible, though, to liken government to bread and water to this degree. This is especially true for Luther.[76] Government involves the human spirit in ways nature does not.[77] First, the devil seems to have very little interest in nature; Satan is interested primarily in maintaining the corruption of the heart and destroying human society by fomenting anarchy. The perversion of nature is primarily an aftershock of warped hearts and corrupt communities. In addition, the exercise of government becomes a spiritual task for Luther at several points. Luther will not concede that Christians should not hold political office because politics is merely a worldly affair, but he claims that it is the responsibility of a called Christian to exercise the duties of public office. Moreover, while the true Christian officeholder who, in faith, upholds justice and peace is on the way to salvation, the official who acts only for self-benefit, destroying justice and peace, is on the way to perdition. The same connection to eternal destiny is present for the obedient subject and the rebel. It is not that one's activity as an official or a subject causes one's salvation or damnation, but spirit, either God's or the devil's, is involved in acts of government in a way that it is not in nature.

If the identification of ordinances of government with gifts of nature is implausible so far as their relation to spirit is concerned, if government involves the spirit, can the purely negative task of governmental sovereignty be defended? Earlier we discovered two teleologies of the spiritual, each of which depended on a particular vantage point. From the perspective of the external, sovereign moment of power, Spirit had an inward *telos*, whereas from the viewpoint of inwardness, the Spirit's *telos* was outward and public. Luther maintains the second of these viewpoints in his reflections on government. He is able thereby to judge good and evil rulers with considerable felicity. But the first perspective, which understands sovereign power as aiming at the heart, is abandoned. The efficacy of government, even though governing is an exercise of spirit, stops at the wall of inwardness. Luther has, in the case of his political theory and only there, locked the heart against the spirit.

The iron curtain that descends between the inward and the external in Luther's political theology is at variance with his broader theology of power.

---

[76] It is true for him in his broader theological project; however, he does think of the ordinance of government as quite close to the natural gifts of God (*Psalm 101*, 193; WA 51:238).

[77] Whether it is possible to maintain a strict dichotomy between the inward and outward even in the case of nature is an open question in light of Luther's emphasis on the bodily, external conditions for the reception of the Spirit.

Far from constituting the theory of the two realms, Luther's political theology in fact tends to contradict it. Here and only here is sovereign power divorced from inwardness; however, it is surely unjust to Luther simply to dismiss his argument without further ado. Luther's division of worldly and spiritual status is designed in large part to make God accessible irrespective of worldly status and to prevent a close association between honor of position and spiritual worth.[78] In the first case, Luther's theological decoupling provides the theoretical center of the doctrine of the priesthood of all believers. In the second, it refuses to respect (or disdain) any person solely on the basis of worldly status. If one wants to open the possibility that government and the external things of the world provide a condition for or an impact on spirit, there is a danger of losing the advantages of the distinction between externality and spirit in Luther's political theology. To all appearances, Luther is right that nobility of spirit is possible and sometimes emerges only under conditions of terrible oppression. He is also correct that every external condition, whether relative comfort or suffering, houses both the magnanimous and the petty.[79] Few external gifts of God cannot be turned to good use, and none can be put to only good use. So far as Luther's argument concludes that external conditions do not and cannot determine the condition of the spirit, there can be little argument with him.[80] Empirical conditions are transcended by the spirit of the person they touch.

Luther says more than this, however. In his political thought, he denies not only the determination of spirit by external conditions but also any influence of the latter on the former. These are different conclusions, and agreement with the first does not necessitate assent to the second. Even if no external occasion determines the spirit, every one has the capacity to influence it, and there is no reason to rule out a priori the possibility that some external conditions and events may be more conducive to spiritual health than others. Indeed, in view of Luther's understanding of the relation between the external world and spirit everywhere except in his political theology, there is reason to suspect such external influence upon inwardness even if one is confined to his thought. If Luther's politics are made to comport with the theology of the two realms and the concept of power that has been developed within it, an influence of earthly authorities on human inwardness should be conceded. At the very least, its possibility must be admitted. For a theology of

---

[78] This is especially clear in his 1531 interpretation of Galatians 2:6 (*Lectures on Galatians, 1535, Chapters 1–4*, 94–100; WA 40[I]:172–82).

[79] Examples of these points are so legion that one need only pay attention to the surrounding world. Two books that speak to this eloquently, but also accomplish much more, are the deeply moving narratives of Langdon Gilkey, *Shantung Compound: The Story of Men and Women Under Pressure* (New York: Harper & Row, 1966); and J. Glenn Gray, *The Warriors: Reflections on Men in Battle* (New York: Harper & Row, Perennial Library, 1970).

[80] This, incidentally, is one of the central implications of Luther's doctrine of double predestination.

power, this has the result that political power can be defined in its pure and ideal sense as the communication of efficacy, along the same lines as power in general, and that the possibility of positive functions of government has been opened. Political power is judged by the same standard as all power. It is one of the many settings of power, subject to the same criteria that apply to power as a whole.

For Luther, too, political power was not identical or determinative of his complete understanding of power. He was able to describe markedly different phenomena as "power" in part because whatever conflict his political concept of power might have with that of other areas of his theology, he understood rule as a segment of power. This should not have allowed him to subsume antagonistic concepts under the general rubric of power, of course, but the opposition between his theories of power is partly lessened by his restriction of spiritual power to that which is connected with and commanded by the Word, of which the New Testament is the determining standard. This is important with respect to his injunction against resistance. Few people whose lungs have been filled with the air of Western-style democracy since birth would support Luther's position with his tenacity. Moreover, it is either ignorant or hypocritical to demand absolute obedience to political authority if one lives in a nation constituted by revolt against rulers. But these reservations change neither the premises of Luther's argument nor their value. If the doctrine of the two realms is theologically fruitful, then in the case of Luther's demand of obedience, we must answer this question: Is the requirement of obedience inseparably linked to the theory of the two realms which produced the definition of power? There is a more specific question to which that can be reduced: Does the theology of the two realms inevitably commit one to Luther's conception of the law? Our answer is that it does not. It is possible to recast the notion of "law" while still maintaining the distinctions of the two realms, justification and sanctification, grace and gift, gospel and law. These basic categories can be accepted without committing one irrevocably to every detail of their execution, particularly when this execution stands in tension with the broader theory.

In order to reformulate the concept of law, a methodological alteration is required. "Law" is clearly an ethical notion in Luther. In the case of the laws of the New Testament, with which we are concerned here, the law's validity is guaranteed simply by the presence of the command in the canonical document.[81] At best, this is a highly questionable ethical framework for our time. We cannot be as convinced as Luther was that Paul's mind is the mind of God in every detail, that Scripture agrees in all of its parts, and so on.[82] More

---

[81] It is not important for us that Luther has his own canon, which tends to exclude, for example, James.

[82] For Luther's position on the intrinsic clarity of Scripture, see *Bondage of the Will*, 89–102 (WA 18:652–61). For Luther, Scripture must be clear or there can be no way to test the accuracy

fundamentally, it is impossible to maintain that the Spirit of God is attached only to Scripture. Tillich's ontological method provides a persuasive alternative to Luther's procedure and will be adopted, in large part, as a basis for understanding the notion of "law." It is unnecessary to embark on a defensc of its validity now. The next two chapters are concerned principally with Tillich's thought, and evidence for the persuasiveness of taking this ontological turn will have to emerge there. Granting for now that ontological reflection is fruitful for understanding power, this much can be said. For ontology, Luther's reading of the command of Romans and First Peter can only be termed "heteronomous," an attempt to disregard or even oppose the structures of being in its ethics. Any "law" must accord with the broader structures of being.[83] Indeed, we accept even Tillich's stronger claim that ethics must be grounded ontologically in order to be more than arbitrary opinion.

If this is so, Luther's assertions with respect to obedience can be evaluated. If law must affirm being, there is no presumptive or necessary validity to a command simply because it is found in the New Testament. Rather, ethics must develop autonomously, given direction by the impact of the Spiritual Presence, in a movement Tillich calls "theonomy," a term "used for the state of culture under the impact of the Spiritual Presence. The *nomos* (law) effective in it is the directedness of the self-creation of life under the dimension of the Spirit toward the ultimate in being and meaning."[84] An evaluation of the validity of Luther's injunction against resistance undergoes a criteriological alteration: it is now subject to the demands of theonomous meaning.[85] Theonomous ethics are based in an expectation and promise of ultimate meaning and include a demand that is relative to the current historical situation.[86]

In the question of resistance, no universal answer concerning its legitimacy is defensible. Rather, the concrete, particular danger of, for example, anarchy must be judged opposite the destruction of meaning accomplished by governmental injustice. One could formulate an opinion of the usual balance of these dangers, but one could not, as Luther does, claim that this balance would hold for all time. The criterion of validity for Luther's position shifts from necessary

---

of doctrine publicly; this would lead to the spiritualist interpretation of Scripture. The "Spirit" must be tested by both inward and external criteria. The difficulty lies not in Luther's demand for a dual test but in his restriction of the external test to Scripture. Luther's response is that only Scripture can make us certain, that is, all human doctrine is uncertain. The resolution of this complex of issues, therefore returns one to a decision about whether Luther's "doctrinaire tendency," discussed briefly in chapter 3, is justified or not.

[83] The necessity of "law" is emphasized also by Tillich: "Freedom and subjection to valid norms are one and the same thing" (*Systematic Theology* [Chicago: University of Chicago Press, 1963] 3:28).

[84] Ibid., 249.

[85] In a sense Tillich opts for the "natural law" side of Luther's ethics if it conflicts with the "scriptural command" side, provided that "natural law" and ontology are not understood as static and unchanging.

[86] This is treated more fully in the following chapters.

affirmation of words of the New Testament to a concrete evaluation of his arguments regarding the immanence and danger of anarchy.[87]

Luther's political theory is criticized on two grounds. The first is internal to the structure of his thought. From that critique, we concluded that the effects of government cannot be restricted to what is external but have an impact on inner life as well, since their external conduct may also be spiritual. The second criticism arises external to Luther's thought. We appropriate from Tillich a method that subjects ethics to a criterion of fulfillment of being and meaning. It is equally important to emphasize what escaped criticism. The distinction between the heavenly and earthly realms is left intact;[88] the critique

---

[87] Luther's position, from this perspective, retains considerable merit. He is frightened by the anarchic character of resistance, for when once the dam of obedience is broken, where does the bloodshed stop? We have witnessed enough revolution to understand the pertinence of Luther's pragmatic judgment, "It is easy to start a fight, but we cannot stop the fighting whenever we want to" (*Admonition to Peace,* 42; WA 18:332). It is, indeed, difficult to imagine a more disastrous situation than one in which everyone is her or his own judge. But we have also seen enough state-sponsored violence to know that if government, the "legitimate authority," is given free rein, the effects of anarchy do not disappear, even if their form is more tyrannical than anarchic. Moreover, we know well that Luther's judgment that the firebreak between isolated acts of disobedience to the sovereign and the complete destruction of worldly order is exceedingly small, and the descent from one to the other exceedingly fast, is an exaggeration that has led to the most brutal repression of difference.

[88] "Intact" if one does not transmute Luther's distinction between the heavenly and earthly realms into the difference between the "churchly" and "cultural." The focus of the doctrine of the two realms is the former, and not two authorities or governments in the earthly realm, church and culture, as Walter Altmann interprets it ("Interpreting the Doctrine of the Two Kingdoms: God's Kingship in the Church and in Politics," *Word and World* 7, no. 1 [Winter 1987]: 43–58). Despite the somewhat more nuanced view of the church in *Luther and Liberation* (pp. x, 69–83), Altmann continues to understand the two realms as primarily a question of the relation of state and church. Heinrich Bornkamm also tends to reduce the relationship between "the kingdom of Christ and the kingdom of the world" to the question of world and gospel (which is also present in the earthly realm) (*Luther's Doctrine of the Two Kingdoms in the Context of his Theology,* trans. Karl H. Hertz, Social Ethics Series 14 [Philadelphia: Fortress Press, Facet Books, 1966], 16). The differentiation of earthly and heavenly may influence decisions about the responsibilities of earthly institutions, but this is not a division of two realms but a distinction of institution, authority, government, and action within the same (earthly) realm. See Steinmetz, *Luther in Context,* 115, for a similar distinction. A superb exposition of the doctrine of the two realms, as distinct from a differentiation of "church" and "state," and its implications for understanding the life of the Christian, is given in Ebeling, *Luther,* 175–209.

To make church and culture the subject of the two realms trivializes Luther's arguments with respect both to the two realms and to ecclesiology. The church stands in the same ambiguous position as the Christian: that is, it participates in both the heavenly and earthly realms. The most that can be said of the "church" is that it is a medium between the two realms, since it functions to transmit the Word, which is the publication of God's grace to the world. Even this, however, does not necessarily apply to a sociologically designated "church" (or else it would have applied to Rome, the church that Luther believed was wholly worldly, and one would be forced to deny that the sociological organization of church is composed of nothing but sinners); instead, "church" is constituted when and where the Word is proclaimed, as Troeltsch points out (*Social Teaching of the Christian Churches* 2:479–80). There is an analogy between these distinctions and "Spirit"

centered only on certain details of Luther's execution of this distinction. Moreover, the definition of power drawn from the exposition of the theology of the two realms remains. Power is still the communication of efficacy, but now this positive view of power is applicable to government.

Although the explication of a concrete political ethic is well beyond our scope, it is important to show the direction the definition of power takes with regard to politics. Power, including governmental power, is not, at bottom, an exercise of domination but a communication of efficacy. Pure domination, for governments also, distorts power because it eliminates the *telos* that is part of the very constitution of power. Sovereignty, which appears as a moment in any presence of power, is not power's end. If the definition of power that has been developed extrapolitically applies to politics, government is liberated from its purely negative tasks of control and domination. It is freed to be judged positively, in terms of the criterion of its communication of efficacy to those upon whom it exercises sovereignty. The same standard applies equally to action which resists government.

Presence and the Body

There is a final issue to introduce before this chapter can be concluded. Two other criteria of power advocated by Foucault were persuasive. Power occurs only when "powers" are present to one another, and this presence must include a bodily element. Luther agrees on both points. The relation of power and presence in Luther's thought has already been explored. The thesis of bodily presence, which qualifies the relation between presence and power, presents a more difficult problem. It reaches its apex in the dispute over ubiquity and Christ's presence in the Lord's Supper. Luther's refusal to specify how this bodily presence is possible makes his doctrine appear tenuous. In the present, it is safe to say that Luther's assertion of real, bodily presence has a standing somewhere between the implausible and the absurd. Not only to us does it appear that way. It seemed nonsensical to the radical reformers as well.

---

and "world." What is "worldly" does not designate a specific location or thing but rather that whatever is under consideration has not been captured by the Spirit.

Moreover, the fundamental presupposition that allows even limited privilege to the church (which is not a simple opposition between the "kingdom of the world" and the "kingdom of God," as we have seen) is that the "revelation" of the Word the church communicates is essentially information. It is not, after all, any externally definable purity; that criterion was exactly what Luther opposed in radical ecclesiology. This notion of revelation as being informative is tied to the privilege of discursive understanding we found problematic in the previous chapter. If it is impossible to accept the latter notion, it is also difficult to accept the former. Although it is well outside the scope of this work to examine this issue in detail, the more productive path is to consider the relation of church to culture on a basis that does not equate revelation with information, as in Tillich's fascinating approach to revelation.

This problem of bodily presence will not be solved here. A successful resolution requires more competence and space than is available. This short-coming certainly limits the persuasiveness of the theology of power being offered, for if power is conceived as ubiquitous, and if it implies the copresence of bodies, at some point an account of how ubiquitous bodily presence can be understood must be rendered. However, the absence of a rigorous argument does not exclude an exposition of the problem's importance. Nor does it prevent an attempt to provide considerable plausibility to Luther's position.

Perhaps the most uncomplicated solution to the problem of the ubiquity of the body of Christ would have been for Luther to deploy the concept of the "spiritual body." Such an answer was available, but it would have brought him within arm's reach of the radicals. The language of "spiritual body" is indeed present in Luther's sacramental theology. However, there are several senses in which this term can be understood, and they must be distinguished. First, there is the basic assertion that Christ's flesh is spiritual, that is, it is born of the Spirit. In this sense, Christ's body is a "spiritual body." Luther's point of disagreement with the fanatics is about whether this spiritual body is also a natural body. For Luther, it is. Spiritual body is not intended as a juxtaposition between spiritual and natural, but between spirit and flesh. A spiritual body does not exclude, but rather requires, a natural body. A possible second sense of "spiritual body," which would posit an exclusivity of spiritual and natural, is rejected. Third, there is the spiritual body that is an effect of the sacrament, encompassing both the spiritual union of Christ with Christian and the communion of love between Christians. To the extent that the sacrament is a prefiguration, it prefigures these unions.[89] But such unities depend on the faithful reception of the Supper and cannot therefore encompass the body of Christ received by all in eating and drinking. This is a crucial bone of contention with the radicals, a bone already broken in effect when Luther removed faith from the sacrament. Luther, on the basis of 1 Cor. 11:27, holds that the reception of the elements of the Supper is common to the unworthy and the worthy, the faithful and the faithless. Common, bodily participation in the Eucharist was, it should be recalled, the ground of the sacrament's double efficacy. Luther's conclusion, in short, is that the ubiquitous body of Christ cannot be reduced to the presence of a spiritual body.

The natural body of Christ is present despite the fact that it is not present in a visible, earthly, or material way. To identify presence with visible presence alone is to say that something can only be present if it is locally present, and this makes a mathematical, "rational" understanding of presence lord over the ways of God.[90] Such a local presence would imply that Christ's flesh is torn to pieces and distributed in parts, corresponding to the pieces of bread; however,

[89] Luther, *Confession Concerning Christ's Supper*, 274–75 (WA 26:411).
[90] Ibid., 179–337 (WA 26:281–478).

Christ's body is not present in the sacrament in such a way, for all communicants receive the entire body of Christ in the Supper.[91]

Because the body of Christ is not present locally in the Supper or elsewhere, Luther is forced to hypothesize other modes of presence that are not local. In addition, he must perform this task while accepting that the nature of a body, and therefore of Christ's body also, is to be finite.[92] Luther argues for two other possible modes of presence in addition to locality. The first is "definitive" presence. There the form of space remains, but it does not enclose the object. Luther's several examples of such a presence include the being of angels and devils, and Christ's passage through the closed tomb. In addition to definitive presence there is "repletive" or supernatural presence. This is possible only for God, since it is a complete presence in all places. Because Christ is united with God in such a way that apart from Christ there is no God, Christ must be capable of being present in this way also. Repletive presence is, it is clear, the greatest presence, since it implies both ultimate transcendence and immanence.[93] The radicals did not object to the omnipresence of God, which Luther explains through repletive, supernatural presence. Nor, for that matter, was their complaint always directed at the presence of Christ in everything, with one important qualification. According to Hedio's report of Marburg, Oeclampadius was willing to admit Christ's presence in the bread according to the divine nature.[94] Luther, however, will not accept such a limitation. The natures of Christ are never present independent of each other; they are united in a single person, and this personal unity means that the natures are indivisible. Therefore, not only is the divinity of Christ omnipresent, but the humanity is also.[95]

It is never quite clear which of the two other modes of presence Luther believes Christ attains in order to be ubiquitous or present in the Eucharist. The protest against inquiry into the mechanics of presence leaves it an open question whether these presences are definitive, repletive, or both.[96] In any case, the argument between Luther and his opponents is whether the body of Christ must be locally present. For Zwingli, the only possible mode of

[91] Luther, *Brief Confession Concerning the Holy Sacrament,* 292 (WA 54:145).

[92] Luther, *Marburg Colloquy and Marburg Articles,* 60, 84.

[93] Luther, *Confession Concerning Christ's Supper,* 215–23 (WA 26:327–36).

[94] Luther, *Marburg Colloquy and Marburg Articles,* 29.

[95] Luther, *Confession Concerning Christ's Supper,* 229 (WA 26:340). The tendency to divide the person of Christ according to the two natures was also Luther's complaint against Zwingli's "damned alleosis." See Reinhold Seeberg, *Text-Book of the History of Doctrines,* vol. 2, *History of Doctrines in the Middle and Early Modern Ages,* trans. Charles E. Hay (Grand Rapids: Baker Book House, 1966) 321; and Sasse, *This Is My Body,* 148–55.

[96] Barclay is correct to note that definitive and repletive presence do not exhaust the possible means of presence of God or Christ, nor does Luther "seek to establish upon such grounds the actual fact of the sacramental presence" (*Protestant Doctrine of the Lord's Supper,* 80).

presence was apparently a local one.[97] All parties agreed on the absurdity of such a local presence. While for Luther's attackers, the presence of a body had to be local, Luther posits additional possibilities.

In support of his contention, Luther has several natural analogies available to him, in addition to the rather miraculous descriptions of definitive presence in particular. A limitation of bodily presence to locality does not explain physical sight, for example, in which objects are present to the eye without being in the eye locally. In a similar vein, Luther makes reference to the relation between physical voice and the ear, the face in a mirror, and the sun, which is in a reflecting lake at every point without being in the lake at all.[98] Finally, he refers to the world as a whole, even the universe. This description has two functions. Initially, Luther uses it much as he uses the examples of sight, voice, and so on. The universe is a body, but it is not in one place.[99] Additionally, this illustration supports his claim that while Christ is omnipresent, this does not endanger the finitude of the body, for Christ is present everywhere in the world—and the world is finite.[100]

It would be difficult, to say the least, to follow Luther's attempts to establish the plausibility of the ubiquity of Christ. Most of the examples he employs are based on an outmoded and unusable physics, or are miraculous acts of God. On the other hand, there is no requirement that Luther's arguments be his only advocates. If his illustrations are not especially helpful for contemporary thought, his central point, that presence and locality are not identical, is not thereby reduced to eccentric raving.

In many respects, Luther's refusal to reduce presence to "local presence" is more credible than his adversaries' identification of the two, especially if one grants the persuasiveness of Foucault's analysis of the spatiality of power.[101] It is important to recall Luther's expansive use of the preposition "in." The Hebrew Scriptures in particular, Luther contended, employed "in" to include, among other prepositions of space, "under," "above," "through," and the like. The restrictive meaning of "in" is the fault of "reason": "Of course, our reason takes a foolish attitude, since it is accustomed to understanding the word 'in' only in a physical, circumscribed sense like straw in a sack and bread in a basket," or "a peasant in his boots or meat in a pot."[102] Once the preposition

---

[97] Luther, *The Marburg Colloquy and the Marburg Articles,* 43, 47, 75, 84. A short and helpful summary of the proceedings at Marburg is Bornkamm, *Luther in Mid-Career,* 638–52.

[98] Luther, *Confession Concerning Christ's Supper,* 217–26, 277 (WA 26:330–38, 414–15).

[99] Luther, *Marburg Colloquy and Marburg Articles,* 60, 68.

[100] Luther, *Confession Concerning Christ's Supper,* 232 (WA 26:343).

[101] There is also a considerable problem with the radicals' view; for them, the body of Christ *is* localized in heaven, as Luther puts it, "sitting like a bird in a bower," and therefore cannot be present in the sacramental elements. If absurdity is to be avoided, siding with the radicals is probably not a wise course.

[102] Luther, *Confession Concerning Christ's Supper,* 230, 320 (WA 26:341, 464). It is not clear why this is a limitation of "reason," since Luther himself is more than willing to give natural illustrations of a broader conception of presence, and these are presumably accessible to reason also.

"in" includes other spatial designations, the possibility arises that framing the sacramental debate around "in" was not the most fortunate decision, particularly since none of the debated scriptural texts employ it.

Luther denies that Christ is present "in" the bread in a local sense. His assertion of the real presence is considerably more plausible if the controlling preposition of the discussion is "to" rather than "in." It is more than somewhat surprising that, of all the alternative renderings of "in" Luther provides, he never uses "to." It is nothing less than astonishing if one reflects on what preposition could unify the variety of expressions he does employ (in, under, above, through, etc.). "To" is an obvious candidate for this task. Moreover, many of Luther's analogies lend themselves to conception in terms of one thing's presence to another. The relation between the voice and the ear, the view and sight, the face and the mirror, and the sun and the lake, are all conceived more adequately as presence of the former to the latter than they are as presence of the former in the latter. Luther's assertion that the believer is "in heaven" lends itself to the same transposition. He does not mean, any more than Calvin did, that Christians are enclosed within the pearly gates, but rather that believers are in God's presence,[103] that is, present to God. Finally, the claim that "the driving force of the universe is not in one place" but in all,[104] a basic assertion of the omnipresence of God, can be rendered as well by saying that God is present to all places and things.

It is not necessary, of course, to replace all other prepositions, relying exclusively on "to." The question is only about an adequate dominant preposition. "In" is especially misleading, for it suggests precisely the localization against which Luther fought. As long as he accepted it as the principal spatial designation, his position was bound to be confusing. If, on the other hand, "to" is made the principal, encompassing preposition, Luther's assertion of alternative modes of presence is more readily apprehended.

Several examples are worth mentioning. Although they are all related to law, this is not an intrinsic limit. One relies on Foucault's discussion of the Panopticon. On the face of it, it would be silly to say that the Panopticon was present "in" the persons its purpose was to watch. Still, it is quite clear that it was always present to the surveyed inmates. The Panopticon's intrinsic deceptiveness consisted in the fact that it actually required that no one need be watching, which meant in turn that the watched began to watch themselves. In this last step, in which watched becomes watcher, in lieu of any real external watcher, it is not too much of a stretch to suggest that "presence to" has in some sense become "presence in." The Panopticon possesses more than its external face; it becomes an inward, self-surveillance mechanism.

If the Panopticon suffers as an illustration because the external mechanism is always visible, which Luther asserts is not true of the "body of Christ,"

---

[103] Luther, *Confession Concerning Christ's Supper,* 232–33, 281–83 (WA 26:343–44, 421–25).
[104] Luther, *Marburg Colloquy and Marburg Articles,* 32.

Foucault's treatment of the alliance between the police and criminal informants does not have the same shortcoming. It is important to repeat that Foucault believes all power is exercised through a bodily presence of "powers." Yet in this case the force of "undercover" informants, or undercover police for that matter, lies precisely in their invisibility. The potential offender never knows if an assumed ally is really a cohort or not. Again, at least part of the point of such operations is to make potential offenders watch themselves. "Presence" becomes, at least in part, invisible.

Even in the case of covert law enforcement, there is a palpable presence of some person to another, even if it does take on a dimension of invisibility. In the instance of the law in general, however, no such palpable, visible, local presence need be assumed. It is simply not true that a visible legal authority is required for most of us to conform to most laws of the land. In general, we do not require the visible presence of a designated legal authority. Even less do we need the written law before our eyes. But two things are quite clear: laws are present to us, even though that presence is not at all visible; and the law has a material, bodily form. Whatever conceptual difficulties we may have with Luther's doctrine of the real presence, we do not experience any such difficulties speaking of the analogous concept of a "body of law." Yet that body is generally invisible, and its presence is rarely "local" in any sense of the term. The nonlocality of the law, combined with the fact that it is really present and is a "body," lends considerable plausibility to Luther's claim that locality and presence are simply not the same. It also gives a certain presumptive validity to his position over against a strict limitation of presence to local presence.

The final example of the law leads into a broader use of the term "body" in our language, a usage as frequent as it is unexamined. Despite our generally physical notion of the "body," we have little or no trouble employing the phrases "body politic" or "social body." Foucault, whose understanding of "body," despite his occasional transcendence of it, is considerably more physical than Luther's, employed the term "social body" with some frequency and considerable ease. The articulation of power on the body, indeed, could not be made a global hypothesis without the introduction of "social body." Foucault slides in and out of this terminology with even less explicit reflection on the meaning of a body not locally present than Luther, perhaps because he had no Zwingli to call him to account. Foucault is certainly not the only thinker to have recourse to language of the social body.[105] Rarely, if ever, does the

---

[105] The common ecclesiological equivalence between church and the "body of Christ" is similar. Luther's use of it is found, for example, in *Christian Nobility*, 130–31 (WA 6:409–10). Ziemke (*Love for the Neighbor*, 43–64) discusses Luther's use of this language at length, although it is never quite clear whether Ziemke thinks that "the body of Christ" was a foundational element of Luther's ecclesiology or simply a concentrated expression for other, more basic elements of it.

Over against the generally conservative, even authoritarian, conceptions of the "social body," in which Luther's understanding certainly stands in large part, lies another element in Luther's thought, namely, that in such an organic conception of society or church, "no member of the

A THEOLOGY OF POWER

use of such terms imply local presence. The closest tie between the social body and local presence in the history of Western thought may be the frontispiece of Hobbes's *Leviathan*. Even in this instance, though, there is a difference between pictorial presentation and political thought. The doctrine of the real presence, understood against the background of our own language, may or may not be persuasive, but it is certainly not absurd.

Although the concept of a bodily presence that is not local, and may not be visible, has not been made conceptually compelling, it does enjoy, by virtue of the examples given, argumentative presumption over against a limitation of bodily presence to locality. This being said, it is obvious that illustration does not constitute argument. The advocacy of a nonlocal bodily presence has not answered the question of what this presence means. It has at best kept the question open, preventing a premature closure of the issue in favor of an identification of body and local presence.

Discussion of Luther's position cannot in fact provide an answer to the meaning of the "real presence of the body of Christ," "social body," or the "body politic." The reason is that the treatment Luther and his adversaries gave to the issue was curiously off center. The debate was conceived, apparently by all sides, as principally a question about modes of presence. We have been faithful to that emphasis, but the question of varieties of bodily presences other than local is simply incapable of resolution if the discussion remains focused around types of presence. Instead, the issue must be approached at a more fundamental level. The root difference between Luther and the radicals concerns nothing less than the nature of the body. Zwingli's contention that the only mode of presence available for a body is local is not a free-floating claim. Luther is right to say it is indebted to a mathematical, quantifiable understanding of presence, but that is not really the issue. Rather, Zwingli limits the body's mode of presence to locality because he understands the body itself as being necessarily local and mathematical.

Luther occasionally touches on this fundamental point, but that is all he does. He maintains, for example, that locality is accidental to the nature of a body. "Place" is merely a mathematical consideration and does not concern the substance of what a body is. The notion of place, moreover, neither determines nor exhausts the notion of presence.[106] This is as far as Luther goes. He does not provide any hypothesis for what the essence of the body is, nor does he discuss the nature of the difference between place and presence. The participants in the sacramental debate occasionally glimpse the central issue, the character of "body." But they soon return to the subsidiary problem of presence without having clarified the fundamental question of the body.[107]

---

body serves itself; nor does it seek its own welfare but that of the other" (*Two Kinds of Righteousness*, 303; WA 2:149).

[106] Luther, *Marburg Colloquy and Marburg Articles*, 32–85.

[107] Even where Luther might be expected to treat the question of what a body is, notably

This criticism of the Reformation debates about the real presence and the ubiquity of Christ applies to the present work as well. The same issue, the nature of the body, is left dangling.[108] What has been accomplished is to note that the thread still hangs; Luther's point is neither ridiculous nor fantastic and has a credibility greater than the restriction of body to precise spatial measurements. The conceptual features of "the body" to which a theology of power refers must be analyzed in greater detail at another time.

With the introduction of this thread, which we will not be able to sew into the cloth of the theology of power, we can summarize the more important features of the definition of power as communication of efficacy which posits itself at the borders. First, power is marked by its character as "gift," using that term more broadly than Luther's technical sense. It includes a moment of sovereignty that communicates an efficacy to the receiver of power which the latter did not possess prior to power's instantiation. Power is always given and received; it is not held. Sovereignty without this communication of efficacy is distorted power, an exercise in domination for its own sake. Second, power's self-positing at the borders implies that power is possessed by neither entity that meets at the border. Nor is power inward or external, so that it could be had; rather, the instantiation of power at the intersection of inwardness and externality has meaning for both of those realms. Power at the borders is incapable of possession, and it cannot be stored; as Arendt argues, it can only happen and then disappear, awaiting another instantiation for its rebirth. If it is still possible to speak of "quantities" of power, albeit imprecisely, this conception of power opposes any zero-sum understanding of power. Rather, power can "increase" to an extent undefinable in advance of the event itself,[109] as broader and/or more intense communications of efficacy.

---

in *Commentary on 1 Corinthians 15,* the issue occupies a small portion of his time and is not terribly enlightening.

[108] James W. Bernauer's article "Beyond Life and Death: On Foucault's Post-Auschwitz Ethic" (*Philosophy Today* 32, no. 2 [Summer 1988]: 128–42) makes a cautionary contribution to the debate, by analyzing the dangers of an organic notion of the "social body," on grounds beyond the classic positions of Hegel and Weber.

[109] The extent of power's "increase" may be undefinable in advance, but it is not infinite. This question of the "increase" of power requires a reintroduction of potentiality and actuality, not as power but as related to it, as chapter 6 argues.

CHAPTER 5

THE BEING
OF POWER

The discussion of Foucault concluded that a definition of power would include the following: First, it would avoid making power definable as domination or external control, which involves several corollaries: power would attain some relation to nonexternal realms of life and would, therefore, have to transcend politics; power would be a productive phenomenon rather than simply an instrument of repression; and power would be defined broadly enough to include both spatial and temporal elements. Second, a theory of power needs to incorporate relations of presence, particularly bodily presence. Third, a theory of power must posit power as ubiquitous. With respect to this last demand, it is clear Luther understands power as omnipresent, not only in his doctrine of the Lord's Supper but more fundamentally in the doctrine of creation *ex nihilo,* which accounts both for the possibility of the ubiquity of Christ's body and the difference between his understanding of power and that of most political theory. It would be irresponsible, however, and inadequate to take the fact that Luther says so as evidence of the truth of his argument. A contemporary defense of power's omnipresence must be forwarded. For this, Paul Tillich's ontological method is particularly fruitful. If the definition of power as communication of efficacy is ontological — that is, if it configures the being of everything that is — then power is ubiquitous, and the linkage between power and the doctrine of creation is validated by an analysis of what it is to be. Nothing can be without a relation to power.

But a showing of the ontological status of power, defined as the communication of efficacy, is not enough. Support for a particular view of what power is must demonstrate not only its plausibility but also its benefits. It is impossible to do this over against all possible options. It is sufficient to argue for a more adequate theory over against alternatives that actually have been advocated.

There are two reasons for the use of Tillich's work: First, the ontological ground of power must be defended, and Tillich provides an important conversational counterpoint to theorists who, in order to eliminate the equation between power and domination, reduce power to an ontic phenomenon. One must decide whether an ontic or ontological approach to power should be pursued. Second, Tillich provides a connection between an ontological conception of power and a theoretical ethic. We must be assured that a theology of power is not just a self-indulgent exercise in the pleasures of thought. It is not necessary that a primarily ontological investigation spell out all of its practical consequences, but it is duty bound to show why the reformulation of a particular ontological concept should concern anyone. Since much of this work has been concerned with political theory, and since the question of the compatibility of the basic definition of power and Luther's political theory has not been resolved fully, ethics supplies a natural area of application. It is important, therefore, to analyze the relationship Tillich establishes between power on the one side and love and justice on the other. This is possible through focusing on Tillich's idea of the locale of power. As with Luther, there is a tension in Tillich's work between a dialectical understanding of power and a "bordering" one; their consequences are quite different.

Preliminary Reflections on Tillich

The setting of tasks to be accomplished in the discussion of Tillich commits us to a thematic rather than a chronological account of Tillich's work. A problem with this approach would arise only if the many writings that span Tillich's long career differ widely on the issue of power. Two changes in Tillich's point of view seem to confirm this difficulty and favor a chronological exposition of Tillich's thought about power.[1]

First, Tillich does modify his conception of ontology and its object. The clearest approach to this revision is to compare Tillich's critique of ontology

---

[1] There are, of course, more than two changes in Tillich's thought over the years, but most of them do not affect his theology of power. For a periodization of Tillich's work, along with mention of other alterations in Tillich's content and approach, see the excellent work of H. Frederick Reisz, Jr., "Paul Tillich's Doctrine of God as Spirit: A Dynamic View" (Ph.D. diss., University of Chicago, 1977), 243–58. Most of these periodic distinctions are quite helpful. The major objection to Reisz's developmental scheme is his assertion that questions of import and meaning become the principal focus of Tillich's thought only in his later years. Although Reisz says that he does not mean these categories were absent from Tillich's work until the doctrine of the Spirit became the theological symbol on which Tillich concentrated, he proceeds sometimes as if this were so. It is impossible to read Tillich, from at least 1919 on, without being bombarded by the questions of meaning and fulfillment. The problem of meaninglessness was always the principal problem of religion in modern culture, and of modern culture itself. It saturates Tillich's discussions of *kairos,* the categories of theonomy, heteronomy, autonomy, courage, history, Christology, and so on. Reisz himself uses an early Tillichian term, "import," in arguing that in his early writings Tillich did not emphasize it. James Luther Adams (*Paul Tillich's Philosophy of Culture, Science, and Religion* [New York: Harper & Row, 1965], 41–61) and John R. Stumme (*Socialism in Theological Perspective: A Study of Paul Tillich, 1918–1933,* Dissertation Series 21 [Missoula, Mont.: Scholars Press, 1978], 71–76) give compelling evidence of the central importance of "meaning" in Tillich's early thought.

in *The Socialist Decision* to his perspective in the *Systematic Theology*.[2] In the former work, ontology's direction is only backward; it asks about the origin of being as it is, the "'whence' of existence." The structures of being to which ontology directs attention are structures of what now is and their dependence on what was. Ontology is concerned with explication of the "powers of origin (*Ursprungsmächten*)"; it is "the final and most abstract version of the myth of origin." Tillich is critical of such a framework because in it "being constitutes the criterion of everything that exists: the power of being (*Seinsmächtigkeit*) is the highest standard. Being is itself the truth and the norm."[3]

---

[2] A review of Tillich's argument in *The Socialist Decision*, and a presentation of its difference from Tillich's later thought, is provided by Langdon Gilkey, *Gilkey on Tillich* (New York: Crossroad, 1990), 15.

[3] Paul Tillich, *The Socialist Decision*, trans. Franklin Sherman (New York: Harper & Row; reprint, Washington, D.C.: University Press of America, 1977), 3, 13, 18, 17–18 (page references are to reprint edition); idem, *Gesammelte Werke* [hereafter *GW*], 2 Band, *Frühe Schriften zum Religiösen Sozialismus*, ed. Renate Albrecht (Stuttgart: Evangelisches Verlagswerk, 1962), 227, 234, 239, 238–39. *The Socialist Decision* is one of the comparatively few places in Tillich's prewar German work in which something like "power of being" occurs. Another is the essays in Paul Tillich, *Religiöse Verwirklichung* (Berlin: Furche-Verlag, 1930), in which *Mächtigkeit* is employed. See esp. "Über gläubigen Realismus" (pp. 68–77) (translated as "Realism and Faith," in Paul Tillich, *The Protestant Era*, abridged ed., trans. James Luther Adams [Chicago: University of Chicago Press, 1957], 68–73); "Natur und Sakrament" (pp. 142–67), translated in *The Protestant Era* (pp. 94–112); "Die Überwindung des Persönlichkeitsideals" (pp. 168–89) (translated as "The Idea and the Ideal of Personality," in *The Protestant Era*, pp. 115–35). In general, the authorized translations of these essays contained in *The Protestant Era* are altered substantially from the original German work.

In relation to social power, Tillich speaks of "Macht des Seins" in *The Socialist Decision* (*GW* 2:229), and yet the difference between the meaning of this phrase and Tillich's later conception of the power of being could not be clearer: being is both "power and powerlessness (*Macht und Ohnmacht*)" (*GW* 2:230), a notion that applies properly to the world of perception, "the original being of *things*" (Paul Tillich, "The Problem of Power," in *The Interpretation of History*, trans. Elsa L. Talmey [New York: Charles Scribner's Sons, 1936], 183; *GW* 2:196; emphasis added). In Tillich's *The State as Expectation and Demand*, in *Political Expectation*, trans. Victor Nuovo, ed. James Luther Adams (New York: Harper & Row, 1971; reprint, Macon, Ga.: Mercer University Press, 1981), 111 (page references are to reprint edition) (*Religiöse Verwirklichung*, 228), *Seinsmacht* is "demonic-destructive." The notion that was to become so determinative for the *Systematic Theology* and much of his American work was largely absent before Tillich left Germany. Part of the reason seems to be the restricted place of ontology.

Even in *The Socialist Decision*, however, Tillich operates with two conceptions of being. The first points backward, and the second incorporates the element of demand for the new in history, which is closer to his later ontological perspective. This second understanding of being allows Tillich to maintain that "*the socialist demand is confirmed by being itself*" (*The Socialist Decision*, 109; *GW* 2:317). This appears to belong to the first conception of ontology, except that it already presupposes that "*justice is the true power of being (Macht des Seins)*. In it the intention of the origin is fulfilled" (*The Socialist Decision*, 6; *GW* 2:317). Note that Tillich is speaking specifically of social power of being.

Resolution of this double nature of being and ontology is in Tillich's contrast between "actual" and "true" origin (*The Socialist Decision*, 6, 141; *GW* 2:229, 345). Emanuel Hirsch's restriction of being's "abyss," for example, to actual powers of origin, is one of the crucial elements in Tillich's criticism of him in "Open Letter to Emanuel Hirsch," in *The Thought of Paul Tillich*, trans. Victor

This sounds as if it could be directed as easily against Tillich's later emphasis on ontology; however, Tillich's argument is directed against ontologies that are not historically conscious. In the first place, ontology as an abstract version of original myth places time under the domination of space. The real "power (*Macht*) of time lies in its irreversible forward motion towards the new, towards the 'Whither.' As long as it does not have this meaning, it is merely a modification of space."[4]

Also associated with the link between ontology and origin is the philosophical focus on "essences." The language of essence is so prominent in Tillich's later work, it is surprising to find a sharp criticism of it in *The Socialist Decision*. The admonition, however, is directed at the same basic point: the traditional "logic of essence is inadequate in the face of historical realities. The 'essence of a historical phenomenon' is an empty abstraction from which the living power (*lebendige Kraft*) of history has been expelled."[5] This is why Tillich hopes the "essential church" overcomes the "ontology of power (*Ontologie der Macht*)."[6] In place of space's dominance over time, Tillich contends for the reality of a history that includes appearance of the new. In place of "essence," Tillich

---

Nuovo and Robert Scharlemann, ed. James Luther Adams, Wilhelm Pauck, and Roger Lincoln Shinn (San Francisco: Harper & Row, 1985), 376–78. Walter A. Weisskopf ("Tillich and the Crisis of the West," in *The Thought of Paul Tillich*, ed. Adams, Pauck, and Shinn, 64) makes the same mistake as Hirsch, albeit from the opposite political direction, when he identifies the "mythical power of [actual] origin" with "dreaming innocence," or true origin. It is just this distinction between the true and the actual that underlies the difference between *Urkräfte* and *Ursprungsmächte*, and is expressed in Tillich's theory of symbols and mediation, as well as his understanding of the Fall. The comment in Tillich, "Open Letter," 377, may indicate that this distinction between the true and actual powers of origin only became clear to Tillich himself in *The Socialist Decision*.

It is interesting that in Paul Tillich, "The Demonic," in *The Interpretation of History*, where the primordial powers of origin, or *Urkräfte*, are the principal topic, the phrase "power of being" appears only in the English version (p. 84). In *GW* 6 Band, *Der Widerstreit von Raum und Zeit: Schriften zur Geschichtsphilosophie*, ed. Renate Albrecht (Stuttgart: Evangelisches Verlagswerk, 1963), 47, Tillich uses *Seinshaftigkeit* rather than any of his more usual terms for "power," namely, *Kraft*, *Mächtigkeit*, or *Macht*. The same is true—and more indicative of Tillich's lack of clarity about the meaning(s) of "power of being"—in "Eschatology and History," in *The Interpretation of History*, 270: "There is no approach to religion at all without what we call theological ontology, the understanding of the Unconditioned or Transcendent as that which gives being to the being, as the transcendent power of being." In *Religiöse Verwirklichung*, 131, "transcendent power of being" is absent; instead Tillich invents a new term, "Protologie" (see also the footnote to the text in ibid., 291), and does not quite decide what the relation is between "protology" and "ontology." "Protology," it appears, is related to *Urkräfte* and true origin. Protology concerns pure being which is not yet history. A similar new introduction of "power" in the English version is seen in a comparison of "The Interpretation of History and the Idea of Christ," in *The Interpretation of History*, 244, and *Religiöse Verwirklichung*, 111–12. The more expansive uses of "power of being" to include what stands behind the actual origin, as well as the increase in *power* of being made possible by history might, therefore, have achieved their final breakthrough between 1933 and 1936. Reisz ("Tillich's Doctrine of God," 252) also locates the crucial turn to "power of being" in *The Interpretation of History*.

4. Tillich, *The Socialist Decision*, 17 (*GW* 2:238).

5. Ibid., 9 (*GW* 2:233).

6. Tillich, "The Problem of Power," 199 (*GW* 2:206).

"must introduce a dynamic concept, in accordance with the character of history. A *concept is dynamic if it contains the possibility of making understandable new and unexpected realizations of a historical origin.* I should like to call such concepts 'principles.'" Though dependence on the powers of origin is not eliminated (the error of empty autonomy), the principle, which incorporates a historical attitude of expectation, transcends an ontology of origin. Tillich maintains:

> The expectation of a "new heaven and a new earth" signifies the expectation of a reality that is not subject to the structure of being, that cannot be grasped ontologically. The old and the new being cannot be subsumed under the same concept of being. The new being is intrinsically unontological. It cannot be derived from the original state. It goes beyond the origin into a second phase, so to speak, the phase of *new in history.*[7]

Some critics of Tillich assume that his own ontological method simply returns to an ahistorical ontology.[8] If he is guilty of asserting such an ontology later in his life, Tillich can be used against himself. But this puts the point the wrong way. Why should ontology be limited to a description of origin? Why can it not include an analysis of the being of new possibility as well? If "[a] principle is the real power (*die reale Macht*) that supports a historical phenomenon, giving it the possibility to actualize itself anew and yet in continuity with the past,"[9] is it not also within the purview of an ontology of the "power of being"? Later, Tillich finds no good reason for the limited view of ontology of *The Socialist Decision,* and in order to account for the reality and power of history, he incorporates time into ontology.

The ontology of the *Systematic Theology* includes the structures of being which make history possible and provide for the possibility of modification in the structures of being themselves. The a priori character of ontological concepts does not imply "a static and unchangeable structure which, once discovered, will always be valid. Structures of experience may have changed in the past and may change in the future."[10] The chance that structures and elements of being will be altered is sufficient evidence that Tillich's ontology

---

[7] Tillich, *The Socialist Decision,* 9, 20 (*GW* 2:233, 241). The definition of "principle" should be kept in mind in discussions of the "Protestant principle."

[8] An excellent review of this literature is found in Reisz, "Tillich's Doctrine of God," 4–9. There is no need to repeat it. Guyton B. Hammond provides the most sustained explication of the vital quality of being-itself when identified with the power of being, as against a lifeless and static ontology (*Man in Estrangement: A Comparison of the Thought of Paul Tillich and Erich Fromm* [Nashville: Vanderbilt University Press, 1965], 96–102; idem, *The Power of Self-Transcendence: An Introduction to the Philosophical Theology of Paul Tillich* [St. Louis: The Bethany Press, 1966], 63). A more recent commentator on Tillich shows that this misreading is persistent. Stumme "wonders if the anticipation of the 'unontological' eschatological reality does not strain the limits of Tillich's own ontological theology" (*Socialism in Theological Perspective,* 98, 240–44). Again, the difference between the ontology Tillich criticizes and his own is not appreciated.

[9] Tillich, *The Socialist Decision,* 10 (*GW* 2:233–34).

[10] Paul Tillich, *Systematic Theology,* vol. 1 (Chicago: University of Chicago Press, 1951), 166.

has little to do with changeless fixation. Exactly by means of the reintroduction of the concept of essence, Tillich is able to include both the spatial and temporal within ontology. In the polar framework of the *Systematic Theology*, they are essentially united. The ontological elements include, among others, the polarity of dynamics and form. The formal pole, "which makes a thing what it is, is its content, its *essentia*, its definite power of being." The dynamic element is experienced as vitality and "implies the tendency of everything to transcend itself and to create new forms."[11] The interdependence of these polar elements means that neither can survive without the other; being is free to include the New Being. Without an ontology that includes the vitality of definite powers of being, moreover, even the common (and sometimes more static) philosophical notion of "degrees of being" is senseless. The concept of degrees of being

> appears to be meaningless if being is identified with existing in time and space. There are no degrees in existing, but an either-or. If, however, being is described as the power of being, the idea of degrees of being loses its difficulty. There are, certainly, degrees in the power of being, namely in the power of taking non-being into one's own self-affirmation.[12]

A final and dramatic indication of the depth to which Tillich's ontology is historical is discovered in his account of the Fall and redemption. It is true that essential humanity is united, mythically, with God in the paradisal situation, but its unity with God is a "dreaming innocence." Paradise is a state of mere potentiality.[13] Actualization of potentiality necessitates a "fall," which is ambiguous in that it separates us from God but at the same time allows the appearance of a definite and formed "us" in the first place. Creation and fall coincide in the actualization of "undecided" potentiality, in the "original fact" of existence.[14] There is, therefore, a certain dissymmetry in Tillich's valuation of creation and redemption. Redemption is not, as in some Christian theology, a mere return to the paradisal state. That is no existence at all. Instead, redemption is the reunification, fragmentary though it may be, of essence and existence.[15] Innocence is not reestablished (an impossibility); instead, existence and essence are fulfilled in redemption. Existential estrangement is conquered,[16] and essential nature loses its character as mere potentiality as it becomes actual. History is not calamity, but a positive condition of salvation: "In Tillich's

---

[11] Ibid., 178, 180–81. The formal pole is what Tillich, in his German work, designated *Seinsmächtigkeit*.

[12] Paul Tillich, *Love, Power, and Justice: Ontological Analyses and Ethical Applications* (London: Oxford University Press, 1954), 40.

[13] Paul Tillich, *Systematic Theology*, vol. 2 (Chicago: University of Chicago Press, 1957), 33; *Love, Power, and Justice*, 112.

[14] Tillich, *Systematic Theology* 2:34–36.

[15] Ibid., vol. 3 (Chicago: University of Chicago Press, 1963), 107, 129.

[16] See esp. ibid., 277–82, 376, although the entire volume emphasizes this point.

understanding the New Being does not consist simply of a return to the starting point, to essence. The new creation includes that which is positive in
existence, namely, freedom and that which is built upon freedom."[17]

The changes in Tillich's formulation of ontology do not, in any case,
demand a chronological approach to his understanding of power. In his early
differentiation between history and ontology, both were real powers. Tillich's
viewpoint changes with reference not to power but to being and ontology.
Being in *The Socialist Decision* did not include the relative non-being of potentiality, which both is and is not.[18] Neither, therefore, could potentiality be a
subject of ontological investigation. This is not to say that Tillich's later change
of mind is not important. It is; it opens the way to a dynamic ontology in
which "power of being" is the basic, ineradicable element of existence. The
basic definition of "power" is, however, not affected by the new conception
of being and ontology. Potentiality was always a power; as *mē on,* or relative
non-being, it is also a power of being.

If the revision in Tillich's view of being and ontology does not demand
chronological treatment of his work, a second factor might: Tillich's alleged
depoliticization after the Second World War.[19] Although the effect of his
different attitude toward politics on a theology of power would be an indirect
one at most, it is still important. It must be shown that Tillich's later thought,
in which the ontology of the power of being takes a larger place on his
intellectual stage, does not reduce unexpectedly the range for political thought.
The usual judgment on Tillich's depoliticization has not, to my knowledge,
attempted to integrate this criticism with the rest of his thought. The isolation of this charge is unfortunate because it leaves a reader wondering about
its significance.

The noncontextual nature of the criticism points to its abstractness.[20] The

[17] Hammond, *Power of Self-Transcendence,* 84; see also Tillich, *Systematic Theology* 1:146, 3:400.
A higher valuation of salvation over against creation is implied in passing by Luther also, in *The
Bondage of the Will.* Still, Luther's usual approach is more circular; redemption is not usually differen-
tiated from a reestablishment of the created state. In the twentieth century, the continuing equa-
tion of salvation and "return to [the] origin" is presented very clearly by Dietrich Bonhoeffer,
Creation and Fall, in *Creation and Fall/Temptation: Two Biblical Studies,* trans. John C. Fletcher (New
York: Macmillan, Collier Books, 1959), 60.

[18] Tillich, *Systematic Theology* 1:172–89. The assertion that *The Socialist Decision* does not include
this is only partly true. There is a hint of its presence when Tillich says: "Being should be called
'dynamic' insofar as it is moving from possibility to reality—it is the not-yet-formed in which,
however, there lies the possibility and the power of form. The dynamic would then be a new
category . . . appropriate to the social situation of revolutionary political romanticism" (*The Socialist
Decision,* 28–29; *GW* 2:249). Tillich's hesitation about this category, as well as his failure to employ
it later in the text, indicates that the full conceptual development and significance of relative non-
being have not occurred.

[19] A critique of Tillich's postwar work on this basis is developed at some length by Stumme,
Socialism in Theological Perspective, esp. 250–55.

[20] The abstractness discussed here is a systematic abstractness, but Langdon Gilkey ("Tillich:
The Master of Mediation," in *The Theology of Paul Tillich,* ed. Charles Kegley [New York: Pilgrim

introduction of the "sacred void" of possibilities for social transformation does not overthrow Tillich's prior emphasis on the *kairos* so much as it expresses his belief that, in his contemporary situation, there was no transformative *kairos*, no historical action charged with eternal significance.[21] *Kairos* is a qualitative concept. One should not call "kairic" a mere interest in dividing the social pie better, although one may call such an interest relatively just and act in its favor, as Tillich did at various times.[22] Transformative *kairoi* appear only when a comprehensive vision of fulfilling meaning appears, that is, when the interest in and possibility of baking a better pie arises. The outline of Tillich's thought does not change in his postwar work; his estimate of the possibilities of the historical situation does. Consequently, criticism of Tillich's depoliticization is only a critique of his conclusion about the possibilities destiny has given us here and now.[23] A special *kairos* is "the juncture of decision and destiny belonging to a particular historical situation."[24] "Sacred waiting" within the

---

Press, 1982], 56–57) points out that Tillich's relative silence on political matters after coming to the United States was partly to avoid a personal abstractness in relation to his work. Tillich recognized that his early political theology did not quite fit the facts of his transposition from Europe to America, either personally or politically. Gilkey (*Gilkey on Tillich*, 205) recalls Tillich's amazement at having been "rescued by a bourgeois, by *the* bourgeois, nation." It is refreshing to encounter a thinker for whom life as it was lived made a difference for philosophical and theological pronouncements. Ronald H. Stone makes a similar point (*Paul Tillich's Radical Social Thought* [Atlanta: John Knox Press, 1980], 112–14). Stone's book is also an excellent summary of the social situation to which Tillich's early thought responded, as is Stumme, *Socialism in Theological Perspective*.

[21] See *Systematic Theology* 3:370–72, on the rarity of transformative *kairoi*. For the claim that the "sacred void" is also a proclamation of the *kairos*, see Paul Tillich, "Reply to Interpretation and Criticism," in *The Theology of Paul Tillich*, ed. Kegley and Bretall, 345–46. Tillich's, "Religion and Secular Culture" (in *The Protestant Era*, abridged ed., 59–61) is especially fascinating because it contains Tillich's self-criticism of his prewar "tinge of romanticism."

[22] See Stone, *Paul Tillich's Radical Social Thought*, 124–30, for examples. If there is a danger in Tillich's emphasis on the *kairos*, it is found in this question of action in spite of the absence of a transforming *kairos*, "whether thus waiting for the distant and unknown *kairos* and guarding ourselves against premature solutions, we may not possibly miss minor assignments of a makeshift nature, which, however uninspiring and preliminary in themselves, could be the earnest and symbol of the coming light in the midst of darkness" (Eduard Heimann, "Tillich's Doctrine of Religious Socialism," in *The Theology of Paul Tillich*, ed. Kegley and Bretall, 324–25).

[23] The pole of destiny is the pole of the *concrete* given (*Systematic Theology* 1:184–85). Destiny limits the possibilities available to historical periods and cultural epochs to, generally, a finite few. But destiny is also the only condition under which freedom can become concrete; otherwise freedom would be empty indeterminacy. For an expansive treatment of the categories of freedom and destiny which shows their fruitfulness for a comprehensive interpretation of history, see Langdon Gilkey, *Reaping the Whirlwind: A Christian Interpretation of History* (New York: Seabury Press, 1976), 159–318.

[24] James Luther Adams, "Tillich's Interpretation of History," in *The Theology of Paul Tillich*, ed. Kegley and Bretall, 307; see also Tillich's discussion of the prophetic attitude and the *kairos* doctrine as the content of that attitude in *Basic Principles of Religious Socialism*, in *Political Expectation*, ed. Adams, 60–61 (*GW* 2:92–94). Prophecy can only issue a demand on the basis of the given. The same point is made in Paul Tillich, "Kairos," in *The Protestant Era*, abridged ed., 48

sacred void is, therefore, a possibility given by Tillich's doctrine of the *kairos*. To wait was, for Tillich, a response to the concrete possibilities offered.[25] In fact, the notion of *kairos* had always implied a waiting attitude[26] and is impoverished if reduced to perpetual activism. This is because our situation relative to the eternal is not a matter of our creation, "a fixed quantity which could be introduced into time";[27] the eternal invades time, not the other way around.[28] As Tillich says, "the given holy cannot be replaced by the posited holy."[29]

One may disagree with Tillich regarding his evaluation of the situation, but there are two points to be made about such disagreement. First, it does not imply a problem with Tillich's conceptual structure but concerns evaluation of the situation to be correlated with that structure. In other words, it is quite possible to challenge Tillich's interpretation of the concrete historical situation from within Tillich's own categories of thought. This is perhaps the highest compliment to Tillich, for it was always his concern to develop a theology that was not frozen but had the dynamism to speak to a changing world. His theological structure carries us beyond his own historical conclusions. Second, it is incumbent upon the challenger to defend a vision of a forceful and kairic invasion of eternity into this time. The demand "Do it better!" must be taken to heart. If Tillich did not see a transforming *kairos* and we do, it is hardly enough to rebuke him without forwarding our own vision

---

(*GW* 6:26). What Tillich believed was "given" was an autonomous culture against which a *kairos* had to be proclaimed, but also an insecurity in that autonomy, which provided an opportunity to proclaim the *kairos* effectively. In the stirring essay "The Protestant Message and the Man of Today," in *The Protestant Era*, abridged ed., 192 (*Religiöse Verwirklichung*, 25), he says, "The man of today . . . *is the autonomous man who has become insecure in his autonomy.*"

[25] The excellent piece by Heimann, "Tillich's Doctrine of Religious Socialism," ascribes even prophetic status to "sacred waiting" (p. 324). Heimann bases this assessment on Isa. 21:11–12:

"Watchman, what of the night?
Watchman, what of the night?"
The watchman says:
"Morning comes, and also the night.
If you will inquire, inquire;
come back again."

[26] Paul Tillich, *The Religious Situation*, trans. H. Richard Niebuhr (New York: Henry Holt & Co., 1932; reprint, New York: Meridian Books, 1956), 176 (page references are to reprint edition) (*GW* 10 Band, *Die Religiöse Deutung der Gegenwart: Schriften zur Zeitkritik*, ed. Renate Albrecht [Stuttgart: Evangelisches Verlagswerk, 1968], 72–73); see also Tillich, "Reply to Interpretation and Criticism," 345–46. An excellent recent defense of the necessity of an attitude of waiting expectation is Tinder, *The Political Meaning of Christianity*.

[27] Tillich, *The Religious Situation*, 176 (*GW* 10:73).

[28] Ibid., 176 (*GW* 10:73).

[29] Tillich, *Basic Principles of Religious Socialism*, 60 (translation modified; *GW* 2:92 reads: "das gegebene Heilige kann nicht ersetzt werden durch das aufgegebene Heilige").

of a more meaningful whole.[30] We too may discover that we must wait for a transforming *kairos* to appear, [31]or we may discover, to Tillich's posthumous delight, that new possibilities have appeared in history. The actual presence of a *kairos* is concrete, a matter of history, and cannot be decided conceptually. The question of *kairic* presence is one of "discernment, not of ontology."[32]

It is not necessary to follow a chronological order in discussing Tillich's theology of power. Neither of the changes in his broader project that might be thought to "periodize" his conception of power does so.

The Ontological Status of Power

For Tillich, the assertion that God is being-itself means that God is the "power of being." In fact, ascription of unconditional power and meaning to God is what removes God from the realm of beings and makes the divine being-itself.[33] The claim that God alone is *a se* "can be said of him only if he is the power of being, if he is being-itself."[34] It is misleading to say, "Power is one of the first of God's attributes,"[35] if one means there could be, even conceptually, an empty container called "God" subsequently filled with power.

---

[30] Stumme does not even attempt this; his critique of Tillich is therefore extremely abstract (*Socialism in Theological Perspective*).

[31] Certainly, we may look to various civil rights movements, which had and continue to have national and international repercussions, as a national candidate for such a *kairos*. Our decisions have felt charged with unconditional import. The question that arises is whether or not this significance may not already be on the wane, whether or not there is degeneration into a mere quest for loose loot and domination instead of a search for a new definition of what it means to be human and just in diverse world and national communities. This danger is beginning to be appreciated by those at the forefront of the movement. Cornel West commented recently, "Now, instead of the civil rights movement being viewed as a moral crusade for freedom, it's become the expression of a particular interest group" (*The New York Times*, 3 April 1991, A1). Moreover, the formal, legislative solutions asked and implemented more and more seem to protect a middle class less in need of protection than the poor, to whom the proffered solutions offer little or nothing.

[32] Langdon Gilkey, personal communication.

[33] Tillich, *Systematic Theology* 1:235–36, 261.

[34] Ibid., 236; see also *Love, Power, and Justice*, 35.

[35] Karl Rahner, ed., *Encyclopedia of Theology: The Concise Sacramentum Mundi* (New York: Crossroad, 1975), s.v. "Power," by Klaus Hemmerle. It is not at all clear that this is Hemmerle's meaning; the quotation actually obscures his direction, which is close to Tillich's in many respects. For its clarity and brevity, Hemmerle's article is superb; it is helpful also as an example of thought about power in contemporary Roman Catholicism, a tradition this book does not examine. The principal, but not unique, shortcoming of the piece is its ambivalence about power's value. Other examples of this equivocation will be examined later. If power is a condition of existence, if it is essentially identical to love, and if beings rightly strive for it, all of which Hemmerle affirms, why say with regret, "the Christian must even be ready on occasion to assume and exercise power, though here too he will only hold it as though he did not (1 Cor 7:29ff)"?

Power is what makes the divine divine; a god without power is a contradiction in terms.[36] Power is, in Luther's terms, not the instrument of God but God's self. Beings' existence depends on participation in the power of being.[37]

Certainly, our definition of power and Tillich's are not identical. Can the assertion that power is the communication of efficacy make the same claim to be the basic ontological ground? The answer can be established by asking: Can anything be without having received, and continually receiving, communications of efficacy? Alternatively, could there be life without the communication and reception of efficacy? The answer to both is negative; therefore, it can be affirmed that being is the power of being. The renunciation of power is indeed the renunciation of life.[38] The ontological status of power and its ubiquity are established simultaneously.

Tillich's claim, and ours, goes beyond the assertion that power is simply an ontological element. Power is not only one ontological component among others, but *the* basic ontological ground. To repeat: Everything has being only because it participates in power, receiving communications of efficacy, and renunciation of all power is renunciation of life. This requires some clarification.

The Alien Legitimation of Power

Some influential contemporary theories of power reduce power to an ontic phenomenon. Ontic positioning of power is, of course, a presupposition of sovereignty theory also. More interesting about certain contemporary philosophies of power is that they "onticize" power in order to save power from an identity with domination. One venture of this sort is Hannah Arendt's severance of power and inwardness. Another objection that can be raised against an argument maintaining that power is the fundamental ontological principle is the suggestion that power depends on something more basic for its being. Although often only implicitly, a frequent candidate for such foundational status is reason. The impact of this competing claim on a theory of power includes, at a minimum, two possibilities. If power is avoidable, or if it can be overcome finally, it is not a structure of being, since it could, in principle, not be. Or if power has its ground outside itself, if it must be supported or

---

[36] This is not true of Christianity alone. G. van der Leeuw persuasively argues that an experience of power gives birth to ascription and awareness of divinity in the history of religions generally (*Religion in Essence and Manifestation,* 2 vols., trans. J. E. Turner [London: George Allen & Unwin, 1938; reprint, Gloucester, Mass.: Peter Smith, 1967]). The typology of religion in Tillich (*Systematic Theology* 1:218–35) is also couched in terms of power.

[37] Tillich, *Systematic Theology* 1:118, 237, 253, 2:167; idem, "The Two Types of Philosophy of Religion," in *Theology of Culture,* ed. Robert C. Kimball (New York: Oxford University Press, 1959), 25–26; idem, "Nature and Sacrament," 110 (*Religiöse Verwirklichung,* 164).

[38] Tillich, "The Problem of Power," 197 (*GW* 2:204–5); *Love, Power, and Justice,* 120.

contained by something else, it is not basic. Many thinkers take just these positions, or some mixture of them.

Only a few of the advocates of the primacy of reason can be considered
here. The discussion is limited arbitrarily to thinkers of this century—Arendt,
Jürgen Habermas, and Bertrand Russell—and special attention is paid to the
philosophies of conversation and persuasion presented by Habermas and
Russell. We begin again with Hannah Arendt. Beside the distinction between
power and individual strength presented earlier, Arendt separates power from
"force," "authority," and "violence." The specific referents of each of these terms
do not concern us here,[39] nor does the descriptive value of some of the differen-
tiations, which is immense.[40] However, the question that was raised in the
previous chapter bears repetition, with a somewhat different twist. How is
it possible that quite opposed phenomena have been related in history? Arendt
posits a continuum between power and violence such that the exclusive
presence of one eliminates the other. If individual strength and power are unable
to coexist (the notion that was criticized earlier), violence as collective strength
is almost always found in combination with power.[41] Authority and force are
also found along this continuum in varying proportions.

What, then, is the continuum along which these ontic realities may be
classed and combined? What is the yardstick by which Arendt preserves the
notion of power as the most desirable state of affairs for political action and
by which violence is treated with the utmost suspicion? The measurement
is not made according to power itself. Why? Because, for Arendt, power stands
in need of legitimacy.[42]

The assertion that power needs legitimation marks a great divide in
political thought and theories of power. As soon as thought questions the
legitimacy of power purely as power, power cannot be the fundamental structure of being but stands in need of validation from elsewhere.[43] One position
is represented by Machiavelli, for whom power cannot be legitimated from

---

[39] For the particulars of these distinctions, see H. Arendt, *On Violence* (New York: Harcourt,
Brace & World, 1970) 35–56; idem, *The Human Condition* (Chicago: University of Chicago Press,
1958) 199–207, although the latter discussion does not include a treatment of "authority."

[40] They are extremely helpful as descriptions and clarifications of the course of recent political
history. *On Violence* contains some of these applications. As examples, her analysis of America's
Vietnam experience rather easily transfers to our involvement with other oppressive states, and
her interpretation of domestic violence against students at Berkeley, with some alterations, helps
one understand more recent FBI investigations of peace groups. Only if such descriptions could
not be executed within our reformulated concept of power (with appropriate terminological
adjustments) would the value of Arendt's analyses argue against our conclusions.

[41] Arendt, *On Violence,* 52.

[42] Ibid.

[43] Foucault identifies need for legitimation as the central distinction between "sovereignty-
theory" and "governmentality-theory" ("Governmentality," *Ideology and Consciousness* 6 [1979]:
5–21). For the first, power is its own end, whereas for the second, power must be given a principle
of legitimacy from elsewhere. Here we are in firm agreement with sovereignty theory.

outside itself, and the other by a venerable line of political theorists from Plato through Marx to nearly all contemporary thinkers.[44] But power is the basic ontological structure. As such, it is incapable of receiving an external legitimation; on the contrary, all that exists receives existence and legitimacy from power. Power itself is legitimate for no other reason than that it is power.

If power requires legitimation, if it is not legitimate because it is power, we must ask, What makes power legitimate? Habermas makes explicit what is implied by Arendt. Power is legitimated by reason. Indeed, power, truly so called, is reason. The mixture of power with other elements along the continuum is judged by pure power, that is, by reason. It is true that Arendt does not say this. For her, the epistemological break between knowledge and opinion

---

[44] For the first option, see Niccolò Machiavelli, *The Prince,* trans. George Bull (Harmondsworth, Middlesex, England: Penguin Books, 1961). An excellent essay on this point is Hanna H. Gray, "Machiavelli: The Art of Politics and the Paradox of Power," in *The Responsibility of Power,* ed. Leonard Krieger and Fritz Stern (Garden City, N.Y.: Doubleday & Co., 1967), 34–53. Machiavelli is almost a lone voice, though not a very soothing one. On the other side, a few representatives are sufficient demonstration. Plato is an ambiguous case. In the early parts of Plato (*Gorgias,* in *The Collected Dialogues of Plato, including the Letters,* Bollingen Series LXXI, trans. W. D. Woodhead, ed. Edith Hamilton and Huntington Cairns [Princeton, N.J.: Princeton University Press, 1961], 248) power may be self-legitimating because it *means* "something good for its possessor." If power is not *the* good, it is at least *a* good. A good treatment of this aspect of Plato is Leonard Krieger, "Power and Responsibility: The Historical Assumptions," in *The Responsibility of Power,* ed. Krieger and Stern, 5–17. Yet Socrates progressively moves away from this assertion, in light of Callicles' identification of power, good, and strength (p. 270). Although Socrates begins his response by attempting to distinguish power and strength, he ends by identifying them, such that power becomes, by the end of the dialogue, neutral in form and more "ruinous" than helpful in content (p. 293). If power retains a relation to the good, the connection is now accidental rather than essential. By the time of *The Republic* (*The Republic of Plato,* trans. Allan Bloom [New York: Basic Books, 1968]), the tension of the *Gorgias* is removed. Political power, at least, requires direction and legitimation from reason. Power is intrinsically dangerous — and actually dangerous the more its exercisers are removed from philosophy.

The approach of the *Republic* is the one canonized in the West. The entire problem for John Locke (*The Second Treatise of Government,* ed. Thomas P. Peardon [Indianapolis: Bobbs-Merrill, Library of Liberal Arts, 1952]), is how to prevent anyone from obtaining too much power or dominion so that government may be legitimate (and rational). The opening question of Jean-Jacques Rousseau (*The Social Contract,* in *The Social Contract and Discourses,* trans. G. D. H Cole, rev. J. H. Brumfitt and John C. Hall [London: J. M. Dent & Sons, 1973], 165) is how the state's power can be made legitimate.

The issue is presented even more starkly in Karl Marx and Friedrich Engels, *The Manifesto of the Communist Party,* in *The Marx-Engels Reader,* 2nd ed., ed. Robert C. Tucker (New York: W. W. Norton & Co., 1978). For Marx and Engels, power cannot be legitimated finally, since it is only "the organized power of one class for oppressing another" (p. 490). Eventually, therefore, political power must be eliminated altogether, since it is ultimately tautological to say that political power is illegitimate. The same opinion is represented in contemporary thought by Steven Lukes (*Power: A Radical View* [London: Macmillan, 1974]), for whom power is always an imposition of the will of the powerful on a powerless victim, whose best interests are always violated in the exercise of power. By definition, therefore, power is incapable of legitimacy. The same is true of M. French, *Beyond Power: On Women, Men, and Morals* (New York: Ballantine Books, 1985); the world must ascend, as the title indicates, beyond power.

is too sharp. Even the unrestricted polis can generate only the power of opinion, which is truly power only if the process of coming to opinion is unrestricted among the equal members of the polis. Arendt's criterion of power, therefore, is plurality. That criterion is not considered, despite its value, because her argument is unique and I have restricted myself to a more common position. Moreover, the criterion of plurality would also have to be analyzed in more detail if it conflicted directly with the definition of power as communication of efficacy. It does not; plurality is not only included in the notion of power as communication of efficacy, but fulfilled in it. The difference with Arendt is this; whereas for her, plurality is the standard which judges power, the conception of power as communication of efficacy maintains that a valuation of plurality emerges from power.

Habermas, however, makes the further argument that the process of reaching agreement is fundamentally presupposed in any notion of reason.[45] Habermas's most explicit reflection on the nature of power occurs in his review of Arendt.[46] To be sure, he wants to include within his theory the elements of competition for and employment of power, elements that include force as a part of power. But power's distortions derive from precisely these elements, since in modern society, communication that could lead to the "forceless force"[47]of consensus is blocked. The impediments to the "ideal situation of discourse (*Sprechsituation*)"[48] in contemporary society lead Habermas to assert that "structural violence is built into political institutions (but not only into them)." Such violence "does not manifest itself as force; rather, unperceived, it blocks those communications in which convictions effective for legitimation are formed and passed on." Habermas explains the formation of ideology, which is based on the illusion of unforced consensus, by means of these warps in the process of reaching unforced agreement. Ideologies in turn allow the generation of "a power which, as soon as it is institutionalized, can also be used against [those who generate it]."[49]

Power is legitimated either ideologically or truly. It is truly legitimate power only if it conforms to the ideal of the unrestricted and unforced process of reaching agreement, and this is the process of reason. Indeed, the very notion of "rationalization" *means* "extirpating those relations of force that are incon-

---

[45] This is clear in all of Habermas's work, from *Knowledge and Human Interests* on (trans. Jeremy J. Shapiro [Boston: Beacon Press, 1971]) and is emphasized especially in *Communication and the Evolution of Society* (trans. Thomas McCarthy [Boston: Beacon Press, 1979]).

[46] Jürgen Habermas, "Hannah Arendt's Communications Concept of Power," *Social Research* 44, no. 1 (1977) (reprinted in *Power,* ed. Steven Lukes [New York: New York University Press, 1986]), 75–93 (page references are to reprint edition).

[47] Ibid., 77. This statement occurs in Habermas's discussion of Arendt, but in the end it is more true of Habermas than of Arendt.

[48] Jürgen Habermas, *Theory and Practice,* trans. John Viertel (Boston: Beacon Press, 1973), 19.

[49] The last trio of quotations are from Habermas, "Hannah Arendt's Communications Concept of Power," 88.

spicuously set in the very structures of communication," and progress is to be measured "against the intersubjectivity of understanding achieved without force, that is, against the expansion of the domain of consensual action together with the reestablishment of undistorted communication."[50] We are brought full circle. If power has a remainder beyond reason, that remainder is domination. In what is not identical to reason, power is only force. Legitimate power is simply the human word of reason. Power is productive, but only through its unification under the superior principles of reason, which alone bring power to its fulfillment and legitimacy.

Much the same conclusion is implied in the now oft-invoked distinction between "coercive" and "persuasive" power, advocated most extensively and clearly by Bertrand Russell.[51] Because of its current popularity, this formulation of power deserves some attention. The differentiation between persuasive and coercive power is underlain by a definition of power as production of intended effects. This has two consequences. First, power becomes purely quantitative;[52] if one is able to achieve more of what one wants, one possesses more power. The second consequence follows: power is concerned with means only but cannot define the ends that are to be attained. Power is a loose cannon that can be aimed in any direction, and it depends on the ship's gunner for its aim. "Naked" power manifests itself in the drive for omnipotence, a solipsistic hunger for total domination.[53]

Into this breach, luckily, steps "persuasive power," which, in its mercy, clothes and transfigures power. Persuasive power "tames" the otherwise wild beast of naked, coercive power. Persuasive power can perform this function because it includes an ethic worthy of attention; it has such worth in turn only because power is not its objective, only its means. What grounds the legitimacy of persuasive power? The answer is pointed: persuasive power is the power of reason. Persuasive power is the greatest power because it seeks not power but reason.[54] Persuasive power attempts to extinguish "irrational belief."[55]

Although the distinction between coercive and persuasive power appears to give a fundamental status to power, appearance is deceptive. "Good" power is ultimately reason, and legitimate and illegitimate power must be judged according to reason's canons. Russell's "ethics of power" obscures more than it reveals; power is engaged in a drama of good cop/bad cop, which continues only so long as the light of reason has not won the day against felonious irrationality. Russell's is not an ethic of power at all, in the sense that ethical

[50] Habermas, *Communication and the Evolution of Society,* 119–20.

[51] Bertrand Russell, *Power: A New Social Analysis* (London: George Allen & Unwin, 1938), 274.

[52] Ibid., 35.

[53] Ibid., 84–107, 271–82.

[54] Ibid., 278–319. The same image of "power taming" is employed by Peter Gay, who asserts that the "supreme problem" of modernity "is the taming of power" ("Burckhardt's *Renaissance:* Between Responsibility and Power," in *The Responsibility of Power,* ed. Krieger and Stern, 183–98.

[55] Russell, *Power,* 314.

principles emerge from analysis of power. Rather, it is an ethic above and against power. As such, it duplicates a common, and predominantly leftist, ambivalence toward power. Pure power is at best a necessary evil, an undesirable element with which reason must ally itself occasionally. Perhaps the classic instance of this ambivalence is found in the *Communist Manifesto:* "Of course, in the beginning," despotic power is required, but only in order the power may finally be abolished.[56] Why this alliance should be necessary if, as Russell says, persuasion is the ultimate power is never clear. Perhaps it is because reason itself must participate in power.

Heteronomy, Autonomy, Theonomy

Tillich's postulate that reason is not the criterion of power because it lacks power of itself makes him a scintillating theoretician of power. Instead, Tillich maintains that humans are "fully rational only on the foundation of, and in interdependence with, nonrational factors."[57] Foucault's disdain for the discourses of truth was based largely on the insight that power produced them. "Truth" is not, as Russell and Habermas believe, a production of autonomous reason and conversation, but is imbued with and created by power and is one of power's effects. For the Foucault of the mid–1970s through the early 1980s, this insight damned both truth and power. The forceless force of consensus is not just illusion; it is also an insidious use of force. Tillich takes a quite different attitude. The dependence of the objective and subjective *logoi* on power condemns neither reason nor power. Indeed, reason attains its greatness as ontological reason, as reason participating in power. Clarification of this point requires treatment of Tillich's concepts of heteronomy, autonomy, and theonomy.[58]

---

[56] Marx and Engels, *Manifesto of the Communist Party,* 490. Tillich responds succinctly: *"In the present, power is opposed by power so that in the future, power can renounce power.* Socialist belief once more shows itself to be a belief in miracles" (*The Socialist Decision,* 76; *GW* 2:290).

[57] Paul Tillich, "The World Situation," in *The Christian Answer,* ed. Henry P. Van Dusen (New York: Charles Scribner's Sons, 1945; reprint, Philadelphia: Fortress Press, Facet Books Social Ethics Series 2, 1965), 13 (page references are to reprint edition). See also "Philosophy and Fate," in *The Protestant Era,* abridged ed., 14–15, in which Tillich places "Logos" within "Kairos"; the latter embraces fate, history, and the event, and is more fundamental than Logos.

[58] A superb and more complete exposition of the relations between this triad of concepts is found in Adams, *Tillich's Philosophy,* 167–75. Gilkey is also helpful (*Gilkey on Tillich,* 3–22). In contrast, an error-filled treatment is contained in Theodore Runyon, "Tillich's Understanding of Revolution" in *Theonomy and Autonomy: Studies in Paul Tillich's Engagement with Modern Culture,* ed. John J. Carey (Macon, Ga.: Mercer University Press, 1984), 274–78. Runyon makes the astonishing claims, without support from Tillich, that it is heteronomy that is without the dimension of depth and that bourgeois society is heteronomous. Tillich's argument is exactly the opposite. Because bourgeois society is autonomous, it lacks relation to the depth of being. Heteronomous forces, which are aware of the depth of existence, attempt to preserve that dimension, but do

Heteronomy and autonomy are originally grounded in, and aspects of, theonomy.[59] A theonomous situation is one in which there is unconditional, eternal import shining through the activities of life and culture. The state of grace, for example, is the appearance of the divine "*through* a living Gestalt which remains in itself what it is. . . . The divine appears through the finite realities as their transcendent meaning. Forms of grace are finite forms, pointing beyond themselves."[60] Culture contains an awareness of its ground and meaningful participation in that which transcends it and seeks to express this participation in its creations.[61] Tillich calls "such a situation 'theonomous,' not in the sense that in it God lays down the laws but in the sense that such an age, in all its forms, is open to and directed toward the divine."[62]

Although it is a historical possibility, at least in fragmentary form, theonomy is not the usual situation; it is certainly not ours. The high Middle Ages was, for example, a period of relative theonomy, in which cultural activities were vessels and expressions of self-transcendent meaning. But theonomy is not attained once and for all.[63] Time changes all—most of all the resources and contents of cultures, and thereby the demands made on a culture. If the life of spirit is essentially historical life, meaning and truth have a history:

> The contents of the historical life are tasks and ventures of the creative spirit. The truth is a living truth, a creative truth, and not a law. What we are confronted with is never and nowhere an abstract command; it is living history, with its abundance of new problems whose solution occupies and fulfills every epoch.[64]

The forms and contents that mediate the eternal ground of meaning at one time and place do not function adequately in all times and places, because reality itself is dynamic and creative.[65] What is "theonomous" is correlated with the

---

so by disregarding autonomous forms' intrinsic significance. True, initially autonomous forms of self-sufficient finitude may come to be imposed by "religious" authority, but then they are no longer autonomous, having sacrificed their own rational principle. Rather, they are heteronomous, but also have a dimension of depth. No social form, including bourgeois society, can be simultaneously heteronomous and without depth, for this contradicts the core meaning of "heteronomy."

[59] Tillich, *Systematic Theology* 1:85, 3:251. A comprehensive late discussion of autonomy, heteronomy, and theonomy is provided in 3:245–82.

[60] Paul Tillich, "The Formative Power of Protestantism," in *The Protestant Era*, abridged ed., 212; *Religiöse Verwirklichung*, 50.

[61] Tillich, *The Religious Situation*, 216 (*GW* 10:91–92); *Systematic Theology* 3:250.

[62] Tillich, "Kairos," in *The Protestant Era*, 44 (*GW* 6:21).

[63] For a brief listing of what Tillich believes were historical manifestations of theonomy, and their disintegration, see *Systematic Theology* 1:85, 3:250. For the significance of the Middle Ages for Tillich's perspective on cultural history, see Adams, *Tillich's Philosophy*, 167.

[64] Tillich, "Kairos," in *The Protestant Era*, 51 (*GW* 6:28); see also Adams, *Tillich's Philosophy*, 60–61.

[65] Tillich, *Systematic Theology* 1:78–79; see also "The Formative Power of Protestantism," in *The Protestant Era*, 214–15 (*Religiöse Verwirklichung*, 53–55).

actual historical situation. The task of clarifying a culture's relation to the eternal ground changes with the components and resources of culture.[66] This is why the "method of correlation" is not simply an optional method. It is not a mere instrument of thought but a requirement laid upon thought (and life) by the interaction of finitude with its infinite ground. One must discern the import of the message for the concrete situation in order to comprehend and be enlivened by the theonomous meaning open to us *now.*[67]

Transformation of the content of the historical situation, with attendant alterations of the range of finite meaning in relation to the eternal ground, opens the door to a domineering heteronomy and sacramentalism[68] on one side and empty autonomy on the other.[69] The fault for the disintegration of a theonomous situation must be laid initially at the door of heteronomous impulses.[70] Contents that expressed theonomous meaning and the media through which they were expressed no longer prove adequate to the changing times. Those forces which drive toward heteronomy try to maintain past forms in the face of dynamic historical destiny. "Religion" in a broad sense, in particular its "priestly" element, binds its adherents to dying and unresponsive contents and media in order to guarantee a relation with the eternal ground of meaning.[71] In short, the finite forms of the sacramental aspect of religion,

---

[66] Tillich, *Systematic Theology* 3:251; "Kairos," in *The Protestant Era*, 38 (*GW* 6:15).

[67] This is the principal reason Tillich can claim that all theology is correlative, whether it recognizes it or not. See David Tracy, "Tillich and Contemporary Theology," in *The Thought of Paul Tillich*, ed. Adams, Pauck, and Shinn, 261–67, for a spirited defense of Tillich's method. Tracy is much more enthusiastic toward Tillich, than in David Tracy, *Blessed Rage for Order: The New Pluralism in Theology* (New York: Seabury Press, 1975), 45–46. An analysis of Tillich's application of the method of correlation, which looks beyond Tillich's schematic statements about it in *Systematic Theology*, is provided in Langdon Gilkey, "The Role of the Theologian in Contemporary Society," in *The Thought of Paul Tillich*, ed. Adams, Pauck, and Shinn, 330–50. An especially interesting presentation is Paul Tillich, "Philosophy and Theology," in *The Protestant Era*, abridged ed., 83–93; Tillich's *Biblical Religion and the Search for Ultimate Reality* (Chicago: University of Chicago Press, 1955) is a sustained treatment of the issues presented more schematically in *Systematic Theology*, vol. 1.

[68] Sacramentalism and its representatives have been grouped under the term "heteronomy." This is permissible, although they have slightly different referents. One might say that sacramentalism refers to the religious object primarily, whereas heteronomy focuses on religious word and law. Sacramentalism and heteronomy are as one in their hardness and inflexibility, and both reveal thereby the same aspect of the demonic. Tillich notes this similarity: "these forms of the demonic . . . are a contemporary power (*Gegenwartsmacht*) in sacramental and orthodox confessionalism" (*Basic Principles of Religious Socialism*, 70 [translation slightly modified; *GW* 2:102]).

[69] The parallels between Tillich's account of the breakup of synthetic theonomy into a "polarity" of autonomy and heteronomy, and his theology of the fall are striking.

[70] For a brief discussion of the collapse of theonomy in the Middle Ages, see Tillich, *Systematic Theology* 1:85.

[71] Tillich, "Kairos," in *The Protestant Era*, 38 (*GW* 6:15); *Systematic Theology* 3:251–52. Not only "religion" is subject to this creedal heteronomy; other "demonisms" of our time, most obviously nationalism, are also heteronomous. See Tillich, *The Religious Situation*, 41–53 (*GW* 10:15–20), in which Tillich identifies both nationalism and capitalism as contemporary demonic forces. They

which once mediated unconditional import to the world, lose their adequacy as correlative symbols. They no longer communicate a message sufficient to the situation of history.[72] Increasing opposition between religion and world, as well as a growing irrelevance of religion to the world, mark a heteronomous situation with respect to explicitly religious spheres.[73] Whenever the core justification for adherence to doctrine or other practices is that my church, my party, my nation, my holy writing, my favorite theologian "says it is so," there predominantly heteronomous forces are at work. Agreement and action proceed not from inner, rational demands but from obedience to abstract and uncomprehended commands.

Still, priestly, sacramental religion demands unconditional obedience to finite forms which, it claims, express the infinite fully; the oppressiveness of religion is due largely to this command to obey finite symbols and laws unconditionally.[74] The demonic aspect of heteronomy is exactly this: heteronomy

----

are heteronomous since they demand rigid adherence to their creeds and symbols, despite the shifting sands of history. In the broader sense of religion as "ultimate concern," these concrete heteronomies are also religious. Witness, for example, efforts to protect the American flag from "desecration." Advocates of such protection often are quite explicit about the religious nature of the symbol. Former Supreme Court nominee Robert Bork is among those who assert that the flag is "sacred." The force of nationalism is even worse when it is combined with explicit "religious" commitment. The disastrous effects of such religious nationalism are clear throughout the world.

Tillich's analysis of capitalism and nationalism as great demonic forces should not be taken as valid for all time, and Tillich did not intend it to be. His view of capitalism in particular was subject to the changing contours of capitalism itself; see Paul Tillich, "Rejoinder," *Journal of Religion* 46, no. 1, pt. 2 (January 1966): 189–91, for his somewhat impatient response to Clark A. Kucheman, "Professor Tillich: Justice and the Economic Order," *Journal of Religion* 46, no. 1, pt. 2 (January 1966): 165–83.

One of the more interesting changes for American readers is a reversal of the status of national principles and those of capitalism. When Tillich evaluated the relation between nationalism and capitalism in *The Religious Situation*, he concluded that capitalism had co-opted nationalism, even though the basic creeds of the two are opposed (*The Religious Situation*, 43, 119–22; *GW* 10:15–16, 48–49). The conflict of principle between nationalism and capitalism was noted earlier by Marx and Engels, *Manifesto of the Communist Party*, 476, 488. In the last decade, opposition between free capitalism and bounded nationalism has become apparent again and, at least in the United States, nationalism is seeking to control the aspects of capitalism that oppose it, as the rising emphasis on "buying American" and the increasingly vociferous opposition to American-based multinational efforts to employ cheaper labor abroad at the expense of employment for Americans show. On the other hand, the proposed North American trade agreement is an effort to transcend national boundaries precisely through international quasi capitalism. Much early opposition to the agreement is cast, unsurprisingly, in nationalist language.

72 This is true even of what were initially autonomous, or even theonomous, forces. The utter collapse of the principle of natural harmony, upon which the persuasiveness of pure capitalism depends, and the failure of capitalist society to recognize this collapse, are examples (*The Socialist Decision*, 51–56; *GW* 2:268–73).

73 Tillich, "Kairos," in *The Protestant Era*, 46 (*GW* 6:23).

74 Tillich, *Basic Principles of Religious Socialism*, 70 (*GW* 2:101–2). David H. Kelsey (*The Fabric of Paul Tillich's Theology* [New Haven: Yale University Press, 1967]) misunderstands what Tillich means by "symbol" in spite of a good presentation of Tillich's thought on symbols. Kelsey equates

substitutes finite form for the infinite itself or, stated in reverse, reduces the infinite to a thing that can be grasped and controlled by those who use the finite forms of religion properly. Heteronomy reduces the forms of grace to objects which can be touched, handled, manipulated, encompassed.[75]

Heteronomy involves domination and the will to dominate. The believer is dominated both internally and externally, while the unbeliever is subjected, at least, to heteronomy's sometimes fanatical desire to dominate. Heteronomous forces, however, do not arise out of pure malice and sadistic will. Tillich's concept of the "demonic" is fascinating because the demonic is not simply "evil."[76] The cardinal mark of the demonic is its inseparable blend of creative and destructive power.[77] Although heteronomous creativity is not possible without destructiveness, neither is heteronomy pure destructiveness.[78]

Any theonomous situation preserves a crucial feature of heteronomy. Heteronomous forces are aware of the unconditional element that gives life and meaning to finite reality.[79] This awareness of ultimacy is, unfortunately, directed to the irretrievable past alone, but in being so directed, heteronomy retains a relation to the powers of origin (*Ursprungsmächte*).[80] What is lacking

---

"symbol" with "holy object" (pp. 127–53), forgetting that a symbol is a *participant* in the infinite which it mediates. Tillich's point is that no object is holy in itself and any object can mediate the holy. The result of Kelsey's error is that he thinks "New Being" arrives from outside the picture of Jesus as the Christ and that the picture of Jesus as the Christ is made to conform to these alien criteria. Kelsey supports an alternative that would, essentially, make Jesus (and perhaps the New Testament) a "holy object."

In the first place, the accusation against Tillich is incorrect because it makes him out to be an idealist. A personal life is as important (which is to say essential) to the appearance of the New Being as works of art are important to the subsequent characterization of artistic "styles," for example. Tillich does not build his Christology merely on "an analysis of the formal properties of the picture" (p. 140). Second, the attempt to make Jesus or any other finite thing "holy" in and of itself is idolatrous, since it substitutes the medium of revelation for its content and identifies the finite thing with the infinite.

75 Tillich, *Systematic Theology* 2:85, 3:379; Paul Tillich, *Protestantism as a Critical and Creative Principle*, in *Political Expectation*, ed. Adams, 24–29 (*GW,* 7 Band, *Der Protestantismus als Kritik und Gestaltung: Schriften zur Theologie I*, ed. Renate Albrecht [Stuttgart: Evangelisches Verlagswerk, 1962], 40–45).

76 Tillich, "The Demonic," 93–96 (*GW* 6:52–54). Tillich claims that Hirsch perverts the depth and force of the concept of "demonic" by identifying "demonic" and "wicked" ("Open Letter to Emanuel Hirsch," 365).

77 Tillich, "The Demonic," 81 (*GW* 6:45 reads: "Immer bleibt die Grundbedeutung erhalten, wenn das Wort noch nicht zum entleerten Schlagwort geworden ist: die Einheit von form-schöpferischer und formzerbrechender Kraft"). See also Paul Tillich, *Dynamics of Faith* (New York: Harper & Row, 1957), 14–16. Obviously, it is this sense, and not that of mere moral disparagement, that is intended in the characterization of nationalism and capitalism as demonic. On capitalism, see Tillich, *Religious Socialism*, in *Political Expectation*, ed. Adams, 50; *GW* 2:177 characterizes capitalism as a "Vereinigung von schöpferischen und zerstörerischen Kräften . . . ."

78 A later use of the concept of the demonic is found in *Systematic Theology* 3:244–45.

79 Ibid., 252; "Author's Introduction," xix.

80 Tillich is not always clear on this point. An analysis of the *Ursprungsmächte* is especially

is a similar awareness of a future-directed demand (*Forderung*).[81] To claim that finite forms capture the infinite with complete sufficiency means that these forms lose their capacity to point to something that transcends, criticizes, and broadens them. In short, heteronomy lacks a "Protestant principle."[82] Still, this should not obscure the fact that there is awareness of divine presence in heteronomy. One feels Tillich's sympathy for the smallness of heteronomous forces, despite their often destructive historical influence.[83] The iron grip with which heteronomy holds its limited symbols and identifies them with the content of the eternal is bound to fail, for history leaves it behind. The travail of heteronomous elements is, finally, that they are unwilling to take the risks of doubt and error implied in the nature of historical decision.[84] Heteronomy may exhibit bravery, but not courage; it cannot accept justification "in spite of" its failures. The astonishing difficulty of accepting this "in-spite-of" character of justification indicates, in intellectual no less than moral matters, the presence of heteronomous drives in most of us, if not all of us.

Heteronomy arises out of a theonomous ground. But it is recognizable only in polar opposition to dissatisfaction with and criticism of the elevation of the finite to unconditional status. Heteronomy is visible as alien law (*heteros nomos*) only when an alternative emerges — the attitude of autonomy.[85] Tillich's use of "autonomy" is double-edged.[86] On one hand, autonomy is simply "obedience to reason, i.e., to the 'logos' immanent in reality and mind. . . . It

---

prominent in *The Socialist Decision,* 13–18 (*GW* 2:234–39); they are the powers of soil, blood, and social group. In *Basic Principles of Religious Socialism,* 59 (*GW* 2:91), these are the same powers associated with the sacramental attitude. See also Gilkey, *Gilkey on Tillich,* 14–15. It is not that heteronomy is only possible on the basis of repristination. There can be a futurist heteronomy as well, of which various strains of Marxism are good examples. See, e.g., Herbert Marcuse, "The Responsibility of Science," in *The Responsibility of Power,* ed. Krieger and Stern, 439–44, in which the attempt to invest science with import is simultaneously an advocacy of the subjection of science's autonomy.

[81] Tillich, *The Socialist Decision,* 4–7 (*GW* 2:228–30), among many places in *The Socialist Decision.* See also "Kairos," in *The Protestant Era,* in which much of Tillich's effort is expended attempting to give the conservative Augustinian philosophy of history a future-directed demand.

[82] The Protestant principle should never be confused with historical Protestantism. In fact, Tillich's question in "The End of the Protestant Era?" (in *The Protestant Era,* abridged ed., 222–33) is whether the Protestant era is at an end. However, this is not the same as the end of the Protestant principle, which could not be overcome because it is an ineradicable part of finitude's relation to the infinite ("Author's Introduction," vii–viii). For a late use of the Protestant principle, see *Systematic Theology* 3:177–87, 243–47, where Tillich identifies this principle as a mark of the Spiritual Presence, directing part of his use of the Protestant principle against Protestantism.

[83] Wilhelm Pauck and Marion Pauck, *Paul Tillich: His Life and Thought* (San Francisco: Harper & Row, 1976), 127.

[84] Tillich's conception of faith, of course, includes doubt as an element in faith itself; see *Dynamics of Faith,* 16–22, 100–101.

[85] Tillich, *Systematic Theology* 3:250.

[86] Adams, *Tillich's Philosophy,* 218.

replaces mystical nature with rational nature. . . . It analyzes everything in order to put it together rationally." Autonomy in this sense is a triumph of rational form and obedience to the logos character of reality. It accepts the task of justice, for example, and demands that the content of legal form be developed out of the historical situation according to norms of law. In this way autonomy is "the dynamic principle of history,"[87] the principle of creativity in culture. It is auto-nomos — it refuses to acquiesce to an alien law merely because it is stated authoritatively. Autonomy insists that it has a right to criticize tradition on the basis of its apprehension of the structures of reality.

In its inception as a distinguishable phenomenon (i.e., in opposition to heteronomy rather than as an aspect of a theonomous situation), the drive to autonomous form may begin as both discovery and "sacralization" of form. According to Tillich, the heritage of contemporary Western society did commence in this way. Mathematical natural science, for instance, "was born out of a desire to know the laws of God's creation, to understand matter as revealing the creator's glory and rationality after it had been regarded since the times of the Greeks as something inferior and anti-divine."[88] Similarly, technical dominion was a way to emancipate humanity from natural demonisms, and capitalism had its source in the discovery and valorization of the individual's creative powers.[89]

Against heteronomous forces which resist the appearance and significance of these forms, autonomy is the face of prophetic criticism; it calls for incorporation of natural forms and the individual into frameworks of meaning and import.[90] In opposing heteronomous alienation, the autonomous spirit "wants to restore the lost presence of the holy through the creation of form."[91] Autonomous spirit knows that its meaning is not self-generated; it is aware that questions of forms' meaning and *telos* cannot be answered from within

---

[87] Tillich, "Kairos," in *The Protestant Era*, 44, 45 (*GW* 6:21, 22). The most sustained reflection concerning autonomous epistemology, a topic beyond the scope of this discussion, is found in Paul Tillich, "Kairos and Logos," in *The Interpretation of History* (*GW*, 4 Band, *Philosophie und Schicksal: Schriften zur Erkenntnislehre und Existenzphilosophie*, ed. Renate Albrecht [Stuttgart: Evangelisches Verlagswerk, 1961]). There Tillich calls the autonomous and culturally dominant way of grasping form "reflexive-explanatory."

[88] Tillich, *The Religious Situation*, 48 (*GW* 10:18). The Jewish-Christian roots of this appreciation of matter are noted in Paul Tillich, *Christianity and Modern Society*, in *Political Expectation*, ed. Adams, 2 (*GW* 10:101).

[89] Tillich, *The Religious Situation*, 48–49 (*GW* 10:18). In addition, Tillich maintains that the bourgeois belief in natural harmony, as long as it lasted, had a religious root (*The Socialist Decision*, 49; *GW* 2:266).

[90] The alliance between the prophetic and autonomous is discovered in the rationality of prophetism, on the one hand (Tillich, *Systematic Theology* 1:141), and the corollary that, for both, the myth of origin is broken (*The Socialist Decision*, 24; *GW* 2:245). This is why Tillich can claim that the relation between bourgeois society and powers of origin is analogous to the relation between prophetic and priestly (*The Socialist Decision*, 54; *GW* 2:271). See also *Protestantism as a Critical and Creative Principle*, 31 (*GW* 7:46).

[91] Tillich, *Basic Principles of Religious Socialism*, 59 (*GW* 2:92).

form itself but depends on form's mediation of meaning which transcends it. This expression of autonomy, in other words, is aware of its participation in the ground of being and is open to the revelation of unconditioned import through form creation. Reason is ontological reason open to, though it cannot produce, an ultimate concern.[92]

Like heteronomy, autonomy is also grounded in theonomy. Recognition, creation, and development of autonomous form are immensely productive and necessary activities. Autonomous activity discloses the "what" that has to be taken into relations of meaning. This is its place within any theonomous situation, and this role cannot be abandoned without transforming theonomy into heteronomy. Tillich is emphatic:

> Theonomy would be destroyed the moment in which a valid logical conclusion was rejected in the name of the ultimate to which theonomy points, and the same is true in all other activities of cultural creativity. There is no theonomy where a valid demand of justice is rejected in the name of the holy, or where a valid act of personal self-determination is prevented by a sacred tradition, or where a new style of artistic creation is suppressed in the name of assumedly eternal forms of expressiveness. Theonomy is distorted into heteronomy in all these examples; the element of autonomy in it is removed — the Spirit is repressed. And then it may happen that autonomy breaks through the suppressive forces of heteronomy and discards not only heteronomy but also theonomy.[93]

"And then it may happen. . . ." The fate of the West was that autonomy did discard theonomy along with heteronomy. The theonomous baby, it will be recalled, is intermingled with heteronomous bathwater in that both are conscious of the presence of the eternal ground. Autonomous reaction disposed of both. In so doing, however, it detached itself from participation in this ground of being and meaning. Autonomy turns its head and manifests a second profile, which Tillich calls the affirmation of "self-sufficient finitude."[94] Valori-

---

[92] Tillich, *Systematic Theology* 1:72–75.

[93] Ibid. 3:251. The degeneration of autonomy is not inevitable, because "autonomy is not necessarily a turning away from the unconditional" ("Kairos," in *The Protestant Era,* 45; *GW* 6:22). "The World Situation," presents the turning point for the West as the transformation from a humanistic autonomy to a technical one. The latter is what degenerates and opens the way for demonic forces. An example of Tillich's analysis of the heteronomous destruction of autonomy in Germany is found in "Open Letter to Emanuel Hirsch," 373–74.

The criticism of Tillich in Victor Nuovo ("On Revising Tillich: An Essay on the Principles of Theology," in *Kairos and Logos: Studies in the Roots and Implications of Tillich's Theology,* ed. John J. Carey [Cambridge, Mass.: North American Tillich Society, 1978], 47) is incorrect on this point. Nuovo argues, he assumes against Tillich, that degeneration of autonomy is not *necessary.* Tillich, however, is clearly in agreement with that claim. There are two sides of autonomy in Tillich's work, and they must be distinguished carefully.

[94] This term is most pronounced in Tillich throughout *The Religious Situation* and *Christianity and Modern Society,* 4 (*GW* 10:102). Later, he defines autonomy as "reason which affirms and actualizes its structure without regarding its depth" (*Systematic Theology* 1:83).

zation of self-sufficient finitude is a less robust aspect of autonomy. Development of form remains its primary endeavor, but the question of form's meaning is severed from its creation. Form becomes its own purpose. No longer does it receive its reason for being from its mediation of transcendent import. The valuation of finite form in and of itself, without relation to spiritual meaning, becomes absolute.[95] Reason is reduced to "technical reason" without significance beyond itself.[96]

Historically, this cast of mind is reflected in full bloom in bourgeois society. The fusion of mathematical natural science, technical dominion, and their methods, led to a situation in which the eternal meaning of that heritage was "filled with unlimited desire for economic power" and reduced to an economic "war of all against all."[97] Tillich's point is broader than his objections to capitalism. What is lost in autonomous society is a sense of form's import and significance, "the question of the meaning of the process which claims the service of all the spiritual and physical human powers."[98] "The process" can be any process which valorizes endless but meaningless activity, not only an economic system. Affirmation of self-sufficient finitude is expressed, for example, by the variety of forms that are claimed to exist for their "own sake." Artistic form, for autonomy, is art for its own sake.[99] The confusion of knowledge and trivia is due in part to pursuit of knowledge for its own sake; merely knowing something gains priority over the meaning of what is known.[100] It is a short and perhaps inevitable step from an impoverished formalism empty of self-transcendent purpose to a vocational autonomy in

[95] Again, the whole of *The Religious Situation,* shows the loss of transcendent meaning in the specific pursuits of contemporary culture and, therefore, in Western culture as a whole. For later presentations of the same point, see Paul Tillich, "The Gospel and the State," *Crozer Quarterly* (Chester, Penn.) 15, no. 4 (October 1938): 260; *Systematic Theology* 3:248. Indeed, the very definition of "theonomy" is "self-transcending autonomy" (Tillich, "Author's Introduction," xii; see also *Christianity and Modern Society,* 6–8; *GW* 10:105–6). See also Roger L. Shinn, "Tillich as Interpreter and Disturber of Contemporary Civilization," in *The Thought of Paul Tillich,* ed. Adams, Pauck, and Shinn, 49–51.

[96] Tillich, *Systematic Theology* 1:53–54, 72–74. Technical reason, to be sure, is an element of ontological, essential reason, but if it is to be meaningful, technical reason must not release itself from the grasp of ontological reason.

[97] Tillich, *The Religious Situation,* 49 (*GW* 10:19).

[98] Ibid., 49, 47–48 (*GW* 10:19, 18). The translation of the latter quotation is modified; the German reads: "die Frage nach dem Sinn dieses alle geistigen und leiblichen Kräfte beanspruchenden Prozesses zu stellen."

[99] An interesting application of Tillich's thought to contemporary literature is provided in Nathan A. Scott, Jr., "Tillich's Legacy and the New Scene in Literature," in *The Thought of Paul Tillich,* ed. Adams, Pauck, and Shinn, 137–55.

[100] The protest against mere curiosity as conforming to the form of knowledge, but missing its purpose, is present in Christianity at least since Augustine. In Tillich's case, mere curiosity is excluded because of his notion of participation. "Concern" implies participation and opposes treating a thing "as a separated object that could be known and handled without concern" (*Systematic Theology* 1:12).

which pride of vocation has no more value than "keeping busy." In this situation, we can surely say, "The forms of the life-process have become completely self-sufficient over against life's depth."[101]

Ontological Power and Legitimacy

The demarcation between the predominance of ontological reason, which is open to revealed import, and technical reason, which affirms the adequacy of pure, independent form, is participation in being-itself. Whereas ontological reason is aware of its participation in transcendent power, technical reason is not. This is why the question of the relation between reason and revelation can be addressed only to ontological reason. If God and revelation are questions delivered directly to technical reason, the answers are confined to relations of means and ends; God winds up as one object among others, and revelation becomes a privileged piece of information. But revelation of eternal import is revelation of the power of being for the world in its concreteness; in order to have significance, form must participate in this power.[102] The empty formalism of self-sufficient finitude is, in its own nature, powerless.

But neither aspect of reason is powerless in its manifestations or it could not be manifest at all; it could not have being, because existence itself depends on participation in the power of being. Concern with form, too, must be related to power. As with many Tillichian concepts, the purely formal concern of reason is two-sided. On one side, reason is what it says it is — concern with form alone. But the subjective *logos* and its apprehension of the immanent structures of reality depend on there being a reality, an objective *logos,* to apprehend. Structures of the mind must unite with structures of reality.[103] The structures of being must first be; being is the fundamental presupposition of reflection. Power of being produces existence. The world may have a *logos* that can be understood, but that *logos* must be posited by power. This would appear to be a fairly uncontroversial claim. It is denied, however, whenever an answer is anticipated to the question, *Why is there something rather than nothing?* If this question is about the origin of existence (and not its purpose) and expects to be answered, we are confronted with another attempt to enshrine reason as the fundamental ontological principle. The question presupposes that a reason — a why for existence — could first be discovered, upon which follow acts of power that produce existents. It implies that being can be derived from

---

[101] Tillich, *The Religious Situation,* 48 (translation slightly modified; GW 10:18 reads: "Die Formen des Lebensprozesses sind völlig selbständig gegenüber der Lebenstiefe geworden").

[102] Tillich, *Systematic Theology* 1:74–129, 2:166–67; *Love, Power, and Justice,* 83. Hammond (*Man in Estrangement,* 88) has a good discussion of the relation between ontological and actual reason, and Gilkey ("The Role of the Theologian in Contemporary Society," 335–40) has a good treatment of ontological and technical reason.

[103] Tillich, *Systematic Theology* 1:75–79.

something other than itself. Tillich is surely right when he responds, "being can only be derived from being."[104] The question Why is there something, and not nothing? is intelligible only if it is taken as the point at which "reason reaches its boundary line, is thrown back upon itself, and then is driven again to its extreme situation,"[105] a question that cannot be answered because "being is the original fact which cannot be derived from anything else."[106] That anything exists is "an astonishing prerational fact,"[107] behind which one cannot go.

The persistent attraction of Why? lies in the fact that, although one cannot go behind being, the question appears to do just that. Finally, however, as anyone well knows who has dealt with a child's dogged question Why? following any statement, the respondent is driven to say, inevitably, "Because that is the way it is." Why is there something rather than nothing? is simply the final stage of the childhood question and permits no answer apart from the one parents are accustomed to giving. If any other answer were given, it would be subject to yet another why and would be therefore meaningless both as question and answer.[108] Being cannot be justified by a reason extraneous to itself.

The reliance of *logos* and its forms on the underivable power of being means that reason, in both its ontological and its technical manifestations, is contained within power. Objectively, acts of power produce beings with a rational structure, including beings that can apprehend those structures. Subjectively, knowledge of rational structure relies on being given an object created through power. Two implications of the conclusion that reason is enveloped in power are important. The first is that we are able to validate retrospectively and ontologically Foucault's assertion that knowledge is contained, from the start, within relations of power. There could be no knowledge developed outside the context of power; both the structures of human reason and the objects about which it develops knowledge already assume power. Truth is generated by power. The second implication follows. It is not possible to develop a criterion of reason outside of power that could "legitimate" power. Any attempt to separate reason from power in order to develop such a criterion is both

---

[104] Ibid., 113.

[105] Ibid. Reisz ("Tillich's Doctrine of God," 154) notes Tillich's debt to Schelling on this point. For Schelling, the why must be resolved on the basis of "will." Tillich's relation to the "voluntarist" tradition is explored by James Luther Adams, "Introduction: The Storms of our Times and *Starry Night*," in *The Thought of Paul Tillich*, ed. Adams, Pauck, and Shinn, 8–14.

[106] Tillich, *Systematic Theology* 1:113.

[107] Tillich, *Courage To Be*, 40.

[108] Tillich, *Systematic Theology* 1:163. Tillich discovers the relation of existence to the eternal exactly here, "at the absolute givenness, the underivability, the inconstruability of the living structure, the non-rational ground on which this structure rests and which comes to expression in the demonic-divine polarity of conflict and social integration, of the will-to-power and love" (*The Religious Situation*, 61–62; *GW* 10:24).

self-deceptive and unproductive. If it expects to have effect, it is already within a complex of power; if it does not, then it is powerless. If reason and power are placed on parallel tracks, there is no principle of reason able to legitimate power from the outside. Power is its own legitimation because any pretence to make it legitimate inevitably participates in power.

If, in spite of its ground in power, reason attempts to separate itself from power, the result is reason's impoverishment. Since Habermas's critical theory has been touched on already, we shall return to it. If the ideal of the ideal speech situation, the forceless force of consensus, supplies the formal criterion for what is and is not rational (and powerful), we may ask Habermas when, or even whether, one may end the unrestricted conversation. When, if ever, is it possible to make a decision about the conversation itself? The same questions apply also to Russell's "persuasive power." In fact, the impasse is even more severe in Russell's case, because persuasive power is not only one power among others, but the greatest power. Of course, no answer to the question of when conversation has lost its usefulness is possible outside the situation in which one finds oneself. But it should be possible to account for and employ power legitimately outside the conversation of reason, unless one wants to commit to the implausible position that *only* the word of reason and action following directly upon unrestricted agreement in the ideal speech situation are valid spheres of action. This indeed seems to be the position of Russell Hanson, who is influenced heavily by Habermas.[109] Hanson is disturbed by the narrowing of possible political options in American political history. But the limitations he describes occurred precisely because members of the political body made decisions about what had to be *done.* Conversations were ended and decisions made. Hanson decries the limitation of our "power-talk" because, it appears, legitimate power lies only in the realm of "talk" or discursive reason. There is no legitimate end to the conversation.

Restricting the realm of legitimate power to "power-talk" is obviously highly abstract. The presumed invalidity of action outside power-talk takes its revenge upon that sphere itself, by making power-talk powerless, without effect outside its own narrow parameters. If Hanson's criterion for rational action is followed, no material action can be taken; nothing can be done outside the sphere of discourse, unless it is possible for discursive reason to develop criteria for its own suspension. Only if the unrestricted conversation could provide such criteria could legitimate nondiscursive action be taken. Otherwise, the pure formalism of the ideal speech situation is a stunning example of powerless autonomy.[110]

---

[109] Russell L. Hanson, *The Democratic Imagination in America: Conversations with Our Past* (Princeton, N.J.: Princeton University Press, 1985).

[110] In "Kairos and Logos," 135–51 (*GW* 4:50–61) Tillich offers a compelling argument against any attempt to separate knowledge and decision. Among other difficulties, it contradicts knowledge's involvement in fate.

Suspension of communication involves a decision that cannot be defended in full by the standards of reason. Decision involves elimination of real possibilities, a limitation inimical to a conversation that attempts to keep all possibilities open. The decision to act outside the discursive format involves a leap. Discursive reason always has one more card to play. The suspension of conversation cannot but feel somewhat arbitrary to discursive reason, since it must be partially external to it.

Moreover, the decision to act by reasoning in discourse instead of acting in some other way is subject to the same leap. Even if it is true that "once participants enter into argumentation, they cannot avoid supposing, in a reciprocal way, that the conditions for an ideal speech situation have been met,"[111] this does not show, as Habermas wants it to, the universal power of reason and the force of unforced consensus. From what source does this "once" come? Even granting that "once" the argument is joined, Habermas is correct, this entry into the conversation itself is not produced by purely rational criteria, and the illusion that it is produces serious difficulties for Habermas's position, as we will see later. Free initiation of conversation is also external to discourse. Refusal to participate in conversation and negotiation is only one reminder of this.[112] Discursive reason cannot justify its own employment, much less its suspension.

The form of rational discourse or conversation is self-sufficient neither in origin nor in end. If it fails to discern its origin in the decision for conversation and persuasion, if it disregards its drive to nondiscursive action, it is left to watch, as fan or protester, the passing parade of a history that does decide for some options against others.[113] The assumed self-sufficient finitude of the conversation, like that of any idea, cannot account fully for concrete decisions, which "imply an element of belief, of hope and daring which cannot be replaced by rational conclusions."[114] Reason, at its best, may tell us what is the case, what we are to do, but it does not say when. "When" is a matter of response to life and can be worked out in advance only rarely, in cases of simple judgments of (usually) little significance. Whatever calculations and judgments are made, seizing the *kairos,* the "right time" to act, is always a matter of venture

[111] Jürgen Habermas, *The Philosophical Discourse of Modernity: Twelve Lectures,* trans. Frederick Lawrence (Cambridge, Mass.: MIT Press, 1987), 323.

[112] It also stretches credulity to assert that such refusal is *de facto* irrational.

[113] Tillich, "Kairos and Logos," 153–54 (*GW* 4:62); see also "The Interpretation of History and the Idea of Christ," 255–56; *Religiöse Verwirklichung,* 120–22. Tillich argues that the attempt to reduce decision to reason is ultimately ahistorical.

[114] Tillich, "The Interpretation of History and the Idea of Christ," 255–56. The translation of this piece is modified substantially from the chapter entitled "Christologie und Geschichtdeutung," in *Religiöse Verwirklichung,* 120–21. *The Interpretation of History* notes that the purpose of the adjustments in this essay and two others was adequacy of presentation to the Anglo-Saxon world. (p. vii).

and risk.[115] One may employ reason in all of these judgments, but reason cannot by itself jump from the side of contemplation to decision. Commonsense judgment knows that decision is closer to the nature of power than contemplation of decision. When one is seized by the situation in such a way that one is unable to decide, unable to act, frozen, we say that that person is "powerless." Decision is a matter of freedom, and the realm of freedom demands inclusion within a conception of power.

Showing that the rational conversation is not self-sufficient confirms the judgment that power is teleological in nature, a communication between areas, and also points to another aspect of self-sufficient finitude. With the rupture between finite form and its infinite ground comes a tendency for finite forms to dissociate from each other.[116] The radical separation of disciplines in the university and indifference of practitioners of one discipline to those in the next building are clear (though far from unique) examples of this phenomenon. The consequence of such self-absorbed specialization is the irrelevance of much academic work not only to other academicians but also to the larger society. The form of discursive action loses its capacity to pass into even other finite forms, notably the realm of nondiscursive action. Whatever power potential may exist in purely discursive action is eviscerated when a *telos* to, and origin in, the concrete situation is ignored.

Decay of self-sufficient rational form is not, however, the final word. To remain within the confines of autonomous form is not an option. Decision and action in freedom do not permit their neglect. Vital forces demand a hearing; origin cannot be effaced in fulfillment.[117] The choice is between infusion of theonomous import into autonomous form and infusion of demonic

---

[115] The clearest exposition of the *kairos* is found in "Kairos." *Systematic Theology* notes the riskiness of kairic judgment (3:364–71). Weisskopf ("Tillich and the Crisis of the West") and Dennis P. McCann ("Tillich's Religious Socialism: 'Creative Synthesis' or Personal Statement?" in *The Thought of Paul Tillich,* ed. Adams, Pauck, and Shinn) both make Tillich into more of a rationalist than he is: Weisskopf by suggesting that Tillich was a rationalist, and McCann by arguing that he should have been. In both cases, the aesthetic, participatory nature of decision is overlooked in favor of "rational" criteria of decision. Tillich does not oppose such criteria (we will see a few of them in the subsequent chapter) but argues they are ultimately insufficient; proclamation of the *kairos* must finally be a "personal statement" which strives to grasp and express the import of our situation. Robert P. Scharlemann gives a good presentation of this point ("Tillich and the Religious Interpretation of Art," in *The Thought of Paul Tillich,* ed. Adams, Pauck, and Shinn, 158–62).

[116] Tillich, *The Socialist Decision,* 85 (*GW* 2:299); "The World Situation," 11.

[117] Tillich, *The Socialist Decision,* 107 (*GW* 2:315). This is the central point in the argument of *The Socialist Decision* as a whole. Tillich advocates a theonomous socialism because he believes autonomous socialism and autonomous bourgeois society are impossible and self-contradictory. Socialism must make "a clear decision for the powers of origin (*Kräfte des Ursprungs*), while rejecting the forces of origin (*Ursprungsmächte*) that have become bourgeois, together with the bourgeois principle itself" (*The Socialist Decision,* 68; *GW* 2:283). Indeed, it was the *Ursprungskräfte* of humanity that shattered the harmony bourgeois society requires (*The Socialist Decision,* 170; *GW* 2:269). See also Tillich, "On the Boundary: An Autobiographical Sketch," in *The Interpretation of History,* 9–10; "The World Situation," 13; *Dynamics of Faith,* 58.

import into the same autonomous form, to the ultimate destruction of form.[118] In Tillich's Germany, the vacuum of meaning left by self-sufficient finitude led to the latter consequence: form was used by what ultimately poisoned and destroyed it—the demonism of the Third Reich.[119] To be sure, this is the contradiction of all political romanticism, which is forced to employ rational form even though its purpose is to destroy those same forms.[120]

Fault for this disaster must be laid squarely at the doorstep of those who have abandoned the meaning of form for pure, and therefore meaningless, formalism. Autonomous form relies for its efficacy on its being related both to the powers of origin it often eschews and to images of fulfillment.[121] Autonomy's second dimension is revealed here; it cannot be, as it professes, concerned finally with form alone, but also must keep contact with the import of form. Autonomy must choose theonomous or demonic import, or have its choice made for it.[122] It will not do, when one form or another has been invaded by demonism, to search for yet another form which can be pure and self-sufficient. For there is no form, once its meaning has died of thirst in a lonely desert, that cannot be overtaken by demonic forces which are at least aware of powers of origin and promise their adherents a fulfillment of repristi-nation. Bertrand Russell's great faith in the form of education as a way to prevent the fanaticisms that give impetus to tyranny must be examined in this light.[123] Can education not also be infused with demonic contents and significance, precisely because it has become an end in itself, directed at mere "knowledge" rather than "wisdom"?[124] Many, if not most, modern tyrants

---

[118] Tillich, *Basic Principles of Religious Socialism,* 86 (*GW* 2:117); see also *Dynamics of Faith,* 77; and "The World Situation," 18.

[119] Carl E. Schorske notes a similar phenomenon occurring between the liberals of nineteenth-century Austria and Schönerer's valorization of the vitality of the past ("Politics in a New Key: Schönerer," in *The Responsibility of Power,* ed. Krieger and Stern, 233–51). This is part of what Schorske maintains constitutes the "new key" that Hitler was to turn into a horrible symphony.

[120] See esp. Tillich, *The Socialist Decision,* 25–26, 42–44 (*GW* 2:246–47, 261–64). Tillich warns his new American audience of the danger of powers surging into the "vacuum" of meaning left by increasingly secular democratic states ("The Gospel and the State," 261).

[121] Tillich, *Basic Principles of Religious Socialism,* 86 (*GW* 2:117); *The Socialist Decision,* 54 (*GW* 2:271).

[122] McCann is succinct: "The socialist decision, in other words, is a choice between socialism and barbarism" ("Tillich's Religious Socialism," 86).

[123] Russell, *Power,* 308–10; see also C. Wright Mills, "On Knowledge and Power," in *Power, Politics, and People: The Collected Essays of C. Wright Mills,* ed. Irving Louis Horowitz (London: Oxford University Press, 1963), 599–613. Despite Mills's concession that education can be a weapon of power at one point, his general position is that the terrible hegemony of power, which controls virtually everything else in America, has left the intellectuals alone and that the knowledge of this group is the best hope for destroying this hegemony. If this seems ludicrous on its face, as surely it is for reasons too numerous to outline, one should not forget Mills's popularity and persuasiveness to a wide audience both inside and outside academic circles.

[124] Tillich notes the emptiness of formal pedagogy in "Religion and Secular Culture," 65; and "The Protestant Message and the Man of Today," 203 (*Religiöse Verwirklichung,* 39).

commit their greatest abuses through the tools of education and especially "re-education" (the reign of the Khmer Rouge stands as the most grotesque recent example), and the ranks of tyrants and malefactors can certainly count many well-educated people in their ranks. The truth of Tillich's observations are not confined to the decade of National Socialism.[125]

In addition to the persuasiveness of Tillich's historical evidence, it is possible to develop conceptual support for his conclusions regarding the necessity of this choice between theonomous and demonic import. In the cases of Russell's "persuasive power" and Habermas's "forceless force," dependence on powers of origin is obvious as soon as the bare form of conversation finds an object about which to converse. Foucault was unable to maintain a playful disposition toward truth, in part because it was impossible to defend the meaningfulness of his work from within such an attitude. In the present case, the choice of a subject about which to converse presupposes participation in the *eros* to knowledge, that is, its import and meaningfulness for its participants.[126]

What is true of the origin of the conversation is true also of its end. Persuasive power is power for something, presumably something external to the event of persuasion itself. That is why coercive power must be exercised occasionally on the unpersuaded. The same can be said of the ideal speech situation. Unlike Hanson, Habermas recognizes the need to suspend the process of reaching agreement in order to act nondiscursively. The critical force of the ideal speech situation, like the critical edge of Tillich's "Protestant principle," is not sufficient.[127] Habermas takes up the question of whether the conversation may be suspended in, as far as I know, only one essay.[128] There he says:

> The groups which look upon themselves as theoretically enlightened (and which Marx in his time identified as the avant-garde of the Communists

---

[125] Nor are they confined to education as a form. Our recent euphoria over "free elections" in Eastern Europe has assumed that the mere structure of an election is the accomplishment of democratic culture. How many tyrants have come to the fore by electoral means only to destroy the electoral process? An especially strong warning against viewing elections as a panacea is Leslie H. Gelb, "The Free Elections Trap," *The New York Times,* 29 May 1991, A23. Unfortunately, no one seems able to imagine an alternative to these potentially dangerous electoral options.

[126] Tillich, *Systematic Theology* 1:72, 95, 176. The assumption of import holds even for those whose role in a conversation is to convince other participants the topic is not significant. The implicit function of such a role is to redirect other participants to more substantive subjects. The only instance in which import is not assumed might be in the case of Kierkegaard's "aesthete," for whom nothing is ultimately serious. The eros of knowledge in this case is exhausted in the pleasure of external conquest of an object or argumentative opponent. Tillich claims that *agapē* conquers "the detached safety of a merely aesthetic *eros*" (*Love, Power, and Justice,* 118).

[127] Tillich, *Systematic Theology* 1:139–40. For Tillich, the "inner dilemma of Protestantism lies in this, that it must protest against every religious or cultural realization which seeks to be intrinsically valid, but that it needs such realization if it is to make its protest in any meaningful way" (*The Religious Situation,* 192; *GW* 10:80). This is why the Protestant principle requires a Catholic substance and a "great *kairos*." Otherwise, the Protestant principle is empty.

[128] Habermas, *Theory and Practice,* 1–40.

or also of the Party) must choose, with a view to their opponents, in each instance between enlightenment and struggle, thus between maintaining and breaking off communication. . . . [In struggle,] the opponent who has been excluded by the breaking off of communication (and also the potential allies) can only be involved virtually.[129]

The criterion for the severance of communication is "rationally" based in the charge that one's opponents are trapped in ideology, and that the "enlightened" are not.[130]

This is a surprising claim for a devotee of unforced consensus.[131] Habermas knows that the discourse of reason participates in a wider environment controlled by the choice between "enlightenment and struggle." This insight obviously calls into question his assertion of identity between power and reason, since the choice of enlightenment or struggle cannot be made by rational criteria alone. Habermas recognizes this. The charge of ideological entrapment, if it involves "strategic action directed to the future . . . cannot be justified in the same manner by reflective knowledge." This is not, however, an isolated problem within the context of Habermas's thought. The hypothesis of the "fictive" superiority of the enlightened, which presumably demands "self-correction"[132] even if hypothetical, as a necessary assumption for action seriously injures central segments of Habermas's critical project. His radical disjunction between rational, legitimate power and the illegitimate power of domination avoids dangerous consequences only if the power of unforced consensus is capable of legitimating and fulfilling power as a whole. Once in the realm of the power of decision and freedom, however, reason's formal criteria cannot fulfill this task; force must be called on as a power superior to reason to compel those trapped in ideological distortion.

Against a narrow pejorative conception of ideology like that employed by Habermas, Tillich notes:

the formal objection must be raised that the assertion of the ideological character of thinking (*ideologische Wahrheitsbegriff*) must allow at least one exception, namely this assertion itself. If this is also nothing but ideology it is only the expression of a special social situation and cannot even try to claim universal validity.[133]

[129] Ibid., 38.

[130] Ibid.

[131] The distrust of any disruption of the conversation in Hanson, *The Democratic Imagination in America,* is more consistent than Habermas's position, but also less interesting.

[132] Habermas, *Theory and Practice,* 39, 40.

[133] Tillich, "Kairos and Logos," 155 (*GW* 4:63). Tillich's specific target is Marx's conception of ideology. A later presentation of Tillich's viewpoint in relation to Marxism, which takes the position that the Marxist and Stalinist use of "ideology" is itself ideological, is found in Paul Tillich, *Christianity and Marxism,* in *Political Expectation,* ed. Adams, 89–96. This essay is interesting for its revealing treatment of Marxism and Tillich's theory of the way in which Marxism could lead to Stalinism. It is also of interest as a later viewpoint on Marxism, which includes many

Habermas exempts considerably more than this. By means of the thin veneer of "virtual participation," certain content-filled political action is excluded from the charge of ideology, even though that action is conducted outside the universal a priori structures of communication, that is, beyond the constructs of consensual reason. It is important to remember that Habermas's persuasive critique of positivism is based largely in its inverse error. What makes positivism untenable as a system of thought is that it cannot account for its own theoretical formulation, which is decidedly nonpositivistic. Positivism can practice but cannot account for its practice.[134] Yet if Habermas is permitted to exempt, for practical purposes, a set of assertions from the charge of ideology and even from the metatheory that made those assertions possible (that is, his theory of communicative rationality can theorize but cannot account for its practices by means of that theory), why is positivism not permitted the reverse error?

This has dire consequences. If positivism is given equal right to be self-contradictory, which seems only fair, then the "enlightened" may be positivists and representatives of instrumental reason. Moreover, if the enlightened, whoever they may claim to be, are permitted the luxury of pure self-contradiction, the standards for who bears enlightenment and who does not are arbitrary, subject to no evaluation at all from reason. Enlightenment becomes a matter of pure force. Habermas's project, which begins by the identification of reason and power, ends with an identification of force and reason once it is thrust into practice.[135] Then truly the way is open for a demonic content which may not only fill the structures of reason, but disregard them entirely in the name of the self-declared superiority of the enlightened. No boundary can be provided for force, no matter how bloodthirsty and rapacious — force that, for its last laugh, can even justify itself in the names of enlightenment and reason. The identification of reason and power collapses under the weight of action and decision. Once the genie is released from the bottle with the "rational" assertion of the ideological imprisonment of one's opponents, the rationality of conversation cannot control it. It is surely true that the supposed basis of the triumphal charge of ideological distortion in pure rationality, a rationality conceptually severed from but nevertheless existentially and ontologically dependent on force, is operative in many of history's greatest campaigns of fanaticism. The belief in the miracle that power can overcome itself by reason blinds its adherents to acts undertaken in the name of that miracle.[136]

---

similarities to but also some differences from Tillich's prewar perspective. Most notably, it makes clear that heteronomy can be futurist.

[134] Habermas, *Knowledge and Human Interests*, 71–90.

[135] This critique also argues, by implication, for a broader, nonpejorative conception of "ideology." As long as "ideology" merely imports condemnation to specific positions, there is no way to resolve its self-contradiction and, finally, its reduction of truth to that force which derives from a smug and self-serving declaration of superiority.

[136] Tillich, *The Socialist Decision*, 76 (*GW* 2:290–91). The bizarre alternation between ineffectual

It is a serious error of ontology if either of two conceptions regarding the relation between reason and power is affirmed: (1) reason and power have no association with each other, or (2) reason is the final and superior power, not a participant in broader power. Exactly because these are ontological errors, they are not mistakes without consequences external to thought. They also influence and limit practice. Power shows that it is broader and greater than reason. If reason denies that it participates in power at all, or affirms its own superiority, it divests itself of any resources for the effective criticism of the more extensive powers and is finally overwhelmed. What disturbs Habermas most of all, that an "investigation of the other of reason [power] would have to occupy a position utterly heterogeneous to reason," turns out to be a self-fulfilling prophecy if his own conception of the relations between power and reason are upheld, because reason cannot hold the *"power* of the keys."[137] Only power can be power. The "taming" of power proves impossible because reason requires instantiation in and by power. Power exceeds reason rather than the other way around. If implacable enemies they are, then power must be victorious.

The result of the severance of reason and power is often an abject fear of powers beyond reason which precludes historical efficacy (as in Hanson as an example of a common leftist attitude),[138] or the absence of rational criteria by which the instances of power could be judged (as in Hobbes and especially Machiavelli as examples of a generally rightist viewpoint). The consequences of affirming the superior power of reason are more complex but frequently take refuge in the same alternatives. When reason discovers that it is not the ultimate power, it lacks the tools with which to reestablish a relation to power exceeding reason. It retreats in fear of those powers or permits the introduction of a principle not only beyond but totally alien and opposed to reason. As often as not, the result is the fanatical employment of any means necessary, no matter how brutal, to achieve a supposedly rational end. This rational covering makes the consequences of an initial faith in the power of reason more insidious than its more truthful Machiavellian counterpart. In either case, the avenging necessity of power permits its cynical and heartless employment. Power becomes pure domination.

If, however, reason emerges from the fundamental ontological principle of power, the situation may turn out quite differently. The excess of power beyond reason is recognized. Reason may, to be sure, claim its place as a participant in power, but it is aware that it is neither identical to the whole of

---

practice and tyrannical policy in political rationalism is not restricted to any special form of government. Its presence in America is demonstrated in Robert W. Tucker and David C. Hendrickson, *Empire of Liberty: The Statecraft of Thomas Jefferson* (New York: Oxford University Press, 1990).

[137] Habermas, *The Philosophical Discourse of Modernity,* 302, 303.

[138] Plato and Locke are classical examples of the same tendency, although Plato makes it clear that the leftist bent of this attitude is more a modern innovation than a necessary outcome.

power, nor the most exalted power. Reason and power are not separated from each other; reason is one of the appearances of power.

Two consequences follow. First, the inner aim of reason, which needs power, is fuller participation in power. Like all that has being, reason seeks its own fulfillment. Reason must seek power in order to fulfill itself. Reason therefore maintains a critical edge against its own powerless manifestations. Second, and paradoxically, the critical power of reason is elevated. Fulfilled power is the communication of efficacy; the production of dominations as ends in themselves, without *teloi* to communications of efficacy, is distorted power. A reason that emerges from and depends on productions of power does not lose the right and obligation to criticize distortions of power. Because it participates in power, it seeks the completion of power in the communication of efficacy. As a manifestation of power, reason drives power's manifestations to their common aim. Reason's criticism of unfulfilled and deformed power is launched precisely in the name of power. This coincidence of objectives affirms Tillich's claim that a valid theonomy does not contradict autonomous form. The way is opened for what can be called truly an ethic of power: the content of ethics and the forms in which that content is expressed emerge from power itself. Fulfilled power is its own criterion, in need of no legitimation from elsewhere. Power does not need legitimation from outside itself, but neither is such external validation possible; power is valid because it is power, because it is what all else requires in order to be, behind or above which nothing could reach in order to legitimate it from outside. Power has been placed firmly on the side of creation, rather than being considered simply an unfortunate result of the Fall. The ground has been claimed allowing the resolution of the perplexing problem of power's geography and permitting an ethic of power to be given a more definitive shape.

CHAPTER 6

THE GEOGRAPHY AND ETHIC
OF POWER

If any account of what it is to have being is an explication of power, the workings of power must be specified more closely. The ontological nature of power has been shown, as has the possibility of overcoming a notion of power as domination. Still, significant issues remain. Of primary importance is what has been termed the "geography of power." The fourth chapter gave a brief synopsis of the importance of this formal question for the content and coherence of a definition of power and made a provisional decision to accept a location of power at the border of encounter. "Border" contains both spatial and temporal components. In addition, the metaphor is designed to preserve power's relation to both inwardness and externality, while overcoming a geography of power that locates power there. If we continue to speak of inner or outer power, such language concerns the effects of power. The problem of power's geography requires solution because Luther could not lay it to rest. Despite the appearance of the idea that power is a phenomenon of the border in Luther, he gives no final judgment about power's site because he is undecided between two alternatives.

Tillich's theology contains a similar equivocation. He too understands power from within the categories of potentiality and actuality, inner posses-sion or external expression.[1] Although the preceding chapter indicated the fundamental importance of power, it did not say what power is for Tillich. That inquiry is for the present. This analysis has both illustrative and constructive value. It illuminates the difficulties of understanding power as potentiality and/or actuality and allows comparison between those alternatives and a treatment of power as a phenomenon appearing at the border of encounter.

First, what Tillich means by "power" must be determined. It turns out that Tillich means a number of things, and these several connotations must be analyzed more closely. An investigation of centered power of being, which is actual with respect to the being whose power it is but potential with respect

---

[1] Paul Tillich, *Love, Power, and Justice: Ontological Analyses and Ethical Applications* (Oxford: Oxford University Press, 1954), 22.

to its external expression, reveals a deep conflict of powers. To overcome the strife that can develop between powers, Tillich resorts to the rational form of justice. He is not satisfied to stop there, however, because justice is a rational form and therefore cannot overcome the conflict of powers completely. Strife between powers is overcome in "creative justice," or love, which has a close affinity with "spiritual power." In the idea of spiritual power a question related to Christology arises — the renunciation of power. In partial opposition to Tillich, an argument is made that affirmation of the possibility of power through its renunciation, or at least including its renunciation, is unnecessarily confusing and tends to vitiate a positive evaluation of power — an evaluation that is necessary if power is the fundamental description of being–itself and of all beings.

The centered conception of power is not, however, the only one Tillich presents. A second strand is discovered in his work, which Tillich does not, in general, recognize as an account of power. This aspect of his work and the variety of positions Tillich takes which depend on it are understood better if power is not centered, but rather a phenomenon of the borders. With respect to Foucault, the intention has been to complete a project he was unable to finish, but in regard to Luther and Tillich, the task is to reconcile aspects of their thought. If the conception of power as border event is carried through, the ground will be laid for a brief statement of the shape of an ethic built upon the foundation of power rather than one placed in the self–contradictory position of controlling or limiting power's emergence.

The Meanings of Power

To discover what Tillich believes power is, it is important to note that, in English, "power" covers a broad range of meaning. So it does also in Tillich's American work. His early German writing, however, usually employs three distinct terms, all of which can be translated as "power" in English and were so "translated" by Tillich himself after crossing the Atlantic. On the one hand, the differentiation of "power" in Tillich's German may avoid the imprecision of English usage. On the other hand, the concentration of meanings within the single term "power" in English affords an opportunity to unite a plurality of senses.

We have focused primarily on the phrase "power of being." A problem appears immediately. Tillich's early uses of this expression in, for example, *The Socialist Decision* and *Religiöse Verwirklichung,* employ *"Seinsmächtigkeit,"* *"Mächtigkeit,"* or *"Seinsmacht."* We already know that the concept of being employed by Tillich at that point referred only to actually existing being. The power of being Tillich designates by *"Mächtigkeit,"* then, relates to the power of existing beings. This is not what is meant by his later use of "power of being" in connection with God, where power of being refers to being–itself, and definitely not an existing thing, no matter how exalted over other existents.[2] In his American work, being-itself is also described as "ground of being," a term that "oscillates between cause and substance and transcends both of them."[3]

Kraft

Being-itself as the ground of being is that in which any existing being must participate in order to have its own specific power of being. The participation of all beings in the power of being implies being-itself is the creative ground of being, underlying and transcending the universe of creatures. In German, Tillich's usual term for this power is "*Kraft.*" Religious *Kraft* is the lifeblood, the inner energy and ultimate meaning of life,[4] at once vital and creative. As vital, the *Kraft* of being is related to powers of origin as "*Urkräfte.*" Vital *Urkräfte* are the formless abyss of being: they "rush out beyond all form into the boundless and yet can enter reality only through form, [they are] the inner restlessness of everything living, the inability to have one's own power to be and grasp one's own being as one's own and come to rest therein."[5] These

---

[2] Tillich's denial that the power of being is an existing thing is almost incessant. He says this as early as "On the Idea of a Theology of Culture," in *What Is Religion?*, trans. William Baillie Green, ed. James Luther Adams (New York: Harper & Row, 1969), 157 (*GW*, 9 Band, *Die Religiöse Substanz der Kultur: Schriften zur Theologie der Kultur*, ed. Renate Albrecht [Stuttgart: Evangelisches Verlagswerk, 1967], 14), in which he gives Kant credit for the argument. Two sustained attacks on the "existence" of God are found in "The Two Types of Philosophy of Religion," in *Theology of Culture*, ed. Robert C. Kimball (New York: Oxford University Press, 1959), 11–25; and *Systematic Theology*, 3 vols. (Chicago: University of Chicago Press, 1951–63) 1:165–66, 173, 190, 204–5.

[3] Tillich, *Systematic Theology* 1:155, 156; see also *Dynamics of Faith* (New York: Harper & Row, 1957), 106.

[4] Tillich, "Kairos," in *The Protestant Era*, abridged ed., trans. James Luther Adams (Chicago: University of Chicago Press, 1957), 43 (*GW*, 6 Band, *Der Widerstreit von Raum und Zeit*, ed. Renate Albrecht [Stuttgart: Evangelisches Verlagswerk, 1963], 20).

[5] Tillich, "The Demonic," in *The Interpretation of History*, trans. Elsa L. Talmey (New York: Charles Scribner's Sons, 1936), 85–86 (translation slightly modified; *GW* 6:48 reads: "die vitalen Urkräfte, die ins Grenzlose über jede Gestalt hinaustreiben und doch nur in der Gestalt zur Wirklichkeit kommen können, die innere Unruhe alles Lebendigen, die Unfähigkeit, seiner selbst mächtig zu sein und das eigene Sein als eigenes zu erfassen und darin zu Ruhe zu kommen"). "*Urkräfte*" should be distinguished from "*Ursprungsmächte*" and "*Macht des Ursprungs*," which are translated as "powers of origin" and "power of origin" (*The Socialist Decision*, trans. Franklin Sherman [New York: Harper & Row, 1977; reprint, Washington, D.C.: University Press of America, 1977], 13; *GW*, 2 Band, *Frühe Schriften zum Religiösen Sozialismus*, ed. Renate Albrecht [Stuttgart: Evangelisches Verlagswerk, 1962], 234–35), and from "*Ursprungskräfte*" (*The Socialist Decision*, 60; *GW* 2:276). The powers of origin of blood, soil, and nation, for example, are conditions for development of a concrete spirit, but they already contain an element of form that *Kraft* lacks. Instead, these "concrete" powers of origin (*The Socialist Decision*, 13; *GW* 2:234) are closer to the symbols of "*Machtwille*" and "*Eroskraft*," which will be discussed later. This is why blood, soil, and nation can become idols; they already have a relation to form, whereas *Urkräfte* purely as such cannot become idols, because they lack form. The relation is the same as that between the power of

vital powers (*vitalen Kräfte*) are the bearers or supports of creaturely being.[6] This is why it is foolhardy for autonomy to try to overcome the powers of origin by pure rationality, for despite those efforts, powers of origin cannot be denied impact; they lie at the base of everything that is.

Powers of origin are also creative. Tillich associates *Kraft* and "creativity" with astonishing frequency.[7] "Creative power" has at least two basic conceptual meanings. First, it corresponds to the symbol of creation and expresses the dependence of being on creative power. In this sense, creative power is the source or condition for the power of any particular being.[8] However, creative power is not restricted to this originary significance. It also denotes the drive of being toward form[9] and self-transcendence.[10] Original creative power is, to be sure, the basis of the creative process of self-transcendence, but creative power also carries that process forward. The two types of creativity are similar but not identical. Powers of origin are an element in all creative power, but creative power also drives toward the concretion and completion of originary powers. In both cases, creative power supports or bears form. Yet concrete forms are not the same as the powers of origin that give birth

---

being-itself and actually existing beings. The latter can only be symbols of the former, which has no "existence" in itself. Similarly, the concrete powers of origin mediate and participate in, but are not the same as, "the power of origin-itself" from which they spring. A helpful discussion of the importance of "participation" is provided in Langdon Gilkey, *Gilkey on Tillich* (New York: Crossroad, 1990), 15.

  6 Tillich, "The Demonic," 78 (*GW* 6:43); see also "The Idea and the Ideal of Personality," 133 (*Religiöse Verwirklichung* [Berlin: Furche-Verlag, 1930], 187).

  7 A few examples are Tillich, *Basic Principles of Religious Socialism*, in *Political Expectation*, trans. James L. Adams and Victor Nuovo, ed. James Luther Adams (New York: Harper & Row, 1971; reprint, Macon, Ga.: Mercer University Press, 1981) 68, 70 (page references are to reprint edition) (*GW* 2:100, 102); "The Demonic," 78–79, 87–89 (*GW* 6:43, 49–50); *The Religious Situation*, trans. H. Richard Niebuhr (New York: Henry Holt & Co., 1932; reprint, New York: Meridian Books, 1956), 49, 52 (page references are to reprint edition) (*GW* 10:18, 20); *Protestantism as a Critical and Creative Principle*, in *Political Expectation*, ed. Adams, 11, 33 (*GW*, 7 Band, *Der Protestantismus als Kritik und Gestaltung: Schriften zur Theologie I*, ed. Renate Albrecht [Stuttgart: Evangelisches Verlagswerk, 1962], 30, 48). In Tillich's American work, the connection between power and creativity is continued. See, e.g., see "The Idea and the Ideal of Personality," 134; *Systematic Theology* 1:180, 200, 237, 251–52; 2:7, 111, 115, 147; 3:22, 31, 112, 200, 274, 283; *Love, Power, and Justice*, 57; "Reply to Interpretation and Criticism," in *The Theology of Paul Tillich*, ed. Charles W. Kegley and Robert W. Bretall (New York: Macmillan, 1961), 341; *The Courage To Be* (New Haven: Yale University Press, 1952), 81, 108.

  8 In addition to the evidence adduced earlier, see *Love, Power, and Justice*, 123–24; *Systematic Theology* 1:237, 262; Paul Tillich, "The Recovery of the Prophetic Tradition in the Reformation," *Faith and Thought* 2, no. 1 (Spring 1984): 14.

  9 Tillich, *Courage To Be*, 81; "The Recovery of the Prophetic Tradition in the Reformation," 13–14; *Systematic Theology* 1:199.

  10 Tillich, "Realism and Faith," 67 (*Religiöse Verwirklichung*, 67–68); *Courage To Be*, 81; *Systematic Theology* 1:178, 191; *The Spiritual Presence*, in *The Eternal Now* (New York: Charles Scribner's Sons, 1963), 84. Guyton B. Hammond gives a good account of the relation between "power of being" and self-transcendence (*Man in Estrangement: A Comparison of the Thought of Paul Tillich and Erich Fromm* [Nashville: Vanderbilt University Press, 1965], 104–6, 139).

to the forms. Instead, creative powers are powers below and within the forms arising from their ground. Without being severed from *Kraft,* at least in its vital manifestations, form implies a specific content distinct from *Kraft.*

The paucity of content which pertains to originary and creative power is worth closer study. *Kraft* underlies, grounds, and is an element within all vital form, but for that very reason it is not identical to form. The situation is structurally similar to the relation between religion and culture. Tillich's opposition to a dualism between religion and culture is grounded in the conviction that vital culture expresses a religious import. The eternal import of cultural creation is not intended explicitly but emerges through the form.[11] Import is not a question of subject matter (this is why "religious art" is not the same as art with a religious subject), but of meaning and significance.[12] Tillich's famous rendering of this point is that religion is the substance of culture, whereas culture is the form of religion.[13] The same can be said of the association between *Kraft* and form. Power of being as *Kraft* is in, with, and under all form and being. One can say with Augustine that God is most remote and transcendent and yet the closest and most inescapable element of being. A corollary is that *Kraft* is ubiquitous. *Kraft* bears and supports all beings, as well as providing them creative motion. If, however, *Kraft* performs these functions, it must also be with all beings. *Kraft* is literally everywhere there is anything.[14] It is the current running deep beneath the restless sea of appearances. *Kraft* embraces creation and God's continuing providence.

The same distinction between *Kraft* and form accounts for the ecstatic and ambiguous character of *Kraft. Kraft* is not form, but it must break through and into form; it can only enter reality in form. *Kraft* is both the drive behind, below, and toward form creation and that which propels form beyond itself. It is the abyss of potentiality. Its nonidentity with form and its corresponding lack of content are why experience of *Kraft* is ecstatic, an experience of power

---

[11] Tillich, *Systematic Theology* 1:149–50; 3:60; see also Nathan A. Scott, Jr., "Tillich's Legacy and the New Scene in Literature," in *The Thought of Paul Tillich,* ed. James Luther Adams, Wilhelm Pauck, and Roger Lincoln Shinn (San Francisco: Harper & Row, 1985), 139–53.

[12] Tillich, *The Religious Situation,* 88–89, 157 (*GW* 10:34–35, 64); "The World Situation," in *The Christian Answer,* ed. Henry P. Van Dusen (New York: Charles Scribner's Sons, 1945; reprint of chap., Philadelphia: Fortress Press, Facet Books, Social Ethics Series 2, 1965) 39–40 (page references are to reprint edition). See also James Luther Adams, *Paul Tillich's Philosophy of Culture, Science, and Religion* (New York: Harper & Row, 1965), 94–95; and Robert P. Scharlemann, "Tillich and the Religious Interpretation of Art," in *The Thought of Paul Tillich,* ed. Adams, Pauck, and Shinn, 157–59. An excellent biographical account of the development of Tillich's perspective on art and its impact on Tillich's attitude of "faithful realism," is provided in Wilhelm Pauck and Marion Pauck, *Paul Tillich: His Life and Thought* (San Francisco: Harper & Row, 1976), 75–79.

[13] Tillich, *Systematic Theology* 3:50; "Author's Introduction," xiii. The idea itself seems to be drawn initially from the experience of art, and applied to other realms on the basis of that experience ("On the Boundary," 49).

[14] "Author's Introduction" (pp. xi–xii) also ties the presence of God to God's power.

beyond categories of finite forms.[15] Ecstasy is ambiguous. In pushing form
beyond itself, *Kraft* is the power of self-transcendence. On the other hand,
ecstasy can lead to the destruction of form. Divine and demonic appear out
of the same creative ground of power. They are differentiated not by their
intrinsic content, for they have no form but only power, but by their effect
on form.[16] The hallmark of demonic power is not that it breaks through finite
form, which divine power does also, but that it breaks through form only
in order to shatter it completely.[17] This is demonic for two reasons. First,
because demonic power is bound to creative power; demonism is defined by
the gordian knot between its creativity and its destructiveness. The knot itself
is demonic, however, because *Kraft* enters reality in form. The demonic uses
what it attempts to destroy. Its power contradicts the very essence through
which it becomes actual. The "demonic is the comprehensive, uniting form
of appearance of the contradiction of essence. It connects the life process to
the bearing powers themselves." It is a "perversion of the creative, and as such
belongs to the phenomena that are contrary to essential nature, or sin."[18] Its
end and limit are in the satanic, which can only be a principle and not a reality

---

[15] Tillich, "The Demonic," 85–93; (*GW* 6:53); *Systematic Theology* 1:21, 79, 218.

[16] Ronald H. Stone notes this criterion of fulfillment of form in Tillich's ethics (*Paul Tillich's Radical Social Thought* [Atlanta: John Knox Press, 1980], 116). This is important in relation to a criteriology of God-language. Tillich's emphasis on symbolic language has been criticized frequently for making all symbols of God equal in value and/or for failing to provide criteria of selection between them. A summary of this discussion is provided in Richard Grigg, *Symbol and Empowerment: Paul Tillich's Post-Theistic System* (Macon, Ga.: Mercer University Press, 1985), 17–29. However, Grigg's treatment of this criticism confuses Tillich's argument. The value of particular symbols cannot be determined outside their concrete use and appearance in a revelatory correlation. Rather, Tillich's own criteria of the value of symbols are existential and pragmatic, namely, whether or not use of a particular symbol points to fulfillment for its receivers and actually has fulfilling effect. (A good summary of the properties of symbols in Tillich's thought is in David H. Kelsey, *The Fabric of Paul Tillich's Theology* [New Haven: Yale University Press, 1967], 42–50, 133–39, although Kelsey claims that pragmatic criteria are woefully inadequate, largely because they open the logical possibility that the picture of Jesus as the Christ could become obsolete.)

Existentially, symbols are less right or wrong (and this includes "attributes" of God) than living or dead (*Dynamics of Faith,* 43, 96–97). A symbol's "rightness" is distinct from its holiness; the holy purely as holy can "destroy us as it can heal us" (p. 16). Symbols are right insofar as they express and represent an ultimate concern that is truly ultimate and holy, and this is a pragmatic judgment that cannot be made outside symbols' concrete use (pp. 96–98). A purely philosophical a priori criteriology of symbols is therefore impossible. One misses the point if one criticizes Tillich for failing to develop such a criteriology or tries to develop one from his theology. Tillich's theology of symbols has little to do with traditional theological efforts to explicate God's attributes.

[17] Tillich, "The Demonic." For a discussion of the marks of the Spirit, see *Systematic Theology* 3:138–245.

[18] Tillich, "The Demonic," 93–94, 93 (*GW* 6:53, 52). The translation of the first quotation is modified. The German reads: "Denn das Dämonische ist die übergreifende, den Lebensprozeß zusammenfassende, mit seinen tragenden Kräften sich einende Erscheinungsform der Wesenswidrigkeit."

because, like total domination, it is the utter obliteration of all form and existence. The correlate of the demonic is the divine, which breaks through form in order to elevate form. Grace is the correlate of demonic possession because in it, too, creative powers burst through form.[19] "The difference," Tillich contends, "is only that the same powers are united with the highest form as grace, as contradict the highest form in the possessed state."[20]

Two points are important. First, *Kraft* is teleological.[21] It intends a relation to form. Second, the criterion of power, as demonic/distorted power on one side, or divine/fulfilling power on the other, is its effect on form. In both these aspects, Tillich's notion of power as *Kraft* harmonizes with the conception of power as communication of efficacy. In the case of demonic power, the domination exercised on form ends there. It belittles and reduces affected being but does so by means of a necessary moment in all power — the external moment of sovereign domination. Divine power, however, while also breaking into form and exercising sovereignty upon it, elevates and fulfills form.

Tillich's view of power is, however, more sophisticated than this. *Kraft* does not exhaust power. The special position of *Kraft* explains the need for a further differentiation of power. *Kraft* is directed toward form. With respect to form, it is potential power, power that accounts for the restlessness of all things. *Kraft* embraces the vital potencies (*vitalen Potenzen*).[22] The descriptive terms used in association with *Kraft* thus far (drive, condition, basis, ground, bearer, support, undercurrent, originary, creative) indicate this potential nature of *Kraft*. The importance of the *Kraft* of being for beings is to provide them

---

[19] Tillich, "The Demonic," 80-88 (GW 6:45-49). Tillich also discusses the demonic in *Systematic Theology* 3:102–6, and there points out the ties between the demonic and the heteronomous. See also H. Frederick Reisz, Jr., "The Demonic as a Principle in Tillich's Doctrine of God: Tillich and Beyond," in *Theonomy and Autonomy: Studies in Paul Tillich's Engagement with Modern Culture*, ed. John J. Carey (Macon, Ga.: Mercer University Press, 1984), 149.

[20] Tillich, "The Demonic," 88 (translation modified); in GW 6:49 this reads: "Der Unterschied ist nur der, daß die gleichen Kräfte als Gnade mit der höchsten Form geeint sind, als Besessenheit der höchsten Form widersprechen." See also "The Idea and the Ideal of Personality, 134 (*Religiöse Verwirklichung*, 188). "Realism and Faith," 80–81 (*Religiöse Verwirklichung*, 83–84), discusses the receiving, or ecstatic, side of this correlation in relation to the "unconditioned power" (*Unbedingt-Mächtigen*). We have avoided consideration of the language of "unconditioned power" because "Reply to Interpretation and Criticism," 340, explicitly denies its validity. Still, the use of *Mächtig* is interesting. From the giving side, *Mächtig* is rendered as *Kraft*. The reason is that ecstasy is a possibility only for a formed being. It is not a symbolic concept like will to power, nor does it designate power without form in itself, as does *Kraft*. Rather, ecstasy and faith take place on the "other side" of form, through the already-formed being rather than on the side of unformed drives or the ground of being. Adams gives a concise description of the meaning of "Unconditioned" in Tillich's early thought (*Tillich's Philosophy*, 197–98).

[21] Tillich, *Systematic Theology* 3:164–65. The teleological power Tillich speaks of here is essential, potential power, or *Kraft*.

[22] Tillich, "The Demonic," 85–86 (GW 6:48).

with inner potentialities and possibilities.[23] The power of being has a dynamic component.[24] The formless potentiality of *Kraft* gains reality through form and is present in beings in order that they may have a power of being of their own, dependent on participation in the *Kraft* of being-itself.[25]

The drive of *Kraft* toward incorporation within form is visible in several places in Tillich's thought. There are, to begin with, the powers that arise out of the *Kraft* of being, the will to power (*Machtwille*) and the power of love. These drives to power and love are based in the nonrational ground.[26] Both these *Kräfte* are present in every creative reality.[27] Since *Machtwille* and *Eroskraft* arise out of the power of being, they are not form either. They are the *mē on,* "the potentiality of being, which is nonbeing in contrast to things that have a form, and the power of being in contrast to pure nonbeing." Like *Kraft* in general, Tillich continues, the will to power and the power of love must be described symbolically:

[23] There is an objection that can be raised. The position taken here is that the relation of God as the power of being to creatures is experienced primarily as the basis of creaturely potentiality. Tillich, however, contends that God is above both potentiality and actuality (*Systematic Theology* 1:245–55). Still, he leans toward the side of potentiality in his conception of God. His objections to the traditional rendering of God as *actus purus* (ibid. 1:180, 246; 2:22; "Reply to Interpretation and Criticism," 339) are an indication of this, and the treatment of God as the ground and power of being is another.

This is not a unique procedure in Tillich's discussion of the unity of the ontological elements in God. For example, he resolves the polarity of freedom and destiny within God more on the side of freedom than destiny: "God is his own destiny" (*Systematic Theology* 1:248). Although one can still speak of God's destiny, this is meant in a quite different sense, and one closer to freedom than "destiny" in regard to beings. For a criticism of the vagueness of Tillich's resolution of the polarities in God, see John Herman Randall, Jr., "The Ontology of Paul Tillich," in *The Theology of Paul Tillich,* ed. Kegley and Bretall, 132–61.

[24] This is argued much more closely in H. Frederick Reisz, Jr., "Paul Tillich's Doctrine of God as Spirit: A Dynamic View" (Ph.D. diss., University of Chicago, 1977), 4–9, 255–80, and "The Demonic as a Principle in Tillich's Doctrine of God," 140, 144. The dynamism of the power of being, which is God, implies the presence of relative non-being (potentiality or *mē on*) in the being of God.

[25] Hammond gives an excellent summary of the meaning of "participation in being-itself" for finitude (*Man in Estrangement,* 139–43).

[26] Tillich, *Basic Principles of Religious Socialism,* 68 (*GW* 2:100). What Tillich calls "irrational" has been rendered as "nonrational." The reason is that one of the connotations attached to "irrational" is "antirational." Tillich does not mean this; instead, "irrational" signifies only that there is no "logically necessary or deductive step" from one condition to another (*Systematic Theology* 2:1). The irrational ground is based in God, who also "creates" structure and form obedient to the *logos.* Certainly, demonic manifestations of the ground may be conditionally antirational, directed to shattering form, but grace unites *Kraft* and the highest form. It is better, therefore, to avoid the non-Tillichian, but almost unavoidable, connotations of "irrational."

[27] Tillich, *Basic Principles of Religious Socialism,* 68 (*GW* 2:100); see also "The Demonic," 91 (*GW* 6:51), where Tillich speaks of "*Eros- und Machttrieb*" rather than "*Liebe und Machtwille.*" In *Basic Principles,* he uses "*Eroskraft*" (pp. 70–71; *GW* 2:102). Guyton B. Hammond correctly notes that beings' "potentialities have their origin in the creativity of the divine life" (*The Power of Self-Transcendence: An Introduction to the Philosophical Theology of Paul Tillich* [St. Louis: The Bethany Press, 1966], 42).

This highly dialectical concept [of potentiality] is not an invention of the philosophers. It underlies most mythologies and is indicated in the chaos, the *tohu-va-bohu,* the night, the emptiness, which precedes creation. It appears in metaphysical speculations as *Urgrund* (Böhme), will (Schopenhauer), will to power (Nietzsche), the unconscious (Hartmann, Freud), *élan vital* (Bergson), strife (Scheler, Jung). None of these concepts is to be taken conceptually. Each of them points symbolically to that which cannot be named. If it could be named properly, it would be a formed being beside other beings instead of an ontological element in polar contrast with the element of pure form. Therefore, it is unfair to criticize these concepts on the basis of their literal meaning.[28]

As *Machtwille* and *Eroskraft, Kraft* enters into form, as the dynamisms and inner potential of a special being. The derivatives of *Kraft* account for the dynamism every living form displays.[29] The abysmal quality of being implies its inexhaustibility (*Unerschöpflichkeit*)[30] and hence creative (*schöpferische*) character. Participation in this inexhaustibility accounts for the "inner infinity of existence," the indwelling of being's inexhaustibility.[31] This is why Tillich can speak of the *Kraft* of particular formations within form, of the *Kraft* of intellect and will, as examples. He can even use *Kraft* to indicate a being's potential to attain external goods, if supported by an inner, subjective *Machtwille.*[32]

For Tillich, the decisive advantage of such formulations is that they prevent the "thingification" of things. If power is recognized within beings, "things are considered more as powers (*Mächte*) than as things."[33] This combats the insidious devaluation of things in autonomy, which refuses to recognize the other's power of being. "Recognition" of the other, the condition of the moral act, is principally recognition of the other's power. Autonomy recognizes things only to submit them to its own will to power. In turn, the result of the desacralization of things, through the deprivation of their inner power of being, leads the subjective will to power to an unending and unbounded will to dominate (*Herrschaftswille*).[34] Autonomy tries to sever things not only from their vertical relation to the ground and transcendence of being but also from the

[28] Tillich, *Systematic Theology* 1:179, 179.

[29] Again, *Kraft* bears and supports form. Tillich's mention of the classical ideal of the relation between body and soul is an instance of the relation of *Kraft* and form. It is concentrated and emanative *Kraft* that forms both soul and body (*Religious Situation,* 141; *GW* 10:59).

[30] Tillich, "The Demonic," 83 (*GW* 6:46–47).

[31] Ibid., 84.

[32] Tillich, *Basic Principles of Religious Socialism,* 77–78 (*GW* 2:109–10).

[33] Tillich, "Kairos," 43 (*GW* 6:20). In "The Idea and the Ideal of Personality," 120–24 (*Religiöse Verwirklichung,* 173–78), Tillich analyzes the process of transformation from a sacramental attitude which presumes the numinous and intrinsic power of things, to an autonomy which robs things of their power and freedom, and therefore, of their sacredness. He believes that the Protestant reformers were guilty of this latter attitude, and the difference between the two points of view is reflected in Tillich's opposition to Luther's understanding of the sacraments ("Nature and Sacrament," 96, 111; *Religiöse Verwirklichung,* 144, 165–66).

[34] Tillich, *Basic Principles of Religious Socialism,* 74 (*GW* 2:106).

horizontal relation to other beings. Autonomy is autonomous in both directions. Autonomy, it was noted earlier, creates an atomistic society.

Mächtigkeit

It is at just this point of recognition that Tillich's concept of power enters a second phase. Recognition is the recognition more of a being than of a potentiality. "Thingification" refers first to a loss of respect for things, and not potentialities, which, after all, are the potentialities of some thing. *Kräfte* in relation to beings are still potentialities; they retain their supporting, grounding, creative, and dynamic functions. *Kräfte* provide dynamism to centered being, the power of which Tillich frequently calls "*Mächtigkeit*." This is the power of form, the "definite power of being" of a being.[35] It is to this definite power of being that Tillich refers with the term "*Seinsmächtigkeit*."[36]

Mächtigkeit is the power of form in existence. All being can be understood as a constantly changing balance of tensions of *Mächtigkeit*.[37] Power as *Mächtigkeit* is the inner, actual power of beings, which in human beings is personal power.[38] Such power is largely a matter of destiny, of being this instead of that.[39]

---

[35] Tillich, *Systematic Theology* 1:178. An extensive early discussion of *Mächtigkeit* is found in *Religiöse Verwirklichung*, 65–87. This piece underwent substantial changes in translation, and a fuller understanding of *Mächtigkeit* in distinction from other terms that are translated as "power" in the English is available in the German version. In fact, the two versions are so different that "Realism and Faith" is somewhat deceptive if taken as an example of Tillich's early thought, although the English version adds a very helpful clarifying paragraph on the different senses of "power of being" ("Realism and Faith," 79).

In relation to these different meanings, Thomas G. Bandy is incorrect to assert that Tillich misspeaks himself when he refers to form as having a power of being, because "'dynamics' is best reserved for the 'power of being'" ("Tillich's Limited Understanding of the Thought of Henri Bergson as 'Life Philosophy,'" in *Theonomy and Autonomy*, 12). This is not the case for Tillich. Power's dynamic element is *Kraft* or, alternatively, the ground or "unconditioned power" (*Religiöse Verwirklichung*, 79–82) of an entity's power of being. Dynamic power of being is neither *Mächtigkeit* nor *Macht*, which are powers nonetheless. To apply a distinction Tillich uses elsewhere, and in an analogous way, in the discussions of Protestant principle and Catholic substance, one can say that *Kraft* is a moving "principle," whereas the forms of power refer to content (Tillich, "On the Idea of a Theology of Culture," 161, 177 [*GW* 9:17, 28–29]; "The Protestant Principle and the Proletarian Situation," in *The Protestant Era*, abridged ed., 163 [*GW* 7:85–86]).

[36] This explains why, when Tillich conceives of ontology as based only on *Seinsmächtigkeit*, he objects that it cannot include history. *Seinsmächtigkeit* is the static, formal pole of existence, lacking the dynamism essential to history.

[37] Tillich, "The Problem of Power," 182 (*GW* 2:195). Note the dependence of *Mächtigkeit* on the *Kraft* of self-transcendence.

[38] Tillich, *Basic Principles of Religious Socialism*, 74–77 (*GW* 2:105–9); *The Socialist Decision*, 98–99 (*GW* 2:307–8).

[39] Tillich, "The Idea and the Ideal of Personality," 115 (*Religiöse Verwirklichung*, 168).

This conception of inner, centered power (which any being has if it is) grounds Tillich's late discussion of the dimensions of being.[40] The power of a being is described in reference to a being's center, to which all other aspects of that being are referred. The specific power of being of the inorganic dimension, the "first condition for the actualization of every dimension," is the actualization of potentiality in "those things in time and space which are subject to physical analysis or which can be measured in spatio-temporal-causal relations."[41] Matter's power of being is the definite power of being of the inorganic. Matter is the center to which analysis of inorganic being is to be referred, whether such an analysis is cognitive, ethical, or religious. With the actualization of organic potentialities, a new dimension of being emerges. The centered power of organic being is spontaneity.[42] In the animal realm, the dimension of self-awareness becomes actualized, while the specific power of the human world is the power of spirit, which makes the historical dimension possible. Tillich explains the manifestation of dimensions in this way:

> Constellations of conditions make it possible for the organic to appear in the inorganic realm. Constellations in the inorganic [sic; Tillich would appear to mean "organic" rather than "inorganic"] realm make it possible for the dimension of self-awareness to become actual, and in the same way constellations under the predominance of the psychological dimension make it possible for the dimension of spirit to become actual.[43]

This description of dimensions of being is intended to avoid, first, a reduction of one dimension to a less rich dimension — materialism, for example, "*is an ontology of death*."[44] Second, Tillich does not want to affirm a dualism that sees the appearance of a particular dimension as a warrant to emasculate, as far as possible, the reality or significance of the dimensions which are

---

[40] Adams has an excellent discussion of Tillich's use as early as 1933 of the dimensions of being (*Tillich's Philosophy*, 100–110). It appears that all the dimensions of being in *Systematic Theology* 3, are present by then; the only difference is that Tillich does not use the term "spirit." Wilhelm Pauck and Marion Pauck claim that Tillich had his basic understanding of the dimensions of being in place even earlier (*Paul Tillich*, 117–18). A suggestive discussion that includes many of Tillich's later "dimensions" can be found in "Nature and Sacrament," 103–6 (*Religiöse Verwirklichung*, 156–59). Although the English version of this work differentiates animal and human life on the basis of "freedom and spirituality," this is absent from the German.

[41] Tillich, *Systematic Theology* 3:19.

[42] This is taken from Tillich's analysis of the relation between force and compulsion in *Love, Power, and Justice*, 47–48. On the basis of *Systematic Theology* 3:19–21, it would be acceptable to say that the specific power of the organic is the power of life; however, earlier (p. 12), Tillich says, "The genesis of stars and rocks, their growth as well as their decay, must be called a life process. The ontological concept of life liberates the word 'life' from its bondage to the organic realm." Therefore, "spontaneity" has been chosen to describe organic power, even though Tillich's discussion of spontaneity does not include an explicit discussion of the dimensions of being, and despite the difficulty this creates for designating the particular power of the vegetative realm.

[43] Tillich, *Systematic Theology* 3:25.

[44] Ibid., 19.

prerequisites of its appearance.[45] The conditions of spirit's reality (the inorganic, the vegetative, and animal self-awareness) must participate in the life of the spirit.[46] The mode of this participation is argued most clearly in the connection between spirit and the psychological center of self-awareness. What Tillich means by "multidimensional unity of life" can be illustrated through his discussion of this relation.[47]

As all "preceding" dimensions make successive ones possible, so the psychological realm conditions the spirit. What is given to self-awareness constitutes the content of both cognitive and moral acts. In a cognitive act, for example, thought lacks an object about which to think without some thing presented to self-awareness. But presentation of such material is not sufficient for an act of knowledge in the proper sense. Knowledge requires the involvement of the personal, spiritual center:

> Without this [psychological] material, thinking would have no content. But in order to transform this material into knowledge, something must be done to it; it must be split, reduced, increased, and connected according to logical, and purged according to methodological, criteria. All this is done by the personal center which is not identical with any particular one of these elements. The transcendence of the center over the psychological material makes the cognitive act possible, and such an act is a manifestation of spirit.

This formulation eliminates two alternative conceptions of the relation of spirit and self-awareness. On the one hand, it precludes reduction of fuller dimensions of life to preceding ones, because the newly emerging center transcends and transforms the dimension out of which it appears. The spiritual center "is not identical with any one of the psychological contents," for then it would be that material and not spirit. On the other hand, a dualism that seeks a radical negation of preceding dimensions is also avoided. As religion is not superimposed on the world as an additional thing that desires the eradication of the world, neither is soul added to body, spirit simply added to self-awareness. Rather, spirit is the center *of* and *within* the psychological material; "the psychological center offers its own content to the unity of the personal center."[48] This means that "the power of the self is its self-centeredness. . . . [I]ts power is the power of a stabilized balance of the elements which are centered in it."[49]

The power of being, of particular beings rather than of being-itself, is the inner, centered power of *Mächtigkeit,* the power of form. As the very center of a being, to which all other dimensions are referred in its inner life, *Mächtigkeit* is actual with respect to that being. Located at the center of a being, however,

---

[45] Paul Tillich, *Die Bedeutung der Gesellschaftslage für das Geistesleben* (*GW* 2:133–38).

[46] Tillich, "Nature and Sacrament," 98 (*Religiöse Verwirklichung,* 147); *Courage To Be,* 83; *Systematic Theology* 3:276, 315–26, 377, 399–401.

[47] Tillich, *Systematic Theology* 3:25–28.

[48] The three preceding quotations are from Tillich, *Systematic Theology* 3:27; see also 1:277–78.

[49] Tillich, *Love, Power, and Justice,* 52.

power is also potential with respect to the external world. External expression of its specific power is not accomplished by the mere fact of its existence. An act is required before its power can be felt. Tillich speaks of the "actualization" of that power[50] which is actual for itself but potential in its expression.

Mächtigkeit, too, has a *telos*. It drives toward external appearance in encounter *(Begegnung)*.[51] Without actualization of power, a being gives up its power of being; it dies and ceases to be. Encounter is where *Mächtigkeit* externalizes itself. The encounter has a double aspect in relation to power. In the first place, it is the condition for actualization of power.[52] The expression of the ontological polarity of individualization and participation in life's self-integration shows this actualizing function. Although self-integration occurs "through the principle of centeredness," the center cannot be preserved unless a being goes out from itself and participates in its environment and world. Failure to participate means that the center "approaches the death of mere self-identity."[53] Although growth must occur through the center, the centered power of form is not sufficient to produce its own growth.[54] In addition to assuming a centered being, self-integration presupposes encounter, without which centered power of being disintegrates.[55] *Mächtigkeit* depends on externalization in order to maintain its power.

The encounter is also where centered power of being meets its limit in resistance of the other.[56] Encounters are therefore the stage on which power is played. Power shows itself by overcoming resistance by some other; in fact, for both individual and social power, conquest of resistance constitutes the basic definition of power.[57] The "other" is a fairly broad notion and can refer metaphorically to aspects of the self as well as external others; it is applied most broadly (and most properly) when Tillich speaks of the overcoming of non-being by being.[58] This idea of power's "proving itself" in triumph over resistance allows Tillich to say that all being can be conceived of as "a constantly changing balance of powers in encounter," or a "balance of tensions of power."[59] In encounter, a centered power of being proves its power in overcoming resistance of the other. Encounter is the locus of the struggle for power,

---

[50] Ibid., 41; *Dynamics of Faith*, 9; *Systematic Theology* 3:164, 268.

[51] Tillich, "The Problem of Power," 182, 195 (*GW* 2:195, 203); *Systematic Theology* 3:308; Tillich, "Love, Power, and Justice," *The Listener*, 2 October 1952, 545.

[52] Tillich, *Love, Power, and Justice*, 36–41.

[53] Tillich, *Systematic Theology* 3:32, 33.

[54] Ibid., 51.

[55] Ibid. 1:177.

[56] Ibid. 1:171; 3:40, 386; *Love, Power, and Justice*, 78–80.

[57] Tillich, *Love, Power, and Justice*, 37, 40, 179; *Systematic Theology* 3:386; *Systematic Theology*, vol. 2, as a whole, interprets the power of the Christ-event as the power to conquer estrangement.

[58] Tillich, *Systematic Theology* 1:236, 250–51, 272–73; 2:125.

[59] Tillich, "The Problem of Power," 182, 183 (*GW* 2:195, 195). Both translations are modified. For the first, the German reads: "einen ständig wechselnden Ausgleich von Mächtigkeiten in der Begegnung"; for the second, "Ausgleich von Mächtigkeitsspannungen."

the field on which formed centers of *Mächtigkeiten* play out their strength.

The fundamental ontological polarity of self and world appears, then, in one of its aspects as a polarity between centered powers of being and encounter. Insofar as power of being is individual and centered, the conception of power presented by Tillich is an atomistic one. But the pole of participation is always present with centered power. As well as providing the limit of centered form and its power, the encounter also provides a condition of its life and opportunity for power's exercise. The double significance of the encounter for centered form also grounds the moral act. A moral act is based in the demand for recognition posed by the very existence of the other.[60] The moral imperative's unconditional form is real because "encounter with another person implies the unconditional demand to acknowledge him as a person." However, "the abstract notion of 'acknowledging the other one as a person' becomes concrete only in the notion of participating in the other one (which follows from the ontological polarity of individualization and participation)."[61] If the association between centered power of being and its encounters is based in the ontological polarities, and hence also in the power of being-itself, the relation between *Kraft* and *Mächtigkeit* must be explored more fully. Before doing so, a third arena of power's appearance should be investigated.

Macht

To this point, the treatment of centered, formal power has been restricted to the power of individual beings, for which Tillich uses the term *Mächtigkeit*. His conception of social power, or *Macht*, is analogous to individual power: *Macht* is *Mächtigkeit* "on the level of social existence."[62] Like *Mächtigkeit*, *Macht* is centered power possessing a will to power and tested in its encounters with other centered powers, whether the "other" denotes another social power or individual powers that resist *Macht*.[63] Like *Mächtigkeit*, centered social power is potential with respect to the external world, "the chance to carry through one's will against social resistance,"[64] and remains hidden unless actualized. The difference between social and individual power of being is this: *Macht*

---

[60] Tillich, *The Socialist Decision*, 6 (*GW* 2:229); "The Gospel and the State," *Crozer Quarterly* (Chester, Penn.) 15, no. 4 (October 1938): 257; *Love, Power, and Justice*, 82.

[61] Tillich, *Systematic Theology* 3:45.

[62] Tillich, "The Problem of Power," 183 (*GW* 2:195). This distinction between *Macht* and *Mächtigkeit* is not always adhered to by Tillich, but in light of their similarity, this is not especially important.

[63] Tillich, *Love, Power, and Justice*, 94–101; *Systematic Theology* 3:340–42.

[64] Tillich, *Love, Power, and Justice*, 36. Note the striking similarity between Tillich's definition of social power ("The Problem of Power," 183 [*GW* 2:196]; and *Love, Power, and Justice*, 110) and that of Max Weber (*Economy and Society: An Outline of Interpretive Sociology*, 2 vols., ed. Guenther Roth and Claus Wittich [Berkeley: University of California Press, 1978] 1:53). See also *The Socialist Decision*, 138 (*GW* 2:342–43).

as social power does not refer to a natural center. The organic, physiological center of individual being is absent from society.[65] Instead, social power is exercised through creation of non-natural centers of leadership. Positions of power (*Machtpositionen*)[66] are not natural structures of power but are created by human beings and occupied by leading groups (*Machtgruppen* or *tragenden Gruppen*).[67] Social power, of course, includes the power of individual beings.

The twofold centering of society accounts for the ambiguity of leadership. Those members of the social group in a position of power are entrusted with representing the group's power of being. At the same time, however, those with social power have their own specific power of being, a *Mächtigkeit* not identical with the interests of the group as a whole.[68] The particularity of the task of representing their own power of being is not left behind in leadership's exercise of social power. That would be impossible. Of course, the specificity of self-representation and self-assertion can gain such ascendency in the employment of social power that its exercise fails to represent the group's power of being.[69] At this point, it is possible that the silent acknowledgment and recognition upon which *Macht* depends are withdrawn due to a loss of confidence that the power of being of the whole is represented adequately by bearers of social power. Centers of social power lose their real power as soon as the inner power of the social group fails to find expression there.[70]

---

[65] Tillich, *Systematic Theology* 3:78, 263; idem, *Shadow and Substance: A Theory of Power*, in *Political Expectation*, ed. Adams, 116–17; see also *Systematic Theology* 3:41, where Tillich notes that lack of a natural center also implies the absence of complete centeredness; and *Systematic Theology* 2:58–59, where he asserts that it is exactly the absence of a natural center which characterizes the social group as a "power structure."

Once again, the question of the meaning and acceptability of the term "social body" arises. Although Tillich does not discuss this metaphor extensively (but see *Systematic Theology* 3:78–79 and *Love, Power, and Justice*, 92–94), his position implies that, although it is dangerous to "personify the group" (*Systematic Theology* 3:312), such a concept is acceptable so long as it is not taken to mean that society has a natural bodily center, as an individual does, and so long as society is not reduced to "body," but includes also a "social spirit" or "spiritual substance of the social group" (*Dynamics of Faith*, 27), manifest in something like a community's vocational consciousness. Tillich, like Luther, does employ the Pauline conception of the "spiritual body" (*Systematic Theology* 3:412–13).

[66] Tillich, "The Problem of Power," 183–84 (*GW* 2:196).

[67] Tillich, *The Socialist Decision*, 52, 60 (*GW* 2:269, 276). These are the groups that give concrete structure to power (*The State as Expectation and Demand*, in *Political Expectation*, ed. Adams, 111; *Religiöse Verwirklichung*, 228). In *Systematic Theology* 3:342, Tillich uses "power structure" rather than "position of power."

[68] Tillich, "The Problem of Power," 184–87 (*GW* 2:196–98); *Systematic Theology* 3:82–84, 263–65.

[69] The possibility of this failure lies in the inevitable transition from actual authority to established authority (*Systematic Theology* 3:83–84). An early and informative treatment of the issue of social and political power is *The State as Expectation and Demand*, 97–114 (*Religiöse Verwirklichung*, 212–32). An excellent review of the question of consent and the basis of power in the assent of the community is in Gilkey, *Gilkey on Tillich*, 17–19.

[70] Tillich, "The Problem of Power," 185–87 (*GW* 2:197–98); *The Socialist Decision*, 137–41 (*GW* 2:342–45).

Responses to this loss of power range anywhere from a smooth replacement of occupants of positions of power to a revolutionary one which may create quite new positions of power, but it is certain in any case that the holders of social power will fall, a judgment confirmed by the astonishing rapidity of recent events in Eastern Europe.[71]

The centered quality of *Mächtigkeit* and *Macht* and their dependence on encounter for the actualization and test of that power raise the question of the relation between centered power and *Kraft*. One side of this collaboration has been described. The condition for appearances of actual centered powers of being (*Macht* and *Mächtigkeit*) is that they are borne and driven by the potential power of *Kraft*, which has its *telos* in form. The question concerning the inverse of this process, of centered power's journey into external actuality, needs further consideration.

The Voyage of Centered Power

Centered power is not a sufficient condition for its own exercise; the unwillingness or inability of definite powers of being to go beyond their center in order to participate in encounter leads to their disintegration and death. To even preserve the center of being, a being must grow. The polarity of dynamics and form is expressed in the self-creation of life. Whereas self-integration "constitutes the individual being in its centeredness," self-creation "gives the dynamic impulse which drives life from one centered state to another under the principle of growth."[72] Self-creativity and destruction relate to the ontological polarity of dynamics and form, which expresses *Kraft* on one side and *Mächtigkeit* and *Macht* on the other. Will to power and the power of love (which Tillich expands beyond Eros to include desire, filiation, and *agape*)[73] drive the actual power of being, which remains potential with respect to the external world, toward the external actuality of that power of being. Will to power and love are implicated again in the transition from potentiality to actuality.

---

[71] Tillich, *Love, Power, and Justice,* 98, 104. Reading Tillich some twenty-five years after his death is occasionally shocking. In *Christianity and the Encounter of the World Religions* (New York: Columbia University Press, 1963), 20, itself a prescient topic, Tillich suggests that Eastern Europe was ripe for a break with the Soviet Union, for "a spiritual victory was never won [there] by the Communist quasi-religion." In his next breath, he suggests that Islam "is not closed to secularism in connection with science and technology, and it is wide open to the entrance of nationalism." In the early 1980s, Iran swung abruptly from one end of this spectrum to the other.

[72] Tillich, *Systematic Theology* 3:51.

[73] Tillich, *Love, Power, and Justice,* 24–34; see also *Systematic Theology* 3:134–38.

The Conflict of Centered Powers

Will to power is, it will be recalled, a symbolic concept. It expresses a being's desire for self-affirmation:

> Nietzsche's "will to power" means neither will nor power, if taken in the ordinary sense of the words. He does not speak of the psychological function called will, although the will to power may become manifest in conscious acts of man, e.g. in the self-control exercised by the commanding will. But basically the will to power in Nietzsche is, as it was in Schopenhauer, a designation of the dynamic self-affirmation of life.[74]

In the polarity of individualization and participation, will to power is an individualizing aspect of *Kraft*. Subjective will to power wills its own self-affirmation. Precisely because it wills *self*-affirmation, however, it is intrinsically unlimited desire. Self-affirmation overcomes the other's resistance to self. Will to power becomes the will to dominate, to eliminate resistance to the self, and is limitless in itself.[75] This is one reason why the twin demonries of nationalism and capitalism are so dangerous.

In the case of twentieth-century nationalism, including the nationalism of democracies, "the sense of national vocation is really present and represents the indissoluble unity of religious faith and national will-to-power." Unfortunately, national will to power does not and cannot include an internal limit to its desire, and therefore "the sense of national destiny . . . contains also the idea that other nations are to be subjected to it. It is essentially universalistic and imperialistic,"[76] a national and democratic will to domination (*Herrschaft*).[77]

Capitalism, for its part, operates on purely formal principles and is thus opened to a filling of the autonomous void by demonic contents. The result is dominance of capital (*Kapitalherrschaft*) over all other contents of culture.[78] The purely formal nature of relations in capitalist society, without reference to the limiting encounter of any inner *Mächtigkeit* of the other, leads to a class struggle, in Tillich's view, because a purely subjective eros and will to power make everything into an instrument or thing to serve its own interest:

---

[74] Tillich, *Love, Power, and Justice*, 36; see also *Courage To Be*, 26–31.

[75] This limitless character of "*Herrschaftwillens*" is noted in considering the situation of the Roman church in the 1920s in *The Religious Situation*, 186 (*GW* 10:77). But the entry of the church into "power politics" is almost inevitable if the church is to take a concrete institutional form (*Systematic Theology* 3:99–100). It is important to note that the will to power is not the same as controlling power. It is rather the desire out of which domination and absolutism arise (*Systematic Theology* 2:55; "The World Situation," 7).

[76] Tillich, *The Religious Situation*, 118, 117 (*GW* 10:47).

[77] Tillich, *GW* 10:47.

[78] Tillich, *The Religious Situation*, 115 (*GW* 10:46).

the purely objective predominance of capital (*Kapitalherrschaft*) . . . , on the one hand, formally gives every individual his due, but on the other, integrates every individual into the system of the rational economic process, in which there are only objective dependent relations but no intrinsic eros and power relationships (*kein inneres Mächtigkeits- und Erosverhältnis*). This system of purely objective power (*Macht*), on the one hand, and purely objective dependence, on the other, led to the class struggle peculiar to the capitalist era. Class struggle is not a universal social phenomenon but the consequence of a rationally formed economic social order in which intrinsic power relations have become extrinsic (*innerer Mächtigkeit zu äußeren Machtbeziehungen geworden sind*). The predominance of capital (*Kapitalherrschaft*) leads necessarily to class struggle, because a purely subjective will founded on eros and power (subjective *Eros- und Machtwille*) takes the rational economic instrument into its service.[79]

Will to power as an expression of *Kraft* bears the definite power of being out of pure inwardness toward its external aim. Precisely in so doing, however, will to power ignores moral demands of recognition. Self-assertion in the will to power is unlimited self-assertion, contained only by others' resistance, which the will to power seeks to overcome, either through subordination or destruction. If unchecked, the drive to individualization seeks elimination of participation. It becomes external domination. If it reaches its limit, and this is the inner contradiction of the will to power's actualization, it can only destroy itself, for life depends on the very participation the will to power seeks to conquer. Tillich discovers this self-contradiction in capitalism, in which acceptance of the principle of economic war of all against all is nonetheless dependent on a basic solidarity of group interests.[80] If capitalism's principle were ever to become fully effective, it would destroy itself, since there would be either no other remaining for the will to power to dominate, or the social relations upon which capitalism depends would be shattered. In our world, wanton destruction of the environment presents us with a concrete instance of the same drive of the will to power to utter tyranny. At the same time, however, were its tyranny complete, it would destroy all other being and therefore itself as well.

In more traditional theological terms, will to power is expressed in the spiritual estrangement Tillich describes as *hubris* and concupiscence.[81] As unlimited desire for self-assertion, human beings make themselves their own center, withdrawing from participation in the divine. We refuse to accept our essential finitude and participation in the infinite with which we are not identical. Hubris is a danger precisely to the "heroes who are great, beautiful, and outstanding, who are the bearers of power and value. . . . By its intrinsic

---

[79] Tillich, *Basic Principles of Religious Socialism,* 78 (*GW* 2:109).

[80] Tillich, *The Religious Situation,* 108–10 (*GW* 10:42–43). This is why creation of destructive ideology, albeit unconsciously, is an important part of social will to power, against which the *Kraft* of the Protestant principle must stand ("The Protestant Principle and the Proletarian Situation," 169–70; *GW* 7:92–93).

[81] On the tie between the will to power and concupiscence, see Gilkey, *Gilkey on Tillich,* 10, 128–31, 161.

dynamics, greatness drives toward *hubris*"; "[a] demonic structure drives man to confuse natural self-affirmation with destructive self-elevation."[82] That structure is the unchecked will to power.

The self-contradiction involved in the boundless will to power is described also in Tillich's use of the symbol "concupiscence," which is not a doctrine about sex, but a symbol for the temptation of the "possibility of reaching unlimited abundance." Concupiscence as related to the will to power is one's attempt to draw "the universe into oneself in terms of the power to use for himself whatever he wants to use." Will to power as self-assertion severs participation in the other and the divine; it does not admit norms by which it can be judged, and therefore "remains unlimited and has demonic-destructive traits."[83]

Concupiscence shows the close tie between love and the will to power. The will to power has desire at its base and contains within itself desire for abundance, which "is the root of love in all its forms."[84] Past this common point of desire, however, the power of love driving from inwardness to externality takes on quite different implications and expression than the will of power. Whereas will to power stands at the limit of individualization, the power of love represents the absoluteness of the participatory pole. Love's recognition of its poverty leads it to seek fullness in the other.[85]

Tillich's later theology of love is the focus here. This later theology is more differentiated than his earlier thought. In the lengthy quotation from *Basic Principles* earlier, Tillich linked erotic will and will to power closely.[86] Later, Tillich finds their common element in desire (*libido*). If love follows its own trajectory from the point of desire, however, its emphasis is on participation. Love seeks reunion of the existentially separated. In its specificity as a quality of love, desire is not desire for pleasure but for "union with that which fulfills the desire." The erotic quality of love transcends desire because it adds the striving "for a union with that which is the bearer of values because of the values it embodies."[87] With this erotic quality, and in polar interdependence with it, comes love's filial property. *Philia* represents the personal pole of love, without which no erotic communion is possible. Unity with the other requires a uniting center through which it can be accomplished. Finally, fulfilled love has an agapic character. The agapic aspect of love cuts into and transforms all other qualities of love; love cuts into love as the manifestation of ultimate reality.[88]

---

[82] Tillich, *Systematic Theology* 2:50, 51; for a slightly different treatment of hubris and concupiscence, see 3:93–94.

[83] Ibid. 2:52, 53, 55.

[84] Ibid. 2:52.

[85] Ibid.; *Love, Power, and Justice*, 29. The same relation between love, poverty, and fulfillment is constitutive of the *eros* to knowledge (*Systematic Theology* 1:95).

[86] See also *The Religious Situation*, 132 (*GW* 10:53–54). It seems that the later distinction between *eros* and *libido* has not been finalized.

[87] Tillich, *Love, Power, and Justice*, 29, 30.

[88] Ibid., 31–33.

There is a curious point in these reflections. In the transition from mere desire to eros and filial love, the requirement of a formed and centered self has been introduced. It is true that desire assumes a centered being, but it does not require a personal center: "Beings without a personal center are without *eros,* although they are not without *epithymia* [desire]." This is why the principal distortions of estranged human love are found where desire has not been transcended. Desire for mere union with the other, in disregard of the power and value the other bears, is "chaotic self-surrender,"[89] an abdication of the personal center upon which the transcending qualities of love depend. If desire is mere subjective desire, ignoring its object and the object's value, the result is self-destruction. In its most radical form, desire is the drive for death, the death instinct. The aim of self-fulfillment is lost in mere desire for union. The participatory pole in its full ascendency, without the pole of individualization, is finally desire for self-annihilation, desire to be taken into the other completely, to rid oneself of one's own centered self.[90] Self-surrender, if it reaches its limit, surrenders its being to another's control. Desire that does not transcend itself ignores the moral demand of recognition as much as an unfettered will to power does, even though in the opposite direction. While will to power refuses to recognize the other as a bearer of power and value, love's desire fails to recognize its own power and value.

The movement of *Mächtigkeit* (and, by analogy, *Macht*), from its own inner center into external reality through the bearing *Kräfte* of love and *Machtwille* has led to a point of deep conflict in Tillich's theology. If either bearing *Kraft* becomes absolute power, centered power of being is destroyed. Without the pole of individualization, the participating being is exterminated because it loses its center, through which participation is possible. Without participation in being, individualization annihilates the other and, ultimately, itself. It is true of the polarities generally that, "the elements of essential being which move against each other tend to annihilate each other and the whole to which they belong"; they create a "structure of destruction."[91]

If this framework stands, what conclusions about power can be drawn? First, Tillich's position has the advantage of pointing out that the greatest intensifications of individualization and participation are also the most dangerous ones: divine and demonic power are in close proximity, and "where the power for good increases, the power for evil increases also."[92] Second, Tillich confirms the ontological self-contradiction of mere domination. Domination, whether as unlimited self-assertion or passive self-surrender, can be effective only so long as it never reaches its *telos,* the extermination of the dominated.

---

[89] Ibid., 31, 68; see also *Systematic Theology* 1:282.

[90] Tillich, *Courage To Be,* 12; *Love, Power, and Justice,* 29; *Systematic Theology* 2:54. This is also the danger of radical forms of mysticism (*Systematic Theology* 3:143).

[91] Tillich, *Systematic Theology* 2:60; *Courage To Be,* 90.

[92] Tillich, *Systematic Theology* 3:373; see also 2:33.

This being said, Tillich's position does not come to rest at this point, where the power of being contains a radical dualism within itself. If it did, the power of being-itself would have to be in relentless combat against the assertion of power by centered beings. It is, however, only in existence, and not essentially, that the way is opened for separation between the poles of individualization and participation. Essentially, the poles are united.[93] Under the conditions of existence, conflict and tension between the poles are possible, even inevitable.[94] If individualization and participation are essentially united, and if the kingdom of God and salvation are symbols for reunion of the separated poles of existence in history and life, then there must be a way to reestablish the essential unity of the polarity within the conditions of existence, upon the ground of the appearance of the New Being under the conditions of existence. Since the poles of individualization and participation have been treated as representing, in part, the will to power and the power of love, the point can be put this way: It must be possible to reunite the powers that drive inner power of being into external world, and so overcome the distortion that occurs when either pole seeks exclusive reign. A principle must be discovered that limits and balances the expressions of *Machtwille* and the desire of love, preventing the "decay" that follows upon their exclusive dominance.[95]

The Ambiguities of Centered Power

Tillich finds this principle in justice. Justice steps into the lacuna between the unlimited demands and expressions of centered powers of being. In the form of justice, the demand of recognition is given its due. It overcomes both the thirst of arbitrary and subjective *Machtwille* and the arbitrary self-surrender of love's desire and is the mediating condition for reuniting love and power.[96] Justice is the rational form that mediates and balances individualization and participation in existence.[97] In bourgeois society, however, justice has been

---

[93] Ibid. 1:171; 2:59–66; 3:401–2.

[94] Ibid. 2:59–78; this is the most complete discussion of the universal conflict of the poles. See also "Reply to Interpretation and Criticism," 343; however, universality and unavoidability of conflict do not imply the necessity of conflict. The threat of polar separation is implied in the structure of being, but its actuality is not (*Systematic Theology* 1:201–2).

[95] Ibid., 149, 154.

[96] Tillich, "Love, Power, and Justice," 545. The value of asceticism is here. It too "puts limits to the endlessness of libido and the will to power and turns them to an acceptance of one's finitude" (*Systematic Theology* 2:82).

[97] The aesthetic emphasis on balance is one-sided. Certainly, health and an equilibrium between the influence of either pole are closely associated in the ontological polarities (*Systematic Theology* 3:277; *Courage To Be*, 79). This has been noted by many commentators. But polar equilibration is not a balance of compromise, but conditions the intensification and preservation of greater manifestations of each polar element. Thus, justice is the citadel through which the road to *eros*, *philia*, and *agapē* must pass. This point is taken up later.

reduced to a merely formal egalitarianism which severs justice from connection with the real individual beings demanding justice.[98] Formal justice allows the material content of society to overcome it and use it for its own ends. When capital becomes dominant, therefore, relations of capital and its possessors to its nonpossessors cannot be controlled by social justice, for these relations have already been declared out of bounds to formal justice. Justice is an autonomous architecture with little or no relation to those between whom it is supposed to mediate. Bourgeois justice, in sum, treats only relations among things considered formally equal in their bearing of power and value.[99] It reflects and accentuates "thingification"; there is little or no connection with actual powers of being.

Tillich believes that a more adequate conception of justice, and an ontologically correct one, must recognize justice's participation in power. Justice must be based on the intrinsic power (*Mächtigkeit*) borne by every being; conversely, justice can be based on intrinsic power of being because degrees of being are susceptible to rational apprehension. Only in this way can valid claims to just treatment be forwarded and decided.[100] Of course, autonomous justice must recognize this, even if this acknowledgment is hidden from it. If one asks, for example, why a person is entitled to just treatment, affirmative answers usually refer to certain human qualities or achievements. But this is precisely a recognition of a demand for justice based on the inner power of

---

An interesting reference to the aesthetics of equilibrium is found in Pauck and Pauck, *Paul Tillich*, 7. The authors claim that balance was Tillich's aesthetic ideal in the architectural creations of his youth. Kelsey (*The Fabric of Paul Tillich's Theology*) takes a potentially very fruitful approach to Tillich, arguing that he is best understood as an aesthetic thinker. Kelsey's presentation is hampered, however, by his attempt to evaluate Tillich by means of nonaesthetic theory of argument, which subordinates aesthetics to external criteria without according aesthetics any independent value.

[98] My thanks to Langdon Gilkey for pointing out that the divorce between justice and the concrete beings to whom it is supposed to apply is not a problem of "bourgeois society" alone; indeed, the problem has been even more severe in Communist nations.

[99] Tillich, *The Religious Situation*, 127–28 (*GW* 10:52). Formal equality as a principle has, for Tillich, only corrective value, although it may be a good and necessary corrective ("Open Letter to Emanuel Hirsch," 381). It cannot be constitutive, because, like autonomy in general, it lacks creative power (*The Socialist Decision*, 142; *GW* 2:346–47). Consequently, its ideal of egalitarianism, formally failing to recognize the impossibility of actual equality (*Love, Power, and Justice*, 45, 59–60; *Systematic Theology* 3:262–63), allows special power groups to dominate without accountability (*The Socialist Decision*, 142; *GW* 2:346–47).

[100] Tillich, "Realism and Faith," 69 (*Religiöse Verwirklichung*, 69–70). Intrinsic power of being is the criterion not only for relations of justice, but also for the symbolic material of the sacraments. Against Luther, Tillich argues that there is natural affinity between the material and its sacramental use. Sacramental elements are symbolic in Tillich's sense; that is, they participate in the power of being they mediate. Just as justice is not solely a creation of the positive law, but must have an ontological basis, so the sacrament is not solely a creation of an arbitrary subjective will, even if the "subject" in this case is God ("Nature and Sacrament," 96, 111; *Religiöse Verwirklichung*, 144, 165–66).

human being,[101] and it requires development of concrete contents of justice which better permit and encourage the emergence of these qualities or achievements.

Tillich's notion of theonomous justice has the decisive advantage of grounding contents of justice in specific powers of being. It opposes radical egalitarianism almost as much as it opposes tyranny, for while the latter refuses to recognize any power outside itself, the former refuses to acknowledge differences in power of being which make some better or worse suited for particular activities than others. The difference between a formal right to just treatment forwarded on the basis of "potential power" cannot be allowed to obscure actual differences between entities with the same potential power. Egalitarianism recognizes only potential power. In this sense, it is only autonomous justice run amok. Moreover, the result of restricting autonomous justice to formal relations of potential equals is quite different from its intention; it means that "the mass of people who are naturally (though not legally) excluded from any serious competition become mere objects of . . . domination."[102]

Egalitarianism is a conceptual option only if power is understood as occasional and relatively infrequent, that is, as strictly political and institutional. It is possible, therefore, for Starhawk to romanticize a golden age of egalitarianism, prior to power-over (especially over women), while at the same time noting that the heroine of the myth that exemplifies the golden age decrees

---

[101] This is why Victor Nuovo is in error in asserting that justice need not be theonomously grounded ("On Revising Tillich: An Essay on the Principles of Theology," in *Kairos and Logos: Studies in the Roots and Implications of Tillich's Theology*, ed. John J. Carey [Cambridge, Mass.: North American Tillich Society, 1978], 47–67). Nuovo maintains that the Kantian basis of morality as human freedom is adequate, and he takes this as an example of autonomous justice. But is not recognition of freedom an acknowledgment of a specific spiritual quality of humanity which demands recognition, and does not Tillich affirm that the structure of the categorial imperative as "a piece of theonomous philosophy" ("Reply to Interpretation and Criticism," 337)? Kant's conception, too, is grounded in the inner power of human being. It is precisely Tillich's point, however, that bourgeois justice does not permit the actualization of human freedom which is demanded even in this quite basic theonomous grounding of justice. What would be required, if freedom is the basic ontological ground of just and fair human relations, are particular contents of justice that can at least precipitate more complete actualizations of human freedom.

[102] "The Idea and the Ideal of Personality," 127; see also *Religious Socialism*, 52–54 (*GW* 2:170–71); *The State as Expectation and Demand*, 107–10 (*Religiöse Verwirklichung*, 224–26). Stone is wrong to assert that "justice" was not a very important concept in Tillich's critique of capitalism (*Paul Tillich's Radical Social Thought*, 119–20). Part of the contradiction of capitalism, we see here, is that the attempt to "autonomize" justice is impossible, and thus certain groups gain an influence that is unjust but is not subject to review by autonomous justice. Stone makes this mistake because he thinks Tillich's exposition of *Mächtigkeit* contemplates only a "natural" equality, whereas for Tillich potential equality did not obscure actual difference in the power of being. Stone leans toward enforcing an egalitarian ideal upon Tillich, with the qualification that Tillich was not an "absolute egalitarian" (p. 127). A good and brief summary of Tillich's position on the formal principle of equality is provided by John R. Stumme, *Socialism in Theological Perspective: A Study of Paul Tillich, 1918–1933*, Dissertation Series 21 (Missoula, Mont.: Scholars Press, 1978), 179–80.

her husband's fate.[103] It is difficult to think of a more dominating act. It is passed over as inconsequential because "egalitarianism" is so restricted as to mean merely, in Michael Mann's words, "Hierarchical differences . . . are not institutionalized."[104] This confinement to institutional analysis is untenable. First, particularly if an egalitarian age is claimed as a moral apex in which all were well pleased, it is difficult to explain why it did not persist. A hypothesis of historical paradise requires account of a historical fall. Second, and more important, to make nonegalitarian institutions the only objects of analysis blinds one to devastating relations of domination below the institutional level. Absence of institutional hierarchy between siblings, for example, should not obscure the fact that domination and submission frequently characterize these relations and many others that are formally equal (one person's declaration of another's fate is a clear instance).

Third, exclusive concentration on the institutional dimension of social relations is a gigantic abstraction whose product is analytic tunnel vision. If its conclusion that domination is per se evil is transferred from institutional analysis to other social relations, as it frequently is, the possibility of a productive relation in which domination is present is ruled out a priori. But there are scarcely any practices or relations in which domination is not only an element, but an intrinsic one, within or outside "institutions." In actual practice, even the most radical egalitarian recognizes that potentiality and formal equality are not final words. Even the egalitarian calls upon others for their particular talents. Egalitarianism is denied as soon as one calls an electrician; formal equality and potentiality yield to a unique, content-laden, expertise. Egalitarianism is cast to the wind when one eats; even if eating is considered a violation of intrinsic justice due the consumed power (as Tillich considers it),[105] consumption forwards a claim to the greater power of being of the consumer. Egalitarianism is "thingification" according to potentiality; particular powers of being are dismissed from consideration. Theonomous justice, on the other hand, is radical de-thingification; beings are viewed as powers rather than things, and justice mediates between the intrinsic claims of these powers in their participation with each other in encounter.

The basis of justice in intrinsic *Mächtigkeit* or *Macht* presents a difficulty to a border geography of power which denies that power is basically inward. That problem is deferred until later; for now the focus is an ambiguity in Tillich's own notion of the association between justice and power. On one hand, justice must participate in power. Justice is borne by concrete spirit.

---

[103] Starhawk, *Truth or Dare: Encounters with Power, Authority, and Mystery* (San Francisco: HarperSan Francisco, HarperCollins, 1987), 45.

[104] Michael Mann, *The Sources of Social Power,* vol. 1, *A History of Power from the Beginning to A.D. 1760* (Cambridge: Cambridge University Press, 1986), 37. Starhawk's agreement with this definition is implicit throughout the first part of *Truth or Dare.* The emergence of "power-over" is the emergence of institutions of domination, particularly military institutions.

[105] Tillich, *Systematic Theology* 3:91; "Love, Power, and Justice," 545.

Justice not only must adjudicate between encountering powers' claims, but its special contents have to reflect the spirit and bear the power of the community in which it is embedded.[106] On the other hand, justice, which is not itself power but a participant in power, provides the criterion that judges and limits expression of inner powers of being.

This is an anomalous situation. Since power is the fundamental ontological concept through which being must be interpreted, power must transcend justice. Justice must be immanent in power.[107] Concrete justice must be borne by the creative *Kraft* of being, or else it cannot be real. Justice has to participate in the potentialities offered by power. Moreover, a concrete form of justice cannot emerge without an actual, centered, positing power.[108] But power also requires justice.[109] As potentialities become centered in actual being and strive for external expression, the possibility of distortion through the tyranny of one form of power must be negated. Justice performs this negating task, and therefore justice must also transcend power, since it is that by which power is judged. To the extent that the potential power of *Kraft* gains content, and to the extent that centered powers of *Mächtigkeit* and *Macht* externalize themselves, the form of justice intervenes to combat "demonic and self-destructive" appearances of "mere power,"[110] and to set power's poles in proper relationship. Put another way, justice balances the results of an exclusivity of the will to power or love as mere desire, for the result of such tyranny is either domination by self or other:

> Justice is the structure without which power would be destructive, and it is the backbone of love without which love would be sentimental self-surrender. In both of them it is the principle of form and measure. Formless love wastes the person who loves and abuses the person who is loved; and formless power destroys, first, other centers of power, and then itself.[111]

Justice must participate in these powers and subdue them into an equilibrium of its own form.

Justice gains its power from the polarity of individualization and participation, rooted in the ontological structure of self and world, while that structure and its polar elements receive normative direction from the form of justice. In effect, justice must stand above power if it is to judge power.

---

[106] The concreteness of any cultural form is emphasized as early as "On the Idea of a Theology of Culture," 155–56 (*GW* 9:13–14); see also "The Problem of Power," 187–90 (*GW* 2:198–200); *The Socialist Decision,* 140, 143 (*GW* 2:344–45, 347); *Love, Power, and Justice,* 80–82.

[107] Tillich, *Love, Power, and Justice,* 67.

[108] Tillich, *The State as Expectation and Demand,* 99 (*Religiöse Verwirklichung,* 214, reads: "Wo keine Selbstmächtigkeit, da is kein Staat; wo keine Macht, Recht zu setzen und durchzusetzen, da ist kein Staat").

[109] Tillich, *The State as Expectation and Demand,* 99 (*Religiöse Verwirklichung,* 214).

[110] Tillich, *Christianity and the Encounter of the World Religions,* 17.

[111] Tillich, *Shadow and Substance,* 118; see also *Systematic Theology* 3:84.

The limit of legitimate power is defined by principles of justice both internal and external to power. As real form, justice participates in the bearing powers of being, but insofar as it mediates the conflict of powers concretely, it must be distinguished from the powers it judges. As actual power, power is not its own criterion but is controlled by rational principles of justice employed to control the unlimited will to self-assertion or self-surrender.

This double relation of justice and power is mapped out early in Tillich's career: "To dissolve the concept of justice into that of power is equally as impossible as to imagine a concept of justice without power."[112] The final sentence of "The Problem of Power" is stunning: "A group can attain inner might only to the degree that it subjects itself to the norm which, transcending power, stabilizes and consecrates all power."[113] Despite alterations in his conception of ontology, Tillich never gives up this position.[114]

Before showing why this is the case, a general outline of the difference between Tillich's view and the concept of power as communication of efficacy at the border of encounter should be included. The notion that power is essentially a communication of efficacy contemplates exactly the dissolution of justice into power. The reason was explained in the last chapter. If justice or fairness stands outside power in any way, the consequence for power is that it tends to become identified with domination. If this is not true of Tillich's treatment of the power of being-itself, it is a danger for his conception of actualization of inner, centered power. The result for justice is that, devoid of extrarational aspects, and therefore devoid of power as well, it cannot exercise any critical right with respect to power. No rational principle has the ability to limit power; this inability applies to rational justice as well. To be sure, Tillich evades this latter consequence by arguing that concrete justice participates in power. But his position here is odd, since the content of justice must be introduced precisely in order to control unfettered exercises of power. It is difficult to see how justice's content, in attempting to mediate the conflict of powers, is still immanent in power. It would be more appropriate to reverse the relation and suggest that since struggles of power are mediated by justice, centered power is contained by the form of justice. The definition of power as communication of efficacy posits a simpler, less sophisticated, and less confusing relation between power and justice or fairness.[115] There is no distinction

---

[112] Tillich, *The Socialist Decision,* 166 (*GW* 2:240).

[113] Tillich, "The Problem of Power," 202 (*GW* 2:208).

[114] That justice is the criterion for power seems so self-evident to Tillich that it is mentioned only casually from time to time. Cultural creation is judged in terms of its "humanity and justice" (*Systematic Theology* 3:331, 335); the fulfillment of history includes the "unambiguous harmony of power and justice," apparently as coequal principles (p. 332). In addition, see *Dynamics of Faith,* 71.

[115] We employ "fairness" instead of "justice" frequently. The reason is that "justice" has become one of the most overused and indefinite concepts in the English language, and now serves largely as a code word for self-interest. It is divorced increasingly from the connotations of "just" and "right." Although "fairness" does not avoid these uses by any intrinsic superiority, it is fresher, less hackneyed, and still accords with the best meanings of "justice."

between varieties of power in terms of their potentiality and actuality, or their inner and outer location, and this permits a single relation between power and fairness. The aspiration is that simplicity is indeed a virtue.

It is necessary to ask why, for Tillich, power cannot contain its own mediating or critical principle. Why is it necessary to introduce justice as arbitrator? The reason is that justice is inherently nonsingular in relation to its objects. That is, justice does not need to be employed in a situation in which there is only one participant but is applied only between beings. Centered power is brought into justice's purview only when it meets another centered power. Justice presupposes encounter; this is not the case with centered power itself. To be sure, power proves itself in encounter, but centered power is inwardly possessed. This has implications for the activity of power and justice in encounter. The encounter is the point at which self-assertion meets resistance from the other. From encounter arises the moral imperative of recognition, and the form and results of recognition are judged by the mediating concept of justice. Power, however, is power precisely because it overcomes another's resistance. In a struggle between powers, power's aim is to overcome resistance so that it can possess power. Struggling powers, asserting themselves, seek triumph over each other. The limitation centered power cannot impose on itself is imposed by justice. The situation is reversed in the case of self-surrendering love. There centered power tries to find its end exclusively in the other. Still, the structure of encounter is framed by the overcoming of resistance, but in this case, the resistance of the self is overcome. The end is complete loss of power by the centered power.

The conclusion is this: If power is centered power, possessed in some measure by a being, it is also directed to the elimination of multiple centers. This is why power cannot be its own normative criterion, for with the ultimate triumph of either will to power or love's self-surrender, power destroys itself. The moral act intervenes to protect multiple centers of power and raises love and the will to power out of polar isolation from each other, opening the way for the greater manifestations of love which presuppose recognition of the other. *Justice must save power from itself.* The moral act, concretized in justice, is related to power in the sense that it is borne by power, but the substantive criteria of morality come from justice rather than power.

The difference between Tillich's theology of power and one which asserts that power is a communication of efficacy comes to this: the framework of centered power, a result of conceiving of power as alternatively potential and actual, cannot bear its own weight. It requires a principle of justice to raise it to higher ground and to preserve it. On the other hand, if power is communication of efficacy, the substantive criteria of justice, fairness, and recognition are implied in the notion of power itself. The reason is that "communication at the border of encounter" includes plurality within itself, an aspect absent in an exposition of "centered power." If there is no other being, there can be no communication and no border, no encounter at all, and therefore no power.

Not only recognition and fairness presume encounter, but power does also and more fundamentally, for without power there is no justice. Encounter is not the stage upon which power is played, but the stage upon which it emerges in the first place. In the private dressing rooms of the theater, there is no power because there is no encounter. Justice has no excess beyond power, but remains always immanent within it.

To prevent the self-destruction of will to power and the self-surrender of love, Tillich employs the rational form of justice. Certainly, justice is not Tillich's final word on the issue. It cannot be final since justice is a rational form; therefore it remains abstract in relation to the particular encounter that demands justice.[116] Proportional justice is a "calculating justice" which "can be measured in quantitative terms." As a rational form, proportional justice is inadequate to the dynamics and unpredictability of the encounter. The bridge to the concrete situation is provided by creative justice, or love, the "creative element" in creative justice. Proportional justice is

> never adequate to [creative justice] because it calculates in fixed proportions. One never knows *a priori* what the outcome of an encounter of power with power will be. If one judges such an encounter according to previous power proportions, one is necessarily unjust, even if one is legally right. Examples of this situation are a matter of daily experience. They include all trespasses of the positive law in the name of a superior law which is not yet formulated and valid. They include struggles for power which are in conflict with indefinite and obsolete rules, and the outcome of which is an increase in the power of being in both the victor and the conquered. They include all those events in which justice demands the resignation of justice, an act without which no human relation and no human group could last. More exactly one should speak of the resignation of proportional justice for the sake of creative justice.[117]

Does the concept of creative justice change essentially the relation between power and form we criticized? Tillich's decision to identify creative justice as the form of love and his assertion that the creative element of justice is love are not simplistic efforts to conceal the frequent conflict between justice and love in Christian theology. Rather, love's access to the concrete situation includes the mediating form of justice in order to prevent love's self-surrender. Within this framework, Tillich can say, "Nothing is more false than to say to somebody: since I love you and you love me, I don't need to get justice from you or you from me, for love eliminates the need for justice."[118] Justice mediates between individualization and participation in order to prevent love's self-obliteration in mere desire. It is therefore the structure through which the higher forms of love appear. Love reaches its heights only by passing

---

[116] Tillich, *The State as Expectation and Demand*, 100, 111–14 (*Religiöse Verwirklichung*, 215, 228–32). This essay is superb in arguing for the necessity of concrete power being the bearer of justice.

[117] Tillich, *Love, Power, and Justice*, 63–64, 83, 64–65; see also *Shadow and Substance*, 122.

[118] Tillich, *Love, Power, and Justice*, 82.

through justice's galvanizing fire, whose flame is one's intrinsic power of being. On the other side, love cuts into justice as revelation cuts into reason.[119] Love is that quality in justice which allows its concrete application and adherence to the *telos* of justice, which is human fulfillment in reuniting love. If renunciation of proportional justice is still a possibility to be valued, as Tillich assures us it is, surrender is not a renunciation of self but its fulfillment. The self is fulfilled by renunciation if surrender mediates the divine presence, if fulfilled form or perfect individuality negates its finitude in order to point to the divine infinite.[120] Self-surrender is desirable, in short, if by it, the finite is a symbol for God's presence.[121]

Justice, therefore, preserves the self, through which love participates in the other. At the same time, love's participation in concrete powers of being allows justice to participate more completely in power. On the one hand, centered power's criterion remains outside itself. Only that power which is in accord with creative justice or reuniting love is to be affirmed. And yet, on the other side, the criterion of reuniting love and creative justice are found in their ability to point to the power of being-itself, or *Kraft*. The triad of Tillich's conceptions of power, as potential, centered, and actual externally, produces a vacillation in his valuation of power and in his ontological claim for power. Power and rational form appear, alternatively, as immanent within each other and as transcendent to each other. The concretion of justice as creative justice does not change this; it only deepens the ambiguity.

---

[119] Ibid., 83.

[120] The surrender of Jesus to the Christ is also the conquest of non-being under conditions of existence. This is the fundamental point of Tillich's Christology. Alexander J. McKelway (*The Systematic Theology of Paul Tillich: A Review and Analysis* [Richmond, Va.: John Knox Press, 1964]) misunderstands Tillich in regard to the sacrifice of Jesus. McKelway interprets this to mean that Jesus is only negated, while for Tillich, the surrender of Jesus to that which is the Christ is also the fulfillment of Jesus in the Christ. The final revelation, for Tillich, is defined by self-surrender without self-loss, by complete self-possession in surrender (Tillich, *Systematic Theology* 1:132–33). As Hammond notes, "one can willingly surrender only that which he fully possesses. The capacity of willing self-sacrifice for a transcendent purpose is a mark of courage and strength, not of weakness" (*Power of Self-Transcendence*, 81; see also *Man in Estrangement*, 169).

[121] In this sense, Jesus as the Christ is the final and ultimate symbol of the divine, because completely transparent to the divine, and "through which the infinite is fully *communicated* to others . . ." (Langdon Gilkey, "The New Being and Christology," in *The Thought of Paul Tillich,* ed. Adams, Pauck, and Shinn, 311). In the Christ-event, there is no confusion between the ultimate and its bearer, and this is why — in principle if not in fact — Christianity cannot become idolatrous. The cross is the principle of its self-criticism (*Dynamics of Faith,* 97–126). The nature of the symbol is to participate in what it symbolizes, pointing to it without being identical with that to which it points. On the representative character of all fulfillment, see *Protestantism as a Critical and Creative Principle,* 20, 25 (GW 7:37, 41–42). The assertion that Jesus as the Christ is the ultimate symbol for the divine is drawn from Tillich's later work and does not account for what Adams (*Tillich's Philosophy,* 267) calls Tillich's "astonishing" denial, in an early piece, of the symbolic character of personal life.

There is another, and closely related, indication of the confusion created by the multiplicity of the meaning of "power" in Tillich's work. The norm of creative justice is exemplified in forgiveness, which renounces the claim to proportional justice in favor of reuniting love.[122] At its limit, does the renunciation of proportional justice also contemplate the renunciation of centered power—in nature, society, or both? Tillich treats this question under the heading of "spiritual power." He is consistent in arguing that exercise of natural and social power, which involves overcoming resistance, requires force and compulsion.[123] Radical pacifism is excluded from the outset, for being must overcome the threat of non-being.[124] Compulsion is an integral element of natural power because natural power is power in conditions of estrangement. There is an ontological unity between power, love, and justice, but in existence this unity has been lost. Power, justice, and love are separated from one another, capable of only fragmentary reunion in history. Among other reasons, power must employ compulsion in this condition of existential estrangement in order to safeguard and make possible justice and love.[125] Compulsory power is a protection against injustice. Power "actualizes itself through force and compulsion."[126] These are the instruments of power. This raises the question of whether or not power may be renounced.

On the one hand, the renunciation of power is identical to the renunciation of life. Compulsion and force are means to overcome non-being's resistance to the power of a form. On the other hand, manifestations of creative justice frequently *do* renounce compulsion. Some of the greatest figures of this century, at least, achieved greatness precisely by renouncing all compulsion. Did they also renounce power? Tillich thinks not. Abdication of natural and social power is not the same as renunciation of all power. Giving up compulsory power can be the greatest power of all: it can be "spiritual power," which operates without and above the ambiguities of compulsion and has its effect through freedom alone. Structurally, spiritual power has considerable affinities with "persuasive power."

Of the many illustrations Tillich could bring to bear to support this point, the most appropriate is Jesus.[127] In a late address, Tillich uses this example:

---

[122] Tillich, *Love, Power, and Justice,* 84–86, 121.

[123] Tillich, "The Problem of Power," 192–96 (*GW* 2:201–4). "Force" is the translation of "*Gewalt.*" The distinction between force and compulsion appears, as far as I know, only in Tillich's later work. Force is a concept restricted to beings without spontaneity, while compulsion is force exercised upon organic beings with the capacity for spontaneous reaction (*Love, Power, and Justice,* 46–48). For our purposes, this distinction makes no substantial difference.

[124] See Tillich, "On the Boundary," 71; *Systematic Theology* 3:387–88.

[125] Paul Tillich, "Love's 'Strange Work,'" *The Protestant* 4, no. 3 (December–January 1942): 72–74; *Systematic Theology* 3:386.

[126] Tillich, *Love, Power, and Justice,* 47.

[127] The power of Jesus as the Christ is centered and internal before it is communicated. Tillich notes that to experience the power of Jesus as the Christ is to experience the "power in him" (*Systematic Theology* 2:125); cf. phrases like the "power of his being" (ibid. 2:157).

"The picture of Jesus shows that the resignation of power can be the greatest power—if the situation demands it. But even of him it was not always demanded. Power through resignation of power is a human possibility, for which one uses the term 'spiritual power.'"[128] It is not necessary to show that the problem of the power of Jesus the Christ is the perennial ground for Tillich's reflections on the renunciation of natural and social power (although one may suspect it),[129] but it is important to note the force of this example for a Christian theology of power.

The New Testament picture of Jesus the Christ is the rock upon which any consistently positive evaluation of natural and social power seems to founder. Luther has little trouble speaking of the weakness of Christ in comparison to the powers of the world, and in this instance does not hesitate to engage in a transvaluation of power: true power is the weakness of Christ and *vice versa*. Tillich too was a christomorphic theologian. In the *Systematic Theology*, not only is Christology the focus of the central volume, but among its five parts "Existence and the Christ" is located squarely in the middle.[130] The center of Christian hope gives up natural and social power.

Tillich cannot be persuaded that the forfeiture of natural and social power is identical with renunciation of power in its entirety. Power itself is not relinquished, for this "would mean resignation of being."[131] Instead, he argues that the concept of resignation of power is a paradoxical one, an affirmation that one only has power through its renunciation.[132] Alternatively expressed, spiritual power makes one's

> natural or social power of being . . . irrelevant. . . . The Spiritual power works through them or it works through the surrender of them. He may exercise

---

[128] Tillich, *Shadow and Substance*, 122. Another example of the same argument, pursued from Jesus' nonanswer to the question of authority, is found in Tillich's fascinating sermon "The Nature of Authority," *Pulpit Digest* 34, no. 186 (October 1953): 25 +.

[129] See the introduction to "The Interpretation of History and the Idea of Christ," 242–43 (*Religiöse Verwirklichung*, 110–11), in which Tillich boldly asserts that no philosophy of history is adequate without reference to Christology. Occasionally Tillich even engages in a radical transvaluation of power. Despite the proclamation that spiritual power is the ultimate power, the cross's power is also ultimate impotence: "in the cross humanity experienced the human boundary-situation as never before and never after. In this power—indeed, in this impotence and poverty—the Protestant church will stand so long as it is aware of the meaning of its own existence" ("The Protestant Message and the Man of Today," 200; *Religiöse Verwirklichung*, 35). It is true that this claim is early in Tillich's career, and prior to the crucial essay "The Problem of Power," but it reappears in English in 1948. The substantial changes from Tillich's original German work do not include any revision of his assertion about power. Spiritual power, it appears, has quite a lot in common with powerlessness.

[130] For a more persuasive and very thorough argument on this point, see Gilkey, "The New Being and Christology," 307–29. Gilkey (*Gilkey on Tillich*, 19) suggests that even Tillich's concept of theonomy is drawn from Christology.

[131] Tillich, *Love, Power, and Justice*, 120.

[132] Tillich, "The Problem of Power," 198 (*GW* 2:205).

Spiritual power through words or thought, through what he is and what
he does, or through the surrender of them or through the sacrifice of himself.
In all of these forms he can change reality by attaining levels of being which
are ordinarily hidden.[133]

There are a number of difficulties with this exposition of the resignation
of power. The first, and least important, is that it is confusing. Only if it is
necessary should recourse be had to a formulation like "power through the
renunciation of power." Yet the very eccentricity of such a phrase leads to the
intuition that such a formula is not necessary. A second problem is more
serious. The analogy between realms or dimensions of being, which Tillich
takes such pains to establish, is seriously threatened by an assertion of the
irrelevance of natural and social power to spiritual power.[134] If natural and
social power are optional for one who possesses spiritual power, could it not
be said that the dimensions of nature and society are irrelevant to the life of
the spirit? To be sure, it can still be claimed that nature and society remain
open to the effects of the spirit,[135] but the assertion could no longer be made
that nature and society always qualify spiritual power. But this is precisely
the dualistic interpretation of the two realms Tillich opposes with tremen-
dous effectiveness and enthusiasm.[136] Tillich accused the German Lutheran
churches of his day of reactionary political conservatism based on this division, and a similar charge against various churches today is supportable.
Moreover, the loss of a necessary connection between spiritual life and life's
other dimensions undercuts Tillich's entire theological program, which is
grounded in the immanence of religion within all nature and culture. His whole
theological and philosophical outlook contradicts the assertion of the optional
character of natural and social power for spiritual power. Yet he is driven to
this position in regard to power because the historical reality of surrender of
centered power undeniably produces unparalleled power for those affected
by it.

The division between spiritual and other powers is made at another point
as well. While natural and social power work through force and compulsion,

---

[133] Tillich, *Love, Power, and Justice,* 120–21.

[134] Tillich prepares for the break between the dimensions of being in relation to power when
he says that only in finite freedom, the human realm, is the distinction between power and force
meaningful (*Love, Power, and Justice,* 7–8). This means that in all nonhuman realms, power is the
same as force. (Thus, *Kraft* unites power and force, since it is prior to all form, even though Tillich
and his translators have usually restricted *Kraft* to "power." Robert Scharlemann has my appreciation
for pointing this out to me.) But if power is communication of efficacy, the distinction between
power and force is not due to finite freedom but is contained in the nature of power itself and
applies to all life. On the other hand, since compulsion is always an element of power, there cannot be power without compulsion, even in the arena of spiritual power.

[135] Tillich, "Nature and Sacrament," 98 (*Religiöse Verwirklichung,* 147, is somewhat different);
Love, Power, and Justice, 120; *Systematic Theology* 3:276.

[136] See esp. Tillich, "The Protestant Principle and the Proletarian Situation," 161–62, 176–81
(*GW* 7:84–85, 99–104); see also Stumme, *Socialism in Theological Perspective,* 217–25.

spiritual power rises above this ambiguity and works only through freedom, "by surrendering compulsion." The argument depends on restricting force and compulsion to external life. Compulsion, in particular, always works in relation to spontaneity. Coercion and compulsion are not the same as force, because they conquer a psychological resistance that "is not calculable, because it is indivisible, constituting an individual being." Spiritual power not only does not work by means of coercion; it even overcomes the compulsions of personality. Tillich puts the difference this way:

> Then what is [spiritual power's] difference from other forms of power? The Spiritual power works neither through bodily nor through psychological compulsion. It works through man's total personality, and this means, through him as finite freedom. It does not remove his freedom, but it makes his freedom free from the compulsory elements which limit it. The Spiritual power gives a center to the whole personality, a center which transcends the whole personality and, consequently is independent of any of its elements.

Tillich is at one with a general unwillingness to apply terms like "coercion" to matters of choice: "No compulsion at all is presupposed in spiritual power."[137]

That resistance is largely unwarranted. Habermas's paradoxical expression "forceless force" is truer to the operation of domination even in matters of choice. Spiritual power is not free of coercion. This is reflected in the common experience of feeling that there is "no choice" but to do something, even if it is physically and socially possible to act in a number of alternative ways. Luther's famous pronouncement "Here I stand; I can do no other," apocryphal or not, is hardly unique to him. The picture of Jesus in Gethsemane, historically accurate or not, strikes a chord because the experience of being forced to make a certain choice *precisely in order to be free* is common to us all. Experience of the powerful coercion of the spirit is not, in its greatest manifestations, a sloppy metaphor, but expresses the really coercive nature of fulfillment of life and freedom in the true, the good, and the beautiful. Conquest of the distorted will of the spirit occurs through Spirit's coercive power. It is not axiomatic that "where there is force there is injustice."[138] Nor is it true to the experience of being driven toward fulfillment, of being grasped by an ultimate concern, to ignore the element of domination contained there.[139]

---

137 Tillich, *Love, Power, and Justice,* 116, 47, 120, 8.

138 Tillich, *Shadow and Substance,* 120.

139 It is difficult to see how Tillich avoids this conclusion. Authority is required in any situation of need ("The Nature of Authority," 27, 30). Yet our neediness and reliance on a gift that is not within our own grasp is certainly not less in matters of the spirit than in aspects of life concerned with physical sustenance, for example. Indeed, in "Author's Introduction" (p. xxv), Tillich says, contrary to his usual position, that Protestantism will make its next step, in accord with the Protestant principle, "unwillingly, . . . forced by a power not its own." This is a more accurate description of the compulsion exercised by Spirit on spirit than is Tillich's attempt to divorce spiritual power and force.

Investigation of the "voyage of centered power" in Tillich's thought has been a long journey in itself. It is helpful to summarize the major arguments. With the introduction of formed and centered power of being, Tillich reintroduces an exposition of power in terms of its quantitative balances in encounters of powers which possess power and engage in an external struggle for more. Moreover, the need for centered power to become actual in the external world through the bearing powers of will to power and love is ambiguous. Form's unlimited desire leads to the conclusion that, if either the pole of individualization (expressed in the will to power) or participation (expressed in the desire of love) dominates exclusively, being is destroyed. The unlimited will to power is directed to unbounded domination of the other. If it succeeds, it destroys the other, and with the other, itself. Love's desire contains an unlimited desire to be dominated and issues finally in surrender of its own being, through which participation in the other is possible at all.

To avoid these consequences, both love's desire and the will to power must be limited. Tillich finds their limitation in encounter, which introduces the rational form of justice as adjudicator between the claims of conflicting powers. Justice mediates between individualization and participation, enabling appearance of the higher forms of love, which presuppose an encounter of self and other. Justice exists in a strange and strained relation with power. On the one hand, it must participate in the bearing power of *Kraft,* or it cannot be. On the other hand, it must limit the desire of centered powers for unqualified self-affirmation or affirmation of the other. The question of the relation of reason and justice to power is thus reintroduced. Rational form is both within and outside power. It is contained within power as *Kraft* and is driven out of its purely rational form toward creative justice, which is justice in service of reuniting love. With respect to the externalization of centered power, however, justice transcends power, since it provides the normative criteria by which actual power is judged. Finally, with the introduction of creative justice, the rational form of justice is again transcended by power, but at the cost of shattering the multidimensional unity of life Tillich affirms throughout his work. This difficulty is exposed in Tillich's strange formulation, "power through the renunciation of power."

There are three points at issue. First, the unity between Tillich's several uses of "power" is unclear. Power as *Kraft* is potential power. As *Mächtigkeit* and *Macht,* power is actual with respect to the being having power, but potential in regard to its external exercise. This duality of power accounts for the abuse of power and the maxim "Power corrupts." Concrete concentration of power in a centered organization provides that organization with relatively limitless possibilities, some or many of which are destructive.[140] The baffling relation between power and justice is due to Tillich's multiple employment of the term "power." If a theology of power is to be successful, its relation to form and

---

[140] Tillich, *The Political Meaning of Utopia,* in *Political Expectation,* ed. Adams, 128 (*GW* 6:160).

its ontological status constant, there must be a basic unity between the various senses of power. This unity is not provided by Tillich.

Second, the source of these vagaries is the formulation of a theory of power within the categories of potentiality and actuality. The transition between centered power's potentiality with respect to its world and its actual power exposes the crux of the problem. Standing behind this difficulty is the failure to provide definite content to the potential power whose aim is form. The formlessness of *Kraft* requires introduction of formed powers of *Mächtigkeit* and *Macht*.[141] These formed powers, actual with respect to themselves but potential with respect to externalization, become subject to the will to power and self-surrender. In addition, such a strategy produces the conceptual puzzle mentioned in the fourth chapter: it contemplates a power that does not imply its own exercise, requiring "use" to be superimposed on the concept of "power" in phrases such as "actualization of power,"[142] "exercise of power,"[143] "use of power," and the like. Moreover, defining power in the language of potentiality and actuality tends inevitably to conceptions of quantities and balances of possessed power which are merely played out on the stage of encounter.[144] The aim of formed power attempting to become actual externally is exclusive power, either of self or other. Avoiding this implication forces the introduction of a principle such as justice, which is supposed to control and limit expressions of formed power. Yet if power is the basic description of being, such an effort is doomed to failure. Instead, a concept of power must be sought which avoids defining it through the ensemble of inner potentiality and external exercise and reconciles the variety of meanings of power.[145]

---

[141] Adams makes a similar point (*Tillich's Philosophy*, 177–78, 255–56, 265–74). He argues that the absence of content in Tillich's notion of the "Unconditioned" clouds the relation between philosophy and theology. The central problem is that Tillich does not tell us what the character of the Unconditioned is, although Adams recognizes the later material criterion of love. Here the root criticism of Tillich lies in the formlessness of *Kraft* and its corresponding lack of content.

Power's formlessness is a feature of Foucault's thought also. Power is a pure relation between forces; the subsidiary "forces" give content to power. Power purely as such is always formless potentiality, entering from the "outside." Gilles Deleuze analyzes this element of Foucault's conception of power in detail (*Foucault* [Minneapolis: University of Minnesota Press, 1988], 74–132).

[142] See the definition of "spirit" as "the actualization of power and meaning in unity" in *Systematic Theology* 3:111.

[143] This phrase occurs in many places in Tillich's work. An explicit connection between domination and the exercise of power is found in *The Socialist Decision*, 48 (*GW* 2:266). References to the "exercise" (*ausüben*) of power are scattered throughout *The Socialist Decision*.

[144] Balances of power are discussed in "The World Situation," 27–28.

[145] We may now deal with the argument forwarded by Reisz in "Tillich's Doctrine of God." Reisz argues that Spirit, and not power, is the broadest and best description of God's activity. The argument assumes that power in and of itself lacks the dimensions of meaning and fulfillment, and that Spirit as the unity of power and meaning completes this requirement better. It is true that "spirit" is that to which the multidimensional unity of life strives, but it is equally true that, prior to the appearance of human life, spirit is a latent capacity in beings, not an actuality.

Finally, and fundamentally, the question is about the definition of power. If power is defined as the possibility or actuality of overcoming resistance, difficulties resembling the two delineated above seem unavoidable. In Tillich's case, too, if power is the conquest of resistance, both in origin and end, power tends to become directionless domination, the aim of which has to be established from outside, from the principle of justice. The intrinsic *telos* of power itself to the communication of efficacy is not acknowledged and must be supplied from elsewhere. The moment of conquest in any performance of power is mistaken for the whole of power.

This criticism of Tillich's theology of power is inadequate in two respects. To begin with, even if it is all true and accurate, there are positive gains in his theory of power. To some extent, the definition of power as communication of efficacy has shown its ability to preserve these advances. Both power's ubiquity and its teleological character are retained. Other points are less clear, and if a theory of power cannot retain the advantages of Tillich's concept of power, that is so much the worse. On the side of power's potentiality, the creative openness of power to the new must be preserved without forcing power into a framework of potentiality and actuality. On the side of centered power, a decisive benefit of Tillich's notion of power as centered within beings is that it provides an ontological ground of justice that surpasses any merely formal, rational justice. Deserting a centered geography of power cannot entail the loss of a concept of theonomous justice. Power's criterion is fulfillment of form and being. If such a standard cannot be discovered within power, there is no advance upon Tillich's view of power; however, confidence that such a criterion is contained within power is implied in the claim that power is the fundamental ontological structure. A related issue is the need to preserve the close unity between divine and demonic power. A theory of power has to account for how it is that the most creative power is also the most dangerous. A hint of an explanation appeared in the analysis of Luther's doctrine of creation. A final insight of Tillich is the point of what is expressed in the formula of "power through its resignation." However clumsy the phrase, it communicates a reality driven home throughout history, and that reality must be incorporated into a theology of power.

Another accusation of one-sidedness consists in this: if Tillich's notion of centered power conflicts with large chunks of his theological project as a whole, it is reasonable to suspect another perspective on power lurking in his work which is more consistent with the aims of his thought. For example, we have concentrated on the element of individuation in the polarity of individuation and participation without exploring sufficiently the polarity in which individuation is involved and without an analysis of the general structure of

---

Spirit's appearance is conditioned by power; spirit can unite power and meaning only if power is already an ontological presence. There is neither concrete meaning nor concrete Spiritual presence without power. Therefore, a decision with respect to power itself cannot be avoided.

Tillich's understanding of "polarity." The symmetry of Tillich's thinking has not been explored and thus, this exposition has been literally one-sided.[146] As with Luther's ambivalence between the alternatives of good works as the fruit of faith and good works as a component of faith, Tillich too has a second view of power.

Tillich, Power, and the Border

This analysis of Tillich's notion of centered power has concentrated on what Tillich himself said about power. The second viewpoint is not one Tillich usually calls a theology of power; we have seen certain intimations of its presence already. In speaking of the relation of proportional justice and creative justice, Tillich said, "One never knows *a priori* what the outcome of an encounter of power with power will be. If one judges such an encounter according to previous power proportions, one is necessarily unjust, even if one is legally right."[147] Tillich maintains the basic structure of centered power, but another element is present. It seems as if power emerges in and through the encounter, as if an encounter is not merely the stage where power is played but is also where power is produced. This permits Tillich to say that the result of such an encounter can be an increase in the power of being of all participants.[148] The possibility that discussion about power can break through the barrier of quantitative "balances of power" and the framework of potentiality and actuality is given here. If power can be increased for all, one may still speak of balances of power, but this does not exhaust what can be said. In surpassing this limit, the restriction of power to a zero-sum game is also overcome. If the encounter is not just a play of preexisting powers, the outcome of which could be predicted if one had sufficient information, then power is not only a matter of inner potentialities expressing and externalizing themselves.

The clearest evidence of the presence of two theologies of power is this statement:

> the power of being becomes manifest only in the process in which it actualizes its power. In this process its power appears and can be measured. Power is real only in its actualization, in the encounter with other bearers of power and in the ever-changing balance which is the result of these encounters. . . . [P]ower of being remains hidden if actual encounters do not reveal it.[149]

---

[146] Nor will we discuss the trinitarian structure of Tillich's later thought. This would be especially relevant to the teleological notion of power advocated in the concept of communication of efficacy. There is a teleological structure in the passage from "Being and God," to "Existence and the Christ," to "Life and the Spirit," finally culminating in "History and the Kingdom." See Gilkey, *Gilkey on Tillich*, 81–173; and Reisz, "Tillich's Doctrine of God."

[147] Tillich, *Love, Power, and Justice*, 64–65.

[148] Ibid., 65.

[149] Ibid., 41.

Tillich collapses two alternatives which should be distinguished. On one hand, power must be real prior to its actualization, for encounter only manifests or uncovers it. In order to reveal something, what is uncovered must have been, albeit concealed, prior to the act of revealing. If what is revealed did not exist previously, then we call such an event "creative," not "revelatory." On the other hand, Tillich claims that power does not exist prior to the encounter. The first alternative implies the centered conception of power upon which Tillich grounds his ontological ethic and his discussion of every thing's power of being. Power *is* prior to an encounter; it is an inalienable part of anything that is, the condition as well as the result of a being's actualization. The second view of power appears to deny power's being apart from its actualization. This second option must be explored.

If there is still an attachment to potentiality and actuality, it may be better to express this second version of power as occupying the transitional space between potentiality and actuality. Power may be better approached as actualization rather than as potentiality. The concept of power as potential led to the notion that power could be possessed without its exercise, expressed by Tillich in the phrase "actualization *of* power." Even in that formulation, however, Tillich seems uncomfortable. Life is alternatively "actuality" and "actualization of potentialities."[150] He vacillates between the constant dynamism implied in "actualization" and the more static notion of "actuality"—between, one might say, process thought and the Greeks.[151] It may well be necessary to preserve both languages. After all, actualization is the actualization of some entity,[152] but it may not be necessary to call all these elements (potentiality, actuality, and actualization) "power." In general, power does not encompass all three in Tillich's work. Rather, he usually restricts "power" to potentiality and actuality, despite the importance of "actualization." If power is a communication of efficacy at the border of encounter, however, it is closer to actualization than it is to either potentiality or actuality, although it is really identical with none of them.

These evidentiary fragments only hint at the presence of a second idea of power in Tillich. The task now is to demonstrate that significant features of Tillich's thought imply that power posits itself at the border of encounter. The objective is less to present Tillich's thought than it is to show how a notion of power emerging at the border arises from within his outlook, even if Tillich himself customarily does not relate these thoughts to power. If "border concepts" can be discovered in Tillich's work, the benefit for the theology of power

---

[150] Ibid., 54; he asserts that life is actualized being. In *Systematic Theology* (1:67) Tillich says that life is being in actuality; however, he retracts that conclusion (1:241–46) and decides that life is better described as actualization rather than actuality. The same ambivalence reappears in *Systematic Theology*, vol. 3, in which Tillich at first (p. 11) maintains that life is the actuality of being, and proceeds in the rest of the volume to concentrate on actualization.

[151] Gilkey, *Gilkey on Tillich*, 90–91.

[152] Tillich, "Reply to Interpretation and Criticism," 339.

presented here is considerable: those insights become implications of the basic definition of power as a self-positing communication of efficacy at the border of encounter. Moreover, a more complete comparison of the consequences of two geographies of power will be possible. The distinction between power at the border and a centered view of power, based in potentiality and actuality or inwardness and externality, will be sharpened and clarified.

Power and Ontological Polarities

Tillich's main conceptual affinity with a decentered view of power lies in his use of the ontological polarities.[153] The structure of his thought depends to a considerable extent on the ontological polarity of self and world. Tillich differentiates the basic polarity of self and world into ontological elements that also are polar. Two of these elemental polarities, individualization/participation and dynamics/form, have received attention. A return to them illustrates the conclusion that the ontological polarities imply a conception of power as a border phenomenon.

Polar elements are essentially united, but are separated in existence. Fulfillment of being depends on their reunion. The destructive implications of separating individualization and participation were explored earlier. If either dominates to the exclusion of the other, being disintegrates. Viewed another way, actually existing beings cannot be without standing between the poles of individualization and participation. Both elements must appear, or neither can. There is "strict interdependence of individuality and participation on the level of complete individualization, which is, at the same time, the level of complete participation"; this corresponds to the interdependence of self and world in which "both sides of the polarity are lost if either side is lost."[154] The poles, therefore, are not self-sufficient but are in fact limiting principles that define not what a being possesses in order to exist but the outer limits between which it must exist. The polarities are more border concepts than dialectical ones, if "dialectic" means movement out of one pole into the other and then a return to the first. That view of dialectic would understand polar elements as relatively independent, even if unfulfilled in their independence, rather than as the outer limit at which being can no longer be.[155] Tillich's assertion that "when individualization reaches the perfect form which we call a 'person,' participation reaches the perfect form which we call 'communion,'"[156]

---

[153] Gilkey, *Gilkey on Tillich*, 31, 81–98.
[154] Tillich, *Systematic Theology* 1:176, 171.
[155] This is not Tillich's understanding of the dialectic of individualization and participation, as is clear in *Courage To Be*, 88–89. However, a centered dialectical position is open to this misinterpretation, so it might be better to avoid the term "dialectic" in regard to power altogether.
[156] Tillich, *Systematic Theology* 1:176; see also *Courage To Be*, 90–92.

does not mean that first one intensifies individuality and then works from there to intensify one's participation. Rather, the perfection of one is achieved in and through the other. Life is lived between the limits of the poles, which have no reality until they are constituted in the area of the border. What occurs between the ideal poles, or at their border, turns back to nourish and create the poles and prevent disintegration of being. This is why fulfillment is reunion of the polar elements between which life is lived.

The point is even clearer in Tillich's exposition of life's self-integration, which plays out the polarity of individualization and participation. The term "center" implies that "there is a periphery which includes an amount of space or, in non-metaphorical terms, which includes a manifoldness of elements. This corresponds to participation, with which individualization forms a polarity." The implication of the other in the very notion of self means that successful self-integration operates by balancing the poles. The contradiction of self-integration is disintegration. Tillich's discussion of this is interesting; disintegration, and its limit in death, are the result of failure to include both individualization and participation in the life process:

> Disintegration means failure to reach or to preserve self-integration. This failure can occur in one of two directions. Either it is the inability to overcome a limited, stabilized, and immovable centeredness, in which case there is a center, but a center which does not have a life process whose content is changed and increased; thus it approaches the death of mere self-identity. Or it is the inability to return because of the dispersing power of the manifoldness, in which case there is life, but it is dispersed and weak in centeredness, and it faces the danger of losing its center altogether—the death of mere self-alteration. The function of self-integration ambiguously mixed with disintegration works between these two extremes in every life process.[157]

The death of self-identity is loss of centered power. Even though power (as *Mächtigkeit* or *Macht*) is supposed to be power of the center, it is not power that can nourish itself. The death of self-alteration is not the death of uniting with the other in desire, but unwillingness to decide for some potentialities rather than others. It participates not in one thing, seeking its own eradication in a single other, but tries to participate in everything, or anything, and loses its center in the play of potentialities, a danger that is increasingly obvious in our culture.[158] The threat mere potentiality poses to power emerges in the existential question:

---

[157] Tillich, *Systematic Theology* 3:33–34.

[158] William R. Rogers thinks it is even a greater problem than narrowness and dogmatism ("Tillich and Depth Psychology," in *The Thought of Paul Tillich,* ed. Adams, Pauck, and Shinn, 112–13). Although this may overstate the case, we do seem to be a culture swinging abruptly from rigidity to utter relativism and back again.

Ann Belford Ulanov argues that our problem is less anxiety of non-being than anxiety of too much being ("The Anxiety of Being," in *The Thought of Paul Tillich,* ed. Adams, Pauck, and Shinn). For Tillich, however, the second is rooted in the first. Concupiscence is grounded in the

How many potentiàlities, given to me by virtue of my being man, *can* I actualize without losing the power to actualize anything in particular? And, How many of my potentialities *must* I actualize in order to avoid the state of mutilated humanity. These sets of questions, of course, are not asked *in abstracto* but always in the concrete form: Shall I sacrifice this that I have for this that I could have?[159]

Power as potential cannot nourish itself either. To reach for endless potentialities destroys power. If potentiality is power, it is power that loses "the power to actualize anything in particular." But it is senseless to speak of power which, on its own, ceases to be power.

Powers of being are fuller the more individualization and participation are balanced and intensified through each other. Being is sustained in the space between the poles, at the border. This applies to all being, from cell to person, the difference being the intensity and breadth of their individualization and participation in and with others. If this is so, why speak of the power of the poles at all? It is better to say that intensity and breadth of power are defined as they appear—in the area between the poles. The poles of individualization and participation have no power of themselves, for they are incapable of their own sustenance. Power is generated in their interaction, when the individualized being meets the other in which it can participate. Neither of the two uses already possessed power, for if a being had power of itself, it would not need another. Instead, the operation of the limiting poles shows that power comes to be between the participants. The emerging power does, of course, reverberate back to the encountering participants and, if it is truly power, communicates efficacy to them.[160] The strict interdependence of the poles means that power must arise on the ground where beings meet. Power emerges between centers, on the border, however wide the space of that border is conceived to be. The limiting poles themselves, in isolation, have no power except the power of disintegration.

The same conclusion can be drawn from analysis of the polarity of dynamics and form. Here again, isolation of either element is fatal. In human

---

attempt to assimilate more and more content into the self, in the hope that a more expansive fortress is less subject to eradication. Fear of being overwhelmed certainly can be the outcome of this thirst. But "what is there" frightens us (pp. 127–28) because its manifoldness and lack of integration into a personal center have the capacity to throw us into the disintegration that approaches non-being. In short, Ulanov reduces Tillich's ontological threat to a series of ontic ones that could, in principle, be overcome in the normal course of existence.

159 Tillich, *Systematic Theology* 3:268–69.

160 One of the more interesting applications of this principle in Tillich's thought is the relation between destiny and freedom. Tillich argues that freedom and subjection to valid norms are identical ultimately. The same can be said of the polarity of destiny and freedom. Freedom is only meaningful—that is, it is distinct from arbitrariness—if it receives and communicates efficacy to the border between itself and destiny, and destiny is only distinct from blind faith if it has a similar relation to the border between itself and freedom. Langdon Gilkey has my appreciation for pointing this out to me.

beings, the polarity of dynamics and form takes shape in the structures of vitality and intentionality. Tillich is careful to note that "there is no vitality as such and no intentionality as such. They are interdependent, like the other polar elements." The self-transcendence stimulated by vitality assumes a self that is transcended, a self that "tends to conserve its own form as the basis of its self-transcendence." Polar elements are limits. No being can restrict its relation to one to the exclusion of the other. The threat posed to a being is just such an exclusive relation:

> Finitude also transforms the polarity of dynamics and form into a tension which produces the threat of a possible break and anxiety about this threat. Dynamics drives toward form, in which being is actual and has the power of resisting nonbeing. But at the same time dynamics is threatened because it may lose itself in rigid forms, and, if it tries to break through them, the result may be chaos, which is the loss of both dynamics and form.[161]

Total loss of either the dynamic or formal pole has the same result: destruction of the centered being.[162] The same is true of the interaction of dynamics and form in society: "The bearers of new tendencies are, then, simultaneously revolutionary, and actually they are always revolutionary, irrespective of whether the overcoming of the old occurs legally or illegally. So considered, every form appears as a temporary balance of polar tensions, out of which new powers and tensions break forth."[163] The choice is between creativity and destruction, but creativity only comes through union of the poles, in a bond between them stretching across their boundaries.

So the question arises again: Is it useful to apply the concept of power to the polar elements since, in fact, they lack any independent power? If the being of beings has its possibility and nourishment between the polar elements, or in a reunification that still preserves their individual character, then power is an event that occurs at the point of contact between dynamics and form, the property of neither element. Power posits itself at the border of the polar elements, belonging to neither but affecting both. Its *telos* is the unity and unification of life; essential power is marked by its communication of efficacy.

As an example of a border concept of power, Tillich's analysis of the polarity of dynamics and form reveals an important characteristic of power's milieu. If power is not possessed by parties to an encounter, there can be no certainty it will appear, or to what extent and intensity it will appear, in any special encounter. Activity intended to generate power always risks failure; conversely, neither are attempts to frustrate more vigorous and broader appearances of

---

161 Tillich, *Systematic Theology* 1:181, 181, 199–200.

162 Ibid. 1:199; *Love, Power, and Justice,* 70, 123; *Courage To Be,* 62.

163 Paul Tillich, *Die Religiöse und Philosophische Weiterbildung des Sozialismus* (*GW* 2:126) reads: "Die Träger der neuen Tendenzen sind dann zugleich die Revolutionäre, und zwar sind sie das immer, ganz gleich ob die Überwindung des Alten rechtmäßig oder rechtzerbrechend geschieht. Von hier aus betrachtet erscheint jede Gestalt als zeitweiliger Ausgleich von Spannungspolaritäten, aus dem neue Kräfte und Spannungen hervorbrechen."

power certain of success. This is because power posits itself between participants and is the possession of no one. Tillich has a great deal to say about
the risk of action, but since he is tied to a centered conception of power, he
does not apply his reflections to the phenomenon of power.[164] But if the unexpected is not merely the result of inadequate calculation or insufficient
information (if, in other words, it is impossible to "reason" oneself to a decision completely), then another factor must have appeared in and through the
encounter, a factor beyond what is calculable from knowledge of the entities
involved in the encounter.

This factor is not, obviously, always fulfilled power defined as the communication of efficacy. It is possible to speak of "increases" or "decreases" in
power by comparing the success of a communication of efficacy with previous
instantiations of power. Just these degrees of power cannot be determined in
advance. An encounter may end in destruction or relative fulfillment. Power
therefore emerges through the encounter, which always includes "a moment
of 'chaos' between the old and the new form, a moment of no-longer-form
and not-yet-form."[165] It arises in the moment of chaos implicit in encounter.
The risk of encounter and action, which Tillich recognizes, is a risk of power,
but not in the sense of putting one's already possessed power at risk. That
would imply that power relations could be precalculated entirely, that the stage
of encounter only plays out and makes manifest balances of intrinsic power.
Rather, encounter is the forum in which power appears in the first place, but
without guaranteeing what expanse of power will emerge through the moment
of chaos and uncertainty.

Events of Power, Risks of History

Because Tillich conceives of power as potential and actual, and because
actual power is centered power, he does not apply his position on the risk
of encounter to a theory of power. But because the ontological polarities are
unrecognized border concepts, he is able to incorporate the venture of
encounter into his theology. Tillich's unacknowledged placement of power
at the border allows inclusion of the element of ultimately incalculable risk,

---

[164] Tillich discusses risk in almost every writing having to do with history or faith, e.g., "Kairos
and Logos" (*GW* 4:43–76); "Open Letter to Emanuel Hirsch," 372; "The Two Types of Philosophy
of Religion," 28–29; *Systematic Theology* 1:103, 144, 152; 3:43, 53–54, 364; "Reply to Interpretation and Criticism," 338, 345; *Love, Power, and Justice*, 55–56; *Dynamics of Faith*, 16–28, 35. None
of these is related to the phenomenon of power. In "The Formative Power of Protestantism" power
is at least mentioned in the context of "daring and risk" (pp. 215–16) but does not refer to the
risk itself. The introduction of "power" in even this limited connection is new to the English
version of the essay; it is not present in *Religiöse Verwirklichung*, 54–57.

[165] Tillich, *Systematic Theology* 3:50. What Tillich says about the chaos implicit in the polarity
of dynamics and form applies equally well to any encounter.

an element he would be unable to introduce if he were persistent in understanding power as either potential or actual. But if it is realized that power appears at the border of encounter, including the border of the polar elements, it is possible to account for the risk of encounter consistently and from within a theory of power.

The chaotic moment generates unforeseeable power. This description merges with another. The risk of power is entwined with its instantiation in a leap. It was mentioned earlier that describing power as a communication of efficacy at the border of encounter implies that power's appearance includes the characteristic of its being a leap for which all preparatory potentialities are inadequate. The leap emphasizes power's self-positing nature, and the notion of "instantiation" indicates that power is not merely spatial but also temporal, moving from one moment to the next; the recognition of this feature of power was derived from an analysis of Luther's disdain for attempts to explain the mechanism of the real presence in the Lord's Supper.

Tillich's thought provides additional illustrations and applications of the confluence between the risk of power and its nature as an event. Pursuit of some of these examples clarifies the difference between potentiality and possibility on the one side, and power on the other.[166] The appearance of a new dimension of life, for example, depends on a constellation of "special conditions" both internal and external to the being in which it appears. But the predominance of a new dimension in a particular type of being depends on a leap, a nonevolutionary (or revolutionary) moment in an evolutionary process. Tillich claims:

> In long periods of transition the dimensions, metaphorically speaking, struggle with each other in the same realm. This is obvious concerning the transition of the inorganic to the organic, of the vegetative to the animal, of the biological to the psychological. This is also true of the transition from the psychological to the dimension of the spirit. If we define man as that organism in which the dimension of the spirit is dominant, we cannot fix a definite point at which he appeared on earth. It is quite probable that for a long period the fight of the dimensions was going on in animal bodies which were anatomically and physiologically similar to those which are ours as historical man, until the conditions were given for that leap which brought about the dominance of the dimension of spirit.[167]

---

[166] Tillich's distinction between "potentiality" and "possibility" (Systematic Theology 3:42) makes no difference here.

[167] Tillich, Systematic Theology 3:21, 26; see also 3:25, 307. Tillich's objection to much European naturalism is based exactly on the failure to recognize this revolutionary moment. To understand the future as merely evolution of preexistent possibilities does not make history at all decisive, for the radically new can never appear (Paul Tillich, "Historical and Nonhistorical Interpretations of History: A Comparison," in The Protestant Era, abridged ed., 19–20; see also "Eschatology and History," 272–77 [Religiöse Verwirklichung, 133–36]). A later and more developed exposition of the same themes is in The Political Meaning of Utopia, 140–54 (GW 6:172–85). The same objection can be lodged against an understanding of power purely as potentialities and actualization, and therefore against Tillich's own explicit theory of power.

The power that produces dominance of a new dimension in beings is not defined by the potentialities or possibilities inherent in them. Instead, power appears both as the leap of a centered being into the space of the border and as the consequences of that leap, neither of which can be predicted completely. If power is the basic ontological fact, it cannot be *subject* to the leap, as it would have to be if power is either potentiality or actuality. Another element, beyond power, would have to appear to actualize or exercise power. Rather, the leap is power.

To be sure, power operates upon the concrete material which is provided by beings, and the possibilities that material creates; however, the moment of power itself, in which a qualitatively different efficacy is communicated to beings as a consequence of the leap of power, is not reducible to their potentialities but involves, beyond those potentialities, a moment that grips and transforms them into a new actuality. Rational description of the mechanics of such a transformation is adequate only to a point. It can specify the material conditions of transformation but cannot guarantee when or whether a transformation will occur. The leap itself is the first appearance of power, and the occurrence of power that affects things in a particular way cannot be assured. The leap into the moment of chaos takes the risk of whether its result is greater power or not. Power's irreducibility to its empirical conditions defines the way in which power transcends any encounter, even while it is immanent in every one.

There are, then, two sides to the leap and risk of power. Viewed from the perspective of the centered being, the leap creates power for the first time. Anything that does not thrust itself outward, into the area of the border, is dead in the broadest sense of that term. Even atomic particles must have a relation with other atomic particles. Anything that has no contact with something else has no existence because it can neither receive communications of efficacy nor communicate efficacy. The power posited in the leap, however, contains risk. The consequences of this power boomerang to the centered being and drive toward other participants in the encounter. Such power, in its consequences, may turn out to be relatively destructive or relatively fulfilling, and on this basis judgments about "increases" or "decreases" in power are made. Power, having appeared, communicates efficacy to participants in a more or less adequate way, making easier or more difficult subsequent appearances of power.

The close tie between these two elements is expressed in Tillich's account of the myth of the Fall. The "dreaming innocence" symbolized by Eden is a state of pure, "non-actualized potentiality." The transition to existence and the estrangement implicit in existence are derived from the effort to bring these potentialities into actuality. This creates the possibility, realized universally, that the essentially united poles of existence become separated from each other: "Actualized creation and estranged existence are identical."[168] So far, Tillich's

---

[168] Tillich, *Systematic Theology* 2:33, 44.

account of essence and the Fall into estranged existence seems to be a straight-forward exposition through the categories of potentiality and actuality.

But Tillich's recognition that, by definition, there is no place in which unactualized potentiality could exist leads him to the claim that the "transition from essence to existence is the original fact." This transition is a "leap" rather than a "structural necessity," but how is this transition possible? The mytho-logical language Tillich uses to grasp the change from essence to existence includes both an inner and an outer dimension. Externally, the "possibility of the transition to existence is experienced as temptation." Temptation tempts something, and the inner correlate of temptation is "aroused freedom," desire to actualize potentialities. Aroused freedom is open to two possibilities: "Man is caught between the desire to actualize his freedom and the demand to preserve his dreaming innocence. In the power of his finite freedom, he decides for actualization."[169]

Tillich is not trying to explain the transition to existence, but to describe it. An "original fact" cannot be explained. But the previous chapter showed that the original fact of existence is the givenness of power, which permits nothing explanatory to get behind it in order to make its "why" open to rational account. This is one reason the creation myth cannot be demythologized.[170] So if the original fact is the movement from essence to existence, the coincidence of moments of creation and fall, and if that original fact is power, then power appears in the moment of transition.

That conclusion may be merely semantic and logical, but it points up again the inadequacy of equating power and potentiality. The essential, potential, but still centered mythological Adam and Eve do not "exist" in this state because the leap in which power appears has not yet been made. However close to the brink of existence Tillich places Adam and Eve, finally "man himself makes the decision and receives the divine curse for it."[171] Decision is a new element in the story. Innocent dreamers do not contemplate deliberatively. The introduction of aroused freedom is intended to describe a newly emerging capacity for decision. But aside from the question of the newness of aroused freedom, which is not an implication of dreaming innocence either, arousal from slumber does not imply the logical necessity of waking.[172] The tran-sition to existence is the original fact because it is the first appearance of power.

---

[169] Ibid. 2:36, 44, 34, 35, 35.

[170] Ibid. 2:29–35. The connection between the literary device of the "half-way" myth and the fact that sin cannot be "explained" is suggested by Gilkey (Gilkey on Tillich, 115–19).

[171] Tillich, Systematic Theology 2:39. A less mythological account of the same process, expounded as the basis for all history, is found in "The Protestant Principle and the Proletarian Situation," 165–66 (GW 7:88).

[172] Hammond says that the Fall "is a necessity of life, not of logic" (Man in Estrangement, 158). This is very insightful, as long as it is clear that "necessity" is being used in two different senses. Hammond's discussion of the relation between Fall and creation in Tillich's work is generally excellent.

Decision is not simply the result of preparation, but an element beyond it—the element of supra- or prerational power.[173] It is not a shortcoming in Tillich's analysis of the biblical story that he does not show an orderly progression of events in which the subsequent is derived from the preceding. He cannot do so because power must finally posit itself, transcending any preceding capacities. It is almost unnecessary to add that this power is ambiguous. It is the original communication and reception of efficacy. It is also the condition for distortion of the ontological polarities through separation of the poles, and the possibility that one or another polar element will destroy life through its exclusive domination.

Both the formation of new dimensions of life and Tillich's account of the fall are structurally similar to Tillich's most important doctrine in his philosophy of history—the doctrine of the *kairos*.[174] The question of the "right time" is implicit in all historical action and, by analogy, in all being. All things take a "risk" of history, of being in the wrong time and being subject to extermination or gradual extinction. Moreover, a leap in evolutionary process is analogous to seizure of a *kairos* at the intersection between a being or group of beings and a cluster of conditions. The same "kairic" element is present in the transition to existence.[175]

The specialized meaning of Tillich's *kairos* doctrine is in his philosophy of history. The structural similarity of this doctrine with Tillich's treatments of life's dimensions and the coincidence of creation and Fall suggest that *kairos* is also a border concept.[176] Again, Tillich's kairic philosophy of history is not tied to his theology of power. The statement that the border character of power is unrecognized in his work but implied in its execution is also true of the concept of *kairos*.

The judgment that a *kairos* is upon us (or that it is not) is chancy. That is because the *kairos,* if it appears through the moment of chaos, is fulfilled power, a communication of efficacy. To claim that kairic power intrudes on

---

[173] Tillich, *Systematic Theology* 3:284.

[174] For the importance of the *kairos* doctrine, see Tillich, "Reply to Interpretation and Criticism," 345; and Gilkey, *Gilkey on Tillich,* 11–12.

[175] The analogy here is structural. "Analogy" also implies differences in the transition to existence and the *kairos*. Langdon Gilkey was helpful in pointing out at least three variances between the two. To begin with, the Fall is universal, whereas a *kairos* is particular both with respect to time and space. Second, the Fall must be expressed partly in myth, whereas this is not necessarily true of the apprehension of a *kairos*. Third, *kairos* involves a relation between freedom and structure, whereas the Fall relies on freedom. To these can be added a fourth difference. The types of freedom involved in the Fall and action within the *kairic* moment differ; the first involves the relatively undeveloped freedom of "dreaming innocence," but seizing a *kairos* involves historical freedom in polar relation with historical destiny.

[176] The difference in emphasis between Tillich's use of "boundary" and "border" and the meaning of these terms in this project is clear from what he says about the doctrine of the *kairos* in "On the Boundary," 57. Tillich, too, considers the notion of the *kairos* to be a "border-concept," but he means this in a sociological/existential sense rather than a technical/philosophical one.

us involves the risk of assessing this time as the "right time," this moment of uncertainty and chaos as a moment of construction rather than decay or destruction. Kairic power therefore refers chiefly to the "when" of action. A *kairos* emerges at the border, "when an old order is passing and a new order is emerging."[177] What is to be done, the content of historical action, depends on its timing. Rational reflection cannot answer this question with certainty but takes a suprarational gamble that this is the time to act, and then acts. Whatever else reason can do, it cannot answer the question When? That question is a matter of concrete response to the "eternal now."[178] Tillich's own political misfortunes show the riskiness entailed in acting on a belief that "now is the time."[179] Equally, failure to seize the possibilities offered by a special time has disastrous consequences; Tillich's early and vociferous opposition to Nazism is vindicated over against those who did not seize the right time to act.

Those judgments are retrospective, and the inability to know at the time one acts is due to the nature of power. Historical power as communication of efficacy is a question held in abeyance until history decides whether that particular time and place were in fact ripe. Historical power appears at the border of the powerful act (itself at the border of inwardness and externality) and the confluence of conditions which determine whether that act is efficacious or not. A greater communication of efficacy is never guaranteed because fulfilled power is not at the discretion of the actor or receiver, but appears of itself. Power is what determines the presence or absence of a *kairos:* power posits a *kairos*.

One may make reflective judgments about whether this kairic power may become available, but one cannot assure it, and this would be true even if one possessed all possible information. Power posits itself and is therefore not ultimately subject to the technical rationality of "information." The risk of action and unforeseen consequences, both powerful and destructive, are not removable features of life. They are not due to defective knowledge, but to knowledge's inability to comprehend power. The last three years offer ample confirmation. The shocking course of world history from 1989 to the present demonstrates the truth of Tillich's claim that the centers of social power "lost" real power when the social group's power failed to find expression in them, and long before their actual demise. Moreover, these same years testify to the transcendence of power over knowledge or reason. From the destruction of the Berlin Wall to German reunification to the utter collapse of the Eastern European bloc and the Soviet Union, momentous events that were utterly

---

[177] Stone, *Paul Tillich's Radical Social Thought,* 49.

[178] Paul Tillich, *The Eternal Now,* in *The Eternal Now* (New York: Charles Scribner's Sons, 1963), 122–32; *Systematic Theology* 3:369–70, 395–96.

[179] The tie between Tillich's doctrine of the *kairos* and his conception of the eternal now is this: the presence and awareness of as well as the response to a particular *kairos* are special kinds of intrusions of the eternal now upon time.

unthinkable within weeks of their occurrence have become routine matters. No amount of foresight or study could have suggested even the possibility of such a fundamental reordering of the world. At the same time, prognostications and hopes that China would be swept along in this flow of events ended abruptly in Tianenmen Square, and the once-cheered revolutions of Eastern Europe have, in some cases, left more corpses than could have been imagined in a nightmare.

Tillich applies this insight of the risk of history to all historical occurrences, even the event of Jesus as the Christ. He takes the historical nature of the manifestation of God in Jesus as the Christ seriously. If the Christ-event is historical, then the risk inherent in all history applies to it. The power of the event of Jesus as the Christ can be destroyed. This claim is quite a shock, and one for which Tillich has drawn fire.[180] His argument is this:

> It could be imagined — and today more easily than ever — that the historical tradition in which Jesus appears as the center would break down completely. It could be imagined that a total catastrophe and a completely new beginning of the human race would leave no memory of the event "Jesus as the Christ."
>
> . . . [T]he end is the moment in which the continuity of that history in which Jesus as the Christ is the center is definitely broken. This moment cannot be determined empirically, either in its nature or in its causes. Its nature may be the disappearance or a complete transformation of what once was historical mankind. Its causes may be historical, biological, or physical. In any case, it would be the end of that development of which Jesus as the Christ is the center. In faith it is certain that for historical mankind in its unique, continuous development, as experienced here and now, Christ is the center. But faith cannot judge about the future destiny of historical mankind and the way it will come to an end. Jesus is the Christ for us, namely, for those who participate in the historical continuum which he determines in its meaning. This existential limitation does not qualitatively limit his significance, but it leaves open other ways of divine self manifestations before and after our historical continuum.[181]

Divine self-manifestation is not exhausted in the historical event of Jesus as the Christ, although that event is the center of our history. Divine power exceeds any of its manifestations. As long as there is anything at all, there is power of being-itself. Historical manifestations of the divine, however, are subject to the risk of history, the limitations of earth, and so on. Because efficacy must be communicated to them and received from them in order for them to persist, power cannot be guaranteed for anything that has being. There are

---

[180] See especially Kelsey (*The Fabric of Paul Tillich's Theology*, 126–53), who argues that Tillich's major failure is that he leaves open the possibility that the saving power of the ultimate could occur through another medium than the picture of Jesus as the Christ. Not only does Tillich leave this door open; he must do so — unless, of course, one wants to assert for all time that if ever the Christ-event is forgotten, God is dead. Tillich's hope is that God is greater than our epoch.

[181] Tillich, *Systematic Theology* 2:99–101.

two reasons for this. In the first place, power is not possessed, but communicated. In the second place, following from the first point, a judgment about the presence or absence of power must refer to the effect of a phenomenon.[182] Tillich is right that the event of Jesus as the Christ can fail to communicate efficacy. It too is subject to the risk of power. The possibility that power can be distorted or cease altogether is given in the nature of power itself and in the contrast between fulfilled and distorted power.

We have shown that major aspects of Tillich's thought are better analyzed as border concepts than as expressions of centered power. The power of the ontological polarities comes not from a "centering" within the poles but from the territory between them. Similarly, the leap of action and the risk of history do not derive their power from the potentialities of centered beings. Rather, the power of action and history are constituted at the border between encountering parties, between inwardness and externality, between potentiality and actuality. It remains to show the ethical implications of this de-centered understanding of power. Before doing so, the results of the investigation to this point should be summarized.

Being Beyond Domination

The argument thus far has been twofold. First, a merely ontic, occasional conception of power is opposed, initially on grounds internal to Christian theology's claim that God is omnipotent, and then through an argument that power is the fundamental ontological element, and is therefore present in all places where there is anything. In addition, the equation of power and domination has been attacked. A collateral thesis of that argument is that it is difficult, if not impossible, to avoid such an equation without reformulating the geography of power, reversing the tradition of theories that see power as centered and conceive of it in the language of potentiality and actuality and of inwardness and externality. If power's form is an inner capacity usable in any direction an actor sees fit, its content can hardly help being understood as domination. At the very least, the result is a conceptual muddle surrounding the question of what actual power is. In any case, the result is a view of power as primarily quantitative in character and capable of possession by beings. In principle, power can be stored like money in the bank, reserved for future exercise. Power exists prior to the encounter of beings, the encounter serving only as the stage upon which previously existing quantities of power are asserted. This reduces radically the contingency of the results of an encounter. Given sufficient information about the quantity of power that is

[182] The criterion of effect upon form is crucial in Tillich's distinction between divine and demonic power. Kelsey's objections to such a criterion could be valid only if power were "possessed" (*The Fabric of Paul Tillich's Theology*).

possessed by a being or group of beings, the outcome of an encounter should be completely predictable.

Moreover, the game of power, performed on the stage of encounter, is conceived of as a balancing of power. Encountering parties meet in order to overcome the resistance of the other, and the end of pure power is therefore the ontologically self-contradictory objective of pure domination. An "ethic of power" crafted on the basis of this understanding of power is not an ethic of power but an ethic against power, an attempt to control the beast of power. A principle alien to power must be introduced to "tame" power, to use Russell's term. Such an ethic is visible in Foucault and in segments of Tillich's work; Luther's valorization of the "weakness of Christ" tends in the same direction.

Finally, treating power through the categories of potentiality and actuality contains two conceptual puzzles, discovered through Tillich, although by no means restricted to his thought. First, the multiple meanings of the term "power" are not reconciled. As potential, power is "capacity," whereas as actual it is domination. In ordinary English usage, the connection between these uses is foggy at best. In Tillich's work, *Kraft* on one side and *Macht* and *Mächtigkeit* on the other have different, and sometimes inconsistent, meanings. Second, the exposition of power as potential creates the possibility that power can exist without ever being used. Consequently, it becomes necessary to add to "power" predicates such as "exercise" and "employ," additives which should be superfluous, contained in the definition of power itself.

The definition of power as communication of efficacy overcomes the identity of power and domination, as well as the centered understanding of power presented through the vocabulary of potentiality and actuality. Christian theology must challenge such an understanding if it is to preserve its claim that God is all-powerful. That power is the basic principle of all being is validated because nothing can exist without continual reception of communications of efficacy. But this theology of power has also tried to give the tradition of political theory its due. A simple transvaluation of power that identifies true power with weakness or meekness is inadequate on several grounds. First, it is irrelevant, since no one actually uses the term "power" this way. No one speaks of ineffectiveness as political power, even if power and weakness are equated for an hour on Sunday. Second, a transvaluation of power merely reverses the conceptual problems without solving them. We would be required to produce a theology of the sovereignty of God, which is now God's weakness, and explain how this weakness, from which the symbols of providence and creation derive, is defensible. Finally, and most important, sovereignty theory is correct as far as it goes. Power does involve sovereignty and domination; even the notion of spiritual power includes compulsion.

Understanding power as communication of efficacy rejects the notion that power can be possessed. Power is neither internal nor external, though it is related to both realms. This decentering of power simultaneously abandons the view that power is capacity, external actuality which dominates, or a combination of the two. Power appears but cannot be held. There is no power separate from its employment; "power" includes the plurality implied in "exercise" through the notion of "communication." It is still possible to speak of quantities of power, greater or lesser power, but those terms are not strictly accurate. A quantification of power refers only to the breadth or intensity of one instantiation of power in comparison with another. Similarly, one can call someone "powerful"; however, this means not that such a person possesses great power but that communications of efficacy occur with great frequency or vividness around such an individual. If there is no power without employment, it is also more easily seen why complete storage of potential is self-destructive. A being with only potential, but no power, could not exist. Pure potentiality is a limit of existence and does not belong to existence. The more that limit is approached, the closer to non-being one is. Only potentialities touched by a broader complex of power have any being at all.

The fact that power entails its exercise explains why the outcome of encounters cannot be predicted with any completeness, regardless of the information one possesses. Power's appearance transcends calculation of capacities and technical reason, in whose structures the elements of information are contained. A useful, although imprecise, example of power's transcendence over all information is the colloquial expression in connection with sports: "On any given day, anything can happen." Information and reason presume regularities in the appearance of power, but power's self-positing may or may not conform to these assumptions. Because power only appears on the same field on which it is played, all history and action involve risk.

The assertion that power is essentially communication of efficacy also breaks through the language of "balances of power," which conceives of power as a zero-sum game. In the analogous, comparative sense delineated above, quantities of power can be discussed, but this no longer implies a finite quantity of power, definable in advance. Rather, power can be increased for all parties in an encounter, to an extent unknown prior to an encounter. The increase of power for one participant does not imply its decrease for another.

These alterations preserve the insights of sovereignty theories. Power includes sovereignty, but the definition of power as the communication of efficacy opposes any theory of power that understands sovereignty as the *telos* of power, or as power pure and simple.[183] If power were domination, one could not say that existence is meaningful at all. Rather, it would have to be understood as a cruel joke in which beings exist only for their destruction. Total

---

[183] Tillich says something quite close to this when he argues that "power that has lost meaning also loses itself as power" (*Systematic Theology* 3:342). What is unclear is whether meaning is added to power from the outside in order to complete it. That meaning seems to be just such an extrinsic supplement is suggested by the earlier discussion of the relation of justice and power, in which justice stands beyond power as its criterion. The definition of power as communication of efficacy alters Tillich's statement to say that "power that has lost meaning loses itself as power because it is already a distortion of the meaning intrinsic to power."

domination implies the end of existence. Power that is mere domination is distorted power, because it takes a moment of power as its completion and fulfillment. The sovereign moment of power is not power's objective. Its aim is the communication of efficacy. God's sovereignty intends the creation and sustenance of creatures or, in other words, their efficacy, and touches them with power in order to communicate efficacy to them. The aim of sovereignty is not exclusive power, but universal power. Fulfilled, essential, and completed power is the communication of efficacy. Distorted power severs an element or moment of power, domination, from the unity in which it is essentially contained.

It has already been shown how this understanding of power eliminates the conceptual quagmire of the addition of "exercise" to power. The problem of the multiplicity of meanings attached to power is also solved. Abandonment of potentiality and actuality as foundations of the definition of power allows the affirmation of a single and unified content of power: the communication of efficacy that occurs at the border of encounter. In whatever realm or form power appears, its content and *telos* are the same.

The notion of communication of efficacy creates questions of its own. Two call for clarification. First, has not the polemic against understanding power as potentiality and actuality erased these categories from philosophical and theological vocabularies? If power is ubiquitous and is not defined by potentiality and actuality, can any place remain for those concepts? If the answer is no, the cure for the theory of power might well be worse than the disease. There can be no question of the usefulness of the language of potentiality and actuality. The same can be said for the value of the terms "inward" and "external." What the redefinition of power implies, however, is only the elimination of these categories as ideas that define power, not their destruction as a whole. Indeed, if power is a communicative event that occurs at the border or intersection of beings in encounter, this directs us to consider the actuality and potentialities of those beings. Power relates to potentiality and actuality, to inwardness and externality, but it is not defined by them. As concepts and realities, they are retained, but they are not power. This is illustrated in Luther's argument regarding the mechanism of the Lord's Supper. Power's self-positing prevented precise description of the mechanics of the sacramental transformation but did not make either the sacramental elements or the recipient worthless or nonexistent. It only meant that neither elements nor communicant had power of themselves.

One can go further. Sacramental elements have potential for a certain type and intensity of power through the Word, if God's promises are to be trusted. It is possible, even necessary, to speak of a potential for power. Otherwise, attempts to communicate efficacy would be random in nature and effect. Power communicates efficacy to something, and something receives that communication. Fulfilled power fulfills those beings between which it appears and to which it is directed. Although it is impossible to define the potential for appearance or reception of power completely in advance of the encounter, it is possible to have some understanding of the limits and potentialities of the beings involved. There is regularity in the structures of beings that can be rationally apprehended and calculated, even if this regularity does not exhaust being. This is why, even though "quantities" of power can be increased in encounter, the extent of this increase is not limitless. Reception or communication of efficacy is efficacious only within the limits of affected beings.

There is a second difficulty with severing power from potentiality and actuality. The claim that potentiality, actuality, inwardness, and externality are not power seems to conflict directly with the position that power is omnipresent. If neither the inner nor outer dimensions of life are, properly speaking, power, is that tantamount to saying that there is a place without power? The suspicion is strengthened by noting the geographical similarity between the border concept of power and Hannah Arendt's claim that power emerges in the "space of appearance."[184] The criticism directed at Arendt was that she reduced power to an ontic reality. The difference from her theory of power was supposed to be that power is related to inwardness.

Clarification of this problem depends on a distinction between presence and identity. God's omnipresence does not mean that everything is God. Similarly, the ubiquity of power does not imply that everything is power. Instead, the power of being is present to all that has being. Nothing can be without a relation to power, without being touched by it. Presence is not identity; in fact, it points to nonidentity. It is a waste of words to say that something is present to itself, if by that one means simply that something is itself. To be present to or for something implies difference from it, since the relationship of presence, in principle, contemplates the possibility of absence. Power's ubiquity, far from making everything identical to power, indicates the distinction between beings and power, which can be obscured if one chooses, as Luther did, the preposition "in" rather than "to."[185] Power must be instantiated on the border of all beings in order for them to exist, but this does not mean that beings are power. The power of being is power impacting upon, not identical with, beings. As the condition for the creation, existence, and sustenance of beings, power also transcends and surpasses them. With these clarifications of the internal ambiguities of the theory of power, the remaining chore is to take up the question of an ethic of power.

---

[184] Hannah Arendt, *The Human Condition* (Chicago: University of Chicago Press, 1958), 199–212.

[185] Tillich also creates some confusion through his attachment to "in"; see, e.g., *Systematic Theology* 3:111–12. Tillich does, however, employ "to" occasionally (*The Spiritual Presence,* 84).

Power and Ethics

Tillich's ontological grounding of ethics has been accepted. His method of correlation is more than a method. If power communicates efficacy, that communication must create or assume the capacity of the receiver of efficacy to receive it. Power that reaches its objective fulfills all parties in encounter, for it reverberates back to them from the border. Despite the evident normative content of this theology of power, it has yet to be shown how the ethical concept of justice can be brought into relation with it and the general shape that an ethic of power would take.

Tillich's grounding of theonomous justice took its departure from structures of centered power. It must be shown how it is possible for an ethic to emerge from within a noncentered understanding of power. In fact, the solution was latent within the discussion of power's relation to potentiality and actuality. Ideas of fairness, of giving all things their due, are constructed on the basis of a reading of reality and inferences regarding beings' potentialities. Such constructions rely on rational apprehensions of power potential. Justice is based in rational assumptions regarding the ability of beings to communicate and receive efficacy, or on their power potential. In political power, leadership is entrusted to those judged able to communicate a certain kind and vitality of efficacy from those communal positions through which power has appeared regularly in the past.

Of course, such preliminary judgments can be incorrect, because of power's surplus in comparison with reason. Tillich is right to say that legality is always abstract and has the capacity to distort true power, even if this insight is not entirely consistent with his centered understanding of power. The encounter may generate power with quite unexpected effects, revealing or creating a situation in which something or someone can communicate or receive efficacy of a different scope and concentration than had been believed. Those events demand a revision in the content of just treatment. In communal leadership, positions that have been surrounded with an aura of power in the past may not serve contemporary needs, or we may find that the power we expected to be instantiated between leadership and populace is not generated. Alternatively, greater power may surround unexpected positions or individuals.

This throws light on the political question of consent and acknowledgment of leadership, or the withdrawal of that consent in resistance. Every thinker with whom this project has been concerned answers this question in one way or another. Two theorists present an especially clear position. Foucault considers resistance the clearest indication that power is not confined to sovereign authority. A more democratic version of the same argument is presented by Elizabeth Janeway, who argues that the withdrawal of consent is preeminent among the "powers of the weak."[186]

The break with a centered conception of power directs us to a different answer. The location of power at the border of encounter with those designated as "leaders," and between all social actors in encounter with each other, retains the pluralistic understanding of power in Foucault and Janeway without affirming that withdrawal of consent or resistance is power of itself. Instead, resistance and withdrawal are precisely refusal to communicate efficacy to structures that require consent and support for their maintenance. To borrow a phrase from Luther, resistance to leadership is the "strange work" of power. It can be justified and defended, certainly, but only on the basis of power's "proper work." In other words, refusal to communicate efficacy must be justified in the name of its own specific power. Indeed, resistance or withdrawal of consent must even seek a concrete *sovereignty,* since this is an ineradicable element of power. It too can be judged in terms of its *telos.* Does it communicate a broader and deeper efficacy than that which it resists? Whatever decision is made (usually, both resistance and support are given in varying degrees), the nature of power itself subjects one to the risk of error.

What applies to the end of what is justified in power's name applies equally to the means employed. Means to an objective are never simply means, but are also independent events of a more or less distorted power. "Conflict between means and ends" is, in part, an erroneous description; the struggle is also between ends. This recognition has several implications for strategies of action. In the first place, an act that is supposed to be instrumental, a means for another end, is also subject to the normative criterion of power. Any act in itself communicates a certain kind and degree of efficacy which is judged by fulfilled power. Moreover, any instrumental action, since it is never merely instrumental, also renders the end sought more or less probable. Action, therefore, is judged according to two complexes of power. The first is according to its own power; the second is in relation to a broader context of power to which it is supposed to be related.

There is often real antagonism between these two complexes of essential power. In addition, there is frequent conflict between the breadth or inclusiveness of power and its depth and intensity. Production of a wider power may be an intolerably shallow power. Our prostration before the altar of "inclusiveness" as a *raison d'être* often results in mush as lifeless in form as it is bland in content—by attempting to include everyone, the product is frequently meaningful to no one. On the other hand, what produces a deep and intense power for a few may not communicate any efficacy to those outside its narrow circle and may, in fact, produce such a power only on the condition that beings external to its power are subject to its domination. The history of religion in all forms affords many examples of this latter ambiguity of power.

---

[186] Elizabeth Janeway, *Powers of the Weak* (New York: William Morrow, 1980).

A theology of power cannot adjudicate a priori either the conflict between the breadth and depth of power or the conflict between means and ends. Fulfilled power includes both the deepest and broadest power, and a judgment upon shallow and noninclusive power.[187] One cannot say that a choice must be made always for one or the other. That choice can be determined only in relation to the situation into which power must enter and is therefore subject to public argument and decision based on criteria more aesthetic than logical.

Still, power may provide a direction for these judgments. For example, all else being equal, nonviolent action is more fulfilling than violent action. The reason for this is that the noblest proponents of nonviolence reject the ultimate exclusivity of power. They seek not the destruction of their opponents but the final participation of those opponents in the broader and deeper power which is sought. Nonviolent action leaves open a breadth of power that is closed in violent conquest — or eradication — of one's enemies. Power's fulfillment, both in breadth and depth, remains possible. Yet this is not a solution that can be advocated universally. The inclusiveness of power sought in this way may be simply impossible, for much depends on the opponents themselves, the media available to the antagonists, and the broader social situation. Moreover, it is easy to imagine the reduction of nonviolent action to "mere" strategy, in which the substance of the message of expansion of the breadth of power is lost. If the message of inclusive love is not felt or communicated by the tactic of nonviolence, it abdicates its claim to superior power. In short, a theology of power cannot reduce event to invariable principle, for such principles outline only the rationally intelligible potentiality for power. Power itself emerges only in the event, which always outruns and exceeds the principle in varying degree and intensity.[188]

It is clear that a strategy of nonviolent action is not renunciation of power. The only circumstance in which it could be considered as resignation of power would be in the event of an utter failure of power to emerge in the encounter in which the strategy is employed. In its intent, and often in its effects, it is exactly the opposite of abjuring power. Nonviolent action intends to produce a deeper and broader power than what has been instantiated previously. Resignation of physical force is not the same as abandonment of power. The power that actually appears is not completely foreseeable, but if nonviolent tactics reach their objective, they generate rather than renounce power. In fact, nonviolent action is, all else being equal and assuming that it is not employed as a cynical device, intrinsically more powerful than violence, for the former leaves open the possibility of power's becoming universal rather than exclusive. If, on the other hand, power is domination, the *telos* of universal fulfillment

---

[187] Tillich's notion of the Spiritual Community is similar; the Spiritual Community is an inclusive community that does not lose its identity (*Systematic Theology* 3:263).

[188] Foucault's somewhat cumbersome term "eventalisation" and Tillich's emphasis on the really "new" reflect the same concern, as does Luther's emphasis on the underivability of the Christ-event.

is not only not given, but actually opposed, since the objective is exclusive power. This is why power must be overcome and conquered by nonviolent action or reason in a sovereignty theory that is uncomfortable with itself. But such a conquest, it has been shown repeatedly, is impossible ontologically.

This line of argument is applicable to the power produced by the event of Jesus as the Christ. For Christian theology, the grounding of ethics in power seems to be an option precluded by the cross. The crucifixion cannot, however, be considered a renunciation of either natural or spiritual power, for this assertion would imply that the crucified one possessed power and then gave it up. This perspective has been ruled out in opting for a decentered geography of power. Instead, the intimate involvement of Jesus' death with the biblical picture of Jesus as the Christ points toward power rather than away from it. The appearance of the possibility of the New Being in history has been one of the world's most fulfilling powers, as well as one subject to distorted use for pure domination.

Tillich locates the finality of the revelation of Jesus as the Christ in the sacrifice of the medium of the person Jesus, which renders the divine ground transparent. Jesus' person disappears in the communication of the message of the New Being and in opening the essential possibility of the New Being under the conditions of existence.[189] If power is not a centered possession of a particular being, then sacrifice of revelatory medium for its content is neither renunciation of power nor assertion of it. Rather, the power of the New Being communicated through the New Testament picture and to the "church" of all ages occurs at the border of encounters between Jesus as the Christ and those with whom Jesus was historically contemporaneous, as well as between the New Testament picture and our reception of it.[190] Jesus is the Christ "only if in fact he does bring the power of the New Being to somebody; that is, he can be called 'the Christ' only if he is received in ecstasy."[191] As transparent medium of the New Being, Jesus as the Christ is "powerful" only in the sense that the picture of this person is surrounded by an aura of power; that is, communications of efficacy emerge from encounters with this picture. The final revelation opens the possibility of "new heaven and new earth," in which the broadest and deepest productions of power are united; the New Being is directed at the universality of the deepest power.

At the same time, this formulation of "new heaven and new earth" makes it clear that power cannot be fulfilled in history. Specification of power's content as communication of efficacy cannot become a frozen system that projects a utopian completion in which power would cease. As long as there is life, there is communication and reception of efficacy. And what is efficacious in

[189] Tillich, *Systematic Theology* 1:128–37; 2:123–24.
[190] Hammond makes a similar point (*Power of Self-Transcendence*, 87–88).
[191] Kelsey, *The Fabric of Paul Tillich's Theology*, 38. As we have seen, Kelsey is finally critical of this position.

a situation will always be new in some sense, sometimes radically new. Power cannot be overcome in history. If it ceases, so do history and life. Power is their ineradicable condition. Far from producing a possible end to history in perfect temporal fulfillment, the "absolutizing of a finite possibility,"[192] the nature of power makes possible criticism of any particular historical present (or any utopian future,[193] which renders the future present to thought) on the basis of its inevitable limitation upon communications of efficacy. Power is, in this sense, a "disappearing" concept.[194] It is always present, but it is also demanded, always immanent and transcendent.[195]

Two further points are in order. First, the New Being's encounter with the world has produced power, and that power has not been limited to "spiritual" power. Tillich's analysis of the dimensions of being is important here. Appearance of a new dimension captures and raises previous dimensions to new possibilities, both fulfilling and distorted. It is impossible to deny that encounter with the picture of Jesus as the Christ has produced effects on body and nature.[196] The power generated in the encounter with Jesus as the Christ is both natural and spiritual.

Second, the assertion that the power of being is communication of efficacy includes a judgment upon weakness. Mere weakness does not dominate, but it is little better for that, since its lack of an element of domination indicates absence of substantial relation to power. Weakness does not dominate, but neither does it communicate efficacy. It is, therefore, not demonic because it lacks power to be demonic. Weakness is the *opposite* of power, domination the demonic distortion of power (but therefore a real power). Insofar as weakness is powerless and fails to communicate or receive efficacy, it is merely worthless.[197] This introduces a needed cautionary note into ethical judgment. Since power is performed and not possessed, all action ventures weakness or distortion into mere domination. It is impossible to be certain whether or not the

---

[192] Tillich, "Open Letter to Emanuel Hirsch," 366.

[193] A fascinating account of utopian thinking and its ontological basis in the distinction between essence and existence is provided in Tillich, *The Political Meaning of Utopia*, 125–80 (*GW* 6:157–210). A comparison of "kairic" and "utopian" thought can be found in the final lecture of that essay and in Paul Tillich, *Kairos und Utopie* (*GW* 6:149–56). The difference between the two is that while utopia projects historical, horizontal fulfillment on the basis of a historical restoration of essence, kairic thinking is oriented to "vertical" fulfillment, which remains impossible in history. The utopian spirit is transformed in kairic thinking. A useful summary of Tillich's relation to utopianism is found in Stumme, *Socialism in Theological Perspective*, 189–91.

[194] This description is borrowed from Robert P. Scharlemann, "Critical and Religious Consciousness: Some Reflections on the Question of Truth in the Philosophy of Religion," in *Kairos and Logos*, ed. Carey, 80–88.

[195] In Tillich's work, the category of demand in unity with presence is presented most forcefully in *The State as Expectation and Demand*, 97–114 (*Religiöse Verwirklichung*, 212–32).

[196] The bodily effects of the Spirit are recognized in Tillich, *Systematic Theology* 3:115.

[197] For a similar, though somewhat sharper, evaluation of "smallness" in contrast to "greatness," see Tillich, *Systematic Theology* 3:88; see also Roger L. Shinn, "Tillich as Interpreter and Disturber of Contemporary Civilization," in *The Thought of Paul Tillich*, ed. Adams, Pauck, and Shinn, 51.

result of one's own leap of power is worthwhile or not. This does not justify inactivity, however, since the results of inaction are also uncertain. Rather, the risk taken in regard to the appearance of power is real, and the gamble of any act must be supported by certainty of one's justification in spite of the possible failure of power to appear. The risk of power must be taken up into "the courage to be."[198] Within this arena of historical risk, the event of Jesus as the Christ can be viewed as the greatest risk of all. It, too, takes the risk of extinction, of eventual weakness.

To this point, exposition of an ethic of power has concentrated on certain possible applications of the theology of power. The more formal aspects of this ethic have not been explored. To a large extent, an investigation of the shape of the ethic of power is also no more than illustrative, because if the risk of action in regard to power is taken seriously, the final proof of an ethic of power is revealed only in its practice. Practice cannot be derived directly from an ontology of power, although practice must be based in it. This said, the conceptual structure of an ethic of power can still be clarified.

It is not that these conclusions are impossible except through a theology of power. What is unique is that this ethic begins from the operation of power. Instead of constructing an ethic that either ignores or attempts to control power, the contention is that a distinctive ethic emerges from power itself. The stronger claim, derived from the conclusion that power is the fundamental ontological element, is this: Any ethic must begin from an understanding of power, for there is no other place from which to start. An ethic that understands itself as not in need of grounding in power is self-deceptive.

The ethical content of fairness, we have seen, is adjudicated through consideration of beings' power potential. The chance of error implicit in such judgments is due to the fact that power potential and power are not the same. Power appears independent of potentiality, at the border of encounter. This geography of power eliminates the need to superimpose a demand of recognition upon power. In a centered view of power, such as Tillich's explicit concept, recognition is external to centered powers. Power is held and possessed, and therefore its *telos* is defeat of resistance to it by centered powers. Its end is domination. The demand for recognition, which is the foundation of the moral act and grounds the interactive concept of justice, attempts to control the unlimited self-assertion of the will to power. Power conceived as communication of efficacy, however, includes recognition in its definition. Power's intrinsic *telos* is communication of efficacy to another being. The other stands within the heart of power from the start. Failure to recognize demands for

---

[198] Tillich, *Courage To Be.* For Tillich, faith and courage are related closely. If "faith, formally or generally defined, is the state of being grasped by that toward which self-transcendence aspires, the ultimate in being and meaning" (*Systematic Theology* 3:130), being grasped in such a way as one is concerned implies that one simultaneously affirms being as meaningful, which carries with it the courage to affirm that meaning in spite of the ambiguities of life.

fairness issued by the other is a distortion of power itself. The end of power in the communication of efficacy is sacrificed for the incomplete, dominating moment of power. Domination, which has its true end in communication of efficacy, becomes an end in itself, refusing the demand of recognition implicit in the nature of power as a whole. Thus, "abuse of power" does not mean that abusers have simply misdirected neutral power to an illegitimate end, which would be the case if power were potentiality. Rather, power's abuse points to a deficiency in the appearance of power itself; power is abused when it is prevented from reaching its own intrinsic aim.

Inclusion of recognition within the concept of power also has implications for the relation of power, justice, and love. If power includes acknowledgment of the other, and if being is essentially power as communication of efficacy, there is no difference between the content of justice and love and the content of power. Justice and love are not external to power, but identical with fulfilled power. Insofar as justice and love are incomplete, they are judged to be so on the basis of the critical criterion of fulfilled power. Fairness and love are simply more concrete expressions of the meaning of the power of being. The contents of justice and fairness are determined by asking the question, What communicates efficacy in this historical situation? The inevitable abstractness and incompleteness of these contents leads love to ask, What communicates efficacy in this particular encounter? The demand laid upon love and justice is generation of power; they seek to overcome distorted or incomplete power.[199] It is still true, however, that power is a more fundamental description of being than either justice or love, for power provides the framework through and in which justice and love attain reality. Both must participate in power in order to be.[200]

The contrast between essential power, in which the element of domination retains its *telos* to and unity with the communication of efficacy, and distorted existential power, in which domination becomes separated from its end, provides the starting point for outlining the general form of an ethic of power. Specification of the power of being as communication of efficacy furnishes the critical standard by which to judge special appearances of power, and criticism of distorted power is issued in the name of this power. Existential power can be said to be estranged, fallen power. Power is distorted when the two elements of power, sovereignty and its *telos* to efficacy, become

---

[199] Frank Guliuzza first pointed out that this understanding of power includes a basic substantive identity with love.

[200] This reverses Tillich's relation between power and love. For him, love is the foundation of power (*Love, Power, and Justice*, 49), whereas our position is that power must be the foundation of love in order for love to appear. Hammond presents a good account of Tillich's argument (*Man in Estrangement*, 159–64); however, Walter M. Horton discovers one place in which Tillich says something quite close to our contention ("Tillich's Role in Contemporary Theology," in *The Theology of Paul Tillich*, ed. Kegley and Bretall, 36).

separated. Sovereignty becomes its own end, losing its essential objective and character as a gift. Pure sovereignty is mere compulsion rather than gift.

It is obvious that on many occasions, separation of power from its end is necessary and relatively desirable. The sovereign element in power may be the only element in a particular encounter, and it may intend precisely limitation or elimination of the efficacy of what it encounters. Separation of power's elements, however, always implies the presence of a distortion in power, either on one side of an encounter or the other, and usually on both. The division of elements implies, in short, a relative absence of justice and love. But justice and love have not arrived on the scene from outside power in order to correct it, limit it, or prevent its abuse. Instead, they have sprung up from within the heart of power itself, as a demand on distorted power to become essential power, that is, to reunite its two immanent elements or, more properly, to fulfill sovereignty by redirecting it to its end, the communication of efficacy.

More specifically, an ethic based on power as the communication of efficacy includes several elements. In the first place, an answer has to be given to the question, *What* is efficacious? Rational ethical reflection on the nature of the good, the just, the right, and so on, as well as more precise anthropological analyses find their place in this question, providing the material of an ethic of power. This content, however, must be qualified by a pragmatic component. It is not enough to ask simply about what the good is. Of equal importance is the question, How is the good to be communicated? A good is irrelevant, powerless, and loses its claim to be good, if it is incapable of being communicated and received.[201] This question of the mechanics of communication is answerable, ultimately, only in practice, in the leap of power into the encounter, even though preliminary reflections about power potentials of certain courses of action may prove helpful, assisted by comprehensive and particular reflection on the cultural, historical, and spatial situation, as has been, of late, the important emphasis of the varied movements which may be classed broadly as "liberationist."

An ethic of power avoids two alternatives. The first is a simplistic pragmatism that advocates "whatever works." The question of what is efficacious is a challenge to such an approach, for it demands that the criterion for what is effective is the good, the essentially powerful. Moreover, since whatever is efficacious must be communicated in order to be power, mere self-interest is not fulfilled power. On the other hand, any abstract utopianism is also impossible, because the pragmatic element of what works is included in an ethic of power. Abstract utopianism, elitist humanism to which only a few have access,[202] and fanatical utopianism in which very few are included, are ruled

---

[201] Tillich's criticism of the powerlessness of idealism and Kantian criticism is based in part on this problem; see *Protestantism as a Critical and Creative Principle,* 19 (*GW* 7:36–37). Criticism cannot be an abstraction which sets itself up against the power of the concretely emerging form.

[202] Tillich's argument regarding the exclusive character of humanism is fascinating (*Systematic Theology* 3:86; "The World Situation," 17). Because of its exclusive nature, the humanist ideal is

out because they fail to actually communicate the efficacious content of their ethic.

In the context of political theory, the point can be put another way. With respect to the political right, which frequently advocates a "realpolitik" that is reduced eventually to self-interest, this theology of power affirms the insight that power is fundamental and unavoidable. It disagrees with the conclusion that dominating power therefore can be used without limit, because it denies that power is possessed and is, therefore, essentially domination. The interest in gaining power is legitimate, but the power that is gained is by nature a universal and not an exclusive power. With respect to the political left, which has a tendency to accept the theory of power presented by the right and then flee from power, the definition of power as the communication of efficacy agrees with its suspicion of pure domination, but disagrees that this is the nature of power. Further, it rejects the conclusion that it is possible to eliminate sovereignty,[203] which remains an element even in persuasive and spiritual power. The leftist ambivalence and fear of power are overcome. In both cases, the tendency to introduce ethical control upon power from outside, or to view power cynically, as divorced from ethics and therefore subject to no judgment and no legitimate limit once the decision is made to employ it, is defeated by the nature of power itself. Power judges its own distortions on the basis of the nature of fulfilled power.

These brief remarks do not serve as the elucidation of an ethic of power. They should indicate the direction and limits such an ethic might take. But it was important to point out the applicability of a theology of power to some more concrete realm of reflection. Ethics does not exhaust these applications, nor has this exposition covered all possibilities in that area. Our purpose is only to make the point that more concrete ethical analyses, as well as in other areas of thought and practice, must take their point of departure from the ubiquitous phenomenon of power.

The theology of power asserts that being is grounded in communication and reception of efficacy, not in domination. The term "asserted" shows a basic limitation to this ontology that cannot be overcome. There is no sense in which a demonstrative proof can be offered that the nature of being is not domination. This requires explanation.

At the beginning of this project, the argument was made that, for Christian faith, defining power as domination was unacceptable. If power is ubiquitous, if it is the unparalleled description of being-itself, then ultimately it must support beings. Communication of efficacy is an ontologically exhaustive description of the power of being. That is, it leaves out no realm

---

self-defeating. The vast majority of humanity is left with no symbols of fulfillment and, receiving nothing from humanism and its ideals, reacts against it. The humanist ideal is valid, but it must both develop and communicate its symbols of meaning to culture at large.

[203] We are, therefore, fundamentally in agreement with Foucault's criticism of Habermas.

of beings, is inescapable as long as there is life, and provides for the fulfillment of being. However, the meaningfulness of existence cannot be affirmed
simply by the statement "this is the way things essentially are." There is no
simple identity of the essential "is" with the existential "ought." That many
do not trust the structures of being is obvious. There are attempts, some heroic
and others petty, to overcome and break these essential structures, and many
simply despair of meaning in being altogether. There are, moreover, no
empirical criteria that come to mind which could "prove" the ultimate meaningfulness of being.[204] For each instance of relative meaning, there are other
instances of relative meaninglessness.

The affirmation of being's ultimate meaningfulness, of its final friendly
intentions toward us, returns us to where we began. In Luther's terms, this
ultimate trust is "faith," or in Tillich's terms, faith requiring courage. The affirmation of the structure of being as meaningful, and with it self-affirmation
as participants in being, is a pronouncement of faith and courage in the
experience of being "grasped by the power of being-itself."[205] Only when faith
and courage enter, beyond and above the evidence that can be adduced by

---

[204] The reformers' doctrine of predestination gains substantial plausibility once reason's inability
to reach faith is recognized, and once predestination is distinguished from determinism. The latter
distinction is clear in Luther's claim that he denies freedom of choice only in what pertains to
salvation or damnation, but not with respect to things of the earthly realm. Luther refuses "quibbles
about temporal bondage, as if this had anything to do with the case" (Luther, *Bondage of the Will*,
197 [WA 18:723]; see also *Bondage of the Will*, 70, 73–74, 87, 103, 107–8, 118–19, 285 [WA 18:638,
641–42, 651, 662–64, 671–73, 781]). Free choice, Luther grants, "does many things, but these
are nonetheless 'nothing' in the sight of God" (*Bondage of the Will*, 239; WA 18:751). Gerhard
Ebeling has an excellent discussion of what Luther's doctrine of the slavery of the will does and
does not mean (*Luther: An Introduction to his Thought*, trans. R. A. Wilson [Philadelphia: Fortress
Press, 1970]).
   For both Luther and Calvin, predestination is spoken of from within the context of faith.
To the one with faith, who realizes that it could not have been attained through "natural" means
of a simple investigation of the evidence, and who realizes that not all find being finally trustworthy,
it is easy to conclude that it is a matter of fate and arbitrariness whether one has this confidence
or not. Faith can hardly seem to have been a personal decision at all. This is the issue: If "'Your
faith has made you well' [Luke 17:19] – do you hear 'your'? Explain it to mean 'you produce faith';
then you have proved free choice" (Luther, *Bondage of the Will*, 232; WA 18:747). Ernst Troeltsch
is correct that the Reformation doctrine of justification is necessarily also a doctrine of predestination
(*The Social Teaching of the Christian Churches*, 2 vols., trans. Olive Wyon [London: George Allen
& Unwin; New York: Macmillan, 1931; reprint, Chicago: University of Chicago Press, 1981]
2:470). Thomas Davis was of considerable help in making this aspect of Calvin's understanding
of predestination clear to me.
   Tillich's somewhat different, but still positive, reinterpretation of Calvin's doctrine of predestination can be found in Tillich, "The Recovery of the Prophetic Tradition in the Reformation." Although he takes the claim in a somewhat different direction, Tillich also asserts that
predestination is sensible only within an existential viewpoint; a nonexistential interpretation
makes "this doctrine an impossibility, and I would say even a demonic blasphemy" (p. 11).
Hammond places Tillich among the predestinarians, at least in a qualified sense (*Power of Self-
Transcendence*, 76).
[205] Tillich, *Courage To Be*, 172; see also *Love, Power, and Justice*, 39.

observation, can ethics grow out of ontology. When the meaningfulness and fulfilling nature of being are affirmed, with or without thematic-discursive religious commitment, then freedom can be, as Tillich says, not mere arbitrariness, but the subjection to valid norms.[206]

It cannot be proved that the nature of being is not domination, even in light of all the destructive consequences that would entail. The genius of Machiavelli's *Prince* lies in forcing a choice upon the reader. Is life ultimately the cynical game of dominating power that Machiavelli describes, or is it not? His position cannot be defeated by demonstrative proofs. Theologically considered, if power is as *The Prince* describes it, the God of creation plays a vicious trick on creatures, creating them only for the final destruction which follows on achievement of power's *telos* to utter domination. Against this, the only answer available is Calvin's:

> the flatterers of princes, immoderately praising their power, do not hesitate to set them against the rule of God himself. Unless [this evil] is checked, purity of faith will perish. Besides, it is of no slight importance to us to know how lovingly God has provided in this respect for mankind, that greater zeal for piety may flourish in us to attest our gratefulness.[207]

The courageous affirmation of the meaningfulness of being presupposes an attitude of worship.

---

[206] Tillich, *Systematic Theology* 3:28–29; see also "The Idea and the Ideal of Personality," 116. Only if being is taken to have fulfilling meaning could the "essential" be taken as a source for norms. Otherwise, there would be no cause to affirm one's essential being rather than destroy it. An affirmation of being, Tillich points out, depends on a prior recognition of the value of essential being, of its belonging to the Divine Life (Tillich, *Systematic Theology* 3:159, 190–91).

Tillich's assertion that love is an ontological structure, that all being evidences desire to reunite with what is separated from it (*Love, Power, and Justice*, 25, 37), appears to hold out the prospect of a more definitive validation of ontological concepts. This is somewhat deceptive. In the first place, Tillich maintains that ontology can be demonstrated only through participation, which rules out a merely detached observatory validation (*Systematic Theology* 1:100–104). In the case of love, Tillich's ontology is validated by the "experience of love fulfilled" (*Love, Power, and Justice*, 27). Similarly, the definition of power as communication of efficacy is validated by the experience of power at its fullest, or not at all. Second, is there convincing evidence available through observation that beings seek reunion any more than they seek separation? For each example of efforts at meaningful reunion that can be adduced in support of Tillich's claim, a counterexample of an attempt in the direction of separation and alienated relations can be found. In making his ontological assertion, Tillich already stands in the "theological circle" (or at least in an empirically unprovable "ontological circle" which can be validated only through participation rather than by any merely external means) insofar as he presupposes the meaningfulness of being. The dependence of ultimate meaning upon decision in freedom is noted in "Eschatology and History," 278–84 (*Religiöse Verwirklichung*, 136–41) and "The Interpretation of History and the Idea of Christ," 247–65 (*Religiöse Verwirklichung*, 114–27). See also Adams, *Tillich's Philosophy*, 215, 225; and Stumme, *Socialism in Theological Perspective*, 176–77. Hammond notes that Tillich's dialectical response to the proofs for God's existence is based on his assumption of the meaningfulness of existence (*Man in Estrangement*, 89). The finally unprovable nature of Tillich's ontology is also noted in McKelway, *Systematic Theology of Paul Tillich*, 103, 106.

[207] Calvin, *Institutes* 2:4.20.1, pp. 1485–86.

Salvific Power

This effort has had two directions. To begin with, the notion that power is domination or control, a conception drawn mostly from political theory, has been criticized. Dissatisfaction with that definition of power has grown steadily in recent years, both inside and outside the field of political philosophy. Certain theologians, too, have expressed the need to develop a different definition of power; however, attempts to reconceive the nature of power have been considerably less successful than the protest against the "orthodoxy" of power. Some of these efforts have been considered explicitly here, while others have not.

The common thread that runs through most contemporary theories of power is their origin in political theory. Because politics is made the exclusive locale of power, the full range and depth of the phenomenon of power are passed over; power is confined to the external dimensions of life and, as in Foucault, power and domination are reidentified to a considerable extent. If domination is rejected as an adequate description of the nature of life, then power is reduced to an ontic phenomenon, as in Arendt. Or, if one is convinced, as Habermas is, that domination is a distortion of power, "true" power tends to be reduced to an ontic phenomenon identical with reason.

The interpretation of power that has been offered here has these main features. Power is affirmed as ubiquitous and unavoidable, the fundamental description of being–itself. Fulfilled power, the ultimate power of being, contains two elements or moments: a moment of sovereignty and a *telos* to the efficacy of those bordering the encounter of power. Sovereignty, far from being domination, appears as a gift that communicates efficacy. Distorted power, on the other hand, maintains the sovereign aspect of power, not as a moment of power but as power complete. Sovereignty loses its end and character as a gift and becomes instead menacing domination. Part of the reason for the prevailing definition of power as domination is that power is viewed as a thing to be had and stored. The notion of "communication of efficacy" does not allow this. Rather, efficacy is communicated at the borders in the mutual, bodily presence of entities; it is instantiated between the participants in encounter and disappears as soon as it appears. Power posits itself in a leap that cannot be known or predicted on the basis of preexistent capacities. Power's appearance can be, figuratively, "more" or "less," but only in comparison to other instantiations of power, not in relation to any possession of power. Finally, some of the implications of this theory of power for ethics were outlined. If the omnipresent power of being is affirmed as an ultimately trustworthy power, shadows of an ethic begin to appear. Instead of power's being completed in exclusive possession, it is fulfilled only as a unity of universal and deep power. Power, insofar as it is essential power, is saving power. The ethical implications of this view emerge from within power itself, rather than being placed in the impossible situation of attempting to control power from the outside.

INDEX